Com
European Politics

Distinctive Democracies, Common Challenges

SECOND EDITION

Edited by

Rory Costello
Associate Professor of Politics
University of Limerick

Neil Robinson
Professor of Comparative Politics
University of Limerick

OXFORD
UNIVERSITY PRESS

OXFORD
UNIVERSITY PRESS

Great Clarendon Street, Oxford, OX2 6DP,
United Kingdom

Oxford University Press is a department of the University of Oxford.
It furthers the University's objective of excellence in research, scholarship,
and education by publishing worldwide. Oxford is a registered trade mark of
Oxford University Press in the UK and in certain other countries

First Edition 2021

Published in the United States of America by Oxford University Press
198 Madison Avenue, New York, NY 10016, United States of America

British Library Cataloguing in Publication Data
Data available

Library of Congress Control Number: 2023915614

ISBN 978-0-19-286644-8

Printed in the UK by
Bell & Bain Ltd., Glasgow

Comparative European Politics

Outline Contents

Detailed Contents

List of Abbreviations

AfD	Alternative for Germany
AKEL	Progressive Party of Working People (Cyprus)
AV	Alternative Vote
CAN	Climate Action Network
CCPI	Climate Change Performance Index
CDA	Christian Democratic Appeal (Netherlands)
CDU/CSU	Christian Democratic Union/Christian Social Union (Germany)
CEE	Central and Eastern Europe
CFSP	Common Foreign and Security Policy
CJM	Climate Justice Movement
CoR	Committee of the Regions
CPP	Comparative Pledges Project
CSDP	Common Security and Defence Policy
CU	Christian Union (Netherlands)
CVP/CD&V	Christian Democratic and Flemish Party (Belgium)
D66	Democrats '66 (Netherlands)
DM	district magnitude
DNP	digitally networked forms of participation
DP	Democratic Party (Luxembourg)
DPS/HÖH	Movement for Rights and Freedoms (Bulgaria)
DUP	Democratic Unionist Party
EAC	European Affairs Committee
EC	European Community
ECB	European Central Bank
ECSC	European Coal and Steel Community
ECJ	European Court of Justice
EDC	European Defence Community
EEAS	European External Action Service
EEC	European Economic Community
EESC	European Economic and Social Committee
ENGO	Environmental non-governmental organizations
ENPP	effective number of parliamentary parties
EP	European Parliament

EPP	European People's Party
ESM	European Stability Mechanism
ESS	European Social Survey
ETA	Basque Homeland and Liberty
EU	European Union
EUGS	EU Global Strategy
Eurozone	term used to refer to the EU member countries that use the Euro as their currency
EVS	European Values Survey
EWM	early warning mechanism
FDI	foreign direct investment
FDP	Free Democratic Party (Germany)
FFF	Fridays For Future
FN	National Front/National Rally (France)
FOE	first-order election
FoE	Friends of the Earth
FPÖ	Freedom Party of Austria
FRONTEX	EU Border and Coast Guard Agency
FYROM	Former Yugoslav Republic of Macedonia
GDP	gross domestic product
GFC	global financial crisis
GHG	Greenhouse gas emissions
GUE/NGL	European United Left/Nordic Green Left
HRVP	High Representative of the Union for Foreign Affairs and Security Policy
IDEA	International Institute for Democracy and Electoral Assistance
IGC	intergovernmental conferences
IMF	International Monetary Fund
ISIS	Islamic State of Iraq and Syria
ISM	Italian Social Movement
JHA	Justice and Home Affairs
KESK	Centre Party (Finland)
KOK	National Coalition Party (Finland)
LR	The Republicans (France)
M5S	5 Star Movement (Italy)
MEP	Member of the European Parliament
MMP	mixed-member proportional
MP	Member of Parliament
MP	Moderate Party (Sweden)

MSI	Italian Social Movement
MSZP	Hungarian Socialist Party
NABU	Nature and Biodiversity Conservation Union
NAM	non-aligned movement
NATO	North Atlantic Treaty Organization
NGO	non-governmental organization
NL	Northern League (Italy)
NORDEFCO	Nordic Defence Cooperation
NPM	New Public Management
NVA	New Flemish Alliance (Belgium)
OECD	Organization for Economic Cooperation and Development
OSCE	Organization for Security and Cooperation in Europe
ÖVP	Austrian People's Party
PA	national public administrations
PCE	Spanish Communist Party
PCF	French Communist Party
PCI	Italian Communist Party
PdCI	Party of Italian Communists
PESCO	Permanent Structured Cooperation
PfP	Partnership for Peace
PIGS	Greece, Ireland, Portugal, and Spain
PIS	Law and Justice (Poland)
PO	Civic Platform (Poland)
PP	Popular Party (Spain)
PQ	parliamentary question
PR	proportional representation
PS	Finns Party (Finland)
PSI	Italian Socialist Party
PSOE	Spanish Socialist Workers' Party
PvdA	Labour Party (Netherlands)
PVV	Party for Freedom (Netherlands)
SAP	Swedish Social Democratic Party
SD	Sweden Democrats
SFP	Swedish People's Party
SMP	Single-Member Plurality
SNP	Scottish National Party
SOE	second-order election

SPD	Social Democratic Party of Germany
STV	Single Transferable Vote
SURE	short-term employment schemes
TCN	third-country national
UKIP	United Kingdom Independence Party
UN	United Nations
UNFCCC	UN Framework Convention on Climate Change
VVD	People's Party for Freedom and Democracy (Netherlands)
XR	Extinction Rebellion

About the Editors

Rory Costello is Associate Professor of Politics in the Department of Politics and Public Administration at the University of Limerick (UL), where he teaches courses on comparative European politics, the European Union, and research methods. Before coming to UL in 2011, he worked at the University of Twente in the Netherlands and at the London School of Economics and Political Science. He received his PhD from Trinity College Dublin in 2009.

Rory specializes in electoral and legislative politics in Europe. His research has appeared in a number of leading political science journals, including the *European Journal of Political Research*, *West European Politics*, *Journal of European Public Policy*, *Party Politics*, *Electoral Studies*, *European Union Politics*, and the *American Journal of Political Science*. His recent work has focused on political representation, voting behaviour, government performance, and party competition.

Neil Robinson is Professor of Comparative Politics in the Department of Politics and Public Administration at the University of Limerick, where he teaches courses on comparative and post-communist politics. Before coming to UL in 2001, he worked at the universities of York and Essex.

Neil specializes in in post-communist politics, particularly the post-communist politics of the former USSR. His research has been published in many journals including the *European Journal of Political Research*, *Political Studies*, *Review of International Political Economy*, and *International Political Science Review*. He has written and edited several books including *Post-Communist Politics* (Prentice Hall, 1997, with Karen Henderson), *State-Building: Theory and Practice* (Routledge, 2007, with Aidan Hehir), *The Sage Handbook of Comparative Politics* (Sage, 2009, with Todd Landman), and most recently *Contemporary Russian Politics* (Polity, 2018).

Notes on Contributors

Patrick Bernhagen Professor of Comparative Politics, Institute for Social Sciences, University of Stuttgart, Germany.

Neil Carter Professor, Department of Politics, University of York, UK.

David M. Farrell Professor, School of Politics and International Relations, University College Dublin, Ireland.

Luke Field Post-Doctoral Fellow, Faculty of Political Science, University of Iceland.

Nuno Garoupa Professor of Law, Antonin Scalia Law School, George Mason University, Arlington, USA.

Paolo Graziano Professor of Political Science, Department of Political Science, Law and International Studies, University of Padua, Italy.

Ruby Gropas European Political Strategy Centre, European Commission, Brussels, Belgium.

Michael Keating Emeritus Professor, School of Social Sciences, University of Aberdeen, Scotland.

Petia Kostadinova Associate Professor, Department of Political Science, University of Illinois, Chicago, USA.

André Krouwel Associate Professor, Department of Communication Science, Vrije Universiteit Amsterdam, the Netherlands.

Conor Little Associate Professor, Department of Politics and Public Administration, University of Limerick, Ireland.

Pedro C. Magalhães Research Fellow, Institute of Social Sciences, University of Lisbon, Portugal.

Shane Martin Anthony King Chair in Comparative Government, Department of Government, University of Essex, UK.

Simona Piattoni Professor of Political Science, Department of Sociology and Social Research, University of Trento, Italy.

Jean-Benoit Pilet Professor of Political Science, Department of Political Science, Université libre de Bruxelles, Belgium.

Tapio Raunio Professor of Political Science, Faculty of Management and Business, Tampere University, Finland.

Alan Renwick Professor of Democratic Politics, Department of Political Science, University College London, UK.

Petra Schleiter Professor of Comparative Politics, Department of Politics and International Relations, University of Oxford, UK.

Simon J. Smith Associate Professor of Security and International Relations, School of Justice, Security and Sustainability, Staffordshire University, UK.

Robert Thomson Professor of Political Science, School of Social Sciences, Monash University, Australia.

Erik Tillman Professor, Department of Political Science, DePaul University, Chicago, USA.

Nikola Tomić, Cybersecurity Research Cluster Lead, Trilateral Research, Ireland.

Anna Triandafyllidou Canada Excellence Research Chair in Migration and Integration, Toronto Metropolitan University, Toronto, Canada.

Angelika Vetter Associate Professor, Institute for Social Sciences, University of Stuttgart, Germany.

Owen Worth Professor, Department of Politics and Public Administration, University of Limerick, Ireland.

Acknowledgements

We would like to thank all our contributors, both to this edition and to the last, for their hard work and for the good grace with which they made changes that either we or the reviewers of the manuscript asked of them. We would like to thank all the people who took the time to review parts of the book, or who looked over all of it, especially William Daniel (University of Nottingham), Giorgos Katsambekis (Institute of Political Research, National Centre for Social Research (EKKE), Greece), and Aris Trantidis (University of Lincoln). We are very grateful to Shane Reynolds for his excellent work on the online resources that accompany this book. Thanks too to our colleagues in the Department of Politics and Public Administration at the University of Limerick who have given us advice on many different aspects of the book from conception through content. Many ideas that have informed the shape of the book came out of our teaching comparative European politics and comparative politics to our students. Much of the time our students were probably not aware of the seeds they were planting but our thanks to them anyway for their inspiration. Any value that this book might have has been enhanced by our editors and the production team at Oxford University Press, for both editions, particularly Grace Howard, Sarah Iles, and Katie Staal. Finally, but not the least in terms of importance, our thanks to Nóirín and Maura for making everything else easier so that we could spend time on this project.

How to Use This Book

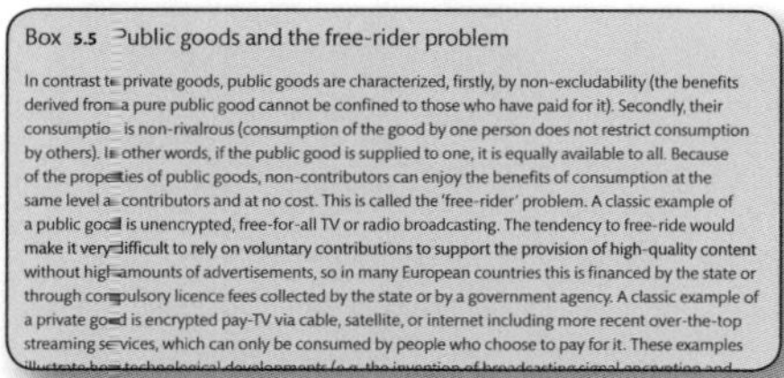

Box 5.5 Public goods and the free-rider problem

In contrast to private goods, public goods are characterized, firstly, by non-excludability (the benefits derived from a pure public good cannot be confined to those who have paid for it). Secondly, their consumption is non-rivalrous (consumption of the good by one person does not restrict consumption by others). In other words, if the public good is supplied to one, it is equally available to all. Because of the properties of public goods, non-contributors can enjoy the benefits of consumption at the same level as contributors and at no cost. This is called the 'free-rider' problem. A classic example of a public good is unencrypted, free-for-all TV or radio broadcasting. The tendency to free-ride would make it very difficult to rely on voluntary contributions to support the provision of high-quality content without high amounts of advertisements, so in many European countries this is financed by the state or through compulsory licence fees collected by the state or by a government agency. A classic example of a private good is encrypted pay-TV via cable, satellite, or internet including more recent over-the-top streaming services, which can only be consumed by people who choose to pay for it. These examples

Boxes

Throughout the book, boxes provide you with extra information on particular topics, while defining and explaining key ideas, helping you to build on what you have learned from the main chapter text.

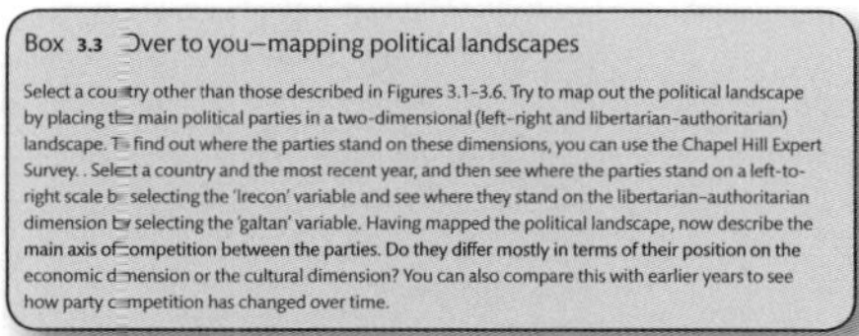

Box 3.3 Over to you—mapping political landscapes

Select a country other than those described in Figures 3.1–3.6. Try to map out the political landscape by placing the main political parties in a two-dimensional (left-right and libertarian-authoritarian) landscape. To find out where the parties stand on these dimensions, you can use the Chapel Hill Expert Survey. . Select a country and the most recent year, and then see where the parties stand on a left-to-right scale by selecting the 'lrecon' variable and see where they stand on the libertarian-authoritarian dimension by selecting the 'galtan' variable. Having mapped the political landscape, now describe the main axis of competition between the parties. Do they differ mostly in terms of their position on the economic dimension or the cultural dimension? You can also compare this with earlier years to see how party competition has changed over time.

Over to you exercise boxes

Over to you exercises in each chapter prompt you to go beyond the textbook, highlighting key political issues in the real world to facilitate critical and reflective thinking, and to help you conduct your own comparative research.

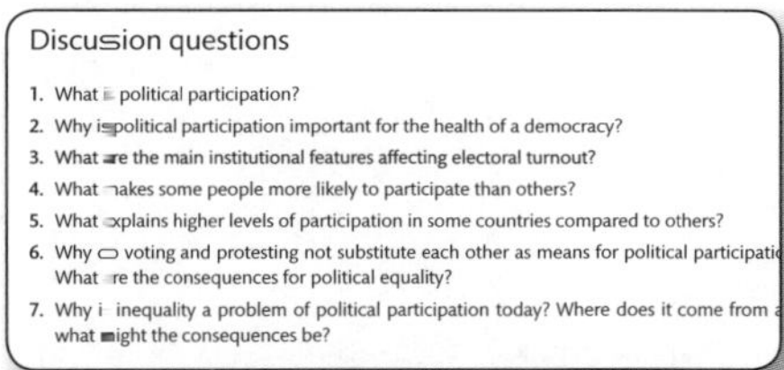

Discussion questions

1. What is political participation?
2. Why is political participation important for the health of a democracy?
3. What are the main institutional features affecting electoral turnout?
4. What makes some people more likely to participate than others?
5. What explains higher levels of participation in some countries compared to others?
6. Why do voting and protesting not substitute each other as means for political participati What are the consequences for political equality?
7. Why is inequality a problem of political participation today? Where does it come from what might the consequences be?

Discussion questions

At the end of each chapter, discussion questions allow you to reflect on the subject matter, apply your knowledge, and critically evaluate what you have learned.

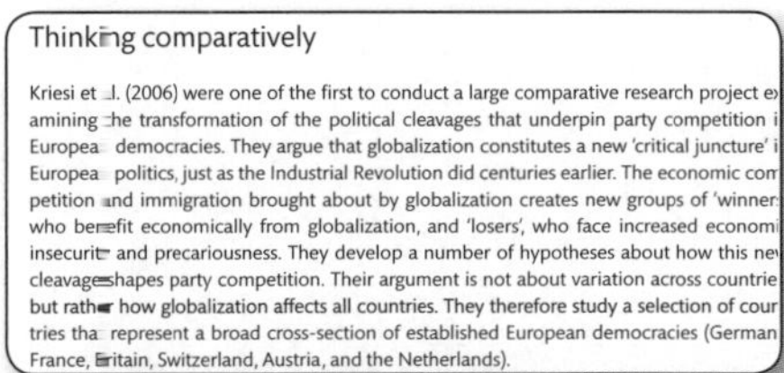

Thinking comparatively

Kriesi et al. (2006) were one of the first to conduct a large comparative research project examining the transformation of the political cleavages that underpin party competition i European democracies. They argue that globalization constitutes a new 'critical juncture' i European politics, just as the Industrial Revolution did centuries earlier. The economic com petition and immigration brought about by globalization creates new groups of 'winner who benefit economically from globalization, and 'losers', who face increased economi insecurity and precariousness. They develop a number of hypotheses about how this ne cleavage shapes party competition. Their argument is not about variation across countrie but rather how globalization affects all countries. They therefore study a selection of cour tries that represent a broad cross-section of established European democracies (German France, Britain, Switzerland, Austria, and the Netherlands).

Thinking comparatively

Thinking comparatively sections at the end of each chapter present examples of comparative research on key topics, so you can learn how to judge theories and hypotheses against the empirical evidence while deepening your understanding of important discourses, debates, and issues.

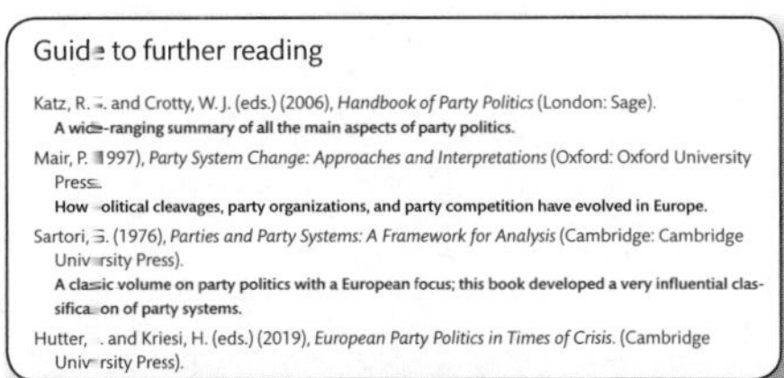

Guide to further reading

Katz, R. S. and Crotty, W. J. (eds.) (2006), *Handbook of Party Politics* (London: Sage).
A wide-ranging summary of all the main aspects of party politics.

Mair, P. (1997), *Party System Change: Approaches and Interpretations* (Oxford: Oxford University Press).
How political cleavages, party organizations, and party competition have evolved in Europe.

Sartori, G. (1976), *Parties and Party Systems: A Framework for Analysis* (Cambridge: Cambridge University Press).
A classic volume on party politics with a European focus; this book developed a very influential classification of party systems.

Hutter, S. and Kriesi, H. (eds.) (2019), *European Party Politics in Times of Crisis*. (Cambridge University Press).

Guide to further reading

Annotated recommendations for further reading at the end of each chapter identify the key literature in the field, helping you to develop your interest in particular topics.

1 Introduction

RORY COSTELLO

1.1 Introduction

In many ways, Europe is the ideal setting for studying democratic politics. It contains several long-standing democracies (fifteen out of twenty of the world's oldest democracies are in Europe (Boix et al. 2013)), along with many countries that democratized in recent decades. Most of these democracies have experienced years of economic and political integration as members of the European Union (EU), have shared histories, and face similar challenges such as migration, climate change, and security. Despite these shared experiences and common challenges, in virtually every aspect of politics—how elections are run, how political power is allocated, how citizens engage with politics—there are important differences between European countries. These differences shape the decisions made by governments, how they respond to the challenges that they face, and ultimately, what life is like for citizens of each country. This makes comparative European politics a particularly rich sub-field of political science. Its democracies are distinctive enough to make comparison worthwhile, yet not so different as to render such comparisons invalid. In the words of a prominent American social scientist, 'Europe remains one of (if not) the most telling examples of why it is important for social science knowledge to be organized in terms of regions as well as nation states or smaller localities or on a global scale' (Calhoun 2003: 18).

Europe has long served both as a source and a testing ground for theories that explain aspects of democratic politics. Some of the most important and enduring insights in comparative politics arose from careful comparisons of European democracies. Early examples include Stein Rokkan's work on the origin of party systems in historical cleavages (e.g. Rokkan 1970), Arend Lijphart's research on consensus or 'consociational' democracies (e.g. Lijphart 1968), Maurice Duverger's arguments regarding the impact of electoral systems on the number of political parties (e.g. Duverger 1954); and Ronald Inglehart's theory on the emergence of 'post-material' values (e.g. Inglehart 1977). In more recent decades, scholars (including the contributors to this volume) have been drawn to comparative European politics to study such themes as democratic consolidation and democratic backsliding; the changing role of the nation state in the context of globalization and European integration; the erosion of mass political engagement and the emergence of new forms of participation; and the rise of populist and far-right parties. All these themes and more will be explored throughout this book.

While political scientists are drawn to European politics because of the potential for comparison, students are often more interested in understanding recent developments on the continent (such as Brexit, the war in Ukraine, or the migration crisis) and their political consequences. This is an equally valid reason to be interested in the subject, and this book aims to equip students to better understand contemporary events and how European governments respond to them. While the first two sections of the book address the building-blocks of democratic politics (elections and representation in Part 1, and the process of government in Part 2), the third part focuses on recent developments that have posed challenges to all or most European democracies.

This chapter explains the overall approach of the book and introduces some of the key concepts in the study of comparative European politics. It begins with an explanation of the geographical coverage of the book (Section 1.2). This is followed by a discussion of the nature of democracy in Europe, highlighting some of the key commonalities and differences between countries (Section 1.3). Section 1.4 introduces some of the challenges facing European democracies that are addressed in the final part of the book. Section 1.5 turns to the question of *how* to study and conduct research on comparative European politics, highlighting some of the main approaches taken by researchers in the field. This will enable readers to better understand the findings from the literature that are discussed throughout the book; it can also be a starting point for students who are interested in conducting their own comparative research in politics. The chapter concludes with a brief outline of the rest of the book (Section 1.6).

1.2 A continent of democracies

Before proceeding, it is worth taking a moment to consider what (or where) exactly Europe is (see Triandafyllidou and Gropas 2015 for an in-depth discussion on this). Although generally classified as a continent, Europe is not a discrete landmass geographically; it is a relatively small part of what is sometimes called the Eurasian continent. The geographical boundaries of Europe are somewhat arbitrary and have changed over time. Today, a collection of geographic features that include the Ural Mountains, the Caspian Sea, and the Black Sea are generally taken as the dividing line between Europe and Asia. Yet even here there are some exceptions: for example, Cyprus, generally considered to be part of Europe, is geographically in the Middle East since it lies below Turkey and is close to the coasts of Lebanon, Israel, and Syria.

Nor is there a clear-cut political boundary to Europe. Several countries (including Russia and Turkey) straddle Europe and Asia, while several other European countries have territories in other continents (for example, the Canary Islands, off the coast of Morocco, which are ruled by Spain; and Greenland, which geographically is in North America but is part of the Kingdom of Denmark) (see Figure 1.1).

The division between Europe and Asia is sometimes seen as primarily cultural and ethnic, but these differences do not follow clear-cut lines either. In medieval times Europe was often

Figure 1.1 Political map of Europe

Source: © Shutterstock By Peter Hermes Furian.

equated with 'Christendom'. The dividing lines between the Christian and Muslim worlds, however, do not follow a neat geographic pattern. For example, countries such as Bosnia-Herzegovina, Albania, and Kosovo are Muslim-majority countries that are geographically within Europe. In any event, for many contemporary Europeans, religion is not as important an aspect of their identity as it was for earlier generations.

More recently, Europe has begun to be equated with the European Union (EU) in the popular mind. However, it is important to stress that Europe is much bigger than the EU. There are twenty-seven member states of the EU, and at least forty-four countries in Europe (depending on how it is defined). Some of these other countries are involved in negotiations to become members of the EU, while others are not. As this is a book about European politics, not EU politics, we do not restrict our focus to member states of the EU.

Our focus is on European democracies, which enables us to side-step some of these debates on the exact boundaries of Europe. We provide evidence and examples from all the countries that are generally acknowledged to be stable democracies. These include the twenty-seven EU member states, plus the UK, Switzerland, Norway, and Iceland. We also consider consolidating democracies, like Serbia and Bosnia-Herzegovina, in some of the chapters that follow.

While Europe today is largely a continent of democracies, this was not always the case. Just three short decades ago, many countries in the central and eastern part of the continent (what was known as the Eastern Bloc—including East Germany, Poland, Czechoslovakia, Hungary, Romania, Bulgaria, Yugoslavia, and Albania) were governed by communist dictatorships, and some (most notably, for this volume, Latvia, Estonia, and Lithuania) were part of the Soviet Union. The collapse of these dictatorships between 1989 and 1991 led to democratic transitions across the region, and also to the re-unification of Germany and the peaceful break-up of Czechoslovakia into the Czech Republic (now officially known as Czechia) and Slovakia. It also led to a series of bloody wars and ethnic conflicts in the Balkans throughout the 1990s, as Yugoslavia broke up into what are now Serbia, Slovenia, Croatia, Bosnia-Herzegovina, North Macedonia, Montenegro, and Kosovo.

Likewise, many Southern European countries were under authoritarian rule as recently as the 1970s. Spain transitioned to democracy in 1977, following nearly four decades of dictatorship under Francisco Franco. Similarly, Portugal established a new democratic constitution in 1976, following the lengthy dictatorship of Antonio Salazar. Democracy was restored in Greece in 1974 after eight years under a military junta. If we go back a bit further, countries such as West Germany, Italy, and Austria transitioned to democracy after World War II, following an extended period under fascist governments.

Table 1.1 lists all of the countries featured in this book, giving the year of the country's transition to democracy (or its most recent transition to democracy in cases where there has been more than one period of democratic rule). These dates come from the dataset on political regimes compiled by Boix et al. (2013; updated in 2020). While there is no universally agreed upon criteria for distinguishing between democracies and non-democracies (see Gallie 1955), Boix and his collaborators categorize countries as democratic if they meet three criteria: the legislature (parliament) is chosen in free and fair elections; the executive (government) is elected either directly or indirectly and is responsible to voters or the legislature; and a majority of adult males are permitted to vote. By today's standards, a country that did not permit women to vote would hardly be considered democratic; this did not become the norm in European democracies until after World War 1 (and in some cases much later—for instance, women did not have the right to vote in Switzerland until 1971).

The transient nature of democracy in much of Europe until recently can be illustrated by the case of Poland. The country was an early pioneer of a very limited form of democracy as far back as the sixteenth century, under a system of elected kings. After a long period of foreign rule (1795–1918), the end of World War I saw the emergence of a modern form of parliamentary democracy in Poland for the first time. However, this was to prove short-lived. A military coup in 1926 put in place an authoritarian regime, and in 1939 Poland was invaded by Nazi Germany and the Soviet Union. After the war, Poland (along with much of Central and Eastern Europe) became a one-party communist dictatorship under the control of the

Table 1.1 Date of most recent democratic transition in each country

Country	Year	Country	Year
Austria	1946	Latvia	1993
Belgium	1894	Lithuania	1992
Bosnia	1992	Luxembourg	1890
Bulgaria	1990	Malta	1964
Croatia	2000	Netherlands	1897
Cyprus	1976	Norway	1900
Czechia#	1993	Poland	1989
Denmark	1945	Portugal	1976
Estonia	1991	Romania	1991
Finland	1917	Serbia	2006
France	1946	Slovakia#	1993
Germany	1945 (1990)*	Slovenia	1991
Greece	1974	Spain	1977
Hungary	1990	Sweden	1911
Iceland	1918	Switzerland	1848
Ireland	1922	United Kingdom	1885
Italy	1946		

Note: # Democratic as part of Czechoslovakia, 1990–93;
* West Germany was democratic from 1945; Germany reunified in 1990.
Source: Boix et al. 2013 (2020).

Soviet Union. Democracy did not return again until 1989, when Poland was at the forefront of the pro-democracy movements that swept the region. Yet the story does not end there. When the Law and Justice Party came to power in 2015, it implemented a number of changes that undermined the independence of the Constitutional Court and led many observers, including the EU, to conclude that the country's status as a fully-fledged liberal democracy was under threat. Such 'democratic backsliding' has also been apparent in some other post-communist countries, most notably in Hungary (see Chapter 10).

Given that many European countries do not have a long unbroken history of democratic government, the fact that the vast majority of countries in Europe are now functioning, stable democracies is quite remarkable. It also highlights the fact that nothing is permanent, and we should not automatically assume that European democracy will continue to flourish. We are currently in the midst of dramatic political changes in several European countries, whereby traditional party systems and political conventions are being overturned.

1.3 The nature of democracy in Europe

People generally associate 'democracy' with the way politics works in their country and assume that things are broadly similar in other democracies. As a student of European politics, you will quickly realize that this is not the case. The most obvious differences between countries concern the 'rules of the game' that define the roles and composition of the political institutions and the relationship between them. These institutional rules also shape the behaviour of politicians, voters, and other political actors, with the result that politics can operate very differently from one country to another. As the subtitle of this book implies, the differences between European countries and the consequences of these differences are important themes in many of the chapters that follow.

First, however, it is important to introduce some of the features that are shared by most European democracies. You will often find the term 'democracy', when used in a European context, prefixed by one or more of the following adjectives: 'representative', 'liberal', 'parliamentary'. The first of these terms ('representative democracy') concerns the role of citizens in the democratic process and is the focus of Part 1 of this book. The terms 'liberal democracy' and 'parliamentary democracy' relate to how countries are governed, which is the focus of Part 2 of the book. Here, these terms are explained as they apply to the European context.

1.3.1 **Representative democracy**

The countries covered in this book are all representative democracies, meaning that citizens elect representatives to make decisions and pass laws on their behalf. The main alternative to representative democracy is direct democracy (most famously associated with ancient Athens). In contemporary Europe, several countries (most notably Switzerland) incorporate important aspects of direct democracy (see Chapter 6), but all of them rely on representative channels for most day-to-day decisions.

There are differing views on what exactly democratic representation entails. A minimalist view is that representative democracy gives citizens a say in who makes the decisions—but what those decisions are is up to the elected leaders (e.g. Schumpeter 1942). However, most people believe that the representative relationship means something more than this: it should give voters a say in *how* their country is governed, as well as who does the governing (e.g. Powell 2004). According to this view, voters elect representatives to pursue particular policy goals, thereby delivering government by the people (to use the phrase of Abraham Lincoln), albeit indirectly and imperfectly.

If elections do give voters influence over government policy, it is political parties that make this possible. Parties typically set out comprehensive policy programmes before the electorate and voters are encouraged to weigh up these alternative programmes when they cast their ballot. The outcome of the election determines the strength of each party in parliament, its prospects for entering government, and ultimately its ability to shape government policy. Furthermore, parties in government have an incentive to try to honour their electoral commitments, because voters can punish them at the next election if they fail to do so. Without cohesive political parties with coherent and distinct policy programmes, it is hard to see how elections could function as a mechanism for channelling voters' policy preferences in any meaningful way.

There are of course significant differences between countries in how the representative process works, and these are explored throughout this book. To highlight one example, some countries have electoral systems that are designed to identify a clear winner—for example, in the UK 'first-past-the-post' system, there is one winner in each constituency, and usually one party ends up winning a majority of seats nationally and forming a single-party government. In this case, the range of alternatives facing voters at election time tends to be quite limited, and for many people the choice boils down to the two main contenders for government (for the past century, these have been the Labour and Conservative parties). Other countries have electoral systems that are designed to produce a parliament that reflects the diversity of opinion among the population. For example, in the Netherlands, parties are allocated seats in proportion to the share of votes they receive across the whole country. This means that voters in the Netherlands are usually able to vote for a party that closely aligns with their views. However, because elections do not deliver a clear winner, the link between elections and government policy (which is based on compromises between parties) is less direct than it is in the UK.

1.3.2 **Liberal democracy**

If a country has free and fair elections, but the elected government introduces laws that systematically discriminate against particular types of citizens (say, based on their religion or ethnicity), should we still consider it to be a democracy? If we return to the criteria used to categorize democracies in Table 1.1, they say nothing about citizens' rights (beyond the right to vote) or equality. However, an important feature of the countries included in this book is that they are all (to at least some degree) liberal democracies. This means that the power of the government is constrained by constitutional rules, which are upheld by an independent judicial system (see Chapter 10). Constitutions define the workings of the political system, such as the division of power among the executive, legislative and judicial branches of government; how these institutions are elected or appointed; and the rules by which decisions are made. They also list the basic rights of citizens, such as a right to a fair trial, freedom of religion, the right to vote, and free speech. Constitutions therefore impose clearly defined limits on the power of the government, including the protection of minority rights.

While there are important differences among countries in terms of what constitutions say, how they are upheld, and how they are modified, liberalism has been a defining characteristic of democracy in Europe. Yet as we have seen, this tradition is under threat in some states where political leaders have sought to override constitutional protections and weaken the independence of the judiciary. The Hungarian Prime Minister, Victor Orbán, famously argued that he wants to build an 'illiberal democracy', and has been accused of undermining the independence of the media and judiciary and the rights of minorities (e.g. European Parliament 2022). Many populist parties in other European countries share Orbán's vision of illiberal democracy, where the will of the majority can be implemented without constraint.

1.3.3 **Parliamentary democracy**

An important distinction in comparative politics is between presidential and parliamentary systems. Presidential systems, as the name suggests, have a president as the head of government who is directly elected and not responsible to the legislative branch. Parliamentary systems, in contrast, have a prime minister as the head of government who is elected by and responsible to the parliament (see Chapters 7 and 9). There is significant geographic clustering of these two regime types: most notably, presidentialism is dominant in the Americas, and parliamentarism is dominant in Europe.

In parliamentary regimes, unlike in presidential systems, there is no clear separation of power between the executive branch (the government) and the legislative branch (the parliament).

Voters do not directly choose their government: rather, they elect the parliament, which then selects the government. If the government (the prime minister and the cabinet) loses the support of the majority in parliament, it can be replaced; and in many countries the prime minister or cabinet can also dissolve parliament by calling an election. This fusion of powers means that parliamentary systems do not suffer from the gridlock that can occur in presidential systems when different political parties control the executive and legislative branches. This places a lot of power in the hands of the prime minister and cabinet, but only so long as they retain the support of the majority in parliament.

With the exception of Cyprus (a presidential regime), all of the countries covered in this book are either parliamentary systems or hybrids in which parliamentarism is an important element. The hybrid systems include Switzerland, where the parliament selects the executive but cannot remove it; and the various countries that have both a directly elected president and a prime minister responsible to parliament, in a system known as semi-presidentialism (see Chapter 7).

1.4 Common challenges

During much of the 1990s and 2000s, a frequently expressed view among young people in affluent European countries was that politics is boring. That sentiment is much less commonly heard today. The reason is that politics is about conflict between competing interests and goals, and across Europe politics is far more polarized and contentious now than it has been for a long time.

In the years following the end of the Cold War there appeared to be a general consensus among the political elite in many countries, supporting a broadly free market approach to economic policy and (in EU member states) a commitment to regional integration through the EU. Some academic commentators began to speak of a 'party cartel', where genuine competition between opposing parties was replaced with consensus and cooperation among the main parties and the silencing of opposing viewpoints (Katz and Mair 1995). This is certainly not the case anymore. Significant differences have emerged between political parties and groups of voters on issues such as immigration, European integration, and climate change. These developments are usually portrayed in a negative light, particularly when it comes to the rise of so-called 'populist' parties that have emerged in many countries to challenge the traditional (or 'establishment') parties. However, this development has also re-invigorated interest in politics in Europe, as can be seen in cross-country surveys. After years of declining election turnout, there are also some tentative signs of a return to the polls. For many Europeans, politics matters more now than it has done in a long time.

An important focus in this book, covered in Part 3, concerns the recent developments that have challenged the political status quo across Europe and created political convulsions in many countries. While there is a geographic dimension to these issues in that they affect some parts of the continent more than others, they are also common challenges for all European countries. In fact, because of globalization and European integration, there is a growing tendency for citizens from around Europe to be concerned with broadly similar sets of issues at any given time. This is clearly shown by the results of regular surveys known as the Eurobarometer conducted in EU member states, where respondents are asked to list the two most important issues facing their country. In the spring of 2013, in the wake of the financial crisis, unemployment was the most or second most frequently cited issue by respondents in almost every member state. By the autumn of 2015 priorities had shifted across the continent; now immigration came up as one of the top two issues in the majority of member states. Unsurprisingly, health was as one of the top issues for respondents in nearly every member state in the winter of 2020, when Europe was the epicentre of the global Covid-19 pandemic. By the summer of 2022, inflation was top of the agenda for citizens in every member state, with prices rising dramatically because of the economic fallout from the Covid-19 pandemic, and because energy prices rose due to the Russian invasion of Ukraine.

While European countries increasingly face common challenges, the political response to these developments has been extremely varied across the continent. The financial crisis led to the rise of radical left-wing parties in some countries, such as Greece, while in others it contributed to the rise of right-wing nationalist and Eurosceptic parties. Some countries, such as Germany, initially responded to the migrant crisis by opening their borders; others, such as Hungary, built fences. When the Covid-19 pandemic hit the continent, some governments (such as Czechia) intervened quickly by placing unprecedented restrictions on personal freedoms in an effort to contain the spread of the virus, while others (such as Sweden) delayed, attempting to keep the economy going and hoping to build up resistance to the disease in the population. The limits on national sovereignty entailed by membership of the EU lead to increasing opposition in the UK, culminating in the Brexit referendum of 2016; while support for European integration in neighbouring Ireland has never been stronger. These differences are not random political outcomes; they are shaped by the underlying political systems and political cultures in each country. This means that the diverse topics covered in this book, such as political institutions, political behaviour, and contemporary challenges, are deeply interlinked.

1.5 Researching comparative politics

Comparative politics is a field of study that is primarily focused on describing and explaining differences and similarities between countries. As we have seen, many aspects of politics (such as electoral systems, regime types, and party systems) vary between countries, so if we want to understand them, we must compare countries.

One reason for conducting comparative political research is to produce systematic descriptions and categorizations of political systems. Indeed, this is an essential first step before moving on to explanatory research. Political systems are complex, involving various institutions of government, constitutional rules, and organizations such as political parties and interest groups that are involved in shaping government decisions. To usefully compare political systems and identify their salient features, a degree of abstraction is necessary. Comparative political scientists often seek to simplify complex reality using typologies. An example is Lijphart's (2012) classification of democracies along a continuum from 'majoritarian' to 'consensus' systems. The former (countries such as the UK and Greece) are characterized by a concentration of power and a confrontational relationship between government and opposition, while the latter (countries such as Switzerland and the Netherlands) are characterized by the dispersal of political power among multiple parties and political institutions, and politics is a process of negotiation and compromise between them. While such typologies are a very useful abstraction and are widely used by political scientists, they are of course simplifications and do not capture all the subtle differences between countries.

Other research in comparative politics is conducted with a view to theory development—that is, coming up with plausible explanations for particular aspects of politics. Detailed studies of one or two countries can lead researchers to propose an explanation for a particular phenomenon, that can later be tested more widely (see Daalder 1987). To return to some of the examples mentioned in the 'Introduction' to this chapter (Section 1.1): the influential theory of how social cleavages shape party systems proposed by Stein Rokkan (discussed in Chapter 3) was originally inspired by his work on his native Norway and comparisons to neighbouring countries; Ronald Inglehart's theory of value change (see Chapter 4) originated in his observations of France and Germany; while Maurice Duverger's 'laws' regarding the effects of electoral systems on the number of political parties (see Chapter 2) were similarly based on close observation of a small number of countries.

A third goal of comparative political analysis is theory testing. Explanations (in any field of study) involve identifying potential causes and effects, and to test these explanations it is necessary to compare. However, the approach to hypothesis testing in comparative politics is often quite different from other disciplines because the causal relationships under investigation cannot be tested using experiments. In an experiment, the causal factor being tested (e.g. a medical treatment) is administered randomly to some cases and not to others. Random assignment ensures that there are no systematic differences between the two groups being compared, so if the researcher observes different outcomes in the two groups, this can be attributed to the effect of the treatment that was administered.

When countries are the focus of analysis, as is the case in comparative politics, experimental manipulation is simply not possible (we cannot, for example, randomly assign different political institutions to different countries). So how do we know that an observed relationship between two things (e.g. the type of electoral system and the number of parties) is not due to some other difference between the countries we are comparing—what is often called a 'confounding variable'? This is a significant problem for explanatory research in comparative politics. A number of strategies are available to mitigate this problem, although the possibility that observed relationships are spurious is never entirely eliminated.

One approach to the problem is known as the 'most similar systems' design. Here, the researcher aims to reduce the potential for spurious relationships by carefully selecting countries that are as similar as possible, while differing with respect to the explanatory factor under investigation. For example, a recent collection of articles (see Kuhlmann et al. 2021) sought to test a hypothesis about how administrative culture shaped the way governments responded to the Covid-19 pandemic. They did this by way of a series of comparisons of similar countries (including Italy and Spain; Belgium and the Netherlands; France, Germany and Sweden; Australia and New Zealand; Hungary and Poland; and South Korea and Japan). By observing consistent patterns of association between the variables of interest (i.e. the type of administrative culture and the nature of the government response to the pandemic) when comparing countries that are similar to one another in many other relevant respects, the authors were able to tentatively conclude that the evidence supports the hypothesis.

Administrative culture (the explanatory factor in the previous example) is not a concept that can be easily quantified, which means that it is difficult to study in more than a handful of countries at a time. However, other factors that might be studied are quantifiable, making it possible for the researcher to examine many countries at once, without going into any great detail on any of them. Continuing with the question of how governments responded to Covid-19, a number of studies carried out statistical analyses using data on all European democracies to try to explain variation in government responses to the pandemic with reference to factors such as government ideology, institutional checks and balances, and public trust in government (e.g. Engler et al. 2021; Toshkov et al. 2022). Expanding the case selection to all European democracies means that the researchers must take account of other differences between the countries that might be driving the results—for example, the number of hospital beds per capita. This type of analysis usually employs statistical techniques to control for such potentially 'confounding' variables.

Large-scale comparative studies such as these have become increasingly common due to the availability of reliable cross-national datasets on various aspects of politics. Prominent examples relevant to comparative European politics include the European Values Survey and the Eurobarometer, which are large-scale opinion surveys regularly carried out across Europe; the Manifesto Project and the Comparative Agendas Project, which collect data on the policy focus of political actors such as parties, parliaments, and the media across countries and over time; the Representative Democracy Data Archive (REPDEM), which collects comparative data on governments, parliaments, and parties across Europe; and the Comparative Constitutions Project, which measures various aspects of constitutions in countries from around the world.

The chapters in this book use the methods of comparative politics to describe and explain the topic at hand. A number of features are also included to help you understand how the study of comparative politics works. This will be of particular benefit if you plan to conduct your own comparative case study as part of your programme of study. The 'Thinking comparatively' box at the end of each chapter describes a relevant piece of research that has been published on the topic, explaining how it was conducted and what the findings were. These examples are designed to help you understand how to evaluate theories against the empirical evidence. Each chapter also includes one or more 'Over to you' boxes, which include suggestions for comparisons that you can carry out yourself to test some of the arguments discussed in the chapter, along with advice on how to go about it (for instance, using some of the comparative datasets described previously). The list of discussion questions at the end of each chapter are designed to help you to assess and apply your understanding of the topic, while the further reading list highlights some of the key writings on each topic.

1.6 Outline of the book

This book provides an introduction to contemporary politics in European democracies. It is broad in scope, both in terms of the topics and the countries covered. It is arranged thematically: each chapter addresses a particular topic and draws on relevant examples from the full range of established European democracies. Each chapter is written by leading scholars who have conducted extensive research on their specific topic.

The book is divided into three parts. The first part deals with the most fundamental element of democratic politics: elections and representation. The central concern of this section is how citizens, either directly or through their representatives, influence political outcomes. It sets out the main practices of how elections work (Chapter 2) and examines the role and behaviour of the main participants in electoral politics, namely political parties and voters (Chapters 3, 4, and 5). It also considers democratic mechanisms that do not rely on the election of representatives, such as referendums and citizens assemblies (Chapter 6). A key focus of this section is not only variation across countries, but also how practices have evolved over time.

The second part turns to what happens after elections have been held, focusing on the institutions and processes of government. Democracies are characterized by a horizontal and vertical division of political power. The horizontal dimension relates to the different branches of central government: the executive branch (Chapters 7 and 8); the legislative branch (Chapter 9); and the judicial branch (Chapter 10). The vertical dimension concerns the different levels of government: central, regional, and local government (Chapter 11); and, in the EU context, the supranational level (Chapter 12). The way in which power is divided among political institutions and levels of government has important implications for how decisions are made and to whose benefit. Furthermore, the degree to which power is centralized or dispersed can affect the robustness of a democratic system.

The third and final section addresses some of the main contemporary problems facing all or most European countries. As we have seen, European countries increasingly must tackle common challenges, either together or individually. This section describes and explains these challenges, examining the deeper structural issues at stake, the political consequences of these developments, and how they have played out across different countries. The section begins by examining economic challenges (including the financial crisis and the impact of Covid-19) (Chapter 13); migration, including the recent refugee crises following the wars in Syria and Ukraine (Chapter 14); climate change, and its impact on policies and politics (Chapter 15); defence and security, including the consequences of the war in Ukraine (Chapter 16); the challenge posed by European integration to traditional models of democracy (Chapter 17); and the growth of radical and populist parties, some of whom constitute a threat to the liberal democratic order (Chapter 18).

It is important to stress that this is a book about the politics of European countries, not a book about the EU. Yet it is impossible to fully understand domestic politics in these countries without considering the EU dimension. There are two chapters in the book specifically on the EU (Chapter 12, which examines how national governments work together at the EU level, and Chapter 17, which assesses the consequences of European integration for the quality of democracy). The impact of the EU on political behaviour, political institutions, and government policies is also examined in many other chapters throughout the book. While the EU dimension is clearly very important (at least for countries that are members of that organization), democratic politics in Europe is still played out primarily at the national level, and national governments remain the primary locus of political power.

Guide to further reading

Mair, P. (ed.) (1990), *The West European Party System* (Oxford: Oxford University Press).

A collection of some of the seminal texts on comparative European politics from leading early figures in the field, including Stein Rokkan, Maurice Duverger, Giovani Sartori, Ronald Inglehart, Otto Kirchheimer, and Hans Daalder.

Dalton, R. J., Farrell, D. M. et al. (2011), *Political Parties and Democratic Linkage: How Parties Organize Democracy* (Oxford: Oxford University Press).

This book systematically examines the role that parties play in representative democracies. Drawing on comparative data on parties and voters, the authors go through each link in the chain connecting voters and government policy, highlighting the critical role played by political parties at each step.

Linz, J. J. and Stepan, A. (1996), *Problems of Democratic Transition and Consolidation: Southern Europe, South America, and Post-Communist Europe* (Baltimore: John Hopkins University Press).

Using the tools of comparative politics, this book seeks to explain the success or otherwise of transitions to democracy that occurred from the 1970s to the 1990s. It includes detailed case studies of democratic transitions in a number of European countries, including Spain, Portugal, Greece, Poland, Bulgaria, Romania, Estonia, and Latvia.

Peters, B. G. (2013), *Strategies for Comparative Research in Political Science* (Basingstoke: Palgrave Macmillan).

This is an accessible text on the theory and practicalities of conducting research in comparative politics. It explains the main goals of comparative research, the logic underpinning the methods of comparative politics, and takes the reader through the key decisions in designing a comparative research project.

References

Boix, C., Miller, M. et al. (2013), 'A complete data set of political regimes', 1800–2007. *Comparative Political Studies*, 46(12): 1523–54.

Calhoun, C. (2003), 'European studies: Always already there and still in formation', *Comparative European Politics*, 1: 5–20.

Daalder, H. (1987), 'Countries in comparative European politics', *European Journal of Political Research*, 15(1): 3–21.

Duverger, M. (1954), *Political Parties: Their Organization and Activity in the Modern State* (London: Methuen Press).

Engler S., Brunner, P. et al. (2021), 'Democracy in times of the pandemic: Explaining the variation of COVID-19 policies across European democracies', *West European Politics*, 44(5–6): 1077–102.

European Parliament (2022), Press Release: 'MEPs: Hungary can no longer be considered a full democracy', available at https://www.europarl.europa.eu/news/en/press-room/20220909IPR40137/meps-hungary-can-no-longer-be-considered-a-full-democracy

Gallie, W. B. (1955), 'Essentially contested concepts', *Proceedings of the Aristotelian Society*, 56: 167–98.

Inglehart, R. (1977), *The Silent Revolution: Changing Values and Political Styles among Western Publics* (Princeton, NJ: Princeton University Press).

Katz, R. S. and Mair, P. (1995), 'Changing models of party organization and party democracy: The emergence of the cartel party', *Party Politics*, 1(1): 5–28.

Kuhlmann, S., Bouckaert, G. et al. (2021), 'Opportunity management of the COVID-19 pandemic: Testing the crisis from a global perspective', *International Review of Administrative Sciences*, 87(3): 497–517.

Lijphart, A. (2012), *Patterns of Democracy: Government Forms and Performance in Thirty-Six Countries* (New Haven, CT: Yale University Press).

Lijphart, A. (1968), 'Typologies of democratic systems'. *Comparative Political Studies*, 1(1): 3–44.

Powell Jr, G. B. (2004), 'Political representation in comparative politics', *Annual Review of Political Science*, 7: 273–96.

Rokkan S. (1970), *Citizens, Elections, Parties: Approaches to the Comparative Study of The Processes of Development* (Oslo: Universitetsforlaget).

Schumpeter, J. A. (1942), *Capitalism, Socialism and Democracy* (New York: Harper and Brothers).

Toshkov, D., Carroll, B. et al. (2022), 'Government capacity, societal trust or party preferences: what accounts for the variety of national policy responses to the COVID-19 pandemic in Europe?', *Journal of European Public Policy*, 29(7): 1009–28.

Triandafyllidou, A. and Gropas, R. (2015), *What Is Europe?* (London: Palgrave Macmillan).

Part 1

Democratic Representation

2 Electoral Systems

JEAN-BENOIT PILET AND ALAN RENWICK

2.1 Introduction

Electoral systems lie at the heart of democratic politics. Modern democracies are built on the logic of representation. That is, the processes of devising, scrutinizing, and choosing between policy alternatives are carried out for the most part not by voters themselves, but by their representatives. Even when voters do become directly involved—as in referendums—agendas and debates are commonly tightly framed by politicians. In democracies, representatives are chosen by means of elections. And the rules governing those elections—the electoral systems—can have profound effects upon outcomes.

So it is crucial to understand what these rules are: what varieties of electoral system can exist. The rules of elections can encompass a huge variety of elements—from who can vote, who can stand for election, and how campaigns are conducted all the way down to the procedures for running a polling station and counting the votes. We cannot address all of these matters here, so we focus on what have been described as the three main dimensions of electoral systems (Farrell 2011): the electoral formula, which defines how votes are translated into seats; districts and district magnitude, which concerns the division of a country into electoral districts and the number of seats in each district; and ballot structure, which shapes the nature of the choice that voters are presented with and how votes are cast. These three dimensions are key in determining how popular wishes are translated into actual political representation.

In addition to describing the key features of electoral systems, we also examine what electoral systems are used today in democracies across Europe. There is tremendous variation, but there are also some clear patterns. Notably, most European democracies employ proportional electoral systems—systems that seek to distribute seats in the legislature across political parties in proportion to the votes that those parties have won. But they often use limited forms of proportional representation, meaning that the degree of proportionality is not necessarily very high and large parties tend to gain some advantage. Another pattern is that electoral systems are becoming increasingly 'personalized': voters have more say than they used to over not just how many seats each party wins, but also which individual candidates fill these seats.

It is important to understand how different electoral systems operate and what systems are used in different places because electoral systems themselves matter: they have effects on political outcomes. These effects are explored towards the end of the chapter (Section 2.5). We begin that section by looking at the effects of the electoral system on the party system: on the distribution of power across political parties. One of the most famous findings in all of political science holds that more proportional systems allow more political parties to prosper. We look at the mechanisms through which this happens and assess the evidence on it. We also consider implications for the nature of government and accountability. Then we examine how electoral systems affect the distribution of power *within* political parties: the degree to which it is parties as collective entities that matter or the individual candidates and politicians within them. This too has profound implications for how democracies operate, particularly for the nature of the relationship between voters and their representatives.

2.2 Electoral formula

The electoral formula is the core of any electoral system. It is the mechanism through which votes are counted and then translated into seats. It determines the model of democracy that lies behind the electoral system and has major effects on politics, not least on the structure of competition among parties and politicians. There are two main families of electoral formulas and therefore of electoral systems: majoritarian and proportional. Beyond these, some systems try to combine aspects of both. We will describe each category in turn.

Majoritarian systems are designed to identify a winner. The logic is straightforward. Voters cast their votes. These votes are counted. A winner is identified and gains whatever is to be allocated—whether that is a seat in the legislature, several seats, or an office such as the presidency.

The simplest example of this logic is the Single-Member Plurality (SMP) electoral system used for general elections in the United Kingdom. Votes are counted in each of 650 constituencies across the country; the candidate with the most votes in each constituency is elected to the House of Commons. There is no minimum number of votes to obtain, or minimum gap between the first and the other candidates running. As its nickname suggests, the system follows a pure first-past-the-post logic.

Other majoritarian systems share the logic of identifying a winner, but use different—often more complex—mechanisms to do so. One argument against SMP is that a candidate could be elected with (sometimes much) less than 50% of the votes. For example, in the UK general elections in 2019, Olivia Blake (Labour) was elected with just 34.9% of the valid votes in her district of Sheffield Hallam: 65.1% of the votes were cast for candidates other than the one eventually sent to Westminster. To avoid such outcomes, several majority electoral systems involve multiple rounds of voting. A minimum threshold for victory is set—most often, 50% of the votes. If a candidate exceeds this threshold in the first round, they are elected. If not, a second round is organized with fewer candidates to ensure that the elected candidates obtain an absolute majority or something close to it. Such 'run-off' systems are used for legislative elections in France and presidential elections in France, Austria, Poland, Portugal, and Romania.

To avoid multiple election rounds while ensuring the winning candidate has wide support, some countries use the Alternative Vote (AV) system. Voters rank the candidates in order of preference (see the ballot paper for the presidential elections in Ireland in Figure 2.1b). If no candidate exceeds 50% of first preferences, the candidate with the fewest votes is eliminated and these votes are transferred to the candidates ranked second on those ballot papers. This continues until a candidate reaches an absolute majority of votes. In Europe, AV is used at the national level only for presidential elections in Ireland (as well as for by-elections for both chambers of the Irish Parliament, the Dáil and the Seanad).

The second main family of electoral formulas are proportional systems. Here, the logic is not to identify a winner, but to give each political party or other group a share of the seats in proportion to its share of the votes. Thus, a party winning 25% of the votes should ideally obtain 25% of the seats. Full proportionality is, however, almost impossible to achieve: if, for example, there are five seats to allocate, 25% of the votes cannot translate into 25% of the seats. Several arithmetic methods can be used to approximate proportionality, each following a slightly different logic.

The family of proportional systems itself divides into two categories: list proportional representation (list PR) and Single Transferable Vote (STV). List PR structures electoral competition among lists of candidates, typically representing different political parties. Votes are counted for each list and the share of votes is translated into a share of seats on the basis of an arithmetic formula. An example of this is the largest remainder formula with the Hare quota. The first step is to calculate the quota, which is the total number of valid votes divided by the

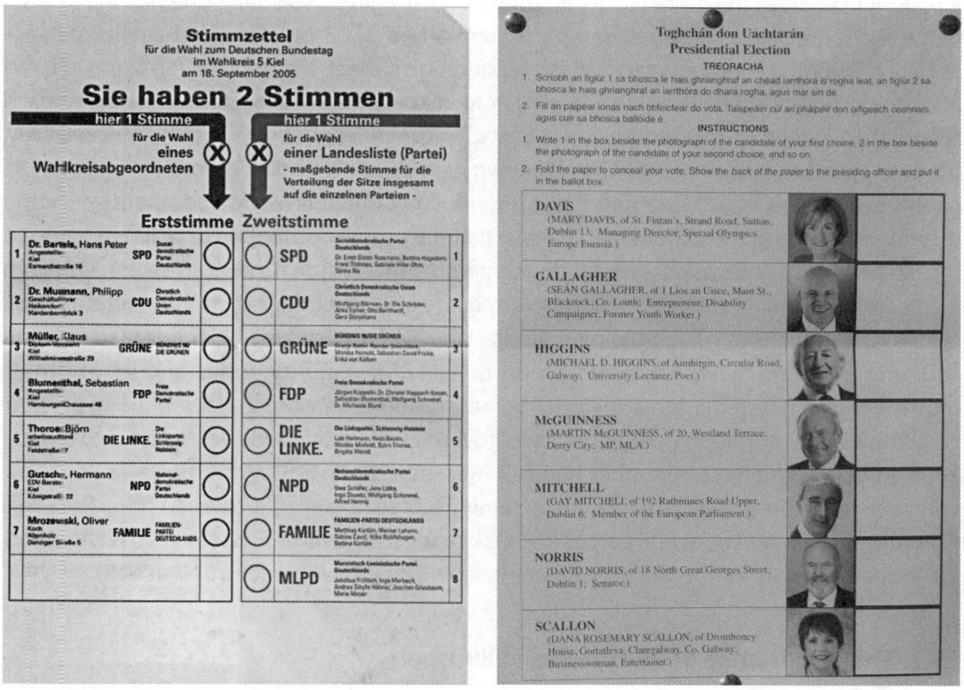

Figure 2.1a Example ballot papers from federal elections in Germany (left), using a mixed-member proportional system; and **2.1b** presidential elections in Ireland (right), using the alternative vote

Source: Bundestagswahl2005_stimmzettel_small.jpg by Schneelocke, Public domain, via Wikimedia Commons; PA Images/Alamy Stock Photo.

number of seats available. Each list (i.e. party) initially receives as many seats as the number of times it has passed the quota: if the quota is 1,000, for example, a list with 5,500 votes get five seats. Then the remainder votes for each party are ranked. Seats that remain to be allocated are distributed to the parties with the largest remainders until all seats are gone.

The other proportional system is STV, used for legislative elections in Ireland and Malta. Voters rank candidates in order of preference (as under AV—see previous, and Figure 2.1b). A quota is calculated (most frequently the Droop quota, which is calculated as follows: quota = (votes/(seats + 1)) + 1). First preferences are counted first, and candidates above the quota are elected. If seats remain to be allocated, surplus votes from candidates already elected are transferred to the second preferences expressed on the ballots. Votes received by last-placed candidates are also transferred. This continues until all seats have been allocated. STV is very similar to AV except in two ways. First, STV works with multimember districts, whereas AV normally uses single-member districts. Second, the quota that a candidate must pass to get elected is 50% of the votes under AV, but lower than that under STV. As a consequence, STV tends to produce more proportional results.

Majoritarian and proportional systems have different logics: identifying a winner versus distributing seats proportionally. These logics have both merits and limitations, as we discuss later (see Section 2.2.1). Some have sought to combine the advantages of both to obtain 'the best of both worlds' (Shugart and Wattenberg 2001; Linhart et al. 2019), leading to the development of mixed electoral systems. Such systems divide seats into two blocs, one allocated following a majoritarian logic, the other using PR. Voters typically have two votes—one relating to each of the two blocs of seats (see the example of Germany in Box 2.1 and the German ballot paper in Figure 2.1a). These systems vary widely, depending on which majoritarian (SMP, run-off, AV) and which PR (list PR, STV) formula is used, how many seats are allocated according to each formula, and whether the two blocs are linked or run independently. In Lithuania and Italy, the two parts are independent (what is known as a 'parallel' mixed system). In Germany, by contrast, as well as in Scotland and Wales, the PR component is used to compensate for the disproportionality of the majoritarian part, so that the overall distribution of seats is as close to the distribution of votes as possible (a 'mixed-member proportional', or MMP, system)—though a process of reform was under way in Germany at the time of writing (Michl and Mittrop 2023).

Finally, another way of combining majoritarian and proportional logics adopted in some countries is the so-called reinforced proportionality (or majority bonus) model. This runs mostly like list PR systems, but a 'majority bonus' is added to ensure that the winning party or coalition obtains a solid majority of seats to govern alone. Italy used such a system between 2005 and 2017: the lower chamber had 617 members; the party or coalition winning most votes was awarded 340 seats, while the remaining 277 seats were allocated to other lists. This system was opposed by several parties and was changed to a mixed system in 2017. A majority bonus also exists for the Greek parliament, as will be explained in further detail.

2.2.1 **The dominance of PR systems in Europe**

Until the late nineteenth century, all electoral systems followed some version of the majoritarian logic: elections focused on choosing individuals rather than representing groups, and these systems offered the natural way of doing that. Majoritarian systems also suited electoral competition between two dominant factions, as operated in most European countries. Yet, over the course of the nineteenth century, two evolutions put pressure on majoritarian systems. First, political parties rose in importance and ties between individual parliamentarians belonging to the same parties strengthened. The lack of any clear connection between the share of votes that a party won and their shares of the seats in legislatures began to cause concern. Second, electoral competition between two camps (often conservatives and liberals) was challenged by the emergence of a third actor: workers' parties (Blais et al. 2005). A proportional logic was better suited to three-party competition. These evolutions prompted various mathematicians and others to devise systems of proportional representation. Most democracies adopted proportional systems for elections to their legislatures in the early decades of the twentieth century, and as new democracies emerged—particularly following the collapse of communism in Eastern Europe in 1989—they mostly pursued the same path. Proportional systems made electoral outcomes far less uncertain. Majoritarian systems survived for the most part only where just a few large parties dominated (on the history and dynamics of electoral system choice see Colomer 2004; Renwick 2010).

As a result of this history, most of Europe's electoral systems are proportional. Majoritarian systems are still used in some large democracies around the globe (India, the USA, Canada, and Australia), but they are rare in Europe, used for legislative elections today only in France and the United Kingdom. As Table 2.1 shows, proportional systems are used in twenty-six of the thirty-one countries that we cover. The great majority of these are

Table 2.1 Electoral systems in national legislative elections in Europe today (2023)

Majoritarian	Intermediate	Proportional	
SMP	**Parallel mixed systems**	**List PR**	**MMP**
United Kingdom	Hungary	Austria	Germany
	Lithuania	Belgium	
Two-round	Italy	Bulgaria	**STV**
France		Croatia	Ireland
	Reinforced PR	Cyprus	Malta
	Greece	Czechia	
	(except May 2023)	Denmark	
		Estonia	
		Finland	
		Iceland	
		Latvia	
		Luxembourg	
		Netherlands	
		Norway	
		Poland	
		Portugal	
		Romania	
		Slovakia	
		Slovenia	
		Spain	
		Sweden	
		Switzerland	

straightforward list systems, but two (Ireland and Malta) use STV, and Germany uses MMP. The remaining four countries use intermediate systems: either parallel mixed systems or so-called reinforced PR.

The dominance of proportional systems does not mean that most European countries have opted for maximally inclusive rules. Rather, they have tried to balance inclusiveness against some containment of the party system. In many cases, what we observe is close to what Carey and Hix called 'limited PR' (Carey and Hix 2011). Such systems sacrifice pure proportionality to promote government stability and accountability. They introduce mechanisms that limit the access of new parties to parliamentary representation in order to avoid over-fragmentation of the party system. The intermediate systems described above do that very clearly. But list PR systems may also incorporate mechanisms to limit proportionality. The two main ones are the division of the country into constituencies of lower district magnitude (fewer than eight to ten seats) and electoral thresholds (see Section 2.3). Most European countries use one or both of these.

2.3 Districts and district magnitude

The second main dimension of the electoral system is the organization of the territory into districts. This element links directly to the logic of territorial representation: the idea that members of parliament represent the nation as a whole, but also the residents of their district in particular.

Some countries in fact allocate all seats in the legislature in just one nationwide district. In the Netherlands and Slovakia, all 150 members of parliament (MPs) are elected this way. But such territorial organization is rare. All other European countries, and the vast majority of countries around the globe, divide their territory into electoral districts that may vary in number, size, shape, and the number of seats to be allocated. The number of seats allocated in each district is crucial for how the system works, and is known as district magnitude (DM).

Almost all majoritarian systems—plurality, run-off, or AV—function with single-member districts, each electing just one representative. The majoritarian logic may be combined with multimember districts, but this is rare. In the 'block vote' system, for instance, voters cast as many votes as there are seats to be allocated and the seats are allocated to those candidates who obtain most votes. This system is used for some local elections in the United Kingdom, where it often allows one party to win all the seats with much less than half of the vote.

Proportional systems, by contrast, require multimember districts: you cannot distribute a single seat proportionally among parties. DMs tend to vary widely both across and within countries. Only Slovenia requires all its multimember districts to be the same size (DM = 11). By contrast, Spain has some districts that send two or three MPs to parliament, while the largest districts, of Barcelona and Madrid, elect thirty-two and thirty-seven respectively.

DM is the main element, alongside the electoral formula itself, that drives an electoral system's effective proportionality. Full proportionality requires large districts. If only a few seats are to be allocated, they cannot be divided among many parties. Spain is the best example: the country is divided into fifty districts, in nineteen of which there are four or fewer seats available. For a long time this allowed the two main parties—the conservative *Partido Popular* and the Spanish Socialist Workers' Party (*PSOE*)—to dominate, capturing the vast majority of the seats with 30 to 40% of the vote each. The largest party could hope to win an absolute majority of the seats with about 40% of the votes. A third party can win a seat in a three-seat district only by securing at least a third of the vote share of the largest party. By contrast, as noted previously, the Netherlands and Slovakia each use a single nationwide constituency electing 150 members of parliament. This allows many parties to gain representation: there were seventeen of them in the Netherlands in 2020, and six in Slovakia in 2020.

As Figure 2.2 shows, low-DM PR is common in Europe. Average DM is below eight—the limit set by Carey and Hix (2011) to define low-magnitude PR—in Austria, Bulgaria, Ireland, Malta Romania, and Spain.

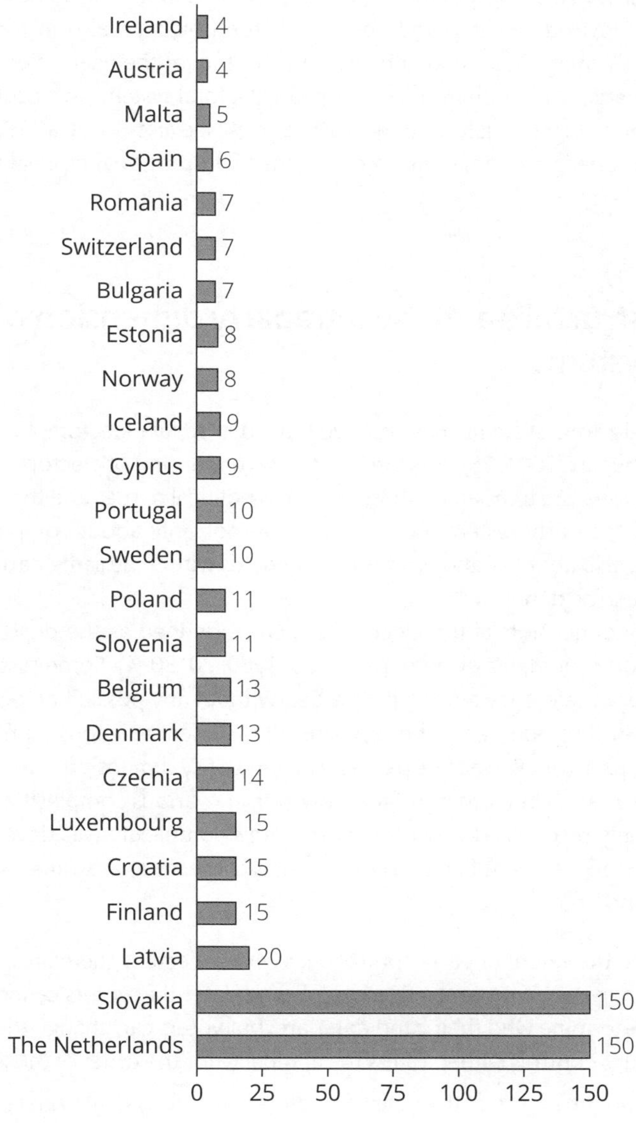

Figure 2.2 Mean district magnitude in list PR countries across Europe

Source: Data from Electoral System Changes in Europe (ESCE) project, at http://www.electoralsystemchanges.eu/.

The other mechanism of limited PR—electoral thresholds—is also widely used across European countries using list PR. A threshold is a percentage of the vote that a party must obtain—either in a district or across the country as a whole—in order to be eligible to receive seats. Such thresholds have often been introduced in list PR countries over recent decades. In 1951, just three countries (of fourteen European democracies using list PR at the time) had an electoral threshold. Only the Netherlands had a national-level threshold, but, at 1%, later lowered further to 0.67%, this can almost be considered token. By 2023, eighteen of twenty-four European democracies using list PR employed some kind of threshold (see Figure 2.3). In particular, all the former communist countries incorporated an electoral threshold in their systems, many of them adopting a 5% threshold (including Poland, Czechia, Estonia, Latvia, Slovakia, Croatia, and Romania). Thresholds are also in use in mixed systems such as in Germany, Italy, and Lithuania. In short, over the years, electoral thresholds moved from a marginal phenomenon in European electoral systems to a central component of electoral democracy, especially in 'new' democracies (see also Bol et al. 2015). This further confirms that Europe is predominantly a continent of proportional representation, but of a limited kind.

2.4 **Ballot structure and the intraparty dimension of electoral systems**

The aspects of electoral systems that we have looked at so far—electoral formula and DM—relate to what Shugart (2001: 25) calls the 'interparty' dimension of electoral systems. That is, they affect how votes are translated into seats across political parties and thereby help define the structure of the party system. But elections are not only about competition between parties. They are also about relations among candidates within the same party: what Shugart names the 'intraparty' dimension.

The intraparty dimension of the electoral system is defined as the degree to which the system focuses on candidates or on parties (Katz 1980: 20, 30–4). Some systems only allow voters to express a preference among the parties, without any possibility to select preferred candidates within these parties. Other systems allow voters to choose among candidates within the same party or even across parties. The intraparty dimension is thus fairly straightforward on the surface. Under that surface, however, are various complexities.

The most widely recognized way of organizing this complexity was developed by Carey and Shugart (1995). They identified two main aspects of the intraparty dimension, which they labelled Ballot and Vote:

- *Ballot* refers to the extent of party control over who is elected. There are three possibilities: parties can present a fixed set of candidates that voters cannot disturb; parties can determine who their candidates are, but voters can change the order of these; or parties control neither access to candidacy nor the order of those candidates.
- *Vote* focuses on the nature of the vote that voters can cast: systems where voters can cast only a vote for a party; those where they can vote for multiple candidates; and those where they can vote only for a single candidate or sub-party list.

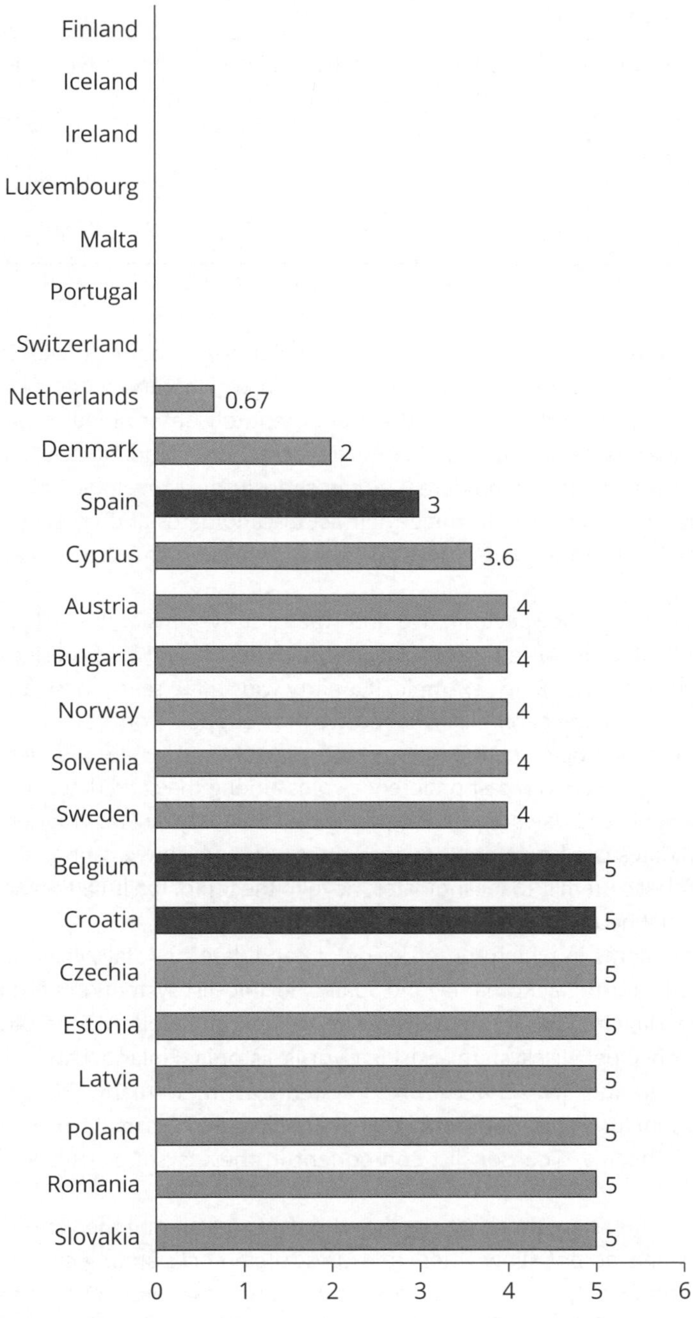

Figure 2.3 Electoral thresholds in list PR countries across Europe (as % of valid votes)

Note: Countries at the top have no legal threshold. In Belgium, Croatia, and Spain (the dark-shaded columns), legal thresholds are applied at district level rather than the national level, which makes it easier for smaller parties to win some seats. In Norway and Iceland, the threshold only applies for compensatory seats (second tier)

Source: Data from Electoral System Changes in Europe (ESCE) project at http://www.electoralsystemchanges.eu/. Figure accurate as of 2023.

Table 2.2 Electoral systems and intraparty candidate ordering

Order determined entirely by parties	Order determined partly by parties and partly by voters	Order determined entirely by voters
Single-Member Plurality (SMP)	Flexible-list PR	Open-list PR
Two-round systems		Single Transferable Vote (STV)
AV		
Closed-list PR		

The crucial element of the *Ballot* dimension in European democracies is the degree to which parties or voters determine the order in which candidates get elected (see Table 2.2). Among the systems where the order is entirely determined by parties, we find most majoritarian systems, such as SMP. Parties select one candidate per district. Voters for that party have no other candidate they can choose. The same logic holds for so-called 'closed-list' systems. Parties determine their list of candidates and voters cannot disturb this. If the party wins three seats, these go to the three candidates ranked highest on the list by the party.

At the other end of the spectrum, we find 'open-list' systems and STV. Parties again select their candidates, but voters have full capacity to decide which of these candidates are elected. Under open-list PR, for example, if a party wins three seats, these are filled by the three candidates from the party's list who receive most support from voters.

Between these two logics are the intermediate 'flexible-list' systems. Parties again put up lists of candidates. Voters can cast preference votes among the candidates. These votes can alter the ranking of candidates defined by parties, but the party rankings matter too. The final order of candidates can be determined in various ways, which we cannot set out in detail here. The simplest system is that candidates move to the top of the list if they secure support from at least a defined proportion of the party's voters.

Closed-list systems in which the ordering of candidates is totally fixed by parties are found in Croatia, Portugal, Romania, and Spain. Flexible-list systems are found in Austria, Belgium, Bulgaria, Czechia, Denmark, Greece, Iceland, the Netherlands, Norway, Slovakia, and Sweden. Open-list systems exist in Cyprus, Estonia, Finland, Latvia, Luxembourg, Poland, Slovenia, and Switzerland. Mixed systems as in Germany, Hungary, Italy, and Lithuania, also include a list component. Lists are closed in Germany, Hungary, and Italy, and open in Lithuania. The non-list component in these systems uses Single-Member Plurality.

On the *Vote* dimension, there are significant differences among the various list systems. Closed-list systems do not allow voters to express preferences among candidates at all. In some open- and flexible-list systems, voters can express one preference for a single candidate (e.g. Austria, Bulgaria, Denmark, Poland, the Netherlands, Slovenia, and Sweden), while in others, voters can indicate several preferences among the candidates on their chosen party's list (e.g. Belgium, Cyprus, Czechia, Iceland, Latvia, Norway, and Slovakia). In Luxembourg and Switzerland, voters can mark as many preferences for candidates as there are seats to be filled, and these preferences can be distributed across different lists (the '*panachage*' system).

Box 2.1 Six European electoral systems

The British electoral system (SMP): the United Kingdom's House of Commons is composed of 650 members. They are all elected in single-member districts (constituencies). The election in each district is won by simple plurality: voters cast a single vote for a single candidate by placing an X next to that candidate's name on the ballot paper; the candidate with the most votes wins.

The French electoral system (majority run-off): the French *Assemblée nationale* has 577 members. They are all elected in single-member districts using a majority run-off system with two rounds of voting. At the first round, voters can cast a single vote for a single candidate by placing a paper ballot with their preferred candidate's name in the ballot box. A candidate is elected if they exceed 50% of the valid votes. If no candidate meets that threshold, a second round is held two weeks later. Only candidates who won the votes of at least 12.5% of all registered voters in the district can run. In most districts, only two candidates run, though there could be three or four in a few districts. Voters again cast a vote for their preferred candidate. The candidate with the most votes wins.

The Dutch electoral system (flexible-list PR): the Dutch *Tweede Kamer* has 150 members, all elected in a single nationwide district. Parties and other groups present lists of candidates. Voters cast a vote for one candidate on one list. Each list securing at least 0.67% of all valid votes wins seats. First, each list receives as many seats as the times it has reached the Hare quota (= votes/seats). The remaining seats are then distributed via the highest averages method.

Seats are then allocated to candidates within lists through a two-step process. First, all candidates whose votes equal or exceed a quarter of the Hare quota are identified. If the number of candidates thereby selected does not exceed the number of seats allocated to the party, all these candidates are elected, and any remaining seats are allocated via list order. If the number of candidates identified at the first step does exceed the number of seats allocated to the party, the candidates with the highest numbers of votes are elected.

The Irish electoral system (STV): the Irish *Dáil* has 160 members, all elected by STV in multimember districts allocating three to five seats. Voters cast a vote by ranking candidates on the ballot from their most to their least preferred (by marking numbers from 1 to as many candidates as they want to differentiate). Valid votes are counted, and a quota is set; quota = (votes/(seats + 1)) + 1. Initially only first preferences are counted. Candidates who reach the quota are elected. If a candidate has more first-preference votes than the quota, surplus votes are transferred to the remaining candidates following the order of preferences marked by voters on their ballot paper. If seats remain to be filled, the candidates with fewest first-preference votes are eliminated and their votes are transferred to the remaining candidates following the order of preferences marked by voters. The procedure of transferring votes continues until all seats for the district are allocated.

The German electoral system (MMP system): the German *Bundestag* has at least 598 members. Of these, 299 are elected in single-member districts under plurality (see the UK system). The other 299 are allocated under list PR in multimember districts corresponding to the states (*Länder*). Each voter has two votes: one for a candidate in a single-member district and one for a closed list at the *Land* level (see Figure 2.1a). Voters are free to combine any candidate with any party. List PR seats are distributed to maximize overall proportionality, by compensating for disproportionalities in the single-member district seats—though only parties with at least 5% of the vote or three single-member district seats nationwide are entitled to receive seats through the party lists. In each *Land*, each party's share of all the seats is calculated on the basis of the list votes using a PR method (*Sainte-Lagüe*). If a party is entitled to more seats than it has obtained through the single-member districts, its remaining seats are filled by the candidates on its list. If a party is entitled to fewer seats than it obtained through the single-member districts, it is allowed to keep the additional seats and the overall size of the *Bundestag* is increased.

(continued...)

This latter provision has led to substantial inflation in the size of the Bundestag in recent years: to 736 seats following the 2021 elections. That has spurred pressure for change, and reforms were in progress at the time of writing in 2023 (Michl and Mittrop 2023).

The Greek electoral system (reinforced proportionality): the Greek Parliament has 300 members. Elections are held under list PR in fifty-nine multimember districts. Voters cast their vote by marking between one and four candidates (depending on DM) from their preferred list. Seats are allocated proportionally in each district. In addition, the largest party receives a bonus of seats—the name 'reinforced proportionality' means not that proportionality is enhanced, but that governments are granted additional legislative strength. Up to the election of 2019, this bonus was worth fifty seats. The bonus was abolished prior to the elections of May 2023, such that this election was contest under a pure proportional system. But a further reform came into force in time for the June 2023 election. The bonus was restored, its size this time varying between twenty and fifty seats depending of the vote share of the largest party.

Turning to non-list systems, in the STV cases (Ireland and Malta), voters can mark and order preferences for as many candidates as they want, and only these preferences determine who is elected. Parties have no control beyond selecting candidates to be listed on the ballot paper. In the majoritarian countries (France and the UK), voters vote for a candidate, not a list. But they have no intraparty choice, as each party presents only one candidate per district.

Recent decades have seen a marked trend towards greater personalization of electoral systems across Europe (Renwick and Pilet 2016; Passarelli 2020). This fits a larger trend towards the personalization of politics in general (Karvonen 2010). The personalizing trend is particularly found in list PR systems. Reforms in this direction have taken place in Austria, Belgium, Czechia, Estonia, Greece, Iceland, Latvia, Lithuania, the Netherlands, Poland, Slovenia, and Sweden. Most changes have involved the ballot dimension, increasing voters' influence over who is elected. Specifically, many countries using lists with limited flexibility have opened them up to a greater degree.

2.5 The main consequences of electoral systems

Electoral systems are much more than neutral technicalities: they also strongly influence how politics works, both during and after elections. In this section, we examine some of the main consequences of electoral systems. We start with their influence on the interparty dimension of electoral competition, before turning to how they may affect the intraparty dimension of politics.

2.5.1 The impact of electoral systems on the interparty dimension of politics

The idea that electoral systems shape interparty competition is far from new. It was most famously stated by the French political scientist Maurice Duverger (1954). 'Duverger's laws' state that:

- simple-majority single-ballot systems (such as SMP) favour two-party systems;
- proportional representation systems favour multiparty systems.

Although these laws have been discussed widely, with divergent findings especially for SMP systems, their logic remains central to understanding how electoral rules shape competition among parties, and consequently the party system. The causal link between electoral and party systems stated by Duverger runs through two mechanisms: the mechanical effect and the psychological effect.

The mechanical effect is the direct and mathematical impact of the electoral rule in how it translates votes into seats. Majoritarian systems such as SMP designate a single winner in each district, therefore limiting mechanically the number of parties gaining parliamentary representation. By contrast, under PR the same distribution of votes almost certainly leads to a wider distribution of seats across parties than under majoritarian rules. In very large districts, as in the Netherlands, parties with tiny vote shares may enter parliament (see Box 2.2).

The mechanical effect can be gauged by examining how real-world proportional systems translate votes into seats. In his reference book comparing thirty-six democracies, Lijphart (1999) did this using Gallagher's (1992) index of proportionality, which summarizes the gaps between parties' vote and seat shares. The smaller the index, the more proportional the system. Figure 2.4 updates this analysis to 2022 and shows that PR systems indeed tend to produce much more proportional outcomes than list systems. The more disproportional systems are majority systems (France and the UK) and those using reinforced proportionality (Italy and Greece). And among PR systems, differences are to be explained for the most part by differences in DM. Spain and Ireland function with more districts of lower DM, reducing the proportionality of the electoral systems compared to countries with larger districts such as Austria, Denmark, or the Netherlands.

Yet, a second mechanism is key to understanding the logic behind Duverger's laws: the psychological effect. This captures 'how parties and voters react to these rules' (Blais and Massicotte 2002: 56). It posits that voters will often be reluctant to vote for a party that has little or no chance of securing a seat. Rather, they cast what political scientists call a *strategic vote* (in contrast to a *sincere vote* for the party they really prefer). Strategic voting is more likely when the electoral system is less proportional and votes for small parties are more likely to be 'wasted'. By contrast, few voters in very proportional systems need abandon their sincere preference, since even small parties have good chances of winning seats. Research confirms that strategic voting is more common in majoritarian than in proportional systems (Abramson et al. 2010). Under PR, it is more common when electoral thresholds are higher (Meffert and Gschwend 2011) or DMs lower (Lachat, Blais, and Lago 2015).

Box 2.2 Over to you—proportionality and district magnitude

The proportionality in the translation of votes into seats is directly influenced by district magnitude—that is, the number of seats to be allocated in the district. The best way to see this is to take the results of an election and vary the district magnitude.

Take the results of one recent election held in a single nationwide district, as in the Netherlands, Slovakia, or Israel. Reduce the number of seats to be allocated down to seventy-five, fifty, twenty-five, and ten. Observe how smaller parties are gradually excluded from seat allocation.

Electoral results in the three countries may be found on the Parties and Elections in Europe website.

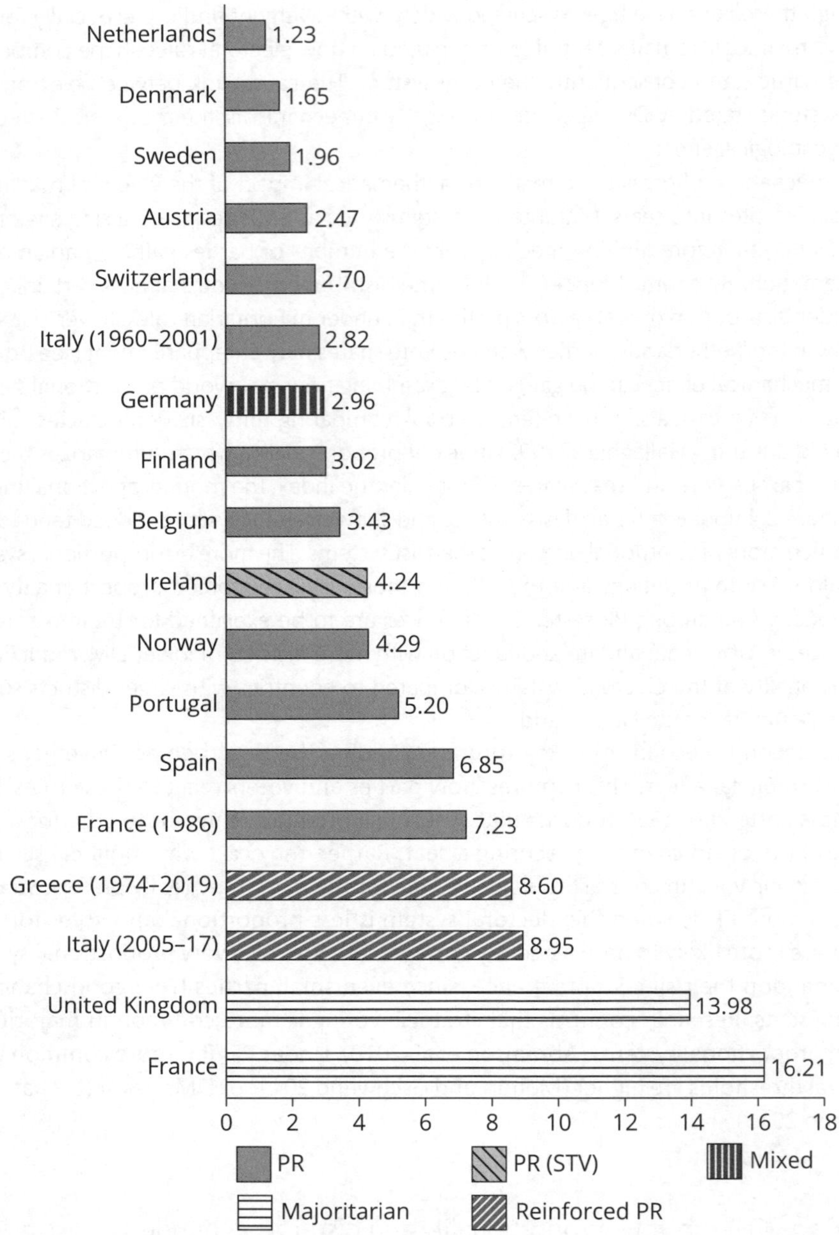

Figure 2.4 Mean value of Gallagher's index of disproportionality for the elections to the lower house of parliament (1960–2022)

Source: Armingeon, Klaus, Virginia Wenger, Fiona Wiedemeier, Christian Isler, Laura Knöpfel, David Weisstanner, and Sarah Engler (2019), Comparative Political Data Set 1960–2017. Zurich: Institute of Political Science, University of Zurich; Gallagher, Michael, (2023), Election indices dataset at https://www.tcd.ie/Political_Science/about/people/michael_gallagher/ElSystems/Docts/ElectionIndices.pdf.

Political parties are also subject to a psychological effect: like voters, they too try to anticipate the mechanical effect of electoral rules and may modify their behaviour accordingly. More proportional systems make it more likely that smaller parties will run, believing they could win some seats, even on a limited share of votes. By contrast, in less proportional systems, politicians could decide not to form new parties or to abandon existing small parties; or small parties could try to form pre-electoral alliances with others to increase their chances of gaining access to parliament (Cox 1997). This logic has been confirmed in studies of real-life elections: for example, Reed (2001) found that the change from a PR system to a mixed-member majoritarian system in Italy in 1993 led to a move towards two-party competition in most electoral districts. Nevertheless, more small parties run for election with little chance of winning than simple theoretical models would postulate (Bol et al. 2018). They might do so, for example, because they want to influence the agenda of the campaign and bring in new issues (see Box 2.3).

The psychological effects on voters and parties tend to reinforce the mechanical effects. These effects combine to explain why, on average, less proportional electoral systems are associated with less fragmented party systems, as well as why reforms towards more proportional systems typically increase party system fragmentation (Ward 2019; Riera 2020). We can see this by looking at the 'effective number of parliamentary parties' (ENPP)—a measure developed by Laakso and Taagepera (1979) capturing the number of parties weighted by their respective electoral sizes. Figure 2.5 shows the average ENPP in each European country between 1945 and 2022. The picture is much messier than in the case of the simple mechanical effect exposed in Figure 2.4: many other factors are involved in shaping the number of parties than simply the electoral system. Thus, some countries with very proportional electoral systems do not have large numbers of parties. But the least proportional electoral systems do tend to be associated with fewer parties.

2.5.2 **The impact of electoral systems on the intraparty dimension of politics**

As posited previously, electoral systems affect the intraparty as well as the interparty dimension of politics. The ballot structure can shape politicians' incentives to cultivate their personal reputations or to burnish the reputations of their parties. Carey and Shugart (1995) posited that systems allowing voters to express preferences for candidates within parties would strengthen politicians' incentives to persuade voters to back them personally. For a candidate, the goal is not only to convince a voter to vote for your party, but also to persuade

Box 2.3 Over to you—strategic desertion and district magnitude

In his theory of electoral systems, Cox (1997) said the number of viable parties in an electoral district is equal to DM + 1, DM being the number of seats available in the district (the district magnitude).

Does this prediction hold up? To test it, select a recent general election held in a European country electing its parliament with multimember districts of varying magnitudes. Verify whether the number of parties running in various districts is indeed equal (or close) to DM + 1.

You can find election results at district level across Europe (and beyond) by visiting the website of the project Constituency-Level Elections Archive, available at http://www.electiondataarchive.org.

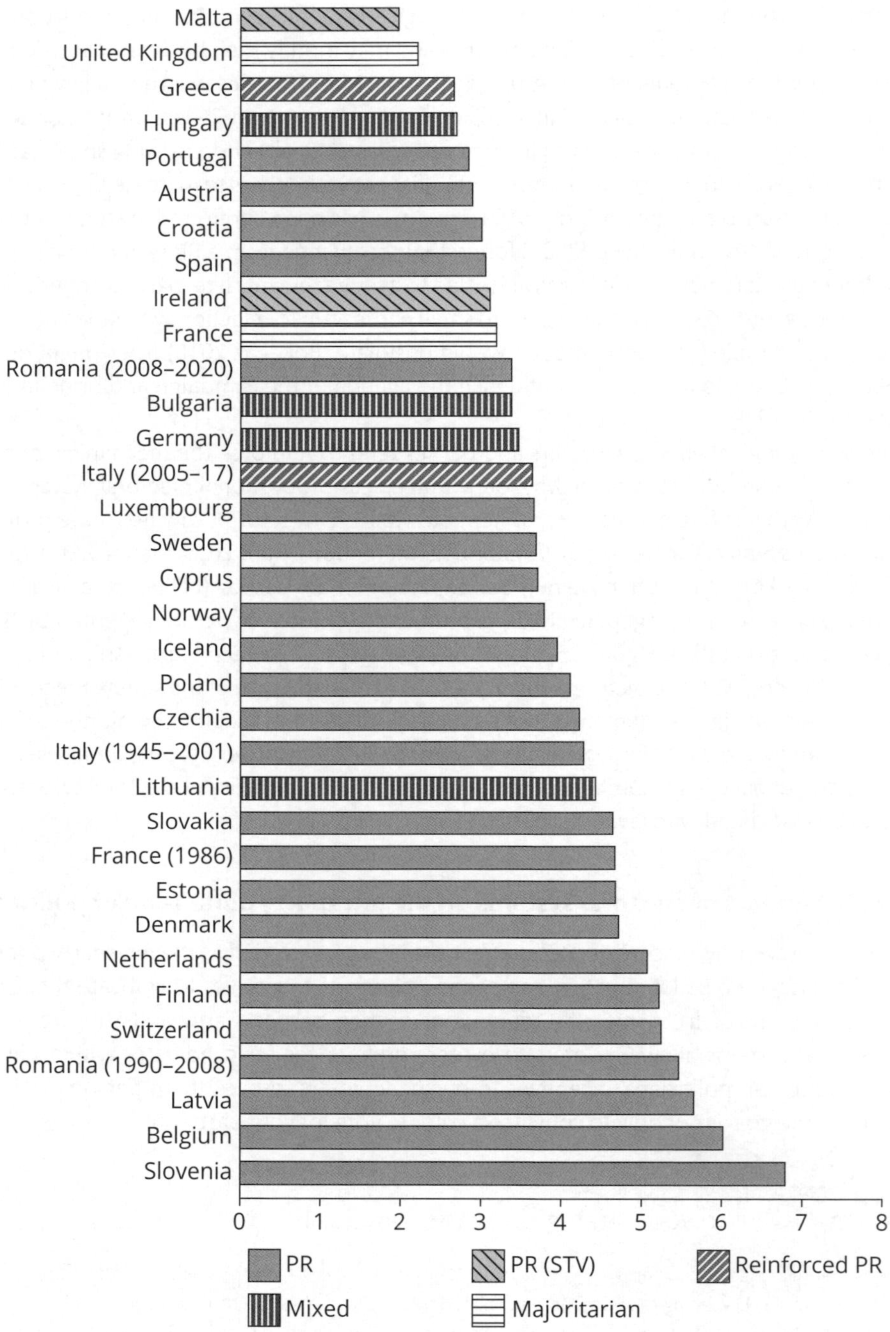

Figure 2.5 Effective number of parliamentary parties (ENPP) for elections to the national lower house of parliament (1945–2022)

Source: Jean-Benoit Pilet, Alan Renwick, Lidia Nunez, Pablo Simon Cosano, and Elwin Reimink, *Electoral System Changes in Europe (1945–2012)*, Database, version 2.0, 2016, available at http://electoralsystemchanges.eu/Public/FilesPage.php?ID=69; reproduced with permission from Nils-Christian Bormann and Matt Golder 'Democratic electoral systems around the world, 1946–2011'. *Electoral Studies*, 32(2): 360–9. Copyright © 2013 Elsevier Ltd. All rights reserved. Available at https://doi.org/10.1016/j.electstud.2013.01.005; Gallagher, Michael, 2023. Election indices dataset at https://www.tcd.ie/Political_Science/about/people/michael_gallagher/ElSystems/Docts/ElectionIndices.pdf.

them to vote for you rather than for your co-partisans. Carey and Shugart (1995) said these incentives are also influenced by DM: greater DM increases incentives to cultivate a personal reputation in open-ballot systems and reduces it in closed-ballot systems. These incentives for candidates to cultivate their personal reputations have consequences during electoral campaigns, but also between them, in parliamentary activities.

Empirical research in list PR systems corroborates these expectations. For example, one study finds that candidates run more personal campaigns in larger districts with open lists (Selb and Lutz 2015). Others find that politicians elected in larger districts with open lists invest more in activities building a personal reputation such as drafting private members' bills in parliament (Bräuninger, Brunner, and Däubler 2012) or spending time connecting with voters in the district (Pilet, Freire, and Costa 2012).

However, these findings are not corroborated when one compares beyond list PR systems, especially across electoral formulas. Notably, it appears that politicians operating in majoritarian systems with single-member districts invest more in cultivating their personal reputations than do their counterparts in list PR systems, even though these systems do not allow voters to express intraparty preferences. Such findings are observed by comparing across countries running elections under SMP and list PR (Zittel 2015) and through comparison of MPs elected from the two parts of mixed systems (Zittel and Gschwend 2008). What is particularly underlined is the greater importance given to constituency representation in single-member majoritarian systems. MPs in such systems act and define themselves primarily as the representatives of their districts in parliament, much more than in PR systems where their role as party foot-soldiers is much more central (Eulau and Karps 1977; Cain et al. 1987; Blomgren and Rozenberg 2012). Such studies agree that electoral systems matter, but exactly what effects they have is often subtle: their impact does not always conform to what we might expect from simple theorizing.

Finally, while we have focused on the impacts of electoral systems on the inter- and intraparty dimensions of politics, the influence of electoral rules extends well beyond the mere distribution of seats. These rules may affect, for example, the representation of social groups (such as women or ethnic minorities—see Bernauer et al. 2015; Lublin and Bowler 2018), the composition and dynamics of government (see Chapter 8), the content of policies adopted (Iversen and Soskice 2006), social inequalities (Han 2015), and the accurate representation of citizens' preferences (Ferland 2021). These effects fall beyond what can be covered in this chapter but are a major agenda for research in political science.

2.6 **Conclusion**

This chapter shows why the study of electoral systems is among the oldest and most prolific fields in political science. Electoral systems vary widely, across a range of different dimensions. And they matter greatly for the character of politics. Whether a country has a two-party system or a multiparty system has a profound effect on the options available to voters at election time and on the nature of governance between elections: on whether governments tend to be formed by one party or several and on structures of accountability for what governments do. Whether a country has a personalized or more party-centred system has deep effects on the relationship between voters and their representatives and how political parties work. It is impossible to understand the politics of a country without understanding its system of election.

For this reason, new articles and books have been published on this topic every year since the 1950s, and more continue to appear. There is innovation in the real world of politics too: Romania passed a new and unique electoral system in 2008 (though it did not last long); Italy has innovated with new systems in 1993, 2005, and 2017; reforms were under consideration in Germany at the time of writing in 2023. In 2007, Estonia became the first country in the world to offer online voting for general elections, and the proportion of voters casting their ballots online has increased in each subsequent election.

Furthermore, there are many important questions about electoral systems still to be answered. In a paper written over a decade ago, two of the leading experts in the field, Shaun Bowler and David Farrell (2009), argued that research should move beyond crudely comparing between majoritarian and proportional systems, or between single-member and multimember systems, and develop more fine-grained analyses looking at the detail of ballot structures, electoral thresholds, and other features. They also said that research should mobilize new methods, including emerging experimental methods.

Scholars have taken these ideas to heart. As you develop your reading on electoral systems, therefore, there is much new work to look out for. Over the coming years, the core ideas set out here will remain important, but new points will also emerge that deserve increasing attention. However democratic politics evolves, electoral systems will remain fundamentally important.

Discussion questions

1. What is meant by the terms 'electoral formula', 'district magnitude', 'electoral threshold', and 'ballot structure'?
2. What is 'electoral proportionality' and how can it be measured?
3. We have seen that the electoral system affects the party system and the nature of governments. But does it also affect the effectiveness of governments and the nature of the policies that are adopted? If so, in what ways? What evidence can you use to examine this empirically?
4. What explains the fact that most European countries have proportional electoral systems?
5. What explains the trend towards greater personalization of electoral systems in recent years?
6. Is it possible to say that some electoral systems are better than others? If so, what is the basis for doing so?

Thinking comparatively

Many of the most discussed consequences of electoral systems concern how they shape voters' behaviour. Most studies of these effects look at the impact of the interparty dimension of these rules, but some also examine the intraparty dimension. The latter approach is taken by Söderlund (2016) in a comparative study of twenty-three countries.

Voters gauge government performance partly in terms of economic outcomes. 'Economic voting' refers to the tendency for voters to reward incumbent governing parties when the economy goes well, and punishing them by voting for opposition parties when economic indicators are negative. But this assumes that voters are only concerned with the interparty dimension of electoral competition. The literature on the personalization of politics (Karvonen 2010) argues that voters also pay attention to the intraparty dimension of electoral politics and to the identity of candidates, independent of the parties they are affiliated to. As a consequence, a voter that is more attentive to candidates would be less likely to cast an economic vote based on the performance of parties in government.

This claim has been tested by Peter Söderlund. He especially examines whether the importance of economic voting is lower in more candidate-centred systems. He first builds on work by Carey and Shugart (1995), Farrell and McAllister (2006), and others to gauge the degree of candidate-centredness of different systems. Then he examines whether the magnitude of the electoral reward (or sanction) for governing parties due to economic performance in the years before an election is smaller under more candidate-centred electoral systems.

His analyses are based upon a study of election results across twenty-three Organisation for Economic Co-operation and Development (OECD) countries between 1961 and 2014 (which represents 294 elections). He finds that, indeed, ruling parties are subject to less electoral punishment for poor economic performances when the electoral system is more candidate-centred. The differences are modest. Nevertheless, they seem to indicate that more candidate-centred electoral systems tend to incentivize voters to pay more attention to the personality, attitudes and behaviours of individual candidates, and less to the policies and performance of political parties. This has important implications for the dynamics of electoral accountability in democracies. This study is also a good example of a body of work examining the importance of candidates in voting behaviour in personalized electoral systems (Bräninger et al. 2012; Zittel 2017; Von Schoultz and Papageorgiou 2021).

Guide to further reading

The best book-length introduction to electoral systems, covering the different types of electoral systems, their effects, and their origins, is Farrell, D. (2011), *Electoral Systems: A Comparative Introduction*, 2nd edn (Basingstoke: Palgrave Macmillan).

A classic, hugely influential, but also very readable analysis of electoral systems and their effects is Lijphart, A. (1994), *Electoral Systems and Party Systems: A Study of Twenty-Seven Democracies, 1945–1990* (Oxford: Oxford University Press).

For analysis that goes beyond the effects of electoral systems on parties and governments to consider impacts on women's representation, ethnic minorities, and constituency service, see Norris, P. (2004), *Electoral Engineering: Voting Rules and Political Behavior* (Cambridge: Cambridge University Press).

A major collection of essays that review the latest research findings on electoral systems, covering a wide variety of themes and also examining electoral systems in a range of particular countries, is Herron, E. S., Pekkanen, R. J., and Shugart, M. S. (2018), *The Oxford Handbook of Electoral Systems* (Oxford: Oxford University Press).

To go deeper into the interparty dimension of electoral systems and their effects on party systems, a harder but very worthwhile read is Cox, G. W. (1997), *Making Votes Count: Strategic Coordination in the World's Electoral Systems* (Cambridge: Cambridge University Press).

For discussion of the intraparty dimension of electoral systems, particularly focusing on patterns of change in European electoral systems, see Renwick, A. and Pilet, J. B. (2016), *Faces on the Ballot: The Personalization of Electoral Systems in Europe* (Oxford: Oxford University Press).

References

Abramson, P. R., Aldrich, J. H., Blais, A., Diamond, M., Diskin, A., Indridason, I. H., Lee, D. J., and Levine, R. (2010), 'Comparing strategic voting under FPTP and PR', *Comparative Political Studies*, 43(1): 61–90.

André, A. and Depauw, S. (2013), 'District magnitude and home styles of representation in European democracies', *West European Politics*, 36(5): 986–1006.

Bernauer, J., Giger, N., and Rosset, J. (2015), 'Mind the gap: Do proportional electoral systems foster a more equal representation of women and men, poor and rich?' *International Political Science Review*, 36(1): 78–98.

Blais, A. and Massicotte, L. (2002), 'Electoral systems', in L. Le Duc, R. G. Niemi, and P. Norris (eds.) *Comparing Democracies 2* (London: Sage Publications): 40–69.

Blais, A., Dobrzynska, A., and Indridason, I. (2005), 'To adopt or not to adopt proportional representation: The politics of institutional choice', *British Journal of Political Science*, 35(1): 182–90.

Blomgren, M. and Rozenberg, O. (eds.) (2012), *Parliamentary Roles in Modern Legislatures* (London: Routledge).

Bol, D., Pilet, J.-B., and Riera, P. (2015), 'The international diffusion of electoral systems: The spread of mechanisms tempering proportional representation across Europe', *European Journal of Political Research*, 54(2): 384–410.

Bol, D., Blais, A., and St-Vincent, S. L. (2018), 'Which matters most: Party strategic exit or voter strategic voting? A laboratory experiment', *Political Science Research and Methods*, 6(2): 229–44.

Bowler, S. and Farrell, D. M. (2009), 'Approaches to the study of electoral system design: Devils, details and experts', paper presented at the ECPR Joint Sessions of Workshops, Lisbon.

Bräuninger, Th., Brunner, M., and Däubler, Th. (2012), 'Personal vote-seeking in flexible list systems: How electoral incentives shape Belgian MPs' bill initiation behaviour', *European Journal of Political Research*, 51(3): 607–45.

Cain, B. E., Ferejohn, J. A., and Fiorina, M. P. (1987), *The Personal Vote: Constituency Service and Electoral Independence* (Cambridge, MA: Harvard University Press).

Carey, J. M. and Shugart, M. S. (1995), 'Incentives to cultivate a personal vote: A rank ordering of electoral formulas', *Electoral Studies*, 14(4): 417–39.

Carey, J. M. and Hix, S. (2011), 'The electoral sweet spot: Low-Magnitude proportional electoral systems', *American Journal of Political Science*, 55(2): 383–97.

Colomer, J. M. (ed.) (2004), *Handbook of Electoral System Choice* (Basingstoke: Palgrave Macmillan).

Cox, G. W. (1997), *Making Votes Count: Strategic Coordination in the World's Electoral Systems* (Cambridge: Cambridge University Press).

Duverger, M. (1954), *Political Parties: Their Organization and Activity in the Modern State* (London: Methuen).

Eulau, H. and Karps, P. D. (1977), 'The puzzle of representation. Specifying components of responsiveness', *Legislative Studies Quarterly*, 2(3): 233–54.

Farrell, D. (2011), *Electoral Systems: A Comparative Introduction*, 2nd edn (Basingstoke: Palgrave Macmillan).

Farrell, D. M. and McAllister, I. (2006), 'Voter satisfaction and electoral systems: Does preferential voting in candidate-centred systems make a difference?' *European Journal of Political Research*, 45(5): 725–49.

Ferland, B. (2021), 'Electoral systems and policy congruence', *Political Studies*, 69(2): 344–65.

Gallagher, M. (1992), 'Comparing proportional representation electoral systems: Quotas, thresholds, paradoxes and majorities', *British Journal of Political Science*, 222(4): 469–96.

Han, S. M. (2015), 'Income inequality, electoral systems and party polarisation', *European Journal of Political Research*, 54(3): 582–600.

Iversen, Torben and Soskice, David (2006), 'Electoral institutions and the politics of coalitions: Why some democracies redistribute more than others', *American Political Science Review*, 100(2): 165–81.

Karvonen, L. (2010), *The Personalization of Politics: A Study of Parliamentary Democracies* (London: ECPR Press).

Katz, R. S. (1980), *A Theory of Parties and Electoral Systems* (Baltimore, MD: Johns Hopkins University Press).

Laakso, M. and Taagepera, R. (1979), 'Effective number of parties: A measure with application to Western Europe', *Comparative Political Studies*, 12(1): 3–27.

Lachat, R., Blais, A., and Lago, I. (2015), 'Assessing the mechanical and psychological effects of district magnitude', *Journal of Elections, Public Opinion and Parties*, 25(3): 284–99.

Lijphart, A. (1999), *Patterns of Democracy* (New Haven, CT: Yale University Press).

Linhart, E., Raabe, J., and Statsch, P. (2019), 'Mixed-member proportional electoral systems–the best of both worlds?' *Journal of Elections, Public Opinion and Parties*, 29(1): 21–40.

Lublin, D. and Bowler, S. (2018), 'Electoral systems and ethnic minority representation', in E. S. Herron, R. J. Pekkanen, and M. S. Shugart (eds.) *The Oxford Handbook of Electoral Systems* (Oxford: Oxford University Press): 159–74.

Meffert, M. F. and Gschwend, T. (2011), 'Polls, coalition signals and strategic voting: An experimental investigation of perceptions and effects', *European Journal of Political Research*, 50(5): 636–67.

Michl, F. and Mittrop, J. (2023), 'Farewell to "Personenwahl": The Traffic Light Coalition's Draft for the Electoral Law Reform in Germany', *Verfassungsblog*, 19 January.

Passarelli, G. (2020), *Preferential Voting Systems* (London: Springer International Publishing).

Pilet, J.-B., Freire, A., and Costa, O. (2012), 'Ballot structure, district magnitude and constituency-orientation of MPs in proportional representation and majority electoral systems', *Representation: The Journal of Representative Democracy*, 48(4): 359–72.

Reed, S. R. (2001), 'Duverger's Law is working in Italy', *Comparative Political Studies*, 34(2): 312–27.

Renwick, A. (2010), *The Politics of Electoral Reform: Changing the Rules of Democracy* (Cambridge: Cambridge University Press).

Renwick, A. and Pilet, J. B. (2016), *Faces on the Ballot: The Personalization of Electoral Systems in Europe* (Oxford: Oxford University Press).

Riera, P. (2020), 'Voting after the change: A natural experiment on the effect of electoral reform on party system fragmentation', *International Political Science Review*, 41(2): 271–86.

Selb, P. and Lutz, G. (2015), 'Lone fighters: Intraparty competition, interparty competition, and candidates' vote seeking efforts in open-ballot PR elections', *Electoral Studies*, 39(3): 329–37.

Shugart, M. (2001), 'Extreme electoral systems and the appeal of mixed member alternative', in M. Shugart and M. P. Wattenber (eds.) *Mixed-Member Electoral Systems: The Best of Both Worlds?* (Oxford: Oxford University Press): 25–53.

Shugart, M. and Wattenberg, M. P. (eds.) (2001), *Mixed-Member Electoral Systems: The Best of Both Worlds?* (Oxford: Oxford University Press).

Söderlund, P. (2016). 'Candidate-centred electoral systems and change in incumbent vote share: A cross-national and longitudinal analysis'. *European Journal of Political Research*, 55(2): 321–29.

Von Schoultz, Å. and Papageorgiou, A. (2021), 'Policy or person? The electoral value of policy positions and personal attributes in the Finnish open-list system', *Party Politics*, 27(4): 767–78.

Ward, D. G. (2019), 'Dynamic effects of electoral laws', *Journal of Elections, Public Opinion and Parties*, 29(3): 402–19.

Zittel, T. (2015), 'Constituency candidates in comparative perspective: How personalized are constituency campaigns, why, and does it matter?', *Electoral Studies*, 39(3): 286–94.

Zittel, T. (2017), 'The personal vote', in K. Arzheimer, J. Evans, and M-L. Beck (eds.) *The SAGE Handbook of Electoral Behaviour* (Thousand Oaks, CA: SAGE Publishing): 668–83.

Zittel, T. and Gschwend, T. (2008), 'Individualised constituency campaigns in mixed-member electoral systems: Candidates in the 2005 German elections', *West European Politics*, 31(4): 978–1003.

3 Political Parties

ANDRÉ KROUWEL

3.1 Introduction

Democratic politics in Europe is dominated by political parties. They structure the choices available to voters; they are the primary channel through which voters are represented in the political system; they organize parliament and form governments. However, political parties across Europe have undergone considerable changes over time. There have been changes in the nature of party organizations, the functions that parties perform, and the relationships between parties and voters. These constitute some of the most significant developments in European politics in recent times, with some going so far as to argue that party democracy in Europe is in crisis (e.g. Mair 2013).

This chapter charts some of the more important developments in European party politics, as well as analysing the contemporary state of party politics. It begins with a discussion of the value of political parties for democracy (Section 3.2), after which it describes the origin of party systems in historical social cleavages and how these cleavages relate to the various party families (Section 3.3). Subsequently, it examines how parties have changed over time in terms of organization, ideology, and electoral appeal (Section 3.4). The chapter then turns to an analysis of contemporary party systems in European democracies, highlighting some recent developments common to many countries, particularly growing polarization and fragmentation (Section 3.5).

3.2 Parties and democracy

Harvard professor Elmer Eric Schattschneider famously argued in 1942 that modern democracy is unthinkable without political parties. Political parties are the principal instrument through which different segments of the population, with the goal of implementing the policies that benefit their interests, compete for political power in legislatures and for control of government. However, political parties are not automatically democratic institutions.

Political parties can be vehicles for repression and ideological propaganda that force citizens into subjugation in totalitarian and authoritarian regimes. Revolutionary parties have liberated people from the shackles of repression, but have also toppled democracies and implemented mass murder. Nevertheless, the omnipresence of political parties in very different political regimes suggests that they perform crucial functions in everyday politics. What are these functions, in particular in large-scale democratic societies? And are political parties a necessary condition for democratic politics?

The most important and defining function of political parties is to structure the electoral process by recruiting, selecting, and then nominating candidates for public office. Parties are the vehicle through which ambitious people come to political power. This *recruitment function* and the subsequent selection of political leaders, parliamentary candidates, and members of the executive are crucial because the quality of the democratic process, of policy making, and policy implementation depends on it. When parties fail in this task, it can lead to a loss of popular support for democratic politics or even an intervention by authoritarian actors that reduce or end democracy. In sum, the recruitment function is the most consequential and defining characteristic of a political party: all other functions to be listed are also executed by other organizations but fielding candidates in an election is what makes an organization an actual political party.

Like environmental organizations, labour unions, associations of business interests, human rights advocacy groups, the military, the state bureaucracy, and many other organizations, political parties develop policy ideas or innovate existing policies. Parties perform this *interest articulation function* when they become the 'institutional translation' of societal demands and interests (Rueschemeyer et al. 1992). Related to interest articulation is the *interest aggregation function*: each policy idea may appeal to specific groups of voters and effective parties try to aggregate these different interests by formulating a coherent view of society, the economy, and the wider world (in other words, an ideology) that is appealing to various social groups. Needless to say, there is substantial variation between parties in their level of aggregation; many political parties only appeal to a small niche of voters or focus on one interest, issue, or social group.

Once candidates have been nominated and policies written down, parties can start campaigning to mobilize for support to implement their ideas. Most political parties use ideological and historical references, colours, symbols, and labels, prior policy successes, historical leaders, training and educational programmes, and propaganda to connect voters to their cause. The symbols and colours help voters to recognize a party's ideological orientation and, in the past, also served to help illiterate voters to recognize their party. Left-wing parties—communist, socialist, and social democratic parties—often use the colour red. The rose is an important symbol for left parties, as are references to labour (like hammers and sickles, indicating the unity between peasants and factory workers). Environmental parties use green and lots of flowers, liberal parties blue and yellow, often including birds, trees, and leaves, while nationalist and extreme-right parties often use colours from the national flag. Parties shape not only individual and collective political identities through these means, but also public opinion to influence what citizens regard as valuable and significant. This *mobilization function*—accruing support for a specific political project—is important because democracy assumes competition between various distinct policy options so that citizens have a choice between viable alternatives at election time. By voting for a party, citizens influence what the next government will do or not do. In an election campaign, political parties are not the only ones forwarding policy proposals or campaigning in favour of or against certain policies. Nevertheless, political parties structure public discourse and give it meaning because they absorb and aggregate policies and ideas into alternatives that can be implemented if the party gains executive power.

Another key function of political parties is to rule by taking control of the executive (see Chapter 8). Not all parties are 'office seeking' and aim for control over the executive: some merely want to advocate an important issue, ideology, or worldview and are not interested in forming or joining a government. However, most of the traditional parties in European democracies—of liberal, conservative, Christian democratic, and social democratic origin—do aim to control government as a single party or in a coalition with other parties. Parties that have often and for long periods been in government include the Conservative Party in Britain and the Christian Democratic Union (*CDU*) in Germany. Social democratic parties have also been in government for long periods, with Tage Erlander of the Swedish Social Democratic Party (*SAP*) serving as prime minister for twenty-three years, while Norway had a social democratic prime minister for seventeen years in Einar Gerhardsen (*Arbeiderspartiet*). The recordholder in a democracy is the leader of the Finnish Centre Party (*KESK*) Urho Kekkonen who was president for almost twenty-six years. Liberal parties have become more powerful over time, leading governments in the Netherlands with Mark Rutte (*VVD*) who became the longest serving Dutch prime minister and in Luxembourg with Xavier Bettel (*DP*) who became head of government in 2013. In this *governing function*, political parties are intermediary agents through which citizens are provided the opportunity to participate in the political decision-making process.

Equally important as taking control of the government is the ability of political parties to perform the role of the *political opposition* against the ones in power. In a democracy, the government needs to be held accountable by parliament and particularly by a strong and credible opposition consisting of one or more parties that could realistically take over government at the next election. There is substantial variation in the capacity of parties to form a stable, purposeful, and effective government or opposition, which is why it is important to assess what types of party organization perform this function and which fail to do so.

While parties can be found in all democracies, there is substantial variation over time and from country to country in what types of party emerge and how all these functions are performed. The next two sections examine the origins of political parties and party systems (Section 3.3) and how the roles performed by political parties have transformed over time (Section 3.4).

3.3 Social cleavages and the origins of party 'families'

Parties are closely associated with the development of modern large-scale democracy, in particular the mobilization of the previously excluded mass population into the political system. Economic and social changes caused by modern capitalism made it impossible to confine politics to a small circle of aristocratic elites. However, the types of political parties that emerged with modern democracy and the nature of party competition vary widely across European democracies. In Scandinavia social democracy has been the dominant political force, competing with a fragmented centre-right of conservative, liberal, religious, and farmers' parties. Christian democrats were often the major political force in Germany, Austria, Belgium, and the Netherlands, primarily competing with social democrats and liberals. In the UK, as well as in France and Spain, the main competitors were a conservative party facing a strong social democratic opponent. How can we explain these differences in European party systems? Why do some countries have a conservative party and others a Christian democratic party and why do we find liberal and social democratic parties in almost all countries? Seymour Martin Lipset and Stein Rokkan (1967) looked deep into European history and found common division lines, or social cleavages, that resulted in the emergence of specific ideological 'party families'. Social cleavages are lines of division within society that are (1) actual primary identities that are felt and experienced by members of society, (2) which groups opposed by the cleavage are aware of and prepared to act upon, (3) that become politically relevant through the creation of formal organizations (trade unions, parties) representing and defending the interests of the group.

Lipset and Rokkan argued that three critical junctures are important to understand both variation and similarities in the emergence of ideological 'party families' that shaped European party systems. The first critical juncture is the Reformation and the 1648 settlement known as the Treaty of Westphalia that largely ended the religious wars, established religious freedoms in Europe, and consolidated the territorial sovereignty of several European states. This state consolidation—albeit not equally successful across Europe—created a tension or *cleavage between the political centre and the periphery*, of which the latter lost some or all of their autonomy in terms of taxation and law making. Centre-periphery cleavages develop where nation building occurs, a process in which minorities with distinct identities are brought under control of the central state. This pitted nationalists and liberals against conservatives and regionalists, creating parties with distinct ideologies on centralization of power, regional autonomy, and tax systems. Particularly in European states with late and weaker state formation, strong regional identities persist to this day, and these regions often demand high levels of autonomy. Such centre-periphery tensions persist today in countries like Spain (with Basque and Catalan separatist movements such as the Catalan *Esquerra Republicana*), the United Kingdom (with Scottish demands for higher autonomy or even independence by the Scottish National Party, *SNP*), and Belgium (with the increasing devolution and federalization of Walloon and Flanders) (see Chapter 11). In some European states, where ethnic or religious groups are geographically concentrated, political parties emerged demanding cultural autonomy, such as the Turkish minority in Bulgaria (Movement for Rights and Freedoms, *DPS/HÖH*) and the Swedish minority in Finland (Swedish People's Party, *SFP*).

The second critical juncture is the National Revolution that resulted in a *cleavage between the (secular) state and the church*, in which religious and more secular groups with a more liberal and left-wing orientation fought a bitter struggle over control of mass education, family life (such as the registration of civil marriage), and the prerogative in making and upholding law and order. The concept of a secular state—resulting from the French revolution of 1789—created tensions far beyond the French borders. Churches—in particular the Vatican—were used to dictating law and public morality and controlling the educational curriculum. In countries that were predominantly Catholic, such as France, Spain, and Italy, a deep church-state cleavage developed between the anti-clerical liberal and radical-left parties versus right-wing religious and conservative parties that sided with the Catholic church. Protestant countries with substantial Catholic minorities, as was the case in the Netherlands and Germany, also witnessed the development of strong Christian democratic parties opposing secular liberal and radical-leftist parties. More to the North—in Scandinavia and Britain—Protestantism had been used as a justification to free the ruling elite from the Roman Catholic dictates of the Vatican, resulting in an official state church status and much lower levels of religious conflict. Scandinavian countries were confessionally very homogeneous and more recently highly secularized, resulting in relatively small Christian parties.

The third critical juncture was the Industrial Revolution, which created two important cleavages: one between agricultural and industrial producers, or the *rural versus urban cleavage*, and another between employers (capital owners) and workers (suppliers of labour), often referred to as the *class cleavage*. Both led to the emergence and consolidation of party families. The rural-urban cleavage pitted dwellers of the agricultural countryside against residents of towns and cities on issues relating to food production, trade, and taxation. Where traditionalism and rural interests came under the threat of modern capitalist production and trade, political parties emerged that specifically defended agrarian interests (for example, farmers' parties in Sweden and Norway, now called the *Centerpartiet* and *Senterpartiet*). On the opposite side of the political spectrum, liberal parties that advocated open markets for international trade were strengthened. The European Union, which heavily supports rural areas with subsidies, structural funds, and a common agricultural policy, has significantly reduced the saliency of this rural-urban cleavage throughout Europe, but it has not entirely disappeared. Sharp differences in economic development and cultural values persist between rural and more urban areas in many European countries, often creating political conflict and mobilization.

The most important cleavage that modern capitalist development created was the class cleavage, in which urban factory workers were pitted against the capitalist elites who controlled the means of production. Workers—exploited by capitalists in order to extract surplus value from their labour—demanded higher wages, better and safer working conditions, and educational opportunities for their children. Workers organized through unions and workers' parties, creating the communist, socialist, and social democratic party families. Where ruling elites forcefully repressed these labour movements and parties and the demands of workers—as in France and Italy—radical socialist and communist parties emerged, such as the French and Italian communist parties (the *Parti communiste français, PCF*, and the *Partito Comunista Italiano, PCI*), and the class cleavage became a dominant political rift. Moderate and reformist centre-left social democratic political parties emerged, and were more easily integrated into the political system, where elites adopted a less confrontational and more cooperative response to worker organization. Table 3.1 summarizes these cleavages resulting from critical junctures in European history.

Table 3.1 Critical junctures, issues, and societal cleavages that structured party systems in Europe

Critical juncture	Critical issues	Cleavage	Party family
Reformation: the 1648 settlement	Consolidation of territorial state, the right to set currencies and levy taxes	1. Periphery versus state-building centre	Conservative, ethnic, linguistic, and regionalist parties
National Revolution	Control over mass education, mass media, civil life (marriage, family affairs), and law and order	2. Church versus secular state	Christian democratic, conservative, and liberal parties
Industrial Revolution	Protection versus modernization and free market enterprise versus workers' rights and state control	3. Rural/agricultural versus urban/industrial interests 4. Workers versus capital owners	Farmers' parties, communist, socialist, and social democratic parties

3.3.1 **Old conflicts frozen in time: Lipset and Rokkan's freeze hypothesis**

Lipset and Rokkan (1967) formulated the *freeze hypothesis* to explain the persistence of these old conflicts in structuring party competition. This hypothesis states that major cleavages would persist since the political parties originating from them, parties like the British Labour and Conservative Parties, remained dominant in European party systems. Party-political loyalties in European democracies had become frozen by the 1920s as the ideologies of new parties that emerged with the extension of the franchise were strongly associated with the cleavage identities. These cleavages provided lasting collective—regional, class, and religious—identities to which political parties could appeal.

The freeze hypothesis became untenable from the late 1960s onwards in the face of the vast transformation of European societies due to unprecedented economic growth, the expansion of higher education, and shifting opinion structures. Traditional cleavages became less and new cleavages more relevant for voting behaviour (Franklin et al. 1992) (see Box 3.1). That does not mean, however, that class and religious differences do not matter anymore. On the contrary, class differences are still relevant, yet have become deeply entangled with differences in educational attainment (Bovens and Wille 2017) and access to housing. Politically significant religious differences between Catholics and Protestants may have declined, but issues related to Islam are among the most salient in most European party systems. The emergence of populist parties in Scandinavian countries, Italy, France, the Netherlands, Germany, Austria, and Spain has put religious-cultural issues at the top of the political agenda. The level of conflict is strongly related to whether the ethnic-religious divisions cut across class and regional differences. If religion, ethnicity, and class are 'cross-cutting' (where each religious group is diverse in terms of ethnicity and class, and vice versa), they can reduce political tensions; if they overlap, political conflict deepens, especially if there is strong geographical separation. Recent transformations of cleavage structures across European democracies are discussed in more detail in Section 3.5, but first we discuss how political parties themselves have changed over time.

Box 3.1 Four hypotheses about the transformation of European cleavage structures

Ever since Lipset and Rokkan (1967) published their theory, a fierce debate ensued on whether these cleavages still structure societies and party systems in Western Europe, or whether these cleavages have profoundly transformed over time. It is possible to distinguish at least four hypotheses:

(1) *The zero-cleavage thesis* (see for example Franklin et al. 1992): these authors argue that the cleavages identified by Lipset and Rokkan no longer explain the current pattern of party competition and voting behaviour. Traditional cleavages have lost meaning and there is no clear new cleavage structure: politics has become largely unstructured, which explains high levels of electoral volatility and fragmentation of party systems.

(2) *The cleavage-stability thesis*: a completely opposite line of argumentation (see for example Bartolini and Mair 1990) argues there is evidence that cleavage politics is alive and well. Those who examine long-term trends in electoral volatility see no sign of a decline of cleavages or a de-alignment of parties: essentially, party systems are stable and traditional parties still dominate parliament and particularly government formation. Moreover, traditional cleavages are still powerful predictors of voting behaviour and this stability in voting patterns indicates that the Lipset and Rokkan freeze hypothesis still stands.

(3) *The cleavage-replacement thesis*: a third line of argumentation (see for example Inglehart 2008) argues that particularly the class cleavage is replaced by a new value cleavage. This new value cleavage divides society between people with materialist values and post-materialist values, and parties adapt to that (see Chapter 4). As new generations grow up in unprecedented economic prosperity and a generous welfare state, feelings of economic insecurity decline. This allows younger generations to become orientated towards non-material values: personal autonomy and freedom, the environment, and cosmopolitanism. Green and libertarian parties become successful among this generation. Some—like Bovens and Wille (2017)—have also framed this as an educational cleavage: younger generations with much higher levels of educational attainment develop vastly different value patterns and party preferences.

(4) Finally, the *cleavage-reboot thesis*: a fourth approach is represented by authors like Giddens (1998); Kitschelt (1994); and Kriesi (1998), who argue that while traditional class and cultural cleavages still structure party competition and voting behaviour, these traditional cleavages have changed in their substance and meaning since the 1960s. The cultural cleavage has absorbed issues like immigration and the role of Islam in Western societies. On the economic dimension, parties and voters become pitted against one another on whether globalization and open borders are good for our economy or whether we should do more to protect existing jobs and workers' rights against the pressures of international capital and labour market flexibility. Environmental issues—such as the human impact on climate change—have also been incorporated in the existing cleavage structure.

3.4 How political parties transformed over time

As we saw in Table 3.1, each critical historical juncture and related cleavage structure resulted in the birth of political parties with different ideological orientations. Parties also differ in terms of their organizational features and patterns of social support. Furthermore, there have been significant changes over time in terms of parties' ideological profile, electoral support, and organizational structure (Krouwel 2012). In this section, these changes are described in terms of a number of key stages in the development of political parties in Europe.

3.4.1 The beginning of party politics: Elite parties

Liberal and conservative parties emerged in the late nineteenth century, before the introduction of mass suffrage (in the UK and France, for example). There was not much organization in these loosely structured '*elite parties*', which consisted of small local caucuses, organized around prominent individuals from the upper classes. Apart from the coordination of voting behaviour of representatives in parliament, there was little national coordination. Extensive extra-parliamentary organization and electoral campaigning were unnecessary as suffrage was limited to the wealthy, propertied male population. The privileged individuals who ran for parliament used their personal financial resources and could contact all potential voters privately since they all came from the same upper echelons of society. In fact, the 'party' was only formed after they entered parliament and consisted primarily of meetings to coordinate voting on bills. These elite parties had no central office or formal membership. These notables usually nominated themselves and their 'party-political' activities were limited to short election periods. While ideological divisions between liberals and religious conservatives were sometimes substantial, no formal party platform was drawn up; the appeal of the party was the individual candidate (or often his family). Logically, the absence of a formal policy programme allowed such individuals a high degree of autonomy in their parliamentary activities (Duverger 1954; Neumann 1956).

3.4.2 The mobilization of the politically excluded lower classes: Mass parties

Mass parties, such as the Social Democratic Party in Germany and the Labour Party in the UK, emerged as a reaction to the political exclusion of large proportions of citizens by the political elite. The lower and middle classes demanded political, social, and economic rights, including voting rights for women, culminating in universal suffrage. Some of the more radical mass parties (like the aforementioned French and Italian communist parties, *PCF* and *PCI*) also demanded sweeping changes in social and economic policies, particularly left-wing parties organizing working-class voters. In response, some traditional elite parties, such as the Conservative Party and Liberal Party in the UK (founded in 1832 and 1859 respectively), adopted similar strategies and organizational formats to these new mass parties, with extensive and active membership organizations and very distinct and well-articulated political ideologies.

In terms of organization, mass parties penetrated deeply into the daily life of their members and established local and regional branches, with a national party leadership. Organizationally, mass parties were in many ways the mirror image of the elite party: traditional elites had political and economic power bases before the formation of their parties, while the lower and middle classes only gained political power through their mass-membership party organizations (Ostrogorski 1902). The main aim of mass parties was to empower the many in order to get their interests represented in politics. Mass parties demanded strong ideological and active commitment from their members, not only during election campaigns, but also continuously and in all spheres of social and economic life (Neumann 1956). Members were also the main financial source, through membership fees, as well as payments for all the services and activities provided by the party. Despite their mass membership, the concentration of power at the helm of the party led to the famous accusation that in mass parties a small and 'unrepresentative oligarchy' exercised central control and dominated decision-making.

This claim was most forcefully made by Robert Michels in 1911. Michels suggested that there was an 'iron law of oligarchy', after studying the internal power structure of the German Social Democrats (*SPD*) and labour unions. According to Michels (1962), even parties most committed to egalitarian and democratic practices become oligarchical, meaning dominated by a small group of leaders.

Mass parties also differed from elite parties ideologically since they typically aimed at the radical redistribution of social, economic, and political resources, and power. As mass parties represented and mobilized specific economic, social, religious, or ethnic groups in society, they developed a coherent ideological vision of the future that was ingrained in all their activities and propaganda. For the leaders of mass parties, it was important to insulate their members from the dominant religious and economic structures of society and develop an alternative, parallel society of ancillary organizations, such as unions, social housing organizations, sports facilities, banks and insurance companies, newspapers, educational institutes, and cultural organizations where all activities were consistent with the party's ideology (Neumann 1956). While there was substantial variation in organizational structures and ideological orthodoxy, mass parties clearly polarized the political landscape by demanding profound changes in economic, social, and foreign policies (Duverger 1954).

3.4.3 **The professionalization of politics: The catch-all party**

After 1945, mass parties slowly professionalized their party organizations and moderated their demands for social and political transformation to appeal to a broader voter base outside their original class or religious core supporters. This transformation of ideological mass parties into politically centrist and moderate *catch-all parties* was facilitated by unprecedented economic prosperity that created a broad middle class made up of skilled manual workers, white-collar workers, and civil servants. Otto Kirchheimer (1966) was the first to describe this transition and in particular referred to this occurring in the German *SPD* and *CDU*, the British Labour Party, the Italian *Democrazia Christiana* (*DC*), and the French *Union pour la Nouvelle République* (*UNR*, Gaullist). As the interests of members of the middle classes converged, polarization between social groups diminished and mass parties slowly diluted their ideology to become catch-all parties, which culminated in a waning of principled opposition and reduced political competition to the question of which party is best at 'managing the state'.

Catch-all parties were also more willing to form coalition governments with former political opponents since this allowed better opportunities to deliver on their policy promises than remaining in opposition. This became possible as former mass parties on both the traditional left and the right accepted a social capitalist model, with rightist parties accepting welfare state arrangements and economic planning and leftist parties no longer demanding the abolishment or substantial revision of capitalism. As a result, alternation in government or cabinet composition no longer automatically resulted in significant policy shifts.

At the organizational level, this transformation of mass parties into catch-all parties made party membership largely redundant. Instead of relying on voluntary activities, catch-all parties adopted more professional election campaigns by employing paid experts. There is also less need for a party press when no clear ideology needs to be propagandized. Many activities that were previously party-based—like education, housing, sports, culture, and health care—were by now brought into general welfare state regimes in almost all European countries and became disconnected from political parties and ideologies. Financially, catch-all parties relied less on membership fees and increasingly on larger corporate and interest group donors, as well as state finance, further reducing the utility of membership. Instead of internal party training and policy development, catch-all parties extracted policy ideas from a range of professional interest groups, which made overall policies more technocratic and less distinctive. Many European political parties still aim to maintain a membership base, however, since state finance is often dependent on membership, and members are still an important pool for political talent development and a source for policy innovation.

In catch-all parties, leaders were no longer selected on ideology or class origin, but on their ability to appeal to many voters, their managerial qualities, and their political pragmatism. Politics became driven by personality and candidate traits, while ideology played a marginal role. A good example is the UK Labour Party under Tony Blair: Blair was a polished media performer and a political centrist who eschewed notions of left and right, claiming that Labour was 'the practical party' that pursued its objectives 'in a measured and non-dogmatic way' (Mair 2013: 93). Consequently the 'personalization' of politics and candidate-centred electoral campaigns—instead of policy-orientated competition—became characteristics of professional electoral catch-all parties (Krouwel 2012).

3.4.4 **The state becomes partisan: The party cartel?**

Over time, the difference between the party organizations and state institutions became blurred as political parties became more and more embedded in and dependent on the state for their human and financial resources. As party programmes became increasingly interchangeable and cooperation between former political enemies became the norm rather than the exception, some critics argued that a political party cartel was formed, which became impenetrable for new political actors and interest groups (Katz and Mair 1995).

The cartel model suggests that political parties collude to monopolize resources and power in an attempt to eliminate political competition. This reduces the democratic function of opposition parties to form a viable alternative to the incumbent government. Cartel parties, the argument goes, coordinate and manage the level of competition among themselves, and disadvantage challenger parties by excluding them from state resources and executive power. While parties previously acted as intermediaries between society and the state, cartel parties meld into the state structures to such an extent that citizens can no longer distinguish between party structures and state structures. They use the rule-making and regulatory state powers to weaken opponents and strengthen cartel members. In this sense, the state becomes 'partisan'.

This argument has received a lot of attention, but such a cartel did not in fact materialize in European democracies. If anything, the opposite of cartelization is visible across European democracies today. Numerous 'outsider' parties—such as Berlusconi's *Forza Italia*, Macron's *La République En Marche*, *Lijst Pim Fortuyn* and Wilders' *Party for Freedom* in the Netherlands, *Podemos* in Spain, and *the Five Star Movement*, *Lega* and *Fratelli di Italia* in Italy, to name just a few examples—have successfully entered European political landscapes and obtained executive power by appealing to ignored sections of the electorate. Radical-right outsider parties use polarizing issues such as immigration to mobilize widespread anti-establishment and anti-elite sentiments. Rather than amicable cartelization, major political opponents within

European party systems seem increasingly hostile to one another as well as towards their radical and populist challengers (Bale et al. 2010). Moreover, the major party families that were supposed to be core members of the cartel, Christian democrats and social democrats, have suffered substantial electoral losses across the European continent, particularly in Belgium, the Netherlands, France, and Italy. In some countries, the traditional political parties have been totally replaced by newcomers, as discussed in Section 3.4.5. Voters are shifting away from moderate, centrist mainstream politics to more radical opponents on all fringes of the political spectrum. Radical and illiberal right-wing populist forces—like the *Rassemblement National* in France, the Progress Party in Norway, or the Danish People's Party—are tearing mainstream, centrist political politics apart (see also Chapter 18).

3.4.5 **Politics incorporated: The emergence of the business-firm party**

Many of the new challenger parties that have emerged across Europe have different organizational structures and more radical ideological orientations compared to mainstream parties and often present themselves as political outsiders. These 'political entrepreneurs' have, at least at their inception, limited or no access to state resources. They rely heavily on resources and strategies from the private sector and commercial mass media channels to promote their message. Some of these 'business-firm parties' directly originate from the private initiative of a political entrepreneur or from the private sector and have, by and large, the structures of a commercial company (Hopkin and Paolucci 1999). One example of a business-firm party originating from an already existing commercial media company was Silvio Berlusconi's *Forza Italia*. Other political entrepreneurs construct a totally new and separate organization like *La République En Marche* of Emmanuel Macron in France, whose financial resources came largely from corporate donors.

Since business-firm parties generate their resources almost exclusively from the private sector, they have very little incentive to build party membership on any meaningful scale. Most campaign tasks will be 'contracted out' to external commercial companies and experts with weak or no ties to the party itself. This is the essence of the business-firm party: all party activities and tasks are conducted under a commercial contract to be delivered to the 'party' (Hopkin and Paolucci 1999: 333). The only individuals with a more permanent stake in the party are the elected officials of the party. Rallies and conferences for members and supporters are still held, but only to show the popularity of the party, its leader(s), and its programme to a wider audience.

In terms of ideology, business-firm parties often have a fierce and radical rhetoric, but their policy platforms are formulated in very vague and ambiguous terms and have relatively few policy details. They are more orientated towards system disruption and marketing of the political leader, and consequently are flexible ideologically and eager to attract support from across broad sectors of society. The electorates of populist versions of entrepreneurial parties often include many from lower- and middle-class voters discontented with traditional politics. This feeling of discontentment is exploited by political entrepreneurs who offer an agenda of both cultural and economic protectionism, including a nativist vision of the welfare state and a strong stance against immigration.

Entrepreneurial business-firm parties signify the all-out 'personalization' of politics. The leader *is* the party; for example, in the UK the Brexit Party leader Nigel Farage was the party's main ideologue and spokesperson, and the party's 2019 electoral campaign centred on him and his personality (see Figure 3.1). This contaminates traditional parties, which feel compelled to transform into leader-centred, media-orientated campaign machines also. Modern political leaders like Trump, Macron, Geert Wilders in the Netherlands, Recep Tayyip Erdogan in Turkey, Viktor Orbán in Hungary, Beppe Grillo in Italy, and Robert Fico in Slovakia all became the core asset of their political movement, much as the presenter or the anchor is the core asset of a media production. This personalization of politics is part of a broader transformation that has been called the 'presidentialization' of parliamentary politics (Poguntke and Webb 2005; Webb and Poguntke 2013). In addition, the influence of social media and 'tabloid' or even 'fact-free' reporting on politics has significantly increased attention to the personal characteristics of candidates, rather than deeper-lying social and economic structures, the actions of political parties, the development and implementation of policies, and long-term political projects.

If political parties no longer aim to clearly identify and articulate political interests of the various social groups, voters become mere clients of parties and simply consume—rather than coproduce—the political 'products' parties offer. During election campaigns, many modern parties simply segment voters into electoral markets that can be micro-targeted with customized messages and online marketing techniques (this was a prevalent feature of the Brexit referendum, for example, when the pro-Brexit campaign used social media data to link anti-European Union (EU) sentiment and issues that prospective voters were personally invested in). Parties create personalized and emotional political messages, rather than substantive and transformative policy proposals. Voters become viewers of a 'political game show' in which they have a limited spectator role only. As in television shows, citizens serve to fill the stands and cheer on the entertainers. Since 1945 active citizenship has been eroded and transformed into a more passive, consumerist, and clientelist relationship (see Chapter 5).

Geert Wilders' Party for Freedom (*PVV*) in the Netherlands is a good case in point. The 'party' is non-existent; it is basically a single man, Wilders. Nobody—not even its parliamentary representatives—can join the party, which does not recognize formal membership. There is no internal democratic procedure for leadership selection or drafting of the party platform; all decisions are taken by the party leader himself. No formal membership means no internal debate on ideas, policies, and tactics, and no means to democratically control the party leadership or hold him accountable. The core feature of a democratic polity—the exchange of ideas—has disappeared. The party is merely an election machine with a financial structure, which produces and promotes only one product: the party leader himself.

3.5 Contemporary cleavage structures and party landscapes

The developments discussed in Section 3.4 have led to profound changes in the nature of party competition across Europe. In this section we will examine the contemporary party landscape in several countries. Party competition in European democracies is usually described in terms of the positions taken by parties on various 'issue dimensions', in particular an economic left-right dimension and the cultural libertarian-authoritarian dimension. Traditionally, conflict over economic redistribution has been most salient, but in recent years the cultural dimension has gained in importance. This section will focus on the location of parties on these two dimensions. Two important trends that can be seen in European party systems over the last two decades should be highlighted. First, *polarization*—increasing ideological distance between political parties, particularly on cultural issues related to immigration and refugees; and second, *fragmentation*—many new parties successfully entering the party system with the simultaneous shrinking of former major parties (see Sartori 1976 for a thoughtful discussion on polarization and fragmentation).

Cultural polarization started in the late 1980s but has accelerated in recent decades and is now dominant in almost all European party systems. Structural economic and demographic changes across European societies resulted in cultural anxieties that have made issues like immigration and asylum for refugees, social and economic integration of migrants, Islam, labour migration, and European integration more salient. For example, Otjes (2015, 2016) shows that the cultural dimension now pits defenders of the national interest and national identity against cosmopolitans, who are more comfortable with multiculturalism and have more fluid identities. A nationalist outlook in life is often combined with authoritarian and anti-elite tendencies, including a strong preference for direct democracy instruments (like referenda), strict law-and-order policies, and the defunding of public cultural institutions (like public broadcasters). This worldview is contrasted with a more internationalist, socially libertarian, and pluralistic outlook among other voters and parties, which has become closely connected with environmentalism and a tendency to support public funding of cultural institutions.

The fragmentation of European political landscapes is primarily visible in the emergence of green, environmentalist parties and right-wing populist, anti-immigration parties. Often right-wing populist parties—such as Le Pen's *Front Nationale*, now *Rassemblement Nationale*—are characterized as extreme right; however—as Figures 3.1–3.6 show—they are not primarily extreme economically, but rather more extreme on the cultural dimension. Their main political orientation is towards an 'ethno-nationalism' that aims to make societies more ethnically homogeneous and return them to traditional values. These parties have sometimes started out as economically right-wing in the traditional sense (pro-free market, anti-welfare), but they have increasingly adopted positions defending the preservation of generic welfare state provisions (such as pensions, health care, child support, unemployment benefits) for the 'native' population. In particular, the previously mentioned *Rassemblement National* of Le Pen is rather left-leaning in terms of its welfare policies and promises of economic protectionism. The *PVV* in the Netherlands, UK Independence Party (*UKIP*) in the UK, and to a lesser extent the *Lega* in Italy and the Sweden Democrats all tend towards a more centrist economic positions but are extreme on the cultural dimension. In all countries discussed in Section 3.5.1, many of the traditional right—Conservative, Christian democrat, and Liberal parties—are actually more right-wing economically than the so-called 'extreme right'.

New entries to the party system are not limited to anti-immigrant parties. On the left we see several newcomers in the shape of green-environmental and radical-left parties such as *Podemos* in Spain, *Syriza* in Greece, the Socialist Party in the Netherlands, *Die Linke* in Germany, and *La France Insoumise* in France. Some of these, like *Syriza* and *Podemos*, are often labelled as left populist parties (see Katsambekis and Kioupkiolis 2019; Charalambous and Ioannou 2019). Green parties have become an important political force in most European party systems as issues related to climate change have grown in importance. In some cases, green parties have even become larger than traditional centre-left social democrats (as occurred in the 2017 Dutch parliamentary elections and recent French elections). In Figures 3.1–3.6, we can see that green parties are typically on the left of the economic divide, and among the most progressive, socially libertarian parties in national political landscapes.

The entry of radical parties on all fringes of the political landscape has impacted on all traditional political party families electorally, but centre-left social democrats seem to be especially vulnerable to populist competition. This is because the centre-left traditionally appealed strongly to lower-educated, working-class voters. Right-wing populists now appeal to this section of the population with a message of resentment against migrants, whose entry at the lower end of the labour market means more competition and the possible suppression of wages for low-skilled workers, as well as pressures on the social housing market and other public services on which labourers and their families rely (see Bale et al. 2010). In addition, social democrats face fierce competition from the radical left-over issues such as affordable housing and health care, anti-austerity and privatization, protection of workers' rights, the costs of education, pensions, and basic income. Social democratic parties across European party systems have been weakened by this fierce competition with green, radical-left, as well as anti-immigration parties.

The traditional centre-right (liberals, conservatives, and Christian democrats) are also vulnerable to competition from far-right anti-immigrant parties. The demand for restrictive immigration and protectionist measures goes against the traditional centre-right defence of the business sector, which favours free markets and labour migration.

3.5.1 **Mapping contemporary European party landscapes: The realignment of party politics**

To better illustrate these developments, we examine contemporary party politics in selected European countries. We map the political landscape in each country on the two issue dimensions discussed previously (economic left-right and cultural libertarian-authoritarian) and describe some of the major recent changes in these party systems. In order to do so, we have collected data on party positions in all countries on salient policy issues based on a close examination of the parties' platforms and political discourse (see for full methodology Krouwel and van Elfrinkhof 2014). Figures 3.1–3.6 relate to a specific election in each country, with each election chosen to illustrate some of the important trends that have occurred more widely across Europe. Although these figures simplify the complexity of electoral competition in many European countries, they do capture the main dimensions of electoral mobilization.

Box 3.2 Over to you—party system change

Select a European country of your choice and examine the electoral results over recent decades. Try to assess the major trends in terms of political parties. Has the party system become more fragmented over time? How many new parties have gained seats and how many splits, mergers or electoral alliances competing under different labels have emerged? Has there been an increase in support for radical parties at the expense of centrist parties? Information on political parties in European countries and their electoral results can be found on the Parties and Elections website.

3.5.1.1 The United Kingdom

Beginning with the UK, the 2016 Brexit referendum put identity, in particular (English) nationalism, at the forefront of political conflict. Traditionally, the two major parties—the Conservatives and Labour—could be linked to the class conflict on the economic left-right dimension. In Figure 3.1 we can clearly see the location of the Labour Party in the left-libertarian quadrant at the time of the 2019 election, together with the Liberal Democrats (Lib Dems) and the Greens (some regional parties, such as the SNP, are also located in this region but are not shown in Figure 3.1). The Conservative party, in contrast, is firmly situated in the right-conservative quadrant.

As in other countries, European integration, immigration, and nationalism have become interlinked in the UK, deepening political and social divisions. By 2009 the UKIP—with political 'entrepreneur' Nigel Farage at its head—had become the second largest party in the European Parliament elections, which use proportional representation, and was an unprecedented upset for the Conservatives. In 2014 UKIP became the largest party in the European election, an achievement Farage repeated with his newly founded Brexit Party in 2019. Despite using the same polarizing narrative over immigration and European integration, UKIP and later the Brexit Party fared much worse in national elections because of the first-past-the-post

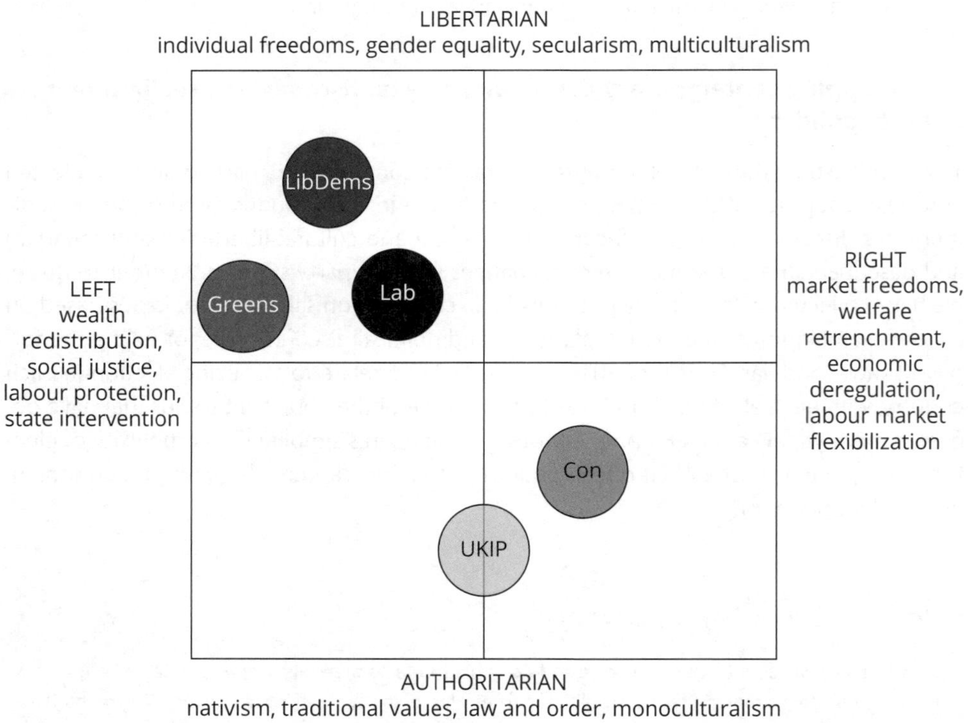

Figure 3.1 Party positions in the UK at the time of the 2019 general election

Source: The data used in this chapter has been developed by Kieskompas (Election Compass) for various European Voting Advice Applications (VAAs); adapted from Friedrich-Ebert-Stiftung. Strategy debates global. Copyright © Friedrich-Ebert-Stiftung at https://www.fes.de/strategy-debates-global.

electoral system (see Chapter 2), but the threat they posed forced the Conservative Party to move to the nationalist pole on issues such as immigration and the relationship with the EU. In the 2019 general election, Nigel Farage decided not to field candidates in many electoral districts after Conservative leader Boris Johnson committed to leaving the EU by 2020. As a result, the Conservative Party won a landslide victory with an eighty-seat majority and the highest vote share for any party since 1979.

3.5.1.2 France

The French political landscape has witnessed significant shifts in recent decades. In 2002 the traditional left-right bipolarity of French politics was shattered when the socialist party presidential candidate (Lionel Jospin) came in third—after the Gaullist Jacques Chirac and the far-right *Front National* (*FN*) leader Jean-Marie Le Pen. Even though Chirac won the second round with a landslide, the emergence of the *FN* transformed party competition in the French Fifth Republic from a main battle between right-wing Gaullists and left-wing socialists into '*tri-partisme*' (i.e. competition between three main parties).

The 2017 and 2022 presidential and parliamentary elections proved even more devastating for the traditional parties since neither the socialist candidate nor the Gaullist/Republican candidate got into the second round, instead both times the run-off was between Emmanuel Macron (who had founded a new party, *La République En Marche* (*LREM*), later renamed *Renaissance*) and Marine Le Pen (who had taken over the right-wing *Front National* from her father, renaming it *Rassemblement National* (*RN*)). Macron won the presidency twice on a centre-right, pro-market economic stance with cultural progressivism and pro-European Union positions (see Figure 3.2). In the 2022 parliamentary elections, many centrist and conservative parties and politicians regrouped in an alliance with Macron's *LREM*, substantially weakening *Les Républicains* (*LR*), yet Macron lost his parliamentary majority. This weakening of the government was the result of the formation of a broad left-wing electoral alliance (which included *La France Insoumise* (*LFI*), the *Parti Socialiste* (*PS*), the communist *PCF*, and the green party *Europe Écologie Les Verts* (*EELV*)), and the huge gains by Le Pen's *RN*, which won eighty-nine seats against eight seats in 2017.

It is clear that the electoral system no longer guarantees a bipolar left-right competition in France. While the left and right divide is still relevant, issues related to economic liberalism, globalization, Europeanization, and cultural liberalism have fragmented both the left-wing and right-wing party block.

3.5.1.3 Italy

Italian politics has been characterized by political instability since 1946, with many governments only managing to stay in office for a short time and frequent alternations in power. However, full party system change took place in the 1990s, when the traditional political parties like the Italian Socialist Party (*Partito Socialista Italiano* (*PSI*)) and Christian Democrats (*DC*) suffered dramatic electoral losses. From 1992 to 2013 the Italian political right orbited around Berlusconi's business firm party *Forza Italia*, but centrifugal forces in the 2013 and 2018 elections disintegrated this right-wing dominance. In the 2013 and 2018 elections a successful anti-system party, the Five Star Movement (*M5S*), gained the largest share of the

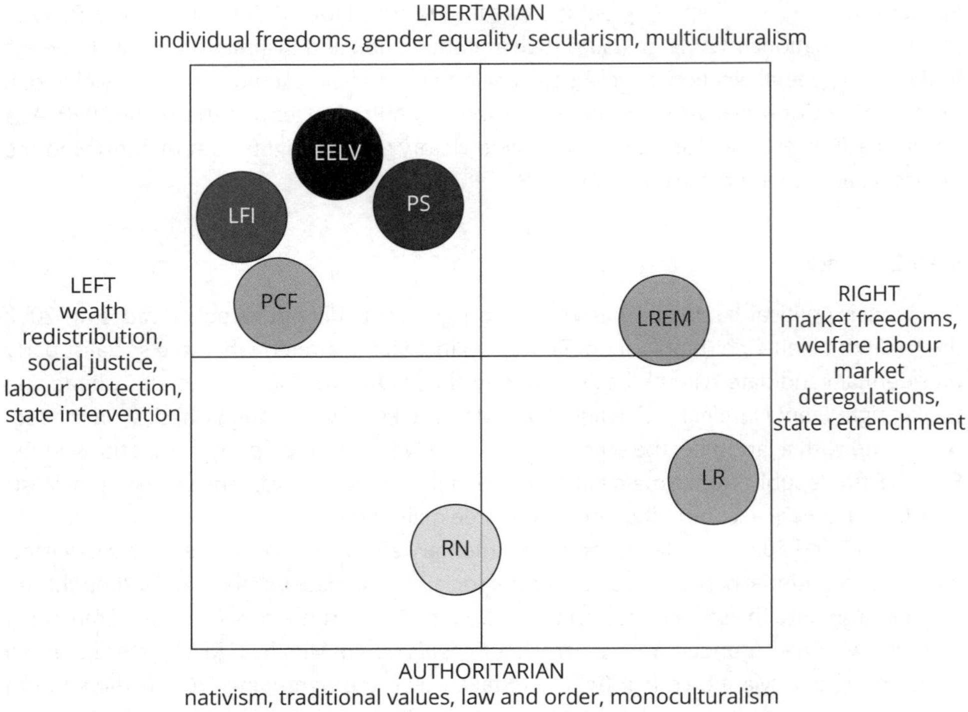

Figure 3.2 Party positions in France at the time of the 2022 presidential and parliamentary election

Source: The data used in this chapter has been developed by Kieskompas (Election Compass) for various European Voting Advice Applications (VAAs); Adapted from Friedrich-Ebert-Stiftung. Strategy debates global. Copyright © Friedrich-Ebert-Stiftung at https://www.fes.de/strategy-debates-global.

popular vote. In addition, the radical right *Lega Nord* became the second largest party in the 2018 election cycle by emphasizing anti-immigrant and anti-EU sentiments. The Five Star Movement has a centrist position on the cultural dimension and a moderate left-leaning economic inclination (see Figure 3.3) because it adopts left-leaning protective stances on economic issues (i.e. the job market, retirement policy, minimum wage, basic income, and taxation), while also incorporating anti-EU rhetoric (*M5S* initially joined an anti-EU European group in European Parliament).

In the 2022 election, *Fratelli di Italia* (Brothers of Italy, (*FdI*)) a direct heir of the Italian fascist tradition led by Giorgia Meloni, gained the largest share of the vote. Meloni's fully populist right-wing coalition, consisting of *FdI*, *Lega*, and *Forza Italia*, represents the normalization of nativist ideas in Italian politics, with a radical right policy profile, including a conspiratorial, anti-science rhetoric during the Covid-19 pandemic. Unlike the fully populist, but unstable and short-lived coalition between *M5S* and *Lega* (2018–19), the Meloni coalition seems more stable. The refugee crisis, the fiscal austerity forced upon Italian governments by the EU, and internal party rifts over policies during the Covid-19 pandemic have all impacted on the party alignment in the Italian political landscape. The political left alliance, the *Partito Democratico*, shifted from the progressive left to the progressive centre. This centrist move created splits with other components of the left. As can be seen in Figure 3.3 there is a clear deviation from

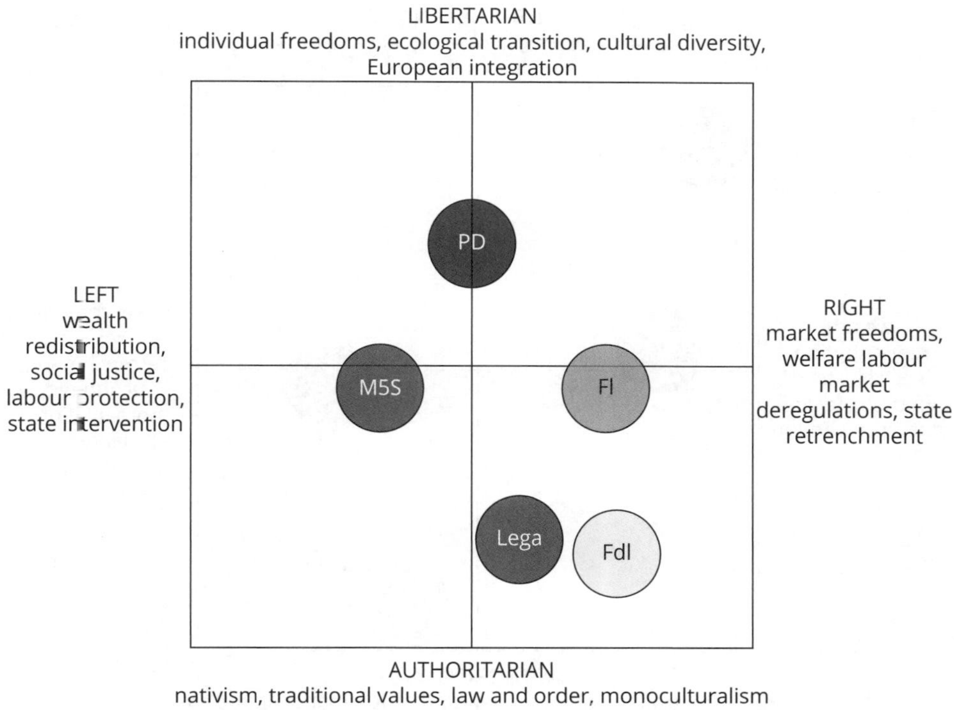

Figure 3.3 Party positions in Italy at the time of the 2022 general election

Source: The data used in this chapter has been developed by Kieskompas (Election Compass) for various European Voting Advice Applications (VAAs); adapted from Friedrich-Ebert-Stiftung. Strategy debates global. Copyright © Friedrich-Ebert-Stiftung at https://www.fes.de/strategy-debates-global.

the traditional left-progressive versus right-wing conservative axis of Italian politics into a realignment of parties based on their stance toward the European Union, immigration related issues and economic and fiscal austerity.

3.5.1.4 Spain

Another Southern European country with a profound transformation in party make-up is Spain. For decades two parties dominated Spanish politics—the conservative-religious *Partito Popular* (*PP*) and the social democratic *PSOE*. This relative stability was shattered in 2015 and 2016, when—after severe street protests against austerity policies—two new parties emerged. These two newcomers—*Podemos* and *Cuidadanos*—swept into third and fourth place with a combined vote share of almost 35% in both 2015 and 2016. The graph of the Spanish political landscape shows that *Unidas Podemos* (*UP*—which includes *Podemos*, and *Izqierda Unidad*, as well as multiple other left parties) occupies a traditional position in the left-progressive quadrant, while *Cuidadanos* is located on the centre-right (Figure 3.4).

The awakening of the centre-periphery dimension over the issue of Catalan independence (see Chapter 11), as well as the emergence of these two newcomers, changed the political logic in Spain. As a result of the strong electoral performance of *Podemos* and *Cuidadanos*, the single-party *PP* government of Mariano Rajoy lost its majority in 2015 and—for the first time in Spanish

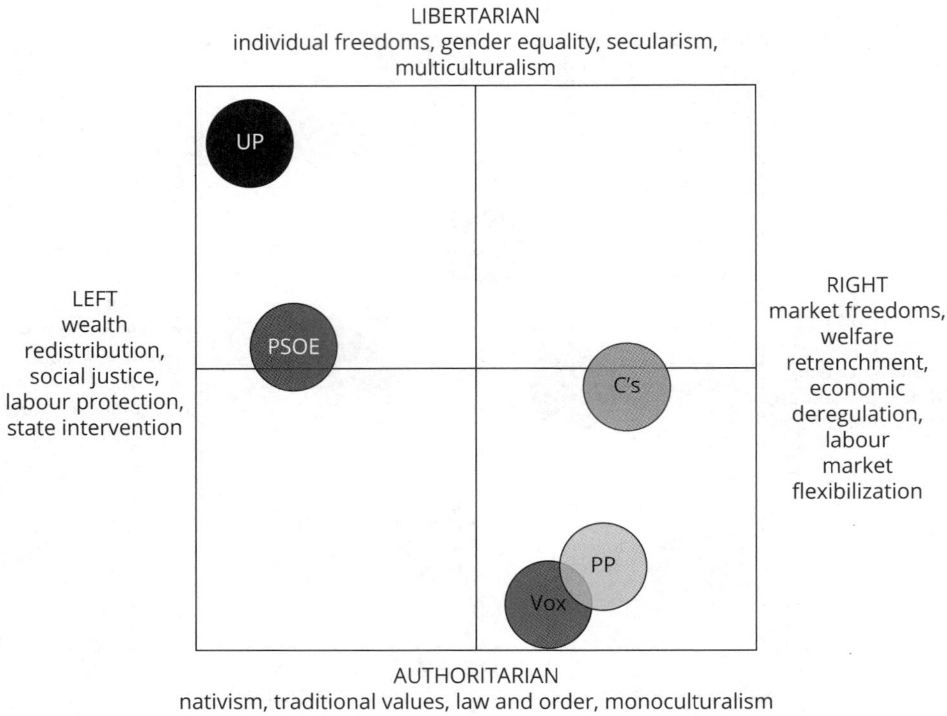

Figure 3.4 Party positions in Spain at the time of the 2019 general election

Source: The data used in this chapter has been developed by Kieskompas (Election Compass) for various European Voting Advice Applications (VAAs); adapted from Friedrich-Ebert-Stiftung. Strategy debates global. Copyright © Friedrich-Ebert-Stiftung at https://www.fes.de/strategy-debates-global.

parliamentary history—was taken down by a constructive 'vote of no confidence' in 2018. The elections of April 2019 did not return a solid majority for *PSOE* or *PP*, but actually provided the opportunity for the anti-immigration party *Vox* to enter parliament as the fifth largest party. A second election was held in November 2019 in a context of fragmentation, electoral volatility and polarization, and the arrival of Pedro Sánchez's government (an unusual coalition of *PSOE*, *Podemos*, and support of pro-independence Catalan parties). This alignment of the left with regionalist parties put wind in the sails of the radical right-wing party *Vox* and the party won 15% of the popular vote. A two-bloc party system was created where left-right differences strongly aligned with approaches to the Catalan conflict, yet fragmentation on both the left and even more on the right made stable majority government problematic.

3.5.1.5 Sweden

Across Europe, cultural polarization occurred over issues related to immigration, particularly regarding Muslim immigrants adhering to Islam. Right-wing extremist and populist parties attack Islam as a religion, which makes conservatives and Christian democrats uneasy. Conservative and Christian democratic ideology and politics are often—albeit loosely—based on Christian principles. This creates a dilemma for the religious centre-right: are they willing to abandon their traditional principles to regain electoral ground lost to the radical right?

Mainstream centre-right (liberal, conservative, and Christian democratic) parties, much like the centre-left social democrats, are also heavily dependent on popular support from the middle classes, who feel increasingly economically precarious and insecure because of globalization and associated economic and cultural changes.

This sense of precariousness is transforming party systems across Europe, with Sweden as a clear example. After 2004 Swedish politics was characterized by 'bloc politics' as parties in parliament created two relatively stable alliances on the left and right. With the entry of the far-right Sweden Democrats (*SD*) in parliament in 2010, the Swedish political landscape was reshaped (Figure 3.5). The *SD* transformed the issue-space of Swedish politics by politicizing cultural issues regarding immigration, thereby changing the national debate and weakening party-voter linkages within the left and right blocs. The increased vote and seat share of the *SD* and other fringe parties such as the Left Party (*V*) in 2018 resulted in an unprecedented political deadlock: neither of the two blocks managed to obtain a parliamentary majority, while both blocks refused to rely on the support of the *SD* for a governing majority. The government formation process was extremely lengthy and difficult by Swedish standards: after several failed attempts by the Swedish Social Democrats (*S*) and Moderate Party (*MP*) to form either a centre-left or centre-right coalition government, a government was formed finally in January 2019 between the Social Democrats, the Greens (*MP*), the Liberals (*L*), and the Centre Party (*C*), shattering the bloc system. In 2022 the

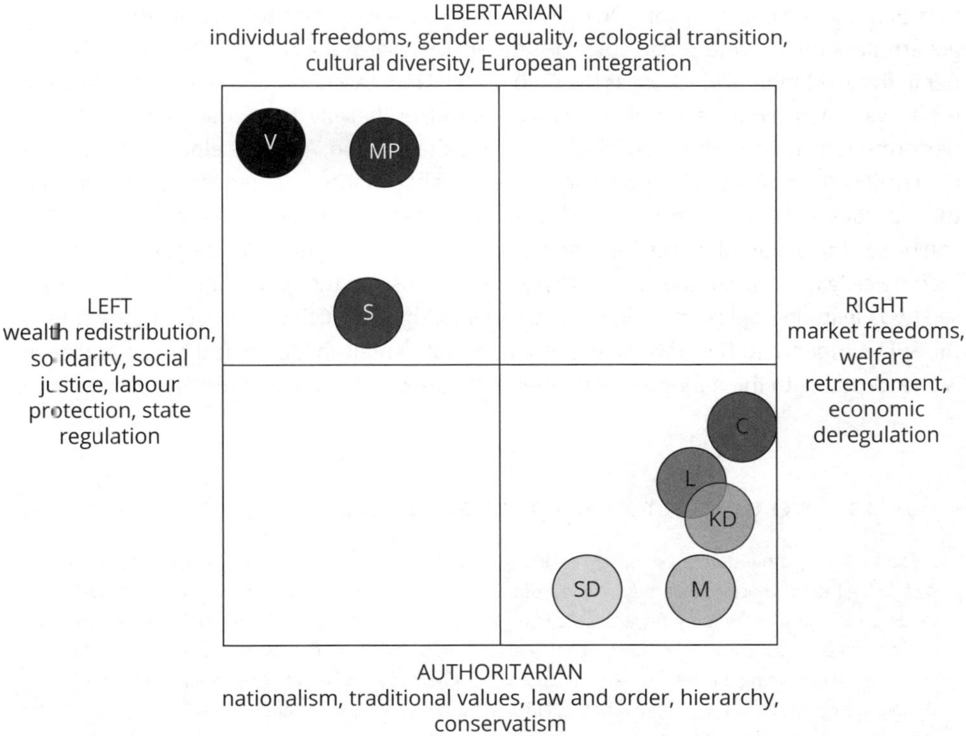

Figure 3.5 Party positions in Sweden at the time of the 2022 general election

Source: The data used in this chapter has been developed by Kieskompas (Election Compass) for various European Voting Advice Applications (VAAs); adapted from Friedrich-Ebert-Stiftung. Strategy debates global. Copyright © Friedrich-Ebert-Stiftung at https://www.fes.de/strategy-debates-global.

mainstream centre-right block abandoned the 'cordon sanitaire' (a policy of non-cooperation) in relation to the radical-right *SD*. A right-of-centre coalition formed consisting of the Moderates, the Christian Democrats (*KD*) and the Liberals, with tacit support from and policy agreement with the *SD*, again breaking the mould of Swedish politics.

3.5.1.6 Germany

Germany was for a long time characterized by political stability and moderation, but the results of both the 2017 and 2021 Bundestag elections showed high volatility. The issue of immigration had dominated the 2017 campaign after Germany's intake of high numbers of refugees in 2015 (see Chapter 14). In 2017, the two major parties, the Christian democrats (*CDU/CSU*) and Social Democrats (*SPD*), both of which (especially the *CDU/CSU*) had been catch-all parties, received their lowest combined vote share since World War II. Moreover, for the first time in twenty-seven years, a new party entered parliament, the far-right Alternative for Germany (*AfD*), which became the third largest party (with 12.6% of the popular vote in 2017). The *AfD* attacked both governing parties on the issue of immigration. The major political parties made a U-turn on immigration, from welcoming large numbers of immigrants in 2015 to entering a competition about who could best limit the number of asylum seekers.

In October 2018, Angela Merkel, chancellor of Germany, announced she would not seek re-election, which weakened the *CDU/CSU* in the run-up to the 2021 elections. Both members of the 'grand coalition' (of *CDU/CSU* and *SPD*) distanced themselves from the last Merkel government under widespread voter dissatisfaction. Olaf Scholz of *SPD* emerged as the winner in the 2021 federal election, as the *CDU* under Amin Laschet was unable to convince voters he was a worthy successor of Angela Merkel and lost heavily. The Green Party (*Die Grünen*) performed strongly, while the *AfD* lost some electoral ground. After the election, the *SPD*, the liberals (*FDP*), and Greens formed a novel 'traffic light coalition', named for the colours of the three parties: red, yellow, and green. This coalition spans widely across the political spectrum can be seen in the graph of the German political landscape (Figure 3.6). There is an enormous ideological gap between the leftist-progressive Greens and the right-wing *FDP*. Basically, we see two clear ideological blocs in German politics: the *FDP*, *CDU/CSU*, *AfD* on one side and the *SPD*, *Grünen*, and *Die Linke* on the other, yet both entail an ideological bloc member that is unacceptable to the major bloc members (*Die Linke* on the left and the *AfD* on the right).

Box 3.3 Over to you—mapping political landscapes

Select a country other than those described in Figures 3.1–3.6. Try to map out the political landscape by placing the main political parties in a two-dimensional (left-right and libertarian-authoritarian) landscape. To find out where the parties stand on these dimensions, you can use the Chapel Hill Expert Survey. Select a country and the most recent year, and then see where the parties stand on a left-to-right scale by selecting the 'lrecon' variable and see where they stand on the libertarian-authoritarian dimension by selecting the 'galtan' variable. Having mapped the political landscape, now describe the main axis of competition between the parties. Do they differ mostly in terms of their position on the economic dimension or the cultural dimension? You can also compare this with earlier years to see how party competition has changed over time.

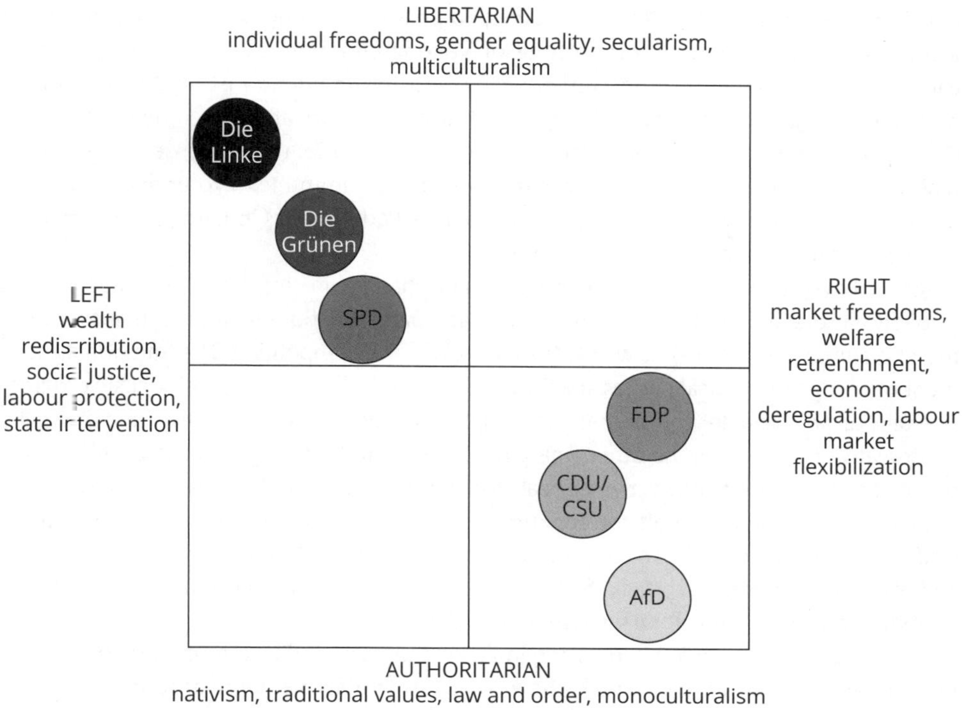

Figure 3.6 Party positions in Germany at the time of the 2021 federal election

Source: The data used in this chapter has been developed by Kieskompas (Election Compass) for various European Voting Advice Applications (VAAs); adapted from Friedrich-Ebert-Stiftung. Strategy debates global. Copyright © Friedrich-Ebert-Stiftung at https://www.fes.de/strategy-debates-global.

3.6 **Conclusion**

In the post-war period after 1945, up until the economic crisis of the late 1970s, ideological mass parties gradually transformed into politically moderate catch-all parties, sharing broadly similar objectives such as full employment, reducing social inequalities by generous welfare state arrangements, and creating economic prosperity for broad lower- and middle-class sections of society. After the crisis of the late 1970s, wages became stagnant or even declined in terms of purchasing power, austerity and welfare state retrenchment undermined middle-class prosperity, while the economy became ever more globalized (Hopkin and Blyth 2019). Over time this has led to a backlash against mainstream parties and economic globalization, resulting in the emergence of more radical challenger and populist parties significantly transforming European party systems. Amidst increasing polarization, declining levels of partisan identification with traditional moderate parties, increased levels of volatility, and ongoing fragmentation, we are witnessing the long-term, structural decline of both social democratic and Christian democratic parties. At the same time, multiple new and successful populist parties have emerged, especially, but not exclusively, from the nationalist right. Voters on the right are generally more inclined to support anti-immigrant politics than left-wing voters, but many social democratic parties have also lost the support of significant proportions of working-class voters who feel that their precarious economic situation is best remedied by reducing immigration. Large sections of the middle classes also feel increasingly 'squeezed' and less secure about their financial future. Centre-right liberal parties (at least those that have avoided splits) and conservative parties have overall fared better electorally, but they are far from immune to voter defection. Very few political parties have escaped electoral fragility. Party politics in Europe, once characterized by stability, is now in significant flux.

As we have seen, there have been significant changes in terms of party organization (broadly a professionalization of campaigning) and party functions (a decline in relevance of membership organizations), as well as the nature of party competition. The traditional alignment of European political parties consisted of economically left-wing and socially progressive parties on one side, and parties with a right-wing economic orientation and a socially conservative mind-set on the other. This pattern seems to be changing. Increasingly we see parties that combine conservative appeals for cultural 'protection' against immigrants with traditional left-wing proposals for economic protection of the native population through welfare state provisions. These parties attack the neoliberal right for allowing open borders and mass immigration and attack the left for defending the economic and political rights of minorities and advocating for a multicultural society.

The rapid changes we are witnessing in European party politics raise many questions. Will this volatility continue, or will a new, long-term pattern emerge around new cleavages? Will the traditional party families—social democrats, Christian democrats, liberals, and conservatives—survive or will new party families develop? Can populist parties form stable governments that can actually implement the policies they profess, or are their political projects impossible to implement? Will voters also become dissatisfied with the inability of right-wing populists to actually 'close' borders and of both right- and left-wing populists to 'protect' the population against economic hardship? Whether European party politics is in crisis, as some have argued, can be debated, but it is certainly in flux. How these changes play out in the coming years will have important implications for European democracies.

Discussion questions

1. What are the main party families in Europe, and what are the main policy differences between them?
2. The main centrist parties in Western Europe—in particular social democrats and Christian democrats—have lost a substantial amount of support. Why do you think these parties have been suffering electoral decline in recent decades and will they recover their prominent position in European party systems?
3. Political parties have transformed substantially over time and new types of party organizations have emerged. Which democratic functions of political parties have declined, and which democratic functions have been better fulfilled by modern political party organizations?

4. What relationship do you see between the ideology of a political party and its organizational structure? And to what extent do elite parties resemble entrepreneurial parties and in what respects do these two party types differ?
5. Can democracy function without political parties?

Thinking comparatively

Kriesi et al. (2006) were one of the first to conduct a large comparative research project examining the transformation of the political cleavages that underpin party competition in European democracies. They argue that globalization constitutes a new 'critical juncture' in European politics, just as the Industrial Revolution did centuries earlier. The economic competition and immigration brought about by globalization creates new groups of 'winners', who benefit economically from globalization, and 'losers', who face increased economic insecurity and precariousness. They develop a number of hypotheses about how this new cleavage shapes party competition. Their argument is not about variation across countries, but rather how globalization affects all countries. They therefore study a selection of countries that represent a broad cross-section of established European democracies (Germany, France, Britain, Switzerland, Austria, and the Netherlands).

To see how the new cleavage has shaped party competition, Kriesi et al. conduct content analysis of newspapers in each country for a series of elections throughout the 1990s and 2000s, identifying the key issues associated with each party in each election. They find that the new cleavage was incorporated into the existing cultural dimension of party competition, and as a result this dimension grew in importance relative to the left–right dimension over time. This was also associated with an increase in party fragmentation, as new parties emerged (such as radical-right parties) that focused on issues such as immigration. Their research sheds light on a common pattern of transformation in party systems over time.

Guide to further reading

Katz, R. S. and Crotty, W. J. (eds.) (2006), *Handbook of Party Politics* (London: Sage).

A wide-ranging summary of all the main aspects of party politics.

Mair, P. (1997), *Party System Change: Approaches and Interpretations* (Oxford: Oxford University Press).

How political cleavages, party organizations, and party competition have evolved in Europe.

Sartori, G. (1976), *Parties and Party Systems: A Framework for Analysis* (Cambridge: Cambridge University Press).

A classic volume on party politics with a European focus; this book developed a very influential classification of party systems.

Hutter, S. and Kriesi, H. (eds.) (2019), *European Party Politics in Times of Crisis.* (Cambridge University Press).

This edited collection includes case-studies from around Europe, examining how party politics has transformed in recent years.

References

Bale, T., Green-Pedersen, C. et al. (2010), 'If you can't beat them, join them? Explaining social democratic responses to the challenge from the populist radical right in Western Europe', *Political Studies*, 58(3): 410–26.

Bartolini, S. and Mair, P. (1990), 'Policy competition, spatial distance and electoral instability', *West European Politics*, 13(4): 1–16.

Bovens, M. and Wille, A. (2017), *Diploma Democracy: The Rise of Political Meritocracy* (Oxford: Oxford University Press).

Charalambous, G. and Ioannou G. (eds.) (2019), *Left Radicalism and Populism in Europe* (London: Routledge).

Duverger, M. (1954), *Political Parties, Their Organization and Activity in the Modern State* (New York: Wiley).

Franklin, M. N., Mackie, T. T. et al. (eds.) (1992), *Electoral Change: Responses to Evolving Social and Attitudinal Structures in Western Countries* (Cambridge: Cambridge University Press).

Giddens, A. (1998), *The Third Way: The Renewal of Social Democracy* (Cambridge: Polity).

Hopkin, J. and Paolucci, C. (1999), 'The business firm model of party organisation: Cases from Spain and Italy', *European Journal of Political Research*, 35(3): 307–39.

Hopkin, J. and Blyth, M. (2019), 'The global economics of European populism: Growth regimes and party system change in Europe', *Government and Opposition*, 54(2): 193–225.

Inglehart, R. F. (2008), 'Changing values among western publics from 1970 to 2006', *West European Politics*, 31(1-2): 130–46.

Katsambekis, G. and Kioupkiolis, A. (eds.) (2019), *The Populist Radical Left in Europe* (London: Routledge).

Katz, R. S. and Mair, P. (1995), 'Changing models of party organization and party democracy: The emergence of the cartel party', *Party Politics*, 1(1): 5–28.

Kirchheimer, O. (1966), 'The transformation of the Western European party systems', in J. La Palombara and M. Weiner (eds.) *Political Parties and Political Development* (Princeton, NJ: Princeton University Press): 177–200.

Kitschelt, H. (1994), *The Transformation of European Social Democracy* (Cambridge: Cambridge University Press).

Kriesi, H. (1998), 'The transformation of cleavage politics: The 1997 Stein Rokkan lecture', *European Journal of Political Research*, 33(2): 165–85.

Kriesi, H., Grande, E. et al. (2006), 'Globalization and the transformation of the national political space: Six European countries compared', *European Journal of Political Research*, 45(6): 921–56.

Krouwel, A. (2012), *Party Transformations in European Democracies* (New York: State University of New York Press).

Krouwel, A. and van Elfrinkhof, A. (2014), 'Combining strengths of methods of party positioning to counter their weaknesses: The development of a new methodology to calibrate parties on issues and ideological dimensions', *Quality and Quantity*, 48(3): 1455–72.

Lipset, S. M. and Rokkan, S. (1967), *Party Systems and Voter Alignments: Cross-National Perspectives* (New York: Free Press).

Mair, P. (2013), *Ruling the Void: The Hollowing of Western Democracy* (London: Verso).

Michels, Robert (1962), *Political Parties: A Study of the Oligarchical Tendencies of Modern Democracy* (New York: Collier Books).

Neumann, S. (ed.) (1956), *Modern Political Parties: Approaches to Comparative Politics* (Chicago, IL: University of Chicago Press).

Ostrogorski, M. (1902), *Democracy and the Organization of Political Parties* (London: Macmillan).

Otjes, S. (2015), 'Hervormen en Herverdelen. Is de links-rechtslijn de enige conflictlijn op het sociaaleconomisch terrein', *Res Publica*, 57(2): 133–58.

Otjes, S. (2016), 'How the Eurozone crisis reshaped the national economic policy space: The Netherlands 2006–2012', *Acta Politica*, 51(3): 273–97.

Poguntke, T. and Webb, P. (eds.) (2005), *The Presidentialization of Politics: A Comparative Study of Modern Democracies* (Oxford: Oxford University Press).

Rueschemeyer, D., Stephens, E. H. et al. (1992), *Capitalist Development and Democracy* (Cambridge: Polity).

Sartori, G. (1976), *Parties and Party Systems: A Framework for Analysis* (Cambridge: Cambridge University Press).

Webb, P. and Poguntke, T. (2013), 'The presidentialisation of politics thesis defended', *Parliamentary Affairs*, 66(3): 646–54.

4 Voting Behaviour

ERIK TILLMAN

4.1 Introduction

Recent years have seen increased electoral volatility. The rise of new parties (especially populist parties, see Chapter 18) and the decline of established parties have raised questions about whether the links between citizens and parties are changing. These questions are important because elections are at the heart of democracy, providing the mechanism by which voters select representatives and governments. How do voters decide which parties or candidates to support? Are citizens most likely to vote for parties that represent their own social groups? Or do citizens seek to select parties that hold positions on the most important issues that are closest to their own? Or is voting mostly about rewarding and punishing the government in power for its performance? Understanding the motivations of voters is important because each of these possible reasons suggests a very different process by which governments are evaluated by voters. This chapter begins by reviewing the main theories that have been put forward to explain voting behaviour (see Sections 4.2 and 4.3 on sociological and rationalist 'models of voting'), before turning to an examination of how voting has changed over time (see Section 4.5) and how it differs between Western and Eastern Europe (see Section 4.6).

4.2 Sociological models of voting

One might assume that most voters make up their minds during election campaigns. Early research provided a different view: many voters have long-term attachments to a political party, so campaigns have little chance to persuade them to vote for another party. Then why do parties invest so heavily in campaigns? One reason is to mobilize their supporters to vote. Also, there are some persuadable voters, whose support could be decisive. This 'minimal effects' argument—which shows that election campaigns reinforce voters' beliefs rather than change them (Berelson et al. 1954)—raises a bigger question: where do voters' political attachments come from? In addition, we observe a mix of similarity and difference across European societies. For example, most European political systems have a social democratic or labour party that traces its origins to a worker's movement of the early twentieth century (see Chapter 3, Section 3.3), suggesting a common pattern. But only some states have regional nationalist parties (for example, the Scottish National Party in the United Kingdom) while others do not (France or Germany). The study of voting behaviour from the perspective of political sociology can help explain these questions.

Political sociology examines the importance of group attachments (to groups like family, local community, occupation, and religion) in shaping political identities and behaviour. Group attachments shape the process of political socialization, by which people develop ideas and beliefs about politics and their role in society and the political system. As individuals grow up, they internalize political values and beliefs from their family, their community and friends, their schools, their religious institutions, and the media. Political parties seek to present themselves as 'the party of' certain groups, such as workers (the UK Labour Party), Catholics (The Maltese Nationalist Party), farmers (Denmark's Liberal Party), or ethnic groups (such as Together for Catalonia in Spain). To the extent they are successful in this aim, the process of political socialization may lead to a durable attachment forming between that party and members of that social group.

4.2.1 **Political cleavages**

Chapter 3 introduced the 'frozen systems' argument (see Section 3.3). Lipset and Rokkan (1967) claim that the national and industrial revolutions of the recent centuries generated a series of political cleavages—namely, a *centre-periphery* cleavage, a *church-state* cleavage, an *urban-rural* cleavage, and an *owner-worker* (or *class*) cleavage. As West European states expanded the franchise in the early twentieth century, political parties sought to integrate new voters into politics—mobilizing and articulating on behalf of their shared identity and interests (Lipset and Rokkan did not include the states of Central and Eastern Europe under communist rule in their study). These parties were typically part of a broader network of social and political organizations that created bonds among members.

Members of each group should vote for parties affiliated with their side of the political cleavage. But how do individuals choose between multiple identities? For example, how would a working-class Catholic vote if Catholics and workers typically vote for different parties? To some degree, it depends on how political cleavages developed in a state and were integrated into the party system so that national history—such as how and when industrialization occurred and the religious history of a country—is important in this argument.

We can still derive some general predictions about political cleavages and electoral behaviour from Lipset and Rokkan's account. First, the class cleavage between owners and workers is typically the most influential. In most states, workers have historically been more likely to vote for social democratic parties. Second, the church-state cleavage is important in many European states. Individuals with strong religious affiliations should be more likely to vote for a party linked to that religious tradition—often a Christian democratic or conservative party. Third, conservative parties often emerged in part to defend the interests of landed elites against the rising influence of urban industrialists. As a result, conservative parties should get more support from voters in rural areas while liberal and social democratic parties are stronger among urban voters. Finally, the centre-periphery cleavage exists in fewer states. In those states, voters who identify more strongly with the peripheral region (that is, those voters who think of themselves as primarily Scottish or Catalonian, for example) should support regionalist nationalist parties in greater numbers.

Do political cleavages still matter today? The frozen party systems described by Lipset and Rokkan in the 1960s have 'melted' significantly since then (see also Chapter 3, Section 3.5). Later in this chapter, we will examine possible reasons for this (see 'Political change?'). Still, political cleavages provide a valuable starting point for understanding the durable attachments between voters and political parties.

4.2.2 **Party identification**

While Lipset and Rokkan were developing their argument about political cleavages, researchers in the United States developed an alternative sociological theory of party attachment (Campbell et al. 1960). In the United States (and some European societies), political cleavages are not strongly related to party support, but many voters still develop durable attachments to a party. The authors' explanation for this puzzle is the concept of *party identification*. Party identification is a durable and affective (meaning that it includes an emotional component) attachment to a political party.

According to this theory, party identification is the main cause of political behaviour: it provides a cue to citizens about important political questions, so party identifiers will normally vote for candidates of their preferred party and adopt their party's positions on major political issues. One's party identity normally remains stable throughout adult life. Thus, it is central to one's political identity, providing a way for citizens to understand and participate in politics despite limited interest or knowledge.

The application of party identification to understand European voting behaviour has yielded mixed results. Figure 4.1 shows the prevalence of party identification in six European countries, comparing those who indicated an attachment to a party and those who do not. Levels of party identification are around 50% in Finland, Germany, and France, but much

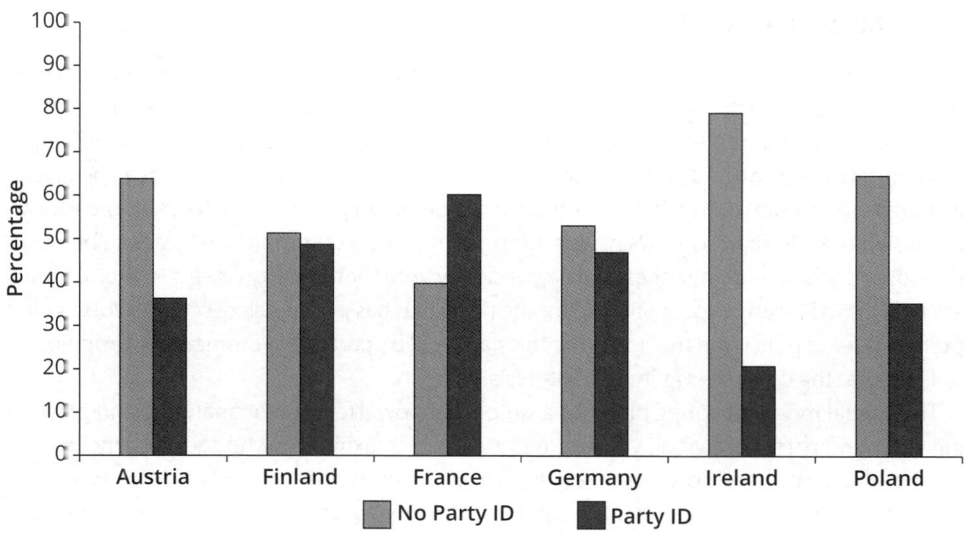

Figure 4.1 Party identification in Europe

Note: The bars show the percentage of respondents in each state who indicate that they feel close to a particular party versus those who do not.

Source: The Comparative Study of Electoral Systems (www.cses.org). CSES MODULE 4 FULL RELEASE [dataset and documentation]. 29 May 2018 version at doi:10.7804/cses.module4.2018-05-29.

lower in Ireland, Austria, and Poland. There are several reasons why party identification is less prevalent in some countries. In multiparty systems (such as in Poland and Austria), parties are easier to form, and there may be multiple parties with similar ideologies and voter profiles; voters are therefore less likely to form a durable attachment to one party. Also, it takes time for party identification to form in new democracies, such as the post-communist states. Finally, party identification is more powerful when the party label (such as 'Labour', 'Conservative', 'Nationalist', or 'Catholic') provides information to voters about candidates that they would otherwise struggle to obtain.

4.3 Rationalist models of voting

While political sociologists were developing group-based account of voting behaviour, other scholars, most notably Anthony Downs, approached the study of voting from the perspective of political economy. Rather than study voters in terms of group attachments, political economists view voters as individuals with preferences about the political outcomes they desire. Political economists assume that voting is rational, meaning that voters will vote to maximize their expected utility (or benefit) from voting.

Rationalist models of voting behaviour assume that voters have preferences about desired political outcomes. These models ignore—or take as given—the process of political socialization that shapes political values. But doing so allows rationalist models to address questions that sociological models cannot about the dynamics of elections. Specifically, why would people switch parties between elections? And how do parties compete to win votes? Sociological theories emphasize the stability of party support over time; rationalist theories focus on the dynamics.

4.3.1 The spatial model

In 1957, Anthony Downs published *An Economic Theory of Democracy*. Downs' analysis uses the concept of the left-right ideological space, establishing the *spatial* model. The spatial model assumes that the entire constellation of policies can be distilled to a single left-right ideological dimension and plotted within that space. Thus, each party and voter can be placed at a single ideal point on the left-right scale, and voters can place themselves and the various parties on the left-right scale. Using this information, voters determine the distance between their own position and that of each party, and they vote for the party closest to them. Voters are *policy maximizers*: a voter will vote for the party that has policies closest to the voter's own preferred set of policies in the hope that this party will be part of government and implement policies that the voter sees as in their interests.

The spatial model of voting provides a simple yet powerful tool for analyzing and predicting voter and party behaviour. While voters are policy maximizers who seek a party that has policies that match their own preferences, Downs assumes that parties are *vote maximizers* that are interested in attracting the support of as many voters as possible. Parties therefore position themselves to gain the largest share of votes possible, given the distribution of voters along the left-right scale and the position of other parties. By modifying assumptions about the ideological distribution of voters and of rival parties, one can derive different predictions about where parties will position themselves. In a two-party system, the rational behaviour for each party is to move to the centre, as close as possible to the median voter. In this way, each party will attract all the voters closer to it than the rival party while splitting the voters in the middle. By contrast, parties in a multiparty system have an incentive to spread out, maximizing their ideological distance from other parties while still retaining a group of loyal voters.

It is important to note that the spatial model rests on major assumptions about voters and parties. First, it assumes that voters and parties share an understanding about the meaning of 'left' and 'right'. While this may seem uncontroversial, remember that the left–right scale may condense multiple dimensions of conflict. Downs believed that voters would focus on parties' economic positions because they lack full information about all the policy positions held by a party. As a result, voters would understand left-wing parties to support increasing state intervention in the economy and right-wing parties to promote a market economy. This assumption may unrealistically diminish the importance of socio-cultural issues, such as attitudes towards gender and reproductive rights.

A second question is whether voters have the necessary knowledge about politics to place themselves and parties on the left–right scale. Consider the distribution shown in Figure 4.2. Why do so many voters place themselves at the midpoint of the scale? One possibility is that they believe that they stand at the middle of the ideological spectrum. But another is that they are uncertain, so they place themselves in the middle when asked in a survey. If voters cannot reliably place themselves or parties on the left–right scale, then it is hard to imagine how they could vote in a manner consistent with the spatial model.

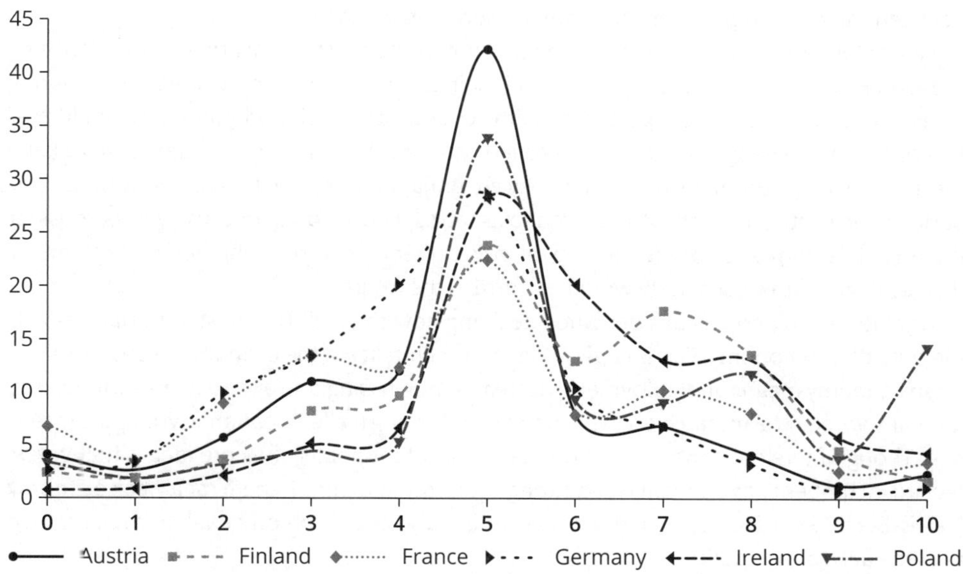

Figure 4.2 Ideological self-placement

Note: The lines show the percentage of respondents in each country placing themselves at each point along the left-right scale where zero indicates 'left' and ten indicates 'right'.

Source: Comparative Study of Electoral Systems, Wave 4.

A final assumption about the spatial model is that voters behave prospectively. In other words, they vote based on their expectations about future party behaviour and outcomes. Although this assumption seems reasonable, it also suggests that voters ignore or downplay parties' past actions. In the spatial model, parties' past behaviour may be important to establish their positions on the left–right dimension, but it is not a direct factor in voting behaviour. If this assumption seems unrealistic, the next model takes the reverse approach.

4.3.2 **Performance voting**

Although the ideological content of parties' positions may be important to voters, there are other issues that do not map out as cleanly onto the ideological spectrum. Consider the state of the economy. Is a strong economy a 'left-wing' or 'right-wing' position? Or what about public safety? Presumably, most citizens prefer to live in communities with low crime. Similar points could be made about issues such as education, foreign policy, health care, and others. On these issues, voters are less interested in the substance of parties' policies (which may be too complex for most voters to understand) but they want a good outcome: a growing economy, good schools, safe streets, and a secure and respected position for their country in the world.

These are known as valence issues. Valence issues are ones on which most voters agree on the goal but disagree about which party is most likely to deliver it. Valence issues contrast with position issues, about which voters and parties have different goals and which form the basis of spatial voting. A prosperous economy is a valence issue, while the level of taxation and social spending is a position issue. However, parties take positions on issues such as taxation or social spending in part to signal their ability to manage the economy, so the difference between valence and position issues can be blurred in practice.

Models of performance voting assume that voters are mostly concerned with valence issues and judge the parties in government on their ability to deliver these policy ends. During an election, voters evaluate the situation in the country and decide whether they would prefer continuity or change. If voters are satisfied with how things are going, they vote to keep the incumbent government in power; if they are unhappy, they vote for the opposition. Thus, performance voting is often also referred to as retrospective voting because voters consider the recent performance of the incumbent government when deciding how to vote rather than evaluating how each party would perform in the future.

What issues do people consider when deciding how to vote? The most important issue is the state of the economy. This is largely due to the centrality of the economy to people's lives: a bad economy means unemployment, decreased purchasing power, and financial insecurity for many voters. The research on the economy and voting (called 'economic voting') is extensive. Though there are controversies on many important points, the core idea is that voters reward incumbent governments for a strong economy and punish them for a weak economy (Lewis-Beck 1988). However, performance voting also occurs on other valence issues, such as crime and foreign policy.

An interesting finding to emerge from economic voting research is that voters are sociotropic: voters judge governments on the state of the national economy rather than their own personal finances (Lewin 1991). Why could this be? One possibility is that voters attribute their own personal (or household) finances to their own actions or local circumstances rather than the government's management of the economy. Another possibility is that voters attribute their financial condition to the government, but unique personal circumstances 'cancel out' when we examine the behaviour of the electorate at large.

One advantage of the performance voting model is that it assumes less of voters than the spatial voting model. Voters do not need to understand the different parties' positions on the major issues or have clear personal preferences. Instead, voters only need to judge whether conditions are getting better or worse and whether the government is responsible for that. While voters are still assumed to be rational, performance voting does not require much knowledge about politics. Performance voting also provides a mechanism for democratic accountability. Because governing parties want to stay in office, they will have an incentive to govern well. Conversely, opposition parties will have an incentive to present themselves as credible alternatives to the incumbents. The result should be competitive pressures to govern well.

There are several limitations to the performance voting model. First, it seems naturally suited for two-party systems, where voters have a clear choice between a governing party and an opposition party. In this case, voters can reasonably conclude that the governing party is responsible for conditions in the country. But it is not as obvious how this model should work in multiparty systems, where coalition or minority governments are common. We explore this problem more in Box 4.1. Clarity of responsibility is reduced when two or more parties share government, because voters cannot be certain about which party deserves credit for conditions, or how they should vote to reward or punish the government (Powell and Whitten 1993).

Theories of performance voting also raise a broader normative question. Performance voting makes sense if governments are responsible for national conditions. If the government had little control over these conditions, then voters would be 'incorrectly' rewarding or punishing them. Various factors—the global economy, natural disasters, international conflicts, and global health crises like Covid-19, which has seen some governments gain support and others lose it—can affect the apparent performance of an incumbent government. Achen and Bartels (2017) argue that voters sometimes reward and punish governments for circumstances beyond their control, which they call 'blind retrospection'. Does it weaken democratic accountability if election outcomes are as much a question of luck as good governance?

Finally, it is important to remember that the distinction between position and valence issues can be blurry. Although it seems straightforward to argue that voters agree on a set of shared goals such as a prosperous economy, safe streets, and good schools, the reality is often that policies aimed at achieving these goals have unequal effects. For example, investors may benefit from one set of economic policies while workers would benefit from another, so each group might evaluate the same economy as performing differently.

4.4 **Evaluating the evidence**

How well do these different models explain voting behaviour in practice? The quick answer is that each contributes partially to our understanding since it depends on what aspect of voting behaviour one hopes to explain. For example, sociological models are more useful to explain why certain groups of voters lean towards specific parties while rationalist models are more helpful when examining changes from one election to the next.

Box 4.1 Clarity of responsibility and performance voting

Performance voting theory suggests that voters should reward the incumbent government when things are going well and punish it when things are going badly. But what if the institutional and political context makes it difficult for voters to assess government responsibility, or to determine how to vote to effect a change? These were the questions raised in a series of studies that introduced the concept of clarity of responsibility. Powell and Whitten (1993) were the first to develop the concept of clarity of responsibility in a study of economic voting. They argued that factors such as the presence of coalition or minority governments, a bicameral legislature, or opposition control of parliamentary committees could diffuse responsibility for national conditions, leaving voters uncertain about whom to hold accountable. In addition, voters in multiparty systems with coalition governments may be unsure about which party to vote for to punish the incumbents and achieve a change in government (Anderson 2000).

Let's explore how clarity of responsibility worked in recent parliamentary elections in three different European states. The 2011 parliamentary elections in Ireland provide an example of high clarity of responsibility. Historically, two main parties—*Fianna Fáil* and *Fine Gael*—dominate its party system. At the time of the 2011 election, *Fianna Fáil* had led the government since 1997, giving it virtually sole responsibility for conditions in the eyes of voters, while *Fine Gael* stood as a clear alternative to form the next government. The election occurred during the European financial crisis and Irish voters punished *Fianna Fáil*, which lost over half of its votes compared to the previous election in 2007 and fell from the largest to the third-largest party. *Fine Gael* emerged as the largest party and led a coalition government until the 2016 election and a minority government until the 2020 election, meaning it had assumed responsibility for the performance of the economy in voters' eyes.

Elections in Finland provide an example of low clarity of responsibility. At the time of the 2015 parliamentary election, the incumbent government was a four-party coalition consisting of the centre-right National Coalition Party (*KOK*), the centre-left Social Democratic Party (*SDP*), and the smaller Swedish People's Party and the Christian Democrats. Responsibility was diffused among four parties, including the largest party of the centre-right and centre-left, respectively. Voters looking for a change could support two larger opposition parties—the Centre Party (*KESK*) or the Finns Party (*PS*)—or one of several smaller parties. The Centre Party became the largest party, increasing its position by fourteen seats in the 200-seat parliament, while the Finns Party became the second largest despite losing a small share of votes and one seat. *KOK* and *SDP* both lost votes and seats. The resulting government led by the Centre Party included *KOK* and *PS*, meaning that only a partial alternation of parties in government occurred. Similarly, the 2019 election led to the formation of a coalition between *SDP*, *KESK*, and three other parties, meaning that *KESK* remained in government despite falling from the largest to fourth-largest party.

What do these elections show? Performance voting is more difficult in low-clarity contexts because it is unlikely that any election will produce a full alternation of power in the next government. And voters may be uncertain about how to vote to punish an incumbent government when they cannot anticipate the outcome of post-election coalition negotiations. Though many political scientists believe that multiparty systems offer advantages over two-party systems, the reduced clarity of responsibility is one possible trade-off.

A deeper answer suggests that each model can explain some part of the puzzle, but larger questions can be revealed. For example, Figure 4.3 shows the relationship between social class and party support among English voters in the 2015 and 2019 British general elections (measured as net Conservative support). Members of managerial and professional classes,

Figure 4.3 Class and party support in Great Britain

Note: The bars show net Conservative Party support (measured as Labour vote subtracted from Conservative vote) among English respondents in each occupational group in the 2015 and 2019 UK general elections.

Source: Source data from British Election Study 2015 Panel Study, Wave 4 and British Election Study 2019 Panel Study, Wave 19 at http://www.britishelectionstudy.com/data/.

as well as the self-employed, and small business owners (SBOs), supported the Conservative Party on balance in both elections. However, workers in routine and semi-routine occupations supported Labour in 2015 but flipped to the Conservative Party in 2019. These patterns are only partially consistent with the claim that the middle classes support conservative parties and working classes support social democratic parties, and the gaps in party support are moderate in size. Thus, group identities like class still shape party support, but their impact is smaller today than it was a generation ago. Also, the composition of the electorate is changing as European societies move from industrial to post-industrial economies. In Box 4.2, we explore the complexities of measuring 'class' in more detail.

Rationalist voting models raise a different set of concerns. Figure 4.4 shows how identifiers of the Conservative and Labour Party evaluated the performance of the British economy over the past year at the time of the 2019 general election. Performance voting suggests that individuals will reward or punish the incumbent Conservative Party based on their evaluation of the economy. But what if partisanship influences how one perceives the economy? Fewer Conservative partisans (27%) believed the economy had worsened than did Labour partisans (73%). Some of this gap could reflect the different economic realities of each party's supporters. However, partisans of the incumbent party are more likely to believe the economy is doing well, while partisans of the opposition parties believe it is doing worse. More generally, the direction of causality is a major concern in rationalist models of voting: do voters evaluate parties based on the issues or performance in government, or do they adapt their issue opinions and performance evaluations to fit their partisanship? The answer seems to be a mixture of both, but controversy remains over the extent to which causality runs in each direction.

Box 4.2 Over to you—social class and voting

Sociological models of voting claim that class membership influences voting behaviour. But how should we measure class? During the mid-century peak of the industrial economy in Western Europe, it was relatively easy to differentiate members of the working class from the middle class. In recent decades, the rise of the service economy has created a wider range of employment roles that cannot be as easily classified, and the weakening of union and community ties mean that workers today are not as embedded in a class-based social network. Thus, it is more difficult to measure class and determine how it affects voting behaviour today.

You can examine this by visiting a national or cross-national survey website that allows online analysis. Some good choices include the European Social Survey or the World Values Survey. For example, the British Election Study website has a 'Data Playground' where you can download data and create charts online. You could analyze the relationship between vote intention ('General election vote intention') and any of several variables that measure class. One possibility is a subjective measure ('Do you ever think of yourself as belonging to any particular class?'). Another option is educational attainment ('Age completed formal education'). A third option is a measure of occupational category ('The National Statistics Socio-economic Classification social class analytic categories'). How would we identify members of the working class using each measure? And does each measure show that members of the working class are more likely to vote Labour? What does this tell you about the relationship between class and voting behaviour in the contemporary era?

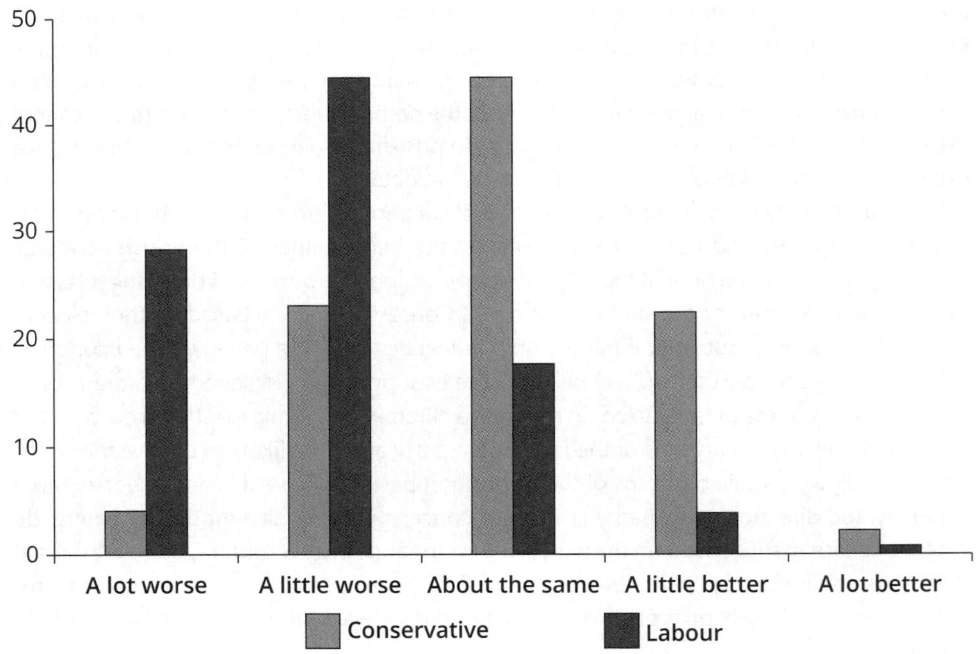

Figure 4.4 Partisanship and evaluations of the national economy

Source: British Election Study 2019 Panel Study, Wave 17, at http://www.britishelectionstudy.com/data.

4.5 Political change?

Section 4.2.1 on political cleavages notes that parties were often part of a larger social network in which individuals were embedded. Religious parties were linked to church and educational institutions that supported and linked members of those communities; social democratic parties were connected to unions and other labour organizations that structured working-class communities. During that era, politics—and much of life—was more 'local' than it is today. Members of religious, class, or ethno-linguistic communities had less opportunity for contact with other groups, which strengthened the influence of political socialization on party loyalties.

But a series of developments that accelerated after World War II changed the situation. The influence of these changes was not lost on Lipset and Rokkan (1967: 55), who noted the threat of the 'welfare state, the spread of the "car and TV" culture, the educational explosion' to the older social and political arrangements. What happened, and what effect did these changes have on electoral behaviour?

The first of these changes was the rapid expansion of the welfare state in the years following 1945. One important welfare programme was the construction of new housing. These new housing estates resulted in the relocation of many residents from dense urban neighbourhoods, which eroded traditional community networks, bringing those residents into contact with other social groups. Second, the greater availability of cars also increased mobility. Third, the rise of television and mass communication provided new outlets for news and entertainment, reducing people's reliance on traditional networks for political information and for social activities. Finally, the expansion of mass education in the post-war years increased 'cognitive mobilization' among younger generations. Cognitive mobilization is theorized as increasing one's ability to think and act independently without cues from trusted social agents. The net effect of these combined changes was to produce an electorate (particularly among the younger post-war generations) that was more independent and less connected to the old social and party networks.

Increased social mobility and cognitive mobilization posed a threat to the traditional social networks and political cleavages that determined voting behaviour. But if the old political cleavages were losing their power, what would replace them? How would post-war generations who came of age in a more socially mobile, prosperous, and educated era decide how to vote? Rival perspectives emerged starting in the 1970s.

4.5.1 Values change and realignment

Political scientist Ronald Inglehart proposed one answer to this question in *The Silent Revolution* (1977) and a series of subsequent books. He argued that an important social and political revolution was occurring in Western societies, resulting in a fundamental shift in how citizens approach politics and develop political loyalties.

The changes of the post-war years had two important consequences. First, the increasing affluence of post-war Western Europe meant that younger generations grew up in an era of relative economic and material security compared to previous generations, and the expansion of welfare state programmes meant that this prosperity was more widely shared.

In addition, the threat of future war between European states diminished after 1945. Growing up in this environment, post-war West Europeans did not confront questions of material security and survival as much as earlier generations. Second, increased cognitive mobilization produced younger generations who were more willing to engage with politics critically rather than deferentially. Higher educational attainment was also accompanied by the growth of non-manual jobs in the service economy, which require greater autonomy and cognitive skills.

These changes led to an intergenerational values shift. Older generations were socialized during times of scarcity (and a greater threat of war), so they prioritized achieving physical and economic security. Inglehart called these 'materialist values'. People with materialist values are motivated by a desire to achieve security in their lives, and they tend to prefer that governments ensure law and order, increase economic prosperity, and keep the country safe. By contrast, younger generations did not face these material concerns. Inglehart argued that they would focus on issues relating to quality of life, individual autonomy and self-expression, and broader questions of social justice—what he called 'post-materialist' values.

This values divide translates into political behaviour, shaping the issues that motivate different groups of voters and putting pressure on existing party systems. The conflict at the heart of these differences pits a desire for greater self-expression and social justice against a desire to ensure economic and social security. Post-materialists tend to demand greater freedom of personal expression and the liberation of those seen as repressed in the existing social and political order (the liberation of women from the oppression of patriarchy, for example). In addition, they push for environmental protection and greater concern for quality of life. Finally, post-materialists demanded greater participation and openness in social and political life. According to Inglehart, post-materialists want a more individualistic and emancipatory society, in contrast to materialists' desire for a society that was secure and prosperous (see Figure 4.5 for a comparison of post-materialist attitudes in different societies).

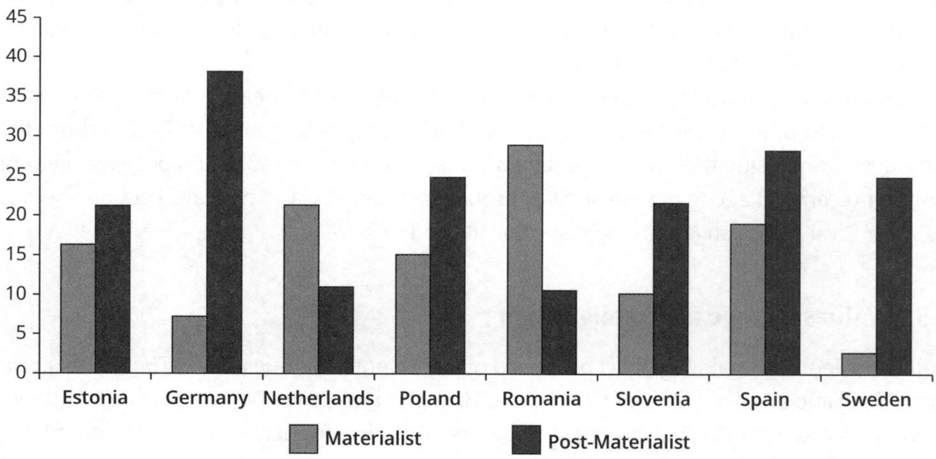

Figure 4.5 Materialist and post-materialist values in selected countries

Note: The bars show the percentage of respondents scoring as materialists and post-materialists, respectively, based on their responses to a four-item battery.

Source: Inglehart, R. et al. (eds.), (2022), World Values Survey: Round Six–Country-Pooled Datafile Version at http://www.worldvaluessurvey.org/WVSDocumentationWV6.jsp. Madrid: JD Systems Institute.

The hypothesized result of these changes is an electoral realignment. A realignment is a fundamental and durable shift in the patterns of which parties people support. Realignments result in a new structure of party competition and voting behaviour. These changes can include voters switching their loyalties from one established party to another; it can also include the creation of new parties—such as green parties—and the collapse of existing parties, or the decline of their vote (for example, the defection of some voters from social democratic to green parties). Though a single 'critical election' may trigger a realignment, they are typically longer-term processes that occur through generational replacement (i.e. younger voters replacing older voters) and a gradual process of voters changing their loyalties.

Has values change triggered a realignment in Western Europe? As the strength of traditional party attachments weakened among new generations, new attachments were formed in their place that were based on values rather than group affiliations. An important result of this values shift was the rise of the 'new left' starting in the 1970s. In contrast to the 'old left', whose roots were in the labour movement, the new left had middle-class origins and emphasized environmental protection and economic and social justice—a strongly 'post-materialist' agenda. The clearest political manifestation of the new left came in the rise of green parties in Western Europe in the 1980s (see Chapter 15), though states with majoritarian electoral systems may have seen the new left become a faction within social democratic parties.

Inglehart's theory of post-materialism has been influential, but it has received various criticisms. One problem is that levels of post-materialism fluctuate more over time than should be expected if these values emerge from early-life socialization. A second criticism suggests that post-materialism largely results from education, rather than affluence, though education may itself be a reflection of affluence. Third, some scholars have questioned whether there is truly a post-materialist value dimension, or whether it is measuring an authoritarian-libertarian dimension that has shifted towards libertarianism as societies have become more affluent.

Box 4.3 Over to you—post-materialist values

Inglehart's theory of values change rests on a socialization hypothesis. He argues that individuals develop post-materialist values when they grow up in economic and physical security, and these values remain durable throughout life. One criticism of this hypothesis is that post-materialist values among adults appear to increase and decrease concurrently with the state of the economy. In other words, people express less post-materialist values during times of economic hardship, which would suggest that these values reflect present conditions and not early-life socialization.

You can test this claim by examining the stability of post-materialist values over time. The World Values Survey contains a materialist–post-materialist value index asked since the 1980s in many European countries. Using the website's 'Online Analysis' tool, you can examine whether post-materialism has become more or less common in each country according to the state of the economy. In particular, you can compare the results from the last survey collected before the start of the global financial crisis in 2008 and the next one collected during the crisis. Did Europeans become more materialist because of the crisis? If so, what does this say about Inglehart's values change argument?

4.5.2 Globalization and realignment

Some political scientists agree that social and economic changes are leading to a realignment of political loyalties, but they do not agree with Inglehart's thesis about post-material values shifts. Instead, they attribute the realignment to the economic and cultural transformations caused by globalization (Kriesi et al. 2008).

Globalization describes the process of opening national borders to trade, investment, services, and migration. Economically, globalization has facilitated the transformation of West European economies from industry and manufacturing towards finance, technology, and services. The result has been a shift in employment from manual jobs in industrial settings to skilled jobs in office settings. This shift has benefited workers with university degrees, while those with lower educational attainment now have fewer job opportunities and reduced earnings potential. Many of the new jobs in finance and technology have clustered in a few major urban areas, such as London or Frankfurt, while traditional industrial employment has declined in other cities, such as the cities of Northern England and Scotland, or the North of France. Thus, globalization has created economic 'winners' among mobile, educated workers while creating 'losers' among manual labourers and residents of industrial areas. Socially and culturally, globalization has been associated with increased migration. Increased migration from developing countries to the Western world is changing national and local demographics while generating debates about national identity and culture.

These transformations are creating a new dimension of political conflict over globalization versus national protection. On one side are those who benefit from globalization and who support a more open and diverse society. On the other side are those who are harmed by globalization and who prefer to preserve a national community. For a realignment to occur, the structure of electoral politics must shift to reflect this new divide rather than older political cleavages. Thus, educated, urban voters should support parties favouring globalization and openness while manual workers and voters in smaller cities should support parties favouring economic and cultural protection.

National party systems have evolved to reflect these shifts (see Chapter 3). Green parties such as The Greens in Germany that represent educated, urban voters have emerged in many countries, while populist radical-right parties, such as *Rassemblement National* in France, promise to protect the national community. Meanwhile, the established parties of the centre-left and centre-right have struggled to balance their traditional economic positions with a new global-national axis of conflict. Social democratic parties, like the UK's Labour Party, have sought to appeal to middle-class, urban voters by embracing globalization and immigration, at the risk of alienating traditional working-class supporters. And conservative and Christian democratic parties, like the UK Conservative Party, attempt to balance support for economic globalization among middle-class supporters with demands for greater protection of national communities among rural and suburban supporters.

Both models of realignment take the transformative social and economic changes of the past several decades as their starting point, and both can point to evidence in their support. But a broader concern remains. Voting behaviour research shows that many voters are not very interested in or knowledgeable about politics, despite gains in cognitive mobilization. As a result, few voters engage meaningfully with complex political issues such as globalization or the environment. Thus, it is unlikely that changing voter attitudes are driving realignment. Instead, realignment is usually an elite-driven process in which party leaders shift their public positions and voters follow their lead over time.

4.5.3 De-Alignment

Theories of de-alignment accept the argument that old political cleavages and loyalties have been eroded by post-war social and economic changes. But they differ from realignment theories in explaining what has replaced those older alignments. De-alignment describes a decrease in the proportion of voters who are attached to a specific party. The result is an increase in floating voters who do not identify with any party but are more likely to switch support between parties from one election to the next (Dalton 2004).

There are several causes of de-alignment. First, increasing cognitive mobilization and social mobility eroded old social attachments without generating new ones. Instead, people became more 'atomized' or self-interested in the post-war years. Second, increasing education produced younger generations of 'critical citizens' who approach politics with greater confidence and less deference towards political elites (Norris 1999). Third, the rise of modern communications, like the internet and social media apps like Twitter, allows voters to obtain political information independent of traditional community and party leaders who managed the flow of political information in previous times.

The result of these developments is a more critical, educated, and detached electorate in which fewer voters are loyal to a party. What will determine voting behaviour instead? First, valence issues and performance voting take on a greater role. Floating voters, who do not identify strongly with a party, are more likely to choose parties based on their performance in office. Second, voters should become more likely to vote for the party that they believe has the most competent leader or candidate(s) in their constituency.

De-alignment has several consequences for elections. First, electoral volatility increases, meaning that there are greater swings in party support from one election to the next, as each party can rely on fewer loyal voters during unfavourable times. Second, participation in politics will become more contingent. Voters may be less willing to perform the traditional work of party loyalists, such as volunteering for campaigns. This contingency may extend to voting itself, leading to reduced and more volatile turnout. Third, reduced attachment to established parties makes it easier for new parties to gain support and enter legislatures. Finally, de-alignment may reduce the incentive for parties to maintain their historical policy or group commitments. If parties cannot rely on the steady support of a group of voters, then they have more incentive to shift positions to appeal to floating voters. Such behaviour can create a vicious cycle if it further repels the shrinking pool of loyal voters.

In short, de-alignment argues that traditional political loyalties are giving way to a new form of politics in which detached and critical voters choose parties based on criteria such as recent performance in office or the quality of leaders. One example of this would be traditional working-class voters abandoning social democratic parties in Germany and the UK for centre-right parties that are seen as better able to manage the economy, or the rise of parties associated with 'strong' leaders like Silvio Berlusconi in Italy or who claim to 'transcend' ideological politics such as Emmanuel Macron in France.

Is this a healthy development for democracy? An optimistic view would be that voters are capable of greater individual engagement with politics, which increases accountability and responsiveness. A pessimistic view might be that campaigns and party leaders can more easily manipulate floating voters, who lack sufficient engagement to hold parties to account. One possibility is that de-alignment has made voters more receptive to populist messages.

4.6 Voting behaviour in post-communist Europe

The discussion so far has drawn on research conducted primarily in Western Europe and North America. During the formative years of voting behaviour research from the 1960s through the 1980s, most of Central and Eastern Europe was under communist rule and lacked free and fair elections.

The transition to democratic systems in the early 1990s raised several questions. First, how would voters develop party attachments when they had no previous experience with electoral politics? Second, how would the post-communist context shape the structure of partisan identities? Post-communist party systems developed in different social and economic contexts than that of West European party systems. Would they reflect similar cleavage structures to those in Western Europe, or would a new series of political cleavages form in post-communist Europe? Finally, would the same fundamentals of voting behaviour still apply as in Western Europe once post-communist realities were taken into account? Or would it be necessary to develop a fundamentally different understanding of voting behaviour in Central and Eastern Europe?

4.6.1 The post-communist context

The collapse of communist regimes led to rapid transformations in Eastern and Central Europe society. Electoral politics developed in the economic and social legacy of communism, so the issues and voting patterns dominating post-communist politics were different than those in Western Europe.

Post-communist Europe underwent a dramatic economic transformation in the 1990s. Communist regimes operated under the principle of a planned economy, in which the communist party leadership determined economic priorities and central state committees translated these priorities into production goals for industry. Communist regimes provided stable employment and economic security for a large share of workers, but many had become economically stagnant by the final years of communism. During the transitions of the early 1990s, state-run factories were privatized, and the post-communist economies opened to foreign competition. The shift to a market economy led to the downsizing and closure of many factories, along with the introduction of new managerial strategies emphasizing profit and efficiency.

Workers and communities experienced disruptions because of this economic transition. Many workers lost their jobs as state-run businesses closed, and communities dependent on employment from a single industry suffered. Although industrial areas in Western Europe had experienced similar challenges in the 1970s and 1980s, the scale of transformation was larger and faster in post-communist Europe. At the same time, the transition created more economic opportunities for enterprising individuals whose options were restricted under the old system. Thus, the transition produced economic winners (people with the skills to navigate economic reform and transfer economic resources like factories that had been state-owned into their own hands, the better educated, and people with political connections) and losers (people who were not able to manage reform or privatize state resources and people such as manual workers and the elderly).

Democratization also created major changes in the social environment. Communist regimes varied in their degree of repressiveness—Romania was more repressive than Hungary, for example—but all were one-party authoritarian systems. The generations who grew up in these regimes were socialized into a system that enforced social and political conformity. Acquiescence and deference were encouraged, while self-expression and protest were not. While West European societies experienced protest movements challenging the status quo in 1968 and later, the communist states were largely cut off from these changes.

4.6.2 **A post-communist alignment?**

The economic context facing post-communist states shaped the development of electoral politics. The creation of economic 'winners' and 'losers' during the transition shaped voting behaviour in post-communist Europe, forming the initial alignment of parties. But the relative newness of the system and the creation and destruction of parties in the early decades hindered the development of party identification.

The post-communist transition benefited individuals who found their opportunities limited under communism while harming those who had worked in protected state-run industries. The 'winners' of the transition included individuals attracted to entrepreneurial and creative occupations and those with advanced education in fields that transferred easily to a market economy. Finally, younger workers were less invested in the old system and had more opportunity to adjust to new economic realities. By contrast, the 'losers' included those who lost jobs because of privatization, those whose job skills did not transfer easily to the new economy, and older workers.

Parties formed to represent the interests of the winners and losers of the transition. New centre-right parties, like Fidesz in Hungary (in the 1990s), Civic Platform in Poland, and the Civic Democratic Party in the Czech Republic, presented the interests of the winners. They favour the market economy, democracy, and the liberalization of society. A key part of the transition was the integration of post-communist states into the Western order, which included membership in the European Union (EU). EU membership was attractive to winners of the transition because freedom of movement provides greater educational and employment opportunities than would be available in their home societies. Thus, centre-right parties tend to appeal to those with higher education and income by supporting the market economy, democracy, and EU membership. Left-wing parties organized around the interests of the losers of the transition. They opposed the transition to a market economy—and particularly the loss of economic protection and solidarity for workers. They further opposed the liberalization of society and EU membership. Thus, left-wing parties tend to appeal to those with lower education and income through support for a return to some variant of the communist economic system and opposition to EU membership (Marks et al. 2006).

This suggests that party loyalties in post-communist Europe are rooted in group identities and interests. These are slightly different than in Western Europe because of the different social and economic history, and they also vary across post-communist states (Kitschelt et al. 1999). But these may not be new political cleavages, because the broader networks of social institutions connecting parties and voters have not formed in these contexts. Instead, modern communications and the disintegration of the old communist social order have produced a more individualistic society such as that seen in contemporary Western Europe. Thus, it makes sense to describe this as a post-communist voter alignment, but there is more debate about whether it constitutes a political cleavage, as will be discussed in Section, 4.6.3.

4.6.3 **Post-Communist values**

Did the relatively lower level of prosperity and the authoritarian political system hinder the development of democratic or post-materialist values in East-Central Europe? The rising popularity of populist parties and leaders in several post-communist states has raised the question about whether democratic values are widely shared among the citizens of these states. The electoral success of Hungarian Prime Minister Viktor Orbán, who has tried to curtail opposition to his rule and who in a 2014 speech called for a new 'illiberal' political system based on a 'different, special', and 'national' approach to democracy, is often taken as one sign of the weakness of democratic values in post-communist Europe.

Figure 4.5 shows a comparison of post-materialist values in several European states. In general, post-materialist values are higher than materialist values in West European states (though the Netherlands is an exception), while the same is less frequently true in post-communist societies. Why might post-materialist values be lower in post-communist societies? A first explanation is that the generations who grew up during the communist era were socialized during an era of relative scarcity, which has shaped their adult worldview. Second, the end of communism led to a rise in inequality and unemployment, especially in the early years of the transition, so individuals who came of age during those years may have experienced rising insecurity. Finally, those who grew up during communism were socialized into a political system that discouraged self-expression or public debate, and their values may reflect that aspect of socialization as well.

Does support for illiberal parties reflect the higher levels of survival values in post-communist Europe? According to Inglehart (2018: 10), survival values prioritize the protection of one's own group, which may result in higher levels of ethnocentrism: the desire to promote one's own national or ethnic group over others. Post-materialism leads to the rise of universalistic values that promote equal concern for all people. A particular area of conflict between leaders like Orbán and his counterparts in Western Europe has concerned the treatment of minorities and refugees. Since coming to power, parties such as Orbán's *Fidesz* have sought to change laws concerning the treatment of minorities and the preservation of national identity and values. They have refused efforts by West European leaders to resettle Middle-Eastern refugees that started with the migrant crises of 2015. It may be the case that these leaders reflect the larger share of survival values of their voters.

4.6.4 **Post-Communist performance voting**

Given the rapid political and economic transition of the 1990s, is performance voting relevant in post-communist Europe? One might expect voters who have little attachment to new political parties to base their vote choice on the performance of parties in power, making economic voting in particular a powerful factor in elections. However, early studies of economic voting found relatively weak results, suggesting that the condition of the national economy had little effect on the vote. While this finding could indicate that citizens of post-communist states did not reward and punish governments for the state of the economy, a better understanding emerges by considering the post-communist context.

In *Regional Economic Voting*, Tucker (2006) argues that economic voting in post-communist states takes place in the shadow of the transition. Voters identify parties as being pro-market (and thus supportive of the transition) or anti-market (and thus opposed to the market transition). Rather than voting simply to reward or punish the incumbents for the state of the economy, voters instead consider those parties' positions regarding the transition. Voters who believe the economy has improved will be more likely to vote for pro-market parties, while voters who think the economy has worsened will be more likely to vote for anti-market parties. In this respect, voters apply a different logic of accountability based on parties' support for the transition to a market economy.

4.7 **Conclusion**

Voting is at the centre of democracy, and understanding why people vote for certain parties is crucial to our understanding of democratic politics. Like most social behaviour, the motivations behind voting are complex. Thus, we have multiple theories of voting, each of which helps us to explain different parts of the puzzle. Sociological theories are valuable for understanding the underlying structure and stability in a country's electoral politics, while rationalist theories are useful for explaining the competitive dynamics.

Recent decades have seen several new changes. First, the erosion of old party loyalties in Western Europe has made elections more volatile and less predictable, leading to debates about re-alignment or de-alignment. Second, the establishment of new democracies in post-communist states allows us to examine the development of voting behaviour among citizens with no prior history of voting. Finally, the rise of populism, the global financial crisis, and the migrant crises have challenged existing party systems (see Chapters 3, 14 and 18). Voting behaviour tends to change gradually as voter loyalties slowly shift and new generations replace old, but the coming decades will see new challenges to established patterns.

Discussion questions

1. What does a high level of party identification in an electorate mean for democratic representation? How would voters hold the government accountable if they vote based on long-term social attachments?
2. Is de-alignment a healthy development for democracy, or is it a trend we should be concerned about?
3. Does performance voting provide a useful mechanism of holding governments accountable, or are the fears about 'blind retrospection' justified?
4. Is globalization creating a new political cleavage in European societies? If so, what are the bonds linking voters together?

Thinking comparatively

How do voters evaluate government performance in a globalized economy? This question has been a central concern in the study of European politics, given the high levels of economic integration among EU member states. If the state of the national economy is shaped more by international than domestic factors, then how should voters evaluate the performance of their own national government? Do voters engage in 'blind retrospection', rewarding and punishing governments for factors beyond their control? One study suggests that voters are able to assess government performance in a globalized economy.

In an article titled 'Benchmarking across borders: Electoral accountability and the necessity of comparison', Kayser and Peress (2012) explore this puzzle. They observe that the international economic growth rate creates a 'benchmark' against which national economies can be compared. If the national economy is growing faster than the international economy, then it is performing better than the global economy, and vice versa. They hypothesize that voters will evaluate their governments on the basis of this 'benchmarked' analysis: they will reward the government when the national economy is outperforming the world economy and punish it when it is underperforming. In other words, voters can distinguish between the international economy (which the government cannot control) and the national economy's divergence from the international economy (which the government can control). They use aggregate election results and survey data from the Comparative Study of Electoral Systems and economic data to test this hypothesis in OECD countries. Their findings are consistent with their hypothesis, suggesting that voters engage in such 'benchmarking' when voting.

But how can this finding be reconciled with arguments about 'blind retrospection'? Kayser and Peress suggest the media plays a role. If national media report on benchmarked national economic performance, then voters can use this information when voting. Still, this finding leaves many questions unanswered. For example, do only relatively sophisticated voters—or perhaps those who work in globalized industries—engage in benchmarking? Also, it is important to remember that national governments may have limited responsibility for national economic over- or underperformance, so rewarding or punishing them for this may still be a form of 'blind retrospection'.

Guide to further reading

Dalton, R. (2004), *Democratic Challenges, Democratic Choices: The Erosion of Political Support in Advanced Industrial Democracies* (Oxford: Oxford University Press).

This book provides one of the most comprehensive accounts of the causes and consequences of voter de-alignment in the advanced democracies, suggesting a wide range of ways by which de-alignment may change both election outcomes as well as democracy itself.

Hellwig, T. (2014), *Globalization and Mass Politics: Retaining the Room to Manoeuvre* (Cambridge: Cambridge University Press).

Hellwig argues that globalization is constraining elected governments, as they must balance between the wishes of their votes and the demands of international market forces. This book examines how parties and voters respond to these growing constraints.

Inglehart, R. (2018), *Cultural Evolution: People's Motivations Are Changing and Reshaping the World* (Cambridge: Cambridge University Press).

After publishing *The Silent Revolution* in 1977, Inglehart produced a series of further studies, each building upon his post-materialism thesis and responding both to critics and ongoing developments. *Cultural Evolution* provides his final elaboration, in which he attempts to explain the rise of right-wing populism in this framework.

Kriesi, H., Grande, E. et al. (2008), *West European Politics in the Age of Globalization* (Cambridge: Cambridge University Press).

In a book that mixes theory with in-depth empirical analyses, Kriesi et al. examine the extent to which globalization is creating a new political cleavage in West European societies.

References

Achen, C. and Bartels, L. (2017), *Democracy for Realists: Why Elections Do Not Produce Responsive Government* (Princeton, NJ: Princeton University Press).

Anderson, C. J. (2000), 'Economic voting and political context: A comparative perspective', *Electoral Studies*, 19(2): 151–70.

Berelson, B., Lazarsfeld, P. and McPhee, W. (1954), *Voting: A Study of Opinion Formation in a Presidential Campaign* (Chicago, IL: University of Chicago Press).

Campbell, A., et al. (1960), *The American Voter* (New York: John Wiley & Sons).

Dalton, R. (2004), *Democratic Challenges, Democratic Choices: The Erosion of Political Support in Advanced Industrial Democracies* (Oxford: Oxford University Press).

Downs, A. (1957), *An Economic Theory of Democracy* (New York: Harper and Row).

Inglehart, R. (1977), *The Silent Revolution: Changing Values and Political Styles among Western Publics* (Princeton, NJ: Princeton University Press).

Inglehart, R. (2018), *Cultural Evolution. People's Motivations Are Changing and Reshaping the World* (Cambridge: Cambridge University Press).

Kayser, M. A. and Peress M. (2012), 'Benchmarking across borders: Electoral accountability and the necessity of comparison', *American Political Science Review*, 106(3): 661–84.

Kitschelt, H., et al. (1999), *Post-Communist Party Systems: Competition, Representation, and Inter-Party Cooperation* (Cambridge: Cambridge University Press).

Kriesi, H., et al. (2008), *West European Politics in the Age of Globalization* (Cambridge: Cambridge University Press).

Lewin, L. (1991), *Self-Interest and Public Interest in Western Politics* (Oxford: Oxford University Press).

Lewis-Beck, M. S. (1988), *Economics and Elections: The Major Western Democracies* (Ann Arbor, MI: University of Michigan Press).

Lipset, S. and Rokkan, S. (eds.) (1967), *Party Systems and Voter Alignments: Cross-National Perspectives* (New York: The Free Press).

Marks, G., et al. (2006), 'Party competition and European integration in East and West Europe: Different structure, same causality', *Comparative Political Studies*, 39(2): 155–75.

Norris, P. (ed.) (1999), *Critical Citizens: Global Support for Democratic Government* (New York: Oxford University Press).

Powell Jr, G. B. and Whitten, G. D. (1993), 'A cross-national analysis of economic voting: Taking account of the political context', *American Journal of Political Science*, 37(2): 391–414.

Tucker, J. A. (2006), *Regional Economic Voting: Russia, Poland, Hungary, Slovakia, and the Czech Republic, 1990–1999* (Cambridge: Cambridge University Press).

5

Political Participation

PATRICK BERNHAGEN AND ANGELIKA VETTER

5.1 Introduction

'Participation' refers to a wide range of citizens' activities, from low-intensity forms such as voting at an election or signing a petition, to more time-consuming and demanding forms such as attending a demonstration or collecting signatures. Most political scientists agree with the view that participation in elections and other forms of political engagement is 'the lifeblood of representative democracy' (Norris 2002: 5). By taking part in elections and in other forms of participation, citizens express diffuse support for the democratic system and provide policymakers with important information about their political preferences. Accordingly, there is widespread concern about citizens' withdrawal from active political involvement in European societies, supposedly manifest in declining electoral turnout, rising anti-party sentiment, and the waning of civic organizations (Poguntke et al. 2015). And while authors have stressed the importance of a free, lively, and valued civil and political society for the successful consolidation of new democracies (Letki 2004), many of the new democracies in Central and Eastern Europe have very low levels of citizen participation by international standards.

This chapter provides an overview of the main modes of citizen participation in politics, especially voting and protesting. We will first look at how turnout at elections and various forms of protest participation have developed in recent decades across European countries and examine the extent to which political participation is in decline (Section 5.2). Second, we will outline the main theoretical explanations for the observed differences in participation between countries and over time (Section 5.3). Third, we consider inequalities and decline in political participation (Section 5.4). And finally, we look at new opportunities for participation at the local level and ask whether these ameliorate or exacerbate existing problems of political apathy and unequal participation (Section 5.5).

5.2 Voting and protesting in Europe

By 'political participation' we mean activities of citizens intended to influence public bodies, their composition, or the decisions they make (cf. Barnes and Kaase 1979: 42) (see Box 5.1). This definition includes a wide range of different forms of political participation. In representative democracies, voting at competitive elections is the most important and widespread form of citizen participation in politics. By influencing who gets to sit in parliament and government, voting affects political decision-making only indirectly and in rather broad terms. The information that is transmitted to political elites by this form of political participation is very simple. Voters can express which party or candidate(s) they support, but not the reason behind their vote choices. This is why in the aftermath of an election there is so much analysis and speculation in the media by political scientists and pundits as to the reasons behind the gains of some and losses of other parties and what they should do differently in order to do better next time. Other activities include writing a petition, on behalf of a group of people, or attending a demonstration in relation to a specific cause. Such activities used to be referred to as 'unconventional' political participation (Kaase and Marsh 1979: 42–5). From the late 1960s onward, participation in these activities has become a common staple of political life in established democracies. These forms of political participation are often on a much smaller scale than, say, national elections. But they convey much richer information concerning the reasons behind them and the demands of the participants. This is most detailed in the context of petitions, which are often accompanied by lengthy analyses of the problem and thorough justification of the remedy proposed by the petitioners. But even participants in street demonstrations often identify very specific problems (e.g. 'too much air pollution') and make very specific demands (e.g. 'ban cars from urban centres'). In this chapter, we refer to these activities as *protest* participation.

Box 5.1 Over to you—forms of political participation

We have defined 'political participation' as activities of citizens intended to influence public bodies, their composition, or the decisions they make. While most scholars agree on these core elements of the concept of participation, some aspects are contested. For instance, Max Kaase and Alan Marsh (1979: 42) suggested that only explicitly 'voluntary activities' count as participation. Moreover, Pippa Norris (2002: 16) argued that political participation is not necessarily directed at public bodies or decision-makers but can encompass activities aimed at influencing the choices and behaviour of fellow citizens, non-governmental organizations, or business corporations. What do you think? Where would you draw the boundaries of what is considered 'political' participation? Consider the following examples:

(1) Is voting at elections still a form of political participation even if it is not voluntary but instead compulsory by law, as is the case in Belgium or Luxembourg?

(2) For many years now, a number of groups have called for a boycott of a major multinational technology company in protest against the company's tax avoidance schemes, support for fossil fuel giants, and firing of activist workers (Ethical Consumer Research Association 2023). What arguments can you find to support the view that people who avoid that particular brand's petrol stations when filling up their tank are acting politically? What arguments would speak against this view of consumer choice as a form of political participation?

5.2.1 **Voter turnout**

Voter turnout can be calculated in different ways. In the US, where many people are not registered to vote even though they would be entitled to, turnout is often calculated as that proportion of the voting-age population that actually voted. In most European countries voter registration is virtually automatic. Therefore, we will take as the denominator the number of voters registered. To describe turnout in European countries, we use data from the International Institute for Democracy and Electoral Assistance (IDEA), an international intergovernmental organization engaged in supporting democracy. Figure 5.1 shows average voter turnout at parliamentary elections between 2010 and 2022 in thirty-five European countries. The average of all thirty-five country turnout rates is 66%. However, there is considerable variation between the countries. Average turnout is particularly high in Luxembourg, Malta, and Belgium. In Luxembourg and Belgium, voting is compulsory, but in Malta it is not. At just 37%, average turnout is lowest in Romania. In Northern Europe, turnout tends to be above average. By contrast, in the younger democracies of Central and Eastern Europe, average turnout barely exceeds 65%.

How has voter turnout developed in recent decades? From the 1960s to the 1990s, turnout declined in most European countries. But there are also countries like Belgium, Denmark, Sweden, and the United Kingdom where turnout remained more or less stable over the decades (Blais 2010). We start our analyses in the 1990s, when free regular elections were introduced in the new democracies of Central and Eastern Europe. Table 5.1 enables us to take a closer look at trends of voter turnout since the early 1990s. The overall picture is that turnout declined in most of the countries under investigation, and in many cases quite considerably so. The decline is most pronounced in the Central and East European democracies, with a fall of twelve percentage points on average, compared to an average decline of only five percentage points in the Western democracies. But there are also notable differences within these two groups: in the West, turnout decreased considerably in Cyprus, France, Greece, Italy, and Portugal. By contrast, the decline has been more modest in Belgium, Ireland, and Germany. In six out of the twenty West-European countries (Denmark, Finland, Luxembourg, the Netherlands, Norway, and Switzerland), turnout actually increased slightly. Variance is also quite large in the younger democracies, ranging from a collapse of turnout (by thirty-nine percentage points) in Romania to a slight increase of four percentage points in Poland.

What explains these differences between countries and the changes in turnout over time? Some of the countries that experienced the sharpest drop in turnout are among those that were severely hit by the financial crisis of 2007–08 and its aftereffects (Cyprus, Greece, and Italy). We might wonder, therefore, whether the decline in turnout reflects citizens' disillusionment with politics. However, other countries, such as Ireland and Spain, also suffered badly from the crisis but experienced only modest decline in turnout. Thus, to understand what might cause the changes in electoral participation, we need theoretical guidance, which we will turn to. But first, we will take a look at citizen participation outside the polling booth.

5.2.2 **Protest participation**

The media frequently report on political protest events, especially if these are large or involve violence. Prominent examples abound: when European governments attempted to contain the fallout of the 2008 financial and economic crisis with the aid of austerity measures that

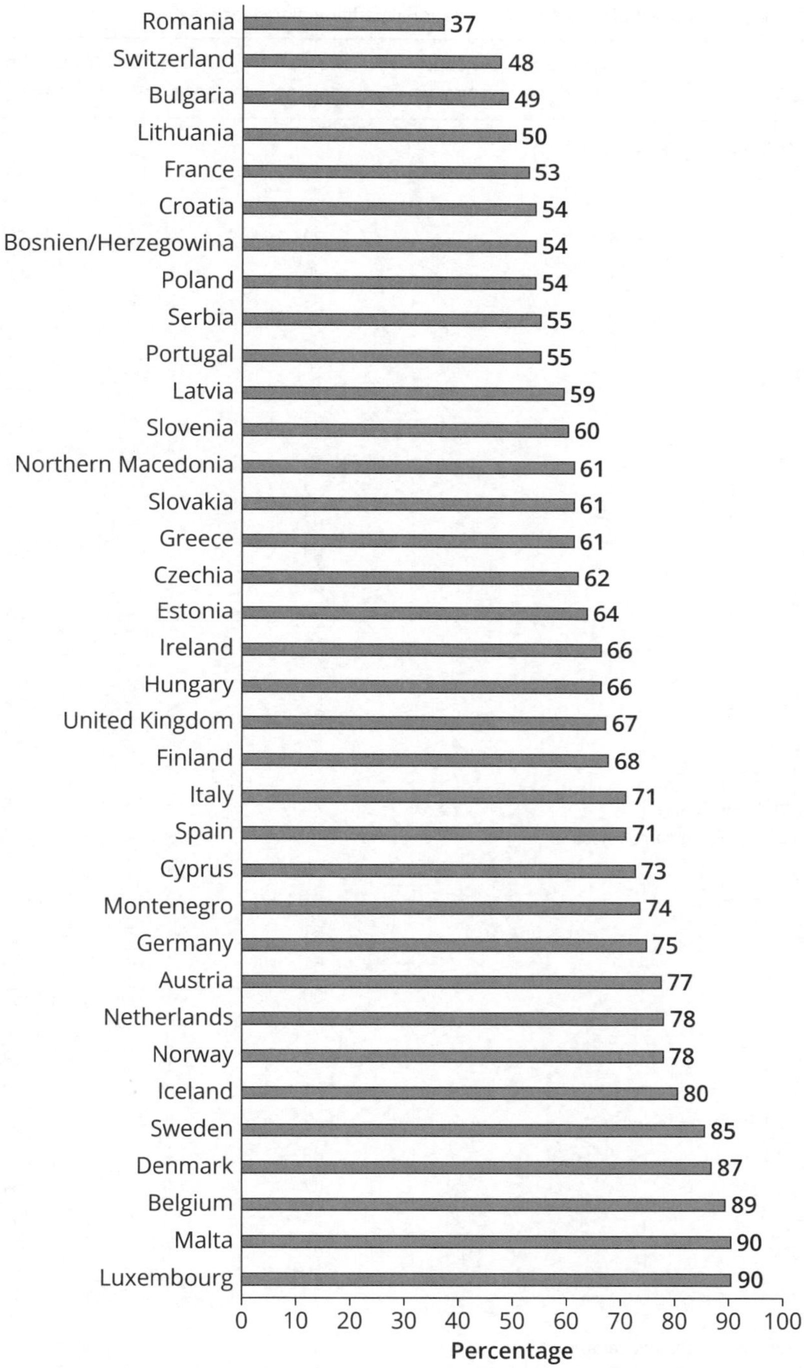

Figure 5.1 Average voter turnout (2010–22) at national parliamentary elections

Note: For countries whose national legislature has two chambers, only the election to the lower chamber is included. If elections are carried out in two rounds (e.g. in France), only the second election round is included.
Source: Source data from International IDEA, voter turnout data at https://www.idea.int/data-tools/data/voter-turnout.

Table 5.1 The development of voter turnout at national parliamentary elections[a]

Country	Means[b] 1990–99	Means[b] 2000–99	Means[b] 2010–22	Mean Difference 1990–2022
West European democracies				
Austria	84	81	77	-7
Belgium	92	91	89	-3
Cyprus	90	90	73	-17
Denmark	84	86	87	+3
Finland	67	66	68	+1
France	68	60	53	-15
Germany	80	76	75	-5
Greece	80	74	61	-19
Iceland	86	85	80	-6
Ireland	67	65	66	-1
Italy	85	82	71	-14
Luxembourg	87	91	90	+3
Malta	96	95	90	-6
Netherlands	76	80	78	+2
Norway	77	76	78	+1
Portugal	65	62	55	-10
Spain	78	73	71	-7
Sweden	85	81	85	0
Switzerland	44	47	48	+4
United Kingdom	75	60	67	-8
West European average	*78*	*76*	*73*	*-5*
Central and East European democracies				
Bosnia-Herzegovina	71	58	54	-17
Bulgaria	67	61	49	-18
Croatia	.	61	54	.
Czechia	78	61	62	-16
Estonia	63	60	64	+1
Hungary	63	69	66	+3
Latvia	72	66	59	-13
Lithuania	53	51	50	-3
Republic of Northern Macedonia	77	63	61	-16
Montenegro	.	69	74	.
Poland	50	47	54	+4
Romania	76	54	37	-39
Serbia	.	61	55	.
Slovakia	84	62	61	-23
Slovenia	74	65	60	-14
Central and East European average	*69*	*61*	*57*	*-12*

Note: [a] See Note to Figure 5.1. [b] Figures have been rounded.
Source: Data from International IDEA, voter turnout data at https://www.idea.int/data-tools/data/voter-turnout.

often hit the most vulnerable members of their countries the hardest, considerable numbers of people took part in peaceful 'anti-austerity' marches, above all in Greece, Ireland, Portugal, Spain, and the UK. In 2018 and 2019, the *yellow vests* movement in France collected over 300,000 signatures to an online petition and organized regular mass demonstrations in Paris and other French cities. Motivated by rising fuel prices and the high cost of living, these protests involved considerable outbreaks of violence. Also since 2018, thousands of school students have taken part in strikes and protests. Known as *Fridays for Future* (FFF), they demand action by governments, businesses, and consumers to contain human-made global warming. FFF has become part of the wider environmental movement, one of several new social movements that have emerged from the 1970s onward (see Box 5.2 and Figure 5.2). And during the Covid-19 pandemic, countries around the world saw protests against the various measures, such as lockdowns, taken by governments to contain the spread of the virus.

The aforementioned protests have enjoyed substantial media coverage. However, most protests are not widely reported; many are small, and the overwhelming majority are non-violent. As a result, systematic data on protest activities are difficult to come by. Given the open, fluid, and sometimes ad hoc character of protests, this is hardly surprising. As a result, researchers seek recourse to survey research (e.g. Rüdig and Karyotis 2013) or event analysis and interviews with protesters (Norris et al. 2005). One important exception to this is online participation through social media. When people engage in online political activity, e.g. by sharing a Tweet on a political issue or signing an online petition, they automatically leave behind a data record that can be used conveniently by social scientists. However, this is not without its own pitfalls (see Box 5.3).

In this section we use data from the last three waves of the European Values Study (EVS), a large-scale, cross-national survey investigating the attitudes and self-reported activities of European citizens. Repeated approximately every nine years in dozens of European countries, the survey provides insights into the ideas, beliefs, preferences, attitudes, values, and opinions of citizens all over Europe.

Box 5.2 New social movements and protest participation

Protest participation is often linked to social movements, and in particular to new social movements. A social movement is defined by della Porta and Diani (2006: 20) as 'a distinct social process, consisting of the mechanisms through which actors engaged in collective action:

- are involved in conflictual relations with clearly identified opponents;
- are linked by dense informal networks;
- share a distinct collective identity'.

They transcend individual organizations and national boundaries. Older examples include the labour movement with its trades unions and left-wing political parties, as well as the women's movement. New social movements include successive waves of feminism as well as various a multifaceted environmental movement. While it should be clear that social movements are not the same as protests, social movements regularly make use of a large repertoire of different forms of protest, such as rallies, demonstrations, vigils, or petitions. For example, the environmental movement provides a social context, in which protest activities such as climate strikes are combined with support for, and membership in, allied political parties (i.e. Green parties). Indeed, Charles Tilly (2004: 3–7) identified the political protest repertoire as a defining element of the concept a social movement.

Figure 5.2 A Fridays for Future demonstration in Munich, Germany, on September 2019

Source: © Timo Nausch/Shutterstock.

Box 5.3 Digitally networked forms of participation

While it is easy to collect data on social media participation, these forms of online political participation are not well researched. One of the reasons for this is that observations of actual online participation are, by definition, not available for those who do not participate online and, furthermore, are rarely accompanied by demographic data that would enable researchers to assess the representativeness of the participants. In one of the few studies tailored to address this problem, Theocharis and van Deth (2018) asked a representative sample of the German population about their political activities, including online activities. The latter include commenting on social media on political or social issues, posting or sharing political links on social media, and encouraging other people to take action using social media. These types of activity form a new and distinct mode of participation, which Theocharis and van Deth call 'digitally networked forms of participation (DNP)'. The authors demonstrate its distinctly political nature by showing that individual participation in DNP can be explained by the same factors that explain the decision to vote or to protest offline. Yet, the authors also found that, despite the impressive rise of social media, the low threshold for involvement offered by platforms such as Facebook and Twitter, and public concerns about 'filter bubbles' and online hate speech, DNP remains a marginal mode of participation. At the same time, the difference between online and offline political participation may be less important that the differences between different types of online or offline participation, respectively (Theocharis et al. (2023)).

Figure 5.3 shows the percentage of people in Europe reporting to have engaged in each of four non-electoral activities at the turn of the millennium (1999–2000), the end of its first decade (2008–10), and towards the end of its second decade (2017–18). We note, first, that relatively low-cost activities, such as signing a petition, are more frequently reported than more

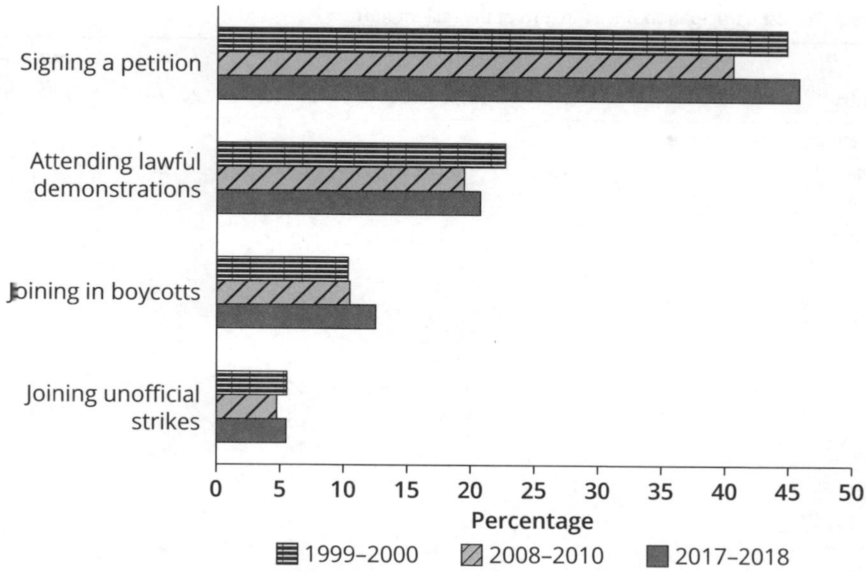

Figure 5.3 The development of non-electoral participation since the turn of the millennium

Note: Respondents were asked about their participation in the following way: "Now I'd like you to look at this card. I'm going to read out some different forms of political action that people can take, and I'd like you to tell me, for each one, whether you have actually done any of these things, whether you might do it or would never, under any circumstances, do it." We coded those respondents as protesters who said they actually have engaged in the respective activity.

Source: European Values Study (EVS), waves 3, 4, and 5. https://europeanvaluesstudy.eu/.

time-consuming ones such as attending a lawful demonstration or potentially costly activities such as joining an unofficial strike. Secondly, during the first decade of the millennium, participation in three types of activities (signing petitions, attending lawful demonstrations, and joining unofficial strikes) incurred a slight decline. However, in all three activities participation levels rebounded by 2017–18. The percentage of people joining boycotts increased gradually from 1999–2000 to 2017–18, suggesting that this form of political consumerism is gaining in importance.

To compare levels of protest participation and their change across European countries, we summarize the various forms of protest participation into a single measure, indicating whether a respondent has reported to have engaged in at least one of the four protest activities at least once in their life. Table 5.2 reports levels of protest participation at the turn of the millennium and towards the ends of the first and second decades, respectively.

The East–West difference in protest participation is even bigger than for voter turnout: at 62% the share of people in Western Europe claiming in 2017–19 to have engaged in at least one of the possible protest activities is nearly twice as big as the respective share of Central and East European respondents (34%). Why do we see such differences? Two decades ago, Berglund et al. (2001: 148–51) suggested that the difference might be due to generational change. In this view, it was above all older respondents 'who have been subjects rather than citizens for most of their lives' and who therefore feel that they are unable to do something about the situation in their respective countries (Berglund et al. 2001: 158). This implies that, following an initial drop, East European societies would eventually see a rise in protest participation. Looking at the changes in protest participation in Table 5.2 supports this view: between 1999–2000 and

Table 5.2 Protest participation since the turn of the millennium[a]

Country	1999–2000	2008–10	2017–18	Difference 1999–2018
West European democracies				
Austria	58	52	60	+2
Belgium	76	67	.	.
Cyprus	.	32	.	.
Denmark	70	75	65	-5
Finland	54	61	53	-1
France	72	74	73	+1
Germany	58	62	70	+12
Greece	65	29	.	.
Iceland	58	63	69	+11
Ireland	64	56	.	.
Italy	63	62	50	-13
Luxembourg	60	65	.	.
Malta	42	39	.	.
Netherlands	68	54	58	-10
Norway	.	77	69	.
Portugal	33	25	23	-10
Spain	37	53	49	+12
Sweden	89	84	75	-14
Switzerland	.	70	74	.
United Kingdom	71	64	73	+2
West European average	*61*	*58*	*62*	*+1*
Central and East European democracies				
Bosnia-Herzegovina	.	26	37	.
Bulgaria	23	14	18	-5
Croatia	41	48	56	+15
Czechia	62	34	45	-17
Estonia	26	25	29	+3
Hungary	17	16	22	+5
Latvia	34	28	26	-8
Lithuania	33	17	21	-12
Republic of Northern Macedonia	.	46	36	.
Montenegro	.	21	48	.
Poland	25	25	41	+16
Romania	21	15	19	-2
Serbia	.	29	35	.
Slovak Republic	59	37	40	-19
Slovenia	37	39	42	+5
Central and East European average	*34*	*28*	*34*	*0*

Note: [a] Cell entries are the percentages of respondents in each country who reported to have engaged in at least one of four activities (signing a petition, joining in boycotts, attending lawful demonstrations, joining unofficial strikes) at least once in their lives.

Sources: IDEA and EVS. Source data from International IDEA, voter turnout data at https://www.idea.int/data-tools/data/voter-turnout; Protest data from EVS (2022). European Values Study 2017: Integrated Dataset (EVS 2017). GESIS, Cologne. ZA7500 Data file Version 5.0.0 at https://doi.org/10.4232/1.13897.

2008–10, protest participation declined in six out of eleven Central and East European countries in our data. However, from 2008–10 to 2017–19, participation rose again in fourteen of the fifteen countries for which data are available. Comparing Tables 5.1 and 5.2, we also note that the overall differences between East and West are rather similar for protest and for voter turnout. Therefore, we will look more closely at the relationship between voting and protesting.

5.2.3 **Voting and protesting**

How do voting and protesting relate to each other? Fuchs and Klingemann (1998) have suggested that voting would decline at the same time, and for the same reasons, as protesting would increase. This points to a substitution process, in which the more established modes of political engagement give way to protest participation. However, as we have seen, voting and protesting both declined during the first decade of the new millennium. An alternative view of political participation perceives protest activity as an extension of, rather than an alternative to, the more institutionalized channels of political engagement such as voting (Verba et al. 1995). In this perspective, voting and protesting are two manifestations of a single phenomenon: citizen participation. Thus, rather than substituting, they might actually reinforce one another. As (van Deth 1997: 11) put it, 'participation breeds participation'. This perspective implies that we should see more protest participation in countries with higher voter turnout.

Combining our data on turnout and protest from Tables 5.1 and 5.2 shows that high turnout tends to go hand in hand with high protest participation (Figure 5.4). The results indicate

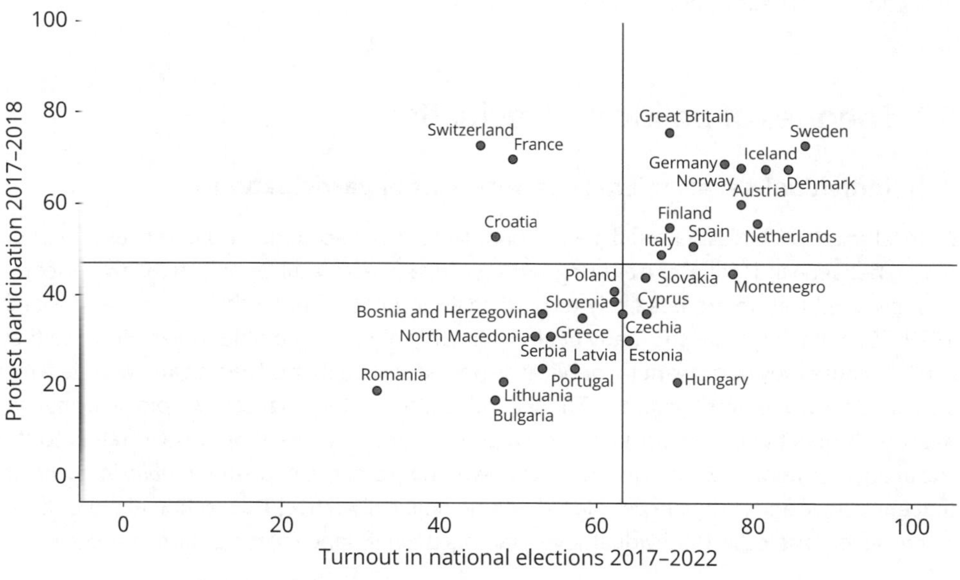

Figure 5.4 The association between voting and protesting at the country level

Note: Data on protest participating are only available until 2018. The measurement of voter turnout has to rely on a longer period because national elections normally take place only every four or five years within a country. The two lines in the graph mark the mean values for voter turnout (63 per cent) and for protest (47 per cent).

Source: IDEA and EVS. Source data from International IDEA, voter turnout data at https://www.idea.int/data-tools/data/voter-turnout; protest data from EVS (2022). European Values Study 2017: Integrated Dataset (EVS 2017). GESIS, Cologne. ZA7500 Data file Version 5.0.0, at https://doi.org/10.4232/1.13897.

Box 5.4 Over to you—are different types of political participation correlated?

In this chapter, we use data from the European Values Study and the International Institute for Democracy and Electoral Assistance (IDEA) to investigate voting and protesting. Another useful resource for researching political participation is the World Values Survey (WVS). Its Online Data Analysis tool allows you to analyse data in your web browser. Using this tool for the most recent round of the World Values Survey (WVS), investigate the relationship between reported voter turnout and online participation ('Political actions online: Signing an electronic petition') for the European countries in the data. Are the different types of political participation related? How strongly? Does the association between voting and online participation depend on the country? If so, what might explain the difference?

that there are, on the one hand, countries where citizens use multiple channels to express their interests. These include Austria, Germany, Great Britain, the Netherlands, and the Scandinavian countries. On the other hand, we find countries with more apathetic societies, where neither high numbers of citizens cast their ballots in elections nor go out on the streets to express their political views. Low levels of engagement are mainly found in Central and Eastern Europe. The correlation between voting and protesting is also found at the individual level: citizens who vote are also more likely to take part in a protest. This means that an explanation for why some people vote but not others might also help us understand why some people are more likely than others to take part in protests. We will review these explanations in Section 5.3, 'Theories of political participation'.

5.3 Theories of political participation

5.3.1 Individual-Level ('micro') determinants of participation

Political scientists have identified a number of factors that account for differences in participation between individual citizens or groups of citizens. Above all, people with lower income and lower education are less likely to participate in politics than others (Kaase and Marsh 1979: 45). But why is that so? Brady et al. (1995: 271) offer a threefold answer: 'Because they can't, because they don't want to, or because nobody asked them'. The first answer refers to a lack of politically relevant *resources*. The second focuses on the level of psychological engagement with politics—it is about people's *values and attitudes*. The third answer refers to the social environment in which citizens decide whether to participate—the *mobilizing contexts* that encourage and stimulate people to become politically active. This section explores these 'micro-level' (also called 'individual-level') factors that influence participation in politics.

5.3.1.1 Resources

Explanations of political participation based on differences in people's resources refer to socio-demographic factors, such as their age, gender, education, and social class (Verba et al. 1978). They are largely the same for voter turnout as for protest participation and predict that men, people of higher socio-economic status, as well as those with higher education levels are more inclined to participate in politics. An exception is age: with increasing age, people are said to be more likely to vote but less willing to turn up at a demonstration. In the 1970s, explanations of civil unrest based on 'relative deprivation' (Gurr 1970) implied that protesters would be drawn primarily from the rank of the socially and economically disadvantaged, who would take to the streets as they perceive elections as unresponsive to their demands. However, the evidence in recent decades supports the alternative view that people are more likely to vote and to protest the better they are equipped with politically relevant resources. This can be seen in the top panel of Table 5.3, which compares the percentages of those voting and protesting for different groups of citizens according to gender, age, education,

Table 5.3 Percentages of voters and protesters by socio-demographic resources, values and attitudes, and mobilizing contexts

		Vote intention	Took part in a protest activity
Socio-demographic resources			
Gender	Female	79	43
	Male	81	49
Age	18–29 years	73	44
	30–49 years	79	50
	50+ years	84	43
Education	Low	77	33
	Middle	79	45
	High	87	63
Household income	Lower	78	39
	Middle	81	47
	Higher	83	55
Values and attitudes			
Satisfaction with the way democracy is developing in country	Not at all satisfied	68	39
	Not very satisfied	78	44
	Rather satisfied	86	50
	Very satisfied	90	51
Materialism/post-materialism	Materialist	77	34
	Mixed	81	48
	Post-materialist	87	67
Mobilizing contexts			
Belonging to a religious organization	Not mentioned	79	44
	Mentioned	89	60
Belonging to a trade union	Not mentioned	79	42
	Mentioned	90	71

Note: Vote intention was measured by the question: 'If there was a general election tomorrow, can you tell me if you would vote?' On the measurement of the protest variables, see description in text.

Source: Fourth wave of the European Values Study, 2008–10, EVS (2022). European Values Study 2008: Integrated Dataset (EVS 2008). GESIS, Cologne. ZA4800 Datafile Version 5.0.0, at https://doi.org/10.4232/1.13841. Unfortunately, the question about vote intention is not included in more recent waves of the EVS.

and household income. Women participate slightly less than men do, although the gender difference in voter turnout is marginal. The role of age depends on the type of participation: voter turnout increases steadily as people get older, but those in the middle age group (thirty to forty-nine-year olds) are most likely to protest compared to younger and older groups. Socio-economic resources (income, educational levels) are strongly related to levels of political participation: people with higher levels of education and higher income are more likely to vote *and* to protest than those with less income and lower education levels, with the differences being more pronounced for protest participation than for voter turnout.

While the reported differences in individual political participation help us explain who is most likely to participate and why, the strong relationship between participation and socio-economic resources also points to a perennial problem of democratic politics in socially and economically unequal societies: the inequality in political participation, with the voices (and interests) of citizens from higher social strata being far more present in politics than those of lower-income groups.

5.3.1.2 Values and attitudes

The aforementioned theory of relative deprivation (Gurr 1970) implies that people are more likely to vote the less satisfied they are with the political situation in their country. A different argument has been proposed by Inglehart (1990), who suggested that increasing societal development and economic security lead to increases in personal skills, greater interest in politics, and shifts in value orientations: narrowly conceived material concerns give way to post-materialist orientations emphasizing self-expression, autonomy, gender equality, and environmental concerns (see Chapter 4). Thus, people who are overall fairly satisfied with the way democracy is playing out in their country should be more likely to be politically active, as satisfaction both reflects and stimulates engagement with the political process. This, in turn, forges increased demands for more participation, in particular for participation that serves the needs and expectations associated with post-materialist value orientations. By contrast, dissatisfied people and those with more materialist value orientations should be more likely to withdraw from politics. The evidence provided in Table 5.3 supports these arguments: satisfaction with democracy and post-materialist value orientations foster participation—voting as well as protesting. Once again, the difference is more pronounced for protest participation than for voter turnout, with post-materialists being about twice as likely as materialists to report a protest activity.

5.3.1.3 Mobilizing contexts

Finally, individuals' social environment can encourage them to a greater or lesser extent to take part in politics. For example, discussing political matters with family members, friends, or neighbours may affect an individual's propensity to become politically active (van Deth 1997). Furthermore, being a member in a civic organization or a trade union may also make people more likely to protest and to vote, as activism of citizens in organizations creates positive externalities for political participation. In organizations like churches, trade unions or sports clubs, people develop their social skills and reinforce trust in one another, as well as widen their cognitive capacities, scope of interest, and other civic virtues. Consequently, people who are active in these civil society organizations are more inclined to engage in various forms of political action, including voting and protesting. According to Dahl (1971: 299), 'joining organisations and participating in politics reinforce one another'. In the bottom panel of Table 5.3 empirical support for this argument is shown for religious organizations and labour unions.

While the individual-level determinants of voter turnout are roughly the same in the East and West, Bernhagen and Marsh (2007) report that the causal mechanism connecting citizens' characteristics with their propensity to join a protest are quite different in the East, compared to the West. Thus, system-level variables may account for some of the differences in political participation. We turn to these in the next section.

5.3.2 **Macro-Level determinants of participation**

While the previous Section (5.3.1) dealt with the differences between people and their individual inclination to participate in politics, participation is also shaped by characteristics of large-scale processes and the political system—the macro level. To see how, it is useful to think of political participation as a form of collective action—after all, elections as well as protests make little sense if only a single person takes part. When people participate in collective action, they contribute to the provision of a public good (Olson 1965; see also Box 5.5). Public goods are desired and can be consumed by many without making the goods scarcer for others. Another important property of a public good is that, once it exists, people cannot be excluded from consuming it. Examples of a public good include clean air, national security, and the legitimacy of the democratic system that mass political participation confers.

Because of the non-excludability, there is a tendency that more people consume the good than are willing to contribute to its production. For example, as long as electoral participation is seen as sufficiently high to support democracy, any one person might prefer to stay at home

Box 5.5 Public goods and the free-rider problem

In contrast to private goods, public goods are characterized, firstly, by non-excludability (the benefits derived from a pure public good cannot be confined to those who have paid for it). Secondly, their consumption is non-rivalrous (consumption of the good by one person does not restrict consumption by others). In other words, if the public good is supplied to one, it is equally available to all. Because of the properties of public goods, non-contributors can enjoy the benefits of consumption at the same level as contributors and at no cost. This is called the 'free-rider' problem. A classic example of a public good is unencrypted, free-for-all TV or radio broadcasting. The tendency to free-ride would make it very difficult to rely on voluntary contributions to support the provision of high-quality content without high amounts of advertisements, so in many European countries this is financed by the state or through compulsory licence fees collected by the state or by a government agency. A classic example of a private good is encrypted pay-TV via cable, satellite, or internet including more recent over-the-top streaming services, which can only be consumed by people who choose to pay for it. These examples illustrate how technological developments (e.g. the invention of broadcasting signal encryption and matching decoders) can lead to a formerly public good becoming privatized: before the arrival of cable, satellite, encryption, and, later on, the internet, it was simply not possible to prevent people from free-riding.

on election day and save the cost of voting (e.g. walking to the polling station on a rainy day, queuing up, or missing the live television coverage of an important sports event), while still enjoying the fruits of the participation of others. Similarly, a group of people might find it in their interest to organize a protest to underscore their common political demands. Yet, as long as it seems likely that enough people attend, each one of them might decide that their attendance is not needed and that they can therefore save themselves the hassle of travelling to the event, perhaps forgoing earnings, or even risking being taunted by protesters from the opposing camp or manhandled by police. It is easy to see how this might lead to a situation in which too few people actually show up at the polling station or protest, even though none of them intends to undermine the common cause. Worse still, if one was to think that insufficient numbers of people are likely to participate in a protest, one would be best off staying at home rather than being one of a sadly small number of protesters whose efforts go unnoticed. However, different institutions and other contextual factors, ranging from compulsory voting rules to the closeness of the election race, can affect the cost-benefit calculus of potential participants. We look at such contexts next.

First, countries' *electoral systems* differ in respect to the expected costs and benefits attached to voting (see Chapter 2). Systems of proportional representation (PR) can be expected, on the one hand, to mobilize voters better than majority systems. The reason for this is that in a PR system fewer votes are 'wasted'. This increases the likelihood of voters to have at least some influence on the outcome of the election. On the other hand, proportional systems tend to be more complicated and therefore demand more of voters, who may have to anticipate various scenarios of coalition governments. The tendency of PR systems to engender coalition governments also decreases the chance of a voter influencing the outcome of the election. Thus, there are conflicting arguments regarding the effect of proportional voting systems on turnout. The evidence seems to support this ambivalent role of PR systems for voter turnout, as any association between the type of electoral system and turnout is far from robust (Stockemer 2017).

Second, *compulsory voting* rules make participation relatively more attractive by increasing the cost of abstaining. Even if not actually enforced, the knowledge that staying at home on polling day is a violation of the law may dwarf the perceived costs of voting—even on a rainy day. Indeed, compulsory voting rules provide a strong and reliable boost to turnout (Smets and van Ham 2013). In Europe, this can be seen in the cases of Belgium and Luxembourg, where voting is compulsory and turnout rates oscillate closely around 90%. With the exception of Malta, no country without compulsory voting comes even close to these turnout levels.

Third, individual voters might expect their vote to make a difference if the election promises to be a close race. Hence, the degree of *electoral competition*, as reflected in the size of the largest party or the gap between the leading two parties, affects voter turnout. Moreover, with higher political competition, parties and candidates invest more in mobilizing potential voters to cast their votes. However, empirical research on the effect of close races has produced mixed findings (Smets and van Ham 2013).

Fourth, individual voters might perceive the importance of their own contribution as higher if the electorate is small. In addition, smaller countries frequently have higher turnout due to closer relations between citizens and representatives and the relatively close geographical distance between citizens and the administrative capital of the country.

Studies have repeatedly found that turnout goes down as the size of the electorate increases (Cancela and Geys 2016).

Finally, not all elections are equally *important*, and citizens should be more willing to incur the costs of voting if something significant is at stake. Arguably the single most important outcome of an election is the formation of the national government. Lacking this function, elections for sub-national parliaments or to the European Parliament are considered less important (see Chapter 17). Reif and Schmitt (1980) have characterized such contests as 'second-order' elections (SOEs), in contrast to the 'first-order' elections (FOEs) leading to national government formation (in parliamentary democracies, FOEs are the elections to the national parliament). The difference in importance has consequences for turnout, which is generally lower at SOEs. However, turnout at SOEs can be pulled up if they are held on the same day as the more important FOEs. Holding different elections (and perhaps referendums) concurrently can also partly address the problem of participatory fatigue said to arise when citizens are asked to go to the polls very frequently, as is the case in Switzerland.

This last factor—importance—also varies across different occasions for protest participation. People are more likely to join a protest when the issue(s) addressed by it matter a great deal to them. This is supported by the finding by Norris et al. (2005) that the specific issue of a protest make a considerable difference to participation.

5.4 What explains the decline in electoral participation?

Can the theories presented in the previous sections help us understand why participation (particularly in elections) has declined in recent decades? The answer is: they can, if we consider generational change. Voter turnout is declining primarily among younger cohorts. Some scholars argue that a broader cultural value change is underway, with younger generations being less interested in politics as well as less likely to conceive of voting as a civic duty (e.g. Inglehart 1990). Related to this, it has been argued that there has been a process of dealignment over time, whereby recent generations of voters are less likely to identify with a political party and are therefore less motivated to vote (Dalton and Wattenberg 2002; see also Chapter 4).

Others argue that lower levels of voting among recent cohorts constitute a persistent footprint of particular elections. Recall that in the previous Section (5.3.2) we discussed how competitive elections stimulate higher turnout. Combined with changes in the voting age, limited competitiveness of elections can have a lasting effect. The voting age was lowered to eighteen in many Western European countries during the 1970s. According to Franklin, this coincided with less competitive elections, which brought a concentration of younger cohorts to experience their first election under unfavourable circumstances. As a result, many of these young voters failed to develop a habit of participation (Franklin 2004). In this view, we should not assume that turnout will inevitably continue to decline; future generations that come of age during periods of intense political competition might be expected to be more politically engaged. Recent research supports the first view, suggesting that young voters are less inclined to vote because their generation is less prone to construe voting as a moral duty and is more sceptical about politicians' responsiveness to their concerns (Blais and Rubenson 2013).

Box 5.6 Explaining voter turnout in selected countries

How can we use the theories presented in this section in the context of individual countries? We will illustrate this here for the cases of Czechia, France, Germany, and Poland. France and Germany belong to the group of West European democracies where we generally find higher turnout, while Czechia and Poland belong to the group of 'younger' democracies in Central and Eastern Europe, where turnout is generally lower (see Figure 5.1 and Table 5.1). Czechia and France are puzzling cases: while we would expect lower turnout rates for Czechia (belonging to the 'younger' democracies), the opposite expectation applies to France. However, turnout rates in both countries deviate from our expectations. Why is this the case?

The differences between France and Germany might reflect differences in the institutional properties of the political systems (Voelkl 2012). Although both countries are 'old' democracies, the institutional contexts of the elections for their parliaments differ significantly. France is a semi-presidential democracy and Germany a parliamentary democracy (see Chapter 7). In France, the president and the national parliament are each directly elected, but the presidential elections are the first- and the elections for the *Assemblée nationale* (the lower chamber of the French legislature) the second-order elections. This might account for the different turnout levels at these elections, with the presidential elections generally showing higher turnout. In Germany, by contrast, the first-order elections are those for the *Bundestag* (the lower chamber of the German legislature). Moreover, the two countries differ in their electoral systems. In France we find a two-round majority voting system, while members of the *Bundestag* are elected using a personalized proportional system, with the latter encouraging higher turnout. Lastly, there are differences between the two countries concerning registration procedures: in Germany, unlike in France, all citizens of voting age are registered automatically, and postal voting is allowed. These institutional differences can account for some of the observed differences in turnout between these two countries.

Let us now turn to the difference in turnout between Poland and Czechia. Both countries have similar institutional arrangements. Therefore, institutional factors can hardly account for the differences in turnout. Low turnout is especially puzzling in Poland, because here the Catholic church helped to maintain civil society during communist rule (Michta 1997). But while Poland had active networks of civic activism before the transition, the country faced serious obstacles when establishing civil society in a liberal democracy (Whitehead 2002). According to Matthes (2016), only a minority of Poles have internalized post-materialist values. These case comparisons show how the individual-level and institutional features introduced in this section can account for some of the differences in turnout.

5.5 What lies ahead: 'Democratic innovations' in local politics?

Given the central role of citizen participation for democracy and the developments in electoral turnout described in this chapter, how can citizens' political involvement be increased? And how can the inequalities in participation described in this chapter be remedied? Some scholars look for answers in new or additional opportunities for political participation (Smith 2009), aiming at a 'stronger' (Barber 1984) or 'participatory' democracy (Pateman 2012). Increasing the opportunities for citizens to participate in political decision-making, especially at the level of local politics, might also help to compensate for a loss of control over national politics in times of globalization. As Dahl (1994: 33) stated already in the early 1990s,

> in the future all democratic countries will be challenged to discover ways of maintaining and strengthening the democratic process as they adapt to transnational forces. . . . In addition, democratic life in smaller communities below the level of the national state could be

enhanced. The larger scale of decisions need not lead inevitably to a widening sense of powerlessness, provided citizens can exercise significant control over decisions on the smaller scale of matters important in their daily lives.

Such 'innovations' in local political participation may include referendums, direct elections to public offices, and deliberative formats for participation, like mini-publics, citizen forums, or round tables (see Chapter 6). For example, directly elected mayors were introduced for London in 2000 (the most high-profile incumbent was the future prime minister Boris Johnson, who was mayor of London from 2008 to 2016), and this has since been introduced in several other UK cities. Similar trends towards the institutionalization of such democratic innovations in local politics can be discerned in different European countries (Vetter et al. 2016). Yet, research on the effects of such 'democratic innovations'—e.g. whether they help to increase political support and strengthen civil society—is still in its beginnings and data on their use are limited (Fournier et al. 2011; Marien and Kern 2017). The verdict is also still out on whether or not these 'innovations' will help to reduce inequality in citizens' participation, and some studies suggest that inequalities tend to persist (see Box 5.7) (Marien et al. 2010; Vetter and Velimsky 2019, referring to local referendums in Germany).

5.6 **Conclusion**

In this chapter, we have introduced the main modes of citizen participation in politics—voting and protesting. We have looked at how turnout at elections and various forms of protest have developed across European countries. Our look at the data has revealed that, over the past two decades, voter turnout has declined in many countries and levels of protest participation have stabilized. While there are overall healthy levels of participation across Europe, there are considerable differences between countries, in particular between East and West European ones. We have also discussed the main factors that account for differences in participation between countries and over time. At the level of the individual, we saw that younger people and those with lower levels of income and education are less likely to participate, while postmaterialist value orientations and membership in organizations increase people's likelihood to take part in politics. Thus, for all forms of participation, we observe considerable inequalities along the lines of social class: the higher up the social ladder, the likelier an individual is to vote and to take part in other forms of political participation. The rise of protest participation

Box 5.7 Over to you—inequalities in participation

Participation is dependent on individual resources, positive attitudes toward the democratic political system, and membership in mobilizing groups or networks. New opportunities for political participation might face the same problems of unequal participation as the 'old' channels of participation. Considering what you have read in this chapter about the relationship between voting and protesting, do you think that new forms of participation can help to overcome old inequalities? Alternatively, would you expect 'new' forms of citizen participation to expand the opportunities mainly for those citizens who are already active? How could these 'new' opportunities be designed to increase participation of groups with lower levels of income, education, or political interest?

that has been observed in the West from the 1980s onward has not led to greater political equality among citizens. On the contrary, social inequalities in protest participation are even more pronounced than those in voting. At the level of the political system, smaller countries and those where voting is compulsory have higher levels of voter turnout, while more important elections and protests draw larger numbers of participants than less important ones. Finally, we have taken a brief look at new opportunities for participation at the local level and asked whether these can help overcome existing problems of unequal participation. It remains unclear to date whether new participatory opportunities, such as mini-publics or citizen forums, will lead to more equal engagement.

Discussion questions

1. What is political participation?
2. Why is political participation important for the health of a democracy?
3. What are the main institutional features affecting electoral turnout?
4. What makes some people more likely to participate than others?
5. What explains higher levels of participation in some countries compared to others?
6. Why do voting and protesting not substitute each other as means for political participation? What are the consequences for political equality?
7. Why is inequality a problem of political participation today? Where does it come from and what might the consequences be?
8. Can 'democratic innovations' help overcome inequalities in political participation?

Thinking comparatively

Hooghe and Quintelier (2014) aim to identify the reasons for the diverging levels and developments of participation in Eastern and Western Europe. Engaging with the literature, they make out two principal explanations. On one side, a 'socialization perspective' argues that citizens of Central and East European countries have been socialized in an authoritarian regime, which effectively discouraged them from fostering a critical attitude towards political elites and from participating in politics. These attitudes and associated behaviours continue beyond the democratic transition of 1989–90. On the other side, an 'experience perspective' holds that Central and East European citizens are persistently confronted with corruption, abuse of power, and illiberal behaviour on the part of political elites. Hooghe and Quintelier want to find out which of these theoretical arguments better explains the difference in political participation between the two regions. To do so, they derive hypotheses specific to each perspective: the socialization perspective implies that the differences between East and West European countries will gradually disappear, as the age groups that still experienced the authoritarian regimes gradually become replaced by younger age cohorts that grew up in democracy. By contrast, the experience perspective implies that current features of the political system, like corruption or ineffective and non-transparent governance, account for low levels of citizen engagement. Using data on over 150,000 respondents collected through the European Social Survey (ESS) in the period 2002–08, the authors test the competing hypotheses from the two theories statistically. They find that, for the period under investigation, it is above all low-income levels, lack of good governance, and high levels of corruption that depress political participation levels, which supports the 'experience perspective'.

Guide to further reading

Birch, S. (2009), *Full Participation: A Comparative Study of Compulsory Voting* (Manchester: Manchester University Press).

This book examines the development as well as the normative arguments for and against compulsory voting. It also assesses the likely effects on electoral campaigns, policy outcomes, and turnout.

Cain, B., Dalton, R. J. et al. (eds.) (2003), *Democracy Transformed? Expanding Political Access in Advanced Industrial Democracies* (Oxford: Oxford University Press).

The authors describe changes in democratic institutions and processes, such as the expansion of referendums, or the introduction of open government provisions, that have the potential to give citizens a greater say in politics. They also consider the larger implication of these reforms for the nature of democracy.

Giugni, M. and Grasso, M. T. (2019), *Street Citizens: Protest Politics and Social Movement Activism in the Age of Globalization* (Cambridge: Cambridge University Press).

Analysing data from seven European countries, the authors explore the antecedents and forms of contemporary protest participation, including the motivations of citizens to take part in demonstrations, mobilizing structures, and perceived effectiveness.

Norris, P. (2002), *Democratic Phoenix: Reinventing Political Activism* (Cambridge: Cambridge University Press).

This book explores various forms of political participation in virtually all countries in the world and analyses the development of citizen participation in politics, including the causes and extent of an alleged decline in civic engagement.

Smith, G. (2009), *Democratic Innovations: Designing Institutions for Citizen Participation* (Cambridge/New York: Cambridge University Press).

This book offers a systematic analysis of diverse democratic innovations like participatory budgeting, electoral reforms, direct legislation, and e-democracy, and draws lessons for the future development of both democratic theory and practice.

Theocharis, Y. and van Deth, J. W. (2017), *Political Participation in a Changing World: Conceptual and Empirical Challenges in the Study of Citizen Engagement* (New York: Routledge).

This book provides a unified account of political participation that facilitates research on both older political activities and newer forms of digitally networked participation.

References

Barber, B. R. (1984), *Strong Democracy* (Berkeley, CA: University of California Press).

Barnes, S. H. and Kaase, M. (1979), 'Conclusion: The future of political protest in Western democracies', in S. H. Barnes, M. Kaase, et al. (eds.), *Political Action: Mass Participation in Five Western Democracies* (London: Sage): 523–36.

Berglund, S., Aarebrot, F. et al. (2001), *Challenges to Democracy* (Cheltenham: Edward Elgar).

Bernhagen, P. and Marsh, M. (2007), 'Voting and protesting: Explaining citizen participation in old and new European democracies', *Democratization*, 14(1): 44–72.

Blais, A. (2010), 'Political participation', in L. LeDuc, R. G. Niemi et al. (eds.), *Comparing Democracies 3:*

Elections and Voting in the 21st Century (London: Sage): 165–83.
Blais, A. and Rubenson, D. (2013), 'The source of turnout decline: New values or new contexts?', *Comparative Political Studies*, 46(1): 95–117.
Brady, H. E., Verba, S. et al. (1995), 'Beyond SES: A resource model of political participation', *American Political Science Review*, 89(2): 271–94.
Cancela, J. and Geys, B. (2016), 'Explaining voter turnout: A meta-analysis of national and subnational elections', *Electoral Studies*, 42: 264–75.
Dahl, R. A. (1971), *Who Governs? Democracy and Power in an American City* (New Haven, CT: Yale University Press).
Dahl, R. A. (1994), 'A democratic dilemma: System effectiveness versus citizen participation', *Political Science Quarterly*, 109(1): 23–34.
Dalton, R. J. and Wattenberg, M. P. (eds.) (2002), *Parties without Partisans: Political Change in Advanced Industrial Democracies* (Oxford: Oxford University Press).
della Porta, D. and Diani, M. (2006). *Social Movements: An Introduction*, 2nd edn (Malden, MA: Blackwell).
Ethical Consumer Research Association (2023), Boycotts Amazon, available at https://www.ethicalconsumer.org/ethicalcampaigns/boycott-amazon (accessed 15 May 2023).
Fournier, P., Van der Kolk, H. et al. (2011), *When Citizens Decide: Lessons from Citizen Assemblies on Electoral Reform* (Oxford: Oxford University Press).
Franklin, M. N. (2004), *Voter Turnout and the Dynamics of Electoral Competition in Established Democracies since 1945* (New York: Cambridge University Press).
Fuchs, D. and H.-D. Klingemann (1998), 'Citizens and the state: A changing relationship?', in H.-D. Klingemann and D. Fuchs (eds.), *Citizens and the State* (Oxford: Oxford University Press): 1–23.
Gurr, T. R. (1970), *Why Men Rebel* (Princeton, NJ: Princeton University Press).
Hooghe, M. and Quintelier, E. (2014), 'Political participation in European countries: The effect of authoritarian rule, corruption, lack of good governance and economic downturn', *Comparative European Politics*, 12(2): 209–32.
Inglehart, R. (1990), *Culture Shift in Advanced Industrial Society* (Princeton, NJ: Princeton University Press).
Kaase, M. and Marsh, A. (1979), 'Political action: A theoretical perspective', in S. H. Barnes, M. Kaase et al. (eds.), *Political Action: Mass Participation in Five Western Democracies* (London: Sage): 27–56.
Letki, N. (2004), 'Socialization for participation? Trust, membership, and democratization in East Central Europe', *Political Research Quarterly*, 57(4): 665–79.
Marien, S. and Kern, A. (2017), 'The winner takes it all: Revisiting the effect of direct democracy on citizens' political support', *Political Behavior*, 40(4): 857–82.
Marien, S., Hooghe, M. et al. (2010), 'Inequalities in non-institutionalized forms of political participation: A multi-level analysis of 25 countries', *Political Studies*, 58(1): 187–213.
Matthes, C. Y. (2016), 'The state of democracy in Poland after 2007: Analyzing the linkage between economic development and political participation', *Problems of Post-Communism*, 63(5–6): 288–99.
Michta, A. A. (1997), 'Democratic consolidation in Poland after 1989', in K. Dawisha and B. Parrott (eds.), *The Consolidation of Democracy in East-Central Europe* (Cambridge: Cambridge University Press).
Norris, P. (2002), *Democratic Phoenix: Reinventing Political Activism* (Cambridge: Cambridge University Press).
Norris, P., Walgrave, S. et al. (2005), 'Who demonstrates? Anti-state rebels, conventional participants, or everyone?', *Comparative Politics*, 37(2): 189–205.
Olson, M. (1965), *The Logic of Collective Action: Public Goods and the Theory of Groups* (Cambridge, MA: Harvard University Press).
Pateman, C. (2012), 'Participatory democracy revisited', *Perspectives on Politics*, 10(1): 7–19.
Poguntke, T., Rossteutscher, S. et al. (2015), 'Introduction: citizenship, participation and democracy in an era of crisis', in T. Poguntke, S. Rossteutscher et al. (eds.), *Citizenship and Democracy in an Era of Crisis* (Abingdon: Routledge): 1–12.
Reif, K. and Schmitt, H. (1980), 'Nine second-order national elections: A conceptual framework for the analysis of European results', *European Journal of Political Research*, 8(1): 3–44.
Rüdig, W. and Karyotis, G. (2013), 'Who protests in Greece? Mass opposition to austerity', *British Journal of Political Science*, 44(3): 487–513.
Smets, K. and van Ham, C. (2013), 'The embarrassment of riches? A meta-analysis of individual-level research on voter turnout', *Electoral Studies*, 32(2): 344–59.
Smith, G. (2009), *Democratic Innovations: Designing Institutions for Citizen Participation* (Cambridge: Cambridge University Press).
Stockemer, D. (2017), 'What affects voter turnout? A review article/meta-analysis of aggregate research', *Government and Opposition*, 52(4): 698–722.
Theocharis, Y. and van Deth, J. W. (2018), 'The continuous expansion of citizen participation: A new taxonomy', *European Political Science Review*, 10(1): 139–63.
Theocharis, Y., Boulianne, S. et al. (2023), 'Platform affordances and political participation: How social media reshape political engagement', *West European Politics*, 46(4): 788–811.
Tilly, C. (2004), *Social Movements, 1768–2004* (Boulder, CO: Paradigm Publishers).

van Deth, J. W. (1997), 'Introduction: Social involvement and democratic politics', in J. W. van Deth (ed.), *Private Groups and Public Life: Social Participation, Voluntary Associations and Political Involvement in Representative Democracies* (Abingdon: Routledge): 1–23.

Verba, S., Nie, N. H. et al. (1978), *Participation and Political Equality: A Seven-Nation Comparison* (Cambridge: Cambridge University Press).

Verba, S., Schlozmann, K. L. et al. (1995), *Voice and Equality: Civic Voluntarism in American Politics* (Cambridge, MA: Harvard University Press).

Vetter, A. and Velimsky, J. A. (2019), 'Soziale Selektivität bei Wahlen und direkt-demokratischen Abstimmungen auf kommunaler Ebene in Deutschland', *Politische Vierteljahresschrift*, 60(3): 487–512.

Vetter, A., Klimovský, D. et al. (2016), 'Giving citizens more say in local government: Comparative analyses of change across Europe in times of crisis', in S. Kuhlmann and G. Bouckaert (eds.), *Local Public Sector Reforms in Times of Crisis: National Trajectories and International Comparisons* (London: Palgrave Macmillan): 273–86.

Voelkl, K. (2012), 'Turnout in parliamentary elections', in O. W. Gabriel, S. Keil et al. (eds.), *Political Participation in France and Germany* (Colchester: ECPR Press): 209–36.

Whitehead, L. (2002), *Democratization: Theory and Experience* (Oxford: Oxford University Press).

6 Beyond Electoral Representation

Direct and Deliberative Democracy

DAVID M. FARRELL AND LUKE FIELD

6.1 Introduction

A common denominator of all democracies is the election of political representatives. This is why democracy is often referred to as 'representative democracy'. As citizens, we get the right to vote every couple of years to decide on whether or not to 'kick the rascals out': for many that is pretty much the sum-total of their involvement with democratic processes. There are, however, other means by which citizens can engage in the political system that move beyond electoral representation, of which the most common—and increasingly so—are referendums, in which citizens are given the opportunity to vote on key policy issues. This chapter explores how and where these operate.

We start with a look at direct democracy, one of the most popular alternatives to representative democracy. The definition of direct democracy has frequently been a contentious issue in both academic and practitioner circles; beyond a broad sense that direct democracy allows citizens to have a direct say on the policies that affect their polity, no standard, fully agreed-upon definition exists. In particular, there is disagreement on the extent to which certain modes of direct democracy are sufficiently 'direct' to qualify for the title. Rather than get bogged down in this normative debate, we have taken the approach of simply focusing on what might be termed 'actually existing direct democracy', i.e. those mechanisms that Altman (2019: 6) describes as 'publicly recognised, institutional process[es] by which citizens of a region or country register their choice or opinion on specific issues through a ballot with universal and secret suffrage'. We focus on the most popular of these mechanisms, the referendum, beginning with an overview of the use of referendums across Europe's democracies, showing how they have become more regular both at national and sub-national level (Section 6.2). We then examine the context in which referendums occur, both in terms of the rules and regulations governing them and also how much scope is given to citizens to control when they are held and what they might be about (Section 6.3). One way of conceiving of referendums, particularly those 'bottom-up' ones that have resulted from citizen petitions, is in terms of the 'voice' they give citizens to influence events in between elections.

We then review the wider range of democratic innovations that, in combination, see democracies move beyond being merely 'vote-centred' representative processes. This includes the relatively recent emergence of yet another form of democracy—'deliberative democracy'—in which citizens are brought into the heart of debates on key policy issues through their involvement in 'deliberative mini-publics' such as citizens' assemblies (Section 6.4).

Referendums and other democratic innovations may not be for everyone. There are questions over whether citizens vote sincerely on the question at hand in a referendum as opposed to using it as an opportunity to express their dissatisfaction with government, whether all citizens are equally willing or able to engage in processes that require some more effort by them, or indeed whether democratic innovations such as citizens' assemblies can ever be 'scaled up' sufficiently to make a real difference to how democracies are run. These concerns are addressed towards the end of the chapter (Section 6.5).

6.2 Referendums

Referendums are a form of decision-making that engages the entirety of an electorate, rather than just elected representatives. In this, they differ from (but exist alongside) the parliamentary representative democracy that comprises the majority of formal European political activity. A referendum is so named because the question at hand is *referred* to the people for an answer: it is sometimes referred to as a 'plebiscite' for the same reason, although this phrasing has fallen out of fashion somewhat in democratic nations because of its association with dictatorial regimes (Beigbeder 2011).

A referendum typically offers a binary set of outcomes. Generally, this will be either to permit or deny a change to some element of public policy, legislation, or a constitutional question. Some variations on this model exist, and are discussed in Section 6.3, but the 'classic' referendum model allows the electorate to either approve or reject a discrete proposal, with one of these options representing maintenance of the status quo.

Referendums are particularly associated with their prevalence in the Swiss political system, which places huge emphasis on direct democracy. Most policy decisions taken at both federal and cantonal (regional) level in Switzerland may be either initiated or vetoed by referendum. However, in other countries, referendums tend to be reserved for significant political questions, such as amending constitutional law, the gain or loss of state territory, or changing treaty status with foreign powers (Qvortrup 2014). There has also been a tendency to refer 'moral questions' to the electorate, with a number of referendums on same-sex marriage rights put to a vote in recent years (such as the referendums in Ireland, Slovenia, and Slovakia in 2015). Historically, the use of referendums has been controversial: lauded by some for their revolutionary potential, critics on both the left and the right have identified their risk

Box 6.1 The pros and cons of referendums

Views are divided over the pros and cons of referendums. Proponents of referendums tend to argue that:

- giving citizens a more direct say on important decisions in between elections enhances democracy, and can add popular legitimacy to these decisions;
- because citizens are given this role there is the added potential that they can become better informed on the issue and perhaps more widely on politics in general;
- by encouraging debate this can help to improve policy outcomes and add greater interest in politics.

However, not everybody agrees. Critics of referendum decision-making identify a number of potential pitfalls, including:

- there is a danger that they can oversimplify complex issues, and limiting voter options to approval or rejection of a proposal may not necessarily reflect public opinion;
- there is a risk of bad decisions made by an uninformed (or misinformed) public (as many 'Remain' voters would claim occurred in the 2016 Brexit referendum in the UK);
- because referendums are decided on a majority decision, there is the potential for the 'tyranny of the majority', where the interests of a minority are not considered or respected, or even actively opposed (Swiss referendums to ban the building of minarets and wearing of face coverings, for example, are often cited as impositions of discriminatory policies by the country's Christian majority on its Muslim minority);
- many referendums experience lower voter turnout relative to elections, particularly when the matter under discussion lacks political salience, which challenges the idea of referendums having a greater popular mandate.

of creating 'tyranny by majority' (ibid.), while others describe their common usage by dictators to apply a veneer of popular legitimacy to autocratic decisions (e.g. Lupia and Johnston 2001). For discussion on the pros and cons of referendums, see Box 6.1.

The use of the referendum method has, in general, become more and more popular since the middle of the twentieth century. Tables 6.1 and 6.2 show the total number of referendums held in thirty-one European countries since the end of World War II: the current twenty-seven member states of the European Union (EU) plus Iceland, Norway, Switzerland, and the United Kingdom. During this period, these thirty-one states have accounted for 7,819 referendums between them: 904 of these referendums have been at the national level.

6.2.1 **The post-communist democracies**

The use of referendums has increased dramatically in the last thirty years compared to the 1945–87 period (LeDuc 2003): as Table 6.1 shows, 587 national referendums were held in the later period, compared to 317 in the earlier. This figure is partly the result of new states emerging after the fall of the Soviet Union (the table includes entries for Croatia, Czechia, Estonia, Latvia, Lithuania, Slovakia, and Slovenia, none of which existed as independent states during the first period of analysis in 1945–87). However, these states collectively account for only eighty-six national referendums in the post-1988 period, meaning that there are other reasons for the surge in referendums.

Table 6.1 European national referendums, 1945–2022

Country	1945–87	1988–2022	Total since 1945
Austria	1	3	4
Belgium	1	0	1
Bulgaria	3	5	8
Croatia	NA	4	4
Cyprus	3	4	7
Czechia	NA	1	1
Denmark	13	7	20
Estonia	NA	4	4
Finland	0	1	1
France	10	7	17
Germany	5	0	5
Greece	5	1	6
Hungary	0	17	17
Iceland	0	8	8
Ireland	12	29	41
Italy	16	63	79
Latvia	NA	10	10
Lithuania	NA	23	23
Luxembourg	0	4	4
Malta	3	3	6
Netherlands	0	3	3
Norway	1	1	2
Poland	5	10	15
Portugal	0	3	3
Romania	1	8	9
Slovakia	NA	19	19
Slovenia	NA	29	29
Spain	5	1	6
Sweden	11	3	14
Switzerland	221	314	535
United Kingdom	1	2	3
TOTAL	317	587	904
Average	13.21	18.94	29.16
Median	3	4	7

Note: Data from the Centre for Research on Direct Democracy (2018) (C2D) website, correct as of March 2023. Only referendums tagged with 'official' status by the C2D are counted. In the case of multiple referendums on independence, only the successful referendum establishing a sovereign and independent state in the country's name is counted. Where multiple options were presented to the electorate in the same referendum, each ballot is treated as a separate entry. 'Germany' includes data from the pre-unification Federal (West) and Democratic (East) Republics as well as the post-1990 unified federal state.

The so-called 'new democracies' themselves show the same variation in appetite for referendums experienced by the more established European democracies. Croatia and Czechia in particular appear towards the less-enthusiastic end of the spectrum, with both holding a low number of referendums, while Estonia's four national referendums and Latvia's ten place

Table 6.2 European sub-national referendums, 1945–2022

Country	1945–87	1988–2022	Total since 1945
Croatia	NA	2	2
Cyprus	0	1	1
France	2	3	5
Germany	28	46	74
Italy	0	9	9
Malta	1	0	1
Spain	6	6	12
Switzerland	2,678	4,107	6,785
United Kingdom	5	21	26
TOTAL	2,720	4,195	6,915
Average	340	466.11	768.33
Median	3.5	6	9

Note: Data from the Centre for Research on Direct Democracy (2018) website, correct as of March 2023. Only referendums tagged with 'official' status by the C2D are counted. Where multiple options were presented to the electorate in the same referendum, each ballot is treated as a separate entry. 'Germany' includes data from the pre-unification Federal (West) and Democratic (East) Republics as well as the post-1990 unified federal state. While municipal referendums are included, some purely consultative local plebiscites (such as the 2019 votes on proposed directly elected mayors for three local authorities in Ireland) are not recorded by the C2D.

them both well below the European average for this period. Slovakia has held almost exactly the average number for a European country in this period, with nineteen, while Lithuania and Slovenia have held far more than the average.

6.2.2 **European Union referendums**

Since 1972, the European Union (EU) has been responsible for forty-eight referendums in member states and countries that are candidates for membership, the latest being held in the UK (2016) and North Macedonia (2018) (Beach 2018; Mendez and Mendez 2017). In many instances, the referendum question was whether or not to accede to the EU, such as the 1972 expansion (Denmark and Ireland approved a decision to join, while Norway declined), the 1994 expansion (Austria, Sweden, and Finland joined, while Norway again declined), and the 2004 enlargement (Czechia, Estonia, Hungary, Latvia, Lithuania, Malta, Poland, Slovakia, and Slovenia all voted to join, while Cyprus joined without holding a referendum). The United Kingdom has twice voted on whether to continue its membership, choosing to remain a member of the European Communities in 1975 and to leave the EU in 2016.

Beyond the question of overall EU membership, the approval of many major European treaties has been subject to a national vote in at least some member states. These include the Single European Act (voted on by Denmark and Ireland), the Maastricht Treaty (voted on by Denmark, Ireland, and France), the Amsterdam Treaty (Denmark and Ireland), and the aborted Constitutional Treaty (voted on by Spain and Luxembourg, who approved it, and

France and the Netherlands, who rejected it). Additionally, Ireland was the sole EU nation to hold a referendum on the Nice, Lisbon, and Fiscal Compact Treaties.

In some instances, EU member states have held referendums on specific EU policy matters. Two of these related to the single currency: Denmark rejected a proposal to adopt the Euro in 2000, while Sweden did the same in 2003. Other examples of referendums on compliance with EU policy can be seen in Denmark (recognizing the European Patent Court in 2014), Greece (refusing the terms of its EU bailout in 2015), the Netherlands (rejecting the EU–Ukraine association proposal in 2016), and Hungary (rejecting EU refugee quotas, also in 2016).

The difference in frequency of EU-related referendums across the member states is probably best explained by whether a provision exists for mandatory or facultative (optional) referendums. With the exception of referendums on whether or not to join the EU, only two states have had mandatory EU-related referendums: Ireland and Denmark. Ireland's Supreme Court ruled in 1986 that the country's requirement of approval by referendum for constitutional change would apply to the proposed Single European Act. This decision has been interpreted to mean that a referendum is required to approve all subsequent major European treaties. Denmark requires referendum approval for any EU treaty that is supported by less than five-sixths of the national parliament; it has run five mandatory and two facultative EU referendums since its accession in 1972 (Beach 2018).

It should be noted that the figure of forty-eight referendums includes a number of referendums held by the same countries on the same topic: Ireland, which voted twice on the Nice (2001 and 2002) and Lisbon (2008 and 2009) Treaties; and Denmark, which voted twice on the Maastricht Treaty (1992 and 1993). The figure does *not* include the considerable number of referendums held in 'third-countries' on matters of cooperation with the EU, which account for eleven national referendums in Switzerland alone.

6.2.3 **Sub-national referendums**

There has been a significant rise in the number of sub-national (or regional) referendums held since 1988 by comparison to the 1945–87 period: as Table 6.2 shows, the more recent period has seen over 1,500 more sub-national referendums than the earlier period. In large part this has been the result of contributions from Germany, which is the second-most prolific user of sub-national referendums after Switzerland; it accounted for two-thirds of all non-Swiss sub-national referendums in the 1945–87 period and over half of all non-Swiss sub-national referendums in the last thirty years.

Germany is not the only country to experience greater recourse to regional referendums since 1988. Italy, which never held a single sub-national referendum between 1945 and 1988, has held nine of them in the thirty years since. The United Kingdom, which has been engaged for the past twenty years or so in a process of devolving power to its regions, has held more than quadruple the number of sub-national referendums since 1988 than it did in the post-war period before (twenty-one compared to five).

It might be assumed that federal states (see Chapter 11) would experience high numbers of sub-national referendums, and indeed, Table 6.2 does feature two countries with federal governments: Germany and Switzerland. However, it should be noted that Belgium and Austria—the only other federal countries in Europe—have not held any sub-national referendums in the post-war period, so it is not a straightforward relationship. Similarly, the other seven countries in Europe to have held sub-national referendums are formally unitary states; that said, several of them—Italy, Spain, and the United Kingdom—have engaged in increasing devolution of powers to their regions, particularly since joining the EU. Arguably, this means that the majority of countries to have held sub-national referendums are either federal or 'federal-like'.

6.3 Do referendums accomplish 'direct democracy'?

In Europe, referendums are used as a complement to representative democracy, not as a replacement. As such, they are not about the creation of a 'perfect' direct democracy, where decisions are taken by citizens unmediated by representative institutions (Budge 1996). It perhaps makes more sense, then, to think of the question in terms of how much more (or less) direct-democratic countries become as a consequence of using referendums. This section considers how much more 'direct democracy' is found in various types of referendums based on the referendum process, the content of referendum questions, and the observable impact of holding referendums.

6.3.1 The referendum process

One of the criteria by which a referendum's direct-democratic value can be considered is the 'who leads?' question. In general, referendums tend to fall along a spectrum of more top-down to more bottom-up. Referendums at the top-down end are generally élite-led: the question may be answered by the people, but its wording is chosen by the government, and campaigns both for and against the proposal are primarily led by established political actors. At the bottom-up end of the spectrum, the voters themselves have far more control over the entire process: generating the referendum question, setting out the rules of the referendum itself, and leading the public campaigns. The more top-down the referendum is, the more it behaves as an addendum to existing representative-democratic structures; the more bottom-up it is, the more it functions as a form of direct democracy.

'Top-down' referendums are generally proposed by governments for one of two reasons: either the government wishes to enact a legal or constitutional change that requires popular approval, or the government is not required to propose the referendum but does so as a means of transferring direct responsibility to the electorate. The latter instance often occurs with referendum questions that are highly sensitive or controversial, where the government may wish to maintain 'clean hands' and not offend large sections of the electorate. It may also be a means to enact a crushing defeat on a proposal that the government (or part of the government) does not support, in which case the government will propose a referendum question and then campaign (or partially campaign) against it. Examples of the latter may include the British referendums on the Alternative Vote electoral system (2011) and Brexit (2016), and the Austrian referendums on nuclear power (1978) and abolishing conscription (2013). The direct-democratic potential in these referendums is evidently somewhat limited: while voters can vote directly on the proposal at hand, they have no role in shaping the referendum question or the answers available. In the majority of cases, the options are limited to approving or rejecting a discrete proposal, with no flexibility or opportunity to amend, which further limits the democratic potential of these measures.

'Bottom-up' proposals (i.e. referendum questions initiated by citizens, rather than governments) take a variety of forms. Their use is not particularly widespread; of the countries in our analysis, only ten have a history of using citizen-generated referendums (Table 6.3). Of these ten, five are post-Soviet 'new democracies': Croatia, Latvia, Lithuania, Slovakia, and Slovenia.

The growth in the use of 'bottom-up' referendums between the two time periods in Table 6.3 is significant, with twice as many held between 1988 and 2022 than in the 1945–87 period (1,567 compared to 729). Of the post-1988 referendums, the 'new democracies' only account for fifty-two such initiatives between them; a figure eclipsed by Italy's own figure of sixty, itself an increase of forty-six on the number used between 1945 and 1987. Hungary has experienced eleven post-1988 citizen-generated referendums, having conducted none in the previous period, while Germany more than doubled its use from eight to seventeen. Only Denmark bucks the trend of the increasing frequency of citizen-generated referendums (having conducted four in the 1945–87 period, it has conducted none in the last thirty years). This general increased usage might be seen as a reaction to the 'hollowing out' of Western representative democracy described by Mair (2013), among others, in the sense that it speaks to the greater ability of citizens to use their 'voice' to influence policy decisions in between elections—something we consider in more detail in the next Section 6.4.

Reidy (2018) identifies three main varieties of citizen-generated referendum. The first of these, citizens' initiatives, allow citizens to propose and vote on legislative or constitutional

Table 6.3 Citizen-led referendums in Europe

	1945–87			1988–2022		
Country	**National citizen-led referendums**	**Sub-national citizen-led referendums**	**Total citizen-led referendums**	**National citizen-led referendums**	**Sub-national citizen-led referendums**	**Total citizen-led referendums**
Croatia	NA	NA	NA	1	0	1
Denmark	4	0	4	0	0	0
Germany	0	8	8	0	17	17
Hungary	0	0	0	11	0	11
Italy	14	0	14	60	0	60
Latvia	NA	NA	NA	7	0	7
Lithuania	NA	NA	NA	11	0	11
Slovakia	NA	NA	NA	14	0	15
Slovenia	NA	NA	NA	18	0	18
Switzerland	110	593	703	245	1,182	1,427
TOTAL	128	601	729	367	1,199	1,567
Average	25.60	120.20	145.80	36.70	119.90	156.70
Median	4	0	8	11	0	13

Note: Data from the Centre for Research on Direct Democracy (2018) website, correct as of March 2023. Only referendums tagged with 'official' status by the C2D are counted. Where multiple options were presented to the electorate in the same referendum, each ballot is treated as a separate entry. 'Germany' includes data from the pre-unification Federal (West) and Democratic (East) Republics as well as the post-1990 unified federal state.

changes. Most commonly found in Switzerland, other European countries to use this method are Hungary, Italy, Latvia, Lithuania, and Germany (at the regional level). Arguably, citizens' initiatives offer the greatest democratic scope in Reidy's typology, as they allow for citizens to actually propose matters, rather than approve or reject a proposal from another actor such as government or parliament. Second, abrogative referendums allow citizens to vote to repeal part or all of an existing piece of legislation. This type of referendum is most commonly associated with Italy, where it can be triggered at the request of 500,000 citizens or five regional councils, but citizens are precluded from abrogating tax laws, budget laws, amnesties, pardons, and laws relating to international treaties. The third variety of referendum in Reidy's typology is the rejective referendum, which allows citizens to vote to veto a proposed piece of legislation. In the European context, rejective referendums are usually associated with Liechtenstein. These varieties offer different levels of democratic value, with the citizens' initiatives having much greater scope for direct control than abrogative or rejective referendums (Uleri 1996). Nonetheless, the option of a veto or removal of parliamentary legislative decisions is still much more directly democratic than the 'top-down' style of referendum.

6.3.2 **The rules of referendums**

The democratic value of referendums is always limited by the rules and restrictions placed on the manner in which they are held. If the process of the referendum is inherently undemocratic, the referendum itself will lose its direct-democratic characteristics. The Venice Commission, an organ of the Council of Europe concerned with promoting 'good' standards of democracy, has outlined a set of rules for 'good practice' during referendums (Venice Commission 2018). The rules themselves are fairly straightforward and common-sense: prohibiting the state from intervening directly in the referendum campaigns, restricting certain forms of financing, and upholding transparency throughout the process are some of its main recommendations. However, as is typically the case for the Council of Europe, its positions are not legally binding and there is little enforcement of these standards across the board.

'Bottom-up' referendums have specific rules that place restrictions on whether the referendum can take place. Generally, this initial hurdle takes the form of a number of signatures that must be applied to a petition in order that a referendum should take place. As Reidy (2018) outlines, the threshold that must be reached varies considerably across countries. For example, Italy and Slovakia require a similar number of signatures to trigger a referendum (500,000 versus 350,000), but given the difference in their populations (59m versus 5.5m), the challenge of securing such a referendum is much greater in Slovakia (where 6.3% of the population must support the proposal to hold a referendum, compared to 0.8% in Italy). As Setälä (2006) describes, this seems to have had a particularly strong impact on whether abrogative or rejective referendums take place, with Italy commonly holding these referendums but relatively few other countries having held them.

The level of regulation on referendum activity varies widely between countries. In their review, Reidy and Suiter (2015) examined the type of regulations in use under four main categories: campaign participation restrictions (mainly relating to campaigning by government, and civil service neutrality); campaign communication rules (including enforced 'balance' or proportional coverage, restrictions on campaign airtime and advertising, and costs); campaign finance regulations (including spending limits, public finance provision, and disclosure laws); and independent electoral management (whether a referendum commission exists, and what it is allowed to do).

These forms of regulation prompt some questions from the direct-democratic perspective. Is more or less regulation better for direct democracy? Is it more complicated than simply 'more' or 'less' being better? Some regulations can throw up oddities that do not necessarily mesh with direct-democratic goals; for example, in Ireland, public broadcasters are compelled to provide equal amounts of airtime to campaigners from both sides of a referendum question. This enforced balance does not have regard to any proportion of views in the country, meaning that one side will often receive much more exposure than its level of support might suggest is appropriate. It is also possible that rules will have unintended consequences. For example, to address the much-discussed issue of low turnout in referendums (see Box 6.1), some countries have introduced a quorum, or minimum turnout requirement for a referendum to pass. Several countries (including Italy, Hungary, Portugal, and Slovakia)

Box 6.2 Referendum rules in different countries

The rules and restrictions on referendum activity vary widely from country to country. Consider the range of approaches in the following examples:

Ireland: because of Ireland's requirement to hold a referendum to approve any constitutional amendment, and the relatively high level of detail in the Irish Constitution, Ireland has held many referendums. There is only provision for two types of referendum: the approval or rejection of a constitutional amendment, and a facultative referendum to break a deadlock between the upper and lower houses of parliament. In practice, only the former has ever been used. There is no provision for a 'bottom-up' referendum. In recent decades, Ireland has appointed referendum commissions to oversee the process of each referendum, including the provision of impartial information. Ireland is also subject to a Supreme Court rule requiring public broadcasters to provide equal airtime to either side of a referendum, referred to as the McKenna Judgement.

Italy: referendums in Italy are extremely common, having held eighty-eight since 1945 (82% of which took place after 1990). Most Italian referendums take place at the national level; however, there is provision for regional referendums as well, with nine of these taking place since 1945. A national 'bottom-up' referendum can be initiated with 500,000 signatures. These are referred to as 'popular' or 'abrogative' referendums, and may be used to abolish existing legislation either partially or entirely. There is no provision for proposing legislation through referendums, nor is any quorum applied.

Slovenia: of the post-Yugoslavian 'new democracies', Slovenia is the most enthusiastic user of the referendum method, having held twenty-nine referendums since gaining independence in 1991. Almost two-thirds of these have been 'bottom-up' referendums, which can be initiated by collecting 40,000 signatures (prior to reforms in 2013, this figure was 5,000). Referendums may propose, veto, or remove legislation; however, for a proposal to pass, the number of voters in favour must be at least 20% of the electorate (irrespective of overall turnout).

Switzerland: of all contemporary European democracies, none has as close a relationship with direct democracy as Switzerland. Referendums are used to decide on a wide range of legislative and policy matters, with the consequence that Swiss citizens often vote three or four times every year. Citizens may initiate a referendum to propose new federal legislation by collecting 100,000 signatures for a petition, and initiate a referendum to veto legislation with 50,000 signatures. Referendums, both 'bottom-up' and 'top-down', also exist at the regional (canton) level. Switzerland imposes a quorum of 40% for results to be valid, and facilitates participation through a variety of means including weekend voting and a generous postal ballot provision.

require a minimum turnout of 50% for a referendum to pass. However, as Aguiar-Conraria and Magalhães (2010) have shown, these rules actually appear to have a depressive effect on turnout, particularly when those on the 'no' side in a referendum campaign encourage people not to vote so as to render the outcome invalid.

One area of regulation that has been met positively is the provision of an independent referendum commission. As discussed by Renwick and Palesa (2019), these bodies offer a means of informing voters about the matter being voted upon, without the bias of supporting a particular outcome. This may take the form of simply running an awareness campaign before the vote, or extend as far as active interventions in the debate by the commission, such as when the chair of Ireland's Referendum Commission intervened in the debate on the 2015 Marriage Referendum to clarify that it would have no impact on surrogacy laws (ibid.). Despite this, commissions—whether specific referendum commissions or general electoral commissions—do not have a role in many European countries, notably being absent from Austria, Czechia, France, Italy, Luxembourg, Slovakia, and Switzerland (Reidy and Suiter 2015). Also, even where referendum commissions are in use for national referendums, they may not be required for use in sub-national referendums.

6.4 **Deliberative democracy**

Electoral representation is predicated on the notion that representatives are elected by citizens. Traditionally the role of the citizen is seen as essentially a passive one, of waiting till the next electoral cycle comes around to decide whether or not to 'vote the rascals out'. As we have seen in the previous Section 6.3, referendums provide an alternative avenue for citizens to express their views on matters of public policy or constitutional reform. That this occurs in between elections is significant, suggesting a more active role for citizens, especially in those increasing number of instances where they are given the possibility to petition for referendums.

This potential for citizen engagement in between elections speaks to a wider debate in political science about whether democracies are being 'transformed' (Cain et al. 2006). While it is undoubtedly true (as discussed in Chapter 5) that voter turnout is declining, it is instructive to note that this is coinciding with citizen engagement in new, less conventional forms of political action. Many people are seeking a more active role in the political system, prepared to challenge (and thereby engage with) existing systems and norms. This amounts to evidence of a *behavioural* shift to a citizenry that is changing in its expectations of the political system and its approach to the system.

There is also growing evidence of widespread *institutional* reform (for details, see Bedock et al. 2012), in large part in reaction to the growing clamour from citizens, and to a large degree driven by parties. Included in the mix of institutional reforms are a series of measures that specifically cater for a citizenry more interested in political action outside of the election cycle. Dalton and his colleagues (2003) refer to this as a 'second wave of democratic reform', personified by the creation of new institutions (such as deliberative mini-publics, discussed later), and the redesign of existing ones (such as local government) with the principal aim of facilitating greater citizen participation, or as Smith puts it, 'to increase and deepen citizen participation in the political decision-making process' (2009: 1).

There is no doubt that when it comes to contemporary democratic institutions things are not as they once were. But this is only to be expected 'when nineteenth-century concepts meet twenty-first century realities' (Warren 2001: 226). Institutions must change and are changing with the times. The emerging new model of democracy is one that is more 'talk-centred' rather than 'election-centred', with citizens being ever more drawn into the policy process in between elections (Steiner 2012: 37).

Table 6.4 illustrates some of the key changes that are associated with this democratic transformation, which include, inter alia: the sheer expansion in the number of things to elect (e.g. Dalton and Gray 2003); citizen-initiated mechanisms of direct democracy (discussed in the previous Section 6.3); reforms within parties (most notably, the greater role of members in selecting leaders and candidates, e.g. Hazan and Rahat 2010; Cross and Blais 2010); more transparent and open administrative processes facilitating greater citizen engagement (Cain et al. 2006); and direct citizen engagement in policy and institutional debates.

The latter relates to a well-established sub-field in democratic theory on deliberative democracy that is now developing quite a firm niche in democratic practice. It is seen most prominently in the case of deliberative mini-publics: small groups of randomly selected citizens, operating according to deliberative principles (including facilitated small-group discussions) and tasked with considering one or a number of important policy, institutional, or constitutional reform issues (Curato et al. 2021). The rationale underlying them is a desire to arrive at the 'best' outcome, through careful and informed deliberation by regular citizens who have no agenda or ulterior motive (in contrast to politicians, whose focus tends to be on re-election) (Farrell and Stone 2020).

These mini-publics can take a range of different forms including citizens' juries, consensus conferences, planning cells, deliberative polls, and citizens' assemblies. As Table 6.5 shows, what they all have in common is that random selection is the mode of recruiting the members (regular citizens), and the mode of operation is deliberation. But in other respects they differ. For instance, citizens' juries and consensus conferences tend to involve small groups of citizens, whereas the other forms of mini-publics such as citizens' assemblies and deliberative polls tend to be larger (thus making them more representative of the wider population). For example, a series of citizens' juries held in Scotland in 2013 and 2014 on the topic of wind farms had between sixteen and eighteen jurors each (Roberts and Escobar 2015), while the Europolis deliberative poll of 2009 brought together 400 randomly selected participants

Table 6.4 A new democratic transformation?

First wave of democratic reform	Second wave of democratic reform
• Introduction of elections to most offices • Mass suffrage extension • Freedom for all parties to compete in elections	• Introduction of elections for more offices (e.g. elected mayors; regional assemblies) • Citizen-initiated mechanisms of direct democracy • Greater competition between and within parties • Greater engagement with administrative processes (e.g. freedom of information) • Direct citizen engagement in policy and institutional debates (e.g. citizens' assemblies, citizens' juries, participatory budgeting)

Source: Reproduced with permission from Farrell (2014). Rights managed by Taylor & Francis.

Table 6.5 Types of mini-public

	Citizens' juries	Planning cells	Consensus conferences	Deliberative polls	Citizens' assemblies
Developed by (first instance)	Ned Crosby (USA, 1971)	Peter Dienel (Germany, 1970s)	Danish Board of Technology (1987)	James Fishkin (USA, 1994)	Gordon Gibson (Canada, 2002)
No. of members	12–26	100–150	10–25	100–500	99–160
No. of meetings	2–5 days	4–5 days	7–8 days	2–3 days	20–26 days
Selection method	Random selection				
Mode of operation	Deliberation				
Result	Collective position report	Survey opinions and collective position report	Collective position report	Survey opinions	Detailed recommendations
Destination of proposal	Sponsor and mass media	Sponsor and mass media	Parliament and mass media	Sponsor (which could be government) and/or mass media	Parliament, government, and referendum

Source: Reproduced from Elstub, S. and McLaverty, P. (2014), *Deliberative Democracy: Issues and Cases* (Edinburgh: Edinburgh University Press). Based on Fournier, P. et al. (2011), *When Citizens Decide: Lessons from Citizen Assemblies on Electoral Reform* (Oxford: Oxford University Press).

from across Europe to debate immigration, climate change, and the EU (Isernia and Fishkin 2014). Another important difference is over the number of meetings, which range from being very short (often single-shot) events, as in the case of citizens' juries and deliberative polls, to being longer, more intensive sessions, most notably in the case of the citizens' assemblies. A third difference of note is the outcome of the mini-public, which ranges from a survey report sent to the media or a private sponsor (as was the case with the Europolis deliberative poll) through to detailed recommendations that are voted on by the wider citizenry in a public referendum (such as the recommendations on abortion from the Irish citizens' assembly).

The most interesting of these experiments are the citizens' assemblies that combine the merits of a large membership, time for intensive and detailed focus on issues, and a significant role in influencing policy outcomes (Reuchamps and Suiter 2016). For Elstub the citizens' assembly is the 'democratically superior mini-public' (Elstub 2014: 172); as Smith notes, '[n]o other randomly selected body has been given the level of influence in the political process' (2009: 75). Table 6.6 sets out five prominent examples: the citizens' assemblies on electoral reform in the Canadian provinces of British Columbia (2004) and Ontario (2007), the Dutch citizens' forum (*BurgerForum*) of 2006, the Irish constitutional convention of 2012–14, and the Irish citizens' assembly of 2016–18 (Farrell et al. 2017, 2018; Fournier et al. 2011). Building on these initiatives, a number of other citizens' assemblies have occurred over the past couple of years, including in France and the UK where citizens' assemblies were set up to examine the issue of climate change (Elstub et al. 2021). Ireland has also seen additional citizens' assemblies on such issues as biodiversity and gender equality. The European Union has also entered this space, with four multinational and multi-lingual 200-member citizens' panels forming the heart of the 2021–22 Conference on the Future of Europe. The growing number of citizens' assemblies and other deliberative mini-publics across the world has prompted the Organization for Economic Cooperation and Development (OECD) to refer to an international 'deliberative wave' (OECD 2020).

Four of the cases listed in Table 6.6 share in common that ordinary citizens were the only members, all selected in a random process; in one case, the Irish constitutional convention, one-third of its members were professional politicians. Meetings occurred at weekends over a number of months, with all five cases having roughly the same number of meeting days (which clearly do not include reading and other activities the members will have been involved with in addition).

The two Canadian cases resulted in referendum questions that went directly to the wider citizenry for consideration, which in both instances were defeated (though in one case in British Columbia, the proposition actually received majority support, but it failed to pass

Table 6.6 Examples of citizens' assemblies

	British Columbia Citizens' Assembly 2004	**Netherlands *BurgerForum* 2006**	**Ontario Citizens' Assembly 2007**	**Ireland Constitutional Convention 2012–14**	**Ireland Citizens' Assembly 2016–18**
Number of members	160 citizens	140 citizens	103 citizens	66 citizens + 33 politicians	99 citizens
Selection method	Pool drawn randomly (stratified) from electoral register; interested people signified their interest; members picked randomly (ensuring gender parity)			Door-to-door recruitment by a market research company of citizens on the electoral register (stratified random)	
Number of topics	1	1	1	8 (+2)	5
Number of meeting days	26	20	24	20	22
Number of recommendations	1	1	1	38	44
Destination of recommendations	Binding referendum	Report to government	Binding referendum	Reports to parliament	Reports to parliament
Outcomes (to date)	Referendum defeated (twice)	Proposal rejected	Referendum defeated	The bulk of the recommendations in train or implemented (including successful referendums on marriage equality and blasphemy)	Successful referendum (abortion); climate change recommendations led to parliament declaring a climate emergency

Sources: Reproduced with permission from Fournier et al. (2011), 'Power to the People?', in *When Citizens Decide: Lessons from Citizen Assemblies on Electoral Reform*. (Oxford, UK: Oxford University Press), DOI: 10.1093/acprof:oso/9780199567843.001.0001. And Farrell, D. M. and Stone, P. (2019). 'Sortition and mini-publics: A different kind of representation', in Rohrschneider R. and Thomassen J. (eds.), *The Handbook of Political Representation in Liberal Democracies* (Oxford, UK: Oxford University Press). In Press.

Box 6.3 Over to you—deliberative mini-publics and referendums

Proponents of deliberative mini-publics talk of their role in helping to improve the referendum process, not least by providing more detail on the wider context underlying the referendum and thus better informing the voters (and politicians). The belief is that this should reduce the risk of a challenge to the outcome of the referendum vote. Does this work in practice? Compare the 2016 Brexit referendum in the UK and the 2018 abortion referendum in Ireland. Both were seen as 'hot', controversial issues for a referendum vote. The Irish vote followed the recommendations of the 2016–18 Irish citizens' assembly, whereas no such process preceded the Brexit referendum. What evidence can you find from the media coverage of the referendums and their outcomes that would support the argument that deliberative mini-publics improve the referendum process? What differences were there in how the vote outcomes were viewed by the losing side?

a super-majority threshold). In the case of the Dutch citizens' forum the recommendation was for only minor changes to the existing electoral system. This was to have been discussed by the government, but the process disintegrated with the collapse of the coalition government. By contrast, both Irish cases have resulted in successful outcomes, most notably the passing of the 2015 marriage equality referendum and the 2018 blasphemy referendum, both following the constitutional convention, and the passing of the 2018 abortion referendum following the citizens' assembly, see Box 6.3 (Reidy et al. 2020).

6.5 **Is direct citizen engagement in between elections for everyone?**

New opportunities for citizens to engage in between elections need citizens to engage. The question is: do they? Two common areas of concern relate to the degree of importance citizens generally might attach to the opportunities given to them to engage in between general elections, and whether these additional opportunities are for everyone. A third area of criticism specific to deliberative mini-publics is that, by their nature as *mini*-publics, they can appear as quite 'exclusive', and as not offering 'much real scope [for] . . . conventional modalities of mass democracy' (Mair 2006: 8). We deal with each of these points in turn.

In the first instance, there is the question of whether citizens place opportunities for engagement in between elections at a lower priority than national elections. This speaks to a prominent debate in European elections research over 'second-order' elections, referring to the phenomenon of elections that are not viewed as having the same importance for voters as 'first-order' elections, such as national parliamentary or presidential elections (see Chapters 5 and 17). According to this perspective, referendums (as one instance of second-order elections) are used by voters to deliver a verdict on the performance of the government of the day, rather than to express an opinion on the issue being voted on.

Assessing the outcomes of four referendums on the Maastricht Treaty (France, two in Denmark, and Ireland), Franklin et al. (1995) found that the likelihood of the referendum passing was best predicted by the popularity of the government of the day, and that voting preferences in the referendum did not correlate strongly with voter opinions on Europe as such. The so-called 'Franklin thesis' has many supporters, but its critics argue that it underestimates the level of voter knowledge and engagement with Europe, particularly as it varies across EU member states. In his rebuttal of the thesis, Svensson (2002) argues that the *issue-voting* perspective (as outlined in Chapter 4) is a much better explanatory model for these referendums. Issue-voting, as the name suggests, holds that voters do in fact approach elections (and referendums) based on the issues salient to those elections, rather than secondary considerations such as support for the government. More recent research on European referendum dynamics has tended to favour the issue-voting explanation over the second-order approach (Holbolt 2009); however, the latter still has its adherents. Furthermore, advocates of the issue-voting explanation do also acknowledge that the effects of issue-voting are more pronounced when there is greater public awareness and debate of the details of the issue at hand, which has not been the case in every referendum (see the following 'Thinking comparatively' Section).

A variant of the 'second-order' thesis which has wider applicability than just to referendums (i.e. it includes all democratic innovations that allow citizens a voice in between elections) is the argument that not all citizens are willing to engage in these processes. The most prominent version of this is Hibbing and Theiss-Morse's (2002) influential argument about 'stealth democrats'—citizens who 'do not want to make political decisions themselves', but rather prefer to leave it 'to those who are assigned to make these decisions'. According to this perspective, the ideals of wider citizen engagement in between elections are fanciful, 'wishful thinking' (2002: 207). A weakness in this argument is that it is based in large part on survey experiments testing hypothetical scenarios on samples of respondents. Real-world examples of citizen engagement in alternatives ways of political participation, such as in deliberative mini-publics, find that, on the contrary, citizens are enthusiastic about the engagement and, furthermore, that 'those most willing to deliberate are precisely those who are turned off by standard partisan and interest group politics' (Neblo et al. 2010: 582).

Then there is the question of whether all citizens are equally capable of engaging in the various forms of democratic innovation such as deliberative mini-publics. We know from voter studies that imbalances in society have an impact on political behaviour. At the heart of the 'new politics' thesis (e.g. Dalton et al. 2004) is an expectation that alternative forms of political participation are concentrated primarily among those who are better educated, more informed, and more interested in politics (see Chapter 5). The logical corollary, therefore, is that we should see this reflected in the members of a mini-public; indeed, this forms the basis for a common criticism of deliberation, namely that the differing capabilities among the participants in a deliberative process result in some dominating over others (e.g. Lupia and Norton 2017; Rosenberg 2014). A response to such criticisms is to point out that in a well-designed mini-public, with well-trained facilitators, many of these problems could be mitigated (see Curato et al. 2017).

A third area of criticism particular to deliberative mini-publics is that 'they are not integrated into the overall system of representative government or democratic institutions, nor do they become part of the regular political cycle in the life of a community' (Pateman 2012: 10). The question is whether mini-publics could realistically be mainstreamed—made more central to the decision-making process in a political system (Dryzek 2010). It might reasonably be asked how small-scale, carefully controlled mini-publics can be scaled up to such an extent to be taken seriously by citizens or the political elite, without becoming unmanageable. Various proposals for mainstreaming have been suggested, perhaps most notably Ackerman and Fishkin's 'deliberation day' (2003)—the idea of a pre-election national holiday to coordinate deliberative events across the country. Another suggested approach is that deliberation should 'go global' (Dryzek 2010), with deliberative exercises giving citizens an opportunity to set the agenda on big questions in international politics, such as environmental protection, human rights, or even global governance.

Recent developments at the regional level in Belgium indicate another way in which deliberative mini-publics can be mainstreamed—by institutionalizing them as permanent fixtures in the political system. In early 2019 the parliament of the German-speaking community of Belgium established the 'Ostbelgien model'—a permanent citizens' assembly consisting of two main parts: a citizens' council (twenty-five randomly selected citizens) which decides on the topics to be considered; and the single-issue citizens' assemblies (of between twenty-five and fifty members randomly selected from the wider population), who make recommendations on the topic they've been asked to consider, which are then sent to the parliament for their consideration (Niessen and Reuchamps 2020). The parliament is obliged to engage seriously with the recommendations (e.g. meetings must be held with the citizens' assembly members to discuss areas of disagreement). The Ostbelgien example was quickly followed by developments of a similar nature in other regional parliaments in Belgium. In December 2019 both the parliament of the Brussels-Capital Region and the French-speaking Brussels parliament adopted new rules giving the parliaments the right to establish deliberative committees comprising a mix of parliamentarians and citizens drawn by lot (Vrydagh et al. 2021).

These Belgian models are sub-national-level experiments that share a desire to institutionalize deliberative mini-publics as added features to their existing systems of representative democracy. It's too early to say how successful they will be, but they have now operated for a number of years and the signs are that they are bedding down. And they are starting to attract interest in other places: permanent citizens' assemblies have now been established in Paris (2021), Brussels (2023), and Milan (2023).

6.6 Conclusion

Democracies are constantly evolving, moving beyond their classic forms as representative systems in which elected representatives represent citizens and the latter's role is limited to determining whether or not to 'kick out the rascals' in each election cycle (Saward 2010). This chapter has examined the increasing ways in which processes have developed to give citizens greater 'voice' in between elections. The most prominent and widespread examples are the use of referendums that over time are used by an ever-greater number of Europe's democracies, and are being used more frequently at both national and sub-national levels. The more 'bottom-up' the referendums are (notably in terms of how much scope is given for citizens to petition to call them), the more we might think of the evolution of a direct form of democracy.

A more recent set of democratic innovations relates to the emergence of deliberative mini-publics, in which random selections of citizens are brought into the heart of discussions over important policy or constitutional matters. While these initiatives are still at an early stage and have not been nearly as widespread in their applications as referendums, they do at least provide a clue to how the 'ecology of democratic institutions' (Warren 2008: 69) could be broadened to allow greater scope for citizen engagement. In John Ferejohn's eyes, initiatives like this could yet provide 'a way to redeem, to some extent, the ancient promise of democracy as a form of popular government—in Lincoln's words, as government "by" the people' (2008: 213). By bringing the people into the heart of the policy process, either as participants in deliberative mini-publics or by giving them a direct vote on a policy matter, Lincoln's dream could well soon be realized.

Discussion questions

1. What are the main challenges posed to representative-democratic structures by referendums? Do they strengthen or weaken representative regimes?
2. Are citizen-led referendums good or bad for democracy?
3. Certain states are much more frequent users of referendums than others. Consider the structural, historical, and political factors that may have led to these preferences.
4. What evidence is there of democracies innovating? Consider whether the examples of democratic reform are sufficient to meet the challenges faced by contemporary democracies.
5. To what extent are all citizens capable of utilizing the 'voice' given to them in contemporary democracies?
6. What are the pros and cons of deliberative mini-publics?

Thinking comparatively

What explains voting in EU referendums? Garry et al. (2005) test the issue-voting perspective versus the second-order perspective by comparing the two referendums held in Ireland on the Nice Treaty. This is a useful comparison because the first referendum, held in 2001, was characterized by a low-key campaign and low levels of public knowledge on the issue, while the repeat referendum held a year later was associated with a more intensive campaign and a more informed electorate. Using survey data to divide voters into cohorts based on factors important to second-order voting (support for government vs. opposition parties) and factors important to issue-voting (supporting or opposing deeper EU integration and enlargement), they found that the issue-voting cohorts were more predictive of voting behaviour than the second-order voting cohorts. The authors conclude that 'both Irish referendums on the Nice Treaty were closer to being processes of deliberation on EU issues than to being plebiscites on the incumbent government'. They also find that issue-voting is particularly important in the context of a high-intensity campaign, such as the second Nice referendum.

Guide to further reading

Aguiar-Conraria, L. and Magalhães, P. C. (2010), 'Referendum design, quorum rules and turnout', *Public Choice*, 144(1)–2: 63–81.

This is an interesting comparative study exploring the impact of referendum design on public engagement in European referendums.

Curato, Nicole, Farrell, David et al. (2021), *Deliberative Mini-Publics: Core Design Features* (Bristol: Bristol University Press).

This book examines the core design features of deliberative mini-publics and their role in the broader policy process.

Fournier, Patrick, van der Kolk, Henk et al. (2011), *When Citizens Decide: Lessons from Citizen Assemblies on Electoral Reform* (Oxford: Oxford University Press).

The definitive study of the first three citizens' assemblies, held in Canada and the Netherlands.

Qvortrup, M. (2014), *Referendums Around the World* (London: Palgrave Macmillan).

This book provides a comprehensive review of referendums in the global context.

Smith, Graham (2009), *Democratic Innovations: Designing Institutions for Citizen Participation* (Cambridge: Cambridge University Press).

This is the key textbook overview of democratic innovations, including thorough treatment of citizens' assemblies and other deliberative mini-publics.

References

Ackerman, Bruce and Fishkin, James (2003), 'Deliberation day', in James Fishkin and Peter Laslett (eds.), *Debating Deliberative Democracy* (Oxford: Blackwell Publishing): 7–30.

Aguiar-Conraria, L. and Magalhães, P. C. (2010), 'Referendum design, quorum rules and turnout', *Public Choice*, 144(1–2): 63–81.

Altman, D. (2019), *Citizenship and Direct Democracy* (Cambridge: Cambridge University Press).

Beach, D. (2018), 'Referendums in the European Union', in William R. Thompson (ed.), *Oxford Research Encyclopedias of Politics* (Oxford: Oxford University Press).

Bedock, Camille, Mair, Peter et al. (2012), Institutional Change in Advanced European Democracies: An Exploratory Assessment. EUI Working Papers, RSCAS 2012/11.

Beigbeder, Y. (2011), 'Referendum', in *Max Planck Encyclopedia of International Law*, [Online] available at http://opil.ouplaw.com/view/10.1093/law:epil/9780199231690/law-9780199231690-e1088. (Oxford: Public International Law).

Budge, Ian (1996), *The New Challenge of Direct Democracy* (Cambridge: Polity).

Cain, Bruce, Dalton, Russell et al. (eds.) (2006), *Democracy Transformed? Expanding Political Opportunities in Advanced Industrial Democracies* (Oxford: Oxford University Press).

Centre for Research on Direct Democracy (2018), *C2D: A database with information on direct democracy institutions such as the referendum and the initiative as well as their use in popular votes*, [Online] available at https://c2d.ch/.

Cross, William and Blais, André (2010), *Politics at the Centre: The Selection and Removal of Party Leaders in the Anglo Parliamentary Democracies* (Oxford: Oxford University Press).

Curato, Nicole, Dryzek, John S. et al. (2017), 'Twelve key findings in deliberative democracy research', *Daedalus*, 146: 28–38.

Curato, Nicole, Farrell, David et al. (2021), *Deliberative Mini-Publics: Core Design Features* (Bristol: Bristol University Press).

Dalton, Russell and Gray, Mark (2003), 'Expanding the electoral marketplace', in Bruce Cain, Russell Dalton et al. (eds.), *Democracy Transformed? Expanding Political Opportunities in Advanced Industrial Democracies* (Oxford: Oxford University Press): 23–43.

Dalton, Russell, Scarrow, Susan et al. (2003), 'New forms of democracy? Reform and transformation of democratic institutions', in Bruce Cain, Russell Dalton et al. (eds.), *Democracy Transformed? Expanding Political Opportunities in Advanced Industrial Democracies* (Oxford: Oxford University Press): 1–20.

Dalton, Russell, Scarrow, Susan et al. (2004), 'Advanced democracies and the new politics', *Journal of Democracy*, 15: 124–38.

Dryzek, John (2010), *Foundations and Frontiers of Deliberative Governance* (Oxford: Oxford University Press).

Elstub, Stephen (2014), 'Mini-publics: Issues and cases', in Stephen Elstub and Peter McLaverty (eds.), *Deliberative Democracy: Issues and Cases* (Edinburgh: Edinburgh University Press): 166–88.

Elstub, Stephen, Farrell, David et al. (2021), *Evaluation of Climate Assembly UK* (Newcastle: Newcastle

University), available at https://www.parliament.uk/globalassets/documents/get-involved2/climate-assembly-uk/evaluation-of-climate-assembly-uk.pdf.

Farrell, David (2014), '"Stripped down" or reconfigured democracy', *West European Politics*, 37: 439–55.

Farrell, David and Stone, Peter (2020), 'Sortition and mini-publics: A different kind of representation', in Robert Rohrschneider and Jacques Thomassen (eds.), *Handbook of Political Representation* (Oxford: Oxford University Press).

Farrell, David, Harris, Clodagh et al. (2017), 'Bringing people into the heart of constitutional design: The Irish Constitutional Convention of 2012–14', in X. Contiades and A. Fotiadou (eds.), *Participatory Constitutional Change: The People as Amenders of the Constitution* (London: Routledge).

Farrell, David, Suiter, Jane et al. (2018), '"Systematizing" constitutional deliberation: The 2016–18 citizens' assembly in Ireland', *Irish Political Studies*, 34(1): 113–23.

Ferejohn, John (2008), 'Conclusion: The citizens' assembly model', in Mark Warren and Hilary Pearse (eds.), *Designing Deliberative Democracy: The British Columbia Citizens' Assembly* (Cambridge: Cambridge University Press): 192–213.

Fournier, Patrick, van der Kolk, Henk et al. (2011), *When Citizens Decide: Lessons from Citizen Assemblies on Electoral Reform* (Oxford: Oxford University Press).

Franklin, M. N., Marsh, M. et al. (1995), 'Referendum outcomes and trust in government: Public support for Europe in the wake of Maastricht', *West European Politics*, 18(3): 101–17.

Garry, J., Marsh, M. et al. (2005), '"Second-order" versus "issue-voting" effects in EU referendums: Evidence from the Irish Nice Treaty referendums', *European Union Politics*, 6(2): 201–21.

Hazan, Reuven and Rahat, Gideon (2010), *Democracy within Parties: Candidate Selection Methods and Their Political Consequences* (Oxford: Oxford University Press).

Hibbing, J. R. and Theiss-Morse, E. (2002), *Stealth Democracy: Americans' Beliefs about How Government Should Work* (Cambridge: Cambridge University Press).

Holbolt, Sara Binzer (2009), *Europe in Question: Referendums on European Integration* (Oxford: Oxford University Press).

Isernia, Pierangelo and Fishkin, James S. (2014), 'The EuroPolis deliberative poll', *European Union Politics*, 15(3): 311–27.

LeDuc, Lawrence (2003), *The Politics of Direct Democracy: Referendums in Global Perspective* (Peterborough: Broadview Press).

Lupia, A. and Johnston, R. (2001), 'Are voters to blame? Voter competence and elite maneuvers in referendums', in Matthew Mendelsohn and Andrew Parkin (eds.), *Referendum Democracy: Citizens, Elites and Deliberation in Referendum Campaigns* (London: Palgrave Macmillan): 191–210.

Lupia, Arthur and Norton, Anne (2017), 'Inequality is always in the room: Language and power in deliberative democracy', *Daedalus*, 146: 64–76.

Mair, Peter (2006), 'Policy-scepticism, party failings, and the challenge to European democracy', Netherlands Institute for Advanced Study in the Humanities and Social Sciences, Uhlenbeck Lecture 24.

Mair, Peter (2013), *Ruling the Void: The Hollowing-Out of Western Democracy* (London: Pluto Press).

Mendez, Fernando and Mendez, Mario (2017), *Referendums on EU Matters: Study* (Brussels: European Parliament: Policy Department for Citizens' Rights and Constitutional Affairs).

Neblo, Michael, Esterling, Kevin et al. (2010), 'Who wants to deliberate—and why?' *American Political Science Review*, 104: 566–83.

Niessen, Christoph and Reuchamps, Min (2020), 'Institutionalizing citizen deliberation in parliament: The permanent citizen's' dialogue in the German-speaking community of Belgium', *Parliamentary Affairs*, 75(1): 135–53.

OECD (2020), *Innovative Citizen Participation and New Democratic Institutions: Catching the Deliberative Wave* (Paris: OECD Publishing).

Pateman, Carole (2012), 'Participatory democracy revisited,' *Perspectives on Politics*, 10(1): 7–19.

Qvortrup, Matt (2014), 'Referendums in Western Europe', in Matt Qvortrup (ed.), *Referendums Around the World* (London: Palgrave Macmillan): 43–64.

Reidy, Theresa (2018), *Citizens' Initiatives.* Paper presented to the Irish Citizens' Assembly, 13 January, [Online] available at https://www.citizensassembly.ie/en/Meetings/Theresa-Reidy-Paper.pdf.

Reidy, Theresa, Suiter, Jane et al. (2020), 'The Irish referendums on marriage equality and abortion', in Julie Smith (ed.), *Palgrave Handbook on European Referendums* (London: Palgrave).

Reidy, Theresa and Suiter, Jane (2015), 'Do rules matter? Categorizing the regulation of referendum campaigns', *Electoral Studies*, 38: 159–69.

Renwick, A. and Palesa, M. (2019), *Doing Democracy Better: How Can Information and Discourse in Electoral and Referendum Campaigns in the UK Be Improved?* [Report] The Constitution Unit, University College London.

Reuchamps, M. and Suiter, J. (eds.) (2016), *Constitutional Deliberative Democracy in Europe* (Colchester, Essex: ECPR Press).

Roberts, Jennifer and Escobar, Oliver (2015), *Involving Communities in Deliberation: A Study of Three Citizens' Juries on Onshore wind FARMs in Scotland,*

Edinburgh (Edinburgh: ClimateXChange and the University of Edinburgh).

Rosenberg, Shawn (2014), 'Citizen competence and the psychology of deliberation', in Stephen Elstub and Peter McLaverty (eds.), *Deliberative Democracy: Issues and Cases* (Edinburgh: Edinburgh University Press).

Saward, Michael (2010), *The Representative Claim* (Oxford: Oxford University Press).

Setälä, M. (2006), 'On the problems of responsibility and accountability in referendums', *European Journal of Political Research*, 45(4): 699–721.

Smith, Graham (2009), *Democratic Innovations: Designing Institutions for Citizen Participation* (Cambridge: Cambridge University Press).

Steiner, Jürg (2012), *The Foundations of Deliberative Democracy* (Cambridge: Cambridge University Press).

Svensson, P. (2002), 'Five Danish referendums on the European Community and European Union: A critical assessment of the Franklin thesis', *European Journal of Political Research*, 41(6): 733–50.

Uleri, Pier Vincenzo (1996), 'Italy: Referendums and initiatives from the origins to the crisis of a democratic regime', in Pier Vincenzo Uleri and Michael Gallagher (eds.), *The Referendum Experience in Europe* (London: Palgrave Macmillan): 106–25.

Venice Commission (2018), *Code of Good Practice during Referendums*, [Online] available at https://www.venice.coe.int/webforms/documents/default.aspx?pdffile=CDL-AD(2007)008rev-cor-e.

Vrydagh, Julien, Bottin, Jehan et al. (2021), 'The deliberative committees between parliamentarians and citizens drawn by lot within the Brussels assemblies', *Weekly Mail/Center for Socio-Political Research and Information*, no. 2492, available at http://hdl.handle.net/2078/245892.

Warren, Mark (2001), *Democracy and Association* (Princeton, NJ: Princeton University Press).

Warren, Mark (2008), 'Citizen representatives', in Mark Warren and Hilary Pearse (eds.), *Designing Deliberative Democracy: The British Columbia Citizens' Assembly* (Cambridge: Cambridge University Press): 50–69.

Part 2

The Process of Government

7 The Executive Branch

PETRA SCHLEITER

7.1 Introduction

The executive branch is composed of two different types of actors: those who are part of the political executive and those who form part of the civil service. The role of the political executive is to govern a country by making policy. Its task is to set strategic priorities, develop policy initiatives, draft corresponding legislation, issue government orders, mobilize support, and oversee policy implementation. Invariably, it takes decisions that have far-reaching consequences for every group in society. It shapes taxation and spending, the scope and quality of public services, the regulation of the private sector, and the maintenance of law and order, and sets priorities in areas such as foreign policy, education, inequality, and immigration. In European democracies, the political executive comprises the prime minister, cabinet, and, where applicable, the president. It is supported by non-elected civil servants who staff government departments and implement government policy. Unlike cabinet ministers, the bulk of the civil service remains in position after general elections and after government changes. Civil servants are expected to serve multiple governments of different political orientations professionally and impartially.

The context in which executives work has evolved over time, with implications for the power to govern. In particular, power has gradually shifted from parliaments to executives. These power shifts have given rise to contemporary debates about executive autonomy. Has the modern executive grown too powerful and autonomous? What are the merits and demerits of the concentration of power within the executive? What factors contribute to the empowerment of executives? Should some powers of executives be constrained, and if so, which? In the discussion that follows, we will return to these questions about executive autonomy at various points.

The chapter begins by describing the role of the political executive in parliamentary and semi-presidential democracies (Section 7.2). We then review the structure of the executive and variations in the powers available to the main actors that constitute the executive branch—the prime minister, cabinet, and, where applicable, presidential heads of state (Sections 7.3 and 7.4). As we shall see, variations in the powers of these actors have consequences for a range of political outcomes, including the probability of intra-executive political conflict, the stability of governments, the effectiveness of governments in legislating and implementing policy, and the electoral performance of political parties (Section 7.5). Next, we turn to the civil service, its functions, and the challenges of controlling it (Section 7.6). The chapter concludes with a return to the question of executive power, autonomy, and its political implications (Section 7.7).

7.2 The constitutional position of the political executive

The political executive is the institution that translates voter choices into policy. It is the nexus by which democracies funnel representation into governance. Cabinets and presidents that form part of the executive are electorally legitimated and accountable in all European democracies. That means that either the elected representatives or voters directly choose who serves in the political executive and hold it accountable. Because different types of democratic constitutions represent voters in different ways, the political executive's composition differs by constitutional format.

In Europe two constitutional formats are prevalent: parliamentary and semi-presidential democracy (see Table 7.1). Under both types of constitutions, the political executive includes a government—headed by a prime minister—that is responsible to a democratically elected parliament. Voters in parliamentary democracies are represented by parliament alone, to which the government is exclusively responsible. Cases in point include Denmark, Estonia, the Netherlands, Spain, and the UK. Voters in semi-presidential democracies elect a president in addition to the parliament to which the government is responsible. Thus, semi-presidential democracies can be defined as systems where a popularly elected president complements the government and prime minister who are responsible to parliament (Elgie 1999). Examples of semi-presidentialism include Austria, the Czech Republic, France, Finland, Latvia, Poland, and Portugal. There is enormous variation in the powers of directly elected presidents in Europe: in some cases, such as France, the president is the most important political leader in the country, while in others, such as Ireland, the president has a very restricted range of powers and generally fulfils a more ceremonial role, while real political power lies with the prime minister. For this reason, some scholars prefer a narrower definition of semi-presidentialism, restricting it to cases where presidents possess 'quite considerable powers' (Duverger 1980). However, what constitutes 'considerable powers' is subject to interpretation and even constitutional powers that appear minor to some observers can prove to be politically consequential. Elgie's (1999) broader definition is therefore employed here.

Some, but not all, parliamentary democracies are republics that feature presidents as heads of state who are indirectly elected by parliament, such as Germany. These presidents may also have some executive powers, although these powers are less extensive, on average, than those of popularly elected presidents in semi-presidential democracies. In contrast, the queens or kings who serve as head of state in parliamentary constitutional monarchies

Table 7.[illegible] Executive type by country

Country	Executive type
Belgium	Parliamentary
Denmark	Parliamentary
Estonia	Parliamentary
Germany	Parliamentary
Greece	Parliamentary
Hungary	Parliamentary
Italy	Parliamentary
Latvia	Parliamentary
Luxembourg	Parliamentary
Malta	Parliamentary
Netherlands	Parliamentary
Norway	Parliamentary
Spain	Parliamentary
Sweden	Parliamentary
United Kingdom	Parliamentary
Austria	Semi-presidential
Bulgaria	Semi-presidential
Croatia	Semi-presidential
Czech Republic	Semi-presidential
Finland	Semi-presidential
France	Semi-presidential
Iceland	Semi-presidential
Ireland	Semi-presidential
Lithuania	Semi-presidential
Poland	Semi-presidential
Portugal	Semi-presidential
Romania	Semi-presidential
Serbia	Semi-presidential
Slovakia	Semi-presidential
Slovenia	Semi-presidential
Cyprus	Presidential (president is head of state and head of government)

Source: http://www.semipresidentialism.com/?p=1053

(such as in the UK and Sweden) do not form part of the political executive because they have purely ceremonial functions.

In parliamentary and semi-presidential democracies, the government is dependent on the confidence of parliament. If a government loses a vote of no confidence in parliament, it must resign (see Chapter 9). That means that in order to form and to stay in office, a government must command the support of a legislative majority. There can be no majority in parliament that opposes the government because such a majority would use its power to vote no confidence to achieve a government change.

The institutional device of the confidence relationship ensures that governments have a *principal–agent relationship* with parliament. In a principal–agent relationship, one person or group, called the *agent*, makes decisions on behalf of another person or group, called the *principal*. The delegation of power from the principal to the agent is the defining feature of the relationship (Lupia 2003). In the relationship between parliament and government, parliament is the democratically elected principal and government is the agent of parliament. Parliament delegates to government the power to devise policy and oversee its implementation, subject to parliamentary accountability (Strøm 2003). One can even think of the government as the most important committee of the legislature (Laver 2006).

The confidence relationship between parliament and government has three consequences. First, it makes political parties central actors in government formation and termination. Second, it ensures that most governments are party-based; that is, composed of politicians who are elected to represent a party in the legislature, although in fairly exceptional circumstances technocratic, non-party governments may be formed. Third, and relatedly, most governments (around two-thirds) have majority status in parliament, in the sense that they are formed by parties that control a majority of the parliamentary seats. This implies that these executives typically have legislative support for their policy goals, precisely because they act on behalf of a parliamentary majority. However, around a third of all European governments have minority status (see Chapter 8). They depend on the tacit support of parties that are not in government but are prepared to support it in office, in return for a degree of influence on government policy (see Box 7.1).

In semi-presidential democracies, the government may additionally be accountable to the president. For instance, following Portugal's transition to democracy, the Portuguese constitution initially (up to 1982) empowered the president to dismiss the cabinet. Such constitutions make the president an additional principal of the cabinet by virtue of their institutional power of cabinet dismissal. This form of semi-presidentialism is referred to as president-parliamentarism (Shugart and Carey 1992), and it effectively ensures that the cabinet has two political masters, with potentially divergent electoral mandates, to which it is accountable. However, only some semi-presidential constitutions grant this power to the president. In Europe most semi-presidential constitutions do not grant the president formal authority to dismiss the cabinet—examples include France, Bulgaria, Croatia (2000-), and Poland. This second sub-type of semi-presidentialism is referred to as premier-presidentialism (Shugart and Carey 1992). In sum, the power to dismiss the cabinet is central in understanding the principal–agent relationships between parliament, president, and the cabinet. However, as we shall see (Sections 7.4 and 7.5), even presidents who are not formally principals of the cabinet can have significant influence on the governance of a country by virtue of their other powers.

Box 7.1 The UK Conservative minority government and the Democratic Unionist Party

In the United Kingdom, in June 2017, the Conservatives reached an agreement with the Democratic Unionist Party (DUP) to back a Conservative minority government led by Theresa May. The deal, which was a consequence of the 2017 general election in which no party won an overall majority of the parliamentary seats, required the ten DUP members of parliament to back the government in key votes including matters of confidence in the government, budget legislation, and all Brexit and security legislation. In return, the DUP secured £1bn of additional funding for Northern Ireland, the part of the United Kingdom in which the party is based.

Box 7.2 The presidentialization of politics

In historical perspective, the power and institutional capabilities of political executives have grown with the expanding functions of the modern European state. Throughout the nineteenth and twentieth centuries, states assumed responsibilities beyond defence and law and order for infrastructure, strategic industries, public services, and eventually public welfare, so that the range and complexity of the policies managed by governments grew. Complemented by suffrage extensions and electoral reforms, this expansion of the state's functions had two consequences: first, it led to the empowerment of the political executive as parliaments and Members of Parliament (MPs) delegated the increasingly complex task of making coherent policy across the growing range of government functions to the cabinet (Cox 1987). Second, it led to the expansion of the institutional capabilities of the executive, as states built sizeable bureaucracies to manage and implement policy in an expanding array of policy areas. In the UK, for instance, the size of the civil service increased from below 100,000 in 1900 to around 800,000 by the end of World War II. This rendered the civil service of modern states larger and expanded its capabilities and complexity beyond the scope of effective parliamentary control, which contributed to the autonomy of the executive from parliament. In short, the rise of the modern state was accompanied by a shift in much of the power to govern from parliament to the executive (see also Chapter 9).

The context in which executives work has continued to change since the end of World War II, with implications for the power to govern. According to Poguntke and Webb (2005), political developments since 1945 have further strengthened the executive vis-à-vis parliament and the prime minister within the executive, a process to which these authors refer as presidentialization. European integration has caused elements of domestic politics to be decided through international negotiations, which is traditionally the domain of leaders (see Chapter 17). The decline in the loyalty of voters to political parties (see Chapter 4) and the increasing focus of the media on leaders have engendered more leader-centric electoral campaigns and growing leader effects in voting behaviour. Jointly, these developments have enhanced the autonomy of prime ministers from the cabinet, their party, and parliament. According to the presidentialization argument, then there has been a shift from collective to individual power and accountability, which has been induced not by legal or constitutional modifications, but by political change within the unaltered frameworks of parliamentary and semi-presidential constitutions. Poguntke and Webb (2005) argue that this concentration of power in the hands of the prime minister has two major drawbacks for democracy: (i) it gives rise to an elitism which contradicts the aspirations of many voters in developed democracies to participate in politics and to influence political decisions; (ii) the empowerment of prime ministers at the cost of cabinets and political parties has left democracies more vulnerable to variations in individual leadership talent by reducing the number of actors who shape and define key strategic political decisions.

A crucial challenge in all democracies lies in controlling the executive to ensure that it acts in accordance with the interests of the people and their elected representatives—that is, parliamentary parties and, where applicable, the president. The issue of executive autonomy, and reforms that aim to limit it, has a direct bearing on this problem. Box 7.2 describes how executive power has grown over time, as part of a process that has been described as the 'presidentialization' of politics in Europe.

7.3 The structure and make-up of the political executive

Armed with this understanding of the political executive, we can turn to its structure and make-up. The government is made up of the prime minister and cabinet. The prime minister is referred to by a range of different titles in European democracies including, for instance, *chancellor* (Germany, Austria), *taoiseach* (Ireland), *minister-president* (Hungary, Latvia), *president of the council of ministers* (Poland), and *prime minister* (Portugal, UK). They are the head of the government and, therefore, the political chief executive. The incumbent of this role sets the strategic direction for government policy, chairs cabinet meetings, coordinates ministers, and represents the government domestically and internationally in meetings with other heads of government at the European level and beyond. As a result, the prime minister is the focus of media attention, and an important aspect of their role is to communicate and defend government policy. Unlike presidents, prime ministers are not subject to constitutional term limits. As a result, it is possible for them to serve multiple successive terms in office. For instance, the German chancellor, Angela Merkel, served four consecutive terms in office following the 2005, 2009, 2013, and 2017 federal elections.

Often, but not always, the prime minister is the leader of the largest parliamentary party, and in coalitions, the premiership is usually claimed by the largest (and therefore dominant) coalition partner. Around 62% of all prime ministers in Europe lead coalition governments; 37% lead single-party governments. In both instances, the survival of the prime minister is contingent on the support of his or her cabinet and of the legislative party or parties supporting it. Prime ministers who lose that support are replaced.

The cabinet is composed of those ministers that head the most important government departments including finance, foreign policy, interior affairs, education, and so on. The ministers that occupy these cabinet posts represent the political party or parties that have formed the government. In coalitions, governing parties typically lay claim to a share of cabinet posts that closely corresponds to the share of legislative support that they contribute to the government (Gamson 1961). Most ministers are drawn from the parliamentary party, though there can be exceptions to this rule. The role of cabinet ministers is to develop policy proposals and to oversee their implementation. In a modern executive, the cabinet does not take collective decisions with respect to every policy issue because the government's functions are too broad, and the issues are technically too complex for non-specialists. However, cabinets have a role as collective bodies to which decisions can be appealed and in which contentious issues are decided (Dunleavy and Rhodes 1990). Hence, cabinet ministers propose and influence government decisions not only through their own portfolio but also through cabinet discussions, in which major disagreements are aired and policy battles fought. Once cabinet agreement is achieved, ministers shepherd the policy through the legislative process to ensure that it is enacted as legislation. Moreover, after it has been legislated, cabinet ministers guide and oversee policy implementation by civil servants.

Many European democracies apply the principle of collective cabinet responsibility for government decisions, once cabinet discussions have concluded and the government has adopted a policy stance. Collective cabinet responsibility requires cabinet ministers to back and defend government policy, even if in private they disagree with that policy. The principle is designed to ensure that the cabinet reaches internal agreement to follow one coherent set of policies. In practice, however, collective cabinet responsibility depends on the prime minister's ability to enforce it by demanding the resignation of ministers who do not abide by it, which is contingent on the political strength of the premier. A prime minister who cannot afford to lose the support of critical factions within his or her party or a critical coalition partner may not be in a position to enforce this type of discipline on ministerial colleagues. The balance of power between prime ministers and their cabinet colleagues depends in part

Box 7.3 A breakdown in collective cabinet responsibility

In 2018, collective cabinet responsibility broke down in the German government as the interior minister Horst Seehofer (Christian Social Union (*CSU*)) disagreed with Chancellor Angela Merkel (Christian Democratic Union (*CDU*)) over immigration policy. Seehofer, who led the *CSU*, the Bavarian sister party of the Chancellor's *CDU*, broke collective cabinet responsibility. He spoke out publicly to oppose Merkel who insisted that immigration required a solution at the European level. He also declared that he was prepared to implement rules to restrict immigration unilaterally and to turn back asylum seekers at the German border if they had already been registered elsewhere in the European Union. The dispute came ahead of Bavarian state elections in which the *CSU*, which at the time commanded an absolute majority in the Bavarian parliament, came under pressure from the far-right Alternative for Germany (*AfD*) amid the refugee influx.

on political circumstances and institutional context (see Section 7.4). Politically 'weak' prime ministers, who struggle to maintain the support of their party or coalition, can find it difficult to maintain cabinet unity and to assert their own authority, while popular prime ministers, who are backed by their party and coalition, are usually better able to settle contentious issues authoritatively (see Box 7.3).

Parliamentary republics (such as Germany) and semi-presidential republics (such as Portugal) complement the cabinet and prime minister with a presidential head of state who forms part of the executive and represents the country diplomatically. Domestically, such presidents are often expected to be a moderating force in national politics and to act as guardians of the constitution. For this reason, some European constitutions explicitly require presidents to serve in a non-partisan capacity and to resign any party membership; others see the president as a political and a partisan figure. To fulfil their international and domestic roles, presidents can be invested with a range of powers (see Section 7.4). Presidents often have a role in the resolution of conflicts within the political system, for instance through their involvement in scheduling referendums, their emergency powers, or powers to decide whether or not parliament should be dissolved, and early elections scheduled. While the majority of Europe's presidential heads of state do not command extensive constitutional power those who are directly elected have, on average, greater powers than those who are not. Nonetheless, all presidents wield a degree of political influence (Tavits 2009). Moreover, individual presidents can be more or less active in fulfilling their role. Hence, the balance of power between the president and cabinet on the one hand, and the president and parliament on the other, can vary with the political and institutional context.

7.4 The institutional powers of the prime minister, cabinet, and president

The opportunities for different executive actors to lead the development of policy and its implementation vary. This section reviews the main institutional powers that the three key actors—the prime minister, cabinet, and president—may have at their command.

Prime ministers are often invested with extensive powers vis-à-vis cabinet and parliament, which allow them to fulfil their central function in coordinating the government and giving its work strategic direction. In relation to the cabinet, prime ministers typically have powers to appoint and dismiss cabinet members. This authority to make final cabinet choices is valuable because it enables prime ministers to choose their own governing team. Of course, these choices must be made within the context of the government's dependence on parliamentary confidence. This means that the cabinet, which a prime minister picks, must command the support of parliament, i.e. of key factions within the prime minister's own party and any coalition partners in addition to supporting parties. To fulfil their function of guiding government activity, prime ministers have the power to chair cabinet meetings as well as discretion to determine the number of ministerial departments and their remit. They also appoint top civil servants. Since their task of coordinating and giving strategic direction to policy across the government is complex and requires extensive information and analysis, premiers are supported by a dedicated administration of their own and by a team of personal advisers. In Germany, for instance, the prime minister (*Bundeskanzler* or *Bundeskanzlerin*) is supported in coordinating the activities of the federal government by the Chancellor's Department (*Bundeskanzleramt*) with 600 members of staff.

In addition, prime ministers may have at their command a range of highly consequential constitutional powers vis-à-vis parliament, including the power to dissolve parliament and to request a vote of confidence in the government. These powers allow chief executives to structure bargaining within government and between government and parliament. Specifically, by threatening an early election or by declaring a vote to be a matter of confidence in the government, they can extract concessions from their own backbenchers, from coalition partners, or from parliamentary parties that fear an early election or the fall of the government. These powers can be used to secure policy compromises and political support for a government (see Box 7.4).

A prime minister's influence on policy is often heightened in the field of foreign policy, where they represent the country diplomatically in meetings with other heads of government. According to Poguntke and Webb (2005), for instance, European integration and European policy processes, which have caused elements of domestic policy to be decided through international negotiations, have strengthened prime ministers in relation to their cabinet colleagues and parliamentary parties. As we have seen, this argument that Europeanization has enhanced the influence and autonomy of the prime minister vis-à-vis other actors within the executive lies at the heart of the view that the politics of European countries have become increasingly presidentialized (see Box 7.2).

The cabinet's role in leading the development and implementation of policy is equally supported by its formal powers. The policy-making function of government is underpinned by the right of legislative initiative. Once a cabinet has developed its legislative programme, individual pieces of legislation are introduced to parliament by ministers. In structuring the bargaining process with parliament over the amendment and adoption of government legislation, cabinets may have powers to guillotine (that is, stop) debates, and to invoke a package vote on a bill, which allows the government to pick what amendments it wishes to accept and which ones it wishes to reject, and to put the bill in that form to an up-or-down vote. Some constitutions also devolve the power to dissolve parliament and to invoke a vote of confidence to the cabinet collectively, rather than concentrating it in the hands of the prime

Box 7.4 Examples of prime ministers' power

In 1993, the British prime minister John Major turned the vote on the Social Chapter of the Maastricht Treaty (the treaty which established the European Union) into a matter of confidence for the government. The government had to obtain support for its policy on the Social Chapter before the European Communities Amendment Act 1993 could come into effect, paving the way for the United Kingdom's ratification of the Maastricht Treaty. By turning government policy on the Social Chapter into a matter of confidence, Major ensured that a defeat for the government would have constituted a vote of no confidence, which would have provoked early elections. This enabled the prime minister to discipline his Eurosceptic backbenchers, who had threatened to defeat the government on the issue.

Finland's prime minister Juha Sipilä conjured the spectre of early elections in June 2017, when he ejected the nationalist Finns Party from his three-party centre-right coalition after the popularity of the Finns plunged and it chose a new anti-immigration leader. Citing differences with the new leader of the Finns in core values, immigration policy, and policy regarding the EU, Prime Minister Sipilä negotiated their replacement by bringing the smaller Swedish People's Party and Christian Democrats into the government.

The Danish Prime Minister Lars Løkke Rasmussen relied on his discretion to dissolve parliament and his party's rising popularity in November 2016 to negotiate an expansion of his parliamentary support, after he had formed Denmark's smallest minority government in forty years. Invoking the risk of a snap election, he ended months of policy battles by striking an agreement between his Liberal Party, the Conservatives, and the Liberal Alliance. The agreement broadened his minority government to a three-party coalition and provided more solid parliamentary support for his agenda of tax cuts and limited public spending.

minister. Both of these powers enable a government to structure the bargaining process with parliament by deploying specific threats (see Box 7.5). In this sense, these powers balance parliament's power to remove the government through a vote of no confidence. These legislative powers make the government the agenda setter in the legislative process.

The policy implementation functions of cabinets are supported by the regulatory powers of governments; that is, the right to issue the directions that are needed to implement legislation. In addition, laws may delegate to cabinet powers to interpret and make policy within the framework of the law through government regulations and ordinances. Some constitutions also grant governments powers to make policy by ordinance or decree in certain areas, as is the case in the French Fifth Republic (1958 to the present). In developing policy proposals, drafting legislation, and overseeing the implementation of policy, government ministers are assisted by their civil service departments.

Of course, the autonomy of the cabinet in shaping legislation and policy may be balanced by other institutions, most notably the countervailing powers of parliament (see Chapter 9). In many European democracies, the power and autonomy of the prime minister and cabinet is also moderated by the president. Presidential power can have two different sources. First, in semi-presidential democracies, where presidents are directly elected by the people (as opposed to indirect election by parliament), popular election is a source of democratic legitimacy and gives the president an electoral mandate that is separate from parliament. Second, presidents (whether directly or indirectly elected) may have legislative and non-legislative constitutional powers (Shugart and Carey 1992).

Box 7.5 Over to you—confidence votes

Many European governments have the power to request a vote of confidence but the precise way in which the procedure is structured varies. Consider the political implications of the following variations among confidence vote procedures.

- Some governments are able to attach a vote of confidence to a specific bill; others are unable to do so. Is a government's power to bargain about parliamentary support for its policies weakened or strengthened by the ability to attach a vote of confidence to a bill?
- In some governments it is the prime minister who can decide whether or not to invoke a vote of confidence; in others it is the cabinet collectively. How does this variation in the confidence vote procedure affect the ability of a prime minister who leads a coalition to bargain with his or her coalition partners about a change of the governing coalition or its termination?
- In some countries the failure of a government to secure parliamentary support for a confidence motion requires the calling of early elections; in others it requires the resignation of the government. How do differences in the consequences of a failed confidence motion affect the ability of the government to use it in bargaining about policy or its ability to stay in power?

Presidential legislative powers are found in semi-presidential and some parliamentary democracies. These powers may include prerogatives to veto legislation, the need for presidential approval to enact legislation or government ordinances, the president's right to introduce legislation, and presidential influence on the process of initiating a referendum. All of these powers give presidents opportunities to shape policy. In addition, presidents may have constitutional powers to affect the formation and termination of the cabinet. This can include the right to name the *formateur*; that is, the person designated to form a government. This is the case for instance in Poland, where normally the president selects the leader of the largest parliamentary party to perform this task. Often presidents also have an influence on the process of dissolving the assembly and calling early elections. Some presidents can reach far into the detailed workings of the government by virtue of their constitutional influence on ministerial selection. For instance, under the Italian constitution, the president may choose to appoint (or oppose) ministers nominated by the prime minister (see Box 7.6).

Presidents (both popularly elected and indirectly elected) are also heads of state who represent the country diplomatically. Several European presidents additionally have the role of commander-in-chief of the armed forces. By virtue of these roles, presidents often have a larger degree of influence on foreign and defence policy than on domestic policy.

Some semi-presidential democracies make the president so powerful that he or she has constitutional primacy over the prime minister as formal head of the executive. France is a case in point. According to the French constitution, the president presides over the council of ministers (that is, government meetings), although presidents often delegate that power to the prime minister. The norm in Europe, however, is that presidents are a moderating force: they influence the work of governments and the policy process, but do not dominate it.

Box 7.6 Government formation in Italy

Italy's president has the constitutional power to nominate the *formateur* (that is, the person who is tasked to form the government) and to approve or oppose the appointment of nominated ministers. After the Italian election in spring 2018, which made the formation of a coalition government composed of the anti-establishment Five Star Movement and the far-right League Party a possibility, the president chose to exercise these powers. President Mattarella disagreed with the potential coalition partners over the appointment as finance minister of Paolo Savona. Savona was known to support the withdrawal of Italy from the Eurozone and President Mattarella refused to approve his appointment. When the parties did not compromise, the president tasked a technocrat, Carlo Cottarelli, to serve as prime minister designate pending an early general election, thus threatening to lock the two parties out of power altogether. This eventually prompted the parties to withdraw their nomination of Savona as finance minister, clearing the path for the government's formation on 31 May 2018. While some were very critical of the president's actions, arguing that he was going against the popular mandate delivered to the Five Star Movement and the League, this example shows how significant powers such as nominating the *formateur* and approving ministerial appointments can be.

7.5 The political implications of the powers of premiers, cabinets, and presidents

The institutional powers available to premiers, cabinets, and presidents shape their opportunities to pursue their goals in three areas: (i) holding office, (ii) shaping policy, and (iii) pursuing their electoral goals. The precise balance of power between the premier, government, and president is therefore enormously consequential. It shapes who is appointed to ministerial and top civil service positions, conditions the policy directions that are chosen, has an impact on how the executive manages elections and its accountability relationship with voters, and affects the risk of conflict between different actors within the executive.

Turning first to office holding, the relative powers of different actors within the executive over ministerial appointments can shape who gets the chance to form a government and who is appointed to ministerial positions. Presidents, for instance, may be able to use their constitutional powers to influence government formation and ministerial appointments (see Box 7.6).

Bargaining over policy is equally shaped by the constitutional powers of executive actors. For instance, a popular prime minister who has constitutional discretion to call snap elections can, to a degree, compensate for weak parliamentary support by using the threat of an early election as a bargaining chip to extract concessions from parties that fear early elections (see Box 7.4).

How constitutional power is distributed among different actors within the political executive has consequences for the representativeness and effectiveness of the executive: broadly speaking, political executives that concentrate extensive power in the hands of a single political actor—in Europe this is most likely to be the prime minister—generate governments and policy outcomes that tend to reflect a narrower, less representative range of interests, because the formal powers of the prime minister enable him or her to avoid compromise and to extract concessions from other parties. For instance, the prime minister in the UK can compensate for political weakness (e.g. if her party does not command a majority in parliament) by making use of her constitutional powers. For the same reason, executives that concentrate power in the hands of the prime minister tend to be able to conclude policy negotiations more expeditiously, other things equal, which can make them more effective. Conversely, constitutions that disperse the power to bargain over office and policy among multiple actors within the executive, such as the Italian constitution, tend to produce more representative outcomes that reflect a broader range of political interests. By the same token, however, they also tend to make the policy process somewhat less effective because it takes longer, on average, to negotiate policy compromise among a broader range of actors and interests.

The dispersion or concentration of power within the executive also has implications for the probability of intra-executive conflict, as the literature on semi-presidential regimes highlights. While constitutions that give a president significant powers to temper the prime minister or government may generate incentives for compromise, they can also engender conflict (see Box 7.7). Scholars of semi-presidentialism have focused particularly on confrontations between presidents and prime ministers. Such conflicts may affect choices regarding government composition, policy, administrative prerogatives to issue executive orders and regulations, reporting within the executive, and the practice of presidential participation in cabinet meetings, among other things. The risk of intra-executive conflict increases when the president and government come from different parties (e.g. Protsyk 2005). Moreover, conflict between presidents and prime ministers is especially likely when prime ministers are politically weak and head a minority government, which suggests that presidents adapt the use of their powers in view of the political opportunities to influence outcomes.

Finally, election-related constitutional powers may additionally give the prime minister, cabinet, or president opportunities to influence the timing of elections (Goplerud and Schleiter 2016). As the literature on opportunistic election timing suggests, the ability to call snap elections gives politicians the opportunity to seek a new mandate in the context of particularly favourable circumstances, for instance when the economy is performing particularly well or when the opposition is unpopular, divided, or unprepared for an election. This skews the electoral playing field in favour of the incumbent and disadvantages opposition parties, which enhances the incumbent's chances of returning to power. According to Schleiter and Tavits (2016), for instance, premiers who have discretion to time elections when they expect to win are on average able to realize a vote-share bonus of five percentage points. Likewise, presidents with powers to influence the timing of parliamentary elections use these

Box 7.7 Conflict between president and government in Poland

In Poland, President Andrzej Duda used his veto power in December 2021 to stimy a controversial media ownership law that critics said was intended to silence a US-owned TV station critical of the government. The law, initiated by the ruling Law and Justice Party (*PiS*) government, would have prevented companies from outside the European Economic Area from controlling Polish media outlets. But critics said the move was intended to attack TVN24, Poland's most watched news channel and a network whose reporters have often been critical of the conservative government.

powers for partisan advantage to promote the electoral fortunes of their allies in government (Schleiter and Morgan-Jones 2018).

In sum, the political implications of the powers of premiers, cabinets, and presidents are vast. The constitutional powers of these actors shape who is appointed to ministerial positions, condition the policy directions that are chosen, impact on the balance between the representativeness and the effectiveness of the executive, affect the risk of intra-executive conflict, and have implications for the conditions under which voters get the chance to hold their government accountable.

7.6 The relationship between the political executive and the civil service

The political executive requires the support of the civil service in order to transform its goals into policy and to ensure their implementation. Weber's (1947) seminal analysis of the bureaucracy stresses this essential function of the civil service in facilitating and implementing the decisions of politicians. His work, however, gives an idealized picture of civil servants, recruited on merit, as faithful instruments that serve politicians to achieve the application of laws and government decrees in an effective and efficient manner. Subsequent work on the civil service has instead focused on problems that may detract from the efficiency and effectiveness of the bureaucracy as a tool of policy development and implementation. This work highlights the potential divergence of bureaucrats' interests from those of their political masters. Politically, it reflects the concerns that are often voiced by ministers about perceived opposition to their policy agenda within the civil service.

Niskanen (1971), for instance, suggests that bureaucrats are motivated by the goal of increasing their budgets. This is because the size of the budget controlled by a particular part of the bureaucracy impacts on the reputation, policy-making capacity, and salaries of the civil servants that work within it. Politically, this argument has been very influential. Niskanen served on the Board of Economic Advisers of the United States (US) President Ronald Reagan and not only influenced the president's agenda, but his thinking has also been cross-nationally influential in motivating efforts to shrink the state since the 1980s.

Similarly, scholars working in the principal–agent tradition have noted that two problems can potentially beset the relationship between civil servants and politicians: adverse selection and moral hazard. Adverse selection refers to the appointment of individuals who may lack the motivation or competence to be effective servants of their political masters. It can become a concern when politicians do not have the power to appoint bureaucrats or when they have imperfect information about the skills and motivations of these bureaucrats. Moral hazard problems may additionally beset the relationship between bureaucrats and politicians. Moral hazard arises when civil servants pursue their personal or political interests instead of acting in the interest of their political masters, because the political executive is unable to fully observe the actions of the bureaucracy.

Note, however, that difficulties in the working relationship between bureaucrats and politicians do not inevitably have their origin in the bureaucracy; rather, they may also lie with the decisions of politicians. Politicians may, for instance, choose to leave the civil service under-resourced and mandates unfunded, or they may issue contradictory policy guidance to civil servants. When policy implementation then falls short of politicians' publicly stated goals, they may shift the blame for these problems to bureaucrats in order to avoid taking political responsibility for their choices.

From the 1980s onward, electoral commitments to improve economic performance and to contain public sector expansion, as well as a growing perception of public bureaucracies as inefficient, have motivated the introduction of New Public Management (NPM) as an approach to control the bureaucracy in many European countries. NPM reforms decentralized the provision of services and aimed to introduce managerialism, competition, and entrepreneurship into the work of the civil service, in part by creating internal markets, splitting up larger agencies into a competing set of smaller ones, and opening up the provision of public services to private providers. Under NPM, performance is assessed against budgetary targets, with audits, benchmarks, and evaluations.

The NPM reforms are often described as having brought a range of benefits to public services including cutting back public expenditure, improving efficiency, effectiveness, and economy within the public sector, heightening transparency in the public sector by defining clear goals that make it possible to hold civil servants accountable, and enhancing the responsiveness of the public sector to its clients. Critiques of NPM have stressed that marketization and privatization are often ineffective ways of providing public goods. Moreover, according to its critics, the fragmentation and privatization of services through NPM has reduced transparency and generated a democratic deficit in the design and provision of services. Likewise, the overriding importance that has been placed on controlling costs in the civil service, and the importance of the profit motive for private providers, can compromise the delivery of actual services.

7.7 Conclusion: Executive autonomy and power

As we have seen in this chapter, the rise of the modern state, changes in voter loyalties, and the demands of European integration have progressively shifted much of the power to govern in Europe from parliament to the executive. This concluding section returns to the implications of this development for governance and executive autonomy, and the challenges this creates for the principal–agent relationships that characterize modern democracies.

On balance, the merits and demerits of the concentration of power within the executive can be summarized as follows. At one level, the concentration of power in modern executives is a necessary response to the demands of governing a state with an extensive range of policy and administrative functions in an increasingly globalized world. Without a political executive and civil service with extensive capabilities, it would simply not be possible to develop coordinated government policies to regulate areas as distinct as education, transport, health, social security, work, pensions, justice, finance, agriculture, security, defence, and foreign affairs.

However, this concentration of power and capabilities in the hands of the executive also gives rise to executive autonomy which creates challenges in ensuring that governments, presidents, and the civil service are subject to appropriate democratic control. In the language of political science, executive autonomy magnifies the principal–agent problems that beset democracies whenever authority is delegated to the executive. Effective controls can ensure that executives act in the interest of citizens rather than pursuing their own personal or political goals. The challenge in designing such controls is to strike a balance so that the controls constrain the executive's ability to act opportunistically in its own interest without compromising its ability to govern effectively.

How then might these powerful executives be appropriately balanced and constrained? In the previous discussion (Section 7.6) we saw the principal–agent problems that may arise between the political executive and the civil service and reviewed the strengths and drawbacks of NPM reforms as a means of addressing these challenges. But principal–agent problems are not confined to the relationship between the civil service and the political executive; they can also arise between the executive and parliament and between the executive and voters.

In theory, European parliaments are the democratic principal of governments, because governments depend on parliamentary confidence: a government that loses parliamentary confidence must resign. As we have seen, however, in practice governments often benefit from a combination of excellent administrative support and formidable institutional powers, which can make it difficult for parliament to stand up to the wishes of the executive. Indeed, some scholars go so far as to describe the rise of executive autonomy as a process that is matched by the 'decline of parliament' (see Baldwin 2004 for a review). According to this argument, the influence of European parliaments over the executive is increasingly illusory. The evidence, however, reveals significant variation. In many European countries the executive's enhanced capabilities are balanced by those of parliament (see Chapter 9).

Despite this significant cross-national variation, however, there have also been consistent trends over time. Most notably, as the capabilities of executives have grown, parliaments, too, have adapted as institutions to retain effective oversight and democratic control over the executive. Constitutional reform initiatives have aimed to rebalance the powers of parliament and the executive. The introduction of the Fixed-Term Parliaments Act (2011) in the UK, for instance, removed the prime minister's power to call early elections at will and placed this power instead in the hands of parliament. Under the Act, an early election is called in two circumstances: (i) if a super-majority of two-thirds of all MPs vote for an early election or (ii) if a government loses the confidence of parliament and parliament does not express its confidence in a government within two weeks. In a similar institutional reform initiative, the Irish Citizens' Assembly recommended in 2018 that the Irish prime minister's discretion to call early elections be curtailed, although this recommendation was not enacted. In France, a committee led by former prime minister Édouard Balladur recommended in 2007 a rebalancing of the powers between parliament and government, and the French Constitutional Court has granted parliament the right to amend government decrees. The French parliament has also been empowered to subject all bills to legislative scrutiny in committee before the plenary session and the length of legislative sessions has been doubled.

Similar reforms have been applied to address the principal–agent problems that can arise from executive autonomy in relation to the interests of the electorate. The concern in this respect is that executives may use their powers for personal or political benefit rather than acting in the public interest. Such opportunities arise, for instance, through the government's ability to control economic policy. Governments are acutely aware that voters hold them accountable for their performance in office, in particular the state of the economy, and with that in mind, incumbents may employ their powers opportunistically to further their re-election goal. A particularly well-documented strategy is the manipulation of the economy to improve voter welfare prior to elections. The literature on political business cycles shows that politicians use monetary and fiscal policy to engineer short-term economic highs prior to elections. Voters observe improved performance prior to elections and reward it electorally, but following the election the economy goes into decline. Overall, this type of self-interested government behaviour is not in the interest of voters because it causes the economy to undergo politically driven cycles of booms and busts, which has welfare-reducing effects. In Europe, successive waves of reforms have progressively constrained the executives' scope to act in this self-interested manner. Notably, the introduction of central bank independence and the Euro have limited the scope for governments to manipulate monetary policy. Similarly, fiscal reforms such as the creation of independent fiscal watchdogs, domestic debt ceilings, and balanced budget rules, along with the European Stability and Growth Pact, increase fiscal transparency and make it harder for governments to engage in self-interested manipulation of the economy.

In sum, this chapter has shown that the challenges of governing modern European democracies have led to a progressive shift of much of the power to govern from parliament to the executive. Moreover, this shift has been underpinned by the development of extensive institutional capabilities within the executive. This has allowed European states to manage an increasing array of functions of the state in an ever more closely integrated international environment, but it has also given rise to new challenges in terms of containing the principal–agent problems that result from executive autonomy. In this concluding section we have seen that it is possible to check the rise of executive autonomy through institutional reforms that reduce its capacity to act in a way that departs from the goals of voters and parliament.

Discussion questions

1. What are the functions of the political executive?
2. Which institutional actors constitute the political executive?
3. Is it better for power to be concentrated or dispersed within the political executive?
4. What strategic advantages can a government derive from the constitutional power to call early elections?
5. What did NPM reforms attempt to achieve? Were they successful?
6. What factors contribute to the empowerment of political executives?
7. Has the modern executive grown too powerful and autonomous?

Thinking comparatively

Some governments have the power to call early elections when they see fit. For instance, Danish parliamentary elections must be held at least every four years, but the prime minister may call early elections at any point within this four-year term. Two contrasting accounts describe what happens when politicians use this discretion to time elections for partisan advantage.

1. Political surfing (Kayser 2005): according to this account, governments can profit from positive shocks to economic performance that are beyond their control or jurisdiction, for instance an upswing in performance that is caused by an international boom. If voters do not distinguish between such shocks and domestic economic performance that the government generated, they mistake the shock for a sign of government competence. This enables politicians to 'surf' the resulting wave of political support by timing elections to coincide with the economic peak in order to improve their re-election chances.
2. Signalling (Smith 2003): this account notes that governments, compared to voters, have better information about the likely trajectory of the economy because they know how competently they manage it. Voters are quite sophisticated. When they observe that a government calls an unexpected early election, they suspect that the economy is about to decline, and that the government is attempting to profit electorally from unsustainably favourable economic circumstances. This encourages voters to punish politicians who attempt to engage in opportunistic election calling for partisan advantage.

These two accounts yield divergent predictions which have been evaluated in a survey-experimental study by Schleiter and Tavits (2016). Amongst other things, this study shows that voters do anticipate a decline in economic performance when they observe an opportunistic election call, but that in the context of a strong economy, the concern about a future economic decline does not outweigh the inclination of the average voter to reward the government for its good performance to date. Hence, it is possible for politicians to benefit from opportunistic election calling, which explains why this strategy is frequently used by governments.

Guide to further reading

Huber, J. D. (1996), 'The vote of confidence in parliamentary democracies', *American Political Science Review*, 90(2): 269–82.

This article offers a seminal discussion of the vote of confidence procedure and its political implications.

Kayser, M. A. (2005), 'Who surfs, who manipulates? The determinants of opportunistic election timing and electorally motivated economic intervention', *American Political Science Review*, 99(1): 17–27.

Some incumbents can use election timing and economic policy tools to improve their re-election chances. How do they deploy these tools? This article addresses that question and analyses the linkages between these strategic choices.

Schleiter, P. and Tavits, M. (2018), 'Voter reactions to incumbent opportunism', *The Journal of Politics*, 80(4): 1183–96.

What conclusions do voters draw when incumbents time elections for partisan benefit? This article addresses that question, using a survey-experimental research design.

Smith, A. (2003), *Election Timing* (Cambridge: Cambridge University Press).

This book explores how UK prime ministers make election timing choices, and how their electoral support develops in response to opportunistic election timing.

References

Baldwin, N. D. J. (2004), 'Concluding observations: Legislative weakness, scrutinising strength?', *Journal of Legislative Studies*, 10(2): 295–302.

Cox, G. (1987), *The Efficient Secret* (Cambridge: Cambridge University Press).

Dunleavy, P. and Rhodes, R. A. (1990), 'Core executive studies in Britain', *Public Administration*, 68(1): 3–28.

Duverger, M. (1980), 'A new political system model: Semi-Presidential government', *European Journal of Political Research*, 8(2): 165–87.

Elgie, R. (1999), 'The politics of semi-presidentialism', in R. Elgie (ed.), *Semi-Presidentialism in Europe* (Oxford: Oxford University Press): 1–21.

Gamson, W. A. (1961), 'A theory of coalition formation', *American Sociological Review*, 26: 373–82.

Goplerud, M. and Schleiter, P. (2016), 'An index of assembly dissolution powers', *Comparative Political Studies*, 49(4): 427–56.

Kayser, M. A. (2005), 'Who surfs, who manipulates? The determinants of opportunistic election timing and electorally motivated economic intervention', *American Political Science Review*, 99(1): 17–27.

Laver, M. (2006), 'Legislatures or parliaments in comparative context?', in B. R. Weingast and Donald A. Wittman (eds.), *The Oxford Handbook of Political Economy* (Oxford: Oxford University Press): 121–40.

Lupia, A. (2003), 'Delegation and its perils', in K. Strøm, C. M. Wolfgang et al. (eds.), *Delegation and Accountability in Parliamentary Democracies* (Oxford: Oxford University Press): 33–54.

Niskanen W. (1971), *Bureaucracy and Representative Government* (Chicago, IL: Aldine-Atherton).

Poguntke, T. and Webb, P. (eds.) (2005), *The Presidentialization of Politics: A Comparative Study of Modern Democracies* (Oxford: Oxford University Press).

Protsyk, O. (2005), 'Politics of intra-executive conflict in semi-presidential regimes', *East European Politics and Society*, 19(2): 135–60.

Schleiter, P. and Tavits, M. (2016), 'The electoral benefits of opportunistic election timing', *The Journal of Politics*, 78(3): 836–50.

Schleiter, P. and Morgan-Jones, E. (2018), 'Presidents, assembly dissolution, and the electoral performance of prime ministers', *Comparative Political Studies*, 51(6): 730–58.

Shugart, M. S. and Carey, J. M. (1992), *Presidents and Assemblies: Constitutional Design and Electoral Dynamics* (Cambridge: Cambridge University Press).

Smith, A. (2003), *Election Timing* (Cambridge: Cambridge University Press).

Strøm, K. (2003), 'Parliamentary democracy and delegation', in K. Strøm, C. M. Wolfgang et al. (eds.), *Delegation and Accountability in Parliamentary Democracies* (Oxford: Oxford University Press): 55–106.

Tavits, M. (2009), *Presidents with Prime Ministers: Do Direct Elections Matter?* (Oxford: Oxford University Press).

Weber, M. (1947), 'Legitimate authority and bureaucracy', reprinted in D. Pugh (ed.) (1984), *Organization Theory* (New York: Penguin): 3–15.

8 Parties in Government

PETIA KOSTADINOVA AND ROBERT THOMSON

8.1 Introduction

Political parties play an essential role in the process of democratic representation. They do this not only by structuring the choice offered to voters in elections (as discussed in Chapter 3), but also by shaping government policy after elections. Many democratic theorists argue that a core function of parties is to translate the wishes of voters as expressed in elections into government policy (Powell and Powell Jr 2000; McDonald and Budge 2005). In this chapter, we examine the role of parties in government, focusing in particular on the question of whether parties provide an effective link between voters and public policy.

Politicians from parties that hold executive office after elections often claim to have a mandate to carry out the promises they made during the previous election campaign. We begin by examining this idea of an electoral mandate (Section 8.2). Despite the intuitive plausibility and widespread appeal of this idea, many political theorists think it is highly problematic. One complicating factor is that in most European democracies, elections rarely if ever produce a single-party majority government. The subsequent Section 8.3 explores how coalition negotiations, in addition to election results, help determine which parties enter government after elections. Which parties form coalitions and how they do so shape the way in which parties affect policies. Section 8.4 reviews three of the main approaches to studying the impact of parties on public policies. The first approach looks at different welfare state models, the second at public spending, and the third at whether parties keep their campaign promises.

8.2 Translating public opinion into policy

Political parties serve as the linkage between voters and government policies by formulating packages of policy proposals and presenting these to voters during election campaigns. Modern democracies are representative democracies, which means that the direct involvement of citizens in policy making, such as through referendums or initiatives, is rare, although becoming more common (see Chapter 6). When parties win government power after elections, their attempts to change policies are justified by the fact that they are representing voters. This idea is found in the *mandate theory* of democracy, a prominent theory of democratic representation. However, this theory can only be applicable under certain conditions, which many would argue seldom apply (Manin et al. 1999).

To achieve representation under the mandate theory of democracy, voters choose among parties that offer alternative policies. Citizens vote for the party whose policies most resemble their own views and preferences. A majority of voters determine the winner(s) of each election, giving them a mandate to govern. The parties in power then work to implement the programs on which they were elected, and to fulfil their mandates (McDonald and Budge 2005). This type of representation is also known as *promissory* representation, because it depends on political candidates making promises to voters and keeping those promises (Mansbridge 2003: 516).

Researchers have studied the extent to which political parties and voters actually behave in the way that mandate theory posits they do (e.g. Naurin et al. 2019). They have also debated the extent to which representation is compromised when weaknesses emerge at any point in the mandate-attribution process. For example, there is substantial evidence that parties tend to emphasize the issues most salient to their voters (Budge and Farlie 1983), while focusing less on other topics. There is also evidence that parties do offer alternatives for voters to choose from, even in newer democracies (Kitschelt et al. 1999). However, the fact that parties in most democracies do not talk about the same topics or address the same policies means that the choice is often unclear.

An example of a typical mandate process in practice was the 2015 general election in the United Kingdom, when the Conservative Party pledged in its manifesto to hold a referendum on European Union (EU) membership. The other parties did not mention the issue of a referendum in their manifestos, but it became clear during the campaign that they would not hold one. The Conservatives held on to government after that election and duly held the referendum in 2016. Regardless of one's view of the merits of the referendum, this course of events is in line with the idea of a mandate. There is a substantial amount of evidence that parties fulfil the majority of their election promises, and we discuss this evidence in more detail later in this chapter (see Section 8.4.3).

Voters are equally important participants in the mandate-attribution process, and the question of how voters select which party to support has generated intense scholarly debates. Some researchers have demonstrated that voters choose parties closest to their own positions (Blais et al. 2001), while others emphasize that why voters select parties depends on whether they are on the same (or different) sides of salient issues, and how strongly they feel about those issues (Rabinowitz and Macdonald 1989). Other scholars argue that citizens pay little attention to politics, lack information about the details of policies, use heuristics (short cuts such as party identification) to select parties, and often cast ballots based on their social identities (Achen and Bartels 2016; see also Chapter 4).

Another contentious issue in relation to mandate representation concerns the legislative majority that emerges from elections, and the extent to which election results can be interpreted as a clear signal. The size of a party's legislative support depends as much on the electoral and party systems (see Chapters 2 and 3) as it does on the breadth of public support for the party. In majoritarian or 'Westminster-type' democracies, named after the seat of the legislature of the United Kingdom, the process of translating public opinion into policy is fairly straightforward. Majoritarian democracies typically have first-past-the-post electoral systems, where a simple plurality of the vote is needed to win elections, and single-member electoral districts produce one representative. These systems tend to lead to two major legislative parties, one of which controls the majority of the seats in the legislature at any given time. These legislative majorities support single-party governments, which creates a clear distinction between winners and losers of elections. However, these governments are often elected on the basis of a minority of votes cast.

The mandate-attribution process is even less obvious in consensus democracies, such as the Netherlands, which try to include as many voters as possible in decision-making. Consensus democracies typically have electoral systems based on proportional representation, where parties offer voters lists of candidates. Voters select among parties, and seats from each multimember district are distributed according to the share of votes that each party receives in the district. These electoral systems are associated with multiple parties in the legislature, and usually no single party holds a majority of seats. Parties then have to agree on how to form a legislative majority in support of a government. If there are not enough votes to do so, minority governments are often formed, but even in the case of governing coalitions, the parties that control the majority could change between elections. For example, after the 2018 Italian election, a coalition government formed comprising the anti-establishment Five Star Movement and the radical right *Lega*. However, *Lega* pulled out of government a year later, and a new coalition involving the Five Star Movement and the centre-left Democrat Party formed without recourse to a new election. In such situations, it is less obvious whether a distinct mandate was transferred from voters to parties, and further, which party's programme the government should implement. In systems where minority or coalition governments are frequent, such as Denmark, the 'clarity of responsibility' (Powell and Whitten 1993) is blurred, making it more difficult for voters to attribute policy outcomes to parties.

8.3 Coalition formation

It is rare that a single party wins an outright majority of the vote and is able to form a government without the support of other parties. More often than not, and especially in consensus democracies, parties need to work together to form coalition governments that involve cooperation between different parties. Table 8.1 illustrates this point by showing the frequency of types of governments that formed across a range of (mostly Western) European democracies, over the period 1944–2020. Single-party majority governments occur rarely or not at all in most of these countries (exceptions include the UK, Greece, and Spain). Minimum-winning coalitions (i.e. coalitions that have a majority, but do not include any surplus parties—see Section 8.3.1) are common in most of these countries, and are particularly frequent in Germany, Iceland, the Netherlands, and Portugal. Surplus majority coalitions (which have more parties than is necessary to control a simple majority in the legislature) are also relatively common, particularly in Belgium, Finland, France, and Italy. Table 8.1 also illustrates that minority governments, in which the governing party or coalition does not have a legislative majority, are widespread. Every European country included in these data has experienced one or more minority government, and such governments occur very frequently in Denmark, Ireland, Italy, Norway, Spain, and Sweden.

Table 8.1 Percentage of different cabinet types selected European democracies, 1944–2020

Country	Minority cabinets[a]	Single-party majority cabinets	Minimum-winning coalitions	Surplus majority coalitions	Non-partisan cabinets
Austria	4	14	75	7	0
Belgium	12	7	40	42	0
Croatia	38	24	14	24	0
Denmark	92	0	8	0	0
Finland	16	0	17	55	12
France	22	5	16	57	0
Germany	10	3	71	16	0
Greece	8	46	13	21	13
Iceland	17	0	72	11	0
Ireland	48	21	24	7	0
Italy	42	0	8	47	3
Norway	64	18	18	0	0
Portugal	32	0	41	14	14
Spain	73	27	0	0	0
Sweden	74	6	19	0	0
The Netherlands	20	0	47	33	0
United Kingdom	7	89	4	0	0
All countries	33	12	28	24	3

Note: Cell entries show percentage of each cabinet type in a given country; rows sum to 100%.
[a] Minority cabinets can be either single-party or coalition governments.
Source: Adapted from Bergman, Torbjörn et al. (eds.), (2021), *Coalition Governance in Western Europe* (Oxford: Oxford University Press), and Bergman, Torbjörn et al. (2021), Party Government in Europe Database (PAGED). Main sponsor: Riksbankens Jubileumsfond (IN150306:1). Available at https://repdem.org.

Considering the frequency with which it occurs, understanding the process of coalition formation is essential to comprehending how parties operate in government and affect policies in consensus systems. Even in majoritarian electoral systems, where single-party governments are the norm, large parties can be seen as coalitions of a range of factions. For instance, most large conservative and social democratic parties (such as the Conservative and Labour parties in the UK) contain quite clearly identifiable factions to the right and left of the political spectrum. Even smaller parties include distinct factions. For instance, green parties often include more radical and pragmatic factions, such as the division between the '*Fundis*' (fundamentalists) and '*Realos*' (realists) in the German Green Party. Differences between such intraparty coalitions can sometimes lead to disagreements when these parties participate in government office.

In the following subsections, we will review the main classical theories of coalition formation. These theories differ considerably in terms of their level of complexity and ambition. Some of the more basic theories (such as the theory of minimum-winning coalitions) simply attempt to explain which combinations of parties are most likely to join together to form a coalition, while other theories (such as the portfolio-allocation model) offer more nuanced insights into the way in which coalition partners formulate government policies.

Box 8.1 The Swiss Federal Council—a unique type of a coalition government?

Switzerland, or the Swiss Confederation as it is officially called, has a remarkable political system that combines elements of strong direct democracy with power-sharing arrangements across the different levels of government and across different government institutions. This system is known as consociationalism. Of particular interest in this chapter is the structure of the Federal Council, the executive branch of the Swiss government. While not officially a 'coalition', the Federal Council resembles one, while also featuring unique set up. The seven members of the Federal Council represent the main political parties from across the political spectrum and reflects the political diversity of the country. As of 2023, the three largest political parties (Social Democratic Party, Swiss People's Party, and The Liberals) each have two members in the Federal Council, while The Centre party has one member. These four parties control 149 out of the 200 seats in The National Council (the lower legislative chamber), making the Federal Council an over-sized majority coalition. The group governs by consensus, which means that government decisions require unanimous support. The seven members of the Federal Council take turns, through one-year terms, as the President of the Federal Council, the equivalent of a rotating 'prime minister'.

Before discussing these theories in more detail, pause for a moment to consider the composition of coalitions of parties that form. The sheer number of possible combinations of governing parties that could theoretically form in a multiparty system is large. A hypothetical legislature with just three parties (parties *a*, *b*, and *c*) has 2^3-1 = 7 possible combinations of parties that could theoretically form a government: each of the three parties on its own (*a*, *b*, and *c*), each combination of two parties (*ab*, *ac*, and *bc*), and the grand coalition of three parties (*abc*). The number of possible combinations increases to fifteen with four parties, thirty-one with five parties, sixty-three with six parties, and 127 with seven parties. With the scale of the analytical challenge in mind, we consider some of the approaches to explaining and predicting coalition formation.

8.3.1 Classical theories of coalition formation

In the face of a complex problem, one approach is to simplify, and classical theories of coalition formation do this. The simplest theory, which might more accurately be described as a 'proposition' or 'baseline' theory, is the idea that the coalition that will form will be 'minimum-winning' (Riker 1962). A *minimum-winning coalition* contains parties with just enough legislative seats to secure a majority, but no more. We would expect minimum-winning coalitions to form if parties are purely office-seeking—that is, motivated by benefits of holding government office. These benefits include the material and financial benefits of being in government as well as the associated prestige. Office-seeking parties may support particular policies, but they only do so in order to win the votes required to enter public office.

This way of thinking about politics can be traced back to Anthony Downs in his influential book, *An Economic Theory of Democracy*, which was published in 1957. In Downs' account, parties do not care intrinsically about policies, but rather use policies strategically to win votes. Voters, on the other hand, do have policy preferences, and will cast their votes for parties that support policies closest to their own preferences. It is widely recognized this this is an oversimplification, not least because parties and politicians very often do care about policy and citizens do not always hold clear policy preferences. Nonetheless, it is remarkable how much of modern-day politics can be explained with these simple assumptions.

Why does the pure office-seeking assumption lead to the proposition that governing coalitions will be minimum-winning? If parties value the benefits of holding office, they will prefer more of these benefits that come with governing to less. Larger coalitions mean that the benefits of office have to be shared among a larger number of parties, thereby leaving fewer benefits for each coalition member. A coalition with a superfluous member would be irrational according to the minimum-winning coalition theory. That superfluous member would reduce the office-related benefits for the other members, without offering any clear gains. Likewise, the office-seeking assumption seems incompatible with minority governments. If parties are purely motivated by attaining office, why would any party support a minority government when they theoretically have the power to bring the government down and force their way into office?

The minimum-winning coalition theory does not predict the exact combination of parties that will form the governing coalition. Usually, several different combinations of parties will meet the criteria for a minimum-winning coalition. This lack of precision is a limitation of the theory. A more refined theory is the idea of *minimum-winning connected coalitions* (Axelrod 1970). The main proposition is that the coalitions that form will consist of parties that command a legislative majority, contain no superfluous members, and are close to—or 'connected to'—each other ideologically. This is a more complex theory since it introduces the idea of parties' policy positions in an ideological space. This is commonly thought of in terms of the left–right dimension that characterizes a large part of politics both in Europe and around the world. Left-wing parties generally advocate policies that invest more public resources in social programmes and that regulate business more stringently, while parties to the right prioritize tax cuts and less regulation of the private sector. The traditional left–right dimension is arguably waning in importance in some countries in recent years, and it is partly being complemented with new political concerns associated with environmentalism, individual rights, and nationalism (see Chapter 3). However, for the purposes of coalition formation, what is important is that the main ideological differences among parties can be summarized in a political space. This way of analysing parties is known as the 'spatial model', which has been described as the 'analytical workhorse' of modern political analysis.

Why would we expect minimum-winning connected coalitions to form? Even if politicians are motivated exclusively by the benefits of office, they need to support policies in order to appeal to voters. Voters choose parties in part based on their policies, but will also punish parties that enter into government and do not deliver on their policy commitments. This threat of electoral punishment gives office-seeking parties a strong incentive to follow through on their campaign promises. If a party is compelled to share government office with another party or parties, it will be better able to deliver policies in line with its campaign promises if its coalition partners advocated similar policies. Moreover, we may relax the assumption that parties are pure office-seekers, and instead recognize that politicians are in fact also at least partly motivated by seeing their preferred policies realized. Politicians and parties that are motivated by policy will prefer to form coalitions with parties that have similar policy goals to them.

Many (though by no means all) coalitions that form in European democracies are indeed minimum-winning connected coalitions. A good example is the German government that formed after the 2017 federal elections. A number of coalition options were explored, including coalitions among parties that were not ideologically adjacent to one another (one such option involved the centre-right *CDU/CSU*, the Greens, and the liberal Free Democrats). However, these options were ultimately rejected because of the insurmountable policy differences between the parties. Eventually, a coalition was formed between the *CDU/CSU* and the centre-left *SPD*—two parties that were ideologically 'connected' and held a majority of seats between them. In general, minimum-winning connected coalitions will include the party that is located in the centre of the policy space (containing the 'median legislator'—described in the next Section, 8.3.2).

8.3.2 **Minority governments**

A distinct line of inquiry relating to government formation focuses on minority governments, where the parties that hold executive office do not command a majority of seats in the legislature (Strøm 1990). For example, the Social Democrats in Sweden formed a single-party minority government after winning only forty-eight out of the 179 seats in the 2019 parliamentary election. The classical models of coalition formation and most contemporary theories do not explain minority governments. This is a significant shortcoming, since approximately one-third of governments in Europe, as well as many governments in other parts of the world, do not control legislative majorities (Field and Martin 2019; see Table 8.1). Minority governments are common in Denmark, Norway, and Sweden, but many other countries also have experience of minority governments.

The conventional wisdom regarding minority governments, particularly in countries in which they are relatively unusual, is that they are unstable, ineffective, and often short-lived. By contrast, theories that explain their occurrence and the available evidence suggest otherwise. According to one model (Crombez 1996), it is a sign of strength rather than weakness when a single party can form a minority government, rather than having to bargain with other parties. Crombez's model states that such parties typically control the *median legislator* and are large, although still control less than half of the legislative seats. The median legislator refers to the member of parliament who is at the mid-point in parliament on the main ideological dimension, such as the left-right dimension. The median legislator's policy position is preferred by a majority of legislators to any of the other policies represented in the legislature. Assuming that parties care about policies rather than the benefits associated with holding government office, they may be induced to support (or at least tolerate) a minority government from the opposition; after all, there would be no majority in favour of any other set of policies.

Comparative research on minority governments distinguishes between minority governments that are 'majorities in disguise', and genuine minority governments (e.g. Strøm 1990). The former are minority governments that have formal or informal support agreements with one or more parties that are not included in the cabinet. For example, after the 2016 Irish general election, *Fine Gael* formed a minority government that involved a deal with the main opposition party, *Fianna Fáil*, who agreed to abstain on key votes. The latter are minority governments that have no such agreements with opposition parties. Instead, they form legislative majorities as needed with different parties, as is often the case in Denmark. Either way, minority governments might be considered as a form of coalition government, even when they consist of a single party in the executive. Minority governments typically have shorter durations than majority governments, but many minority governments last for three or more years. When minority governments do last, they appear to be just as productive as majority governments and are also as likely as majority governments to fulfil governing parties' campaign promises (Thomson et al. 2017). This evidence largely supports the view that the ability of a party to form a minority government is a sign of that party's strong political power rather than its weakness.

8.3.3 **Coalition agreements between parties**

Recent theories of coalition government are concerned not only with which parties come together, but also with how they reach agreements on how to govern. Two key elements of this process are the allocation of ministerial portfolios (see Section 8.3.4) and formulation of coalition agreements. Approximately two-thirds of coalition governments have written agreements among the governing parties, but these vary considerably in form and substance (Müller and Strøm 2008). Post-election coalition agreements in Finland are typically a few hundred words and focus on general principles, while they usually run to tens of thousands of words and include great detail in Belgium and the Netherlands. Lengthy and detailed coalition agreements inevitably take a long time to agree, with Belgian and Dutch coalition formation times being among the longest in the world. Box 8.2 focuses on the coalition formation in the Netherlands in 2017, which lasted 225 days.

Coalition agreements are usually formulated and signed after the elections have taken place. However, pre-election coalitions of parties also occur. For instance, the Swedish Alliance, which was formed in 2004, consisted of four centre-right parties. The Alliance issued a joint manifesto, which was in effect a coalition agreement among the four parties. In Italy too, broad coalitions of parties to the left and right of the political spectrum have formed pre-electoral coalitions and issued joint manifestos. Such pre-election coalitions can affect parties' impact on policies if they enter government after elections. For cabinets composed of parties that signed pre-election coalition agreement, such agreements may provide them with a stronger mandate (Golder 2005), and allow these cabinets 'greater control over legislative policies' (Chiru 2015: 169).

Differences between coalition agreements in their length and detail are associated with distinct views on their significance and function in relation to parties' participation in government. The sceptical view is that these documents are no more than a ritual dance in which parties emphasize general principles and those issues on which they already agree. The sophisticated variant of this sceptical view acknowledges that coalition agreements may contain important policy provisions, but highlights the fact that the agreements themselves are not enforceable without further guarantees. The allocation of senior and junior ministerial portfolios (see Section 8.3.4) may provide such further guarantees that the coalition agreements will in fact be implemented.

A distinct view is that the formulation of the coalition agreement is a stage of crucial importance in the process of coalition government. This importance stems in part from the insulated nature of most negotiations that lead to agreements. At least for the longer and

Box 8.2 Over to you—forming a coalition in the Netherlands

The 2017 Dutch election results precipitated one of the longest-known coalition negotiations in history (225 days). The incumbent *VVD-PvdA* (conservative liberal-social democratic) coalition that had governed from 2012 to 2017 lost its parliamentary majority in the second chamber. As a senior statesperson associated with the *VVD*, which remained the largest party, you have been appointed as *informateur* by the king. The *informateur* is charged with finding sufficient areas of agreement between two or more parties to form a viable governing coalition with a majority of more than seventy-five seats in the second chamber.

Your task is complicated by the significant number of seats gained by the populist anti-immigration right-wing *PVV* (Party for Freedom) led by Geert Wilders. *D66* (a left-leaning liberal party), *CDA* (the mainstream Christian democratic party), *PvdA* (social democrats), *SP* (socialists), *GroenLinks* (a left-wing green party), and the *CU* (a conservative Christian party) all stated that they would not enter into an agreement with the *PVV*. The *CDA* was also reluctant to enter into a coalition without the *VVD*. In addition, *D66* and the *CU* had many conflicts on fundamental ethical issues such as euthanasia.

What coalitions would you explore in which order? How would you structure the negotiations with respect to the formation of the coalition agreement and the allocation of key portfolios? When thinking about this problem, it might be useful to try and order the parties in terms of their overall ideological (left–right) orientation (see Table 8.2).

Table 8.2 Seat-winning parties in the 2017 Dutch general election

Party abbreviation	Brief description	Seats (+/- change)
VVD	Incumbent conservative liberal party. Mainstream centre-right party. Free-market positions on economic issues, liberal on ethical issues.	33 (-8)
PVV	Party for Freedom. Populist anti-immigration anti-European Union right-wing party.	20 (+5)
CDA	Mainstream Christian democratic party. Extensive experience of governing in previous decades.	19 (+6)
D66	Democrats '66. Liberal party. More left leaning than the *VVD* on social welfare issues. Strong proponent of democratic innovations and freedom of choice with respect to euthanasia.	19 (+7)
GroenLinks	Leftist green party.	14 (+10)
SP	Traditional socialist party.	14 (-1)
PvdA	Incumbent mainstream social democratic party.	9 (-29)
CU	Christian Union. A conservative Christian party.	5 (0)
PvdD	Party for the Animals. An animal-rights party.	5 (+3)
50+	A party for the interests of older citizens.	4 (+2)
SGP	A small orthodox Calvinist party.	3 (0)
Denk	Offshoot of the *PvdA* focused on the rights of migrants.	3 (+3)
FvD	Forum for Democracy. A conservative Eurosceptic party.	2 (+2)

more detailed agreements, these negotiations involve months of private meetings between the leaders of different parties behind closed doors. This secretive and secluded setting contrasts with the way in which public policies are usually made, where the wide range of stakeholders affected by a policy lobby intensely to ensure that their views are held. While these stakeholders will surely continue to exercise influence on government, their direct impact on negotiations leading to coalition agreements is generally more muted. This distinct setting allows party elites to formulate agreements that have the potential to affect the direction of government policies significantly. In coalition governments, it is often the agreements—rather than parties' individual manifestos—that form the blueprints for government followed by senior civil servants in the ministries. Moreover, there are strong political norms that compel parties to keep to the commitments they signed up to in coalition agreements.

With such differences in the length, detail, and perspectives on coalition agreements, empirical research has attempted to identify some of the conditions under which coalition agreements play a role in the process of governing. For instance, Moury and Timmermans (2013) examine coalition agreements in Belgium, Germany, Italy, and the Netherlands. They find that these agreements are not confined to general principles or to consensual issues, but also include the coalitions' policy intentions on issues on which the parties vehemently disagreed. Moreover, these policy intentions are generally realized in the form of government policies during the subsequent government periods.

8.3.4 **Ministerial portfolio allocation**

One of the most influential theories of coalition formation is the portfolio-allocation model (Laver and Shepsle 1996). This theory highlights the importance of the allocation of ministerial portfolios among the coalition partners. One of its key assumptions is that parties only agree to join coalitions that can effectively guarantee that the policies laid out in their coalition agreements will be carried out. Providing an effective guarantee is problematic, because coalition agreements are not legally binding documents. Reneging on a coalition agreement may reflect badly on one or more of the parties involved in the coalition, but there are no formal sanctions that can be imposed. The timing of the implementation of policies in government agreements may exacerbate the commitment problem. If a coalition government implements one party's policies early in the governing period, then that party has little incentive to support the implementation of its coalition partner's policies with which it disagrees.

According to the portfolio-allocation model of coalition formation, the allocation of ministerial portfolios gives credibility to coalition agreements. The model proposes that the formulation of coalition agreements and the allocation of ministerial portfolios are interlinked sets of decisions. These decisions are taken in such a way that coalition partners are allocated ministerial responsibilities for those policy areas on which the coalition agreement says that those parties' policies should be implemented. In other words, ministers are charged with implementing their own parties' policies within their own policy portfolios. For example, if a green party and a social democratic party are in a governing coalition and the green party receives the environment portfolio, the model leads us to expect that the government will carry out the green party's environmental policies.

While the portfolio-allocation model of coalition formation is also a simplification, which is a hallmark of all good theories, it has received at least qualified empirical support from a range of studies. When parties participate in coalitions, they generally receive the ministerial portfolios for policy areas to which they attach relatively high levels of salience in their election manifestos. For instance, when green parties participate in government, they almost invariably receive the environmental portfolio. When social democratic parties participate in coalitions, they usually receive the portfolio most relevant to social welfare. When conservative parties participate in coalitions, they usually receive the portfolios most relevant to economic regulation. These patterns indicate that the allocation of portfolios reflects the same exchange-based negotiation outcomes we would expect to find in coalition policy agreements. Ministers have at least some degree of autonomy within their own policy jurisdictions. This ministerial autonomy is partly due to the need for ministers to specialize given the complexity of modern policy making. This specialization makes it unlikely that, say, an agriculture minister will have a sufficient amount of relevant policy expertise to effectively intervene in most policy discussions on, say, welfare policy or housing policy. Ministerial autonomy is also strengthened to the extent that ministers follow the norm that it is generally inappropriate to intervene in the policy areas of other ministers, whether they are from the same party or a different party.

However, other factors undermine the autonomy of ministers in practice. Powerful prime ministers can impose coherence and discipline on cabinets that are disjointed by ministerial divisions. In several countries, it is common to appoint junior ministers from different parties to the ministers as so-called watchdogs of the ministers. Junior ministers usually have their own defined areas of responsibilities and can ensure that a minister charged with implementing policies of another coalition partner does so. Some ministries are also naturally more linked than others in that there are blurred boundary lines between their jurisdictions. This is typically the case, for instance, with agriculture and environment ministries. It is also true for

Box 8.3 Changes of government and 'reshuffles' between elections

Governments often change between elections. This can involve a change in the parties in government, or a change of individual ministers (or indeed prime minister) from within the same party. For example, Italy in the period 1948–91 is often given as an example of a country with rather unstable governments, each lasting on average less than twelve months. In the Italian case, though, a new government meant a change in who was prime minister, often between elections, while the party of the prime minister (Christian Democratic Party) stayed the same. Further, the prime minister's party typically governed in a coalition with the same partners, with the Communist Party always in opposition (Baron 2018). If change in government is understood as new elections or a change in the governing parties, Italy would be among the more stable Western democracies in that period.

Replacing individual members of the cabinet within the same party is typically not considered a change in government, although such frequent changes could hamper a government's ability to deliver policies. Keeping the same ministers in key posts, on the other hand, even if other parts of the government change, can ensure the accumulation of experience and continuity in policy. Research on this question shows that European democracies vary greatly in the extent to which government termination results in a significant replacement of individual ministers (Huber and Martinez-Gallardo 2008). Belgium, Finland, and Italy, for example, are among the countries where ministers are very likely to survive a government termination and keep their portfolios. Ireland stands out as a country with the highest number of both government and individual minister terminations.

ministries of justice and internal affairs. A great deal of recent reforms in central governments have aimed to create more joined-up government. This has included a proliferation of inter-ministerial committees and planning processes.

As described in Chapter 7, there is considerable variation among countries in the extent to which their executive branches are centralized or decentralized, and this can shape ministerial autonomy. Centralized executives generally tend to have more powerful prime ministers and/or more extensive mechanisms that link policy-making processes across different ministerial jurisdictions. Decentralized executives, by contrast, generally give ministers more independence. The UK, France, and Poland are examples of countries with relatively centralized executives, while Belgium, Germany, and Hungary are examples of countries with decentralized executives.

8.4 Policy outputs

Under what conditions do parties' control of governments make a difference to the policies that those governments pursue? Ideals of democratic representation often assume that parties make a difference to government policies. However, in practice, it is often difficult for governing parties to steer public policies in the direction they desire. This section examines three distinct research approaches to assessing the impact of parties on policies. We first focus on how party ideology affects the types of welfare states that have developed across European democracies. We then look at how spending levels in different policy areas can be affected by parties in government. Finally, we examine patterns in the extent to which parties keep their campaign promises when they enter government after elections.

8.4.1 Welfare states

European democracies differ greatly with respect to the social benefits they provide to citizens, in terms of both the generosity and ways in which benefits are provided. These arrangements are commonly referred to as the *welfare state*. While there are multifarious reasons why countries differ with respect to their welfare state models, the role of worker mobilization through political parties, often in coalition with other societal groups, stands out as a prominent factor. The main argument here refers to the impact of parties over a long period of time in establishing certain types of welfare state, rather than the short-term impact of which party is in government at any particular point in time.

Some countries have universal health-care coverage, while others provide this benefit through employers. Retirement ages differ across countries, as does the generosity of pensions. If unemployed, citizens in some countries might receive insurance payments commensurate with their previous salaries, while in other countries unemployment benefits may leave recipients in poverty. Chapter 13 outlines four different models of capitalism found in Europe: the Anglo-Saxon model, where social goods are provided through the market and there is relatively little redistribution of resources; the continental model, featuring a strong tradition of employer-provided social benefits and high levels of redistribution; the Nordic model, with universal rights-based provision for benefits and highly redistributive policies; and the Mediterranean model, which is a hybrid characterized by universal healthcare coverage and work-based provisions for income replacement.

The type of welfare state that has emerged in any given country depends partly on the extent to which rural workers were incorporated into the urban workers' movement and represented by associated political parties. Scandinavian countries had small, capital-intensive farming, where worker mobilization did not threaten the supply of farm labour. This situation was conducive to the formation of coalitions between socialist and farmer parties. This strengthened the labour movement, which made it possible for universal welfare provisions to be introduced. In continental Europe, by contrast, growing worker mobilization was seen as a threat to the labour-intensive farming practices, and such coalitions between social groups were prevented by elites. There, farmers were brought into alliance with conservative parties, isolating the workers' movement, and producing a very different type of welfare system.

The duality of the welfare model found in Southern European states (Italy, Spain, Portugal, and Greece) is due to the presence in these societies of radical communist parties, which were interested in maintaining the support of their electoral base through the employment-related provision of pensions. Facing such competition from the left, more mainstream parties then abandoned the push for full universality of coverage.

Emerging out of several decades of communist rule, with universal, rights-based coverage for health care, education, pensions, and no official unemployment, the welfare regimes in the newer democracies of Central and Eastern Europe do not fit any of the other models. Despite their common pro-market approach during the transition, there is no evidence that these countries resemble a liberal welfare model (Haggard and Kaufman 2008). There are further indications that historical legacies and the influence of their continental European neighbours played a role in shaping the welfare states that emerged across the region during the transition, more so than party ideology (Bohle and Greskovits 2007).

8.4.2 **Spending on particular areas**

Another area of research examines whether the partisan composition of government office affects public spending overall and in particular areas (for a recent review see Potrafke 2017). This is a difficult test for assessing the impact of parties on policies, because most government spending relates to ongoing commitments that were made in the past and that the government of the day is obliged to honour. Moreover, research has shown that most political parties engage in policies leading to political business cycles, expanding the economy through spending before elections (Franzese 2002). Such constraints and behaviour limit the extent to which we expect to see sharp differences between left- and right-wing governments in their spending policies. Nevertheless, parties on the left traditionally draw the majority of their support from social groups that are beneficiaries of higher public spending. Right-wing parties tend to rely on the support from wealthier and business-minded constituencies and generally favour lower budgets and smaller state sectors.

Early studies showed mixed results on the question of whether the type of party that controlled government mattered for total, social, or education spending. Subsequent research clarified the conditions under which party ideology matters for spending. In the early post-WWII years, until the recession years of the 1970s, differences in the ideology of the governing parties resulted in different levels of social spending, with left-wing governments spending more on social services. After 1973, though, the impact shifted from social to total spending, and different types of parties mattered. Right-wing parties reduced the overall size of the state sector, but the ideology of government parties did not have a pronounced impact on social spending (Imbeau et al. 2001). Policies compensating the unemployed are another area where the role of ideology is time dependent. Prior to the 1980s, left-wing governments spent more on unemployment benefits, but this relationship was not observed in the 1980s, when neoliberal policies became widespread. Conversely, government control by right-wing parties did not affect unemployment spending before the 1980s, but they were associated with reductions in subsequent decades (Allan and Scruggs 2004).

One of the puzzles in this area of research concerns the level of government spending in Central and Eastern European countries. No evidence of a partisan effect was found on total social spending across this group of countries. However, the size of some programmes, such as old-age pensions, was larger under centre-right governments than under left-wing governments (Lipsmeyer 2002). Why would parties that espoused economically liberal ideologies accept budgets that increased the role of the state in some sectors of their economies? To understand this, we need to look beyond the immediate association between spending and ideology, and take into account the context of the post-communist transitions. Centre-right parties in the region prioritized other pro-market policies such as privatization that led to sharp increases in unemployment. To tackle these high unemployment rates, such governments also encouraged early retirement, which led to a short-term increase in pension-spending that is seemingly inconsistent with the right-of-centre ideologies.

Compounding this puzzle is the observation that left-wing governments (for example, in Hungary and Poland) tended to spend less on health and education. The explanation for this seeming anomaly is also context dependent. During transition periods, parties on the left needed to prove that they had been transformed from communist parties, and pursuing austerity politics typically associated with the right allowed them to cast themselves in this image. Further, thanks to their loyal electorate, left-wing parties could pursue these policies without fear of electoral repercussion. Right-wing parties, on the other hand, did not face a similar need to legitimize themselves, and they were more vulnerable to electoral accountability because of the volatile electorate (Tavits and Letki 2009).

8.4.3 **Fulfilment of pledges**

Political scientists have also examined the extent to which the promises made by parties during election campaigns are fulfilled or broken after those parties enter government office. Research on pledge fulfilment is a distinct and relatively straightforward way of examining how parties shape policy outputs. Researchers read parties' manifestos or election platforms carefully and extract the promises that can be tested with evidence, such as promises to cut the basic rate of income tax, raise the minimum wage, or increase public spending on health care. They then assess whether these promises were fulfilled and compare rates of pledge fulfilment across different parties, countries, and contexts within countries. Much recent work on campaign pledges has been brought together in the Comparative Pledges Project (CPP; Thomson et al. 2017; Naurin et al. 2019). In the CPP, researchers have gone to considerable lengths to align their definitions and research procedures to arrive at valid comparisons.

The latest evidence from that project covers the fulfilment or breaking of over 20,000 campaign promises made during fifty-seven election campaigns in twelve countries.

The evidence from the CPP shows that in general parties follow through on their campaign promises when they enter into office. Across the twelve countries included in the study, researchers found that governments fulfilled a clear majority of governing parties' pledges at least partially (60% of the 9,133 pledges made by parties that went on to hold government office after the election campaigns). Fulfilment varies significantly depending on a range of factors. One of the most important is whether parties governed alone or as part of a coalition after elections. Single-party governments in the UK, for instance, were found to fulfil 86% of their parties' pledges, while coalition governments in Germany fulfilled 62% of their parties' pledges. This difference between single-party governments and coalition governments was more important than the difference between governments with and without legislative majorities. Swedish single-party minority governments, for instance, also fulfilled a remarkably high percentage, 87%, of the Social Democrats' campaign promises. These findings counter the widespread views held by the general public that parties do not keep their promises and that minority governments are indecisive.

How we interpret the finding that governing parties often keep their campaign promises depends on the significance of what they promise. The qualitative evidence shows that parties' campaign promises include policies that have important consequences for the groups of citizens they affect. For example, manifestos usually contain commitments to change income tax levels to benefit the party's core supporters. Commitments to raise public spending on health care are also common, such as those found in recent UK Conservative and Labour manifestos. As immigration has become a salient electoral issue, more parties have promised to limit net migration. Not all policies involve changes to tax levels, spending priorities, or other readily quantifiable actions and outcomes. Some involve changes to regulations, such as the preservation of natural areas. Moreover, researchers have found that the narrative of major policy changes, such as the neoliberal policies of privatization that began in the late 1970s and gathered pace in the following decades, was foreshadowed by election pledges. At the same time, governments often need to respond to unexpected crises, such as the global financial crisis post-2008 or the Covid-19 crisis of 2020, in ways that they did not anticipate in their previous election manifestos. Indeed, research has demonstrated that governing parties have a harder time fulfilling their election pledges when their countries are more exposed to economic globalization; for instance, the UK Conservative Party's failure to fulfil its famous 2010 pledge to cut net migration to the UK could largely be attributed to the constraints imposed by globalization (Schneider and Thomson 2023). Despite these reservations, parties' campaign promises appear to be substantively important in terms of their effects on groups of citizens.

The likelihood that a party's campaign promises are fulfilled is significantly higher if that party goes on to hold executive office after the elections than if it enters the opposition. Somewhat surprisingly, there are contexts in which the difference between 'winners' and 'losers' in terms of pledge fulfilment is small. For example, in Germany, where we learned that 62% of pledges made by parties in the governing coalitions were fulfilled, 42% of pledges made by the parties that entered the opposition were also fulfilled. Even in the winner-takes-all system of the UK, 20% of opposition parties' pledges were fulfilled. Some of these fulfilled opposition pledges were policies with which the governing parties agreed either explicitly or

Box 8.4 Over to you—campaign promises

The year is 2011. You are an advisor to Nick Clegg, the now former leader of the UK Liberal Democrats, which is the junior party in a coalition government with the Conservative Party following the 2010 UK general election. The Liberal Democrats promised to abolish fees for students in higher education during the previous election campaign. In private, the Conservative prime minister David Cameron has put Nick Clegg under pressure to accept an increase in fees, which would break the Liberal Democrats' campaign promise. *With the information that was available in 2011*, how would you advise the Lib Dem leader? What are the options available to the Lib Dem leader, and what are the costs and benefits of each option? *With the benefit of the hindsight we now have*, how would your advice be different?

implicitly. The way in which we view the fulfilment of opposition parties' pledges depends on our fundamental conception of democracy, as suggested at the beginning of this chapter (Section 8.2). The fulfilment of opposition parties' pledges may be viewed as an anomaly if we adhere to a majoritarian winner-takes-all view of democracy. However, if we adhere to a more consensus-based view of democracy, in which public policies should incorporate as many citizens and affected interests as possible, then we may approve of this pattern. It is worth bearing in mind that in many electoral systems the distinction between winners and losers is blurred at best. Parties that received substantial electoral support arguably represent significant societal interests that should be heard.

Whether we consider promise-keeping to be a good or a bad thing depends partly on our opinions about what was promised. There is a distinction between disapproving of a campaign promise because we consider it unwise or even damaging, but nevertheless recognizing that it may be a legitimate policy, and disapproving of a promise because it violates the fundamental rights of individuals or groups. The latter type of promises are commonly made by populist anti-immigration and anti-Muslim parties in Europe and elsewhere. For example, the 2017 manifesto of the Dutch Party for Freedom included a commitment to 'close all mosques and Islamic schools [and] ban the Koran'. When this is the case, we can argue against the desirability of promise-keeping not only on the basis of the policies themselves, but also on the basis of democratic principles. As we have seen in this and other chapters, democratic representation requires a complex set of principles and practices, and sometimes there are tensions among these. Some of these principles and practices refer to the role of parties in government, which we have focused on in this chapter, but these are best considered in the wider set of democratic institutions discussed in this book.

8.5 **Conclusion**

The impact of governing parties on policies elicits both strong normative reactions (*does my government do what I want?*) and rich scholarly debates (*what types of representation produce what types of party-policy linkages?*). Political parties are central to the effective representation of citizens in modern democracies, and parties are most likely to affect policy through participation in government. Several lessons stand out from the discussions presented in this chapter. (1) The idea of a party mandate, while having widespread appeal, is actually quite problematic in theory and practice. It is usually not the case that election results send clear messages about precisely which policies are supported by public opinion. There is also a range of valid visions of representation, ranging from majoritarian to consensus visions, not all of which incorporate the idea of mandates. (2) The complex process of government formation, including the allocation of ministerial portfolios, determines which parties exert the most influence on government policy. While government formation is complex, there are certain common patterns—for example, governments very often involve the party of the median legislator, often in coalition with other parties that are close to it in the policy space. (3) The type of government formed—whether single-party or coalition, majority or minority—and, more broadly, the nature of the country's democracy in turn shape parties' ability to pursue their policies. (4) Party ideology is a powerful explanation for broad sets of policy outputs, such as welfare states and spending levels. (5) Consistently, across different democracies, the type of government in terms of power-sharing arrangements strongly affects the likelihood of pledge fulfilment by parties in power.

European politics is ever more in flux, with growing anti-establishment sentiments, in part driven by a lack of trust in political parties, and difficult domestic, foreign policy, and global challenges. How parties in government respond to these issues will have implications for the next several generations of voters. Thus, questions regarding the links between election outcomes and government formation, and between government formation and government policy, are vital for discussions about democratic representation.

Discussion questions

1. Why is the idea that elections confer a mandate so widespread? Under what conditions might parties convincingly claim they have a mandate?
2. How do the proponents of majoritarian and consensus models differ in terms of what they consider to be good democratic representation?
3. Why is it often hard to predict which governing coalition will form?
4. To what extent do parties affect the organization and generosity of the welfare state in the countries in which they operate?
5. Are governments in which parties keep higher percentages of their previous campaign pledges more democratic than those in which parties keep fewer pledges? Discuss the reasons that might be given for positive and negative answers to this question.
6. When parties make promises to violate the rights of groups of voters, is the keeping of such promises normatively desirable? Can democracy survive if such promises are routinely upheld by parties in government?

Thinking comparatively

A significant area of research on the intersection between government type and policy outcomes focuses on what scholars have called the 'common pool' problem. Put simply, parties in coalition governments are under pressure to make spending choices in areas most beneficial to their own constituents, leading to higher levels of public spending under multiparty governments than under single-party governments. Bäck et al. (2017) argue that this potential effect of coalition government can be mitigated by the use of comprehensive coalition agreements that set overall spending targets, but this will depend on the context, particularly the power of the prime minister. The researchers tested these arguments using data on government spending from seventeen Western European democracies over three decades. Their cases vary with respect to the use of comprehensive coalition agreements and also in terms of the power of the prime minister, enabling them to test their hypothesis. They find that coalition agreements reduce the effect of government fragmentation on spending only in those contexts where the PM is weak.

Guide to further reading

Dalton, R., Farrell, D. et al. (2011), *Political Parties and Democratic Linkage: How Parties Organize Democracy* (Oxford: Oxford University Press).

A classic study that highlights the crucial mediating role of political parties in the democratic chain of command and control that connects citizens with public policies.

Esping-Andersen, G. (1990), *The Three Worlds of Welfare Capitalism* (Princeton, NJ: Princeton University Press).

A seminal study of the main differences between welfare states and the role of parties in their development.

Lijphart, A. (2012), *Patterns of Democracy: Government Forms and Performance in Thirty-Six Countries* (New Haven, CT: Yale University Press).

One of the most influential books in Political Science, which presents Lijphart's distinction between consensus and majoritarian systems, of which parties are key elements.

Naurin, E., T. R. Royed et al. (eds.) (2019), *Party Mandates and Democracy: Making, Breaking and Keeping Pledges in Twelve Countries* (Ann Arbor, MI: University of Michigan Press).

The largest study to date on the making, breaking, and keeping of campaign promises in different types of governments, including single-party governments and coalitions, both with and without legislative majorities.

References

Achen, C. and Bartels, L. M. (2016), *Democracy for Realists: Why Elections Do Not Produce Responsive Government* (Princeton, NJ: Princeton University Press).

Allan, J. P. and Scruggs, L. (2004), 'Political partisanship and welfare state reform in advanced industrial societies', *American Journal of Political Science*, 48(3): 496–512.

Axelrod, Robert (1970), *Conflict of Interest* (Chicago, IL: Markham).

Baron, D. P. (2018), 'Elections and durable governments in parliamentary governments', *Journal of Theoretical Politics*, 30(1): 74–118.

Bergman, T., Bäck H. et al. (eds.) (2021), *Coalition Governance in Western Europe*. Oxford: Oxford University Press.

Blais, A., Nadeau, R. et al. (2001), 'The formation of party preferences: Testing the proximity and directional models', *European Journal of Political Research*, 40(1): 81–91.

Bohle, D. and Greskovits, B. (2007), 'Neoliberalism, embedded neoliberalism and neocorporatism: Towards transnational capitalism in Central-Eastern Europe', *West European Politics*, 30(3): 443–66.

Budge, I. and Farlie, D. (1983), *Explaining and Predicting Elections: Issue Effects and Party Strategies in Twenty-Three Democracies* (London: Allen & Unwin).

Chiru, M. (2015), 'Early marriages last longer: Pre-electoral coalitions and government survival in Europe', *Government and Opposition*, 50(2): 165–88.

Crombez, Christophe (1996), 'Minority governments, minimal winning coalitions, and surplus majorities in parliamentary systems', *European Journal of Political Research*, 29(1): 1–29.

Downs, A. (1957), *An Economic Theory of Democracy* (New York: Harper).

Field, Bonnie and Martin, Shane (2019), 'Minority governments', in L. Sandy Maisel (ed.), *Oxford Bibliographies in Political Science* (Oxford: Oxford University Press).

Franzese R. J. (2002), 'Electoral and partisan cycles in economic policies and outcomes', *Annual Review of Political Science*, 5: 369–421.

Golder, S N. (2005), 'Pre-electoral coalitions in comparative perspective: A test of existing hypotheses', *Electoral Studies*, 24(4): 643–63.

Haggard, Stephan and Kaufman, R. (2008), *Development, Democracy, and Welfare States: Latin America, East Asia, and Eastern Europe* (Princeton, NJ: Princeton University Press).

Huber, J. D. and Martinez-Gallardo, C. (2008), 'Replacing cabinet ministers: Patterns of ministerial stability in parliamentary democracies', *American Political Science Review*, 102(02): 169–80.

Imbeau, L. M., Petry, F. et al. (2001), 'Left-right party ideology and government policies: A meta-analysis', *European Journal of Political Research*, 40(1): 1–29.

Kitschelt, H., Mansfeldova, Z. et al. (1999), *Post-Communist Party Systems: Competition, Representation, and Inter-Party Cooperation* (New York: Cambridge University Press).

Laver, M. and Shepsle, K. A. (1996), *Making and Breaking Governments: Cabinets and Legislatures in Parliamentary Democracies* (New York: Cambridge University Press).

Lipsmeyer, C. S. (2002), 'Parties and policy: Evaluating economic and partisan influences on welfare policy spending during the European post-communist transition', *British Journal of Political Science*, 32(4): 641–61.

Manin, Bernard, Przeworski, Adam et al. (1999), 'Elections and representation', in Adam Przeworski, Susan Stokes et al. (eds.), *Democracy, Accountability, and Representation* (Cambridge: Cambridge University Press).

Mansbridge, J. (2003), 'Rethinking representation', *American Political Science Review*, 97(4): 515–28.

McDonald, M. D. and Budge, I. (2005), *Elections, Parties, Democracy: Conferring the Median Mandate* (Oxford: Oxford University Press).

Moury, C. and Timmermans, A. (2013), 'Inter-party conflict management in coalition governments: Analyzing the role of coalition agreements in Belgium, Germany, Italy and the Netherlands', *Politics and Governance*, 1(2): 117–31.

Müller, W. C. and Strøm, K. (2008), 'Coalition agreements and cabinet governance', in K. Strøm, W. C. Müller et al. (eds.), *Cabinets and Coalition Bargaining: The Democratic Life Cycle in Western Europe* (Oxford: Oxford University Press).

Naurin, E., Royed, T. R. et al. (eds.) (2019), *Party Mandates and Democracy: Making, Breaking and Keeping Pledges in Twelve Countries* (Ann Arbor, MI: University of Michigan Press).

Potrafke, N. (2017), 'Partisan politics: The empirical evidence from OECD panel studies', *Journal of Comparative Economics*, 45(4): 712–50.

Powell, G. B. and Powell Jr, G. B. (2000), *Elections as Instruments of Democracy: Majoritarian and Proportional Visions* (New Haven, CT: Yale University Press).

Powell, G. B. and Whitten, G. D. (1993), 'A cross-national analysis of economic voting: Taking account of the political context', *American Journal of Political Science*, 37(2): 391–414.

Schneider, C. J. and Thomson R. (2023), 'Globalization and promissory representation', *American Journal of Political Science*, Early view. https://doi.org/10.1111/ajps.12789.

Rabinowitz, G. and Macdonald, S. E. (1989), 'A directional theory of issue voting', *The American Political Science Review*, 83(1): 93–121.

Riker, William H. (1962), *The Theory of Political Coalitions* (New Haven, CT: Yale University Press).

Strøm, K. (1990), *Minority Government and Majority Rule* (Cambridge: Cambridge University Press).

Tavits, M. and Letki, N. (2009), 'When left is right: Party ideology and policy in post-communist Europe', *American Political Science Review*, 103(4): 555–69.

Thomson, R., Royed, T. et al. (2017), 'The fulfillment of parties' election pledges: A comparative study on the impact of power sharing', *American Journal of Political Science*, 61(3): 527–42.

9 Parliaments

SHANE MARTIN

9.1 Introduction

Today, parliaments and the parliamentarians who serve within them are much scrutinized. Some question the degree to which parliamentarians have the interests of the public—rather than their own, narrower, interests—at heart. Many citizens and commentators wonder whether parliaments play any meaningful role in modern politics. A widely discussed theme is the notion of executive dominance (see Chapter 7). Executive dominance can be thought of as the imbalance in the relative power of the executive and legislature where the unevenness favours the executive (Lijphart 1999: 129)—a phenomenon possibly exacerbated by the impact of the Covid-19 pandemic on how governments make decisions during times of crisis, often acting without normal levels of parliamentary oversight and/or relying on delegated authority or emergency powers.

The narrative of executive dominance of legislatures is not new. Ostrogorski (1902) warned that parliaments were being fundamentally weakened by the rise of political parties. Bryce (1921) wrote famously of the decline of parliaments. Highly disciplined parliamentary party groups combined with various executive prerogatives over the legislative process means that the cabinet in European countries commonly dominates decision-making and decision outcomes within the chamber. This de facto dominance allows the cabinet to get the legislation they want, with little opportunity for real parliamentary oversight of the executive. In European Union countries, national parliaments have struggled to adapt as decision- making and influence has shifted further to national executives and the European Parliament (see Chapter 17).

Yet we have been perhaps too quick to dismiss the role of national parliaments in a country's political system. National parliaments across Europe remain the cornerstone of representative democracy. They play central roles in representation, law-making, executive oversight, government formation, and, except for Switzerland, determining how long a government stays in office (Switzerland's federal assembly plays a role in selecting the federal government, but has no power to remove the government; in this sense it is not classified as a parliamentary regime). Many of them adapted quickly and successfully during the Covid-19 pandemic, implementing remote meetings and new ways of working.

This chapter focuses on the structure and functions of national parliaments across Europe. What role are parliaments expected to play and how well do they perform these roles in reality? A theme running throughout this chapter is the question of whether or not we misunderstand parliaments—and in particular their role and function. Often parliaments in Europe are compared and contrasted to the powerful United States (US) Congress. But is it appropriate to compare a parliament in a European country to the parliament of a federal and presidential system like that of the US? We begin with an overview of the basic design of national legislatures around Europe.

9.2 Fundamental design

What does a typical parliament in Europe look like? This is difficult to answer because parliaments are as diverse in design as they are ubiquitous. How parliaments are elected has already been discussed in Chapter 2. In this section, we compare and contrast parliaments based on cameral structure, chamber size, and what can be termed internal legislative organization.

9.2.1 Cameral structure

A parliament's cameral structure describes the number of chambers in the parliament and, in the case of a parliament with two or more chambers, the similarity and differences between the chambers. Unicameral parliaments have only one chamber. Bicameralism means that the parliament has two chambers. Tsebelis and Money (1997: 1) suggest that the 'defining characteristic of bicameral legislatures is the requirement that legislation be deliberated in two distinct assemblies'. Countries such as Demark are now unicameral, whereas they used to be bicameral. Of the thirty-three countries covered here, fifteen are bicameral and eighteen are unicameral (see Table 9.1).

A strong bicameral system has two additional features beyond the mere presence of two chambers. First, to be characterized as a strong bicameral system, the second chamber will have significant formal power in the law-making process, up to and including the power to veto proposed legislation. Second, there is a differentiated membership base when the lower and second chamber are compared. We discuss both in turn.

A second chamber—sometimes referred to as an upper chamber or senate—may provide an extra check on the executive and on the lower chamber, thus allowing for better-considered and more reflective law-making. Second chambers may have the power to veto proposed legislation or the much weaker power to delay (but not stop) proposed legislation. As Russell (2001) notes, requiring a second chamber to scrutinize proposed legislation makes it more likely that any flaws in a bill can be ironed out before it becomes law. The British House of Lords is often considered a revising chamber, in that it typically takes draft legislation from the House of Commons and seeks to improve it. Yet, today the UK House of Lords has lost the ability to veto legislation—at most a bill accepted by the UK House of Commons but rejected by the UK House of Lords can be delayed for one year. Second chambers thus serve as a limit or slowing influence on the ability of the majority in the first chamber to make changes. Some second chambers have more influence within their respective political systems. The German *Bundesrat* and Italian *Senato della Repubblica* are often cited for their influence. The *Bundesrat*

Table 9.1 Parliaments and cameral structures

Country	Name of parliament	Cameral structure	Name of lower chamber	Name of upper chamber
Austria	*Parlament*	Bicameral	*Nationalrat*	*Bundesrat*
Belgium	*Parlement fédéral*	Bicameral	*Chambre des représentants*	*Sénat*
Bosnia-Herzegovina	*Parlamentarna skupština Bosne i Hercegovine*	Bicameral	*Predstavnički Dom*	*Dom naroda*
Bulgaria	*Narodno sabranie*	Unicameral	*Narodno sabranie*	NA
Croatia	*Hrvatski Sabor*	Unicameral	*Hrvatski Sabor*	NA
Cyprus	*Voulī́ tōn Antiprosṓpōn*	Unicameral	*Voulī́ tōn Antiprosṓpōn*	NA
Czech Republic	*Parlament České republiky*	Bicameral	*Poslanecka Snemovna*	*Senat*
Denmark	*Folketinget*	Unicameral	*Folketinget*	NA
Estonia	*Riigikogu*	Unicameral	*Riigikogu*	NA
Finland	*Eduskunta Riksdagen*	Unicameral	*Eduskunta Riksdagen*	NA
France	*Parlement Français*	Bicameral	*Assemblée nationale*	*Sénat*
Germany	*Bundestag*	Bicameral	*Bundestag*	*Bundesrat*
Greece	*Vouli Ton Ellinon*	Unicameral	*Vouli Ton Ellinon*	NA
Hungary	*Országház*	Unicameral	*Országház*	NA
Iceland	*Althing*	Unicameral	*Althing*	NA
Ireland	*Oireachtas*	Bicameral	*Dail Eireann*	*Seanad Éireann*
Italy	*Il Parlamento*	Bicameral	*Camera dei Deputati*	*Senato della Repubblica*
Latvia	*Latvijas Republikas Saeima*	Unicameral	*Latvijas Republikas Saeima*	NA
Lithuania	*Lietuvos Respublikos Seimas*	Unicameral	*Lietuvos Respublikos Seimas*	NA
Luxembourg	*Chambre des députés*	Unicameral	*Chambre des députés*	NA
Malta	*Parlament ta' Malta*	Unicameral	*Kamra tad-Deputati*	NA
Netherlands	*Staten-Generaal*	Bicameral	*Tweede Kamer der Staten-Generaal*	*Eerste Kamer der Staten-Generaal*
Norway	*Stortinget*	Unicameral	*Stortinget*	NA
Poland	*Zgromadzenie Narodowe*	Bicameral	*Sejm Rzeczypospolitej Polskiej*	*Senat*
Portugal	*Assembleia da Republica*	Unicameral	*Assembleia da Republica*	NA
Romania	*Parlamentul României*	Bicameral	*Camera Deputatilor*	*Senatul*
Serbia	*Narodna skupstina*	Unicameral	*Narodna skupstina*	NA
Slovakia	*Narodna rada Slovenskej republiky*	Unicameral	*Narodna rada Slovenskej republiky*	NA
Slovenia	*Slovenski parlament*	(incompletely) Bicameral	*Državni zbor Republike Slovenije*	*Državni svet*
Spain	*Las Cortes Generales*	Bicameral	*Congreso de los Diputados*	*Senado*
Sweden	*Riksdagen*	Unicameral	*Riksdagen*	NA
Switzerland	*Bundesversammlung*	Bicameral	*Nationalrat–Conseil national–Consiglio nazionale*	*Ständerat*
United Kingdom	Parliament	Bicameral	House of Commons	House of Lords

is an important actor because it represents German states at the federal level. The Italian senate has some relatively unique features, including the fact that the Italian government is responsible to, and must be approved by, both the senate and the lower chamber.

All else equal, upper chambers will be most influential when the partisan composition (and majority control) differs across the chambers. Consider, for example, a bicameral system where the same party (or coalition of parties) controls a majority in both the lower and upper chamber. Here—assuming party (or coalition) voting unity within each chamber—the legislative outcomes will likely be the same regardless of the presence or absence of a second chamber. In contrast, a second chamber has more de facto power when the lower-chamber majority does not have a majority in the upper chamber. Then, the parties (or coalitions) who hold the majority in each chamber must engage in inter-cameral bargaining for the legislative process to succeed (assuming the legislative chamber has any formal power). Again, the UK House of Lords is a good example: often the party that controls a majority of seats in the House of Commons lacks a majority in the House of Lords—making policy making more challenging.

The level of similarity or difference between the chambers' partisan composition depends on how the second chamber is selected, and how this differs from the lower chamber's electoral mechanism. Some upper chambers are elected. Other upper chambers are appointed. Some chambers comprise a mix of elected and unelected members. The Irish senate (*Seanad Éireann*) has one of the most unique selection processes, involving a mix of indirect elections and appointment. Forty-three Irish senators are elected by six vocational panels. Selection panels are composed of elected members of local government, members of the lower chamber, and members of the outgoing *Seanad*. Each panel, in theory, represents a particular vocational interest—culture and education, agriculture, labour, industry and commerce, and public administration. A further six senators are elected in an election involving graduates of two universities. Finally, eleven senators are appointed by the prime minister (*taoiseach*).

In a referendum held on 4 October 2013, voters in the Irish Republic were given the opportunity to abolish the *Seanad* but voters rejected the proposal. Some second chambers have been eliminated—for example, in Croatia in 2001. In many countries, the status of second chambers is the subject of significant attention from political elites and voters, with calls for fundamental reform (for example, in Italy). Defenders of bicameralism point to the role of second chambers in improving the quality of deliberation and decisions. Detractors suggest that the second chambers are either redundant (if they mirror the composition of the lower house) or elitist (if they are not democratically elected). As the nineteenth-century political writer Abbé Sieyès is alleged to have said: 'if a second chamber dissents from the first, it is mischievous; if it agrees with it, it is superfluous' (quoted in Campion 1953: 17). Clearly, the benefits of bicameralism versus unicameralism, and the ideal strength of second chambers in a bicameral system, remain a contentious issue.

9.2.2 **Size**

By size of parliament we mean the number of parliamentarians. There is significant variation in the size of the national parliaments among the countries in this book. The country with the fewest national parliamentarians is Bosnia-Herzegovina with fifty-seven parliamentarians. The United Kingdom has the most national legislators of any country in this book—with a total of 1,426 Members of the House of Commons and the House of Lords. Looking at individual chambers, the largest lower chamber is the German *Bundestag* (currently 736 members); the smallest lower chamber is Bosnia-Herzegovina's *Parlamentarna skupština* (forty-two members). The smallest chamber of all is Bosnia-Herzegovina's second chamber with just fifteen members. What determines the size of a parliament? Taagepera (1972) suggests a relationship between the number of legislators and a country's population: the larger the population, the larger the legislature. Such a relationship is intuitively appealing: for representative, communications, and governance purposes, countries with larger populations require more legislators.

9.2.3 **Internal legislative organization**

As with cameral structures and size, parliaments vary significantly in how they are internally organized, including how authority and resources are allocated within the legislature. How a legislature is organized in terms of rules, procedures, and how power and resources are allocated between members is of vital importance in determining where power actually lies. In particular, internal organization may shape the degree to which party leaders control and influence individual members. In some legislatures, power may rest with individual members owing to a highly decentralized organizational structure. In other legislatures, power may rest with leaders (and particular party leaders). The degree to which committees are influential in the day-to-day work of a parliament provides a good indication of where power really lies: with members or with their party leaders.

Committees are frequently cited as amongst the most important internal organizational features of a parliament. Mattson and Strøm (1995: 249) define a committee as 'a subgroup of legislators, normally entrusted with specific organizational tasks'. For example, the German *Bundestag* has twenty-three substantive committees, including the Finance Committee, Defence Committee, a European Union (EU) Affairs Committee, and several 'housekeeping' committees responsible for various aspects of parliamentary administration and governance. Creating a system of committees within parliament and delegating authority away from the main chamber allows for the effective and efficient use of members' time. It can enable members to specialize in particular policy areas, resulting in better legislative activities of benefit to the entire chamber (Gilligan and Krehbiel 1987). However, a competing argument is that committees allow committee members to distribute benefits to their constituents. Benefits could include specific policies favoured by voters in the member's district or so-called 'pork-barrel' projects that involve deputies funnelling public monies towards projects in their constituencies. In this view, members can control policy areas of interest to their constituents (for example, if a member represents a rural district they will seek to sit on an agricultural committee). The more a committee has influence and power, the more members can protect the specific interests of their constituents.

The degree to which individual parliamentarians in European countries could use committee work to represent constituents or directly control government policy is questionable. Committee systems differ across parliaments in their power and significance and the degree to which they are ultimately controlled by parliamentary party groups. Features such as the number of committees, how members are appointed to committees, the formal powers and capacity of committees in the legislative process and to undertake hearings and call

Box 9.1 Over to you—parliamentary committees

Much of the theoretical work on how parliaments work has focused on the nature of committees and why exactly a parliament would choose to work via a system of committees. Some theories suggest committees aid the work of the chamber, allowing specialization and gains from trade. Other theories focus on the electoral payoffs to parliamentarians from their committee work. More recently, scholars have viewed parliamentary committees as a mechanism by which parties in coalition government can monitor each other's ministers—to ensure coalition policy is being implemented. Which approach best captures the actual rationale for committees in European parliaments? To test this, select a parliament with which you are familiar. Describe how committees work in that parliament. How many committees exist? What are the committee portfolios, and do they correspond to government ministries? How are members selected to committees? Do governing parties hold the chairs of committees or are chairs spread across parties? In particular, see if there is a relationship between the partisan affiliation of the government minister (e.g. the agricultural minister) and the partisan affiliation of the committee chair. Try and determine the role of committees in law-making (is there, for example, a 'committee' stage where bills are referred to a specific committee?) and what oversight tools they have at their disposal (can they, for example, call witnesses or undertake pre-legislative or post-legislative scrutiny?).

(perhaps even compel) witnesses, and the match between committee portfolios and government ministries all determine the strength or weakness of a parliament's committee system. By conventional wisdom, Scandinavian parliaments were considered to have strong committees, while the UK and Ireland, in particular, were considered to have weak committees. In Denmark, for example, parliamentary committees play a crucial role in scrutinizing proposed legislation and the work of the government. The Danish *Folketing* has twenty-five committees, each with between seventeen and twenty-nine members. Most of these committees 'shadow' a specific government ministry and can take written or oral evidence for experts and/or relevant groups, as well as table questions to ministers. Today anyone wanting to explore how to measure or enhance parliaments' role and capacity to perform its functions will pay close attention to committee systems, even if they are now the only means by which parliament can work (Martin and Whitaker 2019). It is to these roles and functions of parliament that we now turn.

9.3 Roles and functions

What roles and functions should a national parliament play? Here we discuss four core roles: law-making, a role in determining who is the executive, oversight of the executive in office, and representation. Although methodologically challenging, we will also seek to evaluate how well parliaments actually perform these roles.

9.3.1 Law-making

By almost universal accord, law-making is a central function of any parliament. Norton (2013: 1) even defines a legislature as 'a body created to approve measures that will form the law of the land'. Most parliaments may be limited in what they can legislate for by the country's constitution. To fully understand the influence of a parliament in law-making, it is necessary to explore the degree to which parliaments influence the content of proposed and actual legislation or, alternatively, have become mere rubber-stamps for the preferences and wishes of the executive.

On the one hand, parliaments typically play a crucial role in law-making. With some notable exceptions, laws can only be formally changed by an act of law, passed by a parliament and (where relevant) signed into law by a head of state. Notable exceptions include a role for courts in overturning legislation or interpreting existing laws in a new way (see Chapter 10). Thus, parliament is a real veto player in the legislative process. Only bills that receive the approval of parliament can become law. Votes within a chamber (sometimes referred to as roll-call votes or legislative divisions) are key to the law-making process. Divisions commonly take place in the plenary but can also occur in committees. Parliamentarians may need to cast votes at multiple stages of the legislative process. Some parliaments, for example, consider proposed legislation on three, four, or five separate occasions—often referred to as *stages*. Each stage may provide an opportunity for parliament to reject the bill. Legislators may spend hours, days, or even weeks debating an issue in committees, party caucuses, leadership meetings, and the 'corridors'—and these parliamentary activities are undoubtedly important. But actual decisions are typically made by a formal vote in a plenary session.

The previous simple analysis of the formal legislative process implies that parliament is a key player in law production. Without parliamentary approval, proposed legislation remains that. Towards the end of the chapter, we explore why parliaments may have lost real influence, but for now let us consider how the executive may dominate the law-making process. In many parliamentary systems, the executive controls the legislature's timetable, enjoys a near monopoly on drafting power, and often has at its disposal rights to close debate, reject amendments, or exclusively offer the cabinet's own amendments (see Chapter 7). Rasch (2014: 456) notes that agenda control can involve 'agenda-setting (or generating), blocking (or delaying), and sequencing (or ordering) of alternatives before or until an outcome is reached'.

While the executive may appear to dominate the law-making process, in reality the executive must remain sensitive to the interests and preferences of its supporters in parliament. This may result in a difficult to observe but nonetheless real impact of parliament on policy. Consider, for example, the following scenario. A government proposes a bill, and the bill passes smoothly through the legislative process. While opposition parties (parties with seats in parliament but not represented at cabinet) object to the proposed law, the executive's majority ensure that all votes are won. Can it then be concluded that parliament's role in the legislative process is meaningless? Not necessarily, because the executive (either a single party or a coalition of parties) must be sensitive to the needs of parliamentarians whose votes are needed to win approval. Rationally, an executive would not introduce a bill for which there is insufficient support. Thus, a lack of successful amendments to a bill is no evidence of a lack of parliamentary influence over a bill. Executives anticipate parliament's reaction to a bill, and shape the bill accordingly. Of course, executives do lose bills in parliament, arguably because of a lack of information concerning the interests and preferences of the parliamentarians needed to support the bill.

9.3.2 Government formation

The defining feature of a parliamentary system of government is that the executive 'comes from' and remains 'responsible to' the national parliament. Unlike in a presidential system, voters in a parliamentary system do not elect the executive. Instead, the executive is selected via the parliament. The 'game' of government formation is simplest when a single political party wins a majority of seats in (the relevant chamber of) parliament. A desire to hold executive office means that a majority party is unlikely to decline the right to be the party of government (Müller and Strøm 1999). The formal involvement of the legislature in government formation is often considered merely ceremonial in the presence of a majority party.

However, relatively few elections return a political party with a majority of seats in the legislature. The study of government formation under parliamentarism is primarily focused on understanding and explaining which party or parties form the cabinet in the absence of a majority party (see Chapter 8). Which party or parties get to form the cabinet is a question of obvious substantive and theoretical importance. Which parties govern, and what *type* of cabinet (single party versus multiparty, and majority versus minority), is said to shape public policy. For example, coalition government is often associated with government overspending and budget deficits (e.g., Bawn and Rosenbluth 2006).

To become the executive, or to remain the executive, the government needs the support of a majority of the parliament. Thus, government formation is a core function of parliaments in parliamentary systems. In some political systems, parliament must hold a formal 'investiture' vote, a vote in which they approve the choice of executive (sometimes referred to as positive parliamentarism); in other systems (sometimes referred to as negative parliamentarism) this is not the case. Investiture votes can involve selecting the head of government, members of the cabinet, or the government's policy agenda. Strøm (1990) suggests that the presence of an investiture vote reduces the probability of minority government formation (a cabinet that does not control a majority of seats in the legislature). He argues that minority governments are more likely when governments can survive by building ad hoc policy-based majorities (such as in Denmark). The requirement of a formal investiture vote may impose an immediate and significant hurdle for parties outside of the government since they would have to publicly express their support for the government as a whole (Field and Martin 2022). Some bicameral systems have governments that are invested by both chambers. In Italy, for example, both the House and Senate must vote to confirm the president's choice of prime minister. In fact, Italy represents an interesting case of what we call ex-post *investiture*: a government is appointed (in this case by the president of Italy), comes into office, and then a vote takes place in parliament to accept or reject the government already in place. In contrast, in ex-ante investiture systems, parliament votes to choose a government—who is then appointed by a head of state or similar officeholder. In some parliaments, for example Norway, the government takes power without any investiture vote.

Just as a parliament can have more or less influence in selecting an executive, it can have more or less influence in removing an executive. Three cases are common. In most European countries, parliament can vote to remove a government via a vote of no confidence (see also Chapter 7). A no confidence vote is a vote that, if lost by the executive, requires the executive to resign. This need to have continued confidence is the key definition of a parliamentary system of government: parliament can remove an executive, for whatever reason it likes (the 'for whatever reason it likes' differentiates the confidence procedure in a parliamentary system from an impeachment system in a presidential system). Scholars who bemoan the weakness of parliaments in parliamentary systems often overlook the crucial power of parliament to make and break the executive. Some countries have what is termed a constructive no confidence procedure, where parliament can only remove the executive if it simultaneously appoints a new executive. This is the case, for example, in Germany where a chancellor can only be removed if they are replaced. Finally, in some systems parliament cannot remove the executive. This may be the case (but is not always) in semi-presidential systems. The Swiss case is also relatively unique: the national parliament selects the government but cannot remove it. Because the Swiss parliament cannot remove the executive, most scholars do not classify Switzerland as being a parliamentary system—but neither is it a presidential or semi-presidential system (as the head of government is not directly elected).

9.3.3 **Oversight**

Kreppel (2014: 86) defines parliamentary oversight as 'the monitoring of executive agencies tasked with the implementation of policy decisions, and regular engagement with the political executive to insure it is meeting its commitments to the public and adequately addressing the various policy needs of the country'. Because the government is an agent of the parliament, parliament needs to monitor the activities of both the political executive and the wider bureaucracy. Otherwise, the executive may not act in line with the interests and preferences of parliament. Parliaments typically have a number of tools to enable them to oversee the executive—either the political executive, the bureaucracy, or both. Specific tools to control the executive include: (1) parliamentary questions and interpellations, (2) investigations and hearings, (3) an audit committee or office, and (4) powers to dismiss the executive or individual members of the executive (arguably the ultimate form of oversight).

Parliamentary questions (PQs) are a procedure that permit parliamentarians to formally ask questions of, and receive answers from, members of the executive. PQs are one of the few tools that provide legislators with access to information on the actions and operation of the executive (Martin and Rozenberg 2014). Although the rules governing PQs vary widely, they come in two fundamental forms: oral and written. Oral questions are questions that are verbally asked and verbally answered on the floor of the chamber. Probably the best-known example of oral PQs is Prime Minister's Questions in the British House of Commons. Prime Minister's Questions can provide for political theatre between the executive and opposition (or even the executive and co-partisan parliamentarians). Because oral PQs demand an on-the-spot answer, the respondent needs to have a full command of their area of responsibility. In contrast, written questions are tabled (in writing) by a member and the relevant part of the executive is given a specific period of time to research and furnish a reply—typically also in writing. Interpellations are similar to parliamentary questions, but more extensive, and are analogous to a short debate on the activities of a particular member or part of the executive (Pelizzo and Stapenhurst 2014: 35).

A parliamentary investigation or inquiry refers to the ability of a parliament to undertake a (relatively) detailed examination of some past event or current issue. It is the level of focus and resources that differentiate investigations and inquiries from forms of oversight such as

PQs. Investigations can last from weeks to years. The ability to conduct Parliamentary Inquiries matters. In a comparative study investigating what makes national parliaments more or less powerful, Chernykh et al. (2017) suggest that the power to conduct investigations of the government is one of the most valuable powers a legislative assembly can have. These investigations can potentially uncover significant scandals or cases of maladministration. For example, in 2017, the German parliament concluded a three-year investigation into alleged surveillance of German citizens and the governments of a number of allies by the German Federal Intelligence Service.

Finally in terms of common oversight tools, parliament may be able to audit and conduct an ex-post review of government expenditure and income. In addition to any power over determining the government's budget (the power of the purse), a parliamentary committee or parliamentary audit office may annually review the performance of government departments and related agencies to explore value for money and good governance. In some countries, these public audits are an important mechanism to uncover corruption or other forms of maladministration.

Of course, the ultimate sanction available to a parliament is the power to dismiss the executive. The ability of the legislature to remove the executive for whatever reason it wishes can be conceived of as a responsibility principal—the cabinet is thus said to be *responsible to* the parliament through the no confidence procedure described previously. Strøm (1990) applies agency theory to the operation of Western European parliamentary democracies. From this perspective, parliamentary government can be viewed as a specific chain of delegation. Voters elect representatives to the parliament; parliament selects a cabinet; the cabinet delegates to individual ministers; and ministers in turn delegate to civil servants. Of course, delegation and accountability require each principal to be able to monitor their agent to ensure that the principal's preferences and interests are being fulfilled by the agent. The ability to remove the government is thus the key tool of parliamentary accountability (Strøm et al. 2010). The core aspects of the chain of delegation in a parliamentary system are depicted in Figure 9.1.

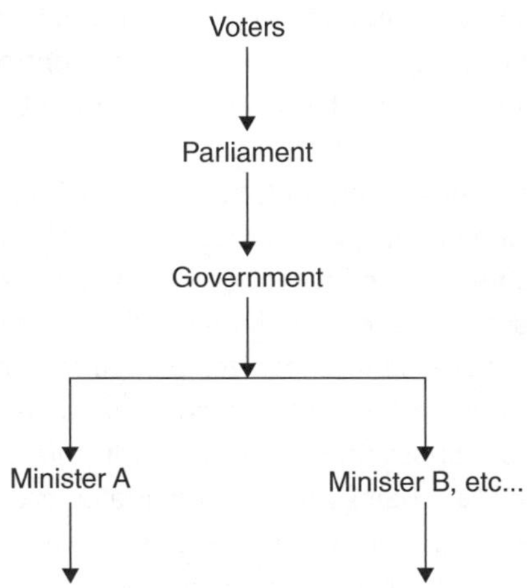

Figure 9.1 The chain of delegation in parliamentary democracy

Source: Adapted from Strøm (2000: 269).

9.3.4 **Representation**

Parliaments, it is often suggested, are the cornerstone of representative democracy. At least in parliamentary systems, voters select parliamentarians to represent their interests and preferences in the political decision-making process. As such, interest representation is an important function of most national parliaments—it is through parliament that the voice of ordinary citizens is channelled. In most European parliaments, legislators represent citizens in a particular geographical district (constituency). The nature and size of this constituency depends in part on the electoral system (see Chapter 2). In some systems a particular region is represented by one parliamentarian; in other cases a district may elect a number of parliamentarians. And of course, in a party-list system, voters may be voting for a party rather than an individual politician. In fact, a country's electoral system significantly impacts the degree to which legislators are representatives of the voters who elected them, or agents of the party to which they are affiliated. In other words, electoral institutions shape patterns of representation and responsiveness in legislatures.

In exploring the relationship between electoral systems and representation, we often talk about candidate-centred versus party-centred electoral systems. In a candidate-centred electoral environment, voters vote for individuals and based on candidates' personal characteristics. In party-centred electoral environments, voters vote for a party or based on a candidate's party affiliation. All else equal, we expect to see more sensitivity by legislators to the interests and preferences of their constituents in countries with more candidate-centred electoral systems. This sensitivity (responsiveness) may come in the form of speaking about and for constituents' policy preferences within the legislative arena or voting in alignment with constituents' interests—for example, legislators represented from rural and farming communities may spend relatively more time discussing agricultural policy and representing the interests of the farming agribusiness sector. But in some political systems representation may involve individual contact between a voter or groups of voters and a legislator—sometimes referred to as constituency case work. Here, legislators may serve as a link between citizens and the government, attempting to obtain redistribution from the government to the member's constituency—a phenomenon known as fiscal particularism or more colloquially as pork-barrel politics. In more party-centred systems, legislators may see themselves less the representative of individual constituents and more the agent of the party leadership.

Ideally, because a legislature has a representative function, it should reflect the make-up of the citizenry at large, at least regarding salient ideological, political, and demographic characteristics. This is what is often referred to as descriptive representation—the ability of national parliaments to represent the interest of female citizens is a good example. Descriptive representation is important because it recognizes particular parts of society and includes them in the representative process. Descriptive representation is important because it leads to substantive representation. Substantive representation refers to the degree to which a particular group's preferences are being represented and considered in the policy process. Substantive gender representation refers to the degree to which women's interests are actively represented within parliament. Phillips (1995) suggests that women are best able to represent the interests of other women; thus, having women parliamentarians is a necessary (but not necessarily sufficient) condition for substantive women's representation. Women understand and are more likely to respond to the interests and preference of fellow women. Despite the near-balanced rate of women to men in the general population, most democratic parliaments around the world have fewer women than men. The data for the countries included in this study are presented in Figure 9.2. The Hungarian Országház and Cyprus's House of Representatives have the joint lowest rate of women parliamentarians, with 14% of women members, followed by the parliaments of Bosnia and Herzegovina and

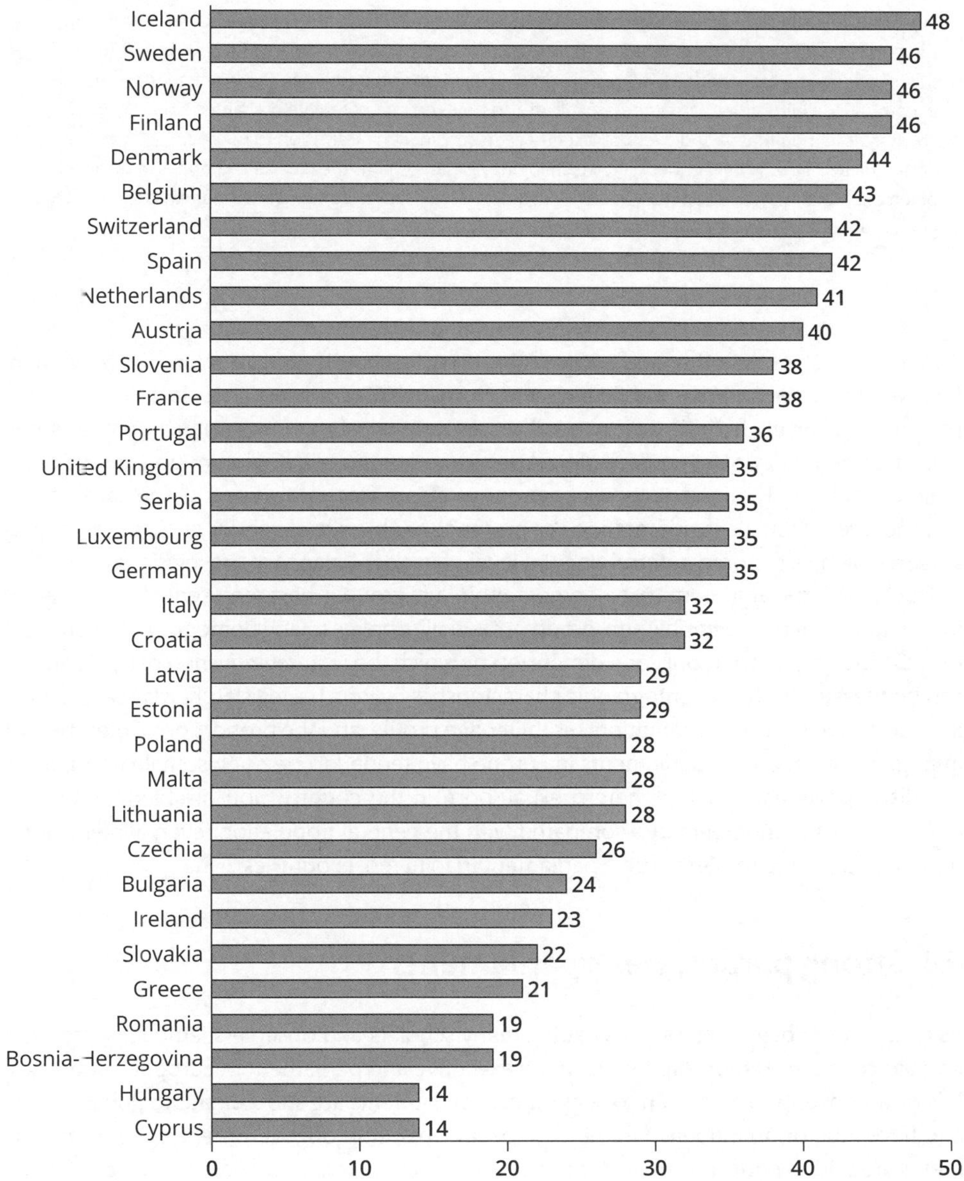

Figure 9.2 Representation of women in national parliaments

Note: Percentage of parliamentarians that are women (lower chamber only in the case of bicameral parliaments).
Source: Adapted with permission from IPU Parline. PARLINE database on national parliaments. © Copyright IPU 2023, at https://data.ipu.org/.

Box 9.2 Over to you—gender balance in parliament

Significant variation exists in the rate of female parliamentarians. What explains this cross-country variation? Some scholars suggest that the choice of electoral system used to elect the parliament impacts the number of female parliamentarians. Other scholars point to the adoption of gender quotas or efforts by political parties to recruit more female candidates. Others still suggest that the role of women in society (for example, the rate of participation of women in the general workforce) explains the supply of, and demand for, female politicians. Which of these explain actual variation in the number of female parliamentarians, across countries but also over time within countries? To test this, select a parliament with which you are familiar. Explore that parliament's current gender balance in comparison with other parliaments. Explore also how the rate of female parliamentarians in your chosen parliament has varied over the last fifty years (or since the transition to democracy for newer democracies). How is the gender balance changing? What explains the level and changes in the level of female parliamentarians? What, if anything, are political leaders doing to encourage more female parliamentarians and what obstacles are faced?

Romania (19%). At the other end of the scale, 48% of Icelandic parliamentarians are women, followed by Sweden (46%), and Finland and Norway (46%), suggesting a clear Scandinavian pattern of relatively high (if still unequal) representation of women in parliament. In some countries, gender quotas require political parties to nominate a minimum percentage of female candidates. The introduction of gender quotas is frequently cited as the cause of increased rates of female legislators and the presence or absence of gender quotas in a political system may be a factor in determining the level of gender balance in the legislature.

The logic of the argument that a demographic sub-group is best represented by someone from within that demographic sub-group potentially applies to any demographic characteristic. Of course, gender is only one dimension by which the *representativeness* of a parliament can be measured. Other demographic characteristics by which a legislature may be assessed include ethnicity, sexual orientation, disability, age profile, and the proportion of members of immigrant origins. Most parliaments in Europe have tended to be not just male dominated, but disproportionately white, heterosexual, born in the country, non-disabled, and much older in terms of members' age compared with the general population (even allowing for a minimum age requirement to be a parliamentarian in most countries).

9.4 Strong parties, weak parliaments

As noted at the beginning of this chapter, many scholars and observers lament a perceived imbalance in the relationship between the executive and parliament in European countries. It is now conventional wisdom to suggest that parliaments are subordinate to governments and have little or no influence in the day-to-day operation of government. Modern parliaments are said to perform a mere 'rubber-stamp' function, readily agreeing to the executive's legislative proposals. The perception is that the executive does what it wants and gets the legislation it wants, particularly if it controls a majority of seats in the parliament (periods of minority government—where the party or parties in cabinet do not between them control a majority of seats in the parliamentary chamber—may temporarily enhance the power of parliamentarians relative to the executive).

Why has the executive become so dominant in parliamentary regimes? Amongst the most prominent explanations is the concept of the *efficient secret*—the combination of executive and legislative leadership in the cabinet. Under parliamentary government the executive comes from and is responsible to parliament. For Bagehot (1867), the cabinet's control of both executive power and (de facto) legislative power in parliamentary regimes contrasts with the situation under presidentialism where the constitutional structure prioritizes a separation of executive and legislative powers, with each branch directly elected. As Bagehot (1867: 48) writes: 'The efficient secret . . . may be described as the close union, the nearly complete fusion, of the executive and legislative powers. No doubt by the traditional theory, as it exists in all the books, the goodness of our constitution consists in the entire separation of the legislative and executive authorities, but in truth its merit consists in their singular approximation'.

But how did the cabinet come to obtain such significant influence in law-making? In a seminal contribution exploring the nineteenth-century British House of Commons, Cox (1987) suggested that an increase in parliamentary business and in particular the volume of legislation arising from industrialization and modernization necessitated a change in parliament's procedural rights. The bottleneck arising from greater volumes for legislation necessitated the erosion of the legislative powers of individual Members of Parliament (MPs)—including the right to introduce bills, control the debate agenda, and make speeches. Such procedural prerogatives passed from individual MPs to party leaders and in particular the cabinet. Strong parties foreshadowed the decline in importance of the individual parliamentarians, and ultimately parliament itself.

Today, unified party group voting tends to be high or very high in most European parliaments. Party voting unity can be defined as the extent to which parliamentarians from the same parliamentary party group vote the same way in floor divisions (Depauw and Martin 2009). The impact of high levels of party voting unity is to make decision-making in the parliament something of a fait accompli. A prime minister with a parliamentary majority and high levels of parliamentary party group voting unity has de facto full control over the legislative process, and anything else parliament does or is supposed to do.

Party voting unity—the basis of a strong party parliament—has one of two fundamental sources. The first is what can be termed parliamentary party cohesion. The second is what can be termed parliamentary party discipline. Because both are fundamental to understanding party voting unity—with consequences for the balance of power between the executive and parliament—we discuss each in turn.

Parliamentary party cohesion is a phenomenon where parliamentarians from the same party share the same set of policy preferences on all policy issues. Thus, cohesion reflects the fact that would-be politicians think carefully about which party to join and ultimately affiliate with a party that shares an individual's policy positions and concerns. Thus, in a multiparty system, a parliamentarian will choose a party that best shares that individual's set of preferences (in a two-party system, it is less likely that a party can be cohesive across multiple policy areas; thus we speak of parliamentary party groups in two-party systems as being ideologically heterogeneous, or 'broad churches'). Ultimately, when it comes to voting on the floor of the chamber, observed voting unity may be caused by high levels of parliamentary party cohesion. If so, members of the same parliamentary party group vote the same way in legislative divisions because they share the same underlying policy and ideological preferences. Occasionally, parliamentarians may switch party to join a party that better reflects their policy preferences and priorities.

Party discipline can be an alternative source of party voting unity. Parliamentary party group discipline refers to the ability of the party leadership to enforce a common voting position within the parliamentary party group, especially where it results in a member not voting in line with his/her own preferences. In practical terms, it is some combination of leadership-induced discipline and ideological cohesion within parliamentary party groups that facilitates the party-based voting that makes the cabinet able to exert such de facto influence over parliamentarians.

Where does party discipline come from? The answer involves carrots and sticks. Perhaps the most important carrot available to the party leadership is the ability to control a parliamentarian's promotion to leadership positions within the party, parliament, and/or government. It could be argued that, once elected, parliamentarians in parliamentary systems are motivated by the desire to gain leadership positions, which they hope will ultimately lead to a ministerial seat (Strøm 1997). The allocation of such political offices—sometimes referred to as 'mega-seats'—is typically at the discretion of the party leader. Mega-seats can include cabinet seats, junior ministerial positions, and offices of extra responsibility within the parliament including the speakership (presiding officer) and committee chairs. In effect, the party leadership can use the potential for promotion within parliament or to the ranks of government as a form of control over individual parliamentarians. The more opportunities exist for promotion, the more parliamentarians will be inclined to obey the party leadership.

Allocation of mega-seats occurs by a variety of means: a strictly non-partisan election involving all legislators as independent voters can occur, either by secret vote or open roll-call. Election of the Speaker of the British House of Commons is an issue for the House as a whole and occurs without involvement of the party leaders. In many other cases, however, the leadership of the parliamentary party group retains formal or effective rights over mega-seat allocation. For example, the prime minister is usually the leader of a political party, and typically enjoys formal control over the allocation of other mega-seats within government, such as ministerial positions. Party leader-centred allocation of mega-seats induces loyalty to the party leadership. In contrast, if the party leadership has no control over the allocation of mega-seats (because of, for example a seniority-based allocation system), individual parliamentarians are much freer to act within the parliamentary arena as they themselves see fit.

If promotion to leadership roles provides a powerful carrot to induce discipline from otherwise 'rebellious' parliamentarians, various sticks may be equally, or even more, powerful tools in the hands of party leaders (and the party whips—the party leadership responsible for ensuring parliamentarians vote along party lines). The strongest stick that may be available to a party leader is the ability to suspend or expel a parliamentarian from the parliamentary party group for voting against the party position. Suspension (or expulsion) does not mean that a parliamentarian loses their seat in parliament—only that they have been removed from membership of the parliamentary party. Any such reaction by the leadership to indiscipline is as extreme as it is effective; a member must weigh voting against the parliamentary party group against their continued membership of the group. In some parties, suspension is automatic for members who break the party whip; in others it is not. In some cases of suspension, a member is automatically readmitted after a period of time; in other cases they have to reapply for membership. In the case of multiple breaches of voting unity, a member may find themselves expelled, although this is clearly a nuclear option.

De-selection as a candidate for the party at the next general election is another powerful tool that the party leadership may have available to discipline members. Candidate selection may be more or less centralized in the party leadership. The more control the party leader exercises over the ability of incumbent parliamentarians to be re-selected as a candidate for the party, the less likely individual parliamentarians will be to exercise autonomy from the party in how they vote in parliament. Likewise, in party-list electoral systems, if a party leader determined an incumbent's placement on the party list, incumbents seeking re-election need to be conscious that voting against the party position in the chamber may result in the leadership moving the member further away from the (prized) top of the list.

Of course, individual parliamentarians may have other incentives to remain loyal to the party leadership or rebel and vote against the party. For example, the distinction between candidate- or party-centred electoral systems discussed previously may also shape legislators' willingness to be disciplined: having to cultivate a personal vote and geographical interests may lead a legislator to break from the party line (Carey and Shugart 1995). It is often assumed that candidate-centred elections (such as elections with open-list electoral systems) promote relatively weak levels of party voting unity and congruence between constituency preferences and representative behaviour, and a strong committee system privileging individual members over political parties. In contrast, party-centred electoral systems (where voters vote for a party rather than an individual candidate) can produce strong party legislatures, making party labels the defining explanation of individual legislative behaviour in many legislatures. In short, whether or not incumbents need to cultivate a personal vote or a party vote defines incumbents' interests and behaviour (Carey and Shugart 1995).

For Huber (1996), one important source of party discipline is the vote of confidence procedure—'an institutional prerogative that permits the government to attach the vote on a specific policy or program to an up or down vote on the government' (Huber 1996: 269). The consequences of this procedure are significant but simple: a government can threaten to dissolve the legislature unless the legislature votes for the government's policies (see Chapter 7). As the government must resign if it loses a vote of confidence, the fate of the cabinet and the legislature is tied directly to the fate of the cabinet's bill, if the cabinet so wishes. Members of the government's legislative coalition face a significant choice: support the government or cause a general election, with all the personal and collective costs and risks associated with this.

9.5 Conclusion

What roles should and do parliaments play within the political system of European countries and how should parliaments be structured to perform the role we want them to perform? Most European democracies today are parliamentary rather than presidential systems. This means that they are designed in such a way that the executive is politically responsible to parliaments, with parliament playing at least a formal role in executive oversight, representation, law-making, and deciding who governs and for how long. Similarly, semi-presidential systems (such as Lithuania, Portugal, Serbia, Romania, and France) share with parliamentary systems the need for the executive to be responsible to parliament.

In terms of oversight, representation, and law-making, developments external to the parliament itself may have the effect of making the executive more influential vis-à-vis parliament in recent decades. Richardson and Jordan (1979) write of 'post-parliamentary democracy' in Europe—with public policy being controlled by executives in consultation with extra-parliamentary entities such as trade unions or interest groups, leaving little room for parliament to influence decision-making and public policy. Globalization, and in some instances regional, economic, and political integration (for example, the European Union), have further challenged the ability of national parliaments to influence the executive's public policy agenda (see Chapter 17). And Pogunkte and Webb (2005: 5) suggest a presidentialization of parliamentary systems—which they define as 'the development of increasing leadership power resources and autonomy within the party and the political executive respectively, and increasingly leadership-centred electoral processes'—further weakens the role of parliament and enhances the role of party leaders. Moreover, the need for public policy to evolve rapidly in times of crisis, such as during a global health pandemic, can further marginalize parliaments from being at the very heart of political decision-making and oversight.

Yet for all the talk of the decline of parliaments, others point to the continued centrality of national parliaments within European countries. Some have suggested that parliaments are more central to political life than heretofore acknowledged (Martin et al. 2014). Much of the 'optimistic' scholarship on the centrality of parliaments has stressed the unobserved but nonetheless significant role that parliamentarians and parliaments exert on the executive's policy agenda. For example, Norton (2013) suggests that the UK parliament has reasserted itself in the twentieth century and is today a 'policy-influencing' legislature. Elections in 2010 and 2017 in the UK resulted in a 'hung' parliament (a parliament where no single political party has a majority of seats). The resulting coalition government (2010–15) and minority government (2017–19) are a reminder of how parliamentary arithmetic can all of a sudden change, and require a heretofore powerful prime minister to caution their agendas. Raunio (2009) suggests that legislatures in Europe have adapted to globalization and European integration, fighting back against extra-parliamentary policy production. Parliaments are ever-evolving institutions with many parliaments around Europe seeking to enhance their capacity.

Moreover, while citizens' confidence in their national legislature may not be particularly strong, such antipathy mirrors the general antipathy to political institutions that has afflicted most European countries. Looking at twelve European countries between 1981 and 2009, Dyrstad et al. (2013: 166) find that 'confidence in parliament follows quiet closely trust in other large institutions, both political and private'. When faced with a choice of abolishing a legislative chamber, otherwise politically disillusioned voters may vote to retain the second chamber, as a 2014 Irish referendum illustrates (MacCarthaigh and Martin 2015). Clearly, then, despite the decades of research suggesting that parliaments are being side-lined and dominated by parties and executives, more recent scholarship has been less willing to 'write off' parliaments, instead pointing to their ongoing, and perhaps even increasing, role in the political system.

Discussion questions

1. What are the most important roles and functions of a national parliament?
2. How can the institutional capacity of a parliament to monitor the government be improved?
3. How does descriptive representation vary across European parliaments, what explains the variation, and why does it matter?
4. How does the formal role of parliament in government formation vary across European parliaments?
5. Why is parliamentary party group voting unity so high in most European parliaments?
6. Do executives really dominate parliaments in Europe?

Thinking comparatively

All parties and legislatures, like most organizations generally, are structured according to some form of hierarchy, such that some MPs are promoted to positions of power in the party, parliament, and/or government, while others continue to sit on the backbenches. Rules—often in a country's constitution—may shape exactly who can serve in cabinet. In some countries, for example, the cabinet or most members of the cabinet must be drawn from the parliament (for example, Ireland), in other countries this is not a requirement (for example, Norway), and in other countries ministerial office may require a parliamentarian to forgo membership of the parliament (for example, France). But beyond any such institutionally imposed boundaries, which MPs become ministers, and why?

Existing research suggests that the probability of promotion to cabinet is related to a parliamentarian's length of time in parliament (seniority), electoral popularity (in preferential electoral systems), education, gender, policy preferences, and other less tangible personal traits (see, for example, Dowding and Dumont 2008).

Smith and Martin (2017) consider one previously unexplored source of potential inequality of opportunity in ministerial selection: the existence of powerful family dynasties in some political systems. Specifically, they investigate whether and how parliamentarians who come from such dynasties, what they call 'legacies', possess advantages over non-legacies in promotion from the backbench to the cabinet.

They distinguish between two types of legacies among MPs: cabinet legacies whose predecessors had experience as cabinet ministers; and non-cabinet legacies whose predecessors never advanced beyond the backbenches. They argue that cabinet legacies should be expected to enjoy a larger advantage over fellow MPs in gaining promotion from the backbenches to the cabinet. This is because cabinet legacies inherit the tacit knowledge, political resources, high-level connections, and family track record in cabinet that helps them to stand out above their co-partisan peers in ministerial selection.

They test their prediction with data from Irish parliamentary elections and cabinets from 1944 to 2016. The results of their analyses reveal that, although cabinet legacies and non-cabinet legacies enjoy equally significant electoral advantages, only cabinet legacies enjoy an advantage in ministerial selection.

This research on political dynasties and ministerial selection points to a potential inequality in access to positions of power in parliamentary systems, with broad implications for our understanding of the development of democracy and representative government.

Guide to further reading

Bäck, H. and Debus, M. (2016), *Political Parties, Parliaments and Legislative Speechmaking* (Basingstoke: Palgrave Macmillan).

Back, H., Debus, M. and Fernandes, J.M. (eds.) (2021), *The Politics of Legislative Debates* (Oxford: Oxford University Press).

Proksch, S. O. and Slapin, J. B. (2015), *The Politics of Parliamentary Debate* (Cambridge: Cambridge University Press).

These three books provide cutting-edge research on the politics of parliamentary speeches. For a long time, scholars studying what members do focused on roll-call votes, committee membership, and constituency service. More recently, technological and methodological developments have allowed scholars to systematically explore parliamentary speeches: which members get to talk and what they say. Of course, a fundamental question remains: who, if anyone, is listening to parliamentary speeches? It could be nobody, but then why would parliaments bother to speak? Most likely, speeches are forms of communication between members, leaders, the party membership, and voters.

Huber, J. D. (1996), *Rationalizing Parliament: Legislative Institutions and Party Politics in France* (Cambridge: Cambridge University Press).

It is generally acknowledged that the framers of France's 5th Republic aimed for a strengthened executive by means of a weakened National Assembly. In this seminal contribution Huber reviews a set of restrictive parliamentary procedures that are assumed to privilege the cabinet in the French legislative process. Huber's work illustrates the co-dependence between parliament and executives in Europe.

Martin, S., Saalfeld, T. and Strøm, K. (eds.) (2014), *The Oxford Handbook of Legislative Studies* (Oxford: Oxford University Press).

This book provides a very detailed overview of research on parliament around the world. Although not limited to European countries, the book explores the theoretical and methodological foundations of legislative studies as well as the structures and functions of parliaments.

Martin, S. and Strøm, K. (2023), *Legislative Assemblies: Voters, Members, and Leaders* (Oxford: Oxford University Press).

This book suggests that all national parliaments face the twin challenges of institutional capacity and accountability to their citizens. In addressing these challenges, assemblies vary in the extent to which they serve the respective interests of three critical sets of actors: their members, party leaders, and voters. The authors identify three ideal types of democratic parliaments—the members' assembly, the leaders' assembly, and the voters' assembly—and analyze national legislative assemblies in the world's sixty-eight most populous democracies in light of these models. Based on extensive new cross-national data, they trace the implications of the three assembly types for the design, internal organization, resources, and powers of democratic national assemblies, develop indices of each assembly type, and score each of the sixty-eight legislative assemblies on these indices.

Rasch, B. E., Martin, S. and Cheibub, J.A.. (eds.) (2015), *Parliaments and Government Formation: Unpacking Investiture Rules* (Oxford: Oxford University Press).

This book seeks to unpack the precise role of parliaments in government formation. The focus of this book is on the parliamentary investiture vote. As noted, investiture consists of a vote in parliament to demonstrate that an already-formed or about-to-be-formed government has legislative support. Surprisingly little has been written on the formal role of parliaments in government formation, despite the centrality of the function.

References

Bagehot, W. (1867), *The English Constitution* (London: Chapman and Hall).

Bawn, K. and Rosenbluth, F. (2006), 'Short versus long coalitions: Electoral accountability and the size of the public sector', *American Journal of Political Science*, 50(2): 251–65.

Bryce, J. (1921), *Modern Democracies* (London: Macmillan).

Campion, L. (1953), 'Second chambers in theory and practice', *Parliamentary Affairs*, 7(1): 17–32.

Carey, J. M. and Shugart, M. S. (1995), 'Incentives to cultivate a personal vote: A rank ordering of electoral formulas', *Electoral Studies*, 14(4): 417–39.

Chernykh, S., Doyle, D., and Power, T.J. (2017), 'Measuring legislative power: An expert reweighting of the Fish-Kroenig Parliamentary Powers Index', *Legislative Studies Quarterly*, 42(2): 295–320.

Cox, G. W. (1987), *The Efficient Secret: The Cabinet and the Development of Political Parties in Victorian England* (Cambridge: Cambridge University Press).

Depauw S. and Martin, S. (2009), 'Legislative party discipline and cohesion in comparative perspective', in D. Giannetti and K. Benoit (eds.), *Intra-Party Politics and Coalition Governments in Parliamentary Democracies* (Abingdon: Routledge).

Dowding, K. and Dumont, P. (eds.) (2008), *The Selection of Ministers in Europe: Hiring and Firing* (Abingdon: Routledge).

Dyrstad K. and Listhaug O. (2013), 'Citizens' confidence in European parliaments: Institutions and issues', in W. Müller and H. Narud (eds.), *Party Governance and Party Democracy* (New York: Springer).

Field, B. N. and Martin, S. (eds.). (2022). *Minority Governments in Comparative Perspective*. Oxford: Oxford University Press.

Gilligan, T. W. and Krehbiel, K. (1987), 'Collective decision-making and standing committees: An informational rationale for restrictive amendment procedures', *Journal of Law, Economics, & Organization*, 3(2): 287–335.

Huber, J. D. (1996), *Rationalizing Parliament: Legislative Institutions and Party Politics in France* (Cambridge: Cambridge University Press).

Kreppel, A. (2014), 'Typologies and classifications', in S. Martin, T. Saalfeld, and K. W. Strøm (eds.), *The Oxford Handbook of Legislative Studies* (Oxford: Oxford University Press): 82–100.

Lijphart, A. (1999), *Patterns of Democracy: Government Forms and Performance in Thirty-Six Countries* (New Haven, CT: Yale University Press).

MacCarthaigh, M. and Martin, S. (2015), 'Bicameralism in the Republic of Ireland: The Seanad abolition referendum', *Irish Political Studies*, 30(1): 121–31.

Martin, S. and Rozenberg, O. (2014), *The Roles and Function of Parliamentary Questions* (Abingdon: Routledge).

Martin, S. and Whitaker, R. (2019), 'Beyond committees: Parliamentary oversight of coalition government in Britain', *West European Politics*, 42(7): 1464–86.

Martin, S., Saalfeld, T. et al. (eds.) (2014), *The Oxford Handbook of Legislative Studies* (Oxford: Oxford University Press).

Mattson, I. and Strøm, K. (1995), 'Parliamentary committees', in H. Döring (ed.) *Parliaments and Majority Rule in Western Europe* (Mannheim: Manheim Centre for European Social Research): 249–307.

Müller, W. C. and Strøm, K. (eds.) (1999), *Policy, Office, or Votes? How Political Parties in Western Europe Make Hard Decisions* (Cambridge: Cambridge University Press).

Norton, P. (2013), *Parliaments in Contemporary Western Europe* (Abingdon: Routledge).

Ostrogorski, M. (1902), *Democracy and the Organization of Political Parties* (Vol. 2) (London: Macmillan).

Pelizzo, R. and Stapenhurst, F. (2014), *Corruption and Legislatures* (London: Routledge).

Phillips, A. (1995), *The Politics of Presence* (Oxford: Clarendon Press).

Poguntke, T. and Webb, P. (eds.) (2005), *The Presidentialization of Politics: A Comparative Study of Modern Democracies* (Oxford: Oxford University Press).

Raunio, T. (2009), 'National parliaments and European integration: What we know and agenda for future research', *The Journal of Legislative Studies*, 15(4): 317–34.

Rasch, B. E. (2014), 'Institutional foundations of legislative agenda setting', in S. Martin, T. Saalfeld and K. Strøm (eds.), *The Oxford Handbook of Legislative Studies* (Oxford: Oxford University Press): 455–80.

Richardson, J. J. and Jordan G. (1979), *Governing under Pressure: The Policy Process in a Post-Parliamentary Democracy* (Oxford: Martin Robertson).

Russell, M. (2001), 'What are second chambers for?', *Parliamentary Affairs*, 54(3): 442–58.

Smith, D. M. and Martin, S. (2017), 'Political dynasties and the selection of cabinet ministers', *Legislative Studies Quarterly*, 42(1): 131–65.

Strøm, K. (1990), *Minority Government and Majority Rule* (Cambridge: Cambridge University Press).

Strøm, K. (1997), 'Rules, reasons and routines: Legislative roles in parliamentary democracies', *The Journal of Legislative Studies*, 3(1): 155–74.

Strøm, K. (2000), 'Delegation and accountability in parliamentary democracies', *European Journal of Political Research*, 37(3): 261–90.

Strøm, K., Müller, W.C. and Smith, D.M. (2010), 'Parliamentary control of coalition governments', *Annual Review of Political Science*, 13: 517–35.

Taagepera, R. (1972), 'The size of national assemblies', *Social Science Research*, 1(4): 385–401.

Tsebelis, G. and Money, J. (1997), *Bicameralism* (Cambridge: Cambridge University Press).

10 Constitutions and Courts

NUNO GAROUPA AND PEDRO C. MAGALHÃES

10.1 Introduction

What is a 'constitution'? One way to answer this question is to define a *constitution*, regardless of whether it is called by that name or not, as a set of written texts with two basic features. First, following the seminal definition by political scientist Samuel Finer (1915–93), a constitution serves to 'regulate the allocation of functions, powers and duties among the various agencies and offices of government, and define the relationship between these and the public' (Finer 1979: 15). Second, a constitution is also the *highest* law, not only in the sense that all ordinary laws, statutes, and regulations need to abide by it but also that the requirements for its approval and amendment are somewhat more stringent that those posed to pass ordinary legislation.

One of the consequences of having a constitution is that certain rights (for example, the right to free speech) will be protected independently of who is in power. Constitutions also make it more difficult for politicians to change the rules of government to benefit themselves, for example by changing presidential term limits or altering the division of power between different branches of government. Therefore, a constitution introduces and imposes constrained government. Constrained government is an important characteristic of liberal democracy; unconstrained government places too much power in the hands of the political branches (the legislature and executive).

Constitutions also introduce risks: too much inflexibility can undermine the effectiveness of public policies and create a danger of rule by those who designed the constitution (the 'founding fathers') or by those who have the role of determining what the constitution means (in most European countries, judges). Therefore, there is a general constitutional dilemma: how much to protect and regulate under the constitution, and how much power to allocate to the people and the institutions entitled to determine the constitutionality of laws and acts of parliament and government. Historically, we find many ways of addressing this dilemma, as discussed in the next Section 10.2.

Constitutions, and the extension of *constitutional review* whereby courts review legislation and decide whether constitutional rights have been violated, vary significantly in Europe (see Sections 10.4 and 10.5). However, constitutional review, at least one that is minimally effective and where courts enjoy at least some guarantees of independence, is usually absent in non-democratic regimes. Several recent developments in Europe have shown precisely that the survival of liberal democracy also hinges on the role of courts, and that old debates about democracy and constitutionalism remain very much alive (see Section 10.3). In countries like Hungary or Poland, for example, reforms have been introduced by the government that limit judicial independence and weaken constitutional review (see Section 10.3.5). Many observers have referred to a movement in the direction of 'illiberal' forms of democracy that have rendered courts too weak to oppose the concentration of political power (e.g. Scheppele 2018; Ginsburg et al. 2018).

There are also dangers associated with the opposite scenario, whereby constitutional courts become too powerful and act more like another political branch of government that is involved in making policy decisions rather than acting as an impartial interpreter of the constitution. As we shall see, however, fears about the 'judicialization of politics' in Europe have been generally exaggerated so far (see Section 10.6 'The political impact of constitutional adjudication').

New debates have also emerged because of European integration (see Section 10.7). Unlike other areas of the world, Europe has strong supranational courts, which are very important in understanding the legal construction and development of protected rights as well as the limits to the political branches of government. Can the European Union (EU) be said to have a 'constitution'? Are constitutions of member states subject to European Union law or case law from the European Court of Human Rights? Opinions vary, and no consensus yet exists on these important issues.

10.2 Constitutions

10.2.1 Historical evolution of constitutionalism in Europe

The oldest written and codified constitution in force is that of the United States. It dates from 1787 and is a short written document with seven articles defining the three branches of government (legislative, executive, and judicial), federalism (the relationship between the federal government and the states), and the procedure for its approval and amendment. Now it also includes twenty-seven amendments (out of thirty-three proposed amendments sent to states for ratification). Furthermore, in the United States, there is 'judicial review': all courts, in the course of their activity in settling disputes and determining the applicable law, are entitled to decide whether statutes conflict with the 'supreme law of the land'—the Constitution—with a Supreme Court enjoying final jurisdiction over such cases.

Constitutionally, Europe looked quite different from the United States (US) in 1787. Today, all European countries have their own constitution. But not all constitutions are the same, and not all were inspired by the American model. European constitutions respond to specific challenges related to a diverse political and social history. It is common to talk about 'waves' of constitutionalism.

A first wave refers to the US Constitution and to several European constitutions of the nineteenth century, some of them still in force, such as in Norway (1814), the Netherlands (1815), Belgium (1831), and Denmark (1849). They limit the power of the government and introduce the rule of law (as guarantor of individual rights against the state).

Second-wave constitutionalism encompasses the period immediately after World War II. It includes countries such as Germany, France, and Italy, and tends to be characterized by the creation of specialized bodies in charge of constitutional review: constitutional courts detached from the regular judiciary put in charge of scrutinizing whether legislation respects the constitution.

Finally, we have third-wave constitutionalism. These are constitutions largely enacted after the 1970s, in the aftermath of right-wing (in Greece, Portugal, and Spain) or communist (in many Central- and Eastern-European countries) dictatorships. They were heavily influenced by the German, French, and Italian experiences, particularly in the adoption of constitutional courts. However, these constitutions also tend to deal more extensively with social and economic rights (such as the right to housing) than those of the second wave.

10.2.2 **Contemporary European constitutions**

Although the definition of 'constitution' stated in the introduction may seem reasonably consensual, the debates around it can become endless. For example, do all European states have a constitution? The answer might seem an obvious 'Yes', but only until we reach British shores. What is called the 'British Constitution' is the result of the accumulation of many laws and unwritten political norms rather than a codified set of legal rules seen as 'the highest law of the land'. This seems to shift the answer to 'No' for the UK. However, that would also ignore two facts.

First, the UK's 'constitution' does contain many written norms. Second, the ways in which constitutions work and are applied rely on informal mechanisms just about everywhere, and not just in the UK. And although the written British constitutional rules can be changed by parliament as any other law—therefore making it 'flexible' rather than 'rigid'—flexibility vs. rigidity in the European context is more a matter of degree than a dichotomy. As we shall see, amending the constitution is only marginally more difficult in some European countries than in the UK. Therefore, for the purposes of this chapter, it is perhaps better to acknowledge that the UK represents a unique case in the European context—although not in the world—whose features, nonetheless, can be placed in a comparative perspective.

European constitutions can be very different from each other in many respects. They vary, for example, in length. While the Constitution of Iceland contains about 4,000 words—the length of, say, a short story—the Constitution of Austria is more than ten times longer—longer, in fact, than any of Shakespeare's plays (*Hamlet* is barely over 30,000 words). This already suggests that some constitutions go into much greater detail than others in specifying rules for the topics they cover.

What topics are those? Following Finer's useful definition stated in the introduction, the first type of rules all constitutions contain concerns 'the relationship between the government and the public'. Such a relationship is normally codified as a set of rights. Rights come in different types. 'Negative rights' are those not to have something done to you, particularly (but not only) by the government. Freedom of speech and from arbitrary arrest, unreasonable search and seizure, or expropriation without compensation fall in this category. Other rights are 'positive', in the sense that they configure individual entitlements to things that need to be provided, especially by the government (thus becoming a constitutional duty for the state). Social and economic rights, for example to health, education, or housing (also known as 'second-generation rights'), are included here. Finally, there are also 'collective rights' (also known as 'third-generation rights'), referring to group entitlements to common goods (minority-language education, cultural heritage, and so on).

These distinctions between types of rights can become slippery very quickly. Some argue that only first-generation or negative rights are really 'rights', as all they require is non-interference, while the remaining ones are subject to the availability of scarce resources and are not always enforceable by courts. Others have noted that rights normally conceived as 'negative' (say, property rights) or 'first generation' (say, voting rights) could hardly be protected without governments using scarce resources to actively 'do things', including registering property and protecting it against usurpation or registering voters and organizing elections. Others still have made a stronger claim in favour of social and economic rights, arguing that, absent the fulfilment of the most basic needs, some 'first-generation' rights cannot be said to be enjoyed at all. Finally, other rights, such as those protecting particular groups from discrimination—defined in terms of ethnicity, religion, nationality, sexual orientation, or gender identity, for example—defy simple classification: while addressing entitlements of social groups (third-generation), they also aim at providing individuals the 'negative right' of freedom from arbitrary and unequal treatment (first-generation). The conceptual and normative discussion could go on much further.

However, we can perhaps draw out two of the most important empirical points. First, European constitutions vary a lot depending on the extent to which they mention and develop these different types of rights. While more than nine out of ten current European constitutional texts explicitly mention, for example, freedom of expression, the notion that there is a right to health care is present in little more than half of them, and only a small number of them specify an attached state duty to provide it. Formalized protection of particular groups from discrimination is also very asymmetric: for example, while the vast majority of constitutions include clauses of equal treatment on the basis of gender or race, only two European constitutions do the same on the basis of sexual orientation and gender identity, with an additional two providing protection based solely on sexual orientation (Raub et al. 2016). In other words, the typical 'first-generation' rights are more universally present in the constitutions of Europe than other types of rights.

Second, the presence of (at least some) social and economic rights has been on an upward long-term historical trajectory, with post-World War II constitutions more likely to adopt extensive catalogues of social and economic rights. Constitutions such as the Portuguese and most of the post-communist countries include rights to education, health, or housing, for example. It is an entirely different question whether the constitutional consecration of those rights leads to their effective protection through measures such as welfare spending. The same can also be said about 'first-generation' rights: freedom of expression or speech are 'protected' in the constitutions of Russia, Belarus, and Azerbaijan, while no specific explicit provision for it exists in the Austrian, Dutch, or French constitutions. The reality of free speech protection in these countries, however, judging from most available cross-national indicators provided by observers such as Freedom House or Reporters Without Borders, suggests that the relationship between the constitutional formalization of a right to free speech and its effective protection is very far from perfect. It is therefore important to keep in mind that constitutions can also serve, in some cases, to describe aspirations, as is often the case with second- and third-generation rights, while in others even first-generation constitutional rights can be little more than legal cheap talk (Ginsburg and Simpser 2014).

The second main type of rules typically contained in constitutions have to do with 'the allocation of functions, powers and duties among the various agencies and offices of government'. This may include the structure of the executive, legislative, and judicial branches, as well as of those of other regulatory and oversight bodies (such as central banks or ombudspersons, for example); rules establishing the powers and competencies of sub-national levels of government and their relationship with the national level; rules determining the election, appointment, retention, and dismissal of all these bodies; and rules about how they make decisions, alone or in combination.

It is here that we normally find the answers to many of the questions that students of comparative politics pose about what makes political institutions different from each other. Is the head of state elected or hereditary? If elected, is she elected by universal suffrage or, for example by parliament (with the latter typically corresponding to a parliamentary system)? If elected by the people, is she the head of the executive (a presidential system) or is there also a prime minister responsible before an elected parliament (a semi-presidential system)? Term limits, electoral systems, second chambers, and the division of authority between regional and central governments are among the myriad of similar topics typically addressed by constitutions with differing amounts of detail.

From this follow two additional functions that constitutions perform. On the one hand, this allocation of functions, powers, and duties determines the extent to which constitutions end up constraining the power of majorities in policymaking, and thus the extent to which protections of the rights of individuals and those of social, cultural, or political minorities that may be already prescribed in the constitution are reinforced (or not). On the other hand, as the works of foremost theorists like Barry Weingast and Russell Hardin have helped us realize, constitutions allow social, economic, and political agents to coordinate around a set of rules that are commonly known and can be credibly presumed to be stable (Weingast 1997; Hardin 1999).

Finally, constitutions contain rules of a third type: those dictating how constitutional rules themselves can be changed. There is great variation here too. The United Kingdom represents one of the cases of greatest flexibility in Europe. Matters such as removing the veto powers and the composition of the House of Lords, creating a Supreme Court, and devolving powers to Scotland and Wales, for example, have been dealt with by approving acts of parliament by majority rule (there were referendums on devolution in Scotland and Wales, but they were not binding). In Sweden, constitutional amendments require only simple majorities in parliament, although two decisions separated by a general election need to be made (binding referendums can also be called, although they are not compulsory). At the other (more rigid) end, amending the Spanish constitution requires the approval of a qualified majority of three-fifths in both lower and upper chambers and, if requested by just 10% of parliamentarians, a referendum, with the rules becoming even more demanding for some sections of the constitution. In Belgium, the two chambers must approve a declaration of constitutional amendment by absolute majority, and elections for those chambers need to be held, followed by the need to pass amendments by a qualified majority of two-thirds in both chambers.

Indices aiming at capturing the rigidity of constitutions, sometimes with not entirely overlapping results, have been devised (Lorenz 2005). In general, more bodies involved in proposing and approving amendments (and with more divergent preferences), the use of qualified majority rules (absolute or even two-thirds or four-fifths majorities), time constraints, requirements for new elections, referendums, and special quorum rules for those referendums are all aspects that, especially if cumulated, can make the constitutional status quo very hard to change.

How flexible or rigid should constitutions be? Extremely flexible constitutions risk defeating some of the very purposes of having a constitution in the first place. Coordination around a structure of government, the perception that governments' commitments to particular courses of action are credible, and the limitation of abuses by majorities seem difficult to obtain under extreme flexibility. Of particular concern is the possibility that such flexibility is used to design entirely new rules that will protect the interests of those who happen to be in power. For example, less rigid constitutions can be more easily changed by current majorities to design electoral rules that favour them or to reduce the political independence of the bodies (judiciaries, constitutional courts, central banks, and the like) that might limit the power of those majorities. The Hungarian 2011 constitution and its 2013 amendments, approved without any other constraint besides a two-thirds majority requirement in a single chamber of parliament, exemplifies the power-aggrandizement risks of a relatively flexible constitution (see Section 10.3.5').

However, extreme rigidity can be problematic as well. Constitutional rules reflect, to a large extent, compromises between existing social and political forces. The inability to amend the constitution in response to changes in the relevance of those forces does not mean that it will survive longer: instead, it may dictate it will end up being subverted and converted into 'window-dressing', or even ultimately overthrown. Studies using the data from the Comparative Constitutions Project show precisely that both extreme flexibility and extreme rigidity are negatively related with the endurance of constitutions (Elkins et al. 2009).

We should be wary of assigning excessive importance to constitutions in terms of their contribution to promote 'good' social, political, or economic outcomes. A particular outcome—democratic stability, prosperity, peaceful resolution of conflicts, high standards of rights protection—can seem to result from a particular constitution but can in fact be caused by the very conditions that made constitutions the way they are in the first place. And yet, constitutions matter. Once a constitution is in place, and if reasonably well-known and seen as legitimate by citizens, political actors considering violating its rules know there will be a likely price to pay—declining public support, electoral punishment, or, ultimately, citizen resistance. Still, this can only be expected if we all know what the constitution actually says. This is where courts step in.

10.3 **Courts**

Because of their legal and political nature, constitutions may sometimes be unclear, vague, imprecise, or ambiguous. They may have been written in a language that induces varying or doubtful interpretations by different political actors. It could be that, in some circumstances, the constitution does not offer clear and determinate guidelines, because not all possible states of the world were predicted by the constitutional drafters. For example, an article in the Irish constitution, introduced by way of a referendum in 1983 and repealed in 2018, established the constitutional right to life of the unborn with due respect to equal right to life of the mother. This, however, immediately raises uncertainty as to what constituted 'a risk to the life of the mother'. In fact, generations change, and semantics evolve. In essence, constitutions are intrinsically incomplete: they do not specify or arrange for what each actor should do in every possible circumstance or in each contingency. Therefore, people can have disagreements over what a constitution says or dictates. When such disagreements exist, there is a need for an institution that addresses this problem.

There are two possible solutions to this quest: legislative supremacy or third-party review. Under legislative supremacy, the legislative body (parliament) decides what the constitution says and therefore, there is no constraint to elected representatives. Under third-party review, a separate institution tells the different branches of government what the constitution says, which inevitably restricts elected representatives. There are a number of alternatives to third-party review. One option is for courts of law to interpret the constitution; that is, exercise constitutional review while also performing judicial review of matters such as criminal law or litigation between private individuals, thus acting as the last court of appeal for non-constitutional matters. A second option is for a specialized body, such as a constitutional court, whose only function is to engage in constitutional review. Or there can be a combination of both of these options: i.e., there is a specialized body such as a constitutional court, but courts of law can also set aside statutes under certain conditions.

In Europe, all these arrangements coexist. As we can see from Table 10.1, most countries have opted for the specialized body model. These are typically known as a constitutional court. In France it is called the Constitutional Council, and Constitutional Law Committee in Finland. Other countries rely on judicial courts such as a high court to perform constitutional review (mainly the Scandinavian countries). Two countries, the Netherlands and the United Kingdom, have legislative supremacy (no formal constitutional review). In the following subsections we first assess the arguments for and against constitutional review, before going on to take a closer look at some of these examples.

10.3.1 **Arguments against and for constitutional review**

There are two distinct arguments against constitutional review (Waldron 2006). One line of reasoning argues that constitutional rights are not necessarily better protected by courts of law than by democratic legislatures. Another argument is that third-party constitutional review of legislation approved by a directly elected parliament lacks democratic legitimacy. Both ideas revolve around the notion that elected representatives, rather than unelected judges, are in a better position to interpret constitutional norms. From this point of view, allowing judges to determine what is constitutional subverts democratic majority rule. At the same time, since judges are not truly neutral (they have their own ideas about the world), constitutional review generates a trend for increasing 'judicialization' of politics, whereby judges and courts become more involved in political decisions (see Section 10.5). This affects democratic legitimacy so, it is argued, legislative supremacy is more adequate.

Table 10.1 Courts and constitutional review in Europe

Constitutional Court	Constitutional Council	Constitutional Law Committee	High Court	Without constitutional review
Austria	France	Finland	Denmark	Netherlands
Belgium*			Estonia	UK
Bosnia-Herzegovina			Greece	
Bulgaria			Iceland	
Croatia			Ireland	
Czech Rep.			Norway	
Germany			Sweden	
Hungary			Switzerland	
Italy				
Latvia				
Lithuania				
Luxembourg				
Malta				
Montenegro				
Poland				
Portugal#				
Romania				
Serbia				
Slovakia				
Slovenia				
Spain				

Note: * Although classified as High Court or Special Senate of the High Court, since May 2007, the institution engaged in constitutional review has been named Constitutional Court (replacing the old Court of Arbitration).

Classified as mixed system because regular courts can also exercise constitutional review.

Source: Reproduced with permission from © Dr. Arne Mavčič. Available at: http://www.concourts.net/tab/tab1.php?lng=en&stat=1&prt=0&srt=0.

The opposing view suggests that, unlike judges, elected representatives do not consider long-term considerations and are prone to respond to partisan interests. Therefore, constitutional review by a third party, such as a constitutional court, is helpful. It imposes effective boundaries to majority rule (hence, preventing the legislative majority from abusing its power). Courts are in a better position to determine which rights are affected or conditioned by the new legislation. Therefore, dialogue between the judiciary and politicians improves legal decision-making and reinforces constitutional rights (Ely 1981).

We also need to explain why elected representatives would be willing to accept constitutional review rather than promote legislative supremacy (Ginsburg and Versteeg 2014). There are four possible explanations for why politicians simply decide to delegate to constitutional institutions the refereeing of possible political conflicts. The first is that politicians are philosophical: they recognize the importance of political and social rights, and the rule of law. The second is that, by accepting constitutional review, politicians are adopting a sort of political insurance strategy: they may lose power in the future and therefore favour a system of constitutional review to minimize possible policy losses when other politicians take power. The third is that politicians realize that there is a need for constitutional review to address possible conflicts across states (in federal systems) or diverse ethnic or religious groups. Creating constitutional review in such cases may create valuable opportunities to shift blame for unpopular decisions away from the political branches of government and onto the judiciary. Finally, politicians may be receptive to the global diffusion of ideas and practices and conform to ongoing international trends.

10.3.2 Legislative supremacy: The cases of the UK and the Netherlands

As we have seen, the UK has a written constitution that is not codified into a single text. The principle of parliamentary sovereignty prevails: no parliament can bind a future parliament or be bound by a previous parliament. Courts of law cannot formally set aside statutes on grounds of their unconstitutionality. Formally, no judge can condemn a law and refuse to apply it on the ground that it is incompatible with the constitution or the fundamental principles of the common law (see Box 10.1).

However, recent developments have empowered the courts in remarkable ways. The Human Rights Act 1998 (which made the European Convention on Human Rights part of the British legal system) and the EC Act 1972 (which made European Union law binding in the UK, until it was repealed in 2019 in the wake of Brexit) are the two special cases. A court can issue a declaration of incompatibility (a statute is inconsistent with UK obligations derived from certain provisions under the Human Rights Act 1998). Once a court has issued a declaration of incompatibility, the law remains the same until the parliament removes the identified incompatibility. For example, the Anti-Terrorism, Crime and Security Act 2001 got into trouble at the Appellate Committee of the House of Lords in 2004, which precipitated new legislation, namely the Prevention of Terrorism Act 2005, in order to fix the underlying problem.

More recently, two constitutional law cases adjudicated by the United Kingdom Supreme Court in 2017 (*Miller v. Secretary of State for Exiting the European Union*) and 2019 (*Miller v. The Prime Minister* and *Cherry v Advocate General for Scotland*), known colloquially as the Miller cases, have been praised and criticized for potentially transforming the principle of parliamentary sovereignty. These two landmark decisions limited the powers of the executive in the context of Brexit legislation (for more details see Section 10.6).

Box **10.1** Common law versus civil law

The 'common law' systems prevalent in the English-speaking world are traditionally dominated by case law, i.e. a set of past judicial rulings to be used as precedents applicable to new situations. Judges are usually appointed after they have distinguished themselves in a professional law-related career and their tenure in office is attached to a specific court. In contrast, civil law systems, with their distant origins in the old Roman law imposed in continental Europe, are rooted in the adoption of 'codes', systematic collections of written articles and customs (such as the French Napoleonic code of 1804 or the German *Bürgerliches Gesetzbuch* of 1900) aimed at replacing the various and contradictory local and feudal charters and customs. This also implies a different role for judges: in civil law systems, we tend to find career judiciaries filled with judges who constitute a professional bureaucracy within the state, are subject to some form of evaluation and promotion from superiors, and whose role is mostly conceived as the application of highly detailed commands emanating from a sovereign parliament.

In the Netherlands, the courts are prohibited from exercising constitutional review (Article 120, 'the constitutionality of acts of parliament and treaties shall not be reviewed by the courts'). However, they can declare that the government has exceeded its authority and nullify measures on those grounds, as well as annul acts of parliament that contravene European treaties. For example, in a landmark decision in 2020 (*Urgenda Foundation v. State of the Netherlands*), the Dutch Supreme Court held that the Netherlands has a positive obligation to take measures for the prevention of climate change.

10.3.3 **The case of Germany**

The current German constitution was enacted in 1949 and it is known as the Basic Law. It is not the first written and codified constitution in German history. However, it reflects the experience with previous constitutions, namely those of the German Empire (1871) and of the Weimar Republic (1919), which formally remained in effect during the Nazi period. A major novelty was the creation of a new body, the Constitutional Court, established in 1951, with the power to declare laws unconstitutional when they do not comply with the Basic Law. The German Federal Constitutional Court (*Bundesverfassungsgericht*) is considered by many scholars to be the world model for third-party constitutional review, particularly for new democracies (Kommers 2006).

This was largely a response to a set of concerns within the German tradition. First, the experience of the Weimar Constitution (1919–33) showed that, in the absence of third-party review, a parliamentary majority could manipulate the constitution to the point of abolishing democracy and replacing it with a dictatorship. In fact, technically, the Weimar Constitution was in place until 1945. Germany is also a civil law country operating under a civil code, with judicial review playing a limited role (see Box 10.1). Given the practical impossibility of completely dismantling a part of the state apparatus that overall had been complacent about repression under the Nazi regime (to say the least), the career judiciary could not be trusted with a task as crucial as reviewing the constitutionality of laws.

Therefore, the new German constitution created a parliamentary-appointed special body, a 'constitutional court', which centralizes constitutional review. Centralization empowers this special body to challenge the political branches of government when needed and enhances the protection of constitutional rights. Ordinary courts of law are denied the authority to set aside statutes when they conflict with the constitution. The German Federal Constitutional Court has the exclusive and final word about federal constitutional disputes. However, it only settles constitutional disputes; it cannot address judicial (these are entertained by the regular courts) or political disputes (which are a matter for the political institutions). Each state of Germany has its own constitutional court to address state-level (sub-national) constitutional disputes.

10.3.4 **The case of France**

Like Germany, France belongs to the civil law family. The French legal system is based on the *Code Napoléon*. A major concern in French legal thinking since the days of the French Revolution and Napoleon has been to avoid the *gouvernement de juges*, or government by judges, an expression coined by Édouard Lambert (1866–1947) to characterize American judges who allegedly make use of personal interpretations of the law rather than of 'the letter and the spirit of the law'.

Consequently, constitutional review by courts of law in France was not a popular idea for a long time. Still today ordinary courts are denied the authority to set aside laws passed by parliament when they conflict with the constitution. In 1958, with the new constitution under President Charles de Gaulle, a new body was created: the Constitutional Council (*Conseil constitutionnel*). However, this third-party body was not designed to be a German-style 'constitutional court' but rather a referee between a strong president and the parliamentary institutions. This role was reinforced with important ancillary functions (such as observing fairness in elections). It has centralized constitutional review since the early 1960s. Until the constitutional amendment of 2008 (to be explained in more detail later; see Section 10.4.1), only 'abstract' review was allowed, i.e. the constitutionality of legislation was only examined without connection to particular legal cases in lower courts.

The French Constitutional Council has two particularities worth noting. First, the former presidents of France are lifetime members of the Council (as of 2023, no former president is a sitting member). Second, appointed members do not need to hold a law degree, although most are lawyers by training.

10.3.5 **The cases of Poland and Hungary**

Many of the former socialist countries opted for a constitutional court in their transition to democracy and capitalism. Like in other post-authoritarian or post-totalitarian contexts, regular courts could not be trusted to exercise effective constitutional review at that stage, since career judges had been trained under the old regime. A new body centralizing constitutional review made more sense to protect individual rights and limit the power of a traditionally strong executive (Sadurski 2014).

Unsurprisingly, concentration of power in strong leaders such as Orbán in Hungary (1998–2002 and 2010 to the present, 2023 at the time of writing) or the Kaczyński brothers in Poland (Lech was president of Poland from 2005 until his death in 2010 and Jarosław has been the leader of the Law and Justice Party since 2003) has led to conflicts and subsequent reforms of the judicial system.

In 2011, Hungary approved a new Fundamental Law. Among many controversial aspects (for example, critics claimed that it violated human rights standards), the new constitution replaced the old Supreme Court with a new institution. This led to a conflict with the President of the old Supreme Court, András Baka. He lodged an appeal against Hungary with the European Court of Human Rights in 2012 (*Baka v. Hungary*). The decision was published in 2014 and largely condemned Hungary for the early termination of the Supreme Court president's mandate in the absence of any possibility for judicial review. At the same time, a new constitutional amendment in 2013 has constrained constitutional review (laws passed by a two-thirds majority cannot be annulled). A new judicial reform was approved by the end of 2018 creating a parallel court system. While the Hungarian government has justified this reform as a mechanism to increase efficiency and quality in administrative litigation, many have considered the new administrative courts as another step in eroding the rule of law.

The Polish Constitutional Court crisis started in 2015 with the late appointment of five judges by the old parliamentary majority, an appointment that was refused by the president of Poland. The new parliamentary majority (after the October election, the Law and Justice Party obtained a large majority) elected different judges who were sworn into office by the president. The Constitutional Court ruled a few weeks later that only three of the five original judges had been lawfully elected. A clash between the Constitutional Court, the president, and the Law and Justice Party majority ensued. By late 2015, the Polish parliament (the *Sejm*) passed a reform of the Constitutional Court changing the appointment mechanism and voting rules in the court. More than thirteen other laws affecting the structure of the Polish judiciary have been passed since then.

These developments have been criticized by international observers as threats to the rule of law and disrespectful to individual rights, thus weakening effective constitutional review in these countries. The EU institutions have voiced concerns that the independence of the judiciary is being undermined in both countries. The European Commission initiated proceedings against Poland in 2017 that could ultimately lead to a suspension of EU voting rights, while in 2018 the European Parliament voted in favour of similar action against Hungary. However, member states avoided voting to determine whether there was 'a clear risk of a serious breach' of the EU common values.

In 2020, the European Commission adopted the Rule of Law Conditionality Regulation, giving the EU the power to withhold funding from member states if they are found to have disregarded the rule of law. After Poland and Hungary challenged the regulation, the Court of Justice of the European Union ruled that the EU could withhold funding so long as the rule of law violations threaten 'the sound financial management of the Union budget.' In 2022, both Hungary and Poland were threatened by the European Commission with withholding funding unless certain pro-rule of law reforms were implemented. In a landmark decision (*Commission v. Poland*), in 2023, the Court of Justice of the European Union adjudicated that Poland's 2019 judicial reforms infringed EU law, after the Commission said that the Polish Supreme Court did not enjoy adequate independence and impartiality. According to the Court, 'the value of the rule of law is an integral part of the very identity of the European Union as a common legal order and is given concrete expression in principles containing legally binding obligations for the Member States.'

10.4 **Centralized constitutional review**

As we have seen, constitutional review is carried out by centralized bodies such as constitutional courts in most European countries. The ideas and legal theories of Hans Kelsen (1881–1973) have shaped the design of most constitutional courts in the Western world. In Kelsen's theory of law, ordinary courts are formally subordinate to the legislative branch, and judges must apply the laws as passed by the legislature. Therefore, ordinary courts cannot perform the role of constitutional review. Hence, in order to effectively restrain the legislature and uphold the constitution, there is a need for an extrajudicial organ. Kelsen suggested a centralized body, a 'constitutional court', separate from the conventional judiciary. This court acts as a negative legislator that has the power to reject (but not propose) legislation.

In fact, as we have seen for the cases of second- and third-wave constitutionalism, the centralization of constitutional review in constitutional courts has been important for democratic consolidation in many European countries that transitioned to democracy following a period of authoritarian rule, such as Spain, Poland, and Hungary. In such cases, the judiciary is often closely associated with the old regime, so an independent constitutional court signals a serious commitment to the democratic ideals enshrined in the new constitution. In the following subsections, we examine the way in which constitutional courts perform constitutional review, consider what happens when there is disagreement within constitutional courts, and look at how judges are appointed to constitutional courts.

10.4.1 **Forms of constitutional review**

The application of the Kelsenian model varies from country to country. On the one hand, there is *abstract review*: it occurs when a constitutional court examines the constitutionality of legislation in the 'abstract': are constitutional norms violated by this piece of legislation? Its main role is to filter out unconstitutional statutes. Abstract review of legislation can be *ex ante*, meaning that it can take place *before* legislation has been promulgated and turned into binding law. However, it can also be *ex post*, i.e. *after* legislation has already become enforceable.

Concrete review is different because it involves private parties who see their constitutional rights affected. One possibility comes from litigation in courts of law. A constitutional issue matters for the specific case being litigated, and the court of law refers the matter to the constitutional court. Another possibility is a direct constitutional complaint to the constitutional court. Usually ombudspersons, non-governmental organization (NGO)s, and other bodies are allowed to file a direct petition when a constitutional right has been violated by a public act or government's action. As for private individuals, there is an effectiveness problem—more generous rules allow more individuals to complain but also increase the likelihood of court congestion.

Concrete and abstract review often coexist in systems with a constitutional court (like in Germany or Spain). Abstract review can also exist in countries where constitutional review is done not by a specialized constitutional court but rather by courts of law: the High Court and Supreme Court of Ireland are empowered to pass judgments both under concrete and abstract constitutional review (if asked by the president). Before the 2008 constitutional amendment, the French Constitutional Council could not exercise concrete review. Now, it can entertain referrals from the Supreme Court and the Supreme Administrative Court under the format of a constitutional question.

Thus, the picture is one of considerable and increasing complexity in European courts, as can be seen in Table 10.2. Some courts only exert one of these types of reviews, but others exert both ex-ante and ex-post abstract reviews, and others still exert both abstract and concrete reviews. Furthermore, many constitutional courts have expanded ancillary powers in different, but important, areas, such as verifying elections, regulating political parties (illegalizing them or auditing their accounts), and other relevant political and administrative functions

10.4.2 **Dissenting in constitutional courts**

Since constitutional courts have multiple judges, their decisions can be written by a single judge on behalf of the entire court, but there is also the possibility of each judge delivering their own opinion. In the United Kingdom, individual opinions are still used while decisions written collectively are standard practice in European constitutional courts. In the latter case,

Table 10.2 European constitutional courts (I)

	Germany	**France**	**Italy**	**Spain**	**Portugal**
Name and year of creation	*Bundesverfassungsgericht* (1951)	*Conseil Constitutionnel* (1958)	*Corte costituzionale della Repubblica Italiana* (1955)	*Tribunal Constitucional de España* (1979)	*Tribunal Constitucional* (1982)
Composition	16	9	15	12	13
Appointment	8 by the *Bundestag* and 8 by the *Bundesrat*	3 each by president, senate, and National Assembly	5 each by president, parliament, and judiciary	4 by congress, 4 by senate, 2 by government, and 2 by judiciary	10 by parliament and 3 by constitutional court
Term duration	12	9	9	9	9
Renewable term	No	No	No	Yes, once (if the previous term was less than 3 years)	Yes, once (before 1997); No (after 1997)
Minimum number of career judges	6	0	5	2	6
Abstract review (ex ante)	Yes	Yes	Only for regional laws	Only for international treaties	Yes
Abstract review (*ex post*)	Yes	No	No	Yes	Yes
Concrete review	Yes	Yes (since 2010)	Yes	Yes	Yes
Published separate opinions	Yes	No	No	Yes	Yes

Source: Websites of the Courts, at https://www.venice.coe.int/webforms/documents/default.aspx?pdffile=CDL-STD(1997)020-e; own research.

however, when there is disagreement over the correct decision, separate opinions by individual judges are also possible. They can be concurring (an opinion written by a single judge or a minority of judges that agrees with the majority decision but expresses different or additional reasons) or dissenting (an opinion written by a single judge or a minority of judges that disagrees with the majority decision).

Separate opinions have a weak tradition in the civil law systems. Constitutional review bodies in France, Italy, Austria, and Belgium simply do not allow them. In Germany, they have been allowed since the 1970s but are, in practice, somewhat rare (dissenting opinions are attached in about 6% of the decisions issued by the German Federal Constitutional Court since 1970, usually involving the most salient political controversies such as abortion or asylum). In other constitutional courts, such as Portugal or Spain, they are cast more often.

10.4.3 **Appointment to constitutional courts**

Around Europe, constitutional judges are appointed by heavily politicized bodies. Inevitably this means that political parties play an active role in the selection and appointment process, which opens avenues of influence in relation to judges. The question of how constitutional court judges are appointed is therefore significant. In some cases, judges are appointed by a supermajority in parliament, which tends to result in more consensual constitutional courts. The variety of mechanisms in place to select constitutional judges is illustrated in Tables 10.2 and 10.3, which give examples from a range of countries.

Conformity between the behaviour of constitutional judges and party interests can come about for two main reasons. First, given that constitutional judges are politically chosen, they tend to exhibit the same preferences as the party that selects them. Second, it is also possible that, when the constitutional judges do not have lifetime appointments or have an eye on potential future gains (regardless of whether the terms are renewable or not), they might want to keep on good terms with the party that selected them, as this might affect their future career opportunities. In other words, judges may be aligned with parties for strategic reasons. Available empirical studies show that party alignment does, to an extent, influence the behaviour of judges in European constitutional courts (Garoupa 2019). However, many other non-political factors also influence judicial behaviour. Furthermore, judges also tend to be interested in maintaining a certain status quo that does not hurt the prestige of the constitutional court, thereby keeping some distance from active party politics.

10.5 The political impact of constitutional adjudication

Several observers have noted tendencies towards a rise in judicial intervention in policymaking and in the 'judicialization of politics', or even the very end of 'legislative supremacy' at the hands of massively empowered constitutional courts (Stone Sweet 2000; Hirschl 2011). The scenario they sometimes have in mind is one of a political system where legislative policymaking is predominantly 'majoritarian' rather than 'consensual' (see Chapter 9), with a single-party cohesive parliamentary majority, a generally veto-free legislative process, and a weak second chamber. In that system, rules regulating access to the constitutional court allow political actors not necessarily aligned with the government—opposition MPs or sub-national

Table 10.3 European constitutional courts (II)

	Austria	Belgium	Poland	Hungary	Czech rep.	Slovakia	Slovenia
Name and year of creation	*Verfassungsgerichtshof* (1953)	*Grondwettelijk Hof* (1980)	*Trybunał Konstytucyjny* (1997)	*Magyar Köztársaság Alkotmánybírósága* (1990)	*Ústavní soud c˘eské republiky* (1993)	*Ústavný súd Slovenskej republiky* (1993)	*Ustavno sodišc˘e Republike Slovenije* (1994)
Composition	14 (plus 6 substitute members)	12 (6 Flemish and 6 French)	15	15	15	13	9
Appointment	By federal government, the national council, or the federal council	By federal parliament	By parliament (lower house)	By parliament	By president and senate	By president and national council	By parliament and president
Term duration	Life (retirement at 70)	Life (retirement at 70)	9	9	10	12	9
Renewable term	–	–	No	Yes, once	Yes, once	No	No
Minimum number of career judges	0	0	0	0	0	0	0
Abstract review (ex ante)	Only for acts of federal entities	No	Yes	Yes	No	No	Only for international treaties
Abstract review (*ex post*)	Yes	Yes	Yes	Yes	Yes	Yes	Yes
Concrete review	Yes	Yes	Yes	Yes	Yes	Yes	Yes
Published separate opinions	No	No	Yes	Yes	No	No	Yes

Source: Websites of the Courts, at https://www.venice.coe.int/webforms/documents/default.aspx?pdffile=CDL-STD(1997)020-e; own research.

governments, for example—to refer bills or laws to the court. Judges are, as we saw, appointed by bodies where parties play a direct or indirect role, and the rules for appointment and retention incentivize a judicial behaviour that has been shown to be at least partly in alignment with the appointing party. In this particular scenario, it turns out that the constitutional court often ends up with a majority of judges appointed by the opposition parties.

What is likely to happen under this scenario? The simple answer is that the court is likely to become a kind of 'third chamber'. Political actors (e.g., opposition Members of Parliament (MPs)) who see legislative policy being set away from their preferences will have the opportunity and the incentive to systematically refer legislation to the court. Ultimately, in such a context, the government may even be forced to engage in 'auto-limitation': it will abdicate from passing its preferred policies in parliament in order to prevent opposition referrals and declarations of unconstitutionality. The case of France since the 1980s is often presented as an illustration of this pattern (Stone Sweet 1992, 2000).

However, this extreme scenario of judicial empowerment is unlikely to be replicated in most European democracies most of the time. There are many reasons for that. First, judges' discretion to interpret and apply the constitution and set policy is never absolute. It is not just the fact that many constitutional commands are unequivocal. It is also that the need to cater to the different audiences that matter for judges—political, but also public, legal, and academic—tends to prevent them from becoming single-minded policy-seekers or mere faithful agents of those who appointed them. For judges, preserving the authority and institutional integrity of a body that needs to secure enforcement of their decisions may even require that public opinion and majority preferences are taken into consideration in decision-making, frustrating the hopes of those who hoped to turn them into pure counter-majoritarian weapons.

Box 10.2 Over to you—comparing constitutions

The Comparative Constitutions Project is a research project providing systematic data about the world's constitutions. Take a look at the project's Constitution Rankings page, which provides information about seven variables characterizing the constitutions of 190 countries: when they were enacted, the amount of topics they cover (their scope), their length, the extent to which they formalize powers for the executive and the legislature, the number of rights they contain, and the extent to which they formally protect judicial independence. Copy the table to a spreadsheet and play around a bit with the variables, using scatterplots and looking for correlations. For example, is there any empirical relationship between, on the one hand, how old constitutions are and, on the other, their scope or length, or even the number of rights they contain? Are older constitutions more or less likely to include rules protecting judicial independence? Consider also how these formal features of constitutions may be related to de facto aspects of political systems. For example, you can collect data from a project like *Varieties of Democracy* (V-Dem Institute), which produces indices based on expert ratings on topics such as the extent to which political systems approximate in practice the ideals of liberal democracy, respect judicial independence, or address material inequalities that may inhibit the exercise of rights and freedoms. Collect some of these variables, add them to your dataset, and explore relationships. For example, how is the formal, constitutional protection of judicial independence related to de facto judicial independence? Do more extensive catalogues of rights seem to be related to the protection of those rights in practice?

Second, even if judges were mere policy-seekers, like the US Supreme Court justices are often argued to be, rules for appointment and retention do not always yield courts whose preferences diverge widely from those of the other key players in the policymaking process, including the main political parties. In many European courts, the situation does not seem so different from that described long ago by the great political scientist Robert Dahl (1915–2014) about the United States: 'the policy views dominant on the Court are never for long out of line with the policy views dominant among the law-making majorities' (Dahl 1957: 279).

Finally, access to the courts varies significantly between countries, from the extreme case of Hungary until 2012, allowing all citizens to trigger abstract review proceedings, to highly restrictive models like Estonia, where not even members of parliament have access to litigation. The central message to be extracted, therefore, is that the extent to which constitutional courts are likely to be empowered as central actors in the policymaking process is likely to vary quite dramatically across contexts and across time. Research in comparative judicial politics still has a lot to tell us about the conditions that favour such empowerment, but what we know from judicial behaviour, judicial appointments, and litigation patterns in some of the best-known systems already suggests that some expectations about a widespread 'judicialization of politics' were probably overblown.

10.6 **Supranational European courts**

There are two important European court systems: the Court of Justice of the European Union (with two separate courts, the Court of Justice and the General Court) and the European Court of Human Rights. The Court of Justice of the European Union observes the interpretation and the application of the treaties of the European Union, including the EU Charter of Fundamental Rights and Freedoms. The European Court of Human Rights hears petitions and issues advisory opinions in the context of the European Convention on Human Rights. At the time of writing, the European Union has twenty-seven member states, and the Council of Europe (that adopted the European Convention on Human Rights) has forty-seven member states.

The enforcement of the decisions of the Court of Justice of the European Union and the European Court of Human Rights in the member states has raised important constitutional questions. When are national constitutional courts subject to European courts? Is European law above national constitutions?

The Court of Justice of the European Union created an important constitutional principle in 1964 in a landmark case, *Flaminio Costa v. ENEL*. It is called supremacy or primacy of European Union law. According to this principle, European Union law prevails over national constitutional law. When there is a conflict between a national constitutional norm and European Union law, the constitutional norm has to be set aside.

Not all European constitutional courts have accepted the supremacy of European Union law that easily. For example, the German Constitutional Court decided in 1986 it would not exercise its jurisdiction where European Union law offered a level of protection for fundamental rights largely equivalent to that provide for by the German Constitution. The obvious consequence is that the German Constitutional Court claims jurisdiction when that level of protections fails the test, therefore rejecting full supremacy of European Union law.

The German Constitutional Court has persisted on this interpretation in several subsequent landmark decisions as recently as 2020 (when questioning the EU bond-buying programme since 2015). Another example is the Irish constitutional practice, on foot of the famous 1986 Crotty decision by the Supreme Court. It requires a constitutional referendum to be held in any cases where a European initiative entails significant change in Irish sovereignty.

The supremacy of European Union law is a limit to constitutional sovereignty. Not surprisingly, it became a major issue in the controversy surrounding the failed treaty establishing a constitution for Europe in 2004. The new treaty explicitly acknowledged this principle. The French and Dutch voters did not ratify the new treaty in 2005. The subsequent Treaty of Lisbon, in 2009, dropped the explicit reference to the supremacy of European Union law.

The supremacy of European Union law was again an important argument in the Brexit referendum in 2016. Paradoxically, Brexit has reinforced the empowerment of British courts in constitutional matters. In a landmark case (*Miller v. Secretary of State for Exiting the European Union*), delivered in 2017, the United Kingdom Supreme Court decided that the executive branch could not initiate the formal withdrawing from the European Union without an explicit vote by the legislative branch. The case had two major constitutional implications in the United Kingdom. First, it redefined the scope of royal prerogatives in matters of foreign affairs. Second, it clarified that the legislatures of Scotland, Wales, and Northern Ireland cannot interfere with such a vote by the UK parliament. The European Union Notification of Withdrawal Act 2017 was subsequently enacted.

With the rise of nationalist, Eurosceptic, and far-right parties in Europe, the role of national constitutional review subject to European courts has become an important and more controversial political aspect. Constitutional exceptionalism (that is, the unique nature of local constitutional arrangements) has been a legal and political argument in the US public debate for a long time. It is now increasingly part of the public debate in many European countries.

10.7 **Conclusion**

Constitutions matter. They perform two essential functions—regulating the branches, offices, and agencies of government and defining the highest law of the country (including fundamental rights). However, constitutional traditions vary across Europe, including examples from the three waves of constitutionalism. Most European countries have constitutional courts to decide the extent to which legislation complies with the constitution. Only two countries, the United Kingdom and the Netherlands, have no formal constitutional review. Still, we have seen that constitutional review takes different forms across Europe, with particular emphasis on the distinction between abstract and concrete review.

There are many longstanding debates regarding the role of constitutions and constitutional review in liberal democracies. For instance, should constitutions be easy or difficult to change? Who should decide on how to interpret the constitution—the legislature, or an independent body such as a constitutional court? How should judges be appointed to constitutional courts in a way that ensures their independence, while avoiding 'government by judges'? The variation that we have seen shows that European countries have arrived at different answers to some of these critical questions, with important implications for how democracy works.

One particularly significant aspect of the European context is the existence of supranational courts such as the Court of Justice of the European Union and the European Court of Human Rights. The enforcement of their decisions in the member states has raised important constitutional questions. While European supranational courts claim that they are above national constitutions, not all constitutional courts accept that view. The dialogue between supranational and national courts in matters of constitutional review is still a controversial matter to some extent, in particular with the rise of national populism and Euroscepticism.

Discussion questions

1. What is a 'constitution'? Why is the British case remarkably different from other European countries?
2. Can we talk about a constitution for the European Union? Would this depend on what we understand by 'constitution'?
3. Most European countries have constitutional review. A few, such as the UK and the Netherlands, do not have formal constitutional review. Does it make a difference? Does it enhance the legislative branch of government?
4. Is there a relationship between constitutionalism and democracy? Does constitutionalism, which implies constraints on government, impede democracy, or is it a necessary condition for democracy?
5. Can constitutional judges in European countries be considered to be politically independent/politically neutral?
6. Is globalization and European integration fostering or hurting constitutionalism in Europe?

Thinking comparatively

Brouard and Hönnige (2017) is an excellent example of comparative research on the role of constitutional courts as veto players. They start from the work of George Tsebelis (2002), who devised a theoretical scheme to compare political systems on the basis of the number, ideological preferences, and cohesiveness of the actors able to exert veto power in legislative policymaking. Tsebelis argued that constitutional courts tend to be 'absorbed' as veto players, meaning that their preferences tend to be within the range of preferences of the other veto players, because of the way they are appointed: by the political veto players themselves. However, Brouard and Hönnige argue that this is not always the case, either because of variations in appointers across systems (not all courts are appointed by veto players) or because of political alternation in the elected branches and the longer terms of constitutional justices (the same court can be absorbed in one moment but not in the next). They compare the United States, Germany, and France, and show that the position of the median justice in the high courts in these countries is not always between that of the remaining veto players. In the US, appointment rules involving both the president and the senate and divided government have historically contributed to a Supreme Court that has been mostly absorbed. Similarly, in Germany, absorption is also frequent, although that depends on the types of legislation and composition of the senate. However, in France, frequent political alternation and a mostly veto-free legislative process put the *Conseil constitutionnel* more frequently at odds with the elected political actors than in the other cases.

Guide to further reading

For comparative studies of constitutional design and performance, see, for example, Ginsburg, T. (ed.) (2012), *Comparative Constitutional Design* (Cambridge: Cambridge University Press); Galligan, D. J. and Versteeg, M. (eds.) (2013), *Social and Political Foundations of Constitutions* (Cambridge: Cambridge University Press); or Ginsburg, T. and Huq, A. (eds.) (2016), *Assessing Constitutional Performance* (New York: Cambridge University Press).

Particularly important has been the Comparative Constitutions Project: Elkins, Z. et al. (2008), *The Comparative Constitutions Project: A Cross-National Historical Dataset of Written Constitutions*. Available at: http://www.comparativeconstitutionsproject.org. One of the major works coming out of that project is Elkins, Z. et al. (2009), *The Endurance of National Constitutions* (New York: Cambridge University Press).

For a more detailed analysis of European experiences, see Stone Sweet, A. (2000), *Governing with Judges: Constitutional Politics in Europe* (Oxford: Oxford University Press). Also Sadurski, W. (2014), *Rights Before Courts: A Study of Constitutional Courts in Postcommunist States of Central and Eastern Europe* (Dordrecht, Netherlands: Springer).

A recent advanced discussion about the role of constitutional courts can be found in Vanberg, G. (2015), 'Constitutional courts in comparative perspective: A theoretical assessment', *Annual Review of Political Science*, 18: 167–85. For authoritarian regimes, largely beyond the scope of this chapter, see Ginsburg, T. and Simpser, A. (eds.) (2013), *Constitutions in Authoritarian Regimes* (New York: Cambridge University Press).

References

Brouard S. and Hönnige, C. (2017), 'Constitutional courts as veto players: Lessons from the United States, France and Germany', *European Journal of Political Research*, 56(3): 529–52.

Dahl, R. A. (1957), 'Decision-making in a democracy: The Supreme Court as a national policy-maker', *Journal of Public Law*, 6(2): 279–95.

Elkins, Z., Ginsburg, T. et al. (2009), *The Endurance of National Constitutions* (New York: Cambridge University Press).

Ely, J. H. (1981), *Democracy and Distrust: A Theory of Judicial Review* (Cambridge, MA: Harvard University Press).

Finer, S. E. (1979), *Five Constitutions: Contrasts and Comparisons* (Atlantic Highlands, NJ: Humanities Press).

Garoupa, N. (2019), 'Constitutional review', in R. D. Congleton, B. N. Grofman et al. (eds.), *Oxford Handbook of Public Choice*, volume 2 (Oxford: Oxford University Press).

Ginsburg, T. and Versteeg, M. (2014), 'Why do countries adopt constitutional review?' *Journal of Law, Economics and Organization*, 30: 587–622.

Ginsburg, T. and Simpser, A. (eds.) (2014), *Constitutions in Authoritarian Regimes* (Cambridge: Cambridge University Press).

Ginsburg, T., Huq, A. Z. et al. (2018), 'The coming demise of liberal constitutionalism?', *University of Chicago Law Review*, 85: 239–55.

Hardin, R. (1999), *Liberalism, Constitutionalism and Democracy* (Oxford: Oxford University Press).

Hirschl, R. (2011), 'The judicialization of politics', in R. E. Goodin (ed.), *Oxford Handbook of Political Science* (Oxford: Oxford University Press).

Kommers, D. P. (2006), 'The federal constitutional court: Guardian of German democracy', *The Annals of the American Academy of Political and Social Science*, 603: 111–28.

Lorenz, A. (2005), 'How to measure constitutional rigidity: Four concepts and two alternatives', *Journal of Theoretical Politics*, 17(3): 339–61.

Raub, A., Cassola, A. et al. (2016), 'Protections of equal rights across sexual orientation and gender identity: An analysis of 193 national constitutions', *Yale Journal of Law and Feminism*, 28: 149–69.

Sadurski, W. (2014), *Rights Before Courts: A Study of Constitutional Courts in Postcommunist States of Central and Eastern Europe*, 2nd edn (Dordrecht, Netherlands: Springer).

Scheppele, K. L. (2018), 'Autocratic legalism', *University of Chicago Law Review*, 85: 545–83.

Stone Sweet, A. (1992), *The Birth of Judicial Politics in France: The Constitutional Council in Comparative Perspective* (Oxford: Oxford University Press).

Stone Sweet, A. (2000), *Governing with Judges: Constitutional Politics in Europe* (Oxford: Oxford University Press).

Tsebelis, G. (2002). *Veto Players: How Political Institutions Work*. Princeton, NJ: Princeton University Press).

Waldron, J. (2006), 'The core of the case against judicial review', *Yale Law Journal*, 115: 1346–406.

Weingast, B. R. (1997), 'The political foundations of democracy and the rule of law', *American Political Science Review*, 91(2): 245–63.

11 Levels of Government

MICHAEL KEATING

11.1 Introduction

Previous chapters have examined the division of power among various branches of central government (Chapter 7, the executive, Chapter 9, legislative, and Chapter 10, judicial branches). There is also a division of power between different *levels* of government—the central government and lower levels such as local and regional government—in every European state. The drawing of boundaries and the distribution of responsibilities among levels of government are central both to the balance of power and to who gains and wins in modern politics. Some states are unitary, while others are federal with a constitutional division of power between the centre and the federal regions. Even within unitary states there are local and regional levels of government. In recent years, there has been a process of rescaling, in which economic and social systems have migrated both upwards to the supranational bodies level (the European Union (EU)) and downwards to local and regional levels. States have responded by restructuring their territorial structures of government, for greater effectiveness in government, in response to demands for more local democracy, and to accommodate cultural and political diversity. In some cases, secessionist movements have emerged, seeking to break away from the state altogether.

This chapter begins by setting out the idealized concept of the integrated nation state. It then reviews the arguments about centralization and decentralization. It examines the levels of government across European states, including municipal, provincial, metropolitan, and regional government. It looks at nationalist movements within states and the way they have sought greater autonomy and even to secede. Finally, it considers issues of rescaling—that is, the shift of power and tasks across different levels—especially in the context of European integration.

11.2 The nation state

Imagine a country with stable boundaries, enclosing a defined territory. Within those boundaries is a community with a shared national identity; an integrated economy; a distinct society; a language; and a culture. There is a single parliament and government, and political parties compete equally across the territory. Shared identity promotes trust among the citizens as well as social solidarity, which underpins a generous welfare state. The boundaries of the nation state confine both business interests and labour movements within them. Unable to move outside these boundaries, they are forced to bargain and reach social compromises. Such is the ideal 'nation-state' that is often used as the basic unit of political analysis.

This idea of the integrated nation state has had a powerful hold on modern political analysis. Indeed, the process of modernization and the rise of government has often been presented as a process of *territorial integration* and *functional differentiation*; that is, government is uniform across the national territory but organized according to tasks such as defence, finance, social security and so on. Traditional local social and economic systems disappeared as they were incorporated into state-wide frameworks. The central state extended its reach into peripheral territories, bringing uniform laws and administration, and extracting taxes. The sociologist Emile Durkheim (1964: 187) wrote that 'we can almost say that a people is as much advanced as territorial divisions are more superficial'. John Stuart Mill (1972) famously argued that free institutions were possible only in unified nations, where the requisite trust was present, and advocated the assimilation of more 'backward' peripheral societies. Yet, in defiance of these predictions of integration, in the early twenty-first century, Scotland and Catalonia have held referendums on seceding from the United Kingdom and Spain respectively (see Box 11.4). Northern Italian regions have voted for more autonomy. Belgium is marked by divisions between Flanders and Wallonia, with Brussels in the middle, and has undergone radical decentralization, becoming a federal state. Even France, long seen as the archetype of centralization, has relaxed its grip over the last forty years. Central European countries have reorganized their systems of local government but with less evidence of decentralization.

Our imaginary nation state is what social scientists call an ideal type: a schematic representation of what a state might look like under certain conditions. In reality, states are complex conglomerations of territories, and their boundaries are by no means clear. They were often formed by the merger of historic territories, which have maintained their old particular features, as the work of Stein Rokkan showed (Rokkan and Urwin 1983). They may be economically integrated or marked by territorial disparities. They may have a single culture and national identity or, like Spain and the United Kingdom, contain competing national projects. Some states are historically centralized (like France and most central European states), while others are federal (like Germany). Even centralized states have various levels of government and administration within them. Only the micro-state of the Vatican City has no territorial sub-divisions.

The question of what levels of government should exist within a state is often politically contentious. This is because it affects the balance of power and control of resources. Decentralization may suit some interests but disadvantage others. Drawing the boundaries of local government units affects whether the rich and poor will get the same services and share their taxes. It may also determine which political party will win the elections. As people move and cities expand or contract, the balance of power may change. So, divisions of government and their boundaries are continually being challenged.

11.3 Arguments for decentralization

Debate about levels of government has focused on three sets of issues: efficiency; community; and equity. These are not purely technical matters, to be resolved on scientific grounds. Rather, they involve important value judgements, and their outcome creates winners and losers.

Efficiency arguments about territorial government go back to the late nineteenth century, as the modern interventionist state expanded its reach beyond the old functions of law and order and taxes. Now it assumed responsibility for roads and bridges, then education, health, urban planning, housing, and social welfare, all of which had to be delivered into local communities. One approach was strictly technical and rational. After the Revolution, France was divided into departments on the basis that a citizen could get from any point in the department to its chief town and back in a day. Other French theorists thought that water basins should be the basis for organizing everything. Classical Management Theory, influential from the late nineteenth century, held there was one best way and one best level to undertake any task. As governments started to plan the economic and physical development of cities, it was argued that they needed larger territorial units, taking in both the city and its hinterland. A key concept here was the labour market or 'travel-to-work' area, connecting life, work, and leisure.

Some scholars argued that larger units are more efficient because they can spread their administrative and overhead costs more widely; this is known as 'economies of scale'. On the other hand, if units become too big, they may start to meet diseconomies of scale as administrators lose knowledge of local conditions and chains of command get too long. Arguments have followed as to the best (or 'optimal') size of unit for delivering a health service; for a school district; for housing; for social services; and for other matters.

More recently, scholars have asked whether these arguments can ever be resolved objectively. Efficiency is a contested concept, and it is by no means obvious what is the optimum level for carrying out specific tasks or even whether there is an optimal level. Efficiency arguments have been associated with a managerial, technocratic, or depoliticized view of the world. It is significant that the study of local government in universities was often assigned to departments of public administration rather than politics. There was also a curious idea that local government should be 'non-political'. Usually this meant that political parties should not be involved, although the issues themselves are inherently political, affecting 'who gets what'. Indeed, changing views about the appropriate structure of government depends on what we want it to do and are themselves political. In the 1960s, when the emphasis was on planning for cities and regions, on extending public services and on redistribution, territorial governments on a larger scale were in vogue. By the 1980s, the intellectual fashion had changed under the influence of 'public choice' thinkers. They defended small governments, arguing that they could enhance efficiency by competing with each other to offer lower taxes and services targeted to local preferences. Local governments would not provide services themselves but contract them with private providers, so they would not have to be large themselves. This linked to New Public Management theories, which emphasize contracting out and competition (Pollitt and Bouckaert 2017).

The second set of arguments about decentralization concerns democracy and community. One strand starts from the primacy of the individual citizen and argues that her desires will be satisfied best if people with the same policy preferences are placed in the same unit. The smaller the unit, the fewer people there are to be satisfied and the more likely it is that they will agree on policies. This draws on Public Choice theory in which the aim is to maximize individuals' preferences for bundles of taxes and services (Ostrom et al. 1988). The matching of people and boundaries is achieved either by drawing the boundaries around the individuals, or by encouraging people to move. Incorporating New Public Management, the units could be small as they would not provide services directly. This is a highly theoretical argument and, in practice, moving both boundaries and people are difficult. There would always be people in the 'wrong' place and finding themselves in a minority. There is also something ethically questionable about encouraging people to segregate into homogeneous communities, whether defined by ethnicity or by class.

A different version of democracy is based less on individuals and more on community. Few countries are completely integrated nation states and sub-state territories often have their own historic cultural, social, or political particularities. Rather than being a collection of self-interested individuals, a political community may be a body of citizens who engage in debate about the common good and make social compromises with each other. Such communities do not need to be homogeneous but rather see themselves as inclusive, open, and multicultural. They may be found at different territorial scales, from the neighbourhood to the large region; indeed, the nation state is itself an example of a territorial political community. The argument for local government that follows is that decisions taken closer to the local political community are more democratic and that policies should be decided at the lowest level consistent with other valid considerations. Local government may also provide greater opportunities for participation (see Chapter 5).

A particular case is that of plurinational states, in which more than one national community has emerged. I put it this way because modern social science recognizes that nations are not entities that can be defined scientifically and clearly distinguished from each other. Nations are, rather, constructed around a number of themes, including history, culture, language, and territory, and are often contested. For many people in Spain, there is a single nation, coterminous with the Spanish state. Others insist that there are four nations (Spain, Catalonia, the Basque Country, and Galicia). Many Catalans insist that they are members of a single nation, Catalonia. Others regard themselves as having a dual identity as Catalan and Spanish. The great majority of people in Scotland regard themselves as Scots but many also see themselves as British. A slightly different case is that of national minorities, who may identify with the people of another state than their own, for example people in Romania who regard themselves as Hungarian, citizens of Northern Ireland who are more Irish than British, or people who find themselves on the 'wrong' side of the border between Denmark and Germany.

One response to such national diversity is to assimilate minorities into the nation state where they live. This has been widely tried, more successfully in some cases (like France) than others (like Spain). The other strategy is to give them a degree of self-government in their own territories, as is now the case in the United Kingdom, Spain, and Belgium. At the limit, states might break up altogether. Following World War I, the central European empires collapsed, producing new nation states. Ireland separated from the United Kingdom as, earlier, Belgium had broken with the Netherlands and Norway with Sweden. In the 1990s Yugoslavia broke up and the Czech Republic and Slovakia separated. Separation, however, rarely produces homogeneous nation states. There are always people left on the 'wrong' side of the border and many people in any case do not have a single identity.

The third set of arguments concerns equity. Modern welfare states are based on the premise that citizens should have equal rights to services and benefits wherever they live. This might be ensured by centralizing everything or alternatively by laying down national standards which local governments would have to meet. Equity arguments have also been used to favour larger units of local government, which can encompass both wealthy and poor neighbourhoods and allow redistribution of tax revenues. In the second half of the twentieth century, this often meant incorporating the wealthy suburbs into the central city, where the poor lived. It was argued that the suburbanites often used the city's public services while avoiding its taxes. Incorporation tended to arouse opposition from both sides. People in the suburbs wanted to keep their wealth and did not want low-income housing brought in. City-centre residents did not want to be outvoted by suburban dwellers who might favour low-level taxes and less generous social services. In the early twenty-first century, well-off professionals have returned to many city centres, changing the politics again. Many of the arguments about the shape of local government have pitched those favouring redistributive politics, who have wanted to keep the wealthy and the poor in the same jurisdiction, against those emphasizing competition among units to drive down costs. The former have tended to favour large units and the latter small ones.

It is tempting to assume that central governments want to keep all the power to themselves and so oppose decentralization, but this is not always the case. Centralized governments may experience congestion as they are obliged to deal with the details of trivial matters and lose sight of the big picture. They will be besieged by local interest groups seeking advantage and risk being 'captured' by them. This was the historic experience of France, where researchers from the 1960s showed that the supposedly monolithic state was in practice penetrated by all manner of local interests. Prefects, officially present in each department to enforce the will of the centre, had to bend to local interests in order to get anything done, while powerful politicians accumulated elected office both at the locality (for example as mayor) and the centre (as MP or minister) in order to dominate both levels. From the 1980s, decentralization proved an attractive way for the central government to regain its own freedom of manoeuvre, concentrating on strategic steering rather than detailed control of the local level.

11.4 Variations on territorial government

While all states divide government into levels, an important distinction is to be made between territorial *administration* and territorial *self-government*. The former exists in states based on the French or Napoleonic model (including Spain, Italy, and Poland), where there has historically been an extensive network of local offices of central government, headed by a centrally appointed official. In France, this is known as the prefect, and we will use this term more generally. The prefect is the representative of the state in the locality but acts as a communication channel in both directions, relaying local concerns back to the centre.

A different tradition is that of local self-government, in which local communities have the responsibility for taking decisions and raising revenue, albeit within limits set by the centre. Local self-government was historically a matter for the privileged classes, including the landowners in the countryside and the merchants in the towns. Voting rights were linked to property ownership and there was a sense, well into the twentieth century, that those who paid the local taxes should have the main say in local government. In the present day, however, local government is elected by universal suffrage in the name of the whole community. Traditions of local self-government have been strong in the United Kingdom, the Nordic countries, and parts of Germany.

In recent years, the differences between the two traditions have been diminishing. The welfare state, with its emphasis on common standards of provision, was a force for centralization after World War II. Common standards were laid down and modern services were rolled out in rural as well as urban areas. Central governments encouraged local governments to expand services, providing subsidies to do so. Poorer areas were given additional help to provide the same level of service as wealthier ones. Since the 1980s, governments have been more concerned to limit local government spending, starting with the United Kingdom but extending to other countries. Yet, alongside this trend to uniformity, Napoleonic countries like France, Spain, and Italy have relaxed centralized control and transferred powers from their field offices to elected local and regional governments.

Germany, Austria, Belgium, and Switzerland are organized on an altogether different model, as federations. Under federalism, there is a constitutional division of power between the federation (central level) and the constituent units, called variously *Länder*, regions, and cantons. A further complication in the Belgian case is that regions co-exist, and partially overlap, with language communities, responsible for matters such as education and social services. In the following sections, these various forms of territorial government are examined.

As each state is free to decide on its own system of territorial government, there is no standard set of institutions. We can, however, usefully distinguish four levels which have historically emerged in most European countries. While the terminology differs from one case to another, we will call this the municipality; the metropolitan level; the province or county; and the 'meso' or regional level.

11.4.1 **The municipality**

The lowest unit of local government across European states is the municipality, based on the local community and known in France, Italy, Spain, and Scandinavia as the commune. These are often ancient units and historically have been very small. During the twentieth century most states sought to consolidate these smaller units into larger ones in the name of viability and efficiency and to provide modern levels of service. The main wave of consolidation in Europe came in the 1960s and 1970s. In West Germany, the number of municipalities was reduced from about 24,000 to 8,500, with similar falls in Spain, Italy, and the Nordic countries. A wave of consolidation in Great Britain brought the number of bottom-tier local governments from around 1,700 to under 350. France stands out as the exception as the local political class were so well represented at the centre that they could preserve their local power bases; there are still over 36,000 communes, more than the rest of the European Union put together. Following the transition to democracy in Eastern and Central Europe, there were initial efforts to establish consolidated local governments, but these tended to fragment into smaller units as politicians sought to establish their own power bases.

Communities based on cities and towns are larger in scale (except in France) and often have traditions of self-government. European cities sometimes enjoyed special privileges in the early modern period as centres of trade and citizenship; some had even been independent states, especially in Italy, Germany, and the Low Countries. They became centres of business and industry in the nineteenth century and were large and wealthy enough to run their own public services and carve out their own sphere of self-government within the state. Cities have remained a key level of territorial government and have consistently resisted being incorporated into higher levels of territorial government. During the 2000s there has been regular debate on the role of cities in economic and social change and about the appropriate form of government. In some countries, city mayors have emerged as important political figures, not only locally but also in national politics.

11.4.2 **Metropolitan government**

The government of large urban areas has been a preoccupation of European states since the nineteenth century. As cities expanded during the Industrial Revolution, they spilled over their jurisdictional boundaries, creating problems for coherent planning, transport, infrastructure, and public services. As the costs of providing services in cities expanded, wealthy taxpayers migrated to the suburbs, where they could control their own municipal governments. One solution to this has been to extend city boundaries to take in the larger area, but this is politically fraught and risks creating units that are too large for democratic participation and the provision of truly local services.

The alternative is metropolitan government, with two tiers: a local level for most service provision and a higher level for strategic planning and major infrastructure. The idea was applied widely from the 1960s, notably in English cities, Barcelona, and the *Randstad* (in the Netherlands). Yet it proved difficult in practice. There were often political rivalries between the two levels, while the metropolitan area did not attract the same loyalty as the historic city. There was confusion about the balance of responsibilities. The division between strategic direction (at the metropolitan level) and detailed policy (at the local level) did not always work as strategic plans are difficult to implement if the main policy instruments are at the local level. As a result, metropolitan governments were widely abandoned from the 1980s, with powers taken up by the centre or returned to the local level. In the 2000s, however, the tide turned again as cities were increasingly seen as centres for economic growth and dynamism. Metropolitan governments were re-established but this time there was more emphasis on cooperation among local governments rather than the erection of a directly elected tier over them. England is illustrative of these trends, with repeated efforts to create a metropolitan level. Metropolitan counties were established by a Conservative government in the 1970s, abolished by another Conservative government in the following decade, and re-invented (as city-regions) by a third Conservative government in the 2000s. These follow the common European model, consisting of associations of existing governments rather than the creation of a wholly new level (see Box 11.1).

11.4.3 **The county or province**

The county or province (department in France) has been used both as a sub-division of central government and as a unit of local government. In France, Italy, and Poland, there are both centrally appointed officials (prefects) and elected department/provincial councils,

> **Box 11.1 Over to you—models of metropolitan government**
>
> Metropolitan government has long been advocated as a means for managing large cities without losing the advantages of smaller units, closer to communities and citizens.
>
> Using the data on the European Metropolitan Authorities website, can you identify common themes in the move towards metropolitan structures? Are the reasons always the same?
>
> What are the main difficulties in setting up a metropolitan level? What conflicts have been experienced? Have metropolitan forms of government proved enduring? Can metropolitan government enhance democracy and accountability? What are the drawbacks of the metropolitan model?

but the latter have progressively taken over more powers and responsibilities. Sweden and Norway have county governors alongside the council, as did Denmark until 2007. Provinces and departments in France, Italy, and Spain were established in the nineteenth century as artificial, functional units intended to replace the historic units (to which people were attached) and thus cement national unity. Over time, however, these units put down roots and attracted local loyalties. They also provided power bases for politicians. So, although since the 1960s they have widely been seen as ill-fitted to modern needs, they have proved resistant to reform. In Germany, the United Kingdom and Scandinavia, there has been some consolidation of the county level into larger units but elsewhere they have co-existed with the new, larger units.

11.4.4 **The meso or regional level**

The final level of government is sometimes called the 'meso' or regional level, lying between the central and local levels. This includes federal states, where a division of powers is entrenched in the constitution (see Box 11.2). Over recent decades, meso government in a non-federal form has spread to formerly unitary states including France, Spain, Italy, Poland and, partially, the United Kingdom. The reasons are twofold: functional considerations; and the management of national diversity.

The emergence of a regional level of government has been associated with the development of the European Union and its own spatial development strategies. As state governments reduced their expenditure and concentration on regional policy, the EU stepped in, with its own programmes, variously known as regional funds, structural funds, and cohesion policy. It also sought to engage local and regional collaborators in the implementation of policy on the ground. From the 1980s, there was a lot of talk about regions bypassing their states in order to go directly to Brussels in search of money and influence and of the emergence of a 'Europe of the Regions', in which regions would be a 'third level' of European government (in addition to the national and supranational levels). In practice, the funding rules make it difficult for regions to get European money by their own efforts, but this did not stop regional politicians from claiming credit for any funds that were spent in their own areas.

Regions were incorporated into European policymaking in two ways in the Treaty on European Union (Maastricht Treaty) of 1992. First, there was provision, at the discretion of member states, for regional ministers to represent the state in the Council of the European Union.

Box 11.2 Federalism in Europe

Federalism is the constitutional division of power between the central and regional levels of government. Each level has its own spheres of responsibility, and there are also areas of shared responsibility between the two levels. Because the division is constitutionally defined, the central government cannot overstep its mark and interfere in areas that are the responsibility of the regional governments, as can happen in unitary (non-federal) states. As well as having political institutions at the regional (or state) level, the regions are also typically represented in central government through the upper house of parliament. In Europe, federal countries include Germany (which consists of sixteen states or *Länder*), Switzerland (with twenty-six states or *cantons*), Belgium (with three language communities and three regions), and Austria (with nine *Länder*). Some other countries, such as Spain and the UK, also have federal features, but they are not formally federal systems.

To take the German example, *Länder* have primary responsible for areas such as education, housing, policing, and culture, while the federal government retains control of issues such as defence, foreign policy, and immigration. On other issues, including welfare, public health, transport, and environmental issues, power is shared between the two levels of government. There is close cooperation between the two levels, especially on issues that involve competences belonging to both. A good example is how German states responded to the Covid-19 pandemic in 2020. The federal government issued guidelines on how to respond, but it was ultimately up to each region which lockdown measures were put in place and when they were lifted. This led to regional differences on issues such as shop openings, travel, and the wearing of face masks. There were also significant regional differences in the response to the crisis in other countries that have federal features. For example, in the UK, where there is less of an overlap in competences between the two levels of government, each of the four nations (England, Scotland, Wales, and Northern Ireland) designed its own strategy for dealing with the crisis, while cooperating where appropriate with the others.

An important proviso was that the regional minister would represent the whole state and not their own region. Second, a Committee of the Regions (CoR) was established, with its membership drawn from local and regional governments. The CoR has gradually extended its rights to be consulted on policy initiatives coming from the Commission but hopes that it might become a third legislative body of the EU (alongside the Council of the EU and the European Parliament) have been disappointed.

While regional or meso level government thus has a technical, functional logic, it has also been used for managing national diversity in Belgium, Spain, the United Kingdom and Italy. In Belgium there is a complex system involving three territorial regions (Flanders, Wallonia, and Brussels) dealing with territorial matters, and three language communities (Flemish, French, and German) dealing with linguistic and personal matters. In Spain, provision was made in 1978 to allow for the establishment of 'autonomous communities'. While this was initially aimed at the 'historic nationalities' of Catalonia, the Basque Country, and Galicia, it was rapidly taken up everywhere, so that the whole country was regionalized. In the United Kingdom, by contrast, devolution extends only to Scotland, Wales, and Northern Ireland. Provisions in the early 2000s for regional government in England lapsed when the first referendum (in the North-East) showed little appetite for it. The UK thus remains highly asymmetrical and attention in England has turned back to the metropolitan city-region concept first tried in the 1970s. The post-war Italian constitution provided for special-status regions for the island and border areas, of which five were eventually set up. Since the 1970s they have co-existed with functionally inspired regions in the rest of the country.

Other countries have resisted using territorial devolution to recognize national diversity, seeing it as a potential threat to national unity. So French regions were mostly drawn to cut across historic cultural provinces or cultural identities: for example, historic Brittany was split between the region of Bretagne and Pays de la Loire, and Normandy was divided into two. The countries of Central and Eastern Europe have been particularly reluctant to base regional government on historic or cultural identities, fearing both separatism (regions breaking away) and irredentism (where regions seek to join a neighbouring country with which they may feel affinity).

There is a legal distinction between federalism (with its constitutional division of power) and regional devolution (a modification of the unitary state). In practice, as regional or meso government has developed, it has in some cases come close to federalism. This is particularly so where the regional level has the power to make laws as opposed to having only administrative powers. Belgium has evolved from a devolved state to one that is officially federal. Successive reforms have sought to federalize Italy, while it has been argued that, in many ways, Spain is federal (Moreno 2001). There are federal features in the devolution settlement in the United Kingdom, although the absence of devolution for England has prevented a thoroughgoing federalization. France, on the other hand, has a much more modest scheme of regional decentralization, in which the regions lack legislative powers.

11.5 **Territorial finance**

A key feature of government, as opposed to mere administration, is tax-raising powers. The form and extent of taxing powers given to local and regional governments vary greatly. Most systems have provision for territorial governments to set their own tax rates. As well as these own resources, local and regional governments in Europe receive grants from central government. Such grants serve a variety of purposes. They provide resources for services meeting national standards; they give additional money to sub-state governments with a lower tax base; and they provide extra for places with greater needs. Sometimes they take the form of earmarked grants, allowing central government to determine the policy as a condition for getting the grant. Alternatively, they can take the form of block grants, within which local governments can set their own priorities. In Germany, there is an elaborate formula intended to allow all areas to provide the same level of services, but this does not avoid arguments over the outcome. In France, on the other hand, there is a mass of specific grants whose overall effect is often unclear. Spain has a series of formulas for redistribution, but these are not always consistent and owe a great deal to political bargaining.

In the post-war years, central governments expanded their support for local government as they sought to extend services across the national territory and, in effect, encourage local governments to spend more. From the 1970s, in the wake of the oil crisis, they started to restrict spending. At the same time, they gave sub-state governments more tax-raising powers, so forcing them to make the difficult choices about spending priorities and the unpopular decisions on taxes. As resources have become scarcer in recent years, there has been increasing conflict about the amount of central support for local government spending and the way it is allocated. There have been repeated efforts to find the best formula for distributing central grants, reconciling local decision-making, equity among regions, and efficiency. The issue of equity, known as 'fiscal equalization', is particularly contested as there are no shared or objective criteria as to what is fair. Whatever the system, those losing out will complain. As the old integrated regionalism gives way to competitive regionalism, wealthy areas are more reluctant to share with the poorer ones, although they still do so to a considerable extent.

11.6 Territorial politics and secession

Territory has now become an important element in political competition. The theme of competition among cities and regions has encouraged parties and leaders to position themselves as defenders of a territorial interest, including the whole of the local population. This allows them to broaden their appeal at a time when class and other traditional forms of political identity have been weakening (see Chapter 4). Such appeals may take the form of protesting about closures of industrial plants or the promise to bring in new investment and jobs. There is a trend to direct election of city mayors and regional government leaders, which encourages such territorial appeals and makes these offices attractive bases of power for ambitious politicians.

There are also increased possibilities for parties pursuing regional autonomy. In the past, these were often seen as characteristic of poor regions, which had been marginalized in the course of modernization; this is the 'revolt of the poor'. Now they are as likely to be found in wealthy regions such as Flanders, Catalonia, or northern Italy, tapping into resentment at having to share their wealth with their poorer compatriots; this is the 'revolt of the rich'. Such movements cut across older left-right alignments and are found across the political spectrum. Regionalism or local nationalism leans to the right in Flanders and northern Italy and to the left in Scotland and Wales, while in Catalonia and the Basque Country it runs all the way from the extreme left to the centre-right. The presence of territorial parties has transformed party competition in such places, forcing the old state-wide parties to incorporate territorial defence and autonomy into their own electoral programmes. This in turn has pushed governments to bring in more decentralization (see Box 11.3).

In some cases, territorial political movements have advanced to the point of demanding the creation of a new state. In 2014 Scotland staged a referendum on a proposal to separate

Box 11.3 Over to you—movements for regional autonomy

Political movements seeking greater regional autonomy exist within several European countries. While these movements may frame their cause in the name of principles of self-determination, in some cases there are also economic motivations at play. Select a region in which a political movement striving for greater autonomy exists. Why do you think they are seeking greater autonomy? Could it be characterized as a 'revolt of the poor' or a 'revolt of the rich', or neither? Henley et al.'s article in *The Guardian*, 'Beyond Catalonia: pro-independence movements in Europe' (17 October 2017) provides a useful map and list of such movements, at https://www.theguardian.com/world/ng-interactive/2017/oct/27/beyond-catalonia-pro-independence-movements-in-europe-map.

from the United Kingdom while remaining in the European Union. In 2017 a similar vote was held in Catalonia on separation from Spain (see Box 11.4). A major difference was that the United Kingdom allowed the Scottish vote and promised to respect the outcome, while the Spanish government refused to recognize the validity of the Catalan exercise. This reflects the conception of the United Kingdom as a union of nations, each of which has, ultimately, a right to go its own way even though all the British political parties are strongly opposed to this happening in practice. Spain's constitution, on the other hand, proclaims the indissoluble unity of the Spanish people. Spanish political parties and the courts have interpreted this to mean that even asking the people of Catalonia whether they want to be independent is impermissible, and that organizing a referendum on independence is a criminal offence. In fact, no constitution in Europe allows for the secession of part of the state and the UK exception is possible because there is no written, codified constitution, allowing the UK parliament great leeway as to what it will permit. Since the 2014 referendum, however, UK governments have refused to allow a second Scottish independence vote.

Secession represents a stark rupture of the state itself rather than a reorganization of government within it. Yet in recent years this distinction has started to blur. In the modern world, and particularly within the European Union, states are not sovereign and independent in the traditional sense. They are subject to global market forces and trading rules, which limit their room for manoeuvre in economic matters. Inside the EU, they have ceded power to European institutions and have to accept the primacy of EU law. Some scholars have argued that we have moved away from the classic idea of sovereignty, in which states recognize no superior authority, towards a post-sovereign dispensation in which power and authority are shared and divided. If this is true in the relationship between states and the EU, it may equally

Box 11.4 Two referendums

Between 2014 and 2017 two independence referendums were held in European Union countries. They present very different characteristics (Cetrà and Harvey 2018).

Scotland: in September 2014 Scotland held a referendum on independence. It was agreed by both UK and Scottish governments and parliaments, which promised to respect the results. It was constitutional and legal. The question was agreed. Both supporters and opponents of independence participated in the campaign. Turnout was 85% and the result was 55 to 45% against independence. The referendum was followed by inter-party negotiations, which produced the Scotland Act 2016, granting Scotland more powers over taxes and welfare and securing the permanence of the Scottish parliament. The outcome was accepted by both sides, although the issue of Scottish independence has not gone away and there are demands for another referendum after Scotland voted to remain in the European Union while the United Kingdom as a whole voted to leave.

Catalonia: in October 2017, the government of Catalonia staged a referendum on independence. This was not agreed with the Spanish government and was ruled to be illegal by the Constitutional Court. Opponents of independence boycotted the campaign and the vote, and the Spanish government sought to stop the vote taking place. Police closed polling stations and evicted voters. Turnout was 43% and 90% of those voted for independence. After the vote, the Catalan parliament declared independence. Ministers were prosecuted and jailed and several fled abroad. The Catalan government was temporarily suspended, and Madrid took direct control of Catalonia.

be true of the position of 'stateless nations' (such as exist in plurinational states, described in Section 11.3) and peoples within states. Self-government then ceases to be a case of acquiring full sovereignty and becomes more a matter of gaining influence and negotiating relationships. So, Ireland can claim to have more influence in the world after it joined the EU, since it is part of a larger bloc and less dependent on its larger neighbour, the United Kingdom.

These considerations have opened the door to 'third-way' proposals for stateless nations, more than mere regional government but less than full independence. Such proposals focus on two issues: symbolic recognition of a territory as having a distinct national identity; and greater political autonomy than enjoyed by other regions. For many years, this was the aspiration of Catalan nationalists, who dreamed of a strong Catalonia within a plurinational Spain. A revised statute of autonomy, adopted in 2006, was heavily amended by the Spanish Constitutional Court in 2010, largely because of objections to the use of the word 'nation' to refer to Catalonia. This was one of the factors pushing Catalan nationalists towards full independence. Moderate Basque nationalists have also sought recognition as a national reality, together with stronger autonomy and a bilateral relationship with Spain. Interestingly, as the Catalan nationalist movement radicalized after 2010, pushing for full independence, the Basque Nationalist Party moved in the other direction, returning to the idea of a special status in Spain after a period in which it had allied with the more radical nationalists.

In Belgium, the New Flemish Alliance (*NVA*) is formally in favour of the independence of Flanders but only in the long term. In the meantime, it argues for a confederal arrangement, in which the constituent parts of the country will have full internal self-government but still cooperate at the Belgian level. *Plaid Cymru*/Party of Wales has used a variety of formulas over the years to argue for self-government falling short of full statehood even as it formally pursues independence.

Scotland appears to be an exception as the Scottish National Party (SNP) does support full independence. Yet since the 1980s this has been placed within the European Union, which entails a certain loss or sharing of sovereignty. For the independence referendum of 2014, the SNP went further, claiming that an independent Scotland would share the monarchy (as indeed do several Commonwealth countries), the pound sterling, and various regulatory institutions. Indeed, they argued that Scotland was currently in six unions with the rest of the UK—political, monetary, monarchical, defence, European, and social—and proposed to withdraw only from the political one.

Contrary to some comment around the time of the Scottish and Catalan referendums, Europe is not rife with secessionist movements. Indeed, the only two places within the EU where there is still significant support for secession are Scotland and Catalonia. There is much more evidence of rescaling, as the relationship among territory, nation, economy, society, and political institutions shifts. 2017 saw referendums in the Italian regions of Lombardy and Veneto for more self-government. Nationalists have made political advances in the French island of Corsica by playing down independence and focusing on resentment of Paris, recognition, and more powers and resources. In Northern Ireland, the settlement of 1998 (the Good Friday or Belfast Agreement) provides for local self-government with power-sharing between the nationalist and unionist communities and links with both the Republic of Ireland and the United Kingdom. It has, for the first time since the creation of the province of Northern Ireland in 1921, provided a form of government acceptable to the two communities, although challenges remain: for instance, the Northern Ireland assembly has been suspended for prolonged periods, and Brexit along with demographic changes in Northern Ireland have reopened the issue of Irish reunification.

Since the 1970s, many European stateless nationalist movements have dreamed of a Europe of the Peoples in which the old states would fade away, allowing smaller units to take their place. This is a utopian vision, which has not come to pass. More realistically, nationalists have sought to carve out a role within European institutions so as to gain both symbolic recognition and more power. This movement linked into the Europe of the Regions theme, although nationalists sought a special position as more than mere regions. In practice, Europe has not provided much sustenance for these ideas. It has insisted on recognition of minority rights as a condition for the accession of new member states in Central and Eastern Europe but has not intervened in Western European cases. European leaders, rather, supported Spain in the face of the Catalan secession attempt in 2017. They have given no support to Scottish independence aspirations even after Scotland voted by a large majority to remain in the EU in the 2016 Brexit referendum, while England and Wales voted to come out. In the Committee of the Regions, stateless nations have no special place and other local and regional representatives argue strongly that they are no different.

Europe has, on the other hand, helped to manage irredentist claims at the borders of states. The European single market and the Schengen scheme have largely eliminated physical borders, allowing the free movement of goods, services, capital, and people (although temporary suspensions were introduced during the migrant crisis that began in 2015, and again during the Covid-19 crisis). It therefore matters less whether a given territory is in one country or another and the opening of borders has encouraged cooperation cross them. Austrian accession to the European Union in 1995 has reduced tensions with Italy over the *Sud Tirol/Alto Adige* region. Fears that, after the fall of communism, Hungary would seek to recover territories lost after World War I have been reduced, even as Hungarian nationalism has grown. The opening of the border between the Republic of Ireland and Northern Ireland, facilitated by the single market, helped the development of the Good Friday Agreement. Brexit, however, resulted in the return of an economic border. While the Northern Ireland Protocol and the Windsor Framework (negotiated between the UK and the EU) allowed Northern Ireland to remain linked to both the EU and the UK markets, the issue remains contentious.

11.7 **Conclusion: Rescaling Europe**

The unitary nation state outlined at the beginning of this chapter was never a reality. States have long been divided territorially and there are governments of various sorts within them. Yet it is not true either that there is a stable hierarchy of levels nested within states. We have identified key levels of government, but these vary greatly from one state to another regarding their size, form, and functions. Recent decades have seen increasing pressures for change in the structure of territorial governments, driven by changes in technology, the economy, society, and politics. In a process of spatial rescaling, functional systems have been migrating to new levels, from the global, through the supranational (European), the state, the regional, and the local. While economic regulation is increasingly a supranational matter, issues of social cohesion may be felt at the level of the local neighbourhood. Identities are no longer (if they ever were) confined to the state level, as old, new, and rediscovered territorial identities emerge in places like Scotland, Catalonia, and Flanders. In northern Italy, a place called Padania was more or less invented from nothing in the 1980s, although it did not have enduring appeal.

While some observers continue to regard this process as a matter of adaptation to functional imperatives, it remains highly political and contested. Consolidation of local governments creates opportunities for some politicians to gain influence while others lose their power bases. The drawing of boundaries includes some citizens and excludes others from the local political community. Scholars have increasingly recognized the importance of territorial institutions for economic development (Keating et al. 2003). With the rise of competitive regionalism, this has become an ever more urgent theme, hence the continued search for new forms. At the same time, there is a debate on whether regions are primarily about economic development or also about social and broader matters.

There is competition among levels of government as each seeks to expand its scope and authority. Thus, French regions have had to find a space between the existing departments and municipalities and the central state. The county or provincial level has long been pronounced redundant as its functions have been taken to new levels, but it remains present as long as it provides a base for politicians. The Spanish and Italian provinces similarly have proved resilient.

The present system of territorial government in European countries was laid down in the expansionary years following World War II, or after transitions to democracy in Southern Europe in the 1980s and Central and Eastern Europe in the 1990s. Devolution in the UK and federalism in Belgium were introduced during relatively good economic times. The economic crisis of 2008 ushered in a period of financial austerity. States have tended to download their budgetary problems to lower levels by cutting support. This has created new tensions between levels of government. It has increased competitions between regions and cities, while wealthier places have complained about transfers to poorer ones. This is happening at a time when interests have come to be constructed and expressed, at least partially, in a territorial mode and institutionalized in the form of regional government, parties, and movements.

The response of regions has been highly asymmetrical. Poorer regions have clung to the central state as their best hope, while wealthy ones press for more fiscal autonomy. So, some struggling cities in western Germany have been asking why their citizens should contribute to transfers to cities in eastern Germany where conditions are actually better, even if, at the *Land* (region) level, the west still appears better off. Some Spanish autonomous communities governed by the conservative *Partido Popular* have called for a reversal of the autonomy process, to give competences back to the centre. In Catalonia, on the other hand, there is broad support across the political parties, business, and trade unions for more regional autonomy. There are similar contrasts between northern and southern Italy, Flanders and Wallonia, and, to a lesser extent, eastern and western Germany.

Social scientists no longer view territory as a mere set of lines on a map. Rather, it has taken on a deeper sociological, economic, cultural, and political meaning. Rescaling means that the map is in continual flux and the meanings themselves are changing. For example, competitive regionalism has given a new economic significance to territory and encouraged politicians to use it to rally support. Decentralization has allowed new levels of democratic deliberation and policymaking to emerge (see Chapter 6). At the same time, it has raised fears of a race to the bottom as some places lose out in global competition. All of this means that territorial government no longer stands on firm foundations. There are continual pressures to redefine territories and to rethink their institutions. Territorial politics and the distribution of power is not a static matter and is not, as emphasized at the beginning of this chapter, a purely technical issue. Both the structure of government and the distribution of resources among territories are at the heart of modern politics and government.

Discussion questions

1. Is the demand for regional autonomy simply a 'revolt of the rich'?
2. What is meant by territorial rescaling?
3. Why is so difficult to reorganize local government?
4. Is there a 'right' level of territorial government for each country and each function?
5. What are the arguments for metropolitan government?
6. Is there a difference between federalism and regional devolution?
7. Do nationalist parties always want their own separate state?
8. How has European integration affected territorial politics in EU member states?

Thinking comparatively

How does European integration influence demands for more autonomy in European regions? The most extreme demand for autonomy is to ask for independence. Cetrà and Liñeira (2018) examine how European political and economic integration have changed demands for sovereignty in four European territories: Catalonia, Scotland, the Basque Country, and Flanders. These four cases are the most prominent examples of sub-state nation-building efforts in Europe. Cetrà and Liñeira argue that European integration has lowered the cost of demanding independence for territories in Europe. Economic integration has given regions access to larger markets and incentivized regional leaders to resist central state institutions and their political projects. They are aided in this by the EU as sub-national units have more opportunities for cooperation beyond the nation state than before, and European institutions can be used to further regional interests in novel ways. This does not mean that Europe has caused calls for independence, however. The main influence on calls for independence is still domestic politics rather than EU politics, but the overall environment in which sub-state nationalism operates has been changed by the experience of EU membership.

Guide to further reading

Congress of Local and Regional Authorities (Council of Europe), at https://www.coe.int/en/web/congress.

Website of the Congress of Local and Regional Authorities, the Council of Europe body that works to develop sub-national democracy in Europe by providing collective forums for representatives from local and regional government and monitoring local and regional elections.

Hooghe L., Marks, G. et al. (2010), *The Rise of Regional Authority: A Comparative Study of 42 Democracies* (London: Routledge).

This book includes the EU states in its analysis of the development of regional government. The book tracks the development of regional authority between 1950 and 2008 and measures how regional authority has grown and seeks to move debates about regional authority beyond debates about centralization versus decentralization to look at the structure of regional politics.

Keating, M. (2013), *Rescaling the European State: The Making of Territory and the Rise of the Meso* (Oxford: Oxford University Press).

An examination of the migration of economic, social, and political systems of action and of regulation to new spatial levels above, below, and across the nation state, in particular to the regional or meso level. Contains historical overviews of territorial differentiation in Europe and a theoretical examination of the concept of territory, as well as how the growth of meso-level politics has been driven by economic, political, and social factors.

Le Galès, P. (2002), *European Cities: Social Conflicts and Governance* (Oxford: Oxford University Press).

A study of the growing importance of cities as centres of governance distinct from national government because of the economic importance and social differences that have developed between cities and national societies. Le Galès argues that cities are becoming collective actors in European politics of great potential.

Loughlin, J., Hendriks, F. et al. (eds.) (2011), *The Oxford Handbook of Local and Regional Democracy in Europe* (Oxford: Oxford University Press).

A comprehensive overview of sub-national democracy in Europe, with chapters on all European states and a comparative overview in its concluding chapter.

Loughlin, J., Kincaid, J. et al. (eds.) (2013), *Routledge Handbook of Federalism and Regionalism* (London: Routledge).

Includes a section on federalism and regionalism in Europe, as well as chapters reviewing theories of federalism and regionalism generally.

Swenden, W. (2006), *Federalism and Regionalism in Western Europe* (Basingstoke: Palgrave).

A detailed study of federalism in Western Europe that takes a thematic approach to the subject, looking at the origins of Western European federal systems, the division of powers between centre and regions, party systems, identity and nationalism, and public policy. Also has case studies of Austria, Belgium, Germany, Spain, Switzerland, and the UK.

References

Cetrà, D. and Harvey, M. (2018), 'Explaining accommodation and resistance to demands for independence referendums in the UK and Spain', *Nations and Nationalism*, 24(4): 1–23.

Cetrà, D. and Liñeira, R. (2018), 'Breaking up within Europe: Sub-state nationalist strategies in multilevel politics', *Journal of Common Market Studies*, 56(3): 717–29.

Durkheim, E. (1964), *The Division of Labour in Society* (New York: Free Press).
Henley, J., Sheehy, F. et al. (2017), 'Beyond Catalonia: Pro-independence movements in Europe', *The Guardian*, 27 October, available at https://www.theguardian.com/world/ng-interactive/2017/oct/27/beyond-catalonia-pro-independence-movements-in-europe-map.
Keating, M., Loughlin, J. et al. (2003), *Culture, Institutions and Economic Development. A Study of Eight European Regions* (Cheltenham: Edward Elgar).
Mill, J. S. (1972), *Utilitarianism: On Liberty and Considerations on Representative Government* (London: Dent).
Moreno, L. (2001), *The Federalisation of Spain* (London: Frank Cass).
Ostrom, V., Bish, R. et al. (1988), *Local Government in the United States* (San Francisco: Institute for Contemporary Studies).
Pollitt, C. and Bouckaert, G. (2017), *Public Management Reform. A Comparative Analysis of New Public Management, Governance and the Neo-Weberian State* (Oxford: Oxford University Press).
Rokkan, S. and Urwin, D. (1983), *Economy, Territory, Identity: Politics of West European Peripheries* (London: Sage).

12 National Governments in the EU Political System

SIMONA PIATTONI

12.1 Introduction

Previous chapters have described how political institutions and the process of government works at the national level in European democracies. For member states of the European Union (EU), this account is incomplete without also considering how governments work together through the EU institutions to produce joint decisions across a broad range of policy areas. This requires an analysis of both how the EU is structured and how decision-making works in practice at the EU level.

It is notoriously difficult to classify the EU political system. Most definitions of the EU must resort to indicating what the EU is not rather than clearly stating what it is: 'neither a state nor an international organization' (Sbragia 1992: 257), 'a mixed federal and confederal system' (Hix and Goetz 2000), 'less than a federation, more than a regime' (Wallace 1983: 403). In part this is due to its unconventional nature—the EU is often referred to as a *sui generis* (i.e. unique) political system (Hix 1994)—but in part also to its constantly changing nature. Very few political systems are in such constant state of flux as the EU. In the course of its not so long existence (the European Economic Community was created by the Treaties of Rome in 1957) it has acquired twenty-two new member states (but also lost one, the UK), giving a current total of twenty-seven, in a process often optimistically indicated as 'widening'. Meanwhile, it has constantly expanded its competences to new policy areas, in a process normally denoted as 'deepening'. Moreover, several other countries have special relations with the EU without being full EU member states: suffice to think of the countries who belong to the European Economic Area (Iceland and Norway) and the European Free Trade Agreement (Liechtenstein and Switzerland), those who have entered negotiation procedures to become member states (the current candidate countries are Serbia, Montenegro, Albania, Moldova, North Macedonia, Ukraine, and Turkey, although negotiations with the latter have stalled) and territories that have a special relationship to the EU by virtue of their being protectorates or former colonies of current EU member states (the so-called outermost regions, former French,

Portuguese, or Spanish colonies, or the overseas countries and territories, such as Greenland and the Faroe Islands, autonomous territories of Denmark).

To make matters even more complicated is the realization that the EU political system does not extend its regulatory and legal reach equally to all member states. Some member states have obtained temporary exemptions from certain obligations (e.g. Sweden could keep in place for several years after accession its monopoly state-owned alcohol-selling shops, *Systembolaget*, which clearly flaunted single market provisions), while others obtained permanent opt-outs and exemptions from entire policy chapters (e.g. Denmark obtained an opt-out to remain permanently outside of the Euro currency). Such is the extent of differentiation within the EU that an entire body of literature has developed theorizing that what characterizes the EU is a process of '*differentiated* integration' (Leruth and Lord 2015; Leruth et al. 2022; Brunazzo 2019), which lately was extended to entertain the possibility that this could in fact be a process of 'differentiated *disintegration*' (Leruth et al. 2019).

While other political systems may also contain special provisions for some of their territories and special exemptions for some of their policies which are then subjected to periodical revisions, the extent of differentiation and change inherent in the European construction is such that the political system of the EU can hardly be compared with those of most national states. In addition, the EU is particularly sensitive to multiple crises that often shape its evolution, so much so that 'integration through crises' (D'Erman and Verdun 2018) is a commonplace understanding of the evolutionary pattern of the EU. While this may be true, it does not make the task of describing and categorizing the political system of the EU any simpler for political scientists. What remains particularly problematic and subject to change is the relationship between the EU and its member states.

What gets configured, then, is a particularly complex kaleidoscope of relations in which virtually all of its elements change simultaneously. Many scholars have converged on a description of the EU as a *multilevel system of governance*, in which multiple governmental levels and non-governmental actors interact differently in different policy areas, giving rise to flexible governance arrangements that do not crystallize into a single permanent and uniform constitutional configuration (Hooghe and Marks 2001; Piattoni 2010). At the centre of this literature is an interest in how policies are made and implemented: how 'governing' takes place in the EU.

To give a sense of how the EU is structured and works, the chapter is organized as follows. In the next Section (12.2), I address the question of how the EU should be conceptualized, and describe the relationship between the main EU institutions, with a particular focus on the role of national governments. In Section 12.3 I compare the EU to national templates such as federal and consociational systems, and also examine how the character of the EU has varied over time and across policy areas. The issues of the effectiveness and legitimacy of this *sui generis* political system will be at the centre of Section 12.4, that discusses how the EU political system calls into question conventional notions of democracy. Section 12.5 concludes.

12.2 How should we conceptualize the EU?

The EU is a political system in which many institutional and non-institutional, individual and collective actors interact—among them, representatives of national governments—but is it a *state*? The fact that it lacks many competences in core, defining state areas—such as defence, law and order, culture and education, taxation—induces some authors to question the very *stateness* of the EU.

The EU lacks both police and military powers, cannot really pursue a cultural and educational policy of its own, and has so far been unable to impose EU-wide taxes of any significance. Even its most remarkable statist traits—a common currency, a common monetary policy, and a common trade policy—are not backed up by a commensurate fiscal power, the capacity to borrow money without the explicit and conditional permission of all member states, and the freedom to enter trade agreements in all possible areas (for example, energy trade is still in the hands of the individual member states). The legal system of the EU is allegedly superordinate to that of its member states—or so it is according to the European Court of Justice (ECJ), which has claimed for itself competence over the extent of its own competences (Weiler 1996; Griller and Ziller 2008)—but this superiority is frequently challenged both by national politicians and by national constitutional courts. What is more important, the EU still lacks a *demos*—a people who share a sense of being part of a political community. So, the EU still appears to be a rather unique construct that does not have the core powers and features that we normally associate with national states.

Yet, this does not prevent it from functioning as a *political system*. EU politics is vibrant and has shown a tendency to become increasingly intertwined with that of the individual member states. If only a few years ago it could be rightfully argued that national public opinion ignored political events in the other member states and that national parliaments were hardly involved in EU policymaking (van der Eijk and Franklin 2007), this is no longer true (see Chapter 17). The long-evoked 'politicization' of the EU has finally occurred. Even if an EU public sphere worthy of this name is still in the making, EU-wide issues are now frequently the subject of public debate in member states (think of the Euro crisis, the refugee crisis and the Covid-19 crisis) and people pay increasing attention to what takes place in other member states (Carreri 2018). The fiscal and budgetary policies of each Eurozone member state—the members that share the common currency, the Euro are matters of national relevance for all other Eurozone member states, and tabs are kept, and scores are given (by the European Commission) on the way in which each of them runs its own economic affairs. In other words, there is a lot of looking over each other's shoulders in the EU, as the political developments and policy choices of the other member states become matters of national relevance.

We need to recall that the EU was born as a system in which national executive representatives would meet to promote their joint and several interests in the Council of Ministers (now known simply as the Council). They were and still are assisted in this task by the Commission, a body of high-level bureaucrats that serves as a secretariat that facilitates policy decisions, suggests new areas of collaboration and oversees and enforces intergovernmental agreements. The Commission's activity is supported by the ECJ, whose task is to adjudicate disputes on the application of EU law between member states, between member states and the Commission, and between individual firms and citizens, on one hand, and EU institutions and member states, on the other (see Chapter 10). Since 1979, a directly elected European Parliament has increasingly shared legislative responsibility with Council and is now co-legislator of most EU legislation. Chief executives of the member states—heads of state and government—also meet periodically to impart political direction to the Union. Their meetings were at first sporadic and informal but, since 1974, they have been scheduled more regularly and, since the Treaty of Lisbon of 2009, the European Council has been formally inserted among the official institutions of the EU and its meetings held a lot more frequently.

As mentioned, the institutional configuration of the EU is rather unique. Legislative, executive, and judicial functions are shared both across EU institutions and between national and EU levels. The legislative function is normally shared between the Council and the European Parliament with different procedures and majorities depending on the issue at hand. They work roughly as the two chambers of a federal system, with the Council expressing the will of the national constituencies and the European Parliament that of the EU people (but, as we shall see, the parallel stops here) (cf. Papadopoulos 2013). Since the Treaty of Lisbon, but much more since the Euro crisis (see Chapter 13), the European Council has been increasingly involved in policymaking in that it made some of the most sensitive decisions and more generally gives political direction to the EU as a whole.

The executive function is also shared by many institutions at different levels. The Commission is administratively responsible just for a handful of policy areas, but much more frequently it oversees the implementation of EU legislation by national and subnational executives. In some rather technical policy areas, moreover, the Commission performs all three functions, finessing the legislative details of 'framework legislation', overseeing its implementation and sometimes also adjudicating disputes among member states or private litigants (e.g. in competition policy). Finally, the ECJ, lately renamed Court of Justice of the European Union to also include the former Court of First Instance, adjudicates disputes that arise from EU legislation. However, it does so when EU institutions or member states or even individual European citizens bring a case to its attention or when the members of national judiciaries ask for its opinion and manage to be heard because of the intrinsic interest of the case. So, not even the judicial function is exclusively lodged at one level.

As can be easily gleaned from the previous information, the institutional architecture of the EU is rather complex as it entails multiple and diverse types of relations between national representatives and EU institutions. Obviously, all EU institutions are made of member states' nationals, but while some of them are expected to represent the interests of the national constituencies, others are supposed to express the voice and will of the EU citizenry as a whole. A distinction is thus drawn between *intergovernmental* and *supranational* institutions in the EU. Intergovernmental institutions are where national governments are represented, and these include the Council and the European Council. Supranational institutions are independent from national governments and include the European Parliament, the Commission, and the ECJ. Consequently, the way in which national representatives relate to these institutions and to one another is rather different in the different institutions. We expect heads of state and government sitting in the European Council and national ministers sitting in the Council to represent the *national interests* of the member states, while the Commissioners, the Chefs de Cabinet, and the functionaries in the Commission, the members of the European Parliament, and the judges and advocates of the ECJ to represent different national sensitivities but *common European values and objectives*. Clearly, this is a somewhat arbitrary distinction as, of course, the members of the national executives also share common European values and objectives. Still, the institutional context in which they operate allows them—in fact, requires them—to pursue, within the framework of EU-level cooperation, their distinctive national interests.

This complex web of interrelations is described in Figure 12.1. This figure distinguishes between national, intergovernmental, and supranational institutions and actors. It also includes actors that can be described as *transnational*, in that they operate horizontally across national

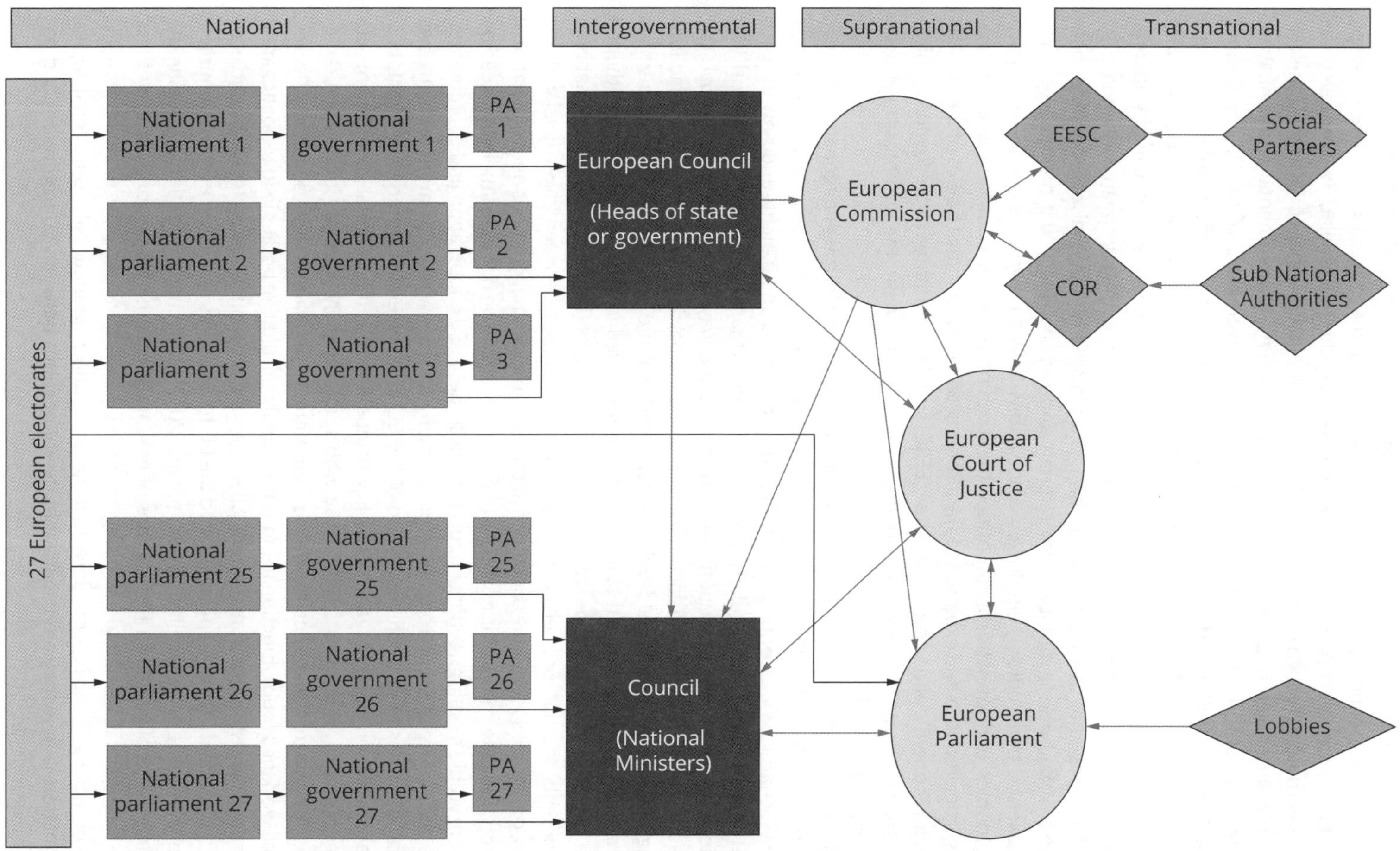

Figure 12.1 Relationship between national and EU institutions

Note: Black arrows = election/legitimation/authorization/oversight; grey arrows = interinstitutional relations/consultation/lobbying.

boundaries. Collectively and severally the citizens of the member states are the sovereigns of this complex political structure. At the national level, the citizens of the twenty-seven EU member states elect parliamentary representatives who in turn elect twenty-seven national governments, which oversee most of the implementation of national and EU policies through twenty-seven national public administrations (PA). Governmental representatives are active also at the EU level in the intergovernmental institutions of the EU, the Council and the European Council. The supranational level includes the European Parliament, which is directly elected by EU citizens and co-legislates with the Council on EU matters. It also includes the ECJ and the European Commission, whose members are nominated by national executives and (in the case of the Commission) approved by the European Parliament. The ECJ, firmly lodged at the supranational level, is addressed by many diverse subjects, both institutional and non-institutional, for referrals and rulings. Finally, the many civil society organizations, trade unions, employers' associations (collectively indicated as 'social partners'), lobbies, and subnational authorities, that span both the trans- and the supranational realms, bring requests and expertise to the attention of the consultative bodies of the EU—the European Economic and Social Committee (EESC) and the Committee of the Regions (CoR)—and pressure to bear upon members of the European Parliament, the Commission and, on occasion, also the ECJ.

In this complex institutional setting, cooperation is achieved through negotiation, but coordination on the distribution of costs and benefits of each policy decision is exceedingly difficult (Scharpf 2000). Conflicts on how to apportion costs and benefits and how to reach shared objectives are more regularly reported by the press than the daily nitty-gritty work that gets done 'in Brussels' to iron out these tensions and find ways in which common goals can be reached to the (partial) satisfaction of all negotiating parties. Therefore, the interactions among different governmental levels are perceived as more conflictual than they perhaps really are. Often negotiations that at one point get blocked in the Council are smoothened by the unobtrusive work of the permanent representatives (i.e. representatives of national governments based in Brussels) or through informal contacts between lower-level working groups, only to be successfully concluded at the next round of negotiations between national ministers. Delicate compromises are chiselled away at a remove from the limelight placed on the more visible meetings, setting important milestones in EU cooperation and coordination.

The complexity of EU policymaking explains why scholars who focus more on high-level political decisions tend to offer a picture of the EU as an essentially intergovernmental organization that only goes as far in its policy competences as the national governments are willing to go (e.g. Moravcsik 1998). Those who study the daily work of Commission directorates, European Parliament legislative committees, permanent representatives' tables, Council working groups, functional and subnational consultative bodies in low-politics areas rather emphasize the 'neo-functionalist' character of the Union based on technical and economic cooperation, where 'spillovers' lead the EU to extend its reach into ever more numerous policy areas (e.g. Sandholtz and Stone-Sweet 2012). Both characterizations are legitimate but run the risk of yielding infinite reruns of the same academic discussions between these highly schematic ways of understanding how the EU works. Moreover, as we have seen, EU decision-making involves both intergovernmental and supranational institutional logics: what matters is how they are balanced in the interactions between EU institutions and national governments.

12.3 National governments in the EU: Two perspectives

It should be clear by now that the EU political system and the place of national governments within it defies simple characterization. This does not mean, however, that we should abandon any attempt to generalize about the complex realities of EU governance. In this section, I will present two main ways of looking at the interactions between national representatives (in whatever capacity they happen to act) and EU institutions, each of which provides useful insights into the nature of the EU. The first is to start from the formal institutional architecture of the EU and compare it to templates from national political systems. This amounts to considering the EU as a federal or a consociational democracy. The second is to distinguish between broad policy areas and analyse each of them as characterized by a particular decision-making mode. To this strand belong the multilevel and network governance characterizations of the EU (Eising and Kohler-Koch 1999; Piattoni 2010) that see the EU as mosaic of different policy regimes. These policy regimes have been more prominent at different points in time, depending on the particular policy issues at the centre of EU-level discussions and negotiations. This has suggested a 'dynamic' theorization of the EU as moving across periods characterized by one type of decision-making mode followed by periods in which a different decision-making mode prevailed. According to this view, EU decision-making functions as a pendulum that swings between extremes often determined by crisis situations or other momentous turning points such as successive enlargement rounds.

12.3.1 National templates

The first way of looking at intergovernmental interactions at the EU level tries to compare the EU to particularly complex national political systems. The most common comparison is drawn with federal systems (see Box 12.1 for a distinction between unitary, federal, and confederal systems).

The interactions that prevail between national representatives at the EU level may be said to resemble more closely those that characterize German cooperative federalism than those that describe American competitive federalism (Scharpf 1988, 2000). Because the EU, just like Germany, cannot directly carry out its own policy decisions but has to use state administrations to this end, and because decisions are usually taken by unanimity (even when unanimous agreement among member states is not formally required—see Box 12.2), states retain a sort of blackmailing power vis-à-vis the centre. Because decisions are normally reached through laborious negotiations, where several items are simultaneously discussed so as to arrive at 'package deals' within which all national representatives find some particularly coveted decisions, they are inclined to accept also the less palatable ones contained in the package. This decision-making stratagem worked brilliantly for the EU for many decades, particularly in pushing forward the Single Market construction, but has become more challenging since Council and European Council meetings have begun address individual items separately and the discussions have become more politicized.

The comparison with German cooperative federalism also serves to highlight some important problems that can emerge when decisions are made jointly by the states who in turn implement those decisions. Decisions made by unanimity cannot be easily modified, as the opposition of just one state suffices to block any change (Scharpf (1988) dubbed this situation

Box 12.1 Unitary, federal and confederal systems

Unitary states recognize a single sovereign—the national people—that is normally represented by a single-chamber parliament. In contrast, federal states recognize multiple sovereigns—the national and the states peoples—who are normally represented in two chambers: in the second, federal chamber sit the representatives of the federated states (see also Chapters 9 and 11). State governments have a certain number of exclusive competences—areas in which they can legislate independently from one another and from the federal centre—and many more shared competences—where legislation can occur only when both levels, represented by the respective chambers, agree. The implementation of decisions can be allocated in various ways, giving rise to different types of federalisms (more or less centralized, more or less cooperative, uniform and differentiated). Federated states may have their own police force and their own judicial circuits as in the United States (US) but cannot autonomously secede nor single-handedly redefine their territories or competences. Just as there are many types of federal states (e.g. parliamentary or presidential), so there are many types of unitary states (think of the UK that has two parliamentary chambers and is a union of fairly distinctive states, although it is classified as a unitary state; or think of regionalized unitary states like Italy and France).

Confederations can be considered as loose federations, but differences run deeper than that. Sovereignty is firmly lodged in the component states and citizens normally obey first and foremost their states' laws. To carry out tasks that are better performed jointly (defence, money, justice), states grant some powers to the confederal centre which, however, is not the depository of a distinct source of sovereignty. Contrary to federal states, confederal states retain the right to secede, and the confederal government is a weak organ mostly representative of the component states. Moreover, while in federations the constitution is a rigid document, in confederations the constitution is a much more flexible document that can be fairly easily amended by the will of the confederal units, often following a direct initiative of the citizens (for a thorough discussion see Burgess 2000, 2006)

Box 12.2 Over to you—voting in the Council

On most matters, the Council of the European Union votes by qualified majority. This means that for a proposal to pass, it must be supported by at least fifteen out of the twenty-seven member states, and those member states must represent at least 65% of the total EU population. However, there is a 'culture of consensus' in the Council which means that every effort is made to reach a unanimous agreement among member states before putting a proposal to a vote.

To examine this, go to the public register of European Council voting results. You can restrict your search (by date, policy area, voting rule, and by the result of the vote) using the search filters. First, restrict your search to votes that are made using the qualified majority rule. You should find that for the vast majority of proposals, there is unanimous or almost unanimous agreement among member states. Why do you think this happens?

Now focus on proposals on which there are divisions in the Council (you can do this by selecting only the 'votes against' option in the voting results search filter). Do you notice any patterns in terms of the types of issues that give rise to divisions, or in terms of which member states most often vote against the agreement? What do you think explains these patterns?

a 'joint-decision trap'). A perfect example of this dynamic is the Dublin regulation (enshrined in a number of agreements signed in Dublin—the so-called Dublin I, II, and II agreements—between 1999 and 2013) which established the rule that the first member state that an asylum seeker enters is responsible for processing that application. These rules seemed like a good idea at the time they were negotiated, when refugee and migration flows were a trickle. These same agreements, however, became particularly penalizing for South-European member states lying at the outer borders of the EU with North Africa and the Middle East when the trickle turned into a flood. Yet despite the obvious shortcomings of the Dublin rules, member states found it very difficult to agree on an alternative solution (see Chapter 14).

Similarly, the deregulatory drive inherent in the full application of the EU's 'four freedoms' (free movement of goods, services, workers, and capital) removes certain national protections in the labour market, while the difficulty of arriving at agreements among member states for regulations at the EU level impedes the development of a common regulations to replace this. This dual asymmetry explains why 'negative integration'—the dismantling of national regulatory systems—is so much easier than 'positive integration'—the construction of a common regulatory system. In the field of social policy, failure to build a European social market economy constitutes a suboptimal result for the Union as a whole as well as for many of its member states (Scharpf 2006). Steps forward have been made both because unanimity is increasingly replaced by (qualified) majority voting in intergovernmental EU institutions and because situations of crisis force decisions that would have been unthinkable in normal times, but the habit of deciding by unanimity still triggers joint decision-making dynamics.

A similar attempt to borrow insights from national interinstitutional dynamics to illustrate EU intergovernmental dynamics has been made by reference to Lijphart's 'consociational democracy' (Lijphart 1976, 1999). In Lijphart's theory, political systems characterized by multiple, overlapping social cleavages (such as the Netherlands and Switzerland) can be held together by the accommodating attitude of their elites. These manage to arrive at consensual decisions by treading carefully on issues that are particularly sensitive for the communities that they represent, by abstaining from regulating particularly sensitive areas, and by striking compromises on issues that are advantageous to all. The communities of Lijphart's theorization are not formal states, but sub-cultural communities ('social segments') that, while sharing very little in terms of a common identity, still find it convenient to regulate jointly a number of economic and political aspects (Bogaards 1998; Bogaards and Crepaz 2002). The accommodating stance of the elites is what allows consociational democracies to thrive and to arrive at common decisions while keeping the communities at a safe distance. In fact, the separation of the communities and the legitimacy of the elites are functional to the latter's ability to negotiate mutually favourable agreements.

A comparable situation existed during the early decades of European integration, when decisions were restricted to relatively non-contentious economic issues that benefited all member states. However, this began to change with the Treaty of Maastricht (1992), which represented a significant deepening of the process of integration. What was once characterized as a 'permissive consensus' (i.e. the public were content to let the political leaders get on with European integration) has turned into an increasingly 'constraining dissensus' (where hostile public opinion increasingly acts as a barrier to integration) (Hooghe and Marks 2009). Nevertheless, the parallel with consociational democracies still holds, and helps to explain how the EU can function as a political system despite a lack of a common political community.

12.3.2 **Policy regimes**

A second way to look at intergovernmental interactions at the EU level is to analyse it policy area by policy area. In this reading, different policy areas are assumed to be inherently more or less prone to unleash hard intergovernmental bargaining or lead to less dramatic negotiations in more secluded institutional venues where supranational institutions and values are more important. Policy areas are often distinguished as belonging to 'high' or to 'low' politics, i.e. areas of intervention that belong to core, defining state competences as opposed to areas that are less vital and essential for the state. The former require the involvement of the uppermost echelons of the bureaucracy and ministerial entourage, while the latter are best handled by lower-level bureaucrats and technical experts.

According to this reading, in policy areas in which national interests play a major role, ministers from national governments are directly involved in intergovernmental negotiations. In some policy areas—such as security and defence policy or budgetary policy—decision-making is prepared by a set of committees and working groups staffed with high-level national experts that operate at a remove from representative democracy but are in close contact with national executives. These include, for example, top-level advisers from the Economy and Finance minister's office in the case of budgetary policy or ambassadors and high-ranking military personnel in the case of security and defence policy. In other technical but less sensitive policy areas—such as agricultural policy, competition policy, or environmental policy—the EU operates through committees staffed with technical experts also nominated by national governments but mostly drawn from national bureaucracies, national universities, and research institutes. Examples thereof are the many committees that decide, for example, on the price of crops or the composition of pesticides that characterize the common agricultural policy. In these committees, intergovernmental bargaining does not involve a clash of 'national interests', but rather reflects scientific or academic convictions often shared across borders in transnational epistemic (i.e. knowledge-based) communities (Joerges and Neyer 2002). The first set of issues are often discussed at length in Council meetings (designated as 'B list' items), while the second set are normally finessed by the permanent representatives and approved without Council discussion (known as 'A list' items).

In addition to distinguishing between policy areas based on the extent to which decisions are made by elected representatives and high-ranking bureaucrats or by technical experts and lower-level bureaucrats, another distinction concerns the extent to which supranational institutions are involved in the policymaking process. The single market operates through the full activation of the supranational institutions of the EU, so much so that it appears to be governed by a 'supranational constitution' (Fabbrini 2013). To this area belong those policy areas in which the 'community method' is applied, entailing the exercise of the Commission's legislative initiative, the exertion of the co-legislative powers of the Council and the European Parliament often deciding on the basis of (qualified) majority voting, and the availability of the full supervisory and adjudicatory activity of the ECJ.

What to say, though, of those momentous decisions—like those made during the Euro crisis (see Chapter 13)—that sidelined both national and European parliaments and were the result of *international* agreements? According to Sergio Fabbrini (2013), the treaty of Maastricht created a parallel 'intergovernmental constitution' in areas pertaining to the

Economic and Monetary Union (EMU). In monetary and, increasingly, also fiscal matters, the Commission is shorn of its power of initiative which has been de facto appropriated by the European Council and has been demoted—but to some extent also elevated—to the level of executor of the will of these intergovernmental bodies, while the supervisory role of the European Parliament and the adjudicating role of the ECJ have been more or less completely sidelined.

The accuracy of this picture, that was heavily shaped particularly by the Euro crisis and the emergency legislation that was enacted to counter it in numerous European Council meetings, sometimes through international agreements that bypassed the more cumbersome procedures of EU law, may be questioned. Still, it is true that particularly during the early phases of the Euro crisis a 'Union method', as it was called by the German Chancellor Angela Merkel, tended to replace the more conventional and supranational 'Community method'. Under the Union method, intergovernmentalism prevails, revealing the unevenness of inter-state power relations. In the EMU, and particularly in the Eurozone, power relations are tilted in favour of the so-called *core countries*—Germany, Austria, and the Netherlands—that have more balanced public accounts, higher primary surpluses, and more favourable credit ratings. They are often backed up in intergovernmental bargaining by so-called *frugal countries*—a different club comprising also Denmark, Finland, and Sweden, that normally back up Germany's conservative stance in monetary matters. Disadvantaged, hence relatively powerless in EMU and Eurozone negotiations, are the *peripheral and southern countries*—Greece, Ireland, Portugal, and Spain—which suffered enormously during the Euro crisis and were at times derogatorily indicated as PIGS.

What is most disconcerting, however, is not so much the rift that was created during the Euro crisis between EU core and peripheral member states, but rather the absence of a representative body that could oversee the decisions made during intergovernmental negotiations and an independent adjudicating body that could review the compatibility of these decisions with the principles of EU law (Fabbrini 2019). The constitutionality of some of the more dramatic decisions made during the Euro crisis—e.g. the decision on the part of the European Central Bank to act as a lender of last resort, a role which had not been envisioned by the original Maastricht treaty—could therefore be challenged and discussed *only* in *national* parliaments and in *national* constitutional courts. For example, the German Constitutional Court was asked to rule on the legitimacy of the German government's decision to contribute to the European Stability Mechanism (ESM) using German taxpayers' money to support programme countries in their effort to correct their imbalances after the Euro crisis. This creates an asymmetry between decisions made at the EU level and democratic and constitutional checks that can be activated only at the national level.

Yet, much of the legislation enacted during the Euro crisis via exceptional mechanisms has been 'normalized' in more recent times. New chapters of far-reaching legislation have been adopted through more conventional mechanisms surpassing even the most sceptical views as to the impossibility of approving EU-wide social legislation. For example, the short-term employment schemes (SURE) programme gave unemployment compensation support to EU workers during the Covid pandemic, and EU bonds backed by the EU budget have been issued to provide fresh resources to those countries that have been most hard hit by the ensuing economic crisis (through the Next Generation EU programme).

12.4 Effectiveness and legitimacy of the EU political system

Just as the interpretations of how the EU political system works differ, so do opinions on its effectiveness and legitimacy. From the previous discussion it is already possible to identify two opposite positions. One position derives the legitimacy of the EU political system from that of the democratically elected governmental representatives who, mainly in the intergovernmental institutions of the EU—the European Council and Council—make decisions on behalf of their national constituencies. The powers of the European Parliament are, at best, an add-on: a nod in the direction of a still-to-come EU democracy if an EU demos were ever to emerge (Moravcsik 2002). The effectiveness of the Union depends on the extent to which national governmental representatives manage to strike intergovernmental agreements that promote their national interests by finding common solutions to common problems. In this view, national sovereignty is only conditionally and temporarily devolved to EU institutions as long as and insofar as doing so serves the several national interests (Moravcsik 1998). However, since EU decisions, being the result of compromises, cannot by definition fully reflect the national interest of any national constituency as formulated at the beginning of the negotiations, national governmental representatives have the task of convincing their constituents that the resulting decisions were in fact opportune and advantageous. National representatives are thus asked to explain and take responsibility for decisions made in Brussels, a task which they are not particularly keen on performing.

The opposite position lodges the legitimacy of the EU in the extent to which an (admittedly still forming) EU demos manages to express its voice and exert its will through the supranational institutions of the EU. The task, and almost mission, of these institutions—the Commission, the European Parliament and the ECJ—is to pursue the general will of the EU demos and provide, at the EU level, the necessary democratic safeguards. This is of course a big challenge and a difficult claim to make: the relationship between the European Parliament and the EU 'government'—if by that we mean the Commission and the many EU agencies that carry out some of the decisions made in Brussels—is not what we would expect in a parliamentary democracy. Despite the attempt to propose party-political candidates for the position of Commission President through the *Spitzenkandidaten* procedure (see Chapter 17), the European Parliament does not yet elect a government as would be the case in national parliamentary democracies. Moreover, large parts of EU legislation are in fact implemented by state administrations over which the European Parliament has no oversight but the ECJ could still sanction in case of failed implementation. Therefore, the legitimacy of the EU in this view depends on the extent to which EU citizens find that EU decisions give voice to their aspirations (input legitimacy) or provide answers to their problems (output legitimacy) (Schmidt 2013; see also Chapter 17).

Neither position then manages to provide a fully convincing argument for the legitimacy of the EU political system nor for its capacity to deliver effective policy decisions. But is it reasonable to expect so much of *any* political system? Are there not, in all democracies, segments of the population that are deeply dissatisfied with the functioning of the political system and question its ultimate legitimacy? In established democracies and in times of normalcy this would not be the case, but a modicum of radical contestation would be present even there and then. Our current times, however, are not times of normalcy, at least judging

Box 12.3 Over to you—EU citizens on the most pressing concerns

To see what European citizens worry about and whether they want the EU to deal with their most pressing concerns, connect to the Eurobarometer web site and access the Standard bi-annual Eurobarometer (e.g. Standard Eurobarometer 98—Winter 2022-23) Check what Europeans worry about (the relevant question is 'What do you think are the two most important issues facing the EU at the moment?') and get a sense for how these concerns have changed over time by looking at earlier surveys (the data cover roughly the last two decades). You will find that Europeans mostly worry about economic issues—whether the financial crisis, as in the 2010s, or rising inflation, more recently. Why do you think this is? What connection is there between the state of the economy and popular confidence in the EU? You may also want to compare the sentiments of the various national citizenries about the future of the EU—whether they are optimistic, pessimistic or neutral—and compare these data with previous Standard Eurobarometers to have a sense of their evolution over time. Through the many Eurobarometers surveys, you will be able to also check EU public opinion on other important issues, such as the war in Ukraine, the energy crisis or the Green Deal.

from the extent to which radical parties are springing up and gaining traction in all European democracies (Kriesi and Pappas 2018). Eurosceptic and populist parties are emerging everywhere in the EU and some of them have managed to gain parliamentary majorities and form governments (see Chapter 18).

The fact of the matter is that EU and national democracies are mutually dependent both for their perceived legitimacy and for their perceived effectiveness so that any comparison or contrast between them is eventually misleading. The attribution of merit and blame for popular or unpopular decisions is objectively difficult and the legitimacy of the system depends on coming to terms with its complexity. In times of heightened interdependence, neither full repatriation of all decision-making powers to national democracies nor complete surrender of sovereignty to supranational organizations are possible or desirable options. The answer rather consists in the laborious search for intermediate solutions and finely crafted cooperation. The possibility must also be entertained that democracy as is normally theorized—as chains of delegation and accountability between the sovereign people and its agents (such as elected representatives) (Curtin 2007)—should be replaced with a more complex notion of democracy that admits multiple sovereigns and intertwined chains of both delegation and accountability (Piattoni 2017). Whether this democracy amounts to a *demoicracy* (Nicolaidis 2013)—a democratic system in which many *demoi* (peoples) decide to govern together, though not as one—or to a *compound democracy* (Fabbrini 2010)—a democracy with multiple separations of power and no decision-making centre—or something else, remains to be seen.

12.5 Conclusion

This chapter charted the difficulty of precisely stating what kind of political system the European Union is by way of comparing it with national political systems, given that it still lacks all the defining traits of a state (although it does have some of them). While comparisons with national systems (such as federalism or consociationalism) do yield important insights, it is impossible to neatly categorize the EU in these terms. This difficulty suggests we should think of it as a system of governance, where bits and pieces of national and supranational institutions cooperate to make and implement decisions on behalf of the national *demoi* as well as on behalf of the budding EU demos. National governmental representatives interact in different ways with one another and with European institutions depending on the policy at hand and the historical moment in which decisions are made. While the potential benefits for states in working together through the EU are clear, the resulting legitimacy of the system and effectiveness of its decisions depend on the extent to which fine-tuned compromises are crafted and relayed to national constituencies as being the best possible solutions for difficult problems.

Discussion questions

1. EU decision-making is sometimes seen as the outcome of intergovernmental negotiations among member states' representatives pursuing their national interests; and at other times it is seen as the product of an inner functional drive that spills from one policy area over to others. Can you identify policy areas or major decisions for which one or the other decision-making mode prevailed?
2. The EU is a very complex, multi-level political system that can hardly be likened to that of any other existing democracy. Still, can institutional or behavioural parallels be drawn between some such formats and the EU? How useful are they?
3. Do you think that the existence of an EU *demos* is a necessary precondition for the creation of an EU supra-state and the establishment of a fully functioning EU democracy? Do you find this scenario likely and appealing, or do you think it is unlikely and undesirable? Explain why.
4. The EU is one of the most complex political systems in the world. Would its democratic temper improve if the European Parliament were given the task to form a European government, as in other parliamentary systems, or if European citizens could directly elect a President of the Commission who would then form their own cabinet, as in presidential systems? Would there be any drawbacks or risks with this?
5. Some argue that EU membership undermines national sovereignty, as states give up power to 'Brussels'. Others counter that member states retain an effective veto on matters of key national interest, and that being part of a powerful block enhances rather than diminishes national sovereignty. What is your view?

Thinking Comparatively

The EU has often been compared to federal states or to consociational (compound) democracies. The chapter has argued that these comparisons can only go so far, yet the exercise may still be useful. The comparison between the EU and the United States (US) is rather common, but it is normally used to mark differences in the evolution of the EU vis-à-vis that of the US or to indicate under what circumstances the EU may be driven to speed up its integration process (Fabbrini 2010). Much recent debate has addressed what may have been a 'Hamiltonian moment' (named after the US Founding Father who collectivized the debt of US states), when in the wake of the Covid pandemic the Next Generation EU programme and particularly its Recovery and Resilience Facility led to the creation of an EU-backed common debt, a step that had been categorically ruled out until then. An uncommon, but arguably more appropriate, comparison could be drawn with India, a democracy in which the diversity of languages and cultures is comparable to that of the EU, but the few remarks in this direction can be found only in the blogs of some think tanks (e.g. Bomassi 2013).

Guide to further reading

Bickerton, C., Hodson, D. et al. (2015), *The New Intergovernmentalism. States and Supranational Actors in the Post-Maastricht Era* (Oxford: Oxford University Press).

This volume theorizes the way in which intergovernmental decision-making has intensified but also changed its nature since the creation of the EMU established with the treaty of Maastricht and even more after the Euro crisis.

Fabbrini, S. (2010), *Compound Democracies. Why the United States and Europe Are Becoming Similar* (Oxford: Oxford University Press).

Starting from the US historical experience, this book suggests that the EU might replicate the evolution of the US towards a federation, given that both have (had) to safeguard the integrity of existing state communities while performing together an increasing number of economic activities.

Wallace, H., Pollack, M. et al. (eds) (2020), *Policy-Making in the European Union*, eighth edn (Oxford: Oxford University Press).

A classic reference on policy-making in the European Union.

Nicolaidis, K. and Howse, R. (eds.) (2001), *The Federal Vision. Legitimacy and Levels of Governance in the United States and the European Union* (Oxford: Oxford University Press).

A collection of first-rate essays that propose highly sophisticated interpretations of the federal features of a 'union of states' like the EU.

References

Bogaards, M. (1998), 'The favourable factors of consociational democracy; A review', *European Journal of Political Research*, 33: 475–96.

Bogaards, M. and Crepaz, M. (2002), 'Consociational interpretations of the European Union', *European Union Politics*, 3(3): 357–81.

Bomassi, L. (2013), 'Europe and India: Not so different after all', *Carnegie Europe*, available at https://carnegieeurope.eu/2013/01/25/europe-and-india-not-so-different-after-all-pub-50738.

Brunazzo, M. (2019), 'The Evolution of EU Differentiated Integration between Crises and Dilemmas', *EUIDEA Research Papers* N. 1, available at https://www.iai.it/sites/default/files/euidea_rp_1.pdf.

Burgess, M. (2000), *Federalism and the European Union: The Building of Europe, 1950–2000* (London: Routledge).

Burgess, M. (2006), *Comparative Federalism. Theory and Practice* (London: Routledge).

Carreri, L. (2018), 'Awakening the sleeping giant? The Euro crisis and EU issue voting in Germany', *Partecipazione e Conflitto*, 11(3): 838–64.

Curtin, D. (2007), 'Holding (quasi-)autonomous EU administrative actors to public account', *European Law Journal*, 13(4): 523–41.

D'Erman, V. and Verdun, A. (2018), 'Introduction: Integration through crises', *Review of European and Russian Affairs*,12(1): 1–16.

Eising, R and Kohler-Koch, B (1999), 'Introduction: network governance in the European Union'. In Kohler-Koch, B. and Eising, R. (eds), *The Transformation of Governance in the European Union* (London: Routledge): 3–13.

Fabbrini, S. (2010), *Compound Democracies. Why the United States and Europe Are Becoming Similar* (Oxford: Oxford University Press).

Fabbrini, S. (2013), 'Intergovernmentalism and its limits: Assessing the European Union's answer to the Euro crisis', *Comparative Political Studies*, 20(10): 1–27.

Fabbrini, S. (2019), *Europe's Future: Decoupling and Reforming* (Cambridge: Cambridge University Press).

Franklin, M. and van der Eijk, C. (2007), 'The sleeping giant: Potential for political mobilization of disaffection in Europe', in van der Brug, W. and van der Eijk, C. (eds), *European Elections and Domestic Politics: Lessons from the Past and Scenarios for the Future* (Notre Dame, IN: University of Notre Dame Press): 189–208.

Griller, S. and Ziller, J. (eds) (2008), *The Lisbon Treaty. EU Constitutionalism without a Constitutional Treaty?* (Vienna: Springer).

Hix, S. (1994), 'The study of the European community: The challenge to comparative politics', *West European Politics*, 17(1): 1–30.

Hix, S. and Goetz, K. (2000), 'Introduction: European integration and national political systems', *West European Politics*, 23(4): 1–16.

Hooghe, L. and Marks, G. (2001), *Multi-Level Governance and European Integration* (Lanham, MD: Rowman & Littlefield).

Hooghe, L. and Marks, G. (2009), 'A postfunctionalist theory of European integration: From permissive consensus to constraining dissensus', *British Journal of Political Science*, 39(1): 1–23.

Joerges, C. and Neyer, J. (2002), 'from intergovernmental bargaining to deliberative political processes: The constitutionalisation of comitology', *European Law Journal*, 3(3): 273–99.

Kriesi, H. and Pappas, T. (eds) (2018), *European Populism in the Shadow of the Great Recession* (Colchester: ECPR Press).

Leruth, B. and Lord, C. (2015), 'Differentiated integration in the European Union: a concept, a process, a system or a theory?', *Journal of European Public Policy*, 22(6): 754–63.

Leruth, B., Gänzle, S., and Trondal, J. (2019), 'Differentiated integration and disintegration in the EU after Brexit: Risks versus opportunities', *Journal of Common Market Studies*, 57(6): 1383–94.

Leruth, B., Gänzle, S. et al. (2022), *The Routledge Handbook of Differentiation in the European Union* (London: Routledge).

Lijphart, A. (1976), *The Politics of Accommodation: Pluralism and Democracy in the Netherlands* (Berkeley, CA: The University of California Press).

Lijphart, A. (1999), *Patterns of Democracy. Government Forms and Performance in Thirty-Six Countries* (New Haven, NJ: Yale University Press).

Majone, G. (1998), 'Europe's "democratic deficit": The question of standards', *European Law Journal*, 4(1): 5–28.

Moravcsik, A. (1998), *The Choice for Europe. Social Purpose and State Power from Messina to Maastricht* (London: Routledge).

Moravcsik, A. (2002), 'In defense of the "democratic deficit": Reassessing legitimacy in the European Union', *Journal of Common Market Studies*, 40(4): 603–24.

Nicolaidis, K. (2013), 'European democracy and its crisis', *Journal of Common Market Studies*, 51(2): 351–69.

Papadopoulos, Y. (2013), *Democracy in Crisis? Politics Governance and Policy* (Basingstoke, UK: Palgrave Macmillan).

Piattoni, S. (2010), *The Theory of Multilevel Governance. Conceptual, Empirical and Normative Challenges* (Oxford: Oxford University Press).

Piattoni, S. (2017), 'The European Union between intergovernmentalism and "shared and responsible sovereignty": The haptic potential of EMU's institutional architecture (The Government and Opposition/Leonard Schapiro Lecture, 2016)', *Government and Opposition*, 52(3):1–27.

Sandholtz, W. and Stone-Sweet, A. (2012), 'Neo-Functionalism and supranational governance', in Jones, E., Menon, A. et al. (eds), *The Oxford Handbook of the European Union* (Oxford: Oxford University Press): 18–33.

Sbragia, A. (1992), *Europolitics: Institutions and Policymaking in the 'New' European Union* (Washington, DC: The Brookings Institute).

Scharpf, F. W. (1988), 'The joint-decision trap: Lessons from German federalism and European integration', *Public Administration*, 66(3): 239–78.

Scharpf, F. W. (2000), 'Notes toward a theory of multilevel governing in Europe', *MPIfG Discussion Paper*, 00/05, available at http://hdl.handle.net/10419/43294.

Scharpf, F. W. (2003), 'Problem-solving effectiveness and democratic accountability in the EU', *MPIfG Working Paper*, 03/01, available at http://hdl.handle.net/10419/41664.

Scharpf, F. W. (2006), 'The joint-decision trap revisited', *Journal of Common Market Studies*, 44(4): 845–64.

Schmitt, V. (2013), 'Democracy and legitimacy in the European Union revisited: Input, output and "throughput"', *Political Studies*, 61(1): 2–22.

Wallace, H. (2010), 'An institutional analysis and five policy modes', in Wallace, H., Pollak, M., et al. (eds.), *Policy-making in the European Union* (Oxford: Oxford University Press): 69–104.

Wallace, W. (1983), 'Less than a federation, more than a regime: The community as a political system', in Wallace, H., Wallace, W. et al. (eds.), *Policy-Making in the European Union*, 2nd edn (London: Wiley and Sons): 403–36.

Weiler, J. (1996), 'European neo-constitutionalism: In search of foundations for the European constitutional order', *Political Studies*, 44(3): 517–33.

Part 3

Common Challenges

13 Politics and Markets

NEIL ROBINSON AND OWEN WORTH

13.1 Introduction

The economy is never far away when we look at any specific collection of policies and issues within European Politics. The ideological battle between the left, which favours greater governmental intervention and investment in the economy, and the right, which believes in less intervention and greater emphasis on market forces, has been a constant issue in European politics over the last one hundred years. Yet politics is such that an economy cannot merely be started from scratch every time a new government comes into office and a move is made on the right-left spectrum. There are certain economic factors—both domestically and internationally—that contribute and shape what a government can achieve in office. This has become more evident for many European states since the advent of the Euro with the supply of money and interest rates being controlled by the European Central Bank (ECB), rather than by the respective state. The financial crisis that began in the late 2000s, and that soon developed into a sovereign debt crisis for many European states as they nationalized the international debts of bad banks, has shown that whilst countries might run their own economic affairs, external conditions have shaped their fiscal capabilities.

In addition to this, a country's size and its historical development play a large role in shaping its economy. Former super-powers such as France and the UK have had a very different historical journey than counties such as Finland or Cyprus and wield far more economic influence internationally. Equally, counties in Eastern Europe have had to go through a transition from communist planned economies just a few decades ago to market economies today. The very different economic journeys that these countries have had means that different constraints on their respective economies are going to be noticeable.

This chapter looks to outline the importance of political economy within comparative European politics by looking at how different economic models account for how states approach their economies. It will outline the different 'varieties of capitalism' that are often put forward to understand how economies are managed (Section 13.2). It will also show the problems and debates that have been thrown up by this categorization (Section 13.3). It will then look at the global financial crisis (GFC) of 2008 and the Covid-19 crisis and their implications for European political economy (Section 13.4).

13.2 Europe's varieties of capitalism

After World War II, Europe was split into two competing economic systems. While the planned socialist economies of East Europe were under Stalin's control, in Western Europe, the Marshall Plan was set up by the United States (US) to aid the re-building of war-torn economies and keep them from drifting towards the Soviet bloc. The US insisted funds would be withdrawn if governments showed any evidence of a pro-Soviet slant. Yet, at the same time, the growth in support for socialism saw the emergence of a set of welfare states in Western Europe. These welfare states were to define European capitalism in ways that were often different to American capitalism with its insistence on individual responsibility within society. As the post-war era developed, different variations of welfare systems emerged that were to form an integral part of each country's economic recovery.

Welfare states were set up in a manner to suit a particular economic system, but other factors also come into play in distinguishing one model of capitalism from another. For example, industrial relations differ from country to country, depending on the degree to which workers protected more through union representation. Some countries opted for a model of government involvement in running of a collection of companies, while others adopted a system that promoted less regulation and greater competition to maximize productivity. Finally, the tax structure of an economy differs vastly across Europe (Esping-Andersen 1996). Differences in taxation are not as straight-forward as they seem: some countries favour relatively high rates of income tax but lower rates for goods or businesses, and others favour the reverse. Where welfare states are extensive and help structure labour markets, and where there is state intervention in the economy and more extensive tax on businesses, the form of capitalism veers toward what Hall and Soskice (2001a: 9) called 'coordinated market capitalism'. Where welfare provision does not affect industrial relations and the government plays a less interventionist role in the affairs of firms the form of capitalism is 'liberal market capitalism'.

Differences across these areas have been used to identify four different models of capitalism within Europe: the *Anglo-Saxon Model*, traditionally favoured in Britain and Anglophone countries; the *Continental Model* or Rhineland model of capitalism, favoured in Germany, the Benelux countries and later in France; the *Nordic Model* that is associated with Scandinavia, and finally, *Mediterranean Capitalism*, which is a hybrid model that that has existed in some Southern European countries. The Anglo-Saxon model is associated with 'liberal market capitalism'. The Continental and Nordic models are different versions of 'coordinated market capitalism', distinguished from one another by their different welfare regimes, fiscal policies, and business-labour partnerships. Finally, we need to consider the forms that capitalism has taken in post-communist countries of Eastern Europe. Table 13.1 summarizes some of the main features of the main European models of capitalism.

13.2.1 **Anglo-Saxon Model**

The origins of the Anglo-Saxon model can be seen in the works of Adam Smith's *Wealth of Nations*, where Smith argues that market competition provides the most effective way of increasing productivity. This view was influential in shaping the British liberal state in the nineteenth century and the development of the American system of capitalism. This view became fashionable again in the 1970s and 1980s in the US, Australia, New Zealand, Canada,

Table 13.1 Varieties of capitalism

	Model			
	Anglo-Saxon	**Continental**	**Nordic**	**Mediterranean**
Regulation of market	Light regulation	Moderate regulation	Light to moderate direct regulation, strong regulation through industrial relations and welfare	Uneven mixture of regulatory regimes
Tax	Aims to set low tax rates for firms and individuals. Tax burdens often fall on individuals rather than firms, through weakly progressive tax systems and indirect taxes like sales taxes	High corporate taxes, progressive income taxes, high welfare contributions	Low corporate taxes/ high income taxes	Low tax take from income taxes despite some high tax rates, high taxes on consumption (sales taxes) and on firms
Industrial Relations	Variable levels of unionization, generally aims to increase labour market flexibility by empowering business over workers	High unionization. Partnership between government, unions and business	High unionization. Partnership between business and unions, strong historical link between unions and government parties	Weak Unionization, uneven patterns of government-union-business cooperation
Welfare System	Safety nets exist, sometimes for historical reasons, but may be weak, and/ or subject to political pressure, to increase labour flexibility	Strong pension, unemployment, health, education and pension systems, although some parts of the welfare system, like pensions, are strained	Strong pension, unemployment, health, education and pension systems. Strong social commitment to inclusive welfare regimes	Uneven welfare provision, mixture of private and public systems

and in Europe, in the UK, and Ireland. Its general premise is that the state should allow the market as much freedom as possible to allow firms to compete amongst each other with the goal of increasing profit margins and growth. Consequently, it favours private property, a low tax base, little regulation of industry and services and a flexible labour market, i.e. a labour market where it is easy to hire and fire workers, where workers move from economic sector and place to place to find employment (Crouch 2009).

In Europe, while the Anglo-Saxon model was historically associated with Britain, the landslide victory of the Labour Party in 1945 brought in a mixed-economic form of development that appeared at odds with the Anglo-Saxon tradition. The welfare state was developed and key industries such as iron and steel, coal, gas and electricity were nationalized. The Bank of England and the transport network also came under public control. This ushered in a period in British history known as the 'post-war consensus' (1945–79). After the election of Margaret Thatcher in 1979 this consensus fractured, and a new economic model was developed that drew far more from the Anglo-Saxon tradition. Industries were privatized, the welfare system trimmed, and higher rates of taxation lowered to try to overcome the economic stagnation of the 1970s.

The Thatcher revolution went some way to re-assert the general principles of the Anglo-Saxon model and Thatcher's well-documented confrontation with trade unions saw their post-war influence reduced, which allowed for greater flexibility in the labour market. However, the welfare-state remained an integral part of the UK social system, with welfare spending still significantly higher than other Anglo-Saxon economies outside of Europe such as the US. While the financial crisis that began in 2008 has seen a further reduction in welfare, the UK still finds itself in the mid-range when it comes to comparisons with other European states. Across the Irish Sea, Ireland is also often identified as an Anglo-Saxon economy and used greater incentives in the 1980s and 1990s to attract foreign investment. Ireland radically reformed its tax base and offered incentives for overseas investors. This would form the basis for Ireland's economy boom in the 1990s that was known as the 'Celtic Tiger', where the reduction of corporation tax paved the way for heavy investment from international technology companies (Coates 2000).

Contemporary Anglo-Saxon economies are often characterized by their focus on the service and knowledge economy, their environment of competitiveness and their flexible labour force. In general, they also have a lower rate of unionization within the workforce. Strategically, incentives for incoming investment are sought by policymakers, such as the reduction of regulations and loopholes to make it an attractive environment for companies and investors.

13.2.2 **Continental Model**

The Continental Model is characterized by partnership between governments and business. Often referred to as Rhineland capitalism due to the success of the West German industrial development after World War II, it looks to combine free market economics with policies driven by the state that aim to provide fair competition within the market and secure favourable conditions for workers (Rhodes and van Appledorn 1997).

The Continental model has its roots in a form of political economy known as 'ordoliberalism'. Ordoliberalism sees the market as the main generator of economic productivity but argues that the market sometimes requires the intervention of the state to maintain levels of productivity during periods of economic stagnation (Bonefeld 2012). Ordoliberalism was influential in the economic outlook of the West German Christian Democrat Party in the 1950s and 1960s. It would also play a significant role in the construction of the European Coal and Steel Community and the European Economic Community (EEC) which formed the basis for the European Union. The Continental Model created a middle ground between competitive market capitalism on the one hand and state-run nationalization on the other, by seeking to build a partnership between the public and private sectors. The model is most associated with Germany, where there is a belief that all employees within industry should feel part of their business and work for a share in its success (known as a Stakeholder Economy). The Continental Model also provides quite stringent regulation for industry and traditionally has high corporation tax rates.

While Germany might be considered the archetypal example of the continental model, other variants include France, which spends more on welfare than Germany and has a more progressive rate of taxation for corporations than Belgium and the Netherlands. One of the problems that the model has incurred in recent years is due to the highly competitive nature of the global economy and the reliance that states have on investment from multinational companies. These companies might not favour investing in a country where regulations and a high tax structure would undermine profits and so in recent years the model has increasingly been diluted. It is very suited to manufacturing, and as Western European countries look to diversify their economies with services and high-tech industries, the model has become even more under threat.

While Germany has looked to adjust the forms of protection and levels of taxation for private investors, France has generally maintained the levels of spending on welfare and at present spends the highest amount on welfare as a percentage of gross domestic product (GDP) of any country in Europe. France has tended to buck the trend of most European countries. In the 1960s it had comparatively one of the most underdeveloped welfare states in Western Europe but gradually it overtook countries that were looking to cut back on spending to the levels that exist today. This contrasts with the UK where the opposite has occurred.

13.2.3 **Nordic Model**

The Nordic Model is geared towards maintaining a high level of state spending on welfare and protection but combines this with light regulation of private enterprises and investment. As a result, it looks to attract overseas investment and has a relatively low level of corporation tax, but this is combined with high rates of income tax that helps to fund the welfare system. Countries that adhere to this model include Sweden and Denmark with Norway providing a specific variation. To a degree, the Nordic Model is seen as reflecting the 'best of both worlds'. Trade unions are highly developed and seen as being able to establish a working partnership with employers, both domestically and internationally (Hilson 2008). Nordic countries are constantly at the top of the market freedom surveys that are carried out across counties, which makes them attractive for international investors. At the same time, the high levels of employment rights and social welfare make them a beacon for left-leaning politicians.

Sweden, perhaps the best example of the Nordic Model, has a progressive rate of income tax, whereby high earners are taxed at a considerably higher rate than those on basic salaries. Corporation tax however is currently just over 20% and in recent years there has been a trend for governments to look to reduce these rates. The partnerships and bargaining that trade unions have with employers and investors means that trust and cooperation can be developed within industry itself and the state does not interfere with negotiations. There is no minimum wage set by the state, but wages are determined through the bargaining process. The private sector dominates economic output within the country with around 90% of companies and resources privately owned. In contrast, Norway has more companies in public hands and the state has a stake in many other companies. It also has invested heavily in natural resources and has gained considerably from its oil reserves.

Despite its merits, the Nordic Model has some shortcomings and in recent years the model has been criticized from the right and the left. For critics on the right, high levels of income tax restrict individual liberties and deter investment. For these critics this would explain why many new technology companies have tended to favour countries such as Ireland and the Baltic states, which have low taxes across the board for the private sector. Those on the left claim that the model only really works if a country has a well-developed political and economic system in the first place. It also relies on a relatively small population in order to work. In recent years increased migration and multiculturalism within Nordic states has been met by resistance from right-wing anti-immigration political parties arguing that the welfare system should only be reserved for the indigenous population.

13.2.4 **Mediterranean Capitalism**

Whether an actual 'model' of Mediterranean capitalism exists is debatable, but there are certain characteristics that are shared among countries such as Spain, Greece, Cyprus, and Portugal. In each of these cases, the welfare state was developed later than others across Europe, partly because of internal problems such as military dictatorship (in the case of Portugal and Spain) or prolonged conflict (in the case of Cyprus). These countries were more dependent on agriculture for longer than Northern European countries and they were not as advanced when their welfare systems were developed. Mediterranean capitalism has been described not as a model, in the sense that it looked to carry out strategic objectives in a particular way to maximize productivity, but more a set of economic policies that formed when they began to develop a market capitalist system (Rhodes 1998).

In Spain, the death of Franco in 1975 saw the country move towards parliamentary democracy and within ten years, membership of the European Economic Community (EEC). Towards the end of Franco's rule, the Spanish state saw considerable economic growth as it looked to support industry, banking, agriculture and tourism and connect with world markets. This was done without calls for labour protection; there were no trade unions in place to push for higher wages and better labour conditions due to the lack of democracy under the regime. By the time democracy arrived in Spain it had an economy that was relatively competitive and had found an international niche in banking and tourism, but its economic infrastructure remained relatively underdeveloped (Lieberman 1995). Spain benefited from funds from the European Union (EU) to develop and what emerged was an economy that appeared to be a more watered-down version of the continental model. Partnerships between government and business were formed and regulations put in place but not to the levels found in Germany and France. Likewise, a welfare system emerged, but this was not as developed as in other countries across the continent.

Income and corporation taxes are not particularly high or low in this model. In recent years Mediterranean countries have looked to develop strategies that were more in line with Anglo-Saxon states to attract investment and gain greater competitiveness. However, by doing this they also became vulnerable to economic collapse, as international investment led to property and credit bubbles. Spain, Cyprus, Portugal, and Greece were all affected by the GFC as these bubbles burst. What this also revealed was just how these economies remained peripheral to Europe as a whole and vulnerable to external market failure. Due to the comparative underdevelopment of their economic infrastructures, Mediterranean countries have tended to focus on specific sectors which might attract investment and lead to short-term growth but are also vulnerable to wider economic collapse.

13.2.5 **Capitalism after communism**

Post-communist forms of capitalism do always not fit neatly into the typology of varieties of capitalism developed to describe the capitalisms of Western Europe. There has been some convergence in Eastern Europe towards the capitalism models of the West, but the process has been uneven across the region due to political, historical, and geographical factors which impacted moves to replace communist central planning with market economy.

The demand for capitalism after the collapse of communism varied across the region. There were constituencies for reform in states like Poland, Hungary and Czechia which had been linked to Western economies under communism through trade and loans (Robinson 2004; Connolly 2013). Geographical proximity to, and historic links with, Western Europe also prompted states like Slovenia and Croatia, and the Baltic states, to embark more rapidly on economic reform when they broke away from Yugoslavia and the Soviet Union respectively. Support for economic change often equated also to support for political reform so that the two processes reinforced one another (Fish 1997; Janos 2000: 385–8). Where the push to democracy was strongest old elites were more completely removed from power and it was easier to introduce reform policies. Once these policies were introduced, they were often not popular because they were associated with the recessions that accompanied the move from communist central planning to a market economy. The governments and parties that introduced reform suffered electorally as a result. However, the electoral losses suffered by parties and politicians associated with economic reform in countries like Hungary, Poland, and Czechia did not lead to the abandonment of reform. Parties and politicians from successor parties to former ruling communist parties, such as the Polish Social Democracy of the Republic of Poland (later part of the Democratic Left Alliance), that succeeded the first generation of reformers in office, moderated reform by slowing it or providing more social protection to groups like the unemployed or pensioners, rather than abandoning it. Pro-reform constituencies were largely absent in states like Bulgaria and Romania, so there was greater political continuity. In Bulgaria, the former communist party renamed itself the Bulgarian Socialist Party and won a majority of seats in the first free elections in 1990. In Romania, large parts of the former communist establishment moved into the National Salvation Front, and it too won a majority in elections in 1990. Consequently, economic reforms were delayed in both states as there was only weak political commitment to economic change.

The complexities of economic change and its entanglement with political change mean that it is not straightforward to transpose the varieties of capitalism typology developed for Western Europe (and other advanced capitalist states) to Eastern Europe (Myant and Drahokoupil 2011: 300–02; Bohle and Greskovits 2012: 10–13). Some have argued that facsimiles of Western models of capitalism have been created in parts of Eastern Europe. Estonia, Latvia, and Lithuania, for example, pursued radical economic reform, and are sometimes described as being close to the Anglo-Saxon model of capitalism. They have low tax rates and their financial sectors have largely been taken over by international banks, and Estonia and Latvia have reformed welfare systems in ways that have encouraged labour market flexibility. Hungary, Poland, and Slovenia have been compared to the Continental Model because there has been more coordination between government and business, and more protection of welfare rights at the expense of labour market flexibility (Buchen 2007).

Others have argued that the differences between post-communist transitional economies are greatest in terms of their fit with the global economy (Bohle and Greskovits 2012; Ban and Adăscăliței, 2022). For Myant and Drahokoupil (2011: 310–12), the main differences between types of post-communist political economy are those between foreign direct investment (FDI)-based economies, peripheral market economies, and oligarchic or clientelistic capitalism. The first set, FDI-based economies, have received large inflows of foreign capital and are exporters of industrial goods. However, they are not highly placed in international production chains: they assemble products for multinational firms that have relocated production to their territories because they are in the EU and have cheaper labour costs. This set includes countries like Poland, Hungary, Slovakia, and Czechia. These economies came closest to raising their economies to the EU averages, but still lagged behind that average. Peripheral market economies are states like Estonia, Latvia, and Lithuania, and some of the small states in what was Yugoslavia. These have received less FDI, have smaller domestic economies (due to small geographic size and populations), and small exports. Much of the growth in these states has come through financial inflows to their liberalized banking sectors. These economies have reformed but are not as integrated into the global economy as the FDI-based economies.

The final set, oligarchic capitalist countries, are, for the most part, states where reform made the least headway and where political and economic power overlap to the detriment of both democratic and market development. Economic competition is limited, and profitable sectors of the economy are dominated by businesses that have political influence. Democratic institutions like political parties and parliaments are weak and this gives powerful economic forces disproportionate political power. This power has often been used to create 'privilege-centered polit[ies]' 'distinguished by highly selective and arbitrary modes of law-enforcement' and corruption (Ganev 2009: 660). This form of capitalism is mostly associated with states that are not in the EU and that were part of the former Soviet Union like Ukraine and Moldova (although both these states are changing to distance themselves from Russia, especially after Russia launched an unprovoked war against Ukraine in February 2022), or are former Yugoslav states, like Montenegro. These unfortunate states might be joined as oligarchic capitalist states by Hungary. The electoral dominance of Viktor Orbán's Fidesz party since 2010 and the subsequent erosion of democracy have seen the development of greater political control over the economy in Hungary and the use of political power to reward supporters and ensure the continued electoral success of Fidesz. From being a leader in developing capitalism Hungary has backslid into a more oligarchic form of capitalism (Magyar 2016; Mihályi and Szelényi 2017: 30–1).

13.3 Are Europe's varieties of capitalism still important?

The idea that different models of capitalism continue to exist in Europe has been questioned in recent years as European economies have been subjected to increased pressure from the international economy. Increasingly, varieties of capitalism appear less as different forms of capitalism and more as different types of neoliberalism. Neoliberalism refers to the free market economic ideas that are often associated with the Anglo-Saxon model of capitalism: privatization, deregulation and less state spending. These ideas have become globally dominant—hegemonic—in the last few decades (Peck 2010). Central to neo-liberalism are the ideas that the private sector rather than the state generates wealth in society and that states should adopt strategies to attract investment to gain a competitive advantage over other economies.

There have been a number of accounts that have criticized the inability of the variety of capitalism literature to adequately account for the supremacy of neoliberalism. These include those from the French Regulation School which understand different forms of capitalism by looking at the accumulation of capital within contrasting regimes and how state and social institutions respond on a national level to regulate these (Boyer and Saillard 2002). This provides a less state-centric and more comprehensive level of analysis and allows for the explanation of change and transformation. Building from this, several other accounts from what is often labelled 'critical political economy' have provided class-based explanations of the supremacy of neoliberalism. Borrowing from the Marxist theorist Nicos Poulantzas, they argue that different variants of capitalism should be understood by looking at the ways that competing fractions of capital interact. Capitalist fractions are formed from different industrial and financial sectors and different types of capital; some capital is 'fixed', i.e. invested in plant, machinery, land, buildings etc., some, like money, can move—'circulate'—easily. Variants of capitalism are shaped by which fractions become prevalent over time within the international capitalist system (Becker and Jäger 2012; Bruff and Ebenau 2014; Jessop and Overbeek 2019). Fractions based on mobile capital have become dominant over the last decades. This rise of mobile capital accounts for how economies have changed over time, and how neoliberalism has become dominant both globally and within Europe. In addition, it can explain the nature of crisis that struck Europe after 2008, and why so many states adopted austerity in response to the crisis (see Box 13.1). In contrast, the traditional variety of capitalism approach described previously was unable to show why so many states opted for austerity, rather than a variety of approaches to the global crisis; indeed, the traditional approach ignored this explanatory inadequacy in the post-crisis environment (Bruff and Horn 2012).

Neo-liberal ideas are often seen as both being spread via economic globalization and as deepening globalization. Both globalization and neo-liberalism stress the need for economies to become more competitive and they work hand in hand to weaken national economic differences. Generally, competitiveness is developed by policy measures that—amongst other things—lower the costs of hiring and firing workers, reduce the tax and welfare burdens on firms to improve a country's attractiveness to investors, remove tariffs and trade barriers, and structure education systems to satisfy employer needs. The need to be competitive under pressure from globalization and neo-liberalism are seen by some analysts as leading to similar policies being adopted in these areas no matter the historical level of coordination within a national economy and its variety of capitalism. The adoption of common policies by European states runs counter to the idea in the varieties of capitalism literature that institutions shape national adaptation to global pressures so that national differences endure and reproduce themselves. Collective bargaining between unions and industries, and the role of the state in managing labour relations, have declined across many European countries, for example, so that whilst there might still be some institutional differences amongst European states that make for different levels of political struggle over policies that affect workers, the practices of economic management and the push for labour market flexibility are common to all states (Baccaro and Howell 2011). So, historical and institutional differences might explain why there were mass strikes and highly confrontational demonstrations by French workers in 2023 when the retirement age was raised, but no comparable protest when the same thing was done earlier in Britain or Ireland. In the end, and despite these different responses to a measure that increased competitiveness, the result was the same: retirement ages rose rather than increased taxes being imposed on businesses to fund pensions for ageing, and longer-lived, populations.

Others have argued that there are both similarities and differences between European forms of capitalism. Historically, it has been argued, Western European capitalism shared a

Table 13.2 GDP growth selected countries, percentages, five-year average, 2001-05, 2006-10, 2011-15, yearly figures 2016-2022

	2001-2005	2006-2010	2011-2015	2016	2017	2018	2019	2020	2021	2022
Austria	1.76	0.64	1.06	2.0	2.3	2.4	1.5	−6.5	4.6	5.0
Belgium	1.94	1.00	1.30	1.3	1.6	1.8	2.2	−5.4	6.1	3.2
Bulgaria	5.70	2.20	1.34	3.0	2.8	2.7	4.0	−4.0	7.6	3.4
Czechia	3.92	1.20	1.74	2.5	5.2	3.2	3.0	−5.5	3.5	2.5
Denmark	1.34	−0.52	1.26	3.2	2.8	2.0	1.5	−2.0	4.9	3.8
France	1.68	0.34	1.04	1.1	2.3	1.9	1.8	−7.8	6.8	2.6
Germany	0.54	0.50	1.68	2.2	2.7	1.0	1.1	−3.7	2.6	1.8
Greece	3.90	−1.36	−3.88	−0.5	1.1	1.7	1.9	−9.0	8.4	5.9
Hungary	4.44	−0.84	2.06	2.2	4.3	5.4	4.9	−4.5	7.1	4.6
Italy	0.92	−0.62	−0.66	1.3	1.7	0.9	0.5	−9.0	6.7	3.7
Netherlands	1.36	0.72	0.78	2.2	2.9	2.4	2.0	−3.9	4.9	4.5
Poland	3.06	3.40	3.12	3.0	5.1	5.9	4.4	−2.0	6.8	5.1
Portugal	0.88	0.28	−0.82	2.0	3.5	2.8	2.7	−8.3	5.5	6.7
Romania	5.66	1.42	2.80	2.9	8.2	6.0	3.9	−3.7	5.1	4.7
Slovakia	5.04	3.52	2.50	1.9	2.9	4.0	2.5	−3.4	3.0	1.7
Spain	3.28	0.18	0.00	3.0	3.0	2.3	2.0	−11.3	5.5	2.5
Sweden	2.62	0.92	2.20	2.1	2.6	2.0	2.0	−2.2	5.1	2.6
United Kingdom	2.42	0.08	1.98	2.2	2.4	1.7	1.6	−11.0	7.5	4.1

Source: Created from data in World Bank 2023; European Commission 2023; and House of Commons Library 2023.

common growth model after World War II. This growth model was based on the expansion of wages, which rose faster than the level of economic growth. This meant there was a transfer of wealth to ordinary people that fuelled growth through the development of mass consumption and the expansion of industries to support it. This growth model collapsed in the 1970s as inflation and unemployment both rose (what was called stagflation). The collapse of the wage-led growth model created similarity amongst European states: they are generally struggling to achieve economic growth. Wages fell in many parts of Western Europe after the 1970s and industries relocated to lower-cost parts of the globe. Some idea of this can be found in Table 13.2, which gives averaged GDP growth rates for five-year periods between 2001 and 2015, and yearly figures thereafter, for a selection of European states. The states that grew most notably in the earliest period in Table 13.2 were East European states that benefitted from inward investment, attracted by lower wages, and were growing from what was a smaller economic base after the transitional recessions that they had experienced in the 1990s. Thereafter most states in Table 13.2 had slower growth and/or negative growth as the GFC took hold in the late 2000s and into the 2010s. When they returned to growth it was slower, dipped into recession during Covid-19 in 2020, before reaching highs after Covid-19 restrictions were eased. Most countries saw some easing-off of growth after 2021 and this easing-off is set to continue over the next few years: the forecast for 2023 for the EU is for a −1% fall in GDP and a fall of −0.23% for the UK (hit by both the common problems Europe faced after Covid-19 and the self-inflicted wound of Brexit), with moderate growth thereafter of about 1.7% in 2024 for the EU and 1% for the UK.

The growth crisis that began for many states after the 1970s is what created the differences between states and their political economies as states adopted different strategies to try to restart growth and fit into the changing global economy (see Baccaro, Blyth and Pontusson 2022a, also Hopkin and Blyth 2019, and Section 13.4). In some cases, they replaced growth based on wage-funded consumption with growth through debt-financed consumption, encouraging citizens to borrow to stimulate their economies. Other states have tried to have exports fuel growth, replacing wage growth with foreign demand as the motor of growth by, amongst other things, driving down domestic costs, including wages. Some states have simply failed to develop or consistently pursue a new growth-based strategy, whilst others have used export growth, wage growth, and borrowing to try to produce a balanced growth model. Finally, some states have developed a 'dependent-led' export model in which they have used their low-cost labour markets to find a niche in the global economy as producers of low-value goods or components for high-value goods produced elsewhere Ban and Adăscăliței (2022: 189). The UK would be an example of debt-financed growth, with Spain and Greece sharing elements of this strategy with high borrowing before the global financial crisis. Germany is an example of export-fuelled growth, Sweden a case of trying to balance growth between wage-led, debt, and export-led, Italy a case of a state that has failed to consistently pursue any growth strategy, and some of the economies of Central and Southern Europe examples of a 'dependent-led' export model (see the case studies in Baccaro, Blyth, and Pontusson 2022b).

There is some cross-over between the varieties of capitalism literature and the idea that growth models are what distinguish between European states in that there is some correspondence between capitalist variant and adopted growth model, in, for example, the UK, Germany, and Sweden. However, the growth model approach and the idea that varieties of capitalism are in abeyance due to globalization and neo-liberalism both point to a larger political problem caused by economic issues, namely the narrowing of political debate over how economies should be organized. Consensus over the need to follow neo-liberal prescriptions or to chase a particular growth model has meant that mainstream politicians have been focussed on a narrow range of technical economic management issues and been less concerned with the needs of voters. In particular, the dominance of neoliberal principles in the global economy has arguably threatened the connection that exists between governments and people, because national control over economic policy has weakened and governments have become unwilling to intervene in the economy to protect their citizens. This is happening just as globalization further shifts things like industrial production away from some of its traditional European bases to countries with less-regulated labour markets and cheaper labour. International markets are seen as having more power than national governments, so popular democratic control of the economy has been eroded. Democracy remains stuck at the nation-state level and globalized economic activity is beyond its control. This has led some commentators to argue that advanced capitalist states have entered an era of 'post-democracy' since a major function of government, economic management, is no longer under democratic control (Crouch 2004, 2015).

13.4 Fifteen years of crisis: Europe, the global financial crisis and Covid-19

Economic crises are not new phenomena in European politics: all European countries have experienced economic crisis, sometimes collectively, sometimes individually. However, the crises that began in 2008– GFC and the Covid-19 crisis—were different in many ways to crises of the past, even to the Great Depression of the late 1920s and early 1930s. The main reason for this difference is the level of economic integration of advanced capitalist economies in the 2000s in comparison to the past.

First, in Europe economic integration was particularly noticeable due to the existence of a common currency, the Euro, that was used by nineteen of the twenty-eight member states of the EU. Having a common currency meant first, that the effects of the crisis were more easily transmitted from one country to another across Europe, even to states that were not a part of the Eurozone. And second, that states were constrained in how they could deal with crisis when they were part of the Eurozone. Having a common currency meant that states could not, for example, devalue their currency to shrink the size of the debts, both government and private, that they owed abroad. This is because national governments did not control their currency, the ECB did. This meant that the political effects of economic crisis were also different to the past. Blame for the crisis and for the policies that were supposed to alleviate crisis were not laid at the feet of national governments alone. Blame was apportioned to both national governments and to the ECB and the European Union. Indeed, national governments were not only blamed for the crisis but also for failing to stand up to 'unelected foreign officials' who were seen as worsening the economic losses of the crisis. In short, the GFC in Europe was not just an economic downturn, an unfortunate but not unusual occurrence, but also a crisis of the idea of coordinated European political and economic action, of European political and economic integration. That the crisis had a pan-European effect does not mean that the experience of crisis was uniform, however. The crisis experience was shaped by the type of capitalism countries had as well as by whether they were members of the Eurozone.

Second, economic interconnectedness meant that the Covid-19 crisis hit Europe and the globe simultaneously and led to lockdowns across Europe and economic contraction. Large amounts of industry and transport, and many service sectors such as entertainment and tourism, closed. Domestic and international trade contracted, and employment, educational, health and transport systems, and international supply chains were disrupted. These problems demanded a huge governmental response. The end of the pandemic did not end the economic effect of Covid. Although the end of the pandemic led to growth economically governments across Europe faced common problems like labour shortages and inflation.

13.4.1 The GFC comes to Europe

There is a large literature on the GFC, and it is impossible to do justice to all of the arguments that have been made about the origins of crisis here (for a fuller account see Tooze 2018). Instead, we will make a few points about the nature of the crisis and how it spread.

The crisis started in the United States (US) because of defaults on subprime mortgages (that is mortgages loaned to borrowers whose ability to meet their mortgage payments was poor).

These mortgages had been bundled together into securities that had been traded between financial institutions. The value of the mortgages had grown due to lax lending by banks and rising house prices. As the value of mortgages grew so too did the size of the market in securities based on mortgages. When people could no longer repay the mortgages the securities on which they were based lost value and financial institutions that were overexposed to them (i.e. that had large holdings of them) were no longer viable. The housing price bubble that had been caused in large part by lending large amounts of money to people who had few means of repaying loans burst, putting further stress on financial institutions that had large amounts of bad debt on their books.

This banking crisis spread from the US to Europe. European banks held US securities, which stressed their balance sheets, and had also engaged in unwise lending that had created property market bubbles in several European countries. As credit from US banks became harder to get, confidence in European banks faltered and these property market bubbles burst. Banks were left with bad debts and losses so that they were unable to meet their obligations to customers. The financial system was on the brink of collapse. European governments were forced, as the US government had been, to take over banks that were 'too big to fail' to try to stabilize the financial system, and the rest of the economy. As they did this what had been a problem in the private financial sector became a public debt problem in many countries since the cost of saving bad banks was borne by state budgets and, eventually, taxpayers and people dependent on state budgets for their income (civil servants, nurses, welfare claimants).

Since some of the countries—most notably Greece, Spain, Portugal, and Ireland—where banks were rescued were members of the Eurozone, and the financial crisis also became a crisis of the common currency and thence a crisis of the EU and European integration.

Politically, there are three things we should note about the crisis at this point. First, there had been a failure of political regulation. Central banks charged with regulating banking sectors had not seen how exposed financial institutions were to the US subprime mortgage crisis. European central banks and governments had also both been happy to see property price rises and construction booms and had done little to stop housing and construction overheating. The crisis was not, therefore, just an economic crisis but cast a shadow on political systems since they had failed to protect their citizens.

Second, the crisis showed that the development of the Euro as a currency had been a flawed process (Mody 2018). No matter what one's opinion about European integration and economic convergence, the crisis made it clear that the currency union had brought very different economies together and then done little to deal with their differences. The Euro had facilitated economic booms in some countries like Greece and Spain, which were in effect able to borrow money more cheaply and in greater amounts than they would have been able to do using their own currencies and without their economies being so closely linked to larger economies like Germany's. This borrowing boosted economic growth but was unsustainable. It might have been avoided if rules about when countries could join the Euro had been better enforced, if there had been better economic coordination between Eurozone countries, of if national governments had not overheated their economies. Since none of these things happened the crisis was, once again, political as well as economic, and it diminished the Euro and EU as projects.

Third, government intervention was seen to favour banks, the wealthy, and 'foreigners' rather than 'ordinary' people, who bore the cost of bank bailouts. Bank debts and losses were not borne by their owners or foreign banks that were owed money by them. Shareholders and bond holders were not 'burned' or forced to take a 'haircut' by losing equity or being forced to settle for a fraction of what they were owed. Instead, debt and loss were passed to the public purse. In countries where the expansion of public debt was massive due to the crisis this was seen as powerful states, particularly Germany, saving their financial institutions to the detriment of smaller, weaker economies like those of Ireland or Greece. Naturally this caused anger at national governments who were seen as sacrificing their people to the interests of the rich and foreign banks at the behest of the EU and the ECB. This helped fuel the rise of anti-establishment parties across Europe (see Chapter 18, also the 'Thinking comparatively' section at the end of this chapter).

The pain of rescuing the financial system was passed on to ordinary EU citizens because the growth in government debt that rescuing the banks incurred led governments to adopt austerity policies. The arguments for and against austerity are summarized in Box 13.1. Whether austerity policies were the right policies to follow cannot be judged here. The effects of these policies, where, however, considerable on the population of most European countries and they had significant political effects. Austerity added to the economic contraction that the GFC caused, contracting welfare states, adding to unemployment and economic hardship generally. The introduction of austerity and economic hardship was, however, different across Europe as we might expect given the differences in the types of capitalism within the continent.

Box 13.1 Austerity

Austerity is a controversial policy (for anti-austerity arguments see Blyth 2013; for an argument that certain forms of austerity work see Alesina et al. 2019). Most often austerity policies take the form of cuts in government expenditure through cutting social services (health, education, housing) and tightening welfare budgets to bring down government debt and budget deficits.

Anti-austerity arguments point out that cutting government spending by reducing the amount of welfare payments made to people (pensions, disability benefits, unemployment benefit, for example), and cutting spending on things like infrastructure, healthcare, policing, or education, takes money out of the economy and reduces economic activity at precisely the time that activity is shrinking anyway. The economy therefore declines faster than it should. Shrinking government spending also hits the poorest and the services they use hardest, which is immoral and wrong-headed. It punishes those that government can most easily effect, public sector workers and the poor and the services they access, as a solution to problems that they did not cause. The poor and public sector workers did not cause a crisis like the one that hit Europe after 2008, bankers did: 'austerity is the idea that the 2008 financial crisis was caused by Wolverhampton [a mid-sized, struggling industrial city in the UK's Midlands] having too many libraries', as the British comedian Alexei Sayle put it. Economically, it is also nonsensical. The poor spend more of their income than the rich. They pump money back into the economy through purchases and consumption. This generates wealth more generally and taxes needed to stop budget deficits growing. Anti-austerity arguments often point out that economies are not like households. A household can lower its debt by cutting back on consumption (buy fewer clothes, cancel a holiday, eat cheaper food) and using the money saved to pay creditors. A national economy cannot do this since its expenditure, public and private, is also in large part its income: if it spends less, it also earns less, which makes paying debt difficult. This problem, critics of austerity argue, is even more acute in a tightly integrated economy like Europe's. Expenditure cuts in lots of states suppress economic activity within and across borders. Cutting the wages of public sector workers in, say Ireland, means fewer Irish people going on holiday in Greece or fewer purchases of Spanish wine, which in turn means fewer Greeks and Spaniards earning enough to buy German cars so that fewer Germans buy Irish butter, and so on.

Pro-austerity arguments often focus on competitiveness and for this reason are often associated with neo-liberalism. Economies that have high debt need to earn revenue to pay this debt down. Paying debt down is best done, it is argued, by becoming more competitive in the global economy. This means driving down costs, particularly costs to businesses like taxes and wages. A country with high debt cannot afford to spend the same amount on welfare, infrastructure etc., unless it taxes more. Since raising taxes adds costs to business the only solution is cutting spending. Cuts to welfare expenditure will also force people to seek work to make up for loss of income. This will mean an increase in the number of people actively seeking work and that will drive down wages as people compete for jobs. An economy that reduces the costs of doing business, it is argued, will be able to compete its way out of debt and crisis. Domestic industry that has lower costs will be able to export since its products will be more competitive (cheaper) than those of foreign rivals. Exports earn revenue, some of which will be invested to create more employment, some of which will be paid to the government as tax. Competitiveness also means that an economy becomes more attractive to foreign investors. Inward investment creates jobs, employed workers pay tax and make purchases, which also generate tax, and this plus export-led growth means the economy can trade its way out of debt and crisis. The anti-austerity response to this is that this might look logical, but it can't be done if everyone is driving down costs through austerity cuts at the same time. If everyone is driving down costs no one gains a trading advantage, and no one can earn their way out of crisis since no one has any money to buy other countries' goods.

13.4.1.1 The GFC in the West

In Western Europe the countries that were hardest hit by the crisis were the countries associated with Mediterranean capitalism and those that had globalized large sections their economies and were as a result susceptible to market volatility. The countries that suffered most therefore, were Portugal, Ireland, Greece, and Spain (PIGS) that had previously been on the periphery of Europe and had historically benefitted from European investment funds (Dainotto 2006). Ireland had been an economic success in the 1990s but its reliance on overseas investment and on a credit bubble that propped up a property boom left it as vulnerable as the Mediterranean states to a global crisis. The PIGS, along with Cyprus, were forced by the 'Troika', the European Commission, ECB, and the International Monetary Fund (IMF), to adopt austerity programmes, to cut their government expenditure and restructure their economies in order to meet the repayments and manage the loans—often referred to as 'bailouts'—that were given to them by the ECB to stabilize their financial systems and allow their economies to function again within the Euro.

Austerity measures were unpopular and led to a growing alienation between many citizens and the state, to popular feelings of economic injustice and precarity that have endured since the crisis (Blyth 2013; Worth 2013). The PIGS might have taken up the most attention within the Eurozone because of their significant bailout programmes and austerity measures. But countries that retained their own currency often needed intervention in order to bailout their banks too. In the UK, the Labour government agreed to recapitalize major banking institutions to avoid their becoming insolvent. After Labour lost power in the 2010 election the

Conservative-Liberal Democrat coalition government introduced a stringent set of austerity measures to reduce the high level of government debt that resulted from the bailout measures. In Iceland, the collapse of the banking system resulted in IMF intervention. However, whilst the Icelandic government accepted an austerity package, it also managed to successfully argue for capital controls as part of its negotiation to protect its economy (Jonsson and Sigurgeirsson 2018). Its ability to control and devalue its own currency as part of this process distinguished its crisis management from those seen within the Eurozone.

The bank bailouts and austerity politics post-crisis have shown that there has been no move towards changing the neoliberal system of economic governance. There was much talk about neoliberalism's popularity being irreversibly damaged by the global crash at the time of the crisis (Gamble 2009). Yet, fiscal discipline, austerity measures and the emphasis on debt reduction have resulted in the belief that the model can survive and sustain recovery (Mirowski 2014).

13.4.1.2 The GFC in the East

The impact of the economic crisis in the new capitalist economies of the East was equally severe. The financial sectors of most East European countries were highly internationalized as banks from Western Europe, from Germany and Austria, had expanded into their financial markets during the 1990s and early 2000s, easily pushing aside most local banks. These banks reacted to the crisis and their exposure to bad debts in their domestic and the US markets by reducing their operations in Eastern Europe. This created a credit crunch, a reduction in the amount of credit available to finance trade and the amount of investment available, so that business activity declined. At the same time demand for goods manufactured in Eastern Europe fell as the global economy shrank. Inward investment also declined as multinationals reduced their operations due to the shrinkage of global demand. These developments further suppressed economic activity.

The solutions and effects of crisis in Eastern Europe were mixed. There was a decline in national income across the board, although the extent of the fall and its duration were mixed (see Myant and Drahokoupil 2012; Connolly 2012). Austerity and the effect on income and employment were hardest in the financialized economies of the Baltics. The FDI-based economies like Poland and Hungary avoided some of the worst of the crisis because their recovery was aided by EU assistance to manufacturing and their ties to the German economy: when it recovered there was more demand for their exports, so they recovered somewhat too. This recovery was not even, however, and there were still political repercussions of the crisis. Overall, the crisis shifted states in the region to more neo-liberal market positions, weakening social contracts and increasing socio-economic inequality (Bohle and Greshkovits 2012: 257).

It also strained some political systems by weakening left-right politics and encouraging populism. This was most noticeable in Poland and Hungary. In both states left-wing parties struggled to honour commitments they had made to welfare expenditure before the crisis began. Even before the crisis, left-wing parties in both Poland and Hungary were forced to make a choice between growth and welfare. In Hungary, for example, the *Magyar Szocialista Párt* (Hungarian Socialist Party (*MSZP*)) managed to retain power in the 2006 elections by promising economic 'reform without austerity'. This promise didn't last beyond the end of the election campaign; an announcement of spending cuts to bring the budget deficit down to 3% of GDP immediately followed the MSZP's coalition retaking office. When the crisis hit welfare promises became even less sustainable and left-wing parties were forced to adopt austerity measures. This undermined their electoral support and raison d'etre. Right-wing parties, like Fidesz in Hungary and the Law and Justice Party in Poland, picked up the votes lost by the left and developed culturally conservative, nationalist, Eurosceptic and xenophobic ideas to tell these voters that the crisis was an existential crisis of the nation rather than an economic one. This enabled them to continue with the same kinds of economic policies, including austerity, whilst laying the blame for national problems and sluggish economic recovery on the EU and migrants (Bohle and Greshkovits 2019).

13.4.2 **The Covid-19 crisis and its economic aftermath**

Europe was still dealing with the fallout of the Euro crisis and the political and social instability left by austerity when a new global crisis in the early months of 2020 presented the continent with a fresh economic challenge. The arrival of the Covid-19 in Europe led to lock-downs across the continent. Lock-downs saw many governments taking the unprecedented step of subsidising businesses and wages of employees in economic sectors that were shut down and which were not seen as being essential services. The EU announced a series of emergency measures including the tearing up of previously stringent rules on fiscal prudency that had been introduced because of the Eurozone crisis. The reaction by governments led to several changes that were hard to imagine before the outbreak.

First, it was widely believed after the GFC that the state would only intervene in the economy to bail out banks in specific instances and this would only be done to re-stimulate the market system. The outbreak of coronavirus has shown us that in specific emergencies this is not the case: the state can intervene in a far more systematic way when necessary.

Second, state intervention has shown that states can drastically alter their course when an external threat arises regardless of what variety of capitalism they have—Anglo-Saxon, Continental—or how far their political economy has been wedded to internationalization and neoliberalism. Some suggested that the measures adopted by states during the outbreak amounted to a 'war economy', where the 'normal' management of the entire economy is suspended to respond to a specific problem (Mulder 2020). Others argued that the reverse was true since employment has been sacrificed, rather than maximized, to achieve a common aim of controlling the spread of disease (Medway 2020). Much of that employment sacrifice was, however, compensated by governments through devices like furlough schemes.

In any case, the coronavirus pandemic has been unique in the sense that it produced an economic downturn that was not financial but was global. To a degree, the coronavirus crisis mirrored economic internationalization's effect on the state. Globalization, whether economic or pandemic, compels states to alter their economies. What this means in the longer term remains to be seen: can the response to Covid-19 be a model for state action to deal with other transnational crises such as the environmental crisis?

At least in the short-term the answer to this question is no. Once states had organized mass vaccination programmes and Covid-19 was contained traditional patterns and concerns of political economy reasserted themselves as governments began to deal with the immediate aftershocks of the Covid crisis. Economic growth restarted as people were released from lock-down (see Table 13.2). This growth brought with it inflation—prices rises—as consumers were

Box 13.2 Over to you—varieties of capitalism after the GFC

One of the leading analysts of the varieties of capitalism literature has argued that whilst the GFC has forced us to think more about the impact of international economic factors on models of capitalism, national models of capitalism are still distinct from one another (Hall 2017). Others would argue that the failure to confront neo-liberalism after the GFC has meant that there is a tendency to convergence between models of capitalism at work that is eroding national models of capitalism.

Which of these positions is true? One way of looking at this issue is to look at indexes of economic characteristics. One of the better indexes is the KOF Swiss Economic Institute Globalisation Index. This index shows the extent to which states are becoming economically more open (imposing fewer barriers to trade, for example), and more socially and politically integrated into global structures. The data can be organized by country or region, and the data goes from 1970 to 2016 (at our last visit).

Pick two countries from the Eurozone (Austria, Belgium, Cyprus, Finland, France, Germany, Greece, Ireland, Italy, Latvia, Lithuania, Luxembourg, Malta, the Netherlands, Portugal, Slovakia, Slovenia, Spain), one from 'old' Europe and one from 'new' post-communist Europe, or one from the North of Europe and one from the South. Look at the KOF Globalization Index and assess how far these counties are converging on a model of globalized political economy. See if there is any other evidence for convergence, or for the retention of national models, by looking at economic data on welfare expenditure from sources like the Organization for Economic Cooperation and Development (OECD) Data Explorer.

freed of lockdown restrictions. Inflation was made worse as global supply chain operations struggled to cope with demand as industrial production restarted. Inflation put pressure on people's living standards as governments and central banks tried to control inflation by raising interest rates. Higher interest rates should mean people spend less, partly because they are incentivized to save and partly because household costs rise as higher interest rates mean things like steeper mortgage payments and increased borrowing costs on loans and credit cards. Inflation was further fuelled by the Russian invasion of Ukraine, which led to increased energy prices, a double blow to household incomes cross Europe because of increased heating and transport costs, and because higher energy prices meant higher prices for goods.

13.5 Conclusion

Political economy has been central to the study of European Politics. The differences between models of capitalism, what states prioritize to try to create economic development and how they manage industrial relations, have all fed into how Europeans have related to each other and to the political systems in which they live. The models of political economy that developed first after World War II, and second after the collapse of the Soviet bloc in the late 1980s continue to evolve. The rise of neoliberalism and development of a global market from the 1970s onwards has meant that models of capitalism have had to adapt to the realities of the international economy. It was thought that the economic crisis that hit Europe after 2008 would bring an end to the dominant economic ideas that had structured European political economy since the 1980s. However, as recovery began—slowly for some, faster for others—the idea that changes in economic organization were inevitable and needed to be fundamental began to fade. In the end, the crisis threw political organization into question more than it did economic organization. The main symptoms of this were the rise of the radical right in places like Hungary and the crisis of the EU that had its most dramatic moment with the 2016 vote in the UK for Brexit. This does not mean that political economy will not evolve further, however. Models of capitalism will change as political change occurs through events like Brexit and the populist surge and will also be shaped by other global developments such as the coronavirus pandemic. Any changes that do take place will be shaped by the past, by the types of capitalism that have existed in Europe, as well as by global economics and politics.

Discussion questions

1. What is considered when defining a variety of capitalism?
2. How important are historical factors in the development of different varieties of capitalism?
3. What are the sources of economic growth in different varieties of capitalism?
4. Are forms of capitalism in Eastern Europe very different to those in Western Europe?
5. Why did the development of the Euro as a common currency make the impact of the financial crisis worse in Europe?
6. Why did the existence of the Eurozone influence hamper or aid European countries responses to crisis?

Thinking comparatively

Hopkin and Blyth (2019) look at the way that shifts in macroeconomic models, changes in how growth is both conceived and brought about, intertwine with political change, with how political parties relate (or not) to voters and organize themselves. A fundamental shift occurred they argue around 1977 when the growth regime that had existed in most of Europe after 1945 changed. The post-war growth regime aimed at creating full employment and encouraged investment in productive activity (industry) over finance and services. It therefore benefitted workers, whose incomes rose and who became mass consumers.

After 1977 and following shocks to European economies which witnessed simultaneous inflation and high unemployment, the growth model changed. Targeting inflation—price rises—was seen as essential to promoting economic growth. Across the board parties came to accept the neo-liberal economic orthodoxies that sought growth through fighting inflation and deregulating finance and services, rather than through investing in industry. Parties reduced their policy commitments to constituents and sought to free themselves of being responsible for meeting constituent demands by putting 'non-political bodies', like central banks, in charge of some policy areas. But this also meant that parties became less able to govern and deal with the problems that were accumulating in the post-1977 growth regime: economic inequality, stalled social mobility, underfunded public services, strained and over-inflated housing markets. They had, quite simply given up on governing and were competing on a narrow range of issues.

This created space for populist parties to enter politics and be competitive. Hopkin and Blyth show that economically populist parties—both right and left—tend to be for state intervention in the economy. This, they argue, explains the steady growth of the populist vote in Europe since the early 2000s. Many voters were fed up with the post-1977 growth regime well before the financial crisis. The financial crisis gave populism a boost, but populism was not created by the crisis. Where that growth regime—and changes in parties—was most notable, in peripheral economies and countries that have an Anglo-Saxon capitalist model, populist vote share has been higher because of economic inequality. Where models of capitalism (continental and Nordic) moderated changes to the growth model and to parties the impact of populism has been less severe, although still noticeable. Populism is 'a demand for action from politicians who have hidden behind the imperatives of market forces and technocratic control of macroeconomic policy' for too long (Hopkin and Blyth 2019: 220).

Guide to further reading

Ebenau, M., Bruff, I. et al. (eds.) (2015), *New Directions in Comparative Capitalisms Research* (London: Palgrave).

Collection that critiques the varieties of capitalism literature for being too narrow, too eurocentric and for not focusing upon the dynamics inherent within the process of international capitalism as a whole.

Hall, P. A. and Soskice, D. (2001b) (eds.), *Varieties of Capitalism: The Institutional Foundations of Comparative Advantage* (Oxford: Oxford University Press).

A highly influential book that outlines the difference between the 'liberal economic' form of market capitalism and the 'coordinated' form of market capitalism. It suggests that national economies largely fit within these two models.

Baccaro, L., Blyth, M. and Pontusson, J. (2022b) (eds.), *Diminishing Returns. The New Politics of Growth and Stagnation* (Oxford: Oxford University Press).

Critiques the variety of capitalism literature and argues that modern capitalism is best characterized by the growth models that states adopt and how this locates them in the global economy. Contains case studies of most European economies.

Peck J. (2010), *The Construction of Neoliberal Reason* (Oxford: Oxford University Press).

Looks at the emergence of neoliberalism as a doctrine and how it rose in the aftermath of the cold war to gain significant influence on how national economies are managed.

Tooze, A. (2018), *Crashed. How a Decade of Financial Crises Changed the World* (London: Allen Lane) and (2021) *Shutdown. How Covid Shook the World Economy* (London: Allen Lane).

Comprehensive history of the global economic crisis that began in 2007, with a discussion of the problems of the Eurozone, and an analysis of the initial impact of Covid-19 on the global economy.

References

Alesina, A., Favero, C. et al. (2019), *Austerity: When it Works and When it Doesn't* (Princeton: Princeton University Press).

Baccaro, L. and Howell, C. (2011), 'A common neoliberal trajectory: The transformation of industrial relations in advanced capitalism', *Politics & Society*, 39(4): 521–63.

Baccaro, L., Blyth, M. et al. (2022a), 'How should we think about modern capitalism? A growth models approach', *Transfer: European Review of Labour and Research*, 28(4): 505–13.

Baccaro, L., Blyth, M. et al. (eds.) (2022b), *Diminishing Returns. The New Politics of Growth and Stagnation* (Oxford: Oxford University Press).

Ban, C. and Adăscăliței, D. (2022), 'The FDI-led growth models of the East Central and South European periphery', in L. Baccaro, M. Blyth et al. (eds.) *Diminishing Returns. The New Politics of Growth and Stagnation* (Oxford: Oxford University Press): 189–209.

Becker, J. and Jäger, J. (2012), 'Integration in crisis: A regulationist perspective on the interaction of European varieties of capitalism', *Competition and Change* 16(3): 169–87

Blyth, M. (2013), *Austerity. The History of a Dangerous Idea* (Oxford: Oxford University Press).

Bohle, D. and Greskovits, B. (2012), *Capitalist Diversity on Europe's Periphery* (Ithaca, NY: Cornell University Press).

Bohle, D. and Greskovits, B. (2019), 'Politicising embedded neoliberalism: Continuity and change in Hungary's development model', *West European Politics*, 42(5): 1069–93.

Bonefeld. W. (2012), 'Freedom and the Strong State: On German Ordoliberalism', *New Political Economy*, 17(5): 633–56

Boyer, R. and Saillard, Y. (2002), *Regulation Theory: The State of the Art*. (London: Routledge).

Bruff, I. and Horn, L. (2012), 'Varieties of capitalism in crisis?', *Competition and Change*, 16(3): 161–8.

Bruff, I. and Ebenau, M. (2014), 'Critical political economy and the critique of comparative capitalisms scholarship on capitalist diversity', *Capital & Class*, 38(1): 3–15.

Buchen, C. (2007), 'Estonia and Slovenia as antipodes', in D. Lane and M. Myant (eds.), *Varieties of Capitalism in Post-Communist Countries* (Basingstoke: Palgrave Macmillan): 65–89.

Coates, D. (2000), *Models of Capitalism: Growth and Stagnation in the Modern Era* (Cambridge: Polity Press).

Connolly, R (2012), 'The determinants of the economic crisis in post-socialist Europe', *Europe-Asia Studies*, 64(1): 35–68.

Connolly, R (2013), *The Economic Sources of Social Order Development in Post-Socialist Eastern Europe* (London: Routledge).

Crouch, C. (2004), *Post-Democracy* (Cambridge: Polity).

Crouch, C. (2009), 'Privatised Keynesian: An unacknowledged policy regime', *British Journal of Politics and International Relations*, 11(3): 382–99.

Crouch, C. (2015), 'The march towards post-democracy, ten years on', *The Political Quarterly*, 87(1): 71–5.

Dainotto, R. (2006), *Europe (in Theory)* (Durham NC: Duke University Press).

Esping-Andersen, G. (ed.) (1996), *Welfare States in Transition: National Adaptions in Global Economies* (London Sage).

European Commission (2023), 'Spring 2023 economic forecast', available at https://economy-finance.ec.europa.eu/economic-forecast-and-surveys/economic-forecasts/spring-2023-economic-forecast-improved-outlook-amid-persistent-challenges_en#:~:text=Upward%20revisions%20for%20the%20euro,0.3%25%20higher%20than%20in%20winter.

Fish, M. Steven (1997), 'The determinants of economic reform in the post-communist world', *East European Politics and Societies*, 12(1): 31–78.

Gamble, A. (2009), *The Spectre at the Feast. Capitalist Crisis and the Politics of Recession* (Basingstoke: Palgrave).

Ganev, V. (2009), 'Postcommunist political capitalism: A Weberian interpretation', *Comparative Studies in Society and History*, 51(3): 648–74.

Hall, P. (2017), 'Varieties of capitalism in light of the Euro crisis', *Journal of European Public Policy*, 25(1): 7–30

Hall, P. and Soskice, D. (2001a), 'An introduction to varieties of capitalism' in P. Hall and D. Soskice (eds.) *Varieties of Capitalism. The Institutional Foundations of Comparative Advantage* (Oxford: Oxford University Press): 1–69.

Hall, P. and Soskice, D. (eds.) (2001b), *Varieties of Capitalism. The Institutional Foundations of Comparative Advantage* (Oxford: Oxford University Press).

Hellman, J. (1998), 'Winners take all: The politics of partial reform in postcommunist transitions', *World Politics*, 50(2): 203–34.

Hilson, M. (2008), *The Nordic Model: Scandinavia since 1945* (London: Reakiton).

Hopkin, J. and Blyth, M. (2019), 'The global economics of European populism: Growth regimes and party system change in Europe', *Government and Opposition*, 54(2): 193–225.

House of Commons Library (2023) GDP – international comparisons: Key economic indicators, available at https://commonslibrary.parliament.uk/research-briefings/sn02784/#:~:text=Compared%20to%20the%20pre%2Dpandemic,2022%2C%20with%20all%20of%202021.

Janos, A. (2000), *East Central Europe in the Modern World* (Stanford: Stanford University Press).

Jessop, B. and Overbeek, H (2019), *Transnational Capital and Class Fractions: The Amsterdam School Perspective Reconsidered* (London: Routledge).

Johnston, A. and Regan, A. (2017), 'Introduction: Is the European Union capable of integrating diverse models of capitalism?', *New Political Economy*, 23(2): 145–59.

Jonsson, A. and Sigurgeirsson, H. (2018), *The Icelandic Financial Crisis: A Study into the World's Smallest Currency Area and its Recovery from Total Banking Collapse* (London: Palgrave).

Lieberman, S. (1995), *Growth and Crisis in the Spanish Economy: 1940–1993* (London: Routledge).

Magyar, B. (2016), *Post-Communist Mafia State. The Case of Hungary* (Budapest: Central European University Press).

Medway, J. (2020), 'The Anti-Wartime Economy' *Tribune*, available at https://tribunemag.co.uk/2020/03/the-anti-wartime-economy.

Mihályi, P. and Szelényi, I. (2017), 'The role of rents in the transition from socialist redistributive economies to market capitalism', *Comparative Sociology*, 16(1): 13–38.

Mirowski, P. (2014), *Never Let a Serious Crisis Go to Waste: How Neoliberalism Survived the Financial Meltdown* (London: Verso).

Mody, A. (2018), *Euro Tragedy. A Drama in Nine Acts* (Oxford: Oxford University Press).

Mulder, N. (2020), 'How the Coronavirus War Economy will change the World', *Foreign Affairs*, available at https://foreignpolicy.com/2020/03/26/the-coronavirus-war-economy-will-change-the-world/.

Myant, M. and Drahokoupil, J. (2011), *Transition Economies: Political Economy in Russia, Eastern Europe, and Central Asia* (Hoboken, NJ: John Wiley & Sons).

Myant, M. and Drahokoupil, J. (2012), 'International integration, varieties of capitalism and resilience to crisis in transition economies', *Europe-Asia Studies*, 64(1): 1–34.

Peck, J. (2010), *The Construction of Neoliberal Reason* (Oxford: Oxford University Press).

Robinson, N. (2004), 'Path dependency, global economy and post-communist change', in N. Robinson (ed.) *Reforging the Weakest Link. Global Political Economy and Post-Soviet Change in Russia, Ukraine and Belarus* (Aldershot: Ashgate): 106–26.

Rhodes, M. (1998), 'Globalization, labour markets and welfare states: A future of 'competitive capitalism' in M. Rhodes and Y. Meny (eds.), *The Future of the Welfare State* (London: Palgrave): 178–203.

Rhodes, M. and van Appledorn, B. (1997), 'Capitalism versus Capitalism in Western Europe', in Rhodes, M., Heywood, P. et al. (eds.), *Developments in West European Politics* (London: Palgrave): 171–89.

Tooze, A. (2018), *Crashed. How a Decade of Financial Crises Changed the World* (London: Allen Lane).

World Bank (2023), Databank: GDP indicators, available at https://databank.worldbank.org/indicator/NY.GDP.PCAP.CD/1ff4a498/Popular-Indicators.

Worth, O. (2013), *Resistance in the Age of Austerity: Nationalism, The Failure of the Left and the Return of God* (London: Zed Books).

14 Migration

ANNA TRIANDAFYLLIDOU AND RUBY GROPAS

14.1 Introduction

Humans have always been mobile and migration patterns have evolved throughout human history. International migration has become a major phenomenon over the course of the past seven decades and its significance has grown for Europe. After centuries of Europeans emigrating to and populating other continents, sustained immigration since the second half of the twentieth century has led to unprecedented levels of diversity and demographic change across Europe. These changes have had significant knock-on social and economic effects, deeply impacting domestic politics, identities, and the European project.

Looking at European Union (EU) member states (where the best comparable data is available), on 1 January 2022, the number of people residing in an EU member state with citizenship of a non-member country was 23.8 million, representing 5.3% of the EU-27 population. In addition, there were 13.7 million persons living in one of the EU member states with the citizenship of another EU member state (Eurostat 2022). Naturally, the percentage of foreigners and foreign-born varies significantly among member states (Figure 14.1).

Immigration has been a sensitive topic in public debate and policy-making. On the one hand, arguments in favour of immigration have underlined the pressing demographic needs of Europe with its ageing population, and the significant contribution that migrants make to the productive capacities of the receiving economies as well as to the social and cultural fabric of receiving countries. Debates have focused on how to attract high-skill migrants or on policies that can improve the participation of migrants in the labour market. Initiatives have been taken to consider the migration heritage of Europe, recognize both the 'native' and migration-related diversity of cultures in Europe and address xenophobia, racism, and discrimination.

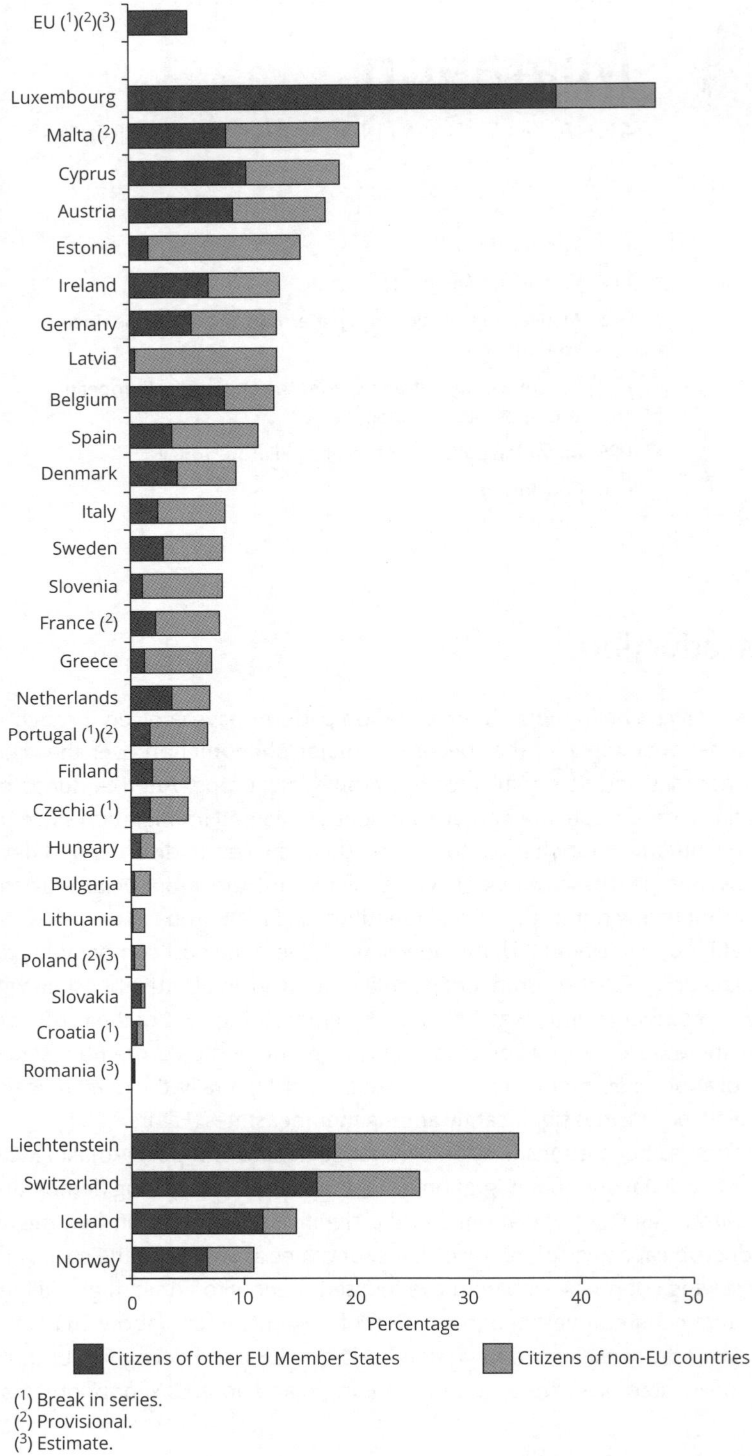

Figure 14.1 Share of non-nationals in the resident population, 1 January 2022, %

Source: Source data from Eurostat (code: migr_pop1ctz). © European Union, 1995–today.

On the other hand, concerns have been raised as regards security and social cohesion, particularly amidst heightened economic insecurity and cultural anxieties. Jihadist terrorism after 2011 and the terrorist attacks in different European cities particularly between 2015–17 (see Chapter 16) raised concerns about the development of 'parallel societies' and led to a growing effort to understand which policies contribute to migrant integration, and which conditions exacerbate inequalities and exclusion and even contribute to violent radicalization. The phenomenon of 'foreign fighters' and the conditions that led young Europeans of migrant background to radicalize, sympathize with Islamic State of Iraq and Syria (ISIS), and leave to fight in Syria and Iraq, even if a tiny minority disconnected from their own ethnic communities (Roy 2016), triggered many policies, research projects, and initiatives aimed at countering radicalization and preventing violent extremism.

Member states with long-established or growing migrant populations increasingly pursued divergent migration, integration, and naturalization policies. For instance, while civic citizenship courses and tests have become mandatory in several countries like the Netherlands, Denmark, and France, the ability to hold dual citizenship has widened, as in the case of Germany. Elections have often served as opportunities to polarize public opinion on matters of identity, religion, and cultural values, and multiculturalism has been declared defunct and failed by some political leaders. And yet policies on the ground have often remained multicultural in essence, accommodating diversity in public life, even political rhetoric has become increasingly securitized and often Islamophobic (Triandafyllidou, Modood, and Meer 2013).

Over the past decade, three important crises have led to migration, asylum and integration policies gaining unprecedented political salience across European countries as well as at the EU level. First, the 'refugee emergency' and border crises of 2015–16 caused by the arrival in Europe of more than a million people fleeing conflicts in Syria and Afghanistan especially; second, the global Covid-19 pandemic in 2020 which brought migration to the fore underlining the importance of 'essential' workers for frontline sectors such as health or agriculture; third, Russia's invasion of Ukraine which led to (as of May 2023), more than 5 million refugees registering for EU Temporary Protection or similar national protection schemes (UNHCR 2023).

This chapter starts by discussing definitions of who is a migrant and how and when migrants can become citizens (see Section 14.2). Following from this, we put recent migration trends into historical perspective (see Section 14.3), looking at the impact that the end of the Cold War has had on migration in Europe, notably in terms of East to West population flows. We examine the effects of the 2008 economic crises and of the post-2011, post-Arab Spring period, the pandemic breakdown of mobility, and the Ukraine invasion, and how these have influenced migration and asylum patterns. We then organize European countries into four groups—old host countries, recent host countries, emigration countries, and small island countries—in relation to the length and nature of their migration experience, as countries of destination, origin, or transit (Section 14.4). Finally, we look at the relationship between migration policies and the politics of migration. This relationship illustrates the tensions that migration-related diversity creates within societies and the different approaches towards integrating such diversity that exist within Europe (see Section 14.5).

14.2 **Who is an immigrant?**

Definitions matter as they frame policies and public discussion of policies and political issues. There have been efforts to achieve some harmonization of data and definitions within the EU. Eurostat data covers almost all countries at least with estimates from 2009 onwards. According to Eurostat:

- immigration is defined as a change of usual residence to another country for a period of at least twelve months. Eurostat tables of *immigrants* usually refer to people who moved to a state in a specific calendar year. They thus provide information on *population flows*;
- the *immigrant population* (stock) of a country encompasses all people who have immigrated and remain in the country regardless of whether or not they have naturalized (i.e. become citizens); they are basically categorized as foreign-born;
- the *foreign population* (stock) of a country includes all persons who have that country as their country of *usual residence*, yet who are citizens of another country (see Figure 14.1);
- data is also collected on the basis of reason for which the first residence permit has been accorded, i.e. for work, for study, for family reunification, or for other reasons that generally cover humanitarian protection (see Figure 14.2).

At the national level, countries frame immigration and collect information in different ways. This means that definitions and data sources may cover different samples, making comparisons between countries difficult and occasionally misleading.

14.2.1 **Migrants or asylum-seekers: Mixed flows and mixed motivations**

Over the past twenty years there has been much discussion about distinguishing migrants and asylum-seekers, and the related questions of mixed flows and mixed motivations. The term mixed flows refers to the flow of people crossing international borders, among whom some are seeking better employment and better income with a view of building a new life for themselves and their children. Others—asylum-seekers—may be fleeing violence and

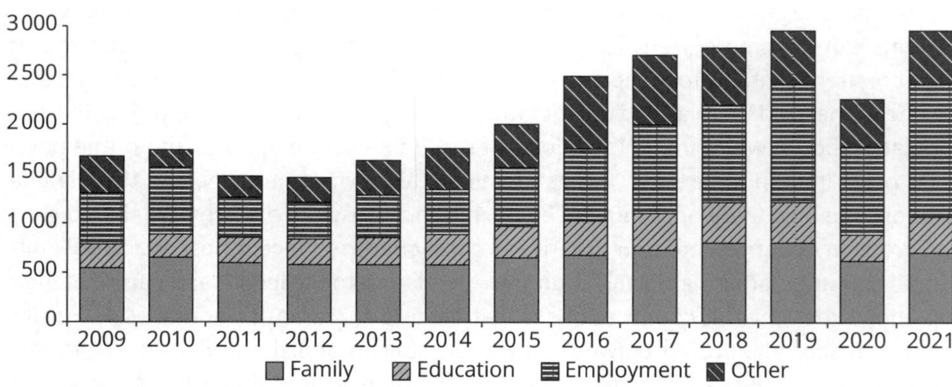

Figure 14.2 Number of first residence permits issued by reason, EU, 2009–21 (1,000 persons)

Source: Source data from Eurostat (code:migr_resfirst). © European Union, 1995–today.

persecution and are in need of international protection. The term mixed motivations refers to people who opt for migrating in search of a better life (also called 'labour migrants' or 'economic migrants') who can be distinguished from refugees (those who seek asylum). However, in reality, the motivations of people who move countries are mixed. A family may leave Afghanistan because they feel unsafe, and because they would like to build a better life for themselves and their children. A young person may leave Morocco both in search of better employment, but also because they may belong to a minority group and hence feel unsafe or discriminated against in their own country. Those with 'mixed motivations' can be conceived as moving *voluntarily* for economic reasons, as well as *forced* because of climate change. These examples illustrate how reality is more complex than existing migration categories and labels. To understand the complex realities of migration, we need to look beyond legal categories that often fall short of capturing real experience.

14.2.2 **Foreign-born and natives, citizenship and naturalization**

The distinction between 'foreign-born' and 'natives' is the most widely used international criterion to identify immigrants in a population (World Bank 2011: xv). It defines immigrants as persons who were born in one country and moved to a new one (regardless of their age when migration happened or the reasons for moving). Foreign-born people though can acquire the citizenship of their destination country. Citizenship acquisition policies differ significantly among European countries and hence 'immigrants' in the sense of 'foreign-born' may be citizens or not.

People can acquire their citizenship either based on their country of birth (*jus soli*, meaning territorial) or through reference to their genealogical origin (*jus sanguinis*, generally characterized as ethno-cultural). Models of ethnic citizenship give preference to ancestry and, hence, to parents' and grandparents' nationality. Models of civic citizenship privilege the place of birth criterion, conferring citizenship to children born in their territory regardless of the nationality of their parents. In general, most citizenship regimes involve a combination of the two elements. In some cases, the *jus soli* principle is applied only if the parents of the child have lived for a certain period in the country, or if the child themself continues to live in that country. In other cases, a pure *jus sanguinis* regime is mitigated by a territorial element: children of foreign parents who are long-term legal residents are given the opportunity to naturalize if they wish to do so.

In all European countries, immigrants have the right to 'naturalize' after a given period. Eligibility for naturalization is defined based on length of stay—which varies from one country to another and is usually between five and ten years of residence in the host country, and under specific conditions which may include socio-economic as well as family status. In some countries, claims to co-ethnic ancestry give rise to preferential paths of naturalization. Let us however illustrate these rules through some relevant examples. Sweden is known for its relatively generous naturalization policy: foreign nationals can become Swedish citizens after five years of legal residence and subject to satisfying specific conditions. These refer mainly to the socio-economic realm (proof of economic independence, employment, stable residence, clean criminal record), and have increasingly included cultural prerequisites such as language competence, familiarity with the customs and traditions of the country of settlement, and/or a feeling of belonging to that country. Acquisition of citizenship via marriage with a Swede or a national of another EU member state is facilitated: if a person is married to a Swedish citizen or living in a registered partnership with or cohabiting with a Swedish citizen, they can apply for Swedish citizenship after three years. In these cases, the couple must have lived together for the past two years. Applicants may or may not keep the citizenship of their country of origin depending on the rules of the particular country they live in, or of their country of origin.

Similarly, to Sweden, in Italy marriage to an Italian gives preferential access to citizenship—two years of legal residence are required for EU citizens and three years for citizens of non-EU countries. By contrast, citizens of non-EU countries with no family ties must have lived for ten years in Italy before they can apply for citizenship. EU citizens with no family ties to an Italian citizen must have lived in the country for only five years.

Another interesting example is Spain, where citizens of Latin American countries can apply for naturalization after only two years of legal residence in Spain. Such preferential treatment recognizes the colonial history of Spain and special historical and cultural ties with Latin American countries. Similarly, Romania provides a path to acquiring Romanian citizenship to nationals of Moldova who can prove their ancestors lived in Moldova (when it was united with Romania in 1918).

14.3 An overview of migration patterns in and to Europe since World War II

The immediate post-World War II period in Europe was characterized by large South to North flows originating from the Northern Mediterranean countries (Greece, Italy, Portugal, and Spain). Western and Northern European countries like Belgium, Britain, France, Germany, and Sweden received significant migration from the South of Europe and the Mediterranean. To differing extents, they also experienced incoming flows from African, Caribbean, and Asian countries. The post-war years were a period of reconstruction and industrial growth in a Europe that was short of labour after the loss of life caused by World War II. Foreign workers moved to fill domestic labour market needs, and were often seen as temporary residents, people who would only reside in their host country for a short period before returning home. The flows of people originating from outside Europe had largely to do with the colonial legacy of the receiving countries, especially in the case of Britain, France, Belgium, and the Netherlands. Immigrants from former colonies were able to take advantage of an open policy towards labour migration and special rights (including in some cases full citizenship rights). These migrations were part of the industrial system of production and were often channelled through active recruitment policies of companies (such as the London Underground) in the receiving societies, and in bilateral agreements between sending and receiving countries.

The migration dynamics in Europe changed in the early 1970s after the oil price shocks, and the subsequent recession. Economic growth had been slowing down in Western Europe, and structural change in labour markets was evident. Unemployment grew, especially in the 'older' industrial economies like the UK and Belgium. Traditional industries such as coal mining and steel declined, and service sectors grew. As the European Economic Community (EEC) pursued policies of economic cohesion and convergence, migration from Southern to Northern Europe gradually declined. By the time Greece, Portugal, and Spain joined the EEC in the early 1980s, there were few migrants from these countries travelling for work to the Northern member states. At the same time, a certain level of industrial development accompanied by a wide expansion of the services sector in Southern Europe created employment opportunities, thereby restricting the 'push' factors to emigration. On the 'pull' side, western and Northern European countries had put a stop to labour migration from the early 1970s onwards, aiming at 'zero immigration'. This equally reduced the flows from Asian and African countries to continental Europe and Britain. Restrictive immigration policies were characteristic of many countries, including Britain and France, as a prerequisite for the successful integration of those already admitted. In other cases, like Belgium, Denmark, and Germany, admissions were restricted in line with the domestic labour market needs while integration remained a non-issue until the 1980s.

While many of the migrant workers indeed returned to their country of origin after some years, a considerable fraction eventually settled in the receiving societies and brought their families over. By way of example, in the period 1955–73, an estimated total of 14 million migrant workers went to the Federal Republic of Germany, for employment, but many left after a few years. After the recruitment stopped in 1973, only approximately 2.7 million foreign workers remained (Vogel and Kovacheva 2014: 148).

Population movements in Central and Eastern Europe (CEE) were severely restricted during the post-war period and until 1989. Labour migration took place on a very limited scale and always through central planning and control. There was some exchange of workers between countries of the communist states in Eastern Europe (such as Albania, Poland, Romania, and Hungary), as well as small-scale incoming migration for labour or study purposes from communist countries in non-European continents (e.g. Vietnam and Cuba) to CEE countries (mainly East Germany and Poland). Outgoing migration from CEE, for instance to western Europe or North America, never stopped completely in spite of the heavy control measures implemented by communist states. Those who left CEE for political reasons quickly found refuge in Western Europe. However, their numbers cannot be compared in terms of magnitude with the large flows from Southern to Northern Europe or from former colonial or developing countries to Western and Northern Europe between the 1950s and early 1970s.

Since the 1980s, the global flow of people has changed again. The integration of the world economy, the globalization of capital and labour, and the rapid development of transport and communication networks contributed to new types of population movements. At the same time, the geopolitical restructuring of Europe after 1989 brought about by the end of the Cold War and the collapse of communist regimes opened new opportunities for temporary or long-term migration within Europe, as well as from developing countries to CEE, not only western Europe.

14.3.1 **Migration in post-1989 Europe**

The demise of the communist regimes in CEE in 1989 made the political landscape more volatile, complex, and uncertain. The closed borders between Eastern and Western European countries were suddenly opened, and many CEE citizens, faced with the dismantling of the economic system and welfare state in their countries of origin, sought better life chances and work opportunities in western and Southern Europe (Wallace and Stola 2001). Similar to citizens from developing countries, people from CEE were integrated into specific niches of domestic labour markets in the EU. The war in former Yugoslavia also created significant flows of intra-European refugees. Many were repatriated soon after the end of the war, but others stayed and successfully integrated (Barslund et al. 2017).

Both the more 'flexible', pro-globalization regimes of the UK and Ireland and the more social protectionist regimes of Germany and the Netherlands introduced new options for temporary legal migration. These efforts contributed to shaping the country-specific forms of migration and living conditions of migrants, but their impact on migration levels has been debatable.

The governments of Southern Europe were unprepared for the influx of migrants after 1989 and particularly after 2011 and the Arab Spring (discussed in the next section, especially 14.3.1 and 14.3.2). Southern European societies, which typically see themselves as mono-cultural and mono-religious, reacted slowly to the presence of immigrants, concentrating mainly on regularization programmes of undocumented workers, and only later in integrating them culturally and politically. The status of undocumented workers has largely been regularized, but political and cultural integration is still limited.

The start of the new century was marked by the 9/11 events and the consequential 'War on Terror' unleashed by the United States (US) government. Indeed, Arab and Asian communities came under intense scrutiny in the wake of the terrorist events in the United States in 2001, but also after the Madrid bombings in 2004 and London bombings in summer 2005. After a period of relative calm, a new wave of terrorist events spread across European cities in 2015–17 raising concerns amongst European citizens as to whether migrant integration has failed (Vertovec and Wessendorf 2010; Triandafyllidou, Modood, and Meer 2011), or whether these events and the rise of international terrorism were the outcome of wider geopolitical transformations and conflicts happening in the Middle East, Southeast Asia, and Sub-Saharan Africa (see Chapter 16). These events magnified anxieties and prejudice towards migration, and perceived 'threats' posed to Western societies' well-being and cohesion. Political rhetoric and scapegoating led to the interchangeable use of the words 'Muslim' and 'immigrant'. Such categorizations and sentiments, needless to say, ignored the rich variety of migrant groups and migration situations across Europe.

At the same time, in the early 2000s, the European Commission and several EU member states announced major shifts in migration policy regarding the recruitment of skilled and unskilled workers from outside the EU. Migration was made easier as concerns grew about shortages of workers in economic sectors where work was onerous or dangerous. Easing the recruitment of migrant workers was seen as a way of making European labour markets more flexible and European economies more competitive (Jordan et al. 2003). To a large extent, demand for labour in the three-D jobs (dirty, dangerous, and demanding) was met by the Eastern Enlargement of the EU in 2004 and 2007, when some former communist countries of Eastern Europe joined the EU. This automatically 'regularized' those citizens of the new EU member states who had already migrated and were working, often in the shadow economy (economic activity unregulated by governmental agencies and laws on things such as worker rights and safety, and that often avoids things like taxation and social security contributions) in the 'older' member states. The Eastern Enlargement further encouraged and facilitated intra-EU labour migration with significant labour flows from Poland, Romania, and the Baltic states in particular to Southern and Western European countries. Many of the EU's old member states initially placed restrictions on new member state citizens' access to their labour markets, thereby limiting the migration of workers from new member states to richer old member states (Trenz and Triandafyllidou 2016). Over time, restrictions on worker mobility from newer EU member states were lifted, but the impacts of this large-scale mobility deeply impacted anti-immigration and anti-EU political narratives and dynamics that contributed to the 'Leave' campaign in the UK's referendum on EU membership a decade later, in 2016.

14.3.2 Migration and asylum at a time of crises

While the early and mid-2000s were marked by economic growth and pro-immigration policies overall, things changed in the 2010s and more specifically after 2008. Europe entered a period of transnational crises that significantly impacted the ways in which European countries manage migration.

The financial crisis that started in 2008 sent shock waves through economies across the globe, increasing unemployment and sovereign debt (see Chapter 13). Portugal, Italy, Ireland, Greece, Spain, Cyprus, Hungary, and Latvia saw their unemployment double between 2010 and 2013 and their economies sink into deep recession with profound social and political consequences. These dramatic economic changes caused, among other things, a slowing down of immigration from non-EU countries to the crisis-ridden Southern EU countries and a modest return flow, especially for migrants from the new EU member states or the Western Balkans (e.g., Albanians from Greece and Italy returning home). They also revived emigration trends from Southern European countries to Northern Europe as well as to overseas destinations like Australia (mainly for the Irish), Angola or Brazil (for the Portuguese), and North America (for all).

Immigration has also been influenced by the popular revolt in North Africa and the Middle East. The spring 2011 revolts (the 'Arab Spring') in Egypt, Tunisia, and Libya, and the civil war which began in 2012 in Syria, have led to important immigration and asylum-seeking flows to Southern European countries, particularly Italy and Greece, which are the geographical steppingstones across the Mediterranean to the EU. Even though the bulk of displaced populations sought refuge across the border in neighbouring states in North Africa and the Middle East, tens of thousands of Tunisians and Sub-Saharan African immigrants arrived from Libya on Italian shores during 2011. These flows receded as EU countries implemented tight border controls and readmission agreements, returning migrants to their country of origin (or last country of transit), and as a measure of political and economic stability returned some to North African and Middle Eastern countries.

The situation rapidly escalated again in 2014 as the conflict in Syria intensified, with dramatically rising migration flows from Türkiye to Greece in 2015. During the 'refugee emergency' between summer 2015 and March 2016, over a million people crossed the Greek/Turkish borders and took the 'Balkan route' towards Austria, Germany, Sweden, and other western and Northern European countries where people largely sought asylum.

While initially the large flows crossing Greece and the Balkans and arriving in Austria and Germany or heading further North to Sweden, were welcomed by European citizens and their governments, the sheer size of the flows (thousands per day for several months) and the pressure on asylum and reception services changed the public opinion rapidly. Fears arose among governments in Germany and Western European countries like the Netherlands that the situation was getting 'out of control'. Central Eastern European countries, starting with

Hungary and followed by Austria, closed their borders in early 2016, causing a domino effect of border closure down to the Greece–North Macedonia land border, thus blocking the migration flows in Greece.

On the initiative of Germany, an agreement between Turkey and the EU was stipulated, the so-called EU–Turkey statement, which encouraged Turkey to control flows from its territory to Greece, while the EU promised in return two large packages of financial assistance (of 3 billion Euros each) to help the country integrate the over 3.6 million Syrian refugees that the country was already hosting (over and above those numbers that crossed to the EU).

These sudden and massive migration and asylum-seeking flows through both the Turkey–Greece and Libya–Italy corridors put significant strain on the EU, as member states showed little solidarity with each other in dealing with the flows. Indeed, according to the Dublin Regulation, an EU law dating back to the 1990s, asylum-seekers who enter EU territory should apply for protection at the first safe country, notably the first EU country, where they set foot. This puts the burden of both first reception and asylum applications' processing on countries at the geographical periphery of Europe, while in effect discouraging secondary movements of asylum-seekers from one EU country to another.

The massive arrivals of summer and autumn 2015 led to a de facto disruption and temporary abandonment of the established Dublin system. Indeed, the EU was divided into three 'camps': the Southern frontline countries that pushed for asylum-seeker redistribution among EU member states, in addition to financial help to deal with migration pressures and new arrivals; the *Visegrád* countries (Czechia, Hungary, Poland, and Slovakia) in the Centre-East, led by Poland and Hungary, which refused to take any refugees; and the Western and Northern countries that sought a balance in between. It should of course be noted that Austria, Germany, and Sweden, which initially welcomed asylum-seekers and later closed their borders, each accepted large numbers of newcomers (200,000 for Austria and Sweden, and over a million in Germany). This was not the case for France, the Netherlands, Belgium, the UK, or Spain. Many EU countries temporarily re-introduced border controls to stem secondary movements from first-arrival countries. Despite the many sustained efforts of the European Commission and the European Council to instil or even impose intra-EU solidarity (through an emergency relocation quota that allowed for Italy and Greece to relocate some of the newly arrived asylum-seekers to other EU countries), at the time of writing in 2023, no long-term relocation mechanism, or 'voluntary solidarity mechanism' has yet been agreed. Efforts underway to reach agreement on the New Pact on Migration and Asylum by 2024 suggest that the relocation of protection seekers will most likely only be possible in small groups, along the flexible solidarity model proposed by the French Presidency of the European Council (Carrera and Cortinovis 2022; Rasche, Welfens, and Engler, 2022). Despite these shortcomings, people in need of protection continue to seek asylum in Europe and except for a brief fall in numbers at the height of the Covid-19 pandemic, asylum applications continue to rise.

In parallel, significant efforts have been made by the European Commission since 2015 to limit irregular arrivals and improve cooperation with the main origin and transit countries, particularly in Africa. This has been a core pillar of the New Pact on Migration and Asylum that was put forward by the von der Leyen Commission in 2020. The EU has integrated migration and forced displacement concerns in its bilateral and regional relations with Morocco, Tunisia, Egypt, Libya, Algeria, Mauritania, Senegal, Niger, Nigeria, Ethiopia, Pakistan, Bangladesh, Iraq, Jordan, Lebanon, Turkey, and the Western Balkans, the African Union, as well as the Rabat, Prague, and Khartoum processes (multinational dialogues between the EU and states in Africa, Central Asia, Balkan states and others on managing migration). As an illustration, relations with Morocco have focused on return, fighting migrant smuggling, as well as developing a Talent Partnership which enhances legal pathways for students, graduates, and skilled workers by better matching labour market needs and skills (European Commission 2023). Such approaches of 'carrots' and 'sticks' have been widely criticized though by civil society and researchers because of their many 'side effects.' Such effects range from the lack of protection afforded to asylum seekers trapped in transit at countries that are unsafe (Kuschminder and Triandafyllidou 2020; Carrera and Geddes 2021; Pacciardi and Berndtsson 2022) to the stiffening of cross border movements and regional economies within Western Africa as the EU imposes rigid border controls in the effort to prevent onward transit migration towards the Mediterranean (Zanker et al. 2020; Mouthaan 2019).

The second major crisis of the last decade has been the Covid-19 pandemic, which brought the globe to a standstill in the period between 2020 and 2022, also highlighted the significant contributions that migrant workers make to the economy and society in crucial sectors like health, care, or agriculture. Those workers that were previously deemed as temporary and 'disposable' became overnight 'essential' (Gahwi and Walton-Roberts 2022). Governments in Germany, Italy, Spain, or Poland for instance mobilized to find appropriate solutions for bringing in migrant workers for agriculture, including chartered flights with few passengers sitting at a safe 'distance', assistance to employers for the quarantine period in appropriate accommodation, and self-isolation (Corrado and Palumbo 2022). However, these measures had less to do with a new sensitivity about the living or working conditions of these temporary foreign workers. Special measures aimed to protect 'essential' work rather than the 'essential' workers (Triandafyllidou and Nalbandian 2020). The concern was also to protect the local community from contagion and a possible outbreak if a migrant worker tested positive for Covid-19. Indeed, safety measures, monitoring, and support only extended through the quarantine period. After it was lifted, there was little follow-up or protection for the migrant workers. The meat industry in several European countries emerged as a pandemic hotspot for instance (Corrado and Palumbo 2022). Similar challenges were faced by care workers in private homes under the pandemic who were confronted with restrictions of their freedom, laid off without notice, and often risked irregular status and expulsion because they were found to be in breach of their stay permit through no fault of their own.

The third major and still ongoing crisis that Europe and the world have faced is Russia's invasion of Ukraine which led to an unprecedented number of people fleeing Ukraine towards neighbouring and more distant European countries as well as Russia and other Eurasian states. This significant refugee crisis led the European Commission to invoke the Temporary Protection Directive (an EU emergency scheme aimed for use in exceptional circumstances of a mass influx to provide quick assistance and reduce pressure on the national asylum systems of EU countries) on 3 March 2022, for all people fleeing the country since Russia began its military invasion on 24 February (European Commission 2022). More than a year later, in May 2023, more than 5 million had registered for Temporary Protection or similar national protection schemes (UNHCR 2023), which provided them with a residence permit, access to the labour market and housing, medical assistance, and access to education for children.

All in all, these developments have shown how migration and asylum are part and parcel of broader socio-economic transformations and political processes and defy tight regulation and strict controls. Beyond the major political, health, and geopolitical crises that have marked the last two decades, several slow onset events are affecting and will further impact migration and asylum flows (including internal displacement) notably the impact of climate change on environmental conditions and local systems of production, as well as the rapid development of advanced digital technologies which have a significant impact on both how states govern migration and on how migrants seek to navigate opportunities and restrictions.

14.4 Different immigration experiences: Organizing European countries into a typology

European countries can be grouped into four sets based on their experiences of migration: (a) old host countries, (b) recent host countries, (c) emigration countries, and (d) small island countries. The first group refers to the traditional host migration countries in the North and West (France, Germany, Belgium, the Netherlands, the UK, Denmark, and Sweden). These countries are generally faced with the challenge of combating the social exclusion and marginalization of second- or third-generation immigrants. These countries are also among the primary destinations of intra-EU mobility, originating mainly from the newer member states.

The second subset includes Southern European countries (Italy, Greece, Spain, and Portugal), Ireland, and Finland. The Southern European countries became migrant hosts in the post-1989 period and received large numbers of asylum-seekers during the 2015 migrant crisis. The immigration experience in these countries has been characterized by the absence of a consistent migration policy. This has led to an increase of undocumented immigration and repeated regularization programmes. Ireland and Finland have been somewhat different as immigration flows started only in the 2000s and in Finland remain contained in numbers. In addition, because of their geographical position, these two countries were less exposed to irregular migration pressures but rather became new destinations for asylum-seekers particularly in the wake of the 2015–16 migration emergency. The new host countries (except for Finland) were hard-hit by the economic crisis that began in 2008 and severe austerity measures also affected the migration landscape. Extremely high unemployment took a negative toll on migrants, pushing many into even more insecure work and living conditions and leading some to consider return migration.

The third subset of countries is constituted by the Central, Eastern, Northeastern, and Southeastern European countries mainly characterized by massive emigration since the 1990s which continues to today and has contributed to substantial depopulation of their rural and remote regions. These countries have since also experienced significant immigration flows from the former Soviet Union countries and from neighbouring nations with which there was a formal relationship—particularly Ukraine, Belarus, Georgia, and Moldova. Since the early 2000s, they have become an attractive destination for entrepreneurs and high-skilled migrants from Western Europe and the US, while immigrants from specific Asian countries have formed ethnic niches in large Central European cities. The outbreak of the Russian war in Ukraine in February 2022 changed their situation once again as overnight, they became transformed into frontline countries that had to respond to the immediate needs of millions of Ukrainians fleeing the war.

Box 14.1 Over to you—comparing experiences with immigration

Select two European countries and compare their recent experiences with immigration. What geographic, historic, economic, or political factors can account for the differences you find? How has immigration affected domestic politics in each country? The Organization for Economic Cooperation and Development (OECD) International Migration Outlook, published each year and available online, provides a detailed overview of recent migration patterns in many European countries. .

Cyprus and Malta are in a category of their own combining a small population, a growing influx of immigrants and asylum-seekers over the past two decades, and continued emigration. Being at the geographic periphery of the EU, they have been exposed to significant irregular migration and asylum-seeking pressures, especially in the wake of the 2011 Arab Spring events.

This grouping of European countries in terms of their immigration history highlights how different countries follow different immigrant integration approaches. Immigrants encounter very different integration prospects and opportunities depending on the country in which they live. Immigrant rights may be linked to their specific country of origin, to their individual status and at the local government level. Formal integration in the labour market has been much slower for those immigrants coming as asylum-seekers, or as dependent family members (particularly women), than it has for labour migrants and foreign students graduating from European universities.

As outlined in Section 14.2, all EU member states distinguish between their own nationals, EU citizens, and developing country nationals. Most EU states have designed a variety of migration status levels for specific groups—temporary workers, asylum-seekers, family members of settled immigrants, immigrants with renewable residence permits, and permanent residents. Each type of permit may encompass a specific set of rights which deviate from citizens' rights, and that change from country to country. Through the single permit and long-term residence directives, the EU has attempted to define minimum conditions. While legal permanent residents sometimes enjoy full equality except for the right to vote in national elections, undocumented workers may be de facto excluded from all rights, or may only be allowed to access specific services such as emergency health care. Asylum-seekers may be restricted in their mobility in various ways ranging from detention and an obligation to live in specified places, to being forbidden to leave a municipality or region, see Box 14.2.

Box 14.2 Migration policies and politics in France and Germany

France: France has historically been a country of immigration with a predominant policy of civic assimilation that stresses loyalty to the French Republic as the basis for assimilation into French society. Migrants were expected to learn French and adopt the political values of the Republic while keeping their religion for their private lives. Acquiring French citizenship was relatively easy for both first- and second-generation migrants, even though tensions arose after the 1980s with regards to migrants' social and political integration. In the 1980s, the *Front National* emerged as a far-right anti-immigrant and racist party, bringing migration to the front-burner of politics.

(continued...)

Faced with massive civil unrest by second-generation immigrant youth in the mid-2000s, the French government reasserted its Republican civic integration model, particularly at the local level through its urban policies (Simon and Sala Pala 2010). It banned religious symbols from schools in 2004 (Kastoryano 2006) and kept its Republican model of assimilation alive.

The *Front National*, renamed *Rassemblement National* (National Rally) in 2018, under the leadership of Marine Le Pen since 2011, has sought to exploit the Republican model by shifting its discourse from racism to a so-called 'patriotic' nativism that emphasizes the importance of love of country, and of French habits and values. Challenging mainstream politics, particularly as she qualified for the second round in both presidential elections of 2017 and 2022 (even though both times being defeated), the party influenced public discourse on migrant integration, national identity, and citizenship.

Against a background of repeated, violent terrorist attacks, the strength of the French Republican model, however, has been seen in the debate over the *Déchéance de Nationalité* (forfeiture of nationality) bill. This notably included stripping terrorism suspects of their French nationality if they have another nationality (because they or their parents originate from a different country, for example). This was brought for discussion in the National Assembly in February 2016, and rejected. The debate testified both to the crisis of French Republicanism (and the risk of shifting to ethnic overtones) and to the re-assertion of the Republican vision of the nation and of national cohesion (Beauchamps 2016).

On the other hand, in 2020, French President Macron spoke repeatedly of religious separatism and of foreign influences within Islam in France, and the need to combat 'radical Islamism' in order to defend the republic and its values. This rhetoric was controversial as for some it unduly stigmatized French citizens of Muslim faith, while for others it offered a welcome clarification of what kind of diversity can be accommodated in the Republic.

Germany: Germany is home to one of the largest Turkish (and hence largely Muslim) immigrant communities in Europe and has experienced significant immigration post-World War II and post-1989 from Southern Europe, Turkiye, former Yugoslavia, and, more recently, Eastern Europe. Germany constitutes a somewhat ambivalent case of a 'reluctant' host country. On the one hand, Germany's leaders have officially acknowledged that Germany is an immigration country and a multicultural society, thereby making integration an important priority. On the other, the restrictive implementation of the liberal citizenship law of 2000 led to a decrease in naturalizations (Schiffauer 2006; Green 2005). After Angela Merkel's famous declaration in October 2010 that 'multiculturalism has failed', Germany has sought to find a 'third-way' approach to integration which emphasizes socio-economic integration of migrants and their children in the labour market and in the education system. Germans of Turkish origin are increasingly represented in public and political life, thus testifying to the civic turn of the German identity. In turn, Germany has re-discovered a stronger sense of integrated national identity (Miller-Idriss and Rothernburg 2012).

There are, however, contrasting tendencies that are felt particularly along the divide between 'Western' and 'Eastern' *Länder* (states). The concerns that divide these Eastern and Western *Länder* include unemployment, voting preferences, and the resurgence in the Eastern *Länder* of strong radical right-wing nationalist movements, such as *Pegida* (Patriotic Europeans Against the Islamization of the Occident). *Pegida* emerged in the wake of the refugee emergency in 2015 (Sorg 2015; Geddes and Scholten 2016). Furthermore, since 2013, Germany has seen the rise of its first overtly nationalist and xenophobic political party since World War II with the *Alternative für Deutschland* (*AfD*). *AfD* initially emerged as an anti-EU party (against the bailouts of Southern European indebted countries) but evolved into an anti-immigrant party after the 2015 refugee emergency, targeting Angela Merkel (chancellor of Germany) and her welcoming approach to refugees. *AfD* won 12% of the national vote in the election of September 2017, becoming the third largest party in Germany's parliament. However, in the election of 2021 *AfD* lost ground, gaining 10% of the national vote and receding again to fourth place in the German political landscape.

14.5 Migration policies and politics in Europe today

Since the late 2000s and during the 2010s we have witnessed in Europe a rise of both anti-immigrant sentiment and populist and extreme right-wing parties (see Chapter 18). Much scholarship has been concerned with explaining the reasons for the electoral success of these parties, seeing migration and globalization as underlying causes of this success. The relationship between migration, migrant integration, globalization, and the rise of anti-immigrant, xenophobic, and racist parties is interactive. In other words, population flows and the restructuring of the welfare state in Europe are real concerns for a significant part of the electorate. Eurobarometer surveys consistently report immigration as one of the principal issues that the EU has to face according to citizens, along with the economic situation, the environment and climate change, unemployment, and the international situation (Standard Eurobarometer 98 2023). While this is an important concern, it has been exploited by far-right populist parties for electoral gains. They have created opportunities for a 'politics of fear' (Wodak 2015) to gain momentum, translating such fear into votes for the populist parties.

In the early 2020s though, there has been significant mobilization in Europe, following from North America, known as the 'Black Lives Matter' movement. Started as a movement against police violence disproportionately affecting Black individuals, the movement has gained currency as a quest for recognition of the persistence of anti-Black racism in both North America and Europe. With regard to its European ramifications, the movement has focused specifically on reckoning with the long history of Black populations in European countries, their colonial histories, and their post-colonial experiences.

It is important to understand and recognize today that historically, European identity has been shaped by colonialism and despite the de-colonization process of the 1960s and 1970s, racial differentiation persists, and Blackness is often stigmatized by politicians and lay people as foreign to Europe and its ethnic makeup (Beaman 2021). This is also particularly pertinent as colonial histories in some European countries (like Italy, Germany, or Sweden) are minimized relative to those of France, the UK, or Belgium which are more openly seeking to come to terms with their colonial pasts (Muvumbi 2021). While this is a matter of higher relevance in Western Europe than Eastern Europe, there are increasing anti-racism and anti-discrimination policies and initiatives aimed at highlighting and valourizing the racial and religious diversity of European populations (Beaman 2021: 110; Skinner 2019).

14.6 Conclusion

Each country in Europe has been affected by migration in different ways. Some have experienced the gradually rising mobility of other Europeans, and others the long-established networks and flows of developing country nationals arriving through a range of migration pathways. In almost all countries, migration has developed into an increasingly divisive issue in domestic politics (Wike et al. 2016). It has played into the left-right political cleavage, but also has been an issue within political families. Changing economic and political landscapes across Europe have blended migration, asylum, free movement, demographic change, the negative effects of globalization, and security together in a mixture that can turn politically toxic. Rising unemployment, the increasing casualization of work (like zero-hours contracts), and wealth inequalities have made it easy for political and populist actors to opportunistically blame incoming workers for precipitating lower labour standards by accepting less attractive conditions of employment, and thereby challenging 'hard-won' welfare systems and societal cohesion.

The rapid rate with which immigration to and within Europe has developed, and its increasingly disorderly patterns have breathed life into far-right political movements, particularly among parts of the population that have been most impacted by issues such as de-industrialization, economic restructuring, and austerity. The rise of anti-immigrant parties into power, or as core opposition parties, has allowed them to dictate the narrative of domestic political debates on immigration, globalization, and Europe, and has re-ignited past prejudices into new expressions of nativism. In turn, this has increasingly challenged Europe's governing institutions and unity between the EU member states, fuelling public discontent with the EU. How European countries and the EU respond to immigration and asylum in the future will have far-reaching implications for politics in Europe.

Current transformations in the world order and the global economy, the increasingly complex food-water-energy security nexus, as well as the intersections between climate change, resource scarcity, urbanization, and the unprecedented pace of technological advances are likely to deeply impact human mobility. Global health crises, concerns about transnational security, and demographic developments will challenge prosperity and stability across the globe. How Europe prepares for and addresses these challenges and opportunities will likely be defining for the European project and will certainly shape the politics and policies of European countries in the decades ahead.

Discussion questions

1. Citizenship acquisition facilitates immigrant integration. Define the *jus soli* and *jus sanguinis* principles for citizenship acquisition and discuss how a more ethnic or more civic definition of citizenship can affect migrants' integration.
2. Compare approaches to migration-related diversity in two EU member states.
3. EU enlargement is often said to have deeply affected migration trends and migration policies in Europe. Discuss in what ways this may be seen to have happened.
4. 'Europe needs immigration'. Do you agree? Discuss this statement.

Thinking comparatively

Attitudes towards immigration and immigrants have become a major fault line in national politics across all European countries between those who see the economic and demographic benefits of migration, and those who view societal change and diversity with more suspicion and unease. In an article already over a decade ago, political scientist Hanspeter Kriesi described attitudes towards migration as a new political cleavage in the making (Kriesi et al. 2012). In the aftermath of the so-called 'migration crisis', governments across Western, Central and Eastern Europe, though historically on the sending side of immigration, faced public resentment against immigrants, while far right anti-immigration parties consolidated their voter base and entered into more government coalitions.

Social research has delved deep into understanding what influences public opinion towards migration in different countries and regions. The real or perceived size of the immigrant population; the demographic composition and the socio-economic characteristics of the immigrant groups; the economic circumstances of the receiving economy; the circumstances in the country of origin; all these contribute to shaping attitudes towards immigration.

In a 2023 study, Lenka Dražanová and Jérôme Gonnot (2003) analyse the composition of migration flows to Western, Central, and Eastern European countries in the period between 2010 and 2019, and attitudes towards migration. They distinguish between migrants' origin, their skill level, and their gender. Their analysis finds that while European Union natives living in regions with a higher share of foreign-born populations are generally less anti-immigrant than those living in regions with a lower share, a short-term increase in the number of immigrants within a given region is associated with more negative attitudes. Moreover, when they tested for gender and origin, their results indicate that male immigrants and those born outside of the European Union are driving most of the negative association between public opinion and changes in the level of immigration in Western European countries, while the educational attainment of migrants makes little difference. While their analysis for Central and Eastern Europe is more limited due to the smaller share of foreign-born immigrants living in those regions, nevertheless, it suggests that inflows of European migrants in Central and Eastern Europe are generally associated with more positive views towards immigration, regardless of their skill level.

Against this background, it is worth reflecting on the following questions: what are the differences and similarities in the attitudes towards migration Western, Southern, and Central Europe? Compare attitudes towards migration in Spain and Belgium, or between the region of Catalonia and that of Flanders for example. How do you explain the differences? Are differences in public attitudes towards migration wider between people living in urban centres and rural areas within the same country, or between people living in urban centres across different countries? How did international migration and intra-EU mobility influence the outcome of the UK referendum on leaving the EU in 2016? What factors contributed to the difference in the kind of political and public response to the arrival of Syrian and Ukrainian refugees in 2015–16 and 2022–23 respectively across Europe?

Guide to further reading

Geddes, A. and Scholten, P. (2016), *The Politics of Migration and Immigration in Europe* (London: Sage).

This second and updated edition offers a review of the interaction between politics and policies of migration in several European countries including France, Germany, and the UK. The book particularly addresses how the European level interacts with the national level of policy making and implementation.

Massey, D. and Arango, J. et al. (1993), 'Theories of international migration: A review and appraisal', *Population and Development Review*, 19(3): 431–66.

The best available review of the main theories on why migration starts and why it continues. Massey and colleagues briefly review the main tenets of each theoretical model.

Mudde, C. (ed.) (2017), *The Populist Radical Right: A Reader* (London: Routledge).

A collection of essays by different authors, thematically organized, this book reviews why and how the populist radical right has risen in Europe and North America, what are its main arguments, and how it affects politics in general and the discourse of conservative parties.

Triandafyllidou, A. and Gropas, R. (eds.) (2014), *European Immigration: A Sourcebook*, 2nd edn (Aldershot: Ashgate).

Covering the EU-28 countries, this book offers an overview of the immigrant population in each country and the main policies governing migration and migrant integration, including citizenship. Each country chapter concludes with a brief overview of discourses on migration and migrant participation in public life. The book also includes a chapter on EU policies.

Triandafyllidou, A., Modood, T. and Meer, N. (eds.) (2011), *European Multiculturalisms* (Edinburgh: Edinburgh University Press).

The first part of this book reviews the main theoretical approaches on multicultural citizenship that are helpful in understanding European realities, while the second part turns to specific dimensions of dealing with diversity such as education, political participation, socio-cultural integration, and the thorny issue of ethnic statistics. The book offers theoretical and comparative insights into European multiculturalism.

Note from the authors

Some sections of this chapter draw on research from pages 2–5 and 8–11 of Triandafyllidou, A., Gropas, R. et al. (2014), 'Introduction', in A. Triandafyllidou and R. Gropas (eds.), *European Immigration: A Sourcebook*, 2nd edn (Aldershot: Ashgate): 1–15. We kindly thank Routledge and Ashgate for granting permission to use parts of that text in this publication.

References

Achilli, L. (2018), 'Why aren't we reforming the Dublin Regulation yet?' *Euractiv*, 25 October 2018, available at https://www.euractiv.com/section/justice-home-affairs/opinion/why-are-we-not-reforming-the-dublin-regulation-yet (accessed 20 December 2018).

Barslund, M., Busse, M. et al. (2017), 'Integration of refugees: Lessons from Bosnians in five EU countries', available at https://www.intereconomics.eu/contents/year/2017/number/5/article/integration-of-refugees-lessons-from-bosnians-in-five-eu-countries.html (accessed 25 June 2020).

Beaman, J. (2021) 'Towards a reading of Black Lives Matter in Europe', *Journal of Common Market Studies*, 59(s1): 103–14.

Beauchamps, M. (2016), 'Denaturalisation: A brief (French) history', *Open Democracy*, 23 April 2016, available at https://www.opendemocracy.net/can-europe-make-it/marie-beauchamps/denaturalisation-brief-french-history (accessed 16 May 2018).

Carrera, S. and Geddes, A. (2021), *The EU Pact on Migration and Asylum in Light of the United Nations Global Compact on Refugees*. (International Experiences on Containment and Mobility and their Impacts on Trust and Rights, Florence: European University Institute).

Carrera, S. and R. Cortinovis (2022), The Declaration on a voluntary solidarity mechanism and EU asylum policy, CEPS In-depth Analysis, https://www.ceps.eu/wp-content/uploads/2022/10/CEPS-In-depth-analysis-2022-04_Voluntary-Solidarity.pdf, [last accessed 14 February 2023].

Corrado, A. and Palumbo, L., 2022. Essential farmworkers and the pandemic crisis: Migrant labour conditions, and legal and political responses in Italy and Spain, in A. Triandafyllidou (ed.) *Migration and Pandemics: Spaces of Solidarity and Spaces of Exception* (New York: Springer): 145–166.

Dražanová, L. and J. Gonnot (2023), Public Opinion and Immigration in Europe: Can Regional Migration

Flows Predict Public Attitudes to Immigration? RSC Working Paper 2023/18, Robert Schuman Centre for Advanced Studies, available at https://cadmus.eui.eu/bitstream/handle/1814/75440/RSC%20WP%202023-18.pdf?sequence=1&isAllowed=y (accessed 9 May 2023).

European Commission (2022), EU invokes Temporary Protection Directive to help those fleeing Ukraine, available at https://ec.europa.eu/migrant-integration/news/eu-invokes-temporary-protection-directive-help-those-fleeing-ukraine_en (accessed 14 February 2023).

European Commission (2023), Report on Migration and Asylum, C(2023) 219 final, Brussels, 12.1.2023, available at https://commission.europa.eu/system/files/2023-01/report-migration-asylum-2022.pdf, (accessed 9 May 2023).

Eurostat (2022), *Migration and Migrant Population Statistics*, available at https://ec.europa.eu/eurostat/statistics-explained/index.php?title=Migration_and_migrant_population_statistics#Migration_flows:_Immigration_to_the_EU_from_non-member_countries_was_1.9_million_in_2020 (accessed 9 May 2023).

Gahwi, L., and Walton-Roberts, M. (2022), Migrant care labour, Covid-19, and the long-term care crisis: Achieving solidarity for care providers and recipients, in A. Triandafyllidou (ed.) *Migration and Pandemics: Spaces of Solidarity and Spaces of Exception* (New York: Springer): 105–121.

Geddes, A. and Scholten, P. (2016), *The Politics of Migration and Immigration in Europe* (London: Sage).

Green, S. (2005), 'Between ideology and pragmatism: The politics of dual nationality in Germany', *International Migration Review*, 39(4): 921–52.

Jordan, B., Stråth, B. et al. (2003), 'Contextualising immigration policy implementation in Europe', *Journal of Ethnicity and Migration Studies*, 29(2): 195–224.

Kastoryano, R. (2006), 'French secularism and Islam: France's headscarf affair', in T. Modood, A. Triandafyllidou, and R. Zapata Barrero (eds.), *Multiculturalism, Muslims and Citizenship: A European Approach* (London: Routledge).

Kriesi, H., E. Grande, et al (2012), *Political Conflict in Western Europe* (Cambridge: Cambridge University Press).

Kuschminder, K. and Triandafyllidou, A. (2020), 'Smuggling, trafficking, and extortion: New conceptual and policy challenges on the Libyan route to Europe', *Antipode*, 52: 206–26. doi: 10.1111/anti.12579.

Miller-Idriss, C. and Rothenberg, B. (2012), 'Ambivalence, pride and shame: Conceptualisations of German nationhood', *Nations and Nationalism*, 18(1): 132–55.

Mouthaan, M. (2019) 'Unpacking domestic preferences in the policy-"receiving" state: The EU's migration cooperation with Senegal and Ghana', *Comparative Migration Studies*, 7: 35.

Muvumbi, A. K. (2023), 'Black Lives Matter in Italy', *European Journal of Women's Studies*, 30(1): 31S–33S.

Pacciardi, A. and Berndtsson, J. (2022), 'EU border externalisation and security outsourcing: exploring the migration industry in Libya', *Journal of Ethnic and Migration Studies*, 48(17): 4010–4028.

Rasche, L., Welfens, N., and Engler, M. (2022) The EU Migration Pact at Two: What Remains of the Fresh Start?, Policy Brief, Jacques Delors Centre at the Hertie School, available at https://www.delorscentre.eu/en/publications/the-eu-migration-pact-at-two (accessed 14 February 2023).

Roy, O. (2016), *Le Djihad et la Mort* (Paris: Seuil).

Schiffauer, W. (2006), 'Enemies within the gates: The debate about the citizenship of Muslims in Germany', in T. Modood, A. Triandafyllidou, et al. (eds.), *Multiculturalism, Muslims and Citizenship: A European Approach* (London: Routledge).

Simon, P. and Sala Pala, V. (2010), '"We're not all multiculturalists yet": France swings between hard integration and soft anti-discrimination', in S. Vertovec and S. Wessendorf (eds.), *The Multiculturalism Backlash: European Discourses, Policies and Practices* (London: Routledge).

Skinner, R. T. (2019), 'Walking, talking, remembering: An Afro-Swedish critique of being-in-the world', *African and Black Diaspora: An International Journal*, 12(1): 1–19.

Standard Eurobarometer 98 (2023), Winter 2022–2023, available at https://europa.eu/eurobarometer/surveys/detail/2872 (accessed 9 May 2023).

Sorg, C. (2015), 'PEGIDA: A post-Nazist uprising?', *Open Democracy*, 26 March, available at https://www.opendemocracy.net/can-europe-make-it/christoph-sorg/pegida-postnazist-uprising (accessed 17 May 2018).

Trenz, H. and Triandafyllidou, A. (2016), 'Complex and dynamic integration processes in Europe: Intra EU mobility and international migration in times of recession', *Journal of Ethnic and Migration Studies*, 43(4): 546–59.

Triandafyllidou, A. and Gropas, R. (2014), 'Concluding remarks', in A. Triandafyllidou and R. Gropas (eds.), *European Immigration: A Sourcebook*, 2nd edn (Aldershot: Ashgate).

Triandafyllidou, A., Modood, T. and Meer, N. (eds.) (2011), *European Multiculturalisms* (Edinburgh: Edinburgh University Press).

Triandafyllidou, A., and Nalbandian, L. (2020). 'Disposable' and 'essential': Changes in the global hierarchies of migrant workers after COVID-19. IOM

Policy Brief, available at https://publications.%20iom.int/books/covid-19-and-transformation-migration-and-mobility-globally-disposable-andessential-changes

Vertovec, S. and Wessendorf, S. (eds.) (2010), *Multiculturalism Backlash: European Discourses, Policies and Practices* (London: Routledge).

Vogel, D. and Kovacheva, V. (2014), 'Germany', in A. Triandafyllidou and R. Gropas (eds.), *European Immigration: A Sourcebook*, 2nd edn (Aldershot: Ashgate).

Wallace, C. and Stola, D. (2001), *Patterns of Migration in Central Europe* (London: Palgrave).

Wike, R., Stokes, B. et al. (2016), 'Europeans fear wave of refugees will mean more terrorism, fewer jobs. Sharp ideological divides across EU on views about minorities, diversity and national identity', Pew Research Center, available at https://www.pewresearch.org/global/2016/07/11/europeans-fear-wave-of-refugees-will-mean-more-terrorism-fewer-jobs.

Wodak, R. (2015), *The Politics of Fear: What Right-Wing Populist Discourses Mean* (London: Sage).

World Bank (2011), *Migration and Remittances Factbook 2011*, 2nd edn (Washington, DC: The World Bank).

UNHCR (2023) Operational Data Portal, Ukraine Refugee Situation, available at https://data.unhcr.org/en/situations/ukraine (accessed 9 May 2023).

Zanker, F., Arhin-Sam, K. et al. (2020), Free movement in West Africa: Juxtapositions and Divergent Interests, MEDAM Policy Brief, 2020/1, June 2020.

15 Climate Politics and Policy

NEIL CARTER AND CONOR LITTLE

15.1 Introduction

Climate change has emerged in recent decades as an open-ended global crisis with varied regional and local manifestations. Emissions of greenhouse gases (GHGs) from fossil fuel production and combustion, agriculture, waste, and other sources have to date warmed the planet by more than 1 degree Celsius above pre-industrial levels. The Covid-19 pandemic and associated restrictions caused a decline in emissions in 2020, but the overall trend continues to be upwards, such that in most years, we emit more GHGs than ever before (UNEP 2022), and atmospheric concentrations of GHGs continue to rise. Some of these gases, including the principal GHG, carbon dioxide, will remain in the atmosphere for several centuries, and this means that further global heating due to past and current emissions is now unavoidable.

Although there are other pressing problems such as biodiversity loss and local environmental pollution, climate change has become the preeminent environmental issue. The United Nations (UN) Environment Programme estimates that globally, we are on track for 2.4–2.6 degrees of warming by 2100, if all existing national pledges are implemented: much higher than internationally agreed targets of 1.5 or 2.0 degrees. If national pledges are not implemented, we are heading for an estimated 2.8 degrees of warming by 2100 (UNEP 2022). The greater the extent of climate change, the greater the risk of uncontrollable, self-reinforcing and irreversible processes, as initial climatic changes trigger tipping points (e.g. polar ice sheets melt, permafrost melts, or rainforests die-back) that entail the release of more GHGs into the atmosphere, and more global heating (OECD 2022).

An effective response to the climate crisis would involve wide-ranging public policy responses and political leadership at subnational, national, and supranational levels. If *climate change mitigation policies* are defined as all policies that influence GHG emissions, then they are multi- and cross-sectoral (encompassing electricity generation, transport, industry, agriculture, building, and many other activities). This remains true even if they are defined more narrowly as those policies that are *intended* to reduce net GHG emissions. *Climate change adaptation policies*—aimed at reducing vulnerability to climate change impacts (like protecting infrastructure from flooding)—have increasingly come to the fore as climate impacts become more imminent and disruptive, presenting another important aspect of governments' responses to climate change (Javeline 2014).

Europe accounts for a significant share of historical GHG emissions: more than one-fifth of historical CO_2 emissions have been produced in the twenty-seven European Union (EU) countries and the UK since 1750 (Ritchie 2019). Given that these emissions remain in the atmosphere for several centuries, this record bears on the question of responsibility for current and future climate change. The EU has begun to turn off the 'tap' of GHG emissions, reducing its annual emissions by more than one quarter between 1990 and 2019. Simultaneously, Europe has increasingly experienced climate impacts: it is warming twice as fast as the global average, and it has experienced heatwaves, droughts, wildfires, flooding, and glacier loss (WMO 2022).

Countries need to work together to respond effectively to the climate crisis. In Europe, the EU has provided a framework for this response, as it has sought to assume a leadership role on climate change (Oberthür and Dupont 2021). Within its own borders, the EU plays a central role in shaping the policy response, both directly, through policy instruments like the EU Emissions Trading System, and indirectly, by setting targets for member states' emissions and other policy outcomes. Perhaps the most prominent example of the latter is the allocation of effort-sharing obligations among its member states so that the EU as a whole can meet its commitments under international climate agreements. In the European Green Deal, launched in late 2019, the EU set itself a net emissions reduction target of at least –55% on 1990 figures for 2030 and a net zero emissions target ('climate neutrality') for 2050.

Beyond its borders, the EU's relatively high level of internal policy ambition and innovation has marked it out as a climate policy leader. It has played a significant regional role (e.g. through enlargement, and through the inclusion of third countries like Norway and Switzerland in EU climate policies). And it has also sought to position itself as a global leader in international negotiations, including on the UN Framework Convention on Climate Change (UNFCCC) in 1992 and on the Kyoto Protocol in 1997, at the Copenhagen Climate Summit in 2009, and on the Paris Agreement in 2015. Its success in this regard has varied, with Copenhagen marking a low point.

Notwithstanding extensive coordination of climate policy efforts within the EU and the wider European region, there are considerable differences between European countries in their political and policy responses. This chapter covers approaches to describing and explaining this diversity, focusing mainly on EU member states. It explores responses in society, in institutional politics, and in government policy outputs and outcomes. It examines the roles of public attitudes (Section 15.2), civil society (interest groups and social movements) (Section 15.3), political parties (Section 15.4), and finally governments (Section 15.5) in addressing climate change. In doing so, it is centred on government climate policy responses and some of the factors that influence those responses in democratic societies. Drawing on recent research, it suggests that each of these play an important role in addressing the problem: government policy matters for climate outcomes, and public attitudes, civil society, and political parties influence governments' responses.

15.2 **Public attitudes**

While each individual may feel that they can do relatively little about climate change (see Box 15.1), political science research tells us that collectively, public attitudes are a powerful force in climate politics. Until recently, we did not have much systematic knowledge about

Box 15.1 Over to you—your environmental footprint

Use the World Wildlife Fund's Footprint Calculator tool to estimate your environmental footprint in terms of tonnes of CO_2 equivalent. To what extent should individuals feel responsible for climate change and other environmental problems, compared to governments and business? How could you reduce your footprint? How can governments (local, national, or supranational) help you to reduce your carbon footprint? Do wealthier individuals bear greater responsibility for environmental problems than poorer individuals? Do governments in wealthier countries bear greater responsibility than those in developing countries?

whether and how public attitudes on climate change and the environment influenced other important outcomes. But recent research has shown that they are a powerful determinant of governments' climate policies (e.g. Anderson et al. 2017; Bakaki et al. 2020). This influence most likely occurs through individuals' attitudes shaping their voting behaviour at elections (and therefore the composition of governments—see Section 15.4), but also their political behaviour between elections (e.g. participation in campaigns or protests—see Section 15.3). For their part, politicians try to avoid the electorate's ire and therefore seek to satisfy public demands. Consistent with this, there is also evidence that public attitudes on the environment shape political parties' environmental policy preferences (e.g. Spoon et al. 2014) and that the environment and climate change are important enough to shape voting behaviour (e.g. Papp 2022).

How can we describe public attitudes towards climate change and environmental problems more generally? While most people value a clean and safe environment, there is in practice substantial variation in individuals' levels of concern about the environment and in their positions on environmental and climate policies. This variation means that the environment is not an issue on which all individuals, policymakers, or political parties agree; indeed, it has been and continues to be the source of much contention, particularly where environmental or climate action entails financial or other costs.

In Europe, public concern about environmental issues has increased over time (Figure 15.1). It dipped during the early stages of the Covid-19 pandemic in 2020, but then recovered quickly. A Special Eurobarometer survey on climate change carried out in Spring 2021, while the Covid-19 pandemic was still a central concern, showed that:

- 78% of respondents believed that climate change was a very serious problem (and 15% 'fairly serious'), similar to before the pandemic;
- 49% believed that climate change was one of the most serious problems facing the world;
- Clear majorities of respondents held governments, the EU, and businesses responsible for climate action, while two in five said that they themselves were individually responsible;
- Three quarters—and more than half of respondents in twenty-six out of twenty-seven EU member states—believed that their national government was not doing enough on climate change (European Commission 2021).

While important, aggregate data indicating rising concern across Europe in recent years belies some substantial variation. Between European countries, there are East-West and

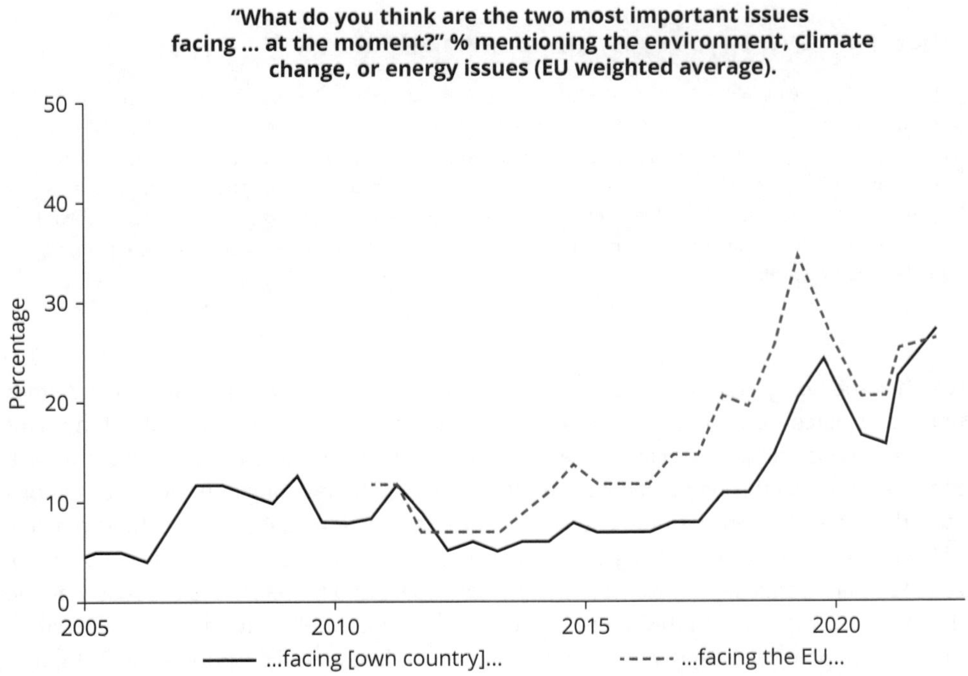

Figure 15.1 Public concern about the environment, climate change, or energy issues in the EU, Autumn 2004–Winter 2021/22

Source: Data from European Commission 2022 at https://europa.eu/eurobarometer/about/other.

North-South differences in public attitudes; public concern in North and West European countries tends to be higher than in Southern Europe and Central and Eastern European countries. This suggests that, among other things, economic factors shape environmental concern, a proposition supported by comparative cross-national research that finds that greater wealth and lower unemployment is associated with greater concern about climate change (Duijndam and van Beukering 2021). Put differently, people on lower incomes prioritize making ends meet. The environment and climate change exists on a crowded public agenda; it remains in many countries a second-tier issue, behind other pressing concerns like the economy, inflation, unemployment, and healthcare (see Box 15.2).

Box 15.2 Over to you—public attitudes on climate change

At the European Commission's Eurobarometer website find a recent survey that includes questions on climate change (you can browse surveys by theme). Examine the survey results. Is there evidence of regional differences in beliefs about or attitudes towards climate change and/or climate action? Is there evidence of change over time (e.g. since the last round of the same survey)? What might explain the differences between countries and changes over time that you observe? Which survey questions do you think are potentially useful for policymakers, and why?

There is also considerable variation between individuals in their attitudes towards climate change and support for climate policies. Support for (and opposition to) climate policies is influenced by ideologies, beliefs (e.g. scientific and religious beliefs) and personal values; by the design of climate policies and how those policies are perceived; and by contextual factors (like trust in government, what others think, and the economy) (Drews and van den Bergh 2016). Bergquist et al.'s (2022) meta-analysis (i.e. an analysis of multiple other studies) of public support for carbon taxes and laws showed that, perhaps surprisingly, gender has no discernible impact on climate policy support, while education and age have only small effects, with better-educated and younger individuals being more supportive of climate policies. In contrast, perceptions of the distributional fairness and the effectiveness of climate policies, and concern about climate change, were important determinants of policy support. The perceived risk and seriousness of climate change, belief in and knowledge of climate change, personal values and left-right political ideology, and trust in institutions also played a role. So, individuals who believe that a policy is fair and effective, who are more concerned and knowledgeable about climate change, who trust in institutions, and who are left-of-centre, younger, and better-educated, are more likely to support climate policies. Significantly, some determinants of public attitudes to climate policy (like values and ideology) are difficult to change, while others (like knowledge) are more manipulable.

While public attitudes shape political action, the reverse is also true: 'top down' political leadership also powerfully shapes public attitudes on climate change. The impact of these 'political cues' has been perhaps most clearly observed in the context of the United States, where polarized party politics has reinforced polarization of public attitudes on climate change (and vice versa), but similar dynamics are evident in Europe. In the context of the political conflict over Brexit in the UK in the 2010s, for example, environmental attitudes shifted away from the consensus that was in evidence only a decade earlier (Kenny 2022). These dynamics exist elsewhere too: Linde's (2020) study of Sweden, Norway, Australia, and New Zealand shows how political parties shape individuals' climate risk perceptions.

15.3 Civil society

Civil society encompasses a wide variety of organizations, including interest groups and non-governmental organizations (NGOs). We can broadly distinguish between those groups that are in favour of more ambitious climate policy (or specific policies) and those who oppose them ('advocates' and 'opponents', in Stokes' (2020) terms). Advocates may include environmental NGOs and 'green' industries (e.g. in the area of renewable energy), while opponents often include (but are certainly not limited to) GHG-intensive industries (e.g. the fossil fuel industry or GHG-intensive forms of agriculture). Civil society plays a vital role in representing interests and ideas in climate politics and can be an important channel through which public attitudes, economic and other interests, and scientific expertise can influence policy.

Increasingly, scholars have brought to the fore the *material* nature of climate politics: that it is a clash over material interests (e.g. Mildenberger 2020). Interest groups operate on the front lines of these conflicts. In some circumstances, interest groups in favour of climate policies have been able to influence policy such that it helps establish a new industry, creating new 'constituencies of interest', and in turn allows them to continue to exert influence on policy. Eikeland and Inderberg (2016) describe how this process happened in Denmark, resulting in strong renewable energy interests successfully resisting the dismantling of ambitious climate and energy policies by a right-of-centre government in the 2000s.

Many of the most powerful economic interest groups have sought to defend the policy status quo in the face of proposals for new or more ambitious climate policies. These interests include representatives of polluting industries, but also quite often trade unions representing the workers who stand to lose out when industries and entire sectors are more heavily regulated or taxed or are even closed (e.g. coal mines). As a result, these powerful economic interests sometimes stand together to oppose climate policies. Mildenberger (2020) has suggested that this results in the 'double representation' of carbon polluters: economic interests in favour of the status quo are always represented—whether the right, representing capital, or the left, representing workers, is in power—and he identifies it as one of the reasons why introducing climate policies has been so difficult. He argues that this advantage is compounded by the fact that carbon polluters have the status quo on their side: as opponents of change, they need only control one veto point, while advocates of change need to steer their proposals past multiple barriers. Yet the preferences of economic interests are not static; they have changed over time. They have increasingly embraced discourses on climate change and sustainability with corporate interests pursuing business-friendly approaches to decarbonization (and 'greenwashing' in some instances) and trade unions demanding a 'just transition' for workers.

The groups in civil society most often associated with climate politics are social movements that focus on environmental and climate policy, and they provide a channel through which public concern about climate change can exert influence. Individuals may join social movements for a range of reasons: to express their concern about climate change, to work with like-minded people, or to support an organization that is trying to shape public debates and to persuade politicians and public servants to change government policies (see Chapter 5).

The environmental movement is large and diverse: it includes a growing number of environmental non-governmental organizations (ENGOs) specifically formed to campaign for action on climate change, such as Climate Action Network (CAN), Fridays For Future (FFF), and Extinction Rebellion (XR). Many other environmental and conservation groups also work extensively on climate change. National conservation groups such as the Nature and Biodiversity Conservation Union (NABU) in Germany, the Royal Society for the Protection of Birds (RSPB) in the UK, or the Dutch *Vereniging Natuurmonumenten* were established long before climate change emerged as a major issue but their focus on the protection of habitats or species—often involving practical conservation work—has led them to emphasize the importance of mitigating and adapting to climate change. Thus, campaigning by the conservation group *Sabima* helped persuade the Norwegian government in 2020 to ban cultivation on peatlands to protect critical carbon sinks (Farstad et al. 2022). Similarly, advocacy groups established to promote a broad environmental agenda through campaigning and lobbying politicians and public servants, including Greenpeace and Friends of the Earth (FoE), have increasingly prioritized climate change. Often, they have done so through the prism of their own established expertise, so campaigning by Greenpeace, for example, has a strong marine focus.

ENGOs come in many shapes and sizes, but one important distinction is between mainstream and grassroots groups. Mainstream groups are often large, centralized, professional organizations that operate as 'insiders' within the political system. They lobby politicians and public officials, give evidence to parliamentary committees, educate the public through in mation campaigns, and seek supportive media coverage. In most countries a handful of su groups (five to ten of them) dominate the environmental and climate movement—attracting most members, employing more staff, and securing the largest budgets. As the urgency of action on climate change has intensified, advocacy groups and conservation organizations have increasingly coalesced. Such coalitions often aim to mobilize their resources more effectively so that they can apply more pressure on governments to ratchet up their climate ambitions and strengthen their policies. Thus, campaigning by Climate Alliance Germany, with 140 member organizations, led to the *Bundestag* passing the Climate Protection law committing to achieving net zero by 2050, supported by a range of sectoral emission limits. Greener UK, a coalition of ten leading environmental organizations, helped persuade the UK government to maintain environmental protections, including on climate change, through the Brexit process.

Some international environmental groups, including Greenpeace and FoE, and broad networks, such as CAN, maintain offices in Brussels to enable them to lobby the European Commission, the European Parliament and member state ministers more effectively. By contrast, grassroots groups are typically informal, bottom-up organizations. Many of these groups are small local groups campaigning against specific unwanted developments such as a proposed new airport, coal mine, or oil well. However, others belong to the wider activist Climate Justice Movement (CJM), a fluid transnational network of individuals and groups, which emerged in response to the continuing failure of global climate summits to deliver the outcomes necessary to mitigate and adapt to climate change. The CJM's moderate wing focuses on securing technical improvements to international treaties, while its radical wing seeks a more fundamental economic, social, and political transformation (sometimes referred to as 'system change') to be secured through bottom-up mass mobilization. Some activists have joined climate camps that encourage discussion about the causes of and solutions to the climate crisis, but two prominent groups, which operate in several countries, are FFF and XR. FFF is a decentralized movement of mostly children and young people seeking to persuade politicians and business actors to embrace the scientific lessons of climate change and act quickly to avert catastrophe. XR, which is more radical, is unconvinced that the existing liberal democratic system can respond effectively to its three core demands of 'Tell the Truth' (about the need for urgent action to address the climate crisis), 'Act Now' (everyone needs to change their behaviour), and 'Decide Together' (a call for a citizens' assembly) (see Box 15.3).

Other social movements have mobilized against climate policies. The *gilets jaunes* ('yellow vest') protests in France during 2018–19 were prompted by widespread opposition to significant increases in fuel tax and inner-city car parking charges, alongside cutting the maximum speed limit on secondary roads. The government of President Macron intended these measures to reduce GHG emissions from transport, but they were widely regarded as disproportionately affecting some of the poorest groups in society who were dependent on their vehicles for work. This populist movement largely consisted of working-class citizens, who took direct action by blocking road junctions, toll booths, and fuel depots across France. While the movement was not explicitly climate-sceptic, the outpouring of anger and frustration that underpinned it was a lesson to policymakers about the potential political consequences of imposing new costs on their citizens in the name of climate policy.

Box 15.3 Varieties of climate protest

Friends of the Earth's (FoE) 'The Big Ask' campaign played a major role in persuading the UK government to introduce the pioneering Climate Change Act 2008 that enshrined ambitious emission reduction targets in law backed by innovative carbon budgets. FoE combined traditional insider methods—getting members to send emails/postcards to their Members of Parliament MPs to persuade them to support the campaign—with an aspirational campaign involving celebrities, gigs, and videos, before, crucially, winning over David Cameron, the newly appointed leader of the opposition Conservative Party; this had important implications for the Labour Government's climate ambitions. Subsequently, FoE rolled out this campaign in several other countries, which contributed to the adoption of Climate Change Acts elsewhere, notably in Finland and Ireland (Carter and Childs 2018).

Client Earth works within the political and judicial system by using the law to fight climate change and protect the environment. It employs around 200 staff in eight national offices, including London, Brussels, Luxembourg, Berlin, Warsaw, and Madrid. One key aim is to use the courts to compel national governments to comply with EU legislation; for example, it challenged the UK and German governments to comply with the Ambient Air Quality Directive, which led to more stringent measures being taken in both countries to reduce pollution from traffic in cities. In Poland, Client Earth was able to prevent the construction of a coal-fired power station by taking action as a shareholder. At subnational level within the UK local planning framework Client Earth often acts as a counterpoint to developers wishing to develop building projects. It also uses corporate and financial law to pursue claims against companies, seeking to leverage the financial risks that climate change imposes on large corporations to encourage them to take action. Thus BP was forced to drop its 'Possibilities Everywhere' advertising campaign when Client Earth claimed it could mislead people into thinking British Petroleum (BP) was a renewables company focused on clean energy even though around 96% of BP's annual expenditure was devoted to oil and gas extraction.

The continuing failure of the UN Framework Convention on Climate Change (UNFCCC) process to achieve effective international climate treaties and the weakness of national government policies has prompted many activists to take more direct action. *Fridays For Future* was inspired by the School Strike for Climate begun by Swedish teenager Greta Thunberg started demonstrating outside the Swedish parliament (the *Riksdag*) in 2018. FFF's strategy involved mobilizing young people through a series of school strikes across many European countries, with around 1.8 million students striking in 120 countries in June 2019. FFF undoubtedly pushed climate change up the political agenda, thereby contributing to the strengthening of EU and national climate policies. One study of parties' responses to FFF in Austria, Germany, and Sweden shows that they follow ideological lines, with green and social democratic parties expressing strong support, and conservative and far right parties responding with varying degrees of opposition (Berker and Pollex 2023).

Fridays For Future uses direct action to shape the policy agendas of politicians and corporate actors—it may try to shame people, but it engages with political elites. In contrast, ER, which has groups in most European countries, rejects traditional methods because, according to one of their co-founders (and contrary to some of the evidence), 'Conventional campaigning does not work. Sending emails, giving money to NGOs, going on A-to-B marches [have] failed to bring about the necessary change' (Roger Hallam, quoted in Berglund and Schmidt 2020: 33). Instead, they embrace unconventional forms of nonviolent direct action involving interventions that involve blocking private and public transport (e.g. roads, trains), and occupying buildings in order to disrupt economic and political activity. This radical form of civil disobedience involving a willingness to break the law and accept the consequences (e.g. arrest by police) means XR is excluded—and excludes itself—from mainstream political institutions and processes. XR's theory of change is based on the idea that if a significant minority of the population (at least 3.5%) gets directly involved in the climate struggle, then change will follow. And while XR generates strong, often vitriolic, criticism from those citizens who are affected (by XR's disruption of transport networks, for example) that outrage also generates extensive media coverage, which XR hopes will encourage others to join their cause.

It is difficult to gauge the impact of ENGO campaigns and actions on climate politics and policy (although see Böhler et al. 2022). Box 15.3 gives examples of different types of activity, both conventional and unconventional, including some examples of 'success'. It is also important to recognize that success can take many different forms, ranging from playing a part in a change of policy to inspiring more people to get involved in climate protests or simply to make changes to their lifestyles.

15.4 **Political parties**

Political parties are another key link in the chain that connects wider society with governments' climate policies and allows society to hold decision-makers accountable for those policies. Just as in society as a whole, climate change has become increasingly salient for parties across Europe, whether they are Green, far right, or mainstream.

Green parties have long been distinct from other political parties in the positions they adopt in favour of climate policies and in the priority they attribute to those policies (Farstad 2018). Indeed, Green parties are at least partly defined by their environmental preferences. But Green parties reject being typecast as single-issue parties that only care about the environment: typically they present left-libertarian programmes combining radical libertarian positions (e.g. on immigration and recreational drugs) with more traditional socialist concerns such as expanding the welfare state and education sector (van Haute 2016).

Since emerging in the 1980s and 1990s Green parties have become well established in Northern and Western Europe—they have met with sustained electoral success in countries including Germany, Finland, Sweden, Luxembourg, and Austria—but have generally struggled to gain a foothold across Southern and Central and Eastern Europe. There is strong comparative evidence that as economic development increases so does the Green party vote share (Grant and Tilley 2019), which suggests that the Greens appeal to citizens in richer liberal democracies where post-material values—progressive views on cultural issues such as immigration and marriage equality, and concern about the environment—are more prevalent (see Chapter 4).

Electoral success has resulted in Green parties increasingly participating in government coalitions. Despite the widespread perception of Green parties as being left-wing, they have entered not just in 'red-green' coalitions with social democratic parties (Denmark, France, Germany, Italy, Sweden) but also coalitions with centrist and/or right-of-centre parties (Austria, Belgium, Czechia, Finland, Ireland, Luxembourg), and dozens more at subnational level. There is mixed evidence from comparative studies concerning the influence of Green parties' participation in government on climate policy: while Jensen and Spoon (2011) show a link between green party participation in government and lower greenhouse gas emissions, Wurster and Hagemann (2018) find Green parties in power at subnational level in Germany had little impact on the growth of renewable energy, and Schulze (2021) observes no Green party effect on the number of climate-energy policies. While Green parties are often allocated the environment/climate ministry, they often receive just a handful of other ministerial portfolios mainly due to their size (Little 2016), and this tends to limit their influence.

For many Green parties, nuclear power presents a dilemma that sits squarely in the domain of climate policy. Pushing for nuclear power to be phased out has been a priority for several Green parties, yet this can create an electricity generation gap that has at times been filled by gas or coal-fired power stations, thereby increasing GHG emissions. Thus, even in Belgium and Germany, the only countries to agree to a nuclear phase-out, the process has taken many decades and is not yet complete. More recently, when Green parties have entered government they have prioritized strengthening framework climate legislation (e.g. the Irish and Swedish Climate Change Acts) and implementing measures such as ecotaxes, guaranteed prices for electricity generated from renewable sources (feed-in tariffs), and investment in renewable energy. However, they have often struggled to exercise influence across a wider range of sectors associated with climate policy, such as transport, agriculture, and food.

In many countries, the *far right* has emerged as the other side of 'new politics', taking positions that are opposed to those of the Greens and the new left on climate change, but also on 'moral' issues like abortion and marriage equality, European integration, and immigration. Far right parties have secured considerable electoral success in recent years right across Europe, often far exceeding the Green party vote, with several far right parties now among the largest parties nationally (see Chapter 18). Far right parties across Europe tend to be climate sceptic. Some explicitly reject climate science (*Alternative für Deutschland* (*AfD*), UK Independence Party), denying the link between human activity and climate change; others mix various climate sceptic claims with a grudging acknowledgement that anthropogenic (i.e. human-made) climate change is happening (Sweden Democrats, Law and Justice Party [Poland]). Either way, far right parties regard climate change as a low priority and they typically urge a cautious (i.e. do little or nothing) approach to the problem. In particular, far right parties are generally critical of 'globalist' multilateral initiatives such as the Paris Agreement and EU climate policies for being ineffective and unjust (Schaller and Carius 2019). Thus, they are hostile to net zero targets and oppose plans to phase out fossil fuels, while some (but not all) far right parties decry the expansion of renewable energy as costly and unreliable. Yet there is variation on some policies: for example, while the French *Ressemblement National* supports energy efficiency measures as a way to address fuel poverty for consumers, the German *AfD* has criticized building insulation as dangerous for limiting air circulation and causing fungal growth (Hess and Renner 2019).

There is clear evidence that strong far right representation in both national legislatures and executives has a negative impact on climate policy (Lockwood and Lockwood 2022) and that government climate policy ambition weakens when far right parties join the government, particularly where those parties control key ministries (Ćetković and Hagemann 2020). Where far right parties do enter government in EU member states there is evidence of an almost immediate increase in GHG emissions (Jahn 2021). Efforts to strengthen EU climate policy are frequently blocked or delayed by groups of states often led by Poland (under the government of the Law and Justice Party), which in early 2023 remained the only EU member state not to agree to a 2050 net zero target. Far right parties in the European Parliament have frequently voted against climate legislation (Schaller and Carius 2019), but probably with little concrete impact on policy ambition. The direct impact of the far right has been limited in several countries by the *cordon sanitaire* whereby established parties agree not to work with far right parties; indeed, this exclusion may have encouraged coalitions to be formed that include Green parties or other parties favouring progressive climate action. However, it is also plausible that the growing electoral success of the far right has constrained the climate ambition of mainstream parties.

Overall, mainstream parties have responded slowly and weakly to the challenge of climate change. Party manifestos give relatively little attention to the issue: one study of manifestos from eighteen countries (fourteen in Europe) between 2009 and 2013 found an average of just 3.3% of each manifesto devoted to climate change (Farstad 2018: 704). There is variation between parties, with climate change being generally (but not exclusively) more salient for left-wing parties than for right-wing parties (Farstad 2018). There is more mixed evidence of a left–right divide in national government climate policy. Tobin (2017) finds that leftist governments are associated with more ambitious climate policy and Schulze (2021; see the Thinking Comparatively section) finds that left-of-centre governments are more likely to bring in 'hard' climate policies (including regulation and taxes) than right-of-centre governments. However, Fankhauser et al. (2015) find no significant difference in the number of laws passed by left-wing and right-wing governments.

The reluctance of mainstream parties to prioritize climate change and to adopt the necessary policy measures is perhaps puzzling, given the scale and urgency of the climate problem. However, in practice parties have many other short-term goals that command immediate attention. Whether dealing with major continent-wide issues like inward migration or the Covid-19 pandemic, or country-specific problems such as managing the economy, political parties all too easily put off addressing the long-term fundamental challenge of transitioning to a carbon-neutral economy. Moreover, they are frequently subjected to strong pressure from business groups and trade unions—which often have close institutional links with mainstream parties—not to implement climate measures such as carbon taxes or regulations that might threaten economic competitiveness. This pressure from economic interests often finds common ground with the wider unpopularity of some climate policies, which may impose considerable costs on certain groups, such as car drivers paying higher petrol taxes or householders required to replace gas boilers with air source heat pumps. Although there is growing public concern about climate change it remains a low priority for most citizens, particularly when voting in national elections, so mainstream parties motivated by vote-seeking incentives are wary of imposing unpopular climate policies that might threaten their electoral support. Instead, mainstream parties frequently pursue an *accommodation* strategy, gradually strengthening their climate programmes to ensure they are not shown up by their main rivals, but unwilling to turn elections into a contest over which party can best deliver progressive climate policies.

15.5 Governments

An effective response to climate change requires every individual and organization to play their part, but perhaps what matters most is government policy. It is often the primary object of influence for social movements, interest groups and political parties, and the subject of debates among the public. Analysing the influence of public attitudes, interest groups, social movements, or political parties on climate policy entails measuring governments' climate policy outputs (actions and inaction) or outcomes (the effects of those outputs). Indeed, measuring climate policy—its ambition, effectiveness, and governments' or countries' climate policy performance—is a research task in its own right.

In the context of climate change, there is little doubt about which *policy outcome* is of primary interest: it is GHG emissions (or GHG emissions net of their absorption by 'carbon sinks'). GHG emissions cause climate change and are therefore at the root of the climate crisis. Yet, even though they are centrally important for the current and future severity of the climate change problem, taking GHG emissions (change in emissions over time, for example; see Table 15.1) as an indicator of a *government's* performance on climate change may be inaccurate and even unfair. It is true that government policies *do* influence GHG emissions (Le Quéré et al. 2019) and that public sector organizations are direct sources of some GHG emissions, but most GHG emissions come from wider society. The sources of these emissions include industries in sectors like energy, transport, and food, and individuals going about their daily lives. As a result, GHG emissions depend on government action and inaction, but they also depend on much more than this; they depend on the responses of societal actors to those actions, and on decisions and behaviour in the wider society and economy that are influenced by a host of other factors.

There is also a broader debate over whether the predominant approach to measuring a country's emissions is a valid measure of a country's climate policy outcomes. Most GHG emissions data report production-based emissions (i.e. emissions produced on the territory of the country), but many argue that consumption-based emissions, taking into account the emissions caused by demand for products and services internationally (e.g. demand for electronics manufactured in Asia), is also a relevant measure of a European country's contribution to climate change. It is also one that would paint developed economy countries in an even poorer light with regard to their historical responsibility and their current performance. For example, a recent study of Ireland showed that its GHG emissions (already relatively high on a per capita basis) would be about 70% higher if imported goods and services were accounted for (De Bruin and Yakut 2022).

If we want to observe how governments act on climate change, a more direct approach is to focus on their *policy outputs* (actions and inaction). There are many hundreds of government policy outputs across all sectors of the economy that can be counted as climate policies; increasingly so, given the progressive integration of climate policy across policy domains. They can be categorized by sector (in electricity generation, transport, agriculture, housing, etc.) and by instrument type (regulations, subsidies, information-provision, etc.). The *Climate Change Laws of the World* database (see e.g. Fankhauser et al. 2015) represents one major effort to record legislative policy outputs. Some outputs are focused domestically (e.g. regulating industrial emissions) while others have an external, international focus (e.g. taking positions on multilateral climate policy proposals).

Even within the EU, there is substantial variation between 'leaders' and 'laggards' on climate policy. As reflected in Table 15.1, the GHG emissions trajectories of European countries are varied. Yet Europe illustrates well that emissions trajectories can be deceptive: in economic terms, West European countries typically have very different starting points in earlier decades than Southern European or Central and Eastern European countries, and this needs to be taken into account when interpreting emissions as an indicator of climate policy performance. Table 15.1 also shows the scores and rankings of European countries in the Climate Change Performance Index (CCPI) 2023, and European countries' varied performance is indicated by their dispersion over almost the full range of rankings. The index focuses primarily on policy outcomes (like emissions and renewable energy uptake) and to

Table 15.1 Climate policy performance in Europe

	GHG emissions ($MtCO_2e$)				CCPI 2023	
Country	**1990**	**2005**	**2019**	**% change 1990–2019**	**Score**	**Rank out of 63***
Austria	66	81	75	+14	51.6	32
Belgium	142	143	116	−19	48.4	39
Bulgaria	81	46	46	−43	49.2	36
Croatia	25	22	18	−28	52	30
Cyprus	5	9	8	+58	49.4	35
Czech Republic	190	140	136	−28	44.2	45
Denmark	78	72	48	−38	79.6	4
Estonia	38	18	14	−63	65.1	9
Finland	58	49	38	−33	61.2	15
France	526	512	413	−21	53	28
Germany	1273	993	793	−38	61.1	16
Greece	101	133	82	−19	57.5	24
Hungary	92	71	59	−36	38.5	53
Ireland	60	76	64	+8	48.5	37
Italy	515	554	377	−27	52.9	29
Latvia	14	5	10	−26	56.8	25
Lithuania	42	18	15	−65	59.2	21
Luxembourg	13	12	10	−19	60.8	17
Malta	3	3	2	−16	60.4	18
Netherlands	226	218	185	−18	62.2	13
Poland	446	355	376	−16	37.9	54
Portugal	60	88	56	−7	61.6	14
Romania	222	119	82	−63	47.1	43
Slovakia	64	45	34	−47	50.1	34
Slovenia	14	13	17	+20	48.2	41
Spain	254	404	277	+9	58.6	23
Sweden	35	34	15	−56	73.3	5
EU 27	**4641**	**4234**	**3367**	**−27**	**60**	**19**
Bosnia and Herzegovina	34	21	25	−27	NA	NA
Iceland	13	13	14	+7	NA	NA
Norway	40	34	32	−20	64.5	10
Serbia	80	31	62	−22	NA	NA
Switzerland	52	52	44	−14	58.2	22
United Kingdom	813	698	459	−44	63.1	11

Note: Data: Climate Watch (2022).
Mt = Megatonnes; CO_2e = CO_2 equivalent;
* top three positions are left empty;
NA = not included in CCPI.
Source: Source data from Climate Watch 2022. Washington, DC: World Resources Institute at https://www.climatewatchdata.org.

Box 15.4 Over to you—national climate change performance

At the end of each year, Climate Action Network and Germanwatch publish the 'Climate Change Performance Index' (CCPI). It gives countries scores on policy outcomes (e.g. GHG emissions, renewable energy share), and on policy outputs, which it asks experts to evaluate, and then it ranks countries on their 'climate change performance' (see Table 15.1).

Look at the most recent set of CCPI results at and find out more about the methodology used to measure countries' climate policy performance at https://ccpi.org/. What indicators is the CCPI composed of? Does it mainly focus on policy outputs or policy outcomes? What are its strengths and weaknesses as a measure of climate policy performance?

Can you think of alternative ways to measure governments' performance or actions on climate change? For ideas, see the Climate Action Tracker website, Bailey and Compston (2013); Bernauer and Böhmelt (2013). Lamb and Minx (2020: table 2) provide an overview of such measures. Many of the studies cited in this chapter also use measures of governments' climate policy outputs or outcomes (e.g. Schulze 2021).

a lesser extent on current policy outputs (government actions). The data reflects the status of Scandinavian countries and some of the larger European countries, like the UK and Germany, as climate leaders. It also reflects the reputations of Southern and Central and Eastern European countries as laggards, but there are also West European countries, like Ireland and Austria, that have also earned reputations as climate laggards. However, the leader-laggard characterization should not be taken too far. The GHG emissions per capita (per person) of several policy 'leaders', such as Finland, Germany, and The Netherlands, are higher than in most member states in Southern and Central and Eastern Europe. And leaders in some sectors can be laggards in others (e.g. a leader in low-carbon electricity generation, but a laggard on agriculture).

Variation in governments' climate policies and in their GHG emissions can be attributed to a wide range of factors. Emissions are primarily driven by economic and demographic factors (e.g. Lachapelle and Paterson 2013). However, policies, institutions, and political factors (like public attitudes, civil society, and political parties, described previously) do also play important roles. Globally, Lamb and Minx (2020) describe how institutions, economic interests, and ideas combine to form 'architectures of constraint', which help to explain why governments' responses have been so inadequate. They identify wealthy, politically stable Organization for Economic Cooperation and Development (OECD) countries (including most EU member states) as those with the largest mitigation potential, but they also suggest that they are underperforming. Likewise, institutional, interest-based, and ideational factors can help to explain variation among European countries (e.g. Tobin 2017; Schulze 2021).

15.6 **Conclusion**

Climate change is in part a political problem. And while it is certainly a global problem, and the continuing climate leadership of the supranational EU remains crucial, many of the key obstacles to effective climate policy lie at national and subnational level. The importance of domestic politics has been underlined by the Paris Agreement, which put in place a 'bottom-up' architecture that relies on governments—rather than a top-down international regime—to take responsibility for setting ambitions and taking action. It means that climate action will continue to be heavily dependent on developments in domestic politics: elections, economic interests, civil society mobilization, and public attitudes, and week-to-week distributive and ideational conflicts over policymaking. The political actors that we have focused on in this chapter are central to domestic climate politics, but there are others we have not touched upon: courts, deliberative assemblies, and individual politicians, for instance, will all play a role in determining whether Europe and the wider world will meet the challenge posed by climate change.

Just as addressing climate change requires scientific, technological, and economic knowledge, addressing the political problem of climate change also requires systematic, empirically grounded knowledge of the political world. In order to map our way through the difficulties and dilemmas that climate change presents, we need knowledge of public policy and of the political obstacles to effective climate action. This kind of knowledge allows policymakers to learn from one another's successes and shortcomings.

Even though climate change is now well-established on the European political agenda, and is sure to remain so, the net zero agenda remains contested. The ongoing development and diffusion of climate science, the increasingly visible changes in weather patterns, and the steady ratcheting up of international treaty obligations will continue to increase pressure on governments to implement more stringent and far-reaching climate policies. Conversely, the increasing costs associated with many decarbonization policies is stimulating protests. This suggests that climate change will become more politicized and, potentially, polarizing in many European countries, as it has in the US and Australia.

Discussion questions

1. Why has the EU tried to play a leadership role in climate politics and what challenges does it face in doing so?
2. In what ways (i.e. through which channels or mechanisms) can public attitudes on climate change influence government policies?
3. What factors might shape the willingness of businesses to support more ambitious climate policies?
4. Compare the different forms of ENGOs campaigning on climate change. Which do you think is the most effective?
5. Why do far right parties tend to adopt climate-sceptic positions? Do they pose a threat to the climate policy ambitions of European countries?
6. Why is it so difficult for governments to *mainstream* climate change across all their activities?

Thinking comparatively

The post-Paris Agreement architecture of climate governance relies heavily on national governments delivering ever more ambitious climate policies. While comparative studies do show a general growth in the number and ambition of climate policies, especially since the late 1990s, substantial cross-national differences exist. This variation between countries is hardly surprising, given that there are good reasons why vote-seeking politicians might not prioritize climate policies, including their low salience in national elections and the potential unpopularity of many climate policies. So when do governments introduce climate policies?

Schulze (2021) addresses this puzzle by asking two questions: do parties matter for climate policy making and is there a link between electoral cycles and climate policy making? He hypothesizes that left-wing governments are more likely to introduce climate policies than right-wing governments, and that the introduction of climate policies is less likely as a national election approaches. He also distinguishes between hard and soft forms of climate policy. 'Hard' policies seek to control the behaviour of citizens and firms through bans, regulations or, for carbon taxes and emissions trading schemes, via significant negative economic incentives. By contrast, the costs imposed by 'soft' policies, such as subsidies, grants and product labelling, are less visible and usually less controversial.

Schulze compares climate policies between 1990 and 2016 for twenty-nine countries (twenty-three of which were in Europe) using the database of the International Energy Agency to count the number of climate measures for each year in the election cycle. The data reveal that, contrary to his expectation, the number of measures grows during the electoral cycle, with the peak year for climate measures the year before an election. In particular, soft policies increase as the election approaches, which suggests that parties may see (some) climate policies as an electoral asset. When ideology is considered, sharp differences are revealed: left-wing governments introduce considerably more hard policies as the election approaches with the opposite happening under centrist and right-wing governments. By contrast, there is no partisan pattern for soft policies. Schulze confirms these findings while controlling for several other factors that might shape the introduction of climate policies, including both domestic variables such as the presence of a Green party in government and economic growth, and external variables such as EU membership.

Thus, despite the constraints facing most governments, it seems parties across the political spectrum deem it politically wise to increase the number of *soft* climate policies as an election approaches, no doubt reflecting growing public concern about climate change. However, only left wing governments see a benefit in increasing the number of *hard* climate policies; indeed, right wing governments reduce the number of hard policies in the run-up to an election. Schulze finds that parties matter for climate policies, and electoral cycles matter too, although not always in the way that he expected.

Guide to further reading

Böhler, H., Hanegraaff, M. et al. (2022), 'Does climate advocacy matter? The importance of competing interest groups for national climate policies', *Climate Policy*, 22(8): 961–75.

This study compares the impact on climate policy of, on the one hand, the mobilization of pro-climate advocacy groups and, on the other hand, groups representing energy-intensive and fossil fuel interests that oppose potentially costly climate measures.

della Porta, D. and Portos, M. (2021), 'Rich kids of Europe? Social basis and strategic choices in the climate activism of Fridays for Future', *Italian Political Science Review*, 53: 24–49.
Drawing on a large survey of Fridays for Future (FFF) activists across fifteen European countries, this article examines their social backgrounds and explores how that shapes their views as to which institutions and strategic approaches can be trusted to tackle climate change.

Lamb, W. and Minx, J. (2020), 'The political economy of national climate policy: Architectures of constraint and a typology of countries', *Energy Research and Social Science*, 64: 101429.
This article applies a comparative political economy approach to explore why countries vary in their commitment to decarbonizing their economies by identifying a range of constraints that hinder the progress of national climate policies.

Lockwood, M. (2018), 'Right-wing populism and the climate change agenda: exploring the linkages', *Environmental Politics*, 27(4): 712–32.
This article seeks to explain why right-wing populist parties tend to adopt climate sceptic positions and oppose policies addressing climate change.

Oberthür, S. and Dupont, C. (2021), 'The European union's international climate leadership: Towards a grand climate strategy?', *Journal of European Public Policy*, 28(7): 1095–114.
This article assesses the EU's contribution to international climate policy. It makes an argument for an EU 'grand climate strategy', involving greater capacity for strategic action, more political coordination and policy integration at the highest levels of its leadership between domestic and international climate policy.

Schaffer, L. M., Oehl, B. et al. (2021), 'are policymakers responsive to public demand in climate politics?' *Journal of Public Policy*, 42: 136–64.
This study shows that the salience of climate policy in the media and the positions of opinions published in national newspapers, which the authors argue are valid proxies for public demand for climate change, influence the number of climate policy measures, both overall and in climate policy sub-fields (e.g. renewable energy, public transport, etc.).

References

Anderson, B., Böhmelt, T. et al. (2017), 'Public opinion and environmental policy output: A cross-national analysis of energy policies in Europe', *Environmental Research Letters*, 12(11): 114011.

Bailey, I. and Compston, H. W. (2013), *Comparing Climate Policies: The Strong Climate Policy Index*, available at http://www.psa.ac.uk/sites/default/files/30_17.pdf

Bakaki, Z., Böhmelt, T. et al. (2020), 'The triangular relationship between public concern for environmental issues, policy output, and media attention', *Environmental Politics*, 29(7): 1157–77.

Berglund, O. and Schmidt, D. (2020), *Extinction Rebellion and Climate Change Activism Breaking the Law to Change the World* (Cham: Palgrave Macmillan).

Bergquist, M., Nilsson, A. et al. (2022), 'Meta-analyses of fifteen determinants of public opinion about climate change taxes and laws', *Nature Climate Change*, 12(3): 235–42.

Berker, L. E. and Pollex, J. (2023), 'Explaining differences in party reactions to the Fridays for Future-movement—a qualitative comparative analysis (QCA) of parties in three European countries', *Environmental Politics*, 32(5): 755–92.

Bernauer, T. and Böhmelt, T. (2013), 'National climate policies in international comparison: The Climate Change Cooperation Index', *Environmental Science & Policy*, 25: 196–206.

Böhler, H., Hanegraaff, M. et al. (2022), 'Does climate advocacy matter? The importance of competing interest groups for national climate policies', *Climate Policy*, 22(8): 961–75.

Carter, N. and Childs, M. (2018), 'Friends of the Earth as a policy entrepreneur: 'The Big Ask' campaign for a UK Climate Change Act', *Environmental Politics*, 27(6): 994–1013.

Ćetković, S. and Hagemann, C. (2020), 'Changing climate for populists? Examining the influence of radical-right political parties on low-carbon energy transitions in Western Europe', *Energy Research & Social Science*, 66.

Climate Watch (2022), *Climate Watch Historical GHG Emissions* (Washington, DC: World Resources Institute), available at www.climatewatchdata.org.

De Bruin, K. C. and Yakut, A. M. (2022), *The Global Emissions Impact of Irish Consumption* [Working Paper]. ESRI, available at https://www.esri.ie/publications/the-global-emissions-impact-of-irish-consumption.

Drews, S. and van den Bergh, J. C. J. M. (2016), 'What explains public support for climate policies? A review of empirical and experimental studies', *Climate Policy*, 16(7): 855–76.

Duijndam, S. and van Beukering, P. (2021), 'Understanding public concern about climate change in Europe, 2008–2017: The influence of economic factors and right-wing populism'. *Climate Policy*, 21(3): 353–67.

Eikeland, P. O. and Inderberg, T. H. J. (2016), 'Energy system transformation and long-term interest constellations in Denmark: Can agency beat structure?', *Energy Research & Social Science*, 11: 164–73.

European Commission (2021), *Special Eurobarometer 513. Climate Change*, available at https://europa.eu/eurobarometer/surveys/detail/2273.

European Commission (2022), *Standard Eurobarometer surveys*, available at https://europa.eu/eurobarometer/about/other.

Fankhauser, S., Gennaioli, C. et al. (2015), 'The political economy of passing climate change legislation: Evidence from a survey', *Global Environmental Change*, 35: 52–61.

Farstad, F. M. (2018), 'What explains variation in parties' climate change salience?' *Party Politics*, 24(6): 698–707.

Farstad, F. M., Hermansen, E. A. T. et al. (2022), 'Explaining radical policy change: Norwegian climate policy and the ban on cultivating peatlands', *Global Environmental Change*, 74: 102517.

Grant, Z. P. and Tilley, J. (2019), 'Fertile soil: Explaining variation in the success of Green parties', *West European Politics*, 42(3): 495–516.

Hess, D. J. and Renner, M. (2019), 'Conservative political parties and energy transitions in Europe: Opposition to climate mitigation policies', *Renewable & Sustainable Energy Reviews*, 104: 419–28.

Jahn, D. (2021), 'Quick and dirty: How populist parties in government affect greenhouse gas emissions in EU member states', *Journal of European Public Policy*, 28(7): 980–97.

Javeline, D. (2014), 'The most important topic political scientists are not studying: adapting to climate change', *Perspectives on Politics*, 12(2): 420–34.

Jensen, C. B. and Spoon, J.-J. (2011), 'Testing the 'Party Matters' thesis: Explaining progress towards Kyoto Protocol targets', *Political Studies*, 59(1): 99–115.

Kenny, J. (2022), 'The Changing Prioritization of Environmental Protection in Britain: 1982–2019', *Government and Opposition* (First View): 1–19. https://doi.org/10.1017/gov.2022.17

Lachapelle, E. and Paterson, M. (2013), 'Drivers of national climate policy', *Climate Policy*, 13(5): 547–71.

Lamb, W. F. and Minx, J. C. (2020), 'The political economy of national climate policy: Architectures of constraint and a typology of countries', *Energy Research & Social Science*, 64: 101429.

Le Quéré, C., Korsbakken, J. I. et al. (2019), 'Drivers of declining CO_2 emissions in 18 developed economies', *Nature Climate Change*, 9(3): 213–17.

Linde, S. (2020), 'The politicization of risk: Party cues, polarization, and public perceptions of climate change risk', *Risk Analysis*, 40(10): 2002–18.

Little, C. (2016), 'Green parties in government', in Van Haute, E. (ed.), *Green Parties in Europe* (London: Routledge): 265–79.

Lockwood, B. and Lockwood, M. (2022), 'How do right-wing populist parties influence climate and renewable energy policies? Evidence from OECD countries', *Global Environmental Politics*, 22(3):12–37.

Mildenberger, M. (2020), *Carbon Captured: How Business and Labor Control Climate Politics* (Boston: MIT Press).

Oberthür, S. and Dupont, C. (2021), 'The European union's international climate leadership: Towards a grand climate strategy?', *Journal of European Public Policy*, 28(7): 1095–114.

OECD (2022), *Climate Tipping Points: Insights for Effective Policy Action*, available at https://doi.org/10.1787/abc5a69e-en.

Papp, Z. (2022), 'Environmental attitudes, environmental problems and party choice. A large-N comparative study', *Political Geography*, 97: 102652.

Ritchie, H. (2019), *Who has contributed most to global CO2 emissions?* Our World in Data available at https://ourworldindata.org/contributed-most-global-co2.

Schaller, S. and Carius, A. (2019), *Convenient Truths. Mapping climate agendas of right-wing populist parties in Europe* (adelphi consult GmbH), available at https://www.adelphi.de/en/publication/convenient-truths.

Schulze, K. (2021), 'Policy characteristics, electoral cycles, and the partisan politics of climate change', *Global Environmental Politics*, 21(2): 44–72.

Spoon, J.J., Hobolt, S.B. and De Vries, C.E. (2014), 'Going green: Explaining issue competition on the environment', *European Journal of Political Research*, 53(2): 363–80.

Stokes, L. C. (2020), *Short Circuiting Policy: Interest Groups and the Battle Over Clean Energy And Climate Policy In The American States* (Oxford: Oxford University Press).

Tobin, P. (2017), 'Leaders and laggards: Climate policy ambition in developed states', *Global Environmental Politics*, 17(4): 28–47.

UNEP (2022), *Emissions Gap Report 2022: The Closing Window—Climate crisis calls for rapid transformation of societies*, (UN Environment Programme), available at https://www.unep.org/emissions-gap-report-2022.

van Haute, E. (ed.) (2016), *Green Parties in Europe* (London: Routledge).

WMO (2022), *State of the Climate in Europe 2021* (World Meteorological Organisation).

Wurster, S. and Hagemann, C. (2018), 'Two ways to success expansion of renewable energies in comparison between Germany's federal states', *Energy Policy*, 119: 610–19.

16

Defence and Security

SIMON J. SMITH AND NIKOLA TOMIĆ

16.1 Introduction

When we look at the external relations of European states—and especially their defence and security policies—we see a wide range of differences. Some states—large and small—are wholly committed to the North Atlantic Treaty Organization (NATO) as being at the core of their national defence. Others—again, large and small—see NATO as important but also look to the European Union (EU) to define and pursue an effective response to various security and defence threats. Still others stand aside from NATO and instead pursue either an independent defence policy or even formal neutrality. These states will frequently prioritize engagement with a range of other multilateral security institutions such as the EU, the United Nations (UN), and the Organization for Security and Cooperation in Europe (OSCE). Within each of these three categories there is still further differentiation between those—large or small, allied, or not—that commit substantial resources to national defence and those that do not. Our goal here is to dive into these debates, to give you a sense of why these differences persist, what has been done to address them, and what are the implications of these differences in a world where security and defence threats are evolving at a rapid pace, including prolonged inter-state war in Europe?

Defence and security are core responsibilities for every state. This does not just apply to borders and territory but is also related to the defence of citizens and their security at home and abroad. It can also be related to the ideas that underpin the state; its democracy and political system, its culture, its society, and its 'way of life' (Buzan 2008). It is important too to appreciate that defence is not just reactive. The aim is not only to respond effectively when threats emerge, but ideally to forestall such threats arising, and so to ensure that the core aspects of the state, its territory, its people, and its ideals, are protected (see Section 16.2). This is normally understood as the concept of *deterrence*.

In all the previous ideas, history matters. States are shaped by many contemporary forces; the interplay of domestic interests, the impact of global economic, political, and strategic forces, and even transnational movements such as those for human rights and demands for climate justice. For each state, however, these forces may be interpreted in profoundly different ways, based on their own histories, geography, and assumptions—particularly their individual *strategic culture* (see Section 16.3.1). A small state, for example, that has been invaded, occupied, and annexed by one of its larger neighbours is likely to have a very different perspective on the world than that of a large former colonial power. Even among similar categories of powers, national differences may be acute. Among smaller European states, for example, why is it that Malta, Ireland, and Austria are outside NATO, while Estonia, Greece, Norway, and the Czech Republic are all committed NATO members? Moreover, as of 2023, Finland has reversed its traditional policy of defence and security 'non-alignment' by formally joining the NATO alliance. Sweden looks likely to do the same.

Size of course matters—but we need to be careful here. It should not be assumed that bigger is better. First, bigger states can be unwieldy, unmanageable, and complex to govern. For their part, smaller states can be nimble, quick, well focused, and determined. Where size does come directly into play is in terms of resources: economic, political, trade, diplomatic, and military—the traditional determinants of 'power'. For many, power rests at the heart of any analysis of defence. As the ancient Greek historian Thucydides, one of the very earliest analysts of war, wrote: 'the strong do what they can and the weak suffer what they must'.

Larger states of course may have much greater material capacity to shape the world around them and—partly because of their historical experience—may also have the political will to wield such resources. Even here, however, the European experience gives pause for thought. Non-material strength also matters. The Soviet Union—and many European empires before it—collapsed, not because of any lack of resources, but because of the weakness of its governance and its failure to deliver to its citizens (Motyl 2001). Thus, the weak will suffer, but weakness can come in many forms.

History, size, and resources are all also contingent on geography. In recent years many scholars have spoken of a 'return' to geopolitics—that geography matters again (Mead 2014). This is partly because of Russia's war of aggression in Ukraine as well as other destabilizing actions in Eastern Europe. Russia's invasion, occupation, and annexation of Crimea (2014) as well as the Donetsk, Kherson, Luhansk, and Zaporizhzhia oblast regions of Ukraine (2022), the role of its troops in Georgia, Moldova, and elsewhere has returned territorial defence firmly to the centre of European defence policy. This is true for many countries in Europe—and not just those sharing a border with the Russian Federation. Territory and geography have always mattered in defence, but we must also take account of new kinds of threats which may derive from states or non-state actors anywhere in the world or domestically, including terrorist attacks and cyber-attacks.

With the end of the Cold War there was an assumption that the rules of the game were changing; that we were moving from a Europe based on division, competing alliances, and defending borders to a Europe of collective security, meeting shared challenges, and dealing more effectively with intangible threats such as injustice, instability, and climate change (Adler 2008). That in turn led to profound changes in European defence policies; with many European states moving from large conscript armies to smaller all-volunteer forces (AVFs) or 'professional armies' and shifting from broad territorial and border defence towards a structure that delivered military forces available for swift overseas deployment on international security missions and peacekeeping. It also meant a substantial—and welcome—fall in defence spending (see Section 16.4).

That shift, however, did not take root. For most European states, the world is a more dangerous place today than it was just twenty-five years ago. The rise of international terrorism, shifting global power balances, and new political challenges to well-established norms of international behaviour have combined to create an era of insecurity and uncertainty. These global and regional forces are affecting all European states, albeit in different ways and to varying degrees as noted previously. Finally, the concepts of security and defence are also changing to include both the traditional state-centric view but also as focus on a mixture of non-state actors, the individual, and what is often termed the 'human security' approach (in which security is defined in terms of the security of individual people, rather than the security of the state), but more recently also the digital, cyber domain, even virtual reality and the 'metaverse' (Europol 2023). Despite all these new developments, states remain the sole legitimate providers of security and defence, which is why this chapter deliberately takes a comparative state-centric approach to illustrate the core issues of defence and security in Europe.

16.2 **What is there to defend and secure: Threat and threat perception**

In 2016, the EU published a 'Global Strategy' (EUGS), its map for the EU's engagement with the rest of the world. It noted that Europe had an incentive to invest in 'the resilience of states and societies to the east stretching into Central Asia, and south down to Central Africa', since '[f]ragility beyond our borders threatens all our vital interests'. In 2022, the EU also published its 'Strategic Compass' to guide the implementation of the security and defence dimension of the EUGS. The European Commission expanded the strategic vision to domestic security, closer to the realm of policing in its EU Security Union Strategy, to include fighting terrorism and organized crime, securing public and cyber space, and critical infrastructure, securing the EU's external borders, investing in security research and innovation, as well as addressing hybrid threats, illegal content online, cybercrime, and modernizing law enforcement.

With the wide-angle lens of the EU, this makes perfect sense. However, the focus seems inward-looking—securing and defending the EU within its borders. Some writers, less polite than the EU, have even spoken of 'arcs of instability' to Europe's East and South—areas of potential volatility with the capacity (by accident or by design) to bring insecurity to Europe at or across its borders. How different do these arcs look from different member state perspectives—situated in the distinct geostrategic regions of Europe from the Baltics, through Central Europe, the Balkans, and the Mediterranean coast, through to the West European heartland and back into the Nordic region? Box 16.1 examines some of these different perspectives.

What the comparison between the six examples in Box 16.1 (to which we will return in the rest of the chapter) is designed to illustrate is that while as a whole 'Europe' may identify—and even prioritize—the nature, shape, and scale of threats in its immediate vicinity, these are seen very differently in respective European capitals. There, the focus can shift both geographically and thematically, depending on the interplay of political parties and domestic interests, history, geography, and the capacity of the state to pursue its interests. It is that variation between national capitals that makes their respective positions towards both territorial and thematic security threats so different.

Box 16.1 Threats and threat perception around the continent—six examples from distinct geostrategic regions

In the Baltic region, in Estonia for example, the core challenges clearly come from the East. As a formerly annexed part of the Soviet Union—with a significant Russian-speaking minority—Estonian security and defence policy planners unsurprisingly focus on Russia. This relates to traditional security issues (military defence), but also to the challenges of potential domestic ethno-national tensions (and their exploitation), and non-traditional challenges such as cyber security, and even 'hybrid warfare' (a combination of cyber and non-cyber, conventional warfare). In Central Europe, Poland has a similar focus—again partly because of its history with Russia—but because of its size, capacity, and geography it is even more focused on traditional territorial defence. The ongoing war in neighbouring Ukraine plays a significant role here. The threat of terrorism is also seen as being acute, with the Polish public ranking it a close second to Russia as an object of security concern.

Further South, in the Balkans, for Serbia in particular, the picture is quite different. As the core successor state of the former Yugoslavia, Serbia has been directly engaged in military conflict in its own region. It has seen itself as a victim of others' aggression while being perceived by several of its neighbours as the aggressor. Today, its priority is a sensitive process of regional peacebuilding with its neighbours as part of its EU membership drive. Serbia's core security threats are, therefore, closer to home and derive from regional instability, terrorism, and threats to the territorial integrity of the Serbian state and to the defence of ethnic Serbs in neighbouring states.

As we move further South, the picture shifts still further. For Greece, regional issues also predominate in its threat assessments. Greece's longstanding disputes with Turkey remain front and centre, with little prospect of their resolution and the ongoing possibility that these might once again spark open conflict. Wider regional issues of instability in the Eastern Mediterranean also feature strongly in Greek security and defence debates, most notably the civil war in Syria and the associated migration and refugee crisis which has imposed huge burdens on the Greek state and people amidst their own economic crisis. In the public mind, migration is also linked to broader fears of terrorism.

Taking a sharp turn north and westwards, perspectives change again. France, as a large, core, Western European state with a permanent seat on the UN Security Council, has both global ambitions and the capacity to pursue them. Threat assessments in Paris encompass the widest possible parameters, from shifting power balances in the Pacific, to stability on the African continent, concerns over recent Russian aggression, climate change, and cyber security. France is also very much concerned with terrorism and its potential to flare up again in Europe. France has been the subject of repeated terrorist attacks on its soil and is actively engaged diplomatically and militarily across North Africa and into the Middle East. The French public and its policymakers traditionally saw Russia as a long-term potential European partner but—given Russian actions in Ukraine, this long-term relationship is being reconsidered.

Further north, Finnish perceptions are shaped by its historic experience and geography. Finland's focus is, therefore, also on territorial security, most especially along its 1,300-km border with Russia. The 'Russia Card', as it is referred to, is a key staple of security and defence debates in Finland. These centre on how the challenge from Russia is best mitigated between effective defence and active diplomacy. As noted previously, the Russian invasion of Ukraine in 2022 changed the calculus in Helsinki and Finland is now a full member of NATO, bringing with it a set of deeper defence and security guarantees. Finnish interests are also directed towards wider regional security; Nordic, Baltic, and Arctic—where Russia again plays a key role in shaping perceptions of both threats and opportunities. Despite joining NATO, Finns still see the security and stability of the EU as a priority, with associated concerns regarding migration and terrorism.

16.2.1 **Territorial threats**

Traditionally, Russia has stood out as the principal territorial threat for many European states. This has been reinforced by the ongoing war in Ukraine and with fears that a Russia-Ukraine war could escalate to a Russia-NATO war. That said, the approach and strategy of European states has varied considerably because of their historical experiences. France, Greece, and Serbia, for example, have—to varying extents—shown a greater comparative level of understanding of Russia's sensitivities and aspirations. Though, once again, the war in Ukraine has impacted on this greatly, especially for France and Greece. By contrast, Estonia, Finland, and Poland—all bordering Russia and sharing comparable experiences of Russian and/or Soviet occupation—have been more sensitive to the prospect of further Russian adventurism and expansion of influence, potentially even beyond the contemporary realities of this in Ukraine and across Eastern Europe.

Territorial security is also an issue with respect to terrorism. The roots of current perceived terrorist threats (Islamic extremism, radical anti-globalism) extend well beyond Europe's borders and the response to this threat encompasses political, diplomatic, economic, and military elements are deployed by European states individually and in concert overseas outside Europe. Moreover, due to advances in technology—such as with commercial drones and explosives—it is conceivable that terrorist organizations could conduct attacks from outside of a targeted state. Securing territorial borders against terrorists is still a priority for all European states, however, but there have been clashes over how that is best managed. There is significant contestation, for example, over handling this at the national level or through shared institutions such as the EU's Schengen system, FRONTEX (the EU's Border and Coastguard Agency), and a web of institutions dedicated to security/judicial cooperation.

As noted previously, France has been at the forefront of efforts to tackle terrorism at home and overseas, and it even invoked Article 42.7 of the Lisbon Treaty on mutual assistance in the aftermath of the 13 November 2015 terrorist attacks in Paris. France has also launched military missions with European and other allies against Da'esh/Islamic State of Iraq and Syria (ISIS) centres in in the Middle East. For Estonia, Greece, Poland, and Serbia, the territorial aspect is focused both on domestic security measures and a renewed focus on border security. This has given rise to challenges in a European context as the EU's *Schengen* system for the free cross-border movement of people has come under pressure because of heavy migrant and refugee flows arising from civil conflicts in Syria and Libya (see Chapter 13).

16.2.2 **Thematic threats**

While territorial threats are perhaps the most obvious on which perceptions between European states vary—again based on history, size, capacity, and geography—there is also considerable variation in what might be termed thematic threats.

On energy security, for example, powerful differences exist over the best strategy to ensure energy independence (Youngs 2009). Many European countries are heavily reliant on Russian gas supplies for heating and electricity generation. Efforts have been made to develop an energy security strategy to reduce this dependence on Russian supplies, with the Baltic states and Finland judged to be the most energy insecure as nearly their entire natural gas consumption was sourced from Russia, either directly or through Belarus. However, things changed dramatically in 2022 as the EU imposed massive and unprecedented sanctions against Russia in response to its invasion and war in Ukraine. The EU has also banned the import of crude oil (from December 2022) and refined petroleum products (from February 2023) from Russia into the EU.

Strategic differences continue to abound. While Estonia is among the least dependent on energy imports in the EU (largely because of its domestic electricity production from shale oil), it is still heavily dependent on Russia for its gas. While Greece has invested heavily and successfully in solar power, it too has a dependence on Russian natural gas and is now a significant transit point for Russia's Turkstream gas pipeline project. Since the imposition of sanctions against Russia, Greece has increased import of gas from other European countries, but its dependence on Russian resources has not been resolved. Poland too depends on Russian gas transhipped through Ukraine and bitterly opposed the building of the Nord-Stream2 Russian-German gas pipeline, designed to free Russia of its dependence on Ukrainian infrastructure. According to the Polish president, it is precisely this which amounts to 'a weapon in the hybrid war being conducted against' Ukraine. In stark contrast, Serbia signed an extended supply deal with Russia for natural gas in 2012 and in 2018 sought rights to the re-export of Russian gas elsewhere in Europe—subject to the development of new pipeline infrastructure. Serbia is still resisting pressures from the EU to impose sanctions on Russia.

On cyber security, subversion and misinformation campaigns using digital technologies, the end goals of European states are similarly aligned, but emphases and priorities differ markedly (Klimburg 2011). The problem with cyber threats is that territorial proximity is not an issue (attacks can be carried out in cyberspace from attackers halfway around the world) and attackers are hard to identify with great certainty. These factors lead to the so-called *attribution problem*. In the context of cyber defence, states need to be sure that an attack originated from another state adversary. Often cyber threat actors are backed by states, and such state-sponsored attacks are often presented as ordinary hacks belonging to day-to-day cybercrime, with the sponsors of attacks denying any involvement. At the same time, especially in war situations, cybercriminals can use conflicts to pursue economic self-interests and launch that can be misconstrued as state-sponsored cyber warfare. For example, Estonian government, web, and media servers collapsed in 2007 under a sustained Russian-based cyber-attack, which followed the controversial removal of a Soviet-era memorial. In the ongoing Russian–Ukrainian conflict, cyberattack activity increased in both countries already in 2014, most likely with the backing of the respective states. One of the most notable cyber-attacks on Ukraine happened in 2015 and caused power cuts (ThreatMon 2023). The attack was attributed to the pro-Russian group Sandworm, which targeted Ukraine's electricity grid. Russia denied involvement in the attack. In 2017, Ukraine was targeted by the infamous Not-Petya ransomware attack, that caused widespread disruptions in Ukraine and other countries and billions of dollars in damage. 'Ukraine's experience highlighted the growing threat of cyber-attacks and the need for countries to take cybersecurity seriously' (ThreatMon 2023). With advancements in technology and skills, cyber threats are going to increase in complexity and devastation. Countries in Europe need to keep investing cybersecurity measures to provide cyber defence and security to their citizens.

In 2010 an EU simulation report found that there were still substantial weaknesses in cross-border collaboration and potentially serious gaps in how member states respond to a cyber emergency, which could result in the collapse or loss of critical national and international networks. In recent years, public debates in Europe have also been consumed by evidence of Russian efforts to subvert and/or influence national elections (France), referendums (the UK), and political systems (Greece, Serbia, Estonia, and France).

When comparing our selected countries, responses to these threats continue to vary quite considerably. Greece, France, and Finland have led EU initiatives designed to develop more active cyber defence measures, increase the sharing of cyber threat intelligence, ensure a higher level of cyber resilience, and improve responses to cyber incidents. These initiatives fall under the broad term of 'cyber defence' and include the prevention and countering of cyber-attacks. Estonia, Finland, and Poland are the most assertive in identifying and tackling what they characterize as active Russian efforts to destabilize national politics. Estonia, with a large Russian-speaking minority, has found itself at the coalface of threats of 'hybrid warfare' (Lanoszka 2016). Working through both NATO and the EU, Estonian officials have spearheaded efforts to combat disinformation and espionage. Poland and Finland are similarly proactive. Poland sponsors a NATO initiative on strategic communications and Finland has established the European Centre of Excellence for Countering Hybrid Threats, which includes French, Polish, and Estonian contributions.

For its part, France's focus on cyber and disinformation is directed more towards Islamic terrorist groups and the dissemination of radical extremism. With a dedicated national action plan and associated strategy, French officials are combating disinformation and propaganda designed to undermine national security. Allegations of Russian funding for French political parties and cyber-attacks against the campaign headquarters (HQ) of President Macron have prompted further initiatives to tackle these issues.

Serbia has a very different perspective. While cyber security is of concern to Serbia, the objects of its concern are very different. For policymakers, cyber security concerns are directed towards regional and local state actors, and criminal and terrorist groups. In the context of Russia and cyber security, Serbia has longstanding good relations with Russia, and the Serbian media is regularly identified as relying heavily on Russian sources for reporting on wider European issues, giving rise to concerns of regional destabilization and the waging of a Russian 'information war'. The Serbian state does not share those concerns since they perceive Russian sources as a counterbalance to pro-European and pro-Western propaganda.

16.3 **How to defend: Reacting to threats**

The previous sections explained why defence is a key policy for states and what types of threats states may face. Perceptions of threats influence their reactions to these threats, but as the following sections (16.3.1 and 16.3.2) will show, states' reactions also depend on (1) existing strategic cultures and ambitions, as well as (2) states' resources and means to react to threats, and their capacity to adapt to the high cost of defence.

16.3.1 **Strategic culture**

Strategic culture can be understood as a set of ideals, military doctrines, patterns of habitual behaviour, and both emotional and cognitive responses within a strategic community (Snyder 1977). Strategic cultures tend to be stable over longer periods of time, making states' reactions to threats more predictable. Proximity of states to certain strategic challenges is a key variable contributing to this stability. Estonia, Poland, and Finland will inevitably be close to Russia, while Serbia and Greece will always be close to Turkey, etc. However, strategic cultures are not set in stone. Large historical events, like world wars, the Cold War, devastating terrorist attacks, or large territorial changes can shift either ideals or emotional and cognitive responses to existing or emerging threats and consequently can lead to changes in strategic cultures.

Strategic cultures differ in terms of states' unique circumstances, but we can distinguish three general strategic cultures: prioritizing national territorial defence, expeditionary ambitions for national interests, and international engagement for collective interests. Strategic cultures are rarely explicitly framed in such terms but can be inferred from critically reading states' national security and defence strategies. All states focus on national territorial defence, but it is the framing of threats and the security environment which reveal how highly territorial defence is prioritized over international engagement or expeditionary engagement in securing national interests. With increased interdependence between European states, there is a development of a Western or European strategic culture defined as 'institutional confidence and processes to manage and deploy military force as part of the accepted range of legitimate and effective policy instruments, together with general recognition of the EU's legitimacy as an international actor with military capabilities' (Cornish and Edwards 2001: 587). It is therefore increasingly difficult to define states' strategic cultures or distinguish between them. Differences, however, can be revealed through comparative analysis.

By looking at our examples and taking the same tour around the continent from Estonia to Finland, we can observe that strategic cultures are somewhat different even between states with similar proximity to the same 'threat' (e.g., Russia or increased migration via the 'Balkan route'). By comparing Estonia to Finland, which is in its immediate neighbourhood, one would presume the same stance towards Russia as a key security concern. This was not the case until recently, however. Estonia's National Security Concept frames Russia's activity in the neighbourhood as 'unpredictable, aggressive and provocative', which directly threatens Estonia's territorial security (Government of Estonia 2017: 4). In contrast, Finland has historically avoided taking sides in conflicts between big powers and aimed to maintain amicable relations with Russia. In its 2012 Security and Defence Policy, Russia is labelled as a 'strategic partner' and 'Finland's biggest trading partner', and 'EU-Russian cooperation in the field of foreign and security policy' was presented as 'an important goal Finland supports' (Prime Minister's Office of Finland 2012: 12). After Russia's annexation of Crimea in 2014, Finland's

Box 16.2 Over to you—comparing security strategies

Strategic culture is a concept rather than an empirical category or explicit state position. Strategic cultures are implicit and require qualitative analysis and interpretation to pinpoint. Find the official security strategies from two European states (the European Defence Agency website is a useful resource) and discuss their respective strategic cultures. Identify and discuss the indicators of the countries' strategic cultures. What are some keywords that reveal the countries' strategic priorities? How are issues framed and prioritized? Is territorial defence the only concern? Are security strategies sufficient to determine the countries' respective strategic cultures? What other sources would you look at?

stance towards Russia changed slightly, and Finland supported EU sanctions against Russia, but for a long time did not openly and explicitly label Russia as a threat to its territorial borders. Finland's official stance changed drastically after the beginning of 2022, when Finland condemned Russia's invasion of Ukraine, and broke from its military block neutrality commitment and applied for NATO membership in May 2022. It became a full NATO member in April 2023. Finland's example is a learning point: even though strategic cultures are generally slow to change, but change can happen within months when a country is faced with immediate danger.

In the South, further examples of strategic cultures that prioritize territorial defence come from Serbia and Greece. With the unilateral declaration of independence by Kosovo, which was historically part of Serbia, Serbia's borders became one of the priorities in defining Serbia's national identity and represent a core security and defence concern for Serbia. Serbia has abandoned any military options for preservation of Kosovo inside its borders. Instead, it relies on diplomatic means to prevent the recognition of Kosovo as an independent state and Kosovo's membership in the UN. Greece supports Serbia's position on Kosovo, i.e., it does not recognize Kosovo as an independent state and shares a strong focus on territorial defence, primarily because of its history of territorial disputes. These include the Turkish invasion of Cyprus in 1974, territorial disputes over sovereign ownership of small islands in the Aegean Sea, and a dispute about the use of the name Macedonia by the new state on its northern border that was created after the breakup of Yugoslavia, which is also the name of a region of Greece (since 2019 the state has been officially known as North Macedonia).

Despite the prominence of territorial defence in our examples of strategic cultures, and the current overwhelming presence of the war in Ukraine in the defence and security discourse in Europe, we must not ignore the gradual shift towards a common European strategic culture that focuses on wider, global security concerns that transcend national borders. While this may not be as surprising for the EU member states from our examples (Estonia, Finland, France, Greece, and Poland), Serbia's EU membership aspirations also influence the state to align its security and defence policy to the EU's Common Security and Defence Policy (CSDP). This is reflected both in Serbia's strategic documents and the deployment of Serbia's military forces to EU crisis management operations worldwide.

Mostly because of its size, military (and nuclear) capabilities, and permanent seat on the UN Security Council, France stands out from the other examples on our list. Its ambitions embedded in its strategic culture also reach further away from the European continent. In its 2013 White Paper on Defence, France openly explains its relationship with the rest of the world: it is present 'in every ocean and in most continents', including its overseas territories, which are of 'economic and strategic importance'. It also boasts about being 'a recognized partner—and often the only European one—for numerous regional organizations' (Republic of France 2013: 14). Its involvement with countries further away from Europe primarily represents an economic interest, but also has a cultural and identity element. It is a matter of national pride, for example, to spread and support the use of the French language around the world. French interest in spreading its influence abroad has roots in the period of its colonial expansion in the nineteenth century, including the establishment of the French Foreign Legion, which is still an active branch of the French military. While the most recent security strategy of France references the situation in Ukraine it also reiterates France's strategic priorities worldwide.

16.3.2 Means and strategies for defence

By comparing strategic cultures of our example states, we can see that larger and wealthier states tend to go beyond territorial and national defence, while smaller and less wealthy states focus more on national or regional security. Strategic culture is therefore strongly correlated with the defence capacities of a state. Defence requires money, and often interests and strategies clash with available resources; although this process can in and of itself lead to military transformation and innovation (Smith 2019). European states vary greatly in their defence spending and available defence infrastructure (military personnel, armaments, vehicles, etc.). Table 16.1, illustrates how wide the resource gaps can be. France has 203,250 active military personnel while Estonia only has a fraction of that. However, Estonia spends 5.2% of its government budget on defence, 1.2% more than France. Finland has a significantly lower percentage of its government expenditures spent on defence (€2.2bn) and a relatively small number of active military personnel (19,250), but its defence readiness is compensated by a large military reserve of around 216,000 people.

Besides these tangible, 'hard-power' resources, states also rely on intangible 'soft-power' resources, in the forms of diplomacy and cultural influence, as well as non-military 'hard power' in the form of economic and trade sanctions or incentives. Often a mixed use of these resources is needed to address the new defence needs of states. The degree to which hard power or soft power is present in states' defence policy varies across Europe and among our six examples, but what is common for all of them is that they incur high costs and state spending.

The available means of a state that can be used for defence shape, and are shaped by, national strategies. We can distinguish three general types of strategies that states can choose from to mitigate the heavy costs of defence policy: (1) military alliances, (2) independent defence, i.e. neutrality/non-alignment, and (3) bi- and mini-lateral cooperation.

Military alliances are the easiest way to mitigate the costs of defence, as states can ask for and rely on help from their allies. European states can be part of several alliances simultaneously, ranging from NATO, to the OSCE and the EU, with its CSDP and Permanent Structured Cooperation (PESCO) frameworks, depending on their respective strategic cultures and historical experiences. States also choose how they will distribute their resources towards these alliances based on the value they attribute to them. NATO is a military alliance with a primary mandate of collective defence; the OSCE specializes in security cooperation, conflict resolution, democracy promotion, and counter terrorism, including the control of arms trade and cyber security. The EU's Common Security and Defence Policy specializes in crisis management, humanitarian intervention, and security sector reform and state-building abroad. Not all countries are members of all of these organizations. Some countries that are NATO and OSCE members are not EU members, like Turkey and Montenegro. On the other hand, not all EU and OSCE members are full NATO members, like Cyprus and Ireland.

Different organizations fulfil different tasks to match different strategic needs of states. However, two of these organizations stand out in the sense that they also fulfil the core strategic needs of a state, namely territorial defence. Only the EU and NATO have a mutual defence clause in their respective treaties (Article 42(7) of the EU's Lisbon Treaty and Article 5 of the North Atlantic Treaty respectively), entailing some obligation of assistance in the event of attack on a member state. While NATO's obligation is firmly institutionalized through an

Table 16.1 Military forces and expenditures

	Active military (approx.)	Reserve military (approx.)	Active paramilitary (approx.)	Total	Defence spending as % of government expenditure (2022)	Defence spending as % of GDP (2022)
Albania	8,000	0	1,000	9,000	5.12	1.58
Austria	22,000	152,000	0	174,000	1.52	0.77
Belgium	29,000	0	5,000	34,000	2.23	1.18
Bosnia-Herzegovina	11,000	0	0	11,000	2.0	0.81
Bulgaria	31,000	3,000	0	34,000	4.06	1.51
Croatia	16,000	0	3,000	19,000	3.93	2.17
Cyprus	15,000	50,000	1,000	66,000	4.52	1.81
Czech Republic	23,000	0	0	23,000	3.17	1.36
Denmark	16,000	46,000	0	62,000	2.93	1.42
Estonia	6,000	28,000	0	34,000	5.34	2.09
Finland	22,000	216,000	3,000	241,000	3.22	1.72
France	203,000	32,000	103,000	338,000	3.43	1.94
Germany	179,000	28,000	1,000	208,000	2.75	1.39
Greece	141,000	221,000	4,000	366,000	7.26	3.69
Hungary	28,000	44,000	12,000	84,000	3.3	1.53
Iceland	0	0	0	0	0	0
Ireland	9,000	2,000	0	11,000	1.03	0.23
Italy	175,000	18,000	182,000	375,000	3.17	1.68
Kosovo	0	0	0	0	0	0
Latvia	5,000	8,000	0	13,000	5.16	2.05
Lithuania	18,000	7,000	11,000	36,000	6.41	2.52
Luxembourg	1,000	0	1,000	2,000	1.6	0.7
Malta	2,000	0	0	2,000	1.22	0.5
Montenegro	2,000	0	10,000	12,000	3.95	1.61
Netherlands	35,000	5,000	6,000	46,000	3.67	1.58
Norway	24,000	39,000	0	63,000	3.78	1.64
Poland	105,000	0	73,000	178,000	5.84	2.39
Portugal	31,000	212,000	44,000	287,000	3.14	1.35
Republic of North Macedonia	8,000	5,000	8,000	21,000	4.59	1.61
Romania	69,000	50,000	80,000	199,000	4.97	1.73
Russia*	1,013,000	2,500,000	710,000	4,223,000	10.35	4.06
Serbia	28,000	50,000	4,000	82,000	5.25	2.28
Slovakia	16,000	0	0	16,000	3.82	1.76
Slovenia	7,000	2,000	6,000	15,000	2.55	1.19
Spain	121,000	15,000	77,000	213,000	3.14	1.47

	Active military (approx.)	Reserve military (approx.)	Active paramilitary (approx.)	Total	Defence spending as % of government expenditure (2022)	Defence spending as % of GDP (2022)
Sweden	30,000	0	1,000	31,000	2.72	1.31
Switzerland	21,000	144,000	0	165,000	2.23	0.76
United Kingdom	150,000	83,000	0	233,000	5.29	2.23

Note: * The figures for active forces and military expenditure change constantly in a war scenario, so this figure cannot be accurately captured.

Sources: Reproduced with permission from Chapter Ten: Country comparisons and defence data. *The Military Balance*, 123(1): 500–5. (2023). Rights managed by Taylor & Francis at https://doi.org/10.1080/04597222.2023.2162724. Information on military spending from the Stockholm International Peace Research Institute (SIPRI), Military Expenditure Database. Available at https://www.sipri.org/databases/milex (accessed 25 May 2022).

integrated military command structure, that of the EU is conditioned by the absence of a commitment to common defence and the 'neutrality' or 'independent defence' posture of several member states. Both clauses were invoked only once to date. Article 5 in NATO was invoked by the European allies in 2001 after the 11 September terrorist attacks on the World Trade Center twin towers in New York and Article 42(7) was invoked by France in 2015 after the 13 November terrorist attacks on Paris.

16.3.2.1 Alliances

Alliances might be beneficial to all their members, especially in terms of sharing the cost of common/mutual defence against outside threats, but within all alliances there are inequalities and issues of leadership, decision-making, financing, and burden sharing. In both NATO and the EU, important decisions on strategy and defence policy are reached by consensus, i.e. all members need to agree on the decision and there should be no objections. In that sense, all members are equal since their voices have the same weight. However, different members have different priorities or different leverage in such deliberations. Larger and wealthier states, usually also founding states, have more leverage (most notably in terms of resources and military expertise). Smaller and newer members tend to develop a specific role within the organization to increase their leverage, but often just 'bandwagon' behind or balance against bigger members to agree or disagree with their proposals (Snyder 1990, 1997).

Traditionally NATO relied on US leadership: the US is the biggest contributor to common defence and has the largest defence budget at its disposal. Across the Atlantic, the European allies, however, had diverging visions on the role of the US in NATO. The main objection to the domination of the US in NATO was voiced by France under President Charles de Gaulle in the 1960s, who argued that the US favoured the UK within the alliance and insisted on more independence of French defence policy within NATO, which led De Gaulle to pull France out of the integrated Military Command Structure of NATO. While still a full member and even contributing troops to NATO missions, France was not part of the command structures that decided on strategy and took operational decisions, until France re-joined the command structure under President Sarkozy in 2009.

De Gaulle's presidency left a great imprint in future relations within NATO and created the so-called Atlanticist–Gaullist divide between strong supporters of US leadership and countries which stress the importance of more independent national defence policies. If we look at the NATO members in our sample of countries, Estonia and Poland are strong supporters of NATO and the leadership role of the US, as they see NATO as key to defending their territories against a potential Russian territorial invasion. France still maintains its Gaullist legacy, although more moderately, especially since the war in Ukraine. It supports and contributes greatly to NATO but pushes for stronger autonomy of European defence. Greece had similar disagreements with the Atlanticists, most notably with the UK and the US during the Cypriot crises in the 1950s and 1960s. As described previously, Greece at the time had an acute military dispute with another NATO member, Turkey. Feeling that the US and the UK were siding with Turkey, Greece also left the military command structure in 1974 and later rejoined in 1980. Greece is still a strong advocate of NATO, as it sees the Alliance as decreasing the likelihood of outright military conflict with Turkey, but also voices its support of more independent European defence.

The EU and its CSDP is the only other obvious choice for an alternative defence structure, especially after the introduction of a mutual defence clause in the 2009 Lisbon Treaty. However, as in NATO, there are disagreements on leadership and the strategic direction a common EU defence policy should take. Major contributors to the CSDP also have concerns over duplication or interference with NATO activities and question the need for a stronger EU defence union when NATO already does the job. A common defence for Europe remains a contested question and is covered in more detailed later in this chapter (Section 16.4 'Defending together: European common defence?').

16.3.2.2 Neutrality and non-alignment

As we have seen, alliances are at first glance useful strategies for national defence considering the heavy cost of defending the state and its citizens from external threats, but at the same time, alliances and their members face some of the challenges described previously. A state can find itself pooling resources and sharing the burden of defence with other allies that benefit much more from the alliance than the state in question. In such cases, states may decide that pursuing an independent defence agenda is more beneficial than joining an alliance. Besides pure rational, economic reasoning, states also opt for independent defence for political reasons.

Even before the Cold War and World War II, certain European states were committed to independent defence and neutrality. Military neutrality thus became a political imperative and represented a core part of national identity. After World War II and the start of the Cold War, the international arena was perceived as bipolar, consisting of 'the West' or 'Western Bloc' represented by the USA and Western Europe and the 'Eastern Bloc' represented by the Soviet Union, Eastern Europe, and several communist states in South-East Asia. The development of distinct 'blocs' in international relations created the need for states to align with one or the other political alliances. Several states, led by Yugoslavia, India, Indonesia, Ghana, and Egypt, decided for an alternative option and established the Non-Aligned Movement (NAM) in 1961. The countries of the movement advocated for independence, territorial sovereignty, and security of non-aligned states in the face of increasingly complex and volatile relations between major powers in the world.

Serbia, as the successor state of Yugoslavia, one of the founders of the NAM, preserved the legacy and reasoning of non-alignment in its strategic culture and remains a militarily neutral state. Serbia's military neutrality is often questioned because of Serbia's strong support for Russia, the import of Russian armaments, and joint exercises between Serbian and Russian militaries. It is, however, difficult to discuss military neutrality in a post-Cold War context of a multi-polar world. When we discuss military neutrality in Europe today, the general benchmark is whether a state is a NATO member or not.

Finland, besides Serbia, in our sample of European states, was another state that believed in independent defence. Finland was in the minority of EU members that are not members of NATO (alongside Austria, Cyprus, Ireland, Malta, and Sweden). Finland's status can be linked to both a strategic culture of pragmatism and self-reliance. Furthermore, during World War II Finland fought both the Soviet Union and Nazi Germany, often having to change sides and choose between equally hostile powers. Its uneasy relationship with the Soviet Union, which Finland perceived as both a potential threat and a stable partner to the East, continued during the Cold War but formally changed after the invasion of Ukraine by Russia in 2022. Finland had been part of NATO's Partnership for Peace programme and had made its armed forces compatible with NATO standards before 2022. It applied for NATO membership in May 2022 and became a member in April 2023. Finland's example shows that a history and strategic choice of military neutrality cannot be sustained in the face of immediate threats to national security and defence.

16.3.2.3 Bilateral and mini-lateral defence cooperation

In the post-Cold War era, with a high degree of political and economic integration and new types of threats, neither old alliances nor independent defence suffice to protect the state. Often the solution is found in the middle ground, in the form of bilateral or 'mini-lateral' defence cooperation (Naím 2009). States can enter these agreements for the same reasons as entering alliances (burden sharing, cost mitigation, etc.), but with greater flexibility and, because of the smaller number of partners, greater simplicity in negotiations. For militarily neutral states, mini-lateral agreements provide the benefits of defence cooperation without the need for the political and resource commitment necessary to join an alliance. Mini-lateral defence agreements are usually entered into by states with a shared territorial context and threat perception, giving most mini-lateral agreements a regional dimension.

All countries on our list belong to one or another regional, mini-lateral initiative. The Nordic Defence Cooperation (NORDEFCO), for example, consists of Finland alongside Sweden, Denmark, Norway, and Iceland, and focuses on sharing information, expertise, and resources to address defence challenges related to the geographic context of the North and High North. NORDEFCO also works in cooperation with another regional mini-lateral cluster of Baltic defence cooperation between Estonia, Latvia, and Lithuania, which aims to increase the interoperability between the defence forces of these three Baltic states.

The desire to hasten NATO and EU membership was the foundation for early regional cooperation among Central Eastern European states. Poland, alongside Hungary, the Czech

Box 16.3 Over to you—comparing defence policies

As we have seen, there is considerable variation in the defence postures and strategies of states across Europe. Patterns here are difficult to identify as multiple variables of history, domestic politics, size/capacity, and geography intersect in many ways. Try to select two comparable European states with very different defence policies in terms of alliance posture, defence expenditure, and strategic ambition, and compare and contrast them. What features stand out that have contributed to each state's defence policy? Can you identify critical historical junctures or crises which shifted national positions? Does the external environment exert pressures on these states either to maintain or to adjust their traditional defence postures? Which factors are more influential—strategic culture and identity or availability of resources?

Republic, and Slovakia, formed a regional cooperation framework known as the Visegrád Group (also Visegrád 4 or V4) in 1991. While cooperation covers different areas like civil society and the environment, the core of the initiative is military and defence cooperation. Serbia and Greece belong to a similar, multifaceted regional cooperation initiative, which was formed in 2008 with the support of the EU—the Regional Cooperation Council. The focus of this initiative is focused on European integration, so the priority fields of cooperation were initially the rule of law, economic cooperation, mobility, and education, but more recently, in 2016, security cooperation intensified. Considering the recent conflicts in the region, defence cooperation currently takes the form of trust building and information sharing at the level of military intelligence.

16.4 Defending together: European common defence?

Considering the wide range of defence strategies that we have identified, and the diverse security interests that underpin them, how is it that more than two dozen European states have committed themselves to a common defence policy and aspire to the creation of a common defence through the European Union? It is important to recall that defence and security have been at the centre of the European project from the start. The very conception of European integration was designed to forestall war on the European continent. The 1952 European Coal and Steel Community (ECSC) was intended to integrate two economic sectors which were not only critical to post-war economic reconstruction but also central to the development of military capacity. The very next proposal was for a European Defence Community (EDC) with a full-blown European army and defence minister (Fursdon 1980). That treaty was negotiated, agreed, and signed by all six of the ECSC members (Belgium, France, the Federal Republic of Germany, Italy, Luxembourg, and the Netherlands) in 1952 but was not finally ratified by the French parliament—not least because of fears of the weakening of French sovereignty implied by the creation of a 'European' army.

While European defence was thereafter defined in Cold War terms and centred on NATO's Atlantic Alliance, pressures on European states to act with greater cohesion internationally strengthened. What could not be agreed, however, was the framework through which this might be pursued. For many European states, led by the United Kingdom but including Denmark, the Netherlands, Norway, and Portugal, nothing could or should be done that would duplicate, complicate, or question the centrality of NATO. For others, led by France but including Belgium and Luxembourg, Europe had to take greater responsibility for itself in the world—even if they themselves were divided over how such cooperation might be governed (exclusively by national governments or including a supranational dimension).

The prospect of Danish, Irish, Norwegian, and UK membership of the European Community (EC) in the late 1960s, the resignation of Charles de Gaulle as French president in 1969, and a 'relaunch' of the European project later that same year opened a window for more cooperation. Following the December 1969 Hague Summit, the six member states of the EC agreed to establish a modest framework for foreign policy cooperation dubbed 'European Political Cooperation'. This amounted to regular meetings among EC foreign ministers and senior foreign ministry officials to discuss foreign policy but not security or defence issues (Nuttall 2000).

With the end of the Cold War, new horizons emerged. The collapse of the Soviet Union freed the countries of Central Europe and newly independent post-Soviet states such as Estonia to make their own foreign policy and defence choices. It also allowed those European states, like Austria, Finland, and Sweden—who had been outside the framework of Cold War military alliances, and who saw EC membership as incompatible with their neutrality—to join the EC. For many, the Balkan wars were a bitter and brutal illustration of the depth of European failure in its own continent. In partial response to these failures, the 1992 Maastricht Treaty—with further treaty revisions in 1997 and 2001—established the European Union and a new policy ambition defined as a 'Common Foreign and Security Policy' (CFSP) and later a CSDP.

Institutional development accelerated as post-Cold War defence spending fell in most European states. NATO expanded and adapted itself to a 'new' security environment which included the territorial defence of its new members across Central and Eastern Europe, a new focus on developing an out-of-area security capacity, such as in Afghanistan, and a new relationship (the Partnership for Peace) with non-members (including Russia) in Europe. As the EU expanded, the Atlanticist centre of gravity grew with new NATO members such as Poland, Hungary, Slovakia, the Czech Republic, and the Baltic states joining the EU in 2004. The EU also began to launch its own military operations under the CSDP with major deployments of troops in Europe and in Africa.

It soon became clear, however, that major differences among European states continued. A bitter split over the 2003 Iraq War accentuated longstanding policy contrasts. European states also lacked some of even the most basic equipment and infrastructure necessary for overseas operations.

CFSP/CSDP was reengineered as part of a much wider reform process which led to the 2009 Lisbon Treaty. This introduced new political structures and a new level of political ambition to defence cooperation. The new post of High Representative of the Union for Foreign Affairs and Security Policy (HRVP) was designed to direct this effort and a new bureaucracy (the European External Action Service (EEAS)) set up to give it effect (Cross 2011). EEAS officials now chaired many of the core political and military committees of CFSP/CSDP.

The UK's 2016 decision to leave the European Union had something of a galvanizing effect on defence debates in Europe. On the one hand, it substantially diminished the military capacity of the EU by upwards of 20 to 25%. On the other, it removed a leading (but by no means the only) opponent of substantially deeper EU military cooperation. As part of the

Box 16.4 Over to you—creating a European army

The European Union is difficult to analyse. It is neither a state nor just another international organization (like NATO or the UN). Because of that, it is something of an outlier in our comparative study of European defence. At the same time, the EU declares itself to have both a Common Foreign and Security Policy as well as a Common Security and Defence Policy and it aspires in its treaties to establish a 'common defence'. Moreover, serious political leaders in both Brussels and in several national capitals have talked about the need to establish a 'European army'. Looking at the diversity of defence policies among European states—even among those sharing the 'common defence' of NATO—to what extent is such an aspiration realizable? Selecting perhaps three European states with very similar defence postures, what is the nature of debates therein towards more integrated defence planning and cooperation? What obstacles do you think exist in the path of the creation of a European army? What do you think the cost/benefit analysis of such a radical defence innovation might be from the perspective of each of those states?

implementation underpinning the EU's 2016 Global Strategy, the HRVP secured member-state agreement in 2017 on a series of sweeping proposals to deepen practical military cooperation and to devote substantial EU money to this end. This included the launch of Permanent Structured Cooperation (PESCO), which allows capable and willing member states to move forward with closer defence integration and avoid getting blocked by other states who did not share the same interests, and 'leaves national sovereignty untouched' (Council of the European Union 2017). By design, PESCO was supposed to be a mini-lateral framework, and followed a more interest-based, technical rationale, which would set it apart from the political and normative alliance under the wider EU CSDP framework. Currently, all EU members have decided to join PESCO, except Malta because of its military neutrality.

16.5 Conclusion

The historical overview of Europe's defence cooperation reminds us of the difficulty with which states surrender a key aspect of their sovereignty, in the form of defence and security policies, to other states, even if the other states have been close allies, and share the same continent, history, and external threats. This chapter concludes as it began—defence and security policies are at the core of the state, and states perceive and react to threats differently. A historical overview also reminds us that after every great event, whether it is the end of World War II or the Cold War, there is always hope for change, lasting peace, and that defence will cease to be crucial to states' existence. However, not only do new times bring new challenges, but old challenges remain.

With globalization, increased interconnectedness, and interdependence, states are closer than ever before. This also brings states' threats closer than ever before. Territorial threats and the defence of national borders remain the key concerns of states, but violent conflicts abroad and the threat to others are increasingly a threat to one's own country. Besides territorial threats, states face thematic threats. Energy concerns and cyber-attacks cut across borders and require joint efforts and (cyber)defence cooperation to address. However, as mentioned earlier, old instabilities have not disappeared. Expansionist and territorial aspirations of large powers have not become a thing of the past, and despite established multilateral organizations and institutions and the existence of international law, states are still faced with the threat of occupation or annexation as the war in Ukraine has demonstrated.

While some of these threats are shared, the reactions of states across Europe can differ significantly. By comparing our six examples, we identified different variables that affect state reactions to threats. States will behave similarly or differently depending on their strategic culture, the availability of resources, and their ability to mitigate the high costs of defence by either joining alliances or mini-lateral initiatives or by mobilizing resources independently and remaining militarily non-aligned. And we have even seen one case, Finland, make the transition from a non-aligned state to a full member of the NATO alliance system in response to a changing security environment. The countries of Europe have been, and still are, greatly involved in and central to global security and defence. Europe, however, is still a fragmented continent. The different military and political constellations that contribute to the defence of the European continent have gradually evolved and cooperated to reach a shared understanding of the world and the threats within. To what extent this shared understanding matches individual countries' understandings remains a question for detailed comparative research, as well as subject to the test of time and challenges to come.

Discussion questions

1. What types of threats do states face in today's world? What are some of the key threats to Europe and its citizens?
2. What are strategic cultures? How do strategic cultures differ across Europe? Is there a common European strategic culture?
3. Using Table 16.1, identify the countries in Europe that spend the most on defence in relation to their government expenditure. Then identify the ones that spend the most in relation to their gross domestic product (GDP). How do these lists correlate?
4. What are alliances? How are they different from mini-lateral defence cooperation initiatives?
5. Why do states opt for military neutrality and non-alignment in an increasingly insecure world and an increasingly costly policy like defence? What might states lose, or gain by joining a military alliance?
6. If defence is at the core of the state, can Europe and European states develop common defence at the continental level without the EU (or another form of entity) becoming a federal, state-like polity?
7. What are the arguments for and against a common European defence?

Thinking comparatively

In this chapter, we hinted at the emergence of a European or Western strategic culture, shared among (Western) European states. We also concluded that strategic culture can be an elusive concept that requires thorough qualitative analysis. The most natural and obvious approach to determine whether European states are developing a shared strategic culture would be to compare national strategic cultures and identify similarities. The study by Stahl et al. (2016) is a good example of such comparative research, as it compares US, French, German, and British reactions to the Russian annexation of Crimea in 2014. Their key question is whether there is a transatlantic security community. A 'security community' is a concept, developed by Adler and Barnett (1998), that tries to explain convergence in states' security and defence policies. The main hypothesis of Stahl et al. is that if a transatlantic security community exists, the reactions of the US, UK, France, and Germany should be similar. The study analyses both quantitative (reaction time, targets, and level of sanctions) and qualitative data (press statements, public speeches, and statements) following the event, and concludes that the reactions of the four states were indeed similar and that a transatlantic security community is possible. The premise of the article, however, was that previous divergences between these states during interventions in Iraq and Libya question the existence of such a security community. The article does not fully explain the absence of divergence in the Russia-Crimea-Ukraine case or why there was divergence before, and how these contradictions affect the development of a transatlantic security community. The article does, however, demonstrate the value of 'thinking comparatively', and argue that a structured comparative approach they employed on the single case study of the Russian annexation of Crimea can be even more effective if used on a series of case studies.

Guide to further reading

Bartels, H. and Kellner, A. M. (2017), *Strategic Autonomy and the Defence of Europe: On the Road to a European Army?* (Bonn: Dietz).

Whitman, R. G., Manners, I. et al. (2017), 'Introduction: Conceptualising the foreign policies of EU member states', in R. G. Whitman, I. Manners et al. (eds.), *Foreign Policies of EU Member States* (London: Routledge).

These two books give country-by-country breakdowns on EU member states' foreign, security, and defence policies. The first volume focuses on responses to the idea of an EU 'army' and the second has a wider focus on foreign policies.

Cottey, A. (ed.) (2017), *The European Neutrals and NATO: Non-Alignment, Partnership, Membership?* (Berlin: Springer).

This edited volume takes an especially useful look at 'neutral' or 'non-aligned' states' defence policies.

Economides, S. and Sperling, J. (eds.) (2017), *EU Security Strategies: Extending the EU System of Security Governance* (London: Routledge).

The added value of this edited volume is that it goes into some considerable comparative depth on the major thematic portfolios in European defence, both regional and sectoral.

Matlary, J. H. and Østerud, Ø. (2016), *Denationalisation of Defence: Convergence and Diversity* (London: Routledge).

This book considers a range of Nordic states with quite different defence policies.

Meijer, H. and Wyss, M. (2018), *The Handbook of European Defence Policies and Armed Forces* (Oxford: Oxford University Press).

This text considers the defence policies of all European states as well as the major thematic issues underpinning European defence and security.

Mérand, F. (2008), *European Defence Policy: Beyond the Nation State* (Oxford: Oxford University Press).

Mérand's analysis is of the roots and nature of defence cooperation in Europe and gives a comprehensive overview of the scale, scope, and direction of defence cooperation among EU member states.

References

Adler, E. (2008), 'The spread of security communities: Communities of practice, self-restraint, and NATO's post-Cold War transformation', *European Journal of International Relations*, 14(2): 195–230.

Adler, E. and Barnett, M. (eds.) (1998), *Security Communities* (Cambridge: Cambridge University Press).

Buzan, B. (2008), *People, States and Fear: An Agenda for International Security Studies in the Post-Cold War Era* (London: ECPR Press).

Council of the European Union (2017), Council Decision (CFSP) 2017/2315 of 11 December 2017 establishing permanent structured cooperation (PESCO) and determining the list of participating Member States, available at https://eur-lex.europa.eu/legal-content/EN/TXT/HTML/?uri=CELEX:32017D2315&from=EN

Cornish, P. and Edwards, G. (2001), 'Beyond the EU/NATO dichotomy: The beginnings of a European strategic culture', *International Affairs*, 77: 587–603.

Cross, M. K. D. (2011), 'Building a European diplomacy: Recruitment and training to the EEAS', *European Foreign Affairs Review*, 16: 447–64.

Europol (2023), *European Union Terrorism Situation and Trend Report* (Luxembourg: Publications Office of the European Union).

Fursdon, E. (1980), *The European Defence Community: A History* (Berlin: Springer).

Government of Estonia (2017), *National Security Concept of Estonia 2017*, available at http://www.kaitseministeerium.ee/sites/default/files/elfinder/article_files/national_security_concept_2017.pdf (accessed 6 August 2018).

Klimburg, A. (2011), 'Mobilising Cyber Power', *Survival*, 53(1): 41–60.

Lanoszka, A. (2016), 'Russian hybrid warfare and extended deterrence in Eastern Europe', *International Affairs*, 92(1): 175–95.

Mead, W. R. (2014), 'The return of geopolitics: The revenge of the revisionist powers'. *Foreign Affairs*, 93(3): 69–79.

Motyl, A. J. (2001), *Imperial Ends: The Decay, Collapse, and Revival of Empires* (New York: Columbia University Press).

Naím, M. (2009), 'Minilateralism: The magic number to get real international action', *Foreign Policy*, 173: 135–6.

Nuttall, S. J. (2000), *European Foreign Policy* (Oxford: Oxford University Press).

Prime Minister's Office of Finland (2012), *Finnish Security and Defence Policy 2012*, available at https://www.bbn.gov.pl/ftp/dok/07/FIN_Finnish_Security_Defence_Policy_2012_Government_Report.pdf (accessed 6 August 2018).

Republic of France (2013), *French White Paper: Defence and National Security*, available at https://ccdcoe.org/uploads/2018/10/White-paper-on-defense-2013-1.pdf (accessed 6 August 2018).

Smith, S. J. (2019), 'Innovating European Defence' in Galbreath, D. J., Mawdsley, J. et al (eds.), *Contemporary European Security* (London: Routledge).

Snyder, G. H. (1990), 'Alliance theory: A neorealist first cut', *Journal of International Affairs*, 44(1): 103–23.

Snyder, G. H. (1997), *Alliance Politics* (Ithaca, NY: Cornell University Press).

Snyder, J. (1977), *The Soviet Strategic Culture: Implications for Nuclear Options* (Santa Monica, CA: Rand Corporation).

Stahl, B., Lucke, R. et al. (2016), 'Comeback of the transatlantic security community? Comparative securitisation in the Crimea crisis', *East European Politics*, 32(4): 525–46.

ThreatMon (2023), In-Depth Analysis on The Roles of Threat Actors and Attacks In The Ukraine-Russia War, Report, 22 March 2023, available at https://threatmon.io/killnet-in-depth-analysis-on-the-roles-of-threat-actors-and-attacks-in-the-ukraine-russia-war/ (accessed 22 June 2023).

White, B. (2017), *Understanding European Foreign Policy* (London: Macmillan).

Youngs, R. (2009), *Energy Security: Europe's New Foreign Policy Challenge* (London: Routledge).

17 Democracy and the EU

TAPIO RAUNIO

17.1 Introduction

Many of the countries covered in this book have joined the European Union (EU) in order to benefit from regional integration (see Chapter 12 for details on how the EU works). But while member states can certainly benefit from EU membership economically and politically, Europe also presents a serious challenge for democracy. A series of reforms to the EU Treaties enacted since the late 1980s have transferred decision-making authority in a broad range of questions to 'Brussels' (which is seen as the heart of the EU). Particularly Eurosceptics—those opposed to the EU—are concerned that deepening integration undermines national democracy. Achieving European-level democracy is no simple task either. The EU brings together twenty-seven countries and close to half a billion citizens, with the member states having their own official languages and political cultures. Hence it is not surprising that many, not least those in the UK who voted for Brexit, claim that EU decisions are taken by 'unelected technocrats' in Brussels. However, for others the solution lies in strengthening democracy in EU institutions, with politicians and scholars advocating for further empowerment of the European Parliament (EP) and more direct democratic accountability of the European Commission, as well as increasing use of majority voting in the Council of Ministers (now known as the Council of the European Union, or simply the Council) and the European Council to facilitate efficient decision-making.

The dilemma facing Europe is of course not a new one. Among the modern classics in political science is *Size and Democracy* by Robert Dahl and Edward Tufte (1973). Exploring the impact of the size of governmental units on democratic performance, Dahl and Tufte showed that so-called 'input legitimacy'—including political participation and interest in politics (see Section 17.2.2)—functioned better in smaller democracies. The history of this line of thinking stretches back to Plato, Aristotle, Montesquieu, and Rousseau, with ancient city-states of Athens or Swiss mountain villages often used as real-world examples of the benefits of small-scale governance. Importantly, Dahl and Tufte also found that larger governmental units were more effective in providing services to the people and in solving societal problems, or what the authors referred to as 'output legitimacy' (see Section 17.2.1). These lessons are highly relevant for understanding the complex relationship between European integration and democracy.

The next section of this chapter discusses the concept of democratic deficit, exploring the process of European integration (17.2). We then examine how citizens can influence EU decision-making through national elections and legislatures (Section 17.3), with the subsequent section focusing on supranational democracy (17.4). We also pay particular attention to EP elections and the selection of the Commission. While both national and European channels of democratic participation face serious challenges, European integration has become more democratic over the years. But there is perhaps a trade-off, with stronger input legitimacy posing an obstacle to efficient decision-making.

17.2 Democratic deficit?

The transfer of policymaking powers from member states to the EU has raised serious concerns about the democratic legitimacy of European governance. Indeed, the image of the EU as a technocratic, supranational apparatus beyond democratic control was one of the key arguments of 'Leave' voters in the 2016 Brexit referendum.

In the context of European integration, the term 'democratic deficit' refers broadly to the weak role of citizens in EU decision-making. A narrower definition focuses on parliaments, pointing to the limited powers of domestic legislatures, and the EP. However, there is no consensus among politicians or scholars about how to address the alleged democratic deficit. Referring to the findings of Dahl and Tufte (1973) mentioned in the introductory section, much depends on whether one believes that the legitimacy of European integration flows from the participation of citizens (input) or from delivering policies that are supported by the people (output).

17.2.1 Output legitimacy

The output legitimacy perspective is often based on the 'no demos' argument. According to 'no demos', EU citizens do not constitute a single nation—they are seen individually as 'the French', the Germans', 'the Italians', 'the Slovenians', and so on. While the term 'nation state' may not adequately reflect the increasingly multicultural nature of most European countries (see Chapter 11), nonetheless EU citizens lack the kind of common identity and political culture found in individual EU member states (or in federal countries such as the United States). There is no EU-wide language, media, or even party system despite the emergence of 'Europarties', parties operating at the European level, and there is no single European 'public sphere', where politicians and citizens can deliberate on issues. Hence the success of European integration depends on its ability to produce 'outputs', public goods (see Chapter 5), or policies that receive support among the public. These could include peace, stability, economic growth, curbing climate change, removal of barriers to trade, a counterweight to globalization and 'excesses of capitalism', or more detailed laws affecting specific policy sectors or occupational groups.

Perhaps the most famous proponent of this line of thinking is Andrew Moravcsik (2002; see also Majone 2005), according to whom the EU in fact is already quite democratic—and is certainly more democratic than other regional intergovernmental organizations in Africa,

Asia, or the Americas (Duina and Lenz 2017). The empowerment of the EP and the central role of national governments in EU decision-making enable citizens to influence decisions, while delegating power to independent central banks, courts, and various regulatory agencies is also common in national politics. Moravcsik also argued that the democratic deficit has facilitated the deepening of integration. More precisely, would people have supported transfers of policymaking powers from their member states to the European Community (EC) and later the EU over the decades had they been given the chance to influence decisions through referendums? As discussed in the next section (17.2.2), the outcomes of various EU-related referendums, including 'Brexit', have been difficult to predict.

A particularly interesting argument relates to the division of authority between the member states and the EU. Moravcsik (2002) emphasizes that issues important to voters—such as taxation and macroeconomic policy, employment, education, or social and health services—remain in the competence of the member states. As a result, the strengthening of supranational democracy (see 17.2.2) would not necessarily bring about more active participation, as long as matters decided by the EU are of secondary importance to the citizens. This argument is certainly logical, but one should note that the powers of the EU cover all policy areas from the funding of cultural projects to the monitoring of national budgets, to the gradual development of the Common Security and Defence Policy (see Chapter 16), not to mention all the internal market, environmental, and external trade legislation. In another key contribution to the debate, Gabel (1998) argued that consensual decision-making between national governments is essential for the legitimacy and survival of European integration for as long as citizens remain primarily attached to their national identities and cultures. In a nutshell, people across the EU should feel that their interests are taken into account in EU decision-making.

17.2.2 **Input legitimacy**

According to the input legitimacy perspective, citizens do not have sufficient possibilities for influencing the direction of European integration or daily EU decisions (Follesdal and Hix 2006; Hix 2008). Democracy entails the idea of accountability, with decision-makers accountable to the voters. In representative democracies this accountability is based first and foremost on regular and free elections, where citizens can choose between competing political parties or candidates. As the EU already possesses significant policymaking authority, it is argued that the link between citizens' preferences and EU policies should become more direct. Moreover, proponents of supranational democracy have argued that regular EU-level elections will over time increase citizens' knowledge of EU issues and may even contribute to the emergence of a European identity—exactly as democracy has strengthened the bond between citizens and the state in countries across the world.

A significant component of democratic deficit is the idea that European integration undermines national democracy (see 17.3.2). As an increasing share of matters are decided at the European level, national-level institutions, particularly domestic legislatures, simply become less important. Crucially, many scholars have argued that national politicians and political parties should bear much of the blame through their failure to publicly discuss EU matters, and for removing the EU from or keeping it out of domestic political competition. Indeed, the lack of domestic debates on Europe is often seen as a significant component of the democratic deficit. For example, the late Peter Mair (2007) saw that European integration contributed to the depoliticization or 'hollowing out' of modern European governance and particularly of national democracy. In another key contribution to the literature, Schmidt (2006) claimed that at the level of the member states there is 'politics without policy' (there is heated political competition in elections, but important policy decisions are increasingly being made elsewhere), while at the European level there is in turn 'policy without politics' (important policy decisions are made, but this is not shaped by competitive elections and party politics). The multilevel structure of European governance, and the interdependence between national and European levels of decision-making, leaves thus little room for genuine debates about alternative policy choices.

How to address the democratic deficit is not an easy question. While those more in favour of European integration typically support the strengthening of EU-level democracy, those opposed to the EU argue that the solution lies in improving democratic accountability at the level of the member states. Referring primarily to the low turnout in EP elections (see 17.4.1) and the lack of a common European identity, Eurosceptic parties across the EU argue that European-level democracy simply does not work. Instead, one should strengthen the powers of national legislatures in EU governance and make more active use of referendums in key integration decisions such as amendments to EU Treaties.

These two paths towards improving input legitimacy can be viewed in terms of 'chains of delegation and accountability' (e.g. Strøm et al. 2003; see also Chapter 9). In the EU context one can separate between the national or intergovernmental chain of delegation and accountability, and the supranational, European chain (Figure 17.1). In the former, citizens (or voters) elect the domestic legislature, which selects and controls the national government that represents the member state in EU institutions. National ministers negotiate on behalf of their countries in the Council, while prime ministers—and in some cases such as Cyprus, France, Lithuania, and Romania, presidents—represent their member states in the European

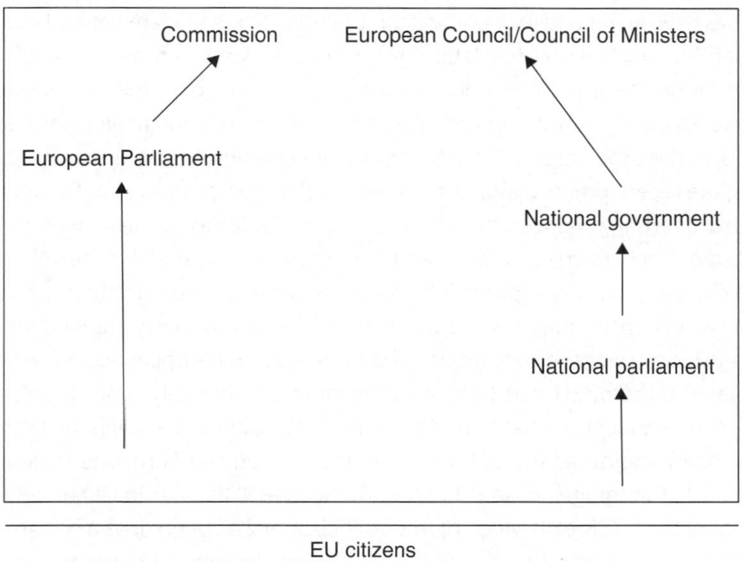

Figure 17.1 Two channels of representation in EU democracy

Council, which is also responsible for Treaty reforms when convening as Intergovernmental Conferences (IGC). In the European chain of delegation and accountability, citizens elect Members of the European Parliament (MEPs), who have a role in scrutinizing the Commission (which forms part of the EU executive branch). What matters for democratic representation is that citizens are offered choices about EU issues in elections and a mechanism for holding the EU executive to account. The next two sections (17.3 and 17.4) examine whether and how these two channels—the national and the European—empower citizens in this way.

17.3 Representation through national institutions

In this section, we examine the national channel for providing input legitimacy in the EU. We begin by examining whether elections to national parliaments offer voters a choice on EU issues. We then turn to the role of national parliaments in EU decision-making, and finally consider the potential for national referendums to give voters a direct say on European integration.

17.3.1 National elections

Existing research indicates that parties do a poor job of offering competing visions of Europe to voters in national elections. The main explanatory factor is that the established national parties, such as the centre-right conservative and centre-left social democratic parties, have an interest in sustaining the prevailing structures of party competition. These national parties are mainly based on the traditional social cleavages recognized in political science literature (such as social class), and parties are often internally divided on EU questions (see Chapter 3). Moreover, surveys show that political parties tend to be more representative of their voters on traditional left-right matters than on issues related to European integration, with parties more supportive of integration than the electorate (Mattila and Raunio 2012). Hence mainstream parties have an incentive to contest the elections along the familiar and safer left-right dimension and to downplay contestation over the EU. Indeed, in most member states these mainstream parties have preferred not to engage in debates over the EU—and where such debates have taken place, this contestation has often benefited smaller parties, including Eurosceptics, at the expense of mainstream governing parties (Szczerbiak and Taggart 2008).

However, the recent politicization (i.e. growing political importance) of European integration has at least partially changed the situation. Already, prior to the challenges facing the EU since the start of the Euro crisis, Hooghe and Marks (2009: 5) argued that 'permissive consensus' (where citizens passively support integration, leaving EU issues to their elected leaders) had given way to 'constraining dissensus', where 'elites, that is, party leaders in positions of authority, must look over their shoulders when negotiating European issues. What they see does not reassure them'. EU questions have become considerably more prominent in national parliamentary elections held since the early 2010s, although it might be better to speak of selective politicization as the debates have focused on the Eurozone bailout packages (see Chapter 13), the refugee crisis (Chapter 14), Covid-19, the war in Ukraine (Chapter 16), or, in the case of the UK, Brexit. Much of this politicization has been driven by various nationalist or populist Eurosceptical parties that have shaken the pro-EU consensus of traditional mainstream parties (see Chapter 18). As a result, many national governments have found

Box 17.1 Over to you—the EU in national elections

It is commonly argued that political parties do not offer citizens meaningful choices over European issues in national parliamentary or presidential elections and that the EU does not feature in the campaigns or in the main television debates between party leaders. Yet the recent politicization of integration together with the rise of various Eurosceptical parties has brought about more contestation over European integration. Choose one recent election from any EU member state or compare recent elections in two or more countries and examine (a) whether parties had distinct positions regarding EU questions and (b) whether the parties and particularly their leaders made active use of the EU in their campaigns. Good sources are parties' election manifestos, the speeches and writings of party leaders or presidential candidates, and the main television debates. (You can find manifestos in the original language on the Manifesto Project Data website. First register (for free), then go to 'Corpus & Documents', where you can either download manifestos or browse documents according to a list of subject areas.)

their freedom of manoeuvre in EU negotiations to be much smaller than before, with the consequence that compromises have been harder to achieve in Brussels. A good example is Finland, where the broad pro-EU partisan consensus was shaken by the populist and Eurosceptical Finns Party in the 2011 elections, in which the party achieved a major breakthrough to national politics. Until then the EU had not featured in election campaigns, but the outbreak of the Euro crisis politicized integration, with the Finns Party and the opposition in general attacking the government for its handling of the bailouts. Following the election, the new Finnish cabinet was under strong pressure not to appear too 'soft' in EU bargaining, demanding, for example, bilateral collaterals for its loans to Eurozone countries, see Box 17.1.

17.3.2 **National parliaments**

Concerns about the democratic deficit of European integration were a key driver behind the increased powers of the EP. The same logic also explains the attention given to the role of national legislatures in EU governance (Rittberger 2005). It is common to argue that domestic legislatures such as the Irish Oireachtas are the cornerstones of European representative democracy, and given their close links with citizens, national Members of Parliament (MPs) more than MEPs can contribute to narrowing the gap between 'Brussels' and European voters. However, according to the so-called 'deparliamentarization' thesis, the gradual deepening of European integration has led to the erosion of parliamentary control over the executive branch. The argument about deparliamentarization is based on constitutional rules and on the dynamics of EU policymaking (Raunio and Hix 2000). The EU member states have transferred policymaking powers to the European level in a significant number of policy areas, and as a result, national parliaments have directly lost influence. After all, it is national governments (not parliaments) that represent their countries in EU negotiations. Domestic legislatures become involved in EU affairs primarily through scrutinizing the Commission's initiatives and through influencing the government that represents the country at the European level, but it can be difficult for national parliaments to force governments to make detailed commitments before taking decisions in Brussels. Considering the dominance of this deparliamentarization thesis in both academic literature and political debate, it is not surprising that national legislatures were often labelled as the main 'losers' or 'victims' of European integration.

Domestic legislatures throughout the EU have nonetheless gradually gained stronger rights in EU governance, both in the context of their own national polities and at the EU level. All national parliaments have a European Affairs Committee (EAC), the main function of which is to coordinate parliamentary handling of EU matters. These committees have been strengthened over time in response to the empowerment of the EU. Other parliamentary committees, such as those dealing with agriculture, environment, and social affairs, have also become more involved in EU affairs, which utilize the policy expertise of a wider range of MPs. There are, however, significant differences between countries in terms of the power of national parliaments vis-à-vis the executive and the strength of the committee system (see Chapter 9), and this shapes the role of national parliaments in EU affairs. For instance, some legislatures such as the Danish *Folketinget* require ministers to appear before the EAC in advance of attending Council meetings, while others focus more on the scrutiny of draft legislative documents (Hefftler et al. 2015; Winzen 2022).

However, the real novelty is the 'early warning system' (EWS) introduced by the Lisbon Treaty in 2009, with the national parliaments assigned the right to monitor the compliance of proposed EU laws with the principle of *subsidiarity*. According to this principle, the Commission should only introduce legislation when EU-level action is more effective than national measures. The subsidiarity principle applies to policy areas where decision-making powers are shared between the EU and its member states. If national parliaments feel that an initiative for a new EU law violates the subsidiarity principle, they can submit reasoned opinions to the Commission. If one-third of national legislatures submit opinions (the so-called 'yellow card'), the Commission must review the proposal. For example, in October 2013 a yellow card was triggered on the proposal to establish the European Public Prosecutor's Office, but in the end the Commission decided to maintain the proposal. The real 'added value' of the EWS is difficult to measure, but clearly many legislatures view it as a worthwhile instrument and appreciate the opportunity to engage in direct dialogue with EU institutions. EWS provides national parliaments with at least some measure of control over EU legislation. It can also improve the quality of EU legislation by forcing the Commission to be more detailed in its justification for new legislative proposals and in general more sensitive to national concerns (Cooper 2019). Beyond EWS, we must not lose sight of the fact that national legislatures are in a sense the gatekeepers of further integration and upholders of national sovereignty, as each member state and its domestic parliament holds veto power over reforms to the EU Treaties.

Scrutiny of EU laws or holding veto power over Treaty amendments may not be the most effective way for national parliaments to contribute to the legitimacy of European governance. Parliamentary debates are a very important means of holding governments to account. While discussions of EU issues are mainly confined to committees, more salient issues such as EU Treaty reforms are also debated by parliaments in plenary, and the recent politicization of integration triggered lively public debates in legislatures across the EU. These debates can help to inform the public about the European political agenda (Winzen et al. 2018). There is considerable variation between the legislatures, with some such as the German *Bundestag* debating EU matters frequently on the floor, while others like the Nordic parliaments and the British House of Commons until the Brexit process preferred to discuss European issues more in the committees.

17.3.3 Referendums

A more direct national channel for citizens to influence European integration, bypassing legislatures and governments, is direct democracy. In two member states, Denmark and Ireland, it is compulsory to hold a referendum when power is transferred to the European level. In other member states referendums are essentially called by national governments, and they have been held only in connection with major integration questions—EC/EU membership, joining the Eurozone and some Treaty reforms. One lesson learned from past EU referendums is their unpredictability: voters across Europe have produced major upheavals for both their own governments and for the EU, and in many cases major embarrassment for political scientists and polling agencies that failed to predict the outcomes. Norwegians have twice rejected EC/EU membership, in 1972 and 1994, while the Danes (2000) and Swedes (2003) voted against their countries adopting the Euro currency. Danes voted against the Maastricht Treaty in 1992, only to approve the Treaty a year later in another referendum after Denmark had negotiated significant opt-outs from the Treaty. Similarly, the Irish voted twice against Treaty reforms, in 2001 and 2008, but like the Danes they changed their minds after Ireland had received promises that the EU would not touch select issues salient to the Irish voters. The Dutch and the French voted in 2005 against the Constitutional Treaty, and in 2016 Britain chose to exit the EU after the 'Leave' side had achieved a narrow victory in the Brexit referendum.

It is thus no surprise that particularly Eurosceptical political forces have called for more active use of referendums in key EU decisions. Direct democracy has its pros and cons (see Chapter 6) that also apply to these EU referendums. On the one hand, as the 48.1% of the population who voted 'Remain' in the Brexit referendum understand, referendums genuinely hand the power to the people. On the other hand, referendum campaigns have often been plagued by exaggerated claims and even outright lies—a situation no doubt facilitated by citizens' low level of knowledge about European integration (Hobolt 2009; Rose 2019).

17.4 Emerging supranational democracy

Given the lack of contestation over Europe in national politics, advocates of supranational democracy have in turn argued that the solution lies in offering citizens genuine choices at the European level. Elections to the EP are the most obvious way in which citizens can have their say. However, for proponents of supranational democracy, this is not enough: European voters should have more say about who wields executive power at the EU level. The main executive arms of the EU are the European Commission and the European Council.

According to Eurobarometers and other public opinion surveys, citizens' knowledge of EU decision-making is very limited—and the current institutional set-up of the EU is certainly complicated. National governments often get the spotlight through taking key decisions in the European Council; the Commission is responsible for initiating new legislation and as the 'guardian of the Treaties' oversees the implementation of the EU's laws and budget, with legislative powers shared between the EP and the Council (see Chapter 12). In most member states the political system is much more straightforward, with the government ruling with the support of the legislature. It is no wonder that citizens find it difficult to grasp where power lies in the EU, and particularly how their vote affects decisions taken at the European level.

Figure 17.2 shows responses to a Eurobarometer question asking whether citizens feel that their voice counts either in national politics or in the EU. The percentage of respondents who feel that their voice counts in the EU varies greatly across countries, from a high of 76% in Denmark to a low of 19% in Estonia, with an average of just over 50% across all member

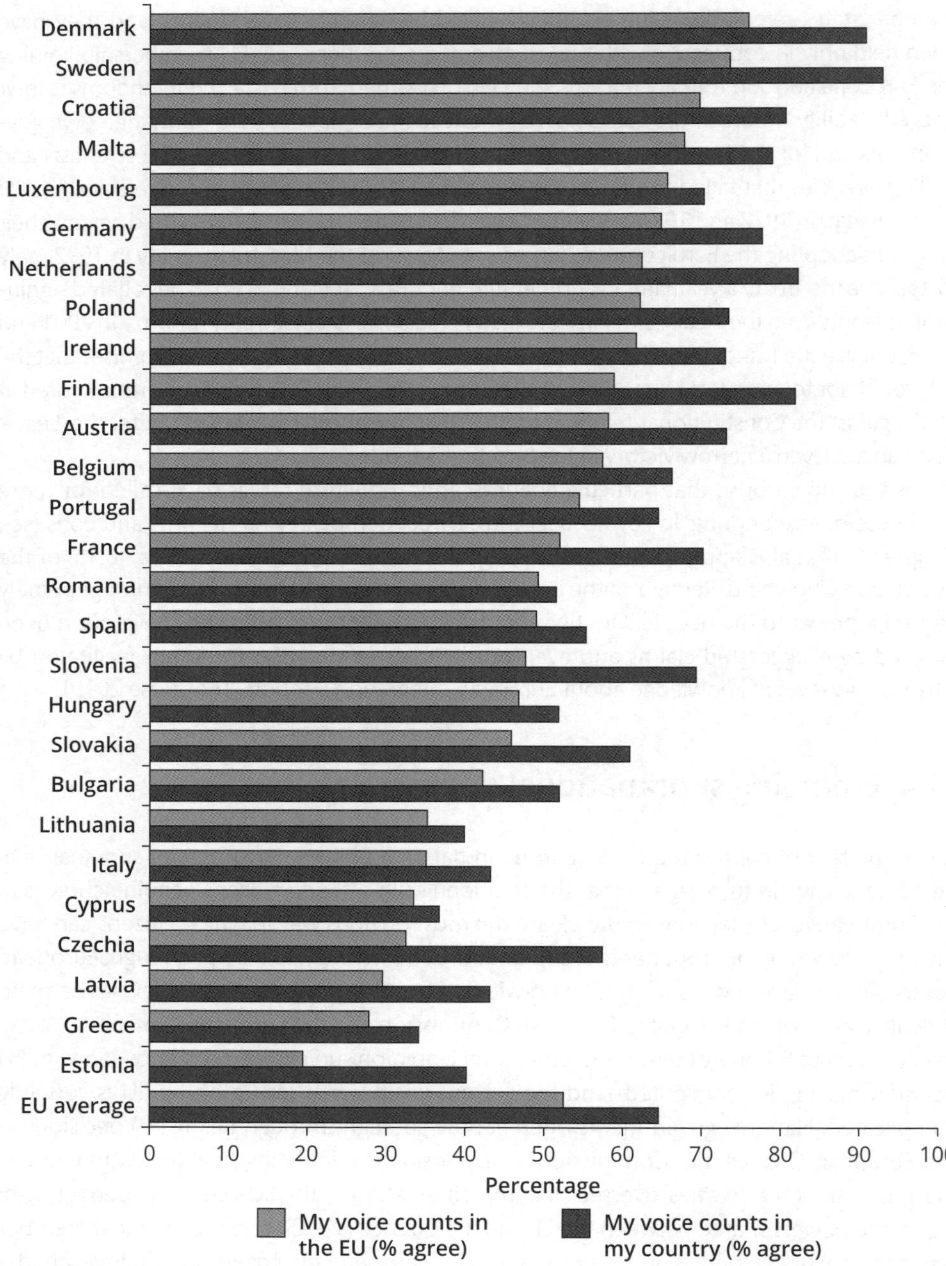

Figure 17.2 Citizen's views on whether their voice counts in the EU and in their country

Source: Eurobarometer 97.3, 2022 at https://search.gesis.org/research_data/ZA7888.

states. But one pattern is clear: in all member states more respondents report that they have a say in their country than in European level decision-making. There is also the widely shared perception of EU decisions being unduly influenced by the thousands of lobbyists working in Brussels. Particularly companies and interest groups with better resources have active contacts with EU institutions, but at the same time lobbying is also strongly present in national politics and it provides an avenue for various stakeholders to have their voice heard in European decision-making (Greenwood 2017).

17.4.1 **European Parliament elections**

Among the various EU institutions, the EP is without a doubt the one that has changed most over the decades (Hix and Scully 2003; Ripoll Servent 2018). It has evolved from a purely consultative body with members seconded from national parliaments to a directly elected chamber vested with significant legislative, scrutiny, and budgetary powers. The Parliament plays a central role in shaping EU laws and budgets and is involved in the appointment and oversight of the Commission. The thrust of legislative work is done in parliamentary committees, in which individual MEPs draft reports that form the basis of the Parliament's resolutions. Importantly, committees and the plenary meet in public and inject much-needed transparency into EU decision-making.

The Parliament has been directly elected since 1979, with 705 seats following the UK's formal exit from the EU in 2020. The literature on Euro-elections has largely been based on the 'second-order' election model, first developed by Reif and Schmitt (1980). According to this analytical framework, second-order elections are less important than first-order elections, with the latter referring primarily to domestic parliamentary or presidential elections. Hence citizens' voting behaviour is more affected by the national first-order context than by factors related to the EP or the EU. The model thus suggests that the EP elections do not really provide an effective link between citizens and EU policymaking.

Turnout is substantially lower than in national parliamentary elections, but it increased up to 51% across EU countries in the 2019 elections. In the previous three elections held after the turn of the millennium (2004, 2009, and 2014), turnout had been between 43 and 46%. Lack of common European identity, low awareness of EU issues, and in general the feeling of 'distance' between voters and Brussels influence turnout, although turnout also declined in national parliamentary elections across most European countries during that period. Particularly Central and Eastern European member states are characterized by lower electoral participation (see Chapter 5). Turnout in EP elections varies significantly between member states: it is high in Belgium and Luxembourg where voting is compulsory, and the all-time low was in Slovakia in the 2014 elections, where only 13% cast their votes. In 2019 turnout was below 30% in Croatia, the Czech Republic, Slovakia, and Slovenia. Turnout has also varied quite strongly over time within individual member states, depending on the particular political context and whether national first-order elections are held simultaneously with the EP elections. As in national elections, highly educated, politically knowledgeable, and pro-European voters are more likely to turn out to vote.

In terms of how parties perform, government parties and larger parties have, in line with the second-order model, suffered losses in EP elections. Voters may experiment with new parties in EP elections, since they know that the elections will not result in major societal changes—at least not in their home country. Consequently, citizens may vote for parties that are a closer match to their own preferences. For example, left-leaning voters that in national elections vote for social democratic parties may vote for the Greens in EP elections. Alternatively, citizens might use EP elections to protest against established mainstream parties. Interestingly, these effects have spilled over into national elections and have contributed to the rise of various smaller parties, notably the Greens and several populist or nationalist parties across the EU. European elections have therefore contributed to the fragmentation of national party systems.

As the second-order model suggests, voting decisions in Euro-elections are heavily influenced by the national party-political environment. The primacy of domestic factors results in part from the strategies of the national parties that control candidate selection and conduct the electoral campaigns. Political parties are often internally divided over the EU, and hence have an incentive to focus on safer domestic themes in their campaigns. However, there is evidence of the increasing importance of the EU as an issue in explaining citizens' voting behaviour. For instance, in the 2014 elections the Euro crisis featured prominently in the campaigns in several member states, with Eurosceptical parties benefiting from the problems facing the EU (Hassing Nielsen and Franklin 2017). Also, in the 2019 elections various cross-national themes—climate change, immigration, Brexit, authoritarian or nationalist tendencies in Europe and beyond—received a lot of attention across the EU (De Sio et al. 2019; Kritzinger et al. 2020; van der Brug et al. 2021; see Box 17.2). Nonetheless, media coverage of the elections and more broadly of what the EP does between the elections tends to be scarce. As a result, Europeans are not really exposed to information about what MEPs do and where parties stand on various issues on the agenda of EU institutions.

Box 17.2 The 2019 European Parliament elections in selected member states

Finland: turnout was 40.7%. Expectations were low ahead of the European elections, as national legislative elections had taken place in mid-April and government formation negotiations coincided with the EP election campaign. However, the campaign revolved around a variety of European issues, not least climate change, and this no doubt benefited the Green League that achieved its best-ever performance in elections with 16.0% of the vote. The winner, however, was the centre-right National Coalition with 20.8%. The Eurosceptical Finns Party captured two seats.

France: turnout was 50.1%. The nationalist and Eurosceptical National Rally (23.3%) finished first just ahead of the liberal, pro-European coalition led by President Macron's *La République En Marche* (22.4%). The Greens achieved a very solid result with 13.5% of the vote. The vote was depicted as a choice between pro-Europeanism and rejection of Europe, but opposition to the EU was probably only one reason why people voted for the National Rally. The French party system has gone through various changes in recent years (see Chapter 2), and these elections produced another poor result for the traditional large parties, the Gaullists and the socialists.

Lithuania: turnout was 52.9%. The leading opposition party, the centre-right Homeland Union (19.7%), sneaked ahead of the two governing parties, the Lithuanian Farmers and Greens Union (12.6%) and the Social Democrats (15.9%). Eurosceptic parties won only one of the eleven seats. The EP elections were completely overshadowed by the second round of presidential elections, also held on 26 May, won by the independent candidate Gitanas Nausėda. The simultaneity of the elections probably also explains the higher turnout.

Poland: turnout was 45.7%, a significant increase from 2014 when only 23.8% cast their votes. The election was basically a contest between the ruling nationalistic Law and Justice Party that has attained international media attention—and is facing sanctions from the EU—on account of violating the EU's rules concerning the impartiality of courts and media, and the European Coalition that brought together various liberal, pro-EU political forces. The former captured 45.4% and the pro-EU coalition 38.5% of the vote. The campaign was dominated by a conservative–liberal cleavage, which will no doubt continue to feature strongly in Polish elections.

United Kingdom: turnout was 36.9%. A strange affair, as the elections were held only on account of Brexit being delayed. Hence Nigel Farage, the main force behind the United Kingdom Independence Party (UKIP), established a new party, the Brexit Party, with the sole goal of making sure that the UK really leaves the EU. Farage's party won the election with a comfortable margin (30.7%). This also galvanized the pro-EU camp, with the Liberal Democrats ending second with 19.8% and the Green Party winning 11.8% of the vote. The result was a blow to the ruling Conservatives that only managed 8.8% of the vote (although the party bounced back to win the national elections held later that year). The other traditionally large party, Labour, did not fare much better with 13.7%.

17.4.2 **European party groups**

Lack of media coverage and limited knowledge of EU decision-making also mean that most citizens probably do not understand how the EP and its party system operate. MEPs sit in transnational party groups, which structure decision-making within the EP (Ahrens et al. 2022). The EP party system has throughout the history of the directly elected Parliament been in practice dominated by the centre-right European People's Party (EPP) and the centre-left Party of the European Socialists (PES; the official group name has been Socialists & Democrats (S&D) since the 2009 elections). Other groupings include the liberals (currently called Renew Europe), the greens (including the regionalists), the radical left, the conservatives, and the Eurosceptics—although particularly the conservative and the Eurosceptical groups have been much less stable in terms of their composition and party names. While the number of Eurosceptic MEPs has grown over time, they remain very much in the minority in the Parliament (Brack 2018; McDonnell and Werner 2020).

Party groups are generally quite cohesive when it comes to voting in the EP, and they are generally much more cohesive than national delegations (that is, all MEPs elected from the same member state). Party cohesion is necessary for the achievement of a group's objectives, and cooperative behaviour inside groups helps individual MEPs in pursuing their own policy goals. As no group has ever held a majority of seats in the Parliament, coalitions among different groups are needed to pass legislation. Often, coalitions form along left–right lines, although pro-/anti-European integration alignments are also common. While party groups dominate decision-making in the Parliament, national interests do nonetheless matter. When an MEP's national party does not agree with the position adopted by the wider EP party group, research shows that the MEP is more likely to follow the voting instructions of the national party (Hix et al. 2007). Moreover, MEPs can use their committee assignments or other tools such as parliamentary questions for advancing the interests of their constituencies (Whitaker 2019).

The main party groups in the Parliament constitute the parliamentary wings of the federations of national parties known as Europarties. National party leaders typically meet under

Box 17.3 Over to you—campaign themes in European Parliament elections

The EP brings together over 700 MEPs across the EU, with these parliamentarians representing almost 200 different national parties. It is commonly argued that domestic politics dominate EP elections, but there are also cross-national issues—such as climate change, immigration, and the future of European integration—that can feature in the campaigns. Choose one or more member states and study (a) to what extent parties campaigned on EU or national issues in the most recent EP elections and (b) to what extent the various EP party group affiliations were featured in the campaigns of the national parties and in the media coverage. Particularly interesting would be to compare Eurosceptic parties with more mainstream pro-EU parties, and to see how their campaigns differed. Good sources are parties' election manifestos, the speeches and writings of party leaders or leading candidates, and news coverage in leading newspapers or social media channels. You can find out more about the 2019 campaign in various countries in the 'Euroflections' European Elections report and in the volume edited by De Sio et al. (2019).

the umbrella of their Europarties in advance of European Council summits, in order to co-ordinate their positions. In this way, Europarties have influenced many important EU policy decisions. Europarties have also introduced membership for individuals, but the drafting of manifestos and selection of leaders and candidates in EP elections remain in the hands of national party elites (e.g. Hanley 2008; Hertner 2019).

Europarties, their EP party groups, and more broadly EU institutions remain distant to most Europeans. To enhance democracy in the EU, some have argued that the EP should become more like a normal parliament that elects a government and holds it to account (Follesdal and Hix 2006; Hix 2008). This could involve linking the appointment of the Commission president to the outcome of EP elections, with Europarties playing a much more direct role in contesting the elections and putting forward candidates for Commission presidency. Alternatively, direct elections could be held for the Commission president, with candidates selected by the Europarties (Decker and Sonnicksen 2011). This would be more akin to a 'presidential' model (such as exists in the United States) than the parliamentary model found in most European countries.

The 2014 EP elections did see some reforms aimed at linking the Commission presidency with the outcome of the elections. Europarties and their EP groups put forward 'lead candidates', or *Spitzenkandidaten*, for the position of Commission president. The EPP won the most seats in the elections, and its *Spitzenkandidat* (Jean-Claude Juncker) was duly appointed as the next Commission president. In the 2019 elections the Europarties again put forward their own lead candidates, who toured across Europe and took part in various public debates. However, the *Spitzenkandidaten* initiative was criticized heavily by Eurosceptics. For example, the British prime minister David Cameron describe it as 'a power grab' by the EP. Ultimately, these critical voices prevailed, as in 2019 the European Council effectively ignored the *Spitzenkandidaten* system and nominated Ursula von der Leyen—who was not the lead candidate of any party group—as the new Commission president (Crum 2023). The European Parliament has also for a long time campaigned in favour of EU-wide transnational lists headed by the *Spitzenkandidaten*, whereby a certain share of MEPs would be elected from such EU-wide party lists. If adopted, voters would have two votes: one for their local or national representatives, and one for the transnational Europarty lists. The hope is that once the Europarties and their EP party groups appear on the ballot paper, voters will pay more attention to them and what they stand for. However, until now some member states have been against such transnational lists.

17.5 Conclusion

How can the EU and European integration become more democratic? The answer depends on what kind of Europe one wants: intergovernmental, supranational, or something in between. For example, increased use of majority voting in the Council facilitates EU decision-making, but for some it simply means further erosion of national sovereignty as their government might be outvoted in Brussels. This chapter has shown that national parliaments are paying more attention to European matters and subjecting their governments to tighter scrutiny; this is good news in terms of the accountability of the Council and European Council. Most citizens may continue to be unaware of what MEPs do, but successive Treaty reforms have transformed the EP from a 'talking shop' to a powerful legislature that injects democracy and transparency into EU decision-making. And perhaps most importantly, questions related to European integration feature more in public discussions, parliamentary debates, and election campaigns than before.

Reflecting similar practices in many member states, the Lisbon Treaty introduced the European Citizens' Initiative where a threshold of one million signatures collected in at least seven EU countries is needed for the initiative for a new law to be submitted to the Commission. However, until now the impact and visibility of the mechanism has been very limited. In 2021–22 the EU even organized a Conference on the Future of Europe with a multilingual digital platform and citizens' panels combined with participation from representatives of national parliaments and EU institutions. Whether such more participatory, bottom-up processes manage to bring European citizens closer to 'Brussels' remains to be seen, but at least in the near future the more conventional routes of participation analysed in this chapter will be the main channels through which citizens can shape EU policies.

Yet for a lot of Europeans these developments do not really matter. For them, political power has drifted beyond democratic control—to market forces, central banks, multinational companies, or to 'Brussels'. These people feel that the opening of borders threatens their way of life and national independence (De Vries 2018). They tend to vote for populist or radical-right parties that oppose the expansion of international authority or the deepening of European integration and—as shown by the Brexit referendum—are not afraid to vote against the EU when given the opportunity. In fact, it is quite logical that Eurosceptical parties focus on national politics. Reforming the EU is difficult, as all key decisions, including Treaty amendments, require unanimity among the member states, whereas achieving victory in national parliamentary or presidential elections can result in significant changes to national integration policy. As Mair (2007: 7) concluded, 'once we cannot organize opposition *in* the EU, we are then almost forced to organize opposition *to* the EU'.

Modern European governance is also characterized by increasing interaction and power-sharing between multiple levels of political authority—from local councils and regions to the national and EU levels to various international organizations (see Chapter 11). Even for informed, politically active citizens, this means blurred lines of accountability, opaque decision-making procedures, and difficulties in identifying who is responsible for the decisions (Hobolt and Tilley 2014). This can also be seen as a trade-off between output efficiency and democratic participation. Intergovernmental cooperation and more broadly EU governance enable member states to collectively address important societal challenges from youth unemployment to migration to questions of international trade and security, and successful bargaining may necessitate confidential exchanges between national governments and EU institutions. Too much democracy or openness can thus be harmful to efficient problem-solving. The multilevel nature of the EU polity also provides multiple access points for influencing politics, and this arguably favours interest groups and companies with better resources.

However, the alternative perspective stresses the importance of public debates and contestation about European integration. The EU with its plethora of languages and national media and political cultures may never constitute a real 'public sphere', and the distance between citizens and Brussels will not go away anytime soon. This implies that the key to addressing the democratic deficit lies at the national level. EU decision-making requires compromises, but this does not mean that domestic debates would be meaningless—quite the contrary. Political parties may have good reasons for avoiding EU debates, but the more politicians discuss and disagree about European issues in public, the better—particularly if these debates are covered by the media. As the recent crises demonstrate, in the short run these debates and increasing contestation over Europe may produce problems for the EU, but in the long run such debates will create the basis for a more democratic Europe.

Discussion questions

1. Citizens across Europe possess limited knowledge of how the EU functions. What would in your opinion be the most effective way of improving citizens' understanding of European integration?
2. Some believe EU governance would become more democratic through further empowerment of the EP, whereas others are in favour of transferring powers back to the member states. What is in your opinion the best way to overcome the EU's democratic deficit?
3. Do you think the selection of the president of the European Commission should become more democratic, for instance by linking it more directly to the outcome of the EP elections or by having separate elections for the position? What are the potential downsides of doing this?
4. Eurosceptical parties have recently increased their presence in European politics, gaining significant victories in both national and European elections. How do you see the impact of such parties on the legitimacy of European and national governance?
5. Do you believe that referendums should be used more actively in EU decision-making? Should such referendums be organized in individual member states or could there also be EU-wide referendums?
6. Each national legislature controls its government that represents the member state in EU decision-making. How does the parliament in your country (or a country of your choosing) become involved in EU affairs? Are EU issues debated in the plenary or are they handled mainly in the committees?

Thinking comparatively

According to the second-order election model, first developed by Reif and Schmitt (1980), the EP elections are less important than national parliamentary or presidential elections. The model is based on three main arguments: turnout is lower in EP elections than in national elections; government parties suffer losses in Euro-elections; and larger parties do worse and smaller parties perform better in EP elections. Covering all EP elections held between 1979 and 2019, Ehin and Talving (2021) ask whether the model still provides a valid framework for understanding voting behaviour in EP elections. They confirm that turnout remains significantly lower in European elections, with also considerable variation between member countries. Governing parties lost votes in comparison with previous national elections, while small parties performed better than in national elections. However, Ehin and Talving also point out that there are exceptions to these general patterns, with much depending on the particular political context within individual countries.

Guide to further reading

Hefftler, C., Neuhold, C. et al. (eds.) (2015), *The Palgrave Handbook of National Parliaments and the European Union* (Basingstoke: Palgrave Macmillan).

This collection shows how each national legislature handles European questions.

Hix, S., Noury, A. G. et al. (2007), *Democratic Politics in the European Parliament* (Cambridge: Cambridge University Press).

Based on a large data set of roll-call votes since the 1979 elections, this book examines how EP party groups vote in the chamber, with particular focus on voting cohesion and coalition formation.

Ripoll Servent, A. (2018), *The European Parliament* (Basingstoke: Palgrave Macmillan).

This book provides an accessible yet analytical introduction to the EP.

Schmidt, V. A. (2020), *Europe's Crisis of Legitimacy: Governing by Rules and Ruling by Numbers in the Eurozone* (Oxford: Oxford University Press).

Focusing on the Eurozone crisis, this book examines the democratic legitimacy of EU decision-making and reflects on the output and input legitimacy of European governance.

Winzen, T. (2017), *Constitutional Preferences and Parliamentary Reform: Explaining National Parliaments' Adaptation to European Integration* (Oxford: Oxford University Press).

This book examines how national parliaments have over time become more involved in EU affairs.

References

Ahrens, P., Elomäki, A. et al. (eds.) (2022), *European Parliament's Political Groups in Turbulent Times* (Cham: Palgrave Macmillan).

Brack, N. (2018), *Opposing Europe in the European Parliament: Rebels and Radicals in the Chamber* (Basingstoke: Palgrave Macmillan).

Cooper, I. (2019), 'National parliaments in the democratic politics of the EU: The subsidiarity early warning mechanism, 2009–2017', *Comparative European Politics*, 17(6): 919–39.

Crum, B. (2023), 'Why the European Parliament lost the *Spitzenkandidaten*-process', *Journal of European Public Policy*, 30(2): 193–213.

Dahl, R. and Tufte, E. R. (1973), *Size and Democracy* (Stanford, CA: Stanford University Press).

Decker, F. and Sonnicksen, J. (2011), 'An alternative approach to European Union democratization: Re-Examining the direct election of the commission president', *Government and Opposition*, 46(2): 168–91.

De Sio, L., Franklin, M. et al. (2019), *The European Parliament Elections of 2019* (Rome: Luiss University Press).

De Vries, C. E. (2018), *Euroscepticism and the Future of European Integration* (Oxford: Oxford University Press).

Duina, F. and Lenz, T. (2017), 'Democratic legitimacy in regional economic organizations: The European Union in comparative perspective', *Economy and Society*, 46(3–4): 398–431.

Ehin, P. and Talving, L. (2021), 'Still second-order? European elections in the era of populism, extremism, and Euroscepticism', *Politics*, 41(4): 467–85.

Follesdal, A. and Hix, S. (2006), 'Why there is a democratic deficit in the EU: A response to Majone and Moravcsik', *Journal of Common Market Studies*, 44(3): 533–62.

Gabel, M. J. (1998), 'The endurance of supranational governance: A consociational interpretation of the European Union', *Comparative Politics*, 30(4): 463–75.

Greenwood, J. (2017), *Interest Representation in the European Union*, 4th edition (Basingstoke: Palgrave Macmillan).

Hanley, D. (2008), *Beyond the Nation State: Parties in the Era of European Integration* (Basingstoke: Palgrave Macmillan).

Hassing Nielsen, J. and Franklin, M. N. (eds.) (2017), *The Eurosceptic 2014 European Parliament Elections: Second Order or Second Rate?* (Basingstoke: Palgrave Macmillan).

Hefftler, C., Neuhold, C., et al. (eds.) (2015), *The Palgrave Handbook of National Parliaments and the European Union* (Basingstoke: Palgrave Macmillan).

Hertner, I. (2019), 'United in diversity? Europarties and their individual members' rights', *Journal of European Integration*, 41(4): 487–505.

Hix, S. (2008), *What's Wrong with the European Union and How to Fix It* (Cambridge: Polity Press).

Hix, S. and Scully, R. (eds.) (2003), 'The European Parliament at fifty', *Journal of Common Market Studies*, 41(2): (special issue).

Hix, S., Noury, A. G., and Roland, G. (2007), *Democratic Politics in the European Parliament* (Cambridge: Cambridge University Press).

Hobolt, S. B. (2009), *Europe in Question: Referendums on European Integration* (Oxford: Oxford University Press).

Hobolt, S. B. and Tilley, J. (2014), *Blaming Europe? Responsibility without Accountability in the European Union* (Oxford: Oxford University Press).

Hooghe, L. and Marks, G. (2009), 'A postfunctionalist theory of European integration: From permissive consensus to constraining dissensus', *British Journal of Political Science*, 39(1): 1–23.

Kritzinger, S., Plescia, C. et al. (eds.) (2020), *Assessing the 2019 European Parliament Elections* (London: Routledge).

Mair, P. (2007), 'Political opposition and the European Union', *Government and Opposition*, 42(1): 1–17.

Majone, G. (2005), *Dilemmas of Integration: The Ambiguities and Pitfalls of Integration by Stealth* (Oxford: Oxford University Press).

Mattila, M. and Raunio, T. (2012), 'Drifting further apart: National parties and their electorates on the EU dimension', *West European Politics*, 35(3): 589–606.

McDonnell, D. and Werner, A. (2020), *International Populism: The Radical Right in the European Parliament* (London: Hurst).

Moravcsik, A. (2002), 'In defence of the "democratic deficit": Reassessing legitimacy in the European Union', *Journal of Common Market Studies*, 40(4): 603–24.

Raunio, T. and Hix, S. (2000), 'Backbenchers learn to fight back: European integration and parliamentary government', *West European Politics*, 23(4): 142–68.

Reif, K. and Schmitt, H. (1980), 'Nine second-order national elections: A conceptual framework for the analysis of European election results', *European Journal of Political Research*, 8(1): 3–44.

Ripoll Servent, A. (2018), *The European Parliament* (Basingstoke: Palgrave Macmillan).

Rittberger, B. (2005), *Building Europe's Parliament: Democratic Representation beyond the Nation-State* (Oxford: Oxford University Press).

Rose, R. (2019), 'Referendum challenges to the EU's policy legitimacy – and how the EU responds', *Journal of European Public Policy*, 26(2): 207–22.

Schmidt, V. A. (2006), *Democracy in Europe: The EU and National Polities* (Oxford: Oxford University Press).

Strøm, K., Müller, W. C. et al. (eds.) (2003), *Delegation and Accountability in Parliamentary Democracies* (Oxford: Oxford University Press).

Szczerbiak, A. and Taggart, P. (eds.) (2008), *Opposing Europe? The Comparative Party Politics of Euroscepticism: Volumes I and II* (Oxford: Oxford University Press).

van der Brug, W., Gattermann, K. et al. (eds.) (2021), 'No longer second-order? Explaining the European Parliament elections of 2019', *Politics*, 41(4): (special issue).

Whitaker, R. (2019), 'Case of "You Can Always Get What You Want"? Committee assignments in the European Parliament', *Parliamentary Affairs*, 72(1): 162–81.

Winzen, T. (2022), 'The institutional position of national parliaments in the European Union: Developments, explanations, effects', *Journal of European Public Policy*, 29(6): 994–1008.

Winzen, T., de Ruiter, R., and Rocabert, J. (2018), 'Is parliamentary attention to the EU strongest when it is needed the most? National parliaments and the selective debate of EU policies', *European Union Politics*, 19(3): 481–501.

18

Populism and Its Challenges to Democracy

PAOLO GRAZIANO

18.1 Introduction

The expansion of research on populism over the past few years has been quite remarkable. At the end of 2010 a Google Scholar search with the keyword 'populism' would register about 100,000 entries. By September 2022 the total number of entries for populism was almost 500,000, an impressive five-time growth in populism research in twelve years.

There is a reason for this expansion of scholarly interest: populist political claims have been increasingly used by politicians in democratic and nondemocratic regimes (see, among many other examples, the *International Political Science Review* Special Issue devoted to world populism and more specifically the 'Introduction', Hadiz and Chryssogelos 2017). Donald Trump's Presidency in the United States (US) seemed to be very illustrative of a political success facilitated by a powerful populist rhetoric, and one that was dangerous for democracy for some political scientists (see Lieberman et al. 2019; Skonieczny 2021). In many other parts of the world, populism seemed to become 'the only game in town'. In short, populism has become a world phenomenon.

Populism has developed significantly in the European Union (EU) and in Europe as well. Brexit, for example, has been described as a populist-fuelled political process that represented one of the major changes (if not the largest change ever) in EU politics (Browning 2019). Indeed, Brexit could be seen as the most successful result of right-wing (or exclusionary) populist parties since it represented a call for action for people against the EU, which was portrayed as a non-representative organisation headed by an evil elite. Beyond the United Kingdom, several other European political systems have been increasingly affected by populist parties or movements and in some countries populist success gave birth to populist governments (for example, Poland, Hungary, Spain, Italy, Greece). Finally, Euroscepticism and populism in several countries have been interconnected, since populism has

Figure 18.1 An exemplar of a populist variant? UKIP's leader Nigel Farage campaigning for Brexit using an exclusionary anti-immigration message

Source: Alex MacNaughton/Alamy Stock Photo.

lowered the trust of EU citizens towards national and EU institutions, especially between 2007–13, see Figure 18.1 (on the relationship between Euroscepticism and populism see Taggart and Pirro 2021).

Until quite recently populism has been studied primarily as a phenomenon regarding a) 'right-wing' parties and b) parties in opposition. However, since 2010, first in Hungary and Poland, and more recently in Greece, Italy, and Spain, populist parties have become even more pivotal in political systems. In short, populism has changed political competition and has posed new challenges to decision-making processes in various EU countries.

This chapter will first introduce the concept of populism (Section 18.2), map the populist parties active in European countries (Section 18.3), illustrate the reasons of their success (Section 18.4), examine populist parties in government (Section 18.5), and look in more detail at the cases of Hungary and Poland, where populist parties in power are posing serious threats to democratic rule. The chapter concludes with some remarks on the future of populism and populist parties in European countries.

18.2 Understanding populism

The recent wave of studies on populism has provided multiple definitions of populism. Broadly speaking, these definitions generally converge in seeing its focus on the people and on its antagonistic relationship with political, economic, and cultural elites as populism's core feature. They often consider people's aspirations to be betrayed by corrupt political elites and suspect that a conspiracy against the people is taking place (Taggart 2004). The central role of the people in politics is generally associated with a claim that ruling elites have betrayed the people and abused their power so that there is a need to restore peoples' sovereignty (Mény and Surel 2002). The differences between definitions of populism are how this description of the relationship between elites and people is classified, and how it is seen as shaping populist organization and leadership.

For some claims about the relationship of the people and elites are a form of political *rhetoric* that appeals to the power of the common people in order to challenge the legitimacy of the current political establishment and is marked by the unscrupulous use (and instrumentalization) of widespread public anxiety and disenchantment (Abts and Rummens 2007: 407). For others these claims make up the thin-centred or weak *ideology* of populism (Mudde 2004; Albertazzi and McDonnell 2008) that holds society to be ultimately separated in two homogeneous and antagonistic groups: 'the pure People' (generally conceived as monolithic) versus 'the corrupt elite', and argues that politics should be an expression of the *volonté générale* (general will) of the people (Mudde 2004: 543; for a critique, see de la Torre and Mazzoleni 2019). These readings of society (and politics) clearly simplify the relationship between represented and representatives: the representatives should represent the 'people' as a unitary group, but instead the elite—either economic or political, or both—represent the people's 'enemies' and prevent 'the people' from being adequately represented. Finally, according to a socio-cultural approach (Ostiguy 2018; Moffitt 2015), populism is a *political style* and a specific form of relationship. This reading of populism is inspired by the work of Laclau (1977, 2005) who sees populism as a political and social discourse in which disparate and marginalized (in their own eyes at least) social interests are bound together as a political force using an 'empty signifier', the notion of the 'people'. An 'empty signifier' is a political construct that is used to create popular or social identities and that has no essential meaning, i.e. there is no fixed definition of what a term represents, and it can be associated with different social interests by political actors to bind them together to develop their political support. The 'people' is an empty signifier since it can be defined as a 'class', as a group of 'natives', or as a group of 'nationalistic' individuals, or even simply those not in the elite.

Populism's search for 'true' representation of the people against the elite shapes it as a movement and can give it a particular communicative style. Populism is often associated with charismatic and personalistic leadership. This style of leadership represents the populist idea that there should be no intermediaries between leaders and the led. It can emphasis the role of the leader as a true 'saviour' who alone, and against elite opposition, can rescue the people from crisis. Such charismatic and personalistic leadership means that leaders can have full controls over the organization of a populist party or political movement (Kriesi 2018).

Despite populism's focus on the people who the 'people' are remains ambiguous. Müller calls the notion of the people a 'metapolitical illusion' (Müller 2016: 18). Competing interpretations try to clarify who 'the people' are, some seeing the people in terms of national identity, class, or sovereignty (Mény and Surel 2002), others referring to a 'heartland', a place in which a virtuous and unified population resides in the populist imagination (Taggart 2004; Mudde 2004). Different definitions of 'the people' have led to the identification of different types of populism—or 'populist variations', in Laclau's (2005) term. Clearly, from a *historical perspective*, populism has varied substantially—from the US People's Party (a nineteenth-century left-wing agrarian party) to contemporary populist parties. For this reason, some scholars—especially those focusing on Latin America (for example, Weyland 2003)—have introduced the notion of 'neopopulism', which better differentiates contemporary phenomena from the ones of the late nineteenth century. Another analytical distinction has been made following a more focused *political perspective*: populist parties (or movements) may vary—be inclusionary or exclusionary—on material, political, and symbolic dimensions (Mudde and Rovira Kaltwasser 2013: 158–65). The material dimension regards 'the distribution of state resources, both monetary and non-monetary, to specific groups in society'; the political dimension refers to 'political participation and political contestation', since one of the key elements of populist parties and movements is to ask for greater ways for the people to participate; the symbolic dimension is linked to 'setting the boundaries of "the people" and (. . .) "the elite"'. Put differently, the distinction between 'inclusionary' and 'exclusionary' populist parties depends on resource distribution (for example, welfare benefits granted to residents or citizens), on the beneficiaries (for example, residents or citizens) of desired greater political participation and on the definition of people (for example, individuals who happen to be in a given political space or individuals who are natives of the country). These variants are particularly important as they allow to identify substantial differences among different populist parties or movements. For example, SYRIZA and *Podemos* have been seen as closer to the inclusionary ideal-type (Stavrakakis and Katzambekis 2014; Ramiro and Gomez 2016; Font et al. 2022), whereas the French nationalist *Front National* (now *Rassemblement National*) and several other Western parties have been categorized as exclusionary (Betz 2001; Caiani and Grazian 2019).

Box **18.1** Italy: The 'promised land of populism'

Italy has become the 'promised land of populism' (Tarchi 2015) due to the long-lasting nature of its 'political crisis', caused not only by growing dissatisfaction with democracy but also with declines in institutional trust of the national government and Parliament, and political actors (mainstream parties). Post-war Italy can be described as a permanently dissatisfied and divided society. The dominant post-war political coalition included social groups that had supported fascism. There was no alternation in power and the Italian Communist Party was never in government despite securing almost 35% of the vote during the 1970s. The possibility that the Communist Party could be part of a government was seen as a threat to the Western bloc and this made Italy a special victim of the Cold War period. The end of the Cold War, the discrediting of communism as a left alternative, and the collapse of political coalitions that had been held together by fear of communism, led to great electoral volatility and substantial changes in the Italian party (and political) system (Morlino and Tarchi 1996). The 're-orientation' of the party system in a populist direction became especially visible in early 1994 with the launch of a new populist party of *Forza Italia* (Forward Italy). Another party, labelled as 'regional populist' (McDonnell 2006), already existed: the *Lega Nord*. Founded in 1991, the *Lega* became increasingly right-exclusionary populist, especially after a change of leadership (2013) and after it changed its name to *Lega* (2017), abandoning its 'regionalist' focus to become a national party. Two other populist parties were founded around 2010: the Five Star Movement, a populist party founded in 2009 by a comedian (Beppe Grillo), and *Fratelli d'Italia* (Brothers of Italy), a radical right or exclusionary political party in 2012 founded by former members of Italian Social Movement (*MSI*), the neofascist party that was successor to Mussolini's National Fascist party. *Fratelli d'Italia* is led by Giorgia Meloni, one of its founders, who is the prime minister of Italy at the time of writing.

The other two types of crises (economic and cultural, see Section 18.4) also need to be considered to understand the birth of new parties and their growing success in Italy. The 2008–09 financial and economic crisis hit Italy hard and gave rise to growing resentment towards the EU. In times of economic uncertainty, Italy's growing migrant population (around 0.5% in 1990 and around 9% in 2021) has increasingly become a target of populist parties, especially of those with a clear exclusionary nature (*Lega* and *Fratelli d'Italia*). *Lega*, for example, used a very successful slogan in the 2018 elections, 'Italians first' (*Prima gli italiani*), which helped secure an impressive vote increase in the national elections for the party—from around 4% in 2013 to almost 18% in 2018. The success of the populist parties made Italy one of the few EU countries (together with Greece, Hungary, and Poland) where populist parties have been in government in leading positions for several years, and the current government (2022) is the first Western Europe right-exclusionary populist government.

18.3 Mapping populist parties in Europe

One of the first difficult exercises in comparative European politics in recent years has been to identify what populist parties are and how they may be differentiated from 'mainstream' parties. On recent collective effort, Rooduijn et al. 2019, considered all EU members plus Iceland, Norway, Switzerland, and the United Kingdom (thirty countries in total) for the 1989–2020 period to distinguish between right and left populist parties, which Rooduijn et al. call far-right and far-left parties. Here we will just call them right-exclusionary and left-inclusionary parties since they vary in their radicality and are not all anti-systemic like some other small far-right and far-left groups like out-and-out fascist parties on the far right (the British National Party, for example, or the National Democratic Party of Germany) or Trotskyite or Maoist parties on the far left (like *Lutte Ouvrière*, Workers' Struggle, in France, or in Portugal the *Partido Comunista dos Trabalhadores Portugueses/Movimento Reorganizativo do Partido do Proletariado*, Portuguese Workers' Communist Party/Re-Organized Movement of the Party of the Proletariat). The parties examined by Rooduijn et al. needed to have either won a) at least one seat or b) at least 2% of the votes in national parliamentary elections. Their list has been peer-reviewed by more than eighty academics, well-known populism experts, to further validate the results. As shown in Table 18.1, the total of populist parties is 121: 41 are populist, sixty are right-exclusionary populist and twenty are left-inclusionary populist.

In broad terms, the differences between right and left can be connected to the distinction between inclusionary and exclusionary populism presented above. Both variants of populism engage in an antagonistic discourse where the 'people' are fighting against 'the elite' (the economic and—when populist are not in power—the political establishment). However, their definition of the people varies substantially since nativist tones are present in the right or exclusionary types of populism whereas a more encompassing definition of 'the people' is offered by left or inclusionary types (see, for example, the Spanish left or inclusionary populist party Podemos, which considers immigrants to be part of the 'people'; Sanders et al. 2017). Not only parties may be different, but also electorates may present differences. For example, beyond showing low levels of political trust, in the Dutch case right supporters show low immigration tolerance, whereas voters of left parties are in favour of more (generalized) income equality (Rooduijn and Akkerman 2017). Other studies—focusing primarily, but not only, on

Table 18.1 Populist parties in thirty-one European countries

	Populist	Populist right	Populist left	Total populist parties
Austria	2	2		4
Belgium	1	3		4
Bulgaria	4	5		9
Croatia	1		4	5
Cyprus			1	1
Czech Republic	2	4		6
Denmark		3		3
Estonia	1	2		3
Finland	1	1		2
France		2	1	3
Germany		1	1	2
Greece	1	3	4	8
Hungary		5		5
Iceland	3			3
Ireland			1	1
Italy	4	3		7
Latvia	2			2
Lithuania	6	1		7
Luxembourg	1			1
Netherlands	2	3	1	6
Norway	1	1		2
Poland	1	4		5
Portugal		1		1
Romania	1	3		4
Slovakia	4	3	1	8
Slovenia	2	2	1	5
Spain		1	3	4
Sweden		2		2
Switzerland	1	4		5
United Kingdom		1	2	3
Total	*41*	*60*	*20*	*121*

Source: Source data from Rooduijn, M. et al. (2019). 'The PopuList: An Overview of Populist, far right, far left, and Eurosceptic Parties in Europe', available at www.popu-list.org.

radical right populist electorates—suggest that a 'populist voter' does not exist, i.e., that there are no distinctive socio-economic characteristics that allow us to single out who will be a populist voter (Rooduijn 2018), although almost all populist electorates that have been studied are characterized by higher political distrust than voters for non-populist parties. The one and only common feature that European populist electorates share, therefore, is *high political distrust*—well captured by the 'anti-elite' rhetoric which can be found in both right (or exclusionary) and left (or inclusionary) populist political parties. Beyond this common trait there are also specific factors that account for populist party success that are connected to broader political, economic, and cultural crises.

Box 18.2 Over to you—judging populist parties and what kind of populism they represent

Read the most recent party manifestos in a European country of your choice and grade them in terms of a) 'populist intensity' (how populist they are); b) types of populism ('inclusionary', 'hybrid', or 'exclusionary'). You can select cases from The PopuList website. The part manifestos can be found on the Manifesto Project Data website.

For a), you can select words that you consider linked to populism and do a word count using free online and easy to use programmes (such as Yoshikoder) to see how frequently they occur. For an example of how to use manifestos to look at how parties can be classed as a type of populism look at Nuria Font et al. (2021) 'Varieties of Inclusionary Populism?', *Government & Opposition*, 56(1): 163–83.

18.4 Explaining populist success: The role of multiple crises

Where does the current wave of populism come from? The most important (and successful) populist parties have been created—or rebranded—fairly recently as populist parties grew in importance in European countries only after the 1990s, and especially towards the end of 2000s (Caiani and Graziano 2019). Why and how has this happened? As elsewhere, and particularly in Latin America, populism typically occurs where there is economic crisis (Laclau 1977; Roberts 1995; Stavrakakis et al. 2017). Populism can also be fuelled by crises that are political or cultural in origin (Brubaker 2017; Caiani and Graziano 2019). All these forms of crisis have played a role in developing populism in Europe. First, between 2007 and the beginning of the Covid-19 pandemic in early 2020, political trust towards both political parties and public institutions has been following a negative trend. In 2008, the financial and economic crisis hit Europe hard, and was especially severe in some countries. Finally, the 2015 refugee crisis heightened anti-immigration sentiments, making populist appeals, especially from right-exclusionary populists, much more powerful (Hangartner et al. 2019; Algan et al. 2017). Clearly, we need to take a closer look at how these types of crises have unfolded over the past thirty years and what their relationship to populist politics might be.

18.4.1 Political crisis

There is a considerable debate in the literature on the extent to which the rise of (mainly radical-right) populist parties should be understood as part of a broader realignment of party systems. The main argument is that the European party system long-lasting restructuring has provided political space for new parties able to mobilize around less structured political cleavages, such as economic insecurity and immigration. Political crisis deals first with the shortcomings of *representative democracy* that—according to Kriesi and Pappas (2015)—has undergone a 'structural crisis of representation'. Over the past decades, European countries have witnessed a weakening of traditional party identities and changing party functions. Mainstream parties have progressively lost electoral ground to new populist challengers that have been better able to represent the 'losers of globalization', people who have fallen behind economically since they cannot adapt to economic transformation, and/or who feel threatened by greater cultural diversity (Kriesi 2014, 2018). Furthermore, mainstream parties (both on the left and on the right) have increasingly become similar in their political proposals, leaving substantial political space to non-mainstream parties (Spoon and Klüver 2019)—often populist parties.

Political crisis, therefore, is a key factor that explains the recent reinvigoration of populism across all Europe, given that contemporary democracies are representative democracies, where political parties act as the main agents of representation. Put differently, and following this reading, the main explanation for the strength of populism is that mainstream (and 'old') parties have not been capable of representing voters who have either decided not to vote anymore (i.e. abstain), or who have decided to vote for 'challenger' parties, especially those parties mobilizing around an 'anti-establishment' agenda. Furthermore, especially in some European countries where the Cold War had 'frozen' the political landscape (such as in Italy, where a relatively successful—but always in opposition—Communist Party was able to capture the preferences of 'anti-establishment' voters), the collapse of communist political regimes created political opportunities for new political parties wanting to leave behind conventional right-left politics. Furthermore, political crisis was even more evident in those cases where communist political regimes had collapsed all together: it is not by chance that it is especially in Central-Eastern European countries that populist parties have been particularly numerous and successful.

Globalization and post-industrialization (i.e. the end of the mass industrialization which characterized European countries since the end of the eighteenth century) have led to a decline in class voting and partisan identification, increased political alienation among certain segments of the population, and reduced trust in the political elite. This interpretation is rooted in the view that political parties are increasingly uncapable of mobilizing voters: not only do voters vote less, but they are also less interested in becoming party members and—if they decide to vote—they select 'new' (anti-establishment, i.e. populist) parties.

18.4.2 **Economic crisis**

Another argument is that economic crises facilitate the emergence and success of populist parties (Hernández and Kriesi 2016; Moffit 2015; Stavrakakis and Katzambekis 2014; Ramiro and Gomez 2016; Vasilopoulou et al. 2014). Additionally, as highlighted by Arzheimer (2009: 273) with respect to the radical right, 'the extreme right will benefit from high levels of immigration and unemployment'. According to 'relative deprivation' theories (i.e. the idea that people may feel 'deprived' if others in the same political community are better off), economically vulnerable individuals are 'more likely to develop feelings of anomic and relative deprivation which then lead them to populism' (Spruyt et al. 2016: 342). Moreover, economic crises increase political discontent toward representative institutions, two factors strongly related with populism. However, there are also studies showing that poor economic performance (including growth, unemployment, and inflation rates) does not explain the success of radical right-wing populist parties (Arzheimer and Carter 2006). Some scholars emphasize that economics may matter for the fortune of populist parties but only under certain contextual circumstances related to the party competition, such as the positioning of the other parties on the issue (Arzheimer 2009). Put differently, the evidence regarding the role of poor economic performance in explaining populist success is rather mixed.

Beyond poor economic performance, economic determinants of populism have also been connected to economic globalization in the form of changing patterns of international trade (especially the rise of China as a manufacturing power), or financial globalization (Rodrik 2021). Countries beyond European (and other Western) democracies like China have become increasingly competitive and this has advanced de-industrialization processes in European countries and the emergence of new loci of economic power. According to Rodrik, 'empirical evidence leaves no doubt that globalization has played a significant role in the rise of populism in recent years' (Rodrik 2021: 162), especially with reference to right-wing or exclusionary populism. Globalization—in times of economic crisis, as for example the recession experienced between 2008 and 2009—has created a diffuse sense of economic insecurity, even in countries like Sweden where the economic crisis was not particularly acute in comparative terms (on Sweden, see Dal Bò et al. 2019).

18.4.3 **Cultural crisis**

A last set of crisis-related explanations for the success of populist parties is linked to cultural factors. This approach sees the rise of populist parties as a reaction against a wide range of rapid cultural changes that erode the values and customs of Western societies (Inglehart and Norris 2019). This explanation may be problematic because, among other things, 'cultural backlash' refers to several, potentially unrelated issues, such as anti-immigrant attitudes, mistrust of global and national governance, support for authoritarian values and left-right ideological self-placement (see Schäfer 2022). Moreover, the post-materialist silent revolution (i.e. the change of cultural values of Western democracies' citizens away from concerns about economic issues towards things like identity politics, multiculturalism, social liberalism around marriage, family, and sexuality) dates to the 1960s and 1970s and until very recently populist parties have not been as successful as they currently are. However, if we focus on attitudes towards migration and we consider the 'cultural insecurity' that might derive from growing migration flows, then we find numerous supportive studies in the literature linking cultural crisis to populism.

Several studies address the cultural crisis explanation by focusing on the cultural threat posed by 'immigration', including aspects such as anti-immigrant attitudes and migrants' presence within the domestic political community. There is strong support in the literature for the cultural grievance explanation at the individual level based on immigration: several studies have shown that anti-immigrant attitudes are positively related to radical right populist support (Lubbers and Scheepers 2002; van der Brug and Fennema 2007; Norris 2005; Ivarsflaten 2008). Furthermore, and as has already been outlined, radical right populist parties perform well when they mobilize over immigration grievances (Ivarsflaten 2008). However, the hypothesis linking immigration with populism is weakened by research findings that show that the 'level of immigration (. . .) has a statistically significant negative relationship with right populist vote share', i.e. more immigration does not translate automatically into more votes for exclusionary populist parties (Roberts 2017: 18). Vadlamannati and Kelly (2017: 30), using panel data on twenty-seven Organization for Economic Cooperation and Development (OECD) countries from 1990 to 2014, also found 'no direct effect of refugee flows in explaining electoral support for populist-right parties'. It can be argued, therefore, that looking just at immigration figures is not sufficient to understand the impact of the phenomenon on

Box 18.3 Over to you—crisis and the emergence of populism

Select one European country and identify the reasons explaining the success of one or more populist parties by focusing on potential explanatory factors associated with the political, economic, and cultural crises discussed in this section. You may select one or more indicators to verify which has greater explanatory potential in the selected cases. You can pick a case from The PopuList website at popu-list.org.

populist voters. Citizens' 'subjective' perceptions also need be considered. Populists can benefit from a 'migration crisis' that they themselves declare to exist no matter what the actual number of migrants might be. Populists, in other words, can 'perform' a migration crisis by talking the issue up so as to activate their voter's subjective (and negative) perception of what is going on in their society. In this way, populist political actors can construct specific 'failure stories' in line with people's sentiments and transform them into a perceived crisis rather than populism's emergence being a reaction to a pre-existing crisis (Moffitt 2015).

To conclude on the role of the crises: it is difficult to single out only one factor (or one crisis) that convincingly provides a general explanation of populist parties' success. The most convincing arguments at present on the rise of populism stress that multiple crises (political, economic, cultural) have induced electorates to increasingly consider and vote for challenger parties that are seen as 'anti-establishment' in political, economic, and cultural terms. Which parties have reacted to crisis, and how, varies. In some cases, parties were already in the political system, for example, the right populist exclusionary party *Front National*—now *Rassemblement National* (National Rally)—in France, founded in the early 1970s. Parties like the *Rassemblement National* became more successful in the 2000s as they re-oriented their ideology, making it increasingly 'thin', although still embedded in nationalism, to broaden their political appeal as crises overlapped and multiplied. Others have mobilized over the crises and entered the political scene with a specific 'populist' political project, for example, the left-inclusionary populist party Podemos in Spain, created in 2014 by political scientists who detected a political space not covered by other political parties after the great recession that followed financial crisis in the late 2000s.

18.5 **Populist parties in government: A challenge to all and a threat to some democracies**

In South and Latin America, populists have been in government since the 1940s. Until the late 1990s and early 2000s, populist parties in government were very rare in Europe, and even after their recent electoral growth only a limited number of populist governments have been formed (Caiani and Graziano 2022). Only Greece had a significant and relatively long-lasting (eight years) populist government before the 2000s. In a comparative study on populists in government (covering European countries such as Greece, Italy, and Hungary and Latin American ones such as Argentina, Peru, Venezuela, and Ecuador), Pappas (2019) identifies common features of populist governments. Populist governments stimulate further political polarization of their societies. Beyond this, populists in government 'colonize the state by appointing party loyalists at all levels of bureaucracy; 2) launch a massive assault on liberal institutions; 3) set up a new constitutional order that replaces institutions of horizontal accountability with others more vertical in nature' (Pappas 2019: 73). This picture of populist government better describes the Latin American and Hungarian cases where democracy might not be fully consolidated, than, say, the Italian case, which was a consolidated democracy by the 1990s. Several studies have born this out. A study by Albertazzi and Mueller (2013), which looked at European countries such as Austria, Italy, Poland, and Switzerland, concluded that it 'must be acknowledged that, although very dangerous to the *liberal* element of contemporary European democracies, populism is also well embedded in the rules and procedures of electoral democracy' (Albertazzi and Mueller 2013). In other words, in some European cases populism does not represent a threat to democracy since populist parties accept democracy's procedures and rules. Their time in office, however, can make politics less tolerant and socially progressive, i.e. accepting of social differences and lifestyles. Likewise, Albertazzi and McDonnell (2015), in a study that looked at Italy (*Popolo della Libertà*—People of Freedom—and *Lega Nord*) and Switzerland (Swiss People's Party), showed that populist parties adapt, make good use of the governmental power, and endure electoral loss. They did not, as some had predicted, disappear after poor governmental performances. These studies show that populism can constitute an opportunity for democracies since it allows citizens to find parties that will represent them using democratic rules and procedures. In turn this can provide greater overall satisfaction with democracy and/or trust in institutions and political parties. On the other hand, some recent studies have shown that right-wing exclusionary populist parties may constitute a threat to democracy, or impact the quality of democracy, whereas there is much less evidence that left-wing (or inclusionary) populist parties do (Ruth-Lovell and Grahn 2022; Vittori 2022).

Over the past decade two countries have become particularly problematic with respect to both the quality of democracy and its survival with populists in power: Hungary and Poland. Both countries are new democracies and have been ruled by exclusionary populist government for over a decade (Hungary; Batory 2016) and almost a decade (Poland; Stanley and Cześnik 2019). In both countries, populist governments have defined the 'people' in contrast to the EU elites and for this reason are defined by scholars as 'Eurosceptic populist' (Csehi and Zgut 2021). Furthermore, in both cases the ruling populist parties only consider 'natives' as belonging to the 'people'. The 'people', they argue, need to be defended from migrants who may disrupt traditional (i.e. religious, pro-family) values, and these concerns can be seen in welfare reforms adopted in both countries (Lendvai-Bainton and Szelewa 2021).

Pirro and Stanley (2022) argue that an 'illiberal playbook' has been followed by the Hungarian and Polish governments over the past decade. This 'playbook' unfolds over three key stages or 'gradations of illiberal policy change with respect to the rule of law': *forging*, *bending*, and *breaking*. The first stage, forging, 'reflects the fact that illiberal actors often seek to make changes that break substantially with a mainstream consensus without necessarily challenging the rule of law. These areas of change will vary by context. In the case of populist radical right parties, there is likely to be an emphasis on morality (. . .) and memory politics' (Pirro and Stanley 2022: 90). Stage two, bending is a type of policy change 'consistent with the letter of the law, but in contradiction to its spirit. It involves the reinterpretation or disabling of existing legislative constraints in ways that are not procedurally illegal but that defy or subvert liberal-democratic norms' (Pirro and Stanley 2022: 90–1). The final stage, breaking, occurs when 'legislative actions are contrary to both domestic and international law, constituting a direct breach of the constitutional order and of liberal-democratic principles' (Pirro and Stanley 2022: 90). The two countries have gone through all three stages and become examples of 'de-democratization' or 'democratic backsliding' in Europe.

In Hungary, the most important populist party FIDESZ (which is an acronym for Alliance of Young Democrats) was founded in 1988. Initially, the party was 'a significant player in the liberal camp of democratic opposition', but under the leadership of Viktor Orbán, the party turned into a 'conservative catch-all party around the mid-1990s', winning the elections in 1998 (Batory 2016: 286). After two electoral defeats in 2002 and 2006, the party turned increasingly populist and has been ruling as a 'populist-party-in-government' since 2010. The populist rule has given birth to a 'de-democratization' process (Bogaards 2018; Batory 2022) or to 'democratic backsliding' (Bakke and Sitter 2020) which can be seen with respect to key elements of a consolidated democracy: free media, independent civil society, free and fair elections, rule of law (separation of powers). Since 2010, the Orbán's government has transformed state-run media into a 'propaganda machine by populating editorial boards and oversight organs' with people loyal to the FIDESZ. 'Orbán's allies took control of most national and regional newspapers' (Bakke and Sitter 2020: 26) as well, reducing, if not ending, any sort of media pluralism. With respect to civil society, the government led by Orbán limited the independence of the universities (the Central European University was forced to relocate to Vienna), restricted religious organizations by taking away their legal status in 201, which reduced the number of churches supported economically by the government, and stigmatized local non-governmental organizations (NGOs) for receiving foreign funds. The electoral process has been heavily manipulated under FIDESZ's rule. Constituency boundaries were redrawn, appointment rules of the electoral commission were changed, fair electoral competition was highjacked by allowing more electoral campaign opportunities for the government and limiting the campaign opportunities for the opposition. Such manipulation led the Organization for Security and Co-operation in Europe to define the 2014 and 2018 elections as free but not fair (Bakke and Sitter 2020: 27). Finally, Orbán changed the constitution, secured increasing governmental control over the judiciary and used parliamentary procedures to decrease debate and scrutiny of new legislation. All these measures weakened the separation of powers in Hungary. More recently, the Hungarian government has been under scrutiny by the EU institutions and sanctions (i.e. cuts in EU funds) for not respecting the rule of law have been requested by the European Commission. The Covid-19 pandemic created a number of challenges to FIDESZ and its hold on power, but the most recent elections (2022) gave Orbán a strong majority (a *supermajority* of over two-thirds of parliamentary seats, enough to allow constitutional changes to be made), although with a declining popular support (Batory 2022). Orbán's success can be connected to emergency legislation introduced in early 2020 further reducing the political spaces for party and civil society opposition, which made their voice difficult to hear during the electoral campaign. Currently, Hungary is considered internationally as an 'illiberal democracy' because of its decade-long 'de-democratization' or 'democratic backsliding'. This process was managed by a radical right exclusionary populist government and demonstrates how populism can challenge young and non- yet-consolidated democratic regimes.

Poland is another country where populism became mainstream during the 1990s (Stanley and Cześnik 2019). PiS (Law and Justice) has been the most successful party, governing for a short period in 2005–07 and thereafter obtaining a growing electoral success. After 2015,

PiS, following the Hungarian example, 'enacted a deliberate and painstakingly sequenced assault on the constitutional structure, the power and autonomy of discrete institutions of state, and the rights and freedoms of individuals and social groups' (Pirro and Stanley 2022: 92). More specifically, with respect to media freedom, the Polish government—although it did not manage to go as far as Hungary in terms of ownership restructuring—used state advertising funds and subsidies to support favourable media and adopted a series of measures aimed limiting the civil society critical of PiS. Furthermore, the free and fair nature of elections has been limited by the PiS government taking control of the electoral process through the unilateral appointment of the National Electoral Office. Finally, although lacking the Hungarian supermajority, the Polish government has severely reduced the autonomy of the judiciary and civil service. PiS installed loyalists in important public positions in the civil service, state intelligence, the general prosecutor's office, state companies, and bodies involved in public procurement (Bakke and Sitter 2020: 26–8). In the words of two experts on the Polish political situation:

> PiS is a case of radical populism: it has transformed itself from a relatively moderate party (. . .) to a populist radical right movement whose reach extends beyond the conventional bounds of party politics. Although it had to moderate its electoral appeal at times in order to gain support from more centrist voters, having gained a majority, it has embarked on a radical process of elite replacement and system change.
>
> (Stanley and Cześnik 2019: 85)

Finally, both countries have recently questioned the superiority of EU law paving the way towards what is labelled as a 'legal exit' from EU regulations. For example,

> Poland's constitutional tribunal has taken major step towards a 'legal Polexit' with far-reaching consequences for Warsaw's funding and future relations with the bloc. The tribunal, whose legitimacy is contested after multiple appointments of judges loyal to PiS, said some provisions of EU treaties and EU court rulings clashed with Poland's highest law, adding that EU institutions act beyond the scope of their competences
>
> (*The Guardian*, 7 October 2021, online edition)

Both the Polish and the Hungarian cases have shown what the consequences of populist parties in power may be when a) democracy is still not considered the only viable political system option—i.e. democracy is not yet fully consolidated; and, b) radical right or exclusionary policies are adopted and implemented, not only isolating specific 'outgroups' (former elites, migrants, sexual minorities) but also changing the nature of the political regime from a democratic one to an illiberal democratic—if not autocratic—one, i.e. going through all the stages of forging, bending, and breaking identified by Pirro and Stanley (2022).

18.6 **Conclusion**

Populist parties have been on the rise over the past decade and have increasingly challenged the status quo. Through a very basic, elementary but quite successful appeal to the 'people' against the elite (often, also European institutions), exclusionary or radical right and inclusionary or radical left populist actors have 'performed' (Moffit 2015) various crises and managed to increase their electoral appeal, both at the national and at the European level. However, if we take a closer look at the dynamics of populist success, we realize that only a limited number of populist parties have played governmental roles at the national level, and within EU institutions their success has been limited politically. Only the populist governments in Central and Eastern Europe (especially Hungary and Poland) have truly challenged traditional domestic and—growingly—EU decision-making. Both the Hungarian and the Polish governments—still led by exclusionary (or radical right) populist parties in early 2023—are against some of the fundamental principles at the heart of the EU (such as human rights). As for the other exclusionary political parties, however, their challenges to both domestic democratic decision-making and the EU political system have been limited and contained.

Inclusionary (radical left) populist parties in government (such as SYRIZA, partially the Five Star Movement and Podemos, which is progressively losing some of its populist features; see Mazzolini and Borriello 2021), have never posed serious challenges to liberal democracy. They may have formulated, approved and implemented controversial policies (as in the case of the Five Star Movement's *reddito di cittadinanza*, a conditional cash-transfer, i.e. an economic benefit provided only under specific conditions), but they have never gone against the democratic traits of domestic political systems. What may be seen as distinctive of radical left or inclusionary populist parties is that they have been very critical of specific European policies (although not the EU per se) when in opposition but have become increasingly less critical once in government. For example, one of the most successful inclusionary (radical left) populist parties, Greece's SYRIZA, watered down its Euroscepticism because '[w]hen the party entered government, it became clear that Greece was not in a strong negotiating position vis-à-vis the troika and could not therefore obtain the concessions it had hoped for' (Vasilopoulou 2018: 324). Likewise, another inclusionary populist party, the Italian Five Star Movement, can be seen more as 'Euroconfused' rather than 'Eurosceptic' (Salvati 2019).

In conclusion, although it does seem that populist parties are here to stay, there is a clear distinction to be made between a) varieties of populism; b) the nature of the democratic regime (consolidated or non-consolidated); c) their relationship with the EU and European decision-making. Not all the populist parties pose the same threats to democracies: whereas inclusionary or radical left populist parties do not seem to be problematic, exclusionary or radical right populist parties can determine a 'democratic backsliding', as in the case of Hungary and Poland where governments have been led by exclusionary, radical right populist parties for several years. The more consolidated the democratic regime is, the less probable it is for populist parties (even in government) to erode the democratic nature of the regime; once again, both Poland and Hungary are 'young' democracies and therefore have not yet been capable of becoming fully consolidated. Finally, all populist parties are highly critical of the EU, but their criticism is usually less strong once they are in government.

Discussion questions

1. How can populism be defined?
2. What are the different types of populist parties?
3. What are the main factors which can be used to explain the emergence and success of populist parties in European countries?

4. What are the conditions that must be met for populism to become a risk to democracy? Provide examples.
5. What political strategies could mainstream parties adopt to contain the success of populist parties?

Thinking Comparatively

Studying populist political parties in a comparative fashion is not easy. It is not by chance that many contributions have traditionally focused on definitional issues (what is populism?) and were limited as in-depth qualitative studies. The recent development of databases (such as the Global Populism Database and popu-list.org) and broader comparative research designs have allowed us to 'think comparatively' in a more systematic manner. One example of this comparative approach is a research project conducted by two Dutch scholars, based at Radboud University (Nijmegen) who in 2018 launched an expert survey aimed at providing a 'way of measuring parties' populism using expert surveys that allow for precise interval-level measurement of populism, encompasses the full range of political parties in twenty-eight European countries that recognizes the multidimensionality of the concept of populism' (Meijers and Zaslove 2021: 374). The authors conducted a study based on a survey fielded between April and June 2018. 'In total, 861 invitations were sent to country experts in the twenty-eight countries with expertise in party politics. Experts have been selected on the basis of publications records in Web of Science as well as biographical information. In the end, the survey has 294 recorded responses (. . .)' (Meijers and Zaslove 2021: 382). The results of the survey are of particular interest since they do confirm the added value of a 'continuous' measurement and not a dichotomous one (i.e. populist or not). More specifically, the results show that a 'fine-grained, continuous measure of populism allows us to identify and differentiate between parties with low, moderate and high levels of populism' (Meijers and Zaslove 2021: 398), allowing—for example, with reference to Italian case analysed in Box 18.1—to appreciate the difference between Forza Italia! (Go Italy!) and *Lega*, the former 'moderately' populist the latter 'highly' populist.

Guide to further reading

Mudde, C. and Rovira Kaltwasser, C. (2017), *Populism: A Very Short Introduction* (Oxford: Oxford University Press).

A basic reader for who would like to know more about populism—especially in terms of its definition and development.

Mény, Y. and Surel, Y. (eds.) (2002), *Democracies and the Populist Challenge* (Basingstoke: Palgrave).

A very useful collection of essays focusing on the re-emergence of populist parties in Europe.

Ionescu, G. and Gellner, E. (eds.) (1969), *Populism: Its Meanings and National Characteristics* (London: Weidenfeld and Nicolson).

A classic introduction to populism: an edited volume based on the papers presented at a path-breaking 1967 London School of Economics (LSE) conference which focused on what was defined as a 'spectre haunting the world'.

Rovira Kaltwasser, C., Taggart, P. et al. (eds.) (2018), *Oxford Handbook of Populism* (Oxford: Oxford University Press).

A comprehensive review of definitions and approaches to populism and types of populist partis and movements, its relationship to other political phenomena like democracy and nationalism, and overviews of populism across the globe.

References

Abts, K. and Rummens, S. (2007), 'Populism versus democracy', *Political Studies*, 55(2): 405–424.

Albertazzi, D. and McDonnell, D. (2008), *Twenty-first Century Populism: The Spectre of Western European Democracy* (Basingstoke: Palgrave Macmillan).

Albertazzi, D. and Mueller, S. (2013), 'Populism and liberal democracy: Populists in Government in Austria, Italy, Poland and Switzerland', *Government & Opposition*, 48(3): 343–71.

Albertazzi, D. and McDonnell, D. (2015), *Populists in Power* (London: Routledge).

Algan, Y., Guriev, S. et al. (2017), 'The European trust crisis and the rise of populism', *Brookings Papers on Economic Activity, 2017*(Fall): 309–400.

Arzheimer, K. (2009), 'Contextual factors and the extreme right vote in western Europe, 1980–2002', *American Journal of Political Science*, 53(2): 259–75.

Arzheimer, K. and Carter, E. (2006), 'Political opportunity structures and right-wing extremist party success', *European Journal of Political Research*, 45(3): 419–43.

Batory, A. (2016), 'Populists in government? Hungary's "system of national cooperation"', *Democratization*, 23(2): 283–303.

Batory, A. (2022), 'More power, less support: The Fidesz Government and the Coronavirus pandemic in Hungary', *Government and Opposition*, First View: 1–17, doi.org/10.1017/gov.2022.3.

Bakke, E. and Sitter, N. (2020), 'The EU's *Enfants Terribles*: Democratic backsliding in Central Europe since 2010', *Perspectives on Politics*, 20(1): 22–37.

Betz, H.-G. (2001), 'Exclusionary populism in Austria, Italy and Switzerland', *International Journal*, 56(3): 393–420.

Bogaards, M. (2018), 'De-Democratization in Hungary: Diffusely defective democracy', *Democratization*, 25(8): 1481–99.

Browning, C. S. (2019), 'Brexit populism and fantasies of fulfilment', *Cambridge Review of International Affairs*, 32(3): 222–44.

Brubaker, R. (2017), 'Why populism?', *Theory and Society*, 46(5): 357–85.

Caiani, M. and Graziano, P. (2019), 'Understanding varieties of populism in times of crises', *West European Politics*, 42(6): 1141–58.

Caiani, M. and Graziano, P. (2022), 'The three faces of populism in power: Polity, policies and politics', *Government and Opposition*, 57(4): 569–88

Csehi, R. and Zgut, E. (2021), '"We won't let Brussels dictate us": Eurosceptic populism in Hungary and Poland', *European Politics & Society*, 22(1): 53–68.

Dal Bò, E., Finan, F. et al. (2019), *Economic Losers and Political Winners: Sweden Radical Right*, manuscript, February.

de la Torre, C. and Mazzoleni, O. (2019), 'Do we need a minimum definition of populism? An appraisal of Mudde's conceptualization', *Populism*, 2(2): 79–95.

Font, N., Graziano, P. et al. (2022), 'Varieties of inclusionary populism? SYRIZA, Podemos and the Five Star Movement', *Government & Opposition*, 56(1): 163–83.

Hadiz, V. R. and Chryssogelos, A. (2017), 'Populism in world politics: A comparative cross-regional perspective', *International Political Science Review*, 38(4): 399–411.

Hangartner, D., Elias, D. et al. (2019), 'Does exposure to refugee crisis make natives more hostile?', *American Political Science Review*, 113(3): 442–55.

Hernández, E., and Kriesi, H. (2016), 'The electoral consequences of the financial and economic crisis in Europe', *European Journal of Political Research*, 55(2): 203–24.

Inglehart, R. F. and Norris, P. (2019), *Cultural Backlash: Trump, Brexit and Authoritarian Populism* (Cambridge: Cambridge University Press).

Ivarsflaten, E. (2008), 'What unites right-wing populists in Western Europe? Re-Examining grievance mobilization models in seven successful cases', *Comparative Political Studies*, 41(1): 3–23.

Kriesi, H. (2014), 'The populist challenge', *West European Politics*, 37(2): 361–78.

Kriesi, H. and Pappas, T. S. (eds.) (2015), *European Populism in the Shadow of the Great Recession* (Colchester: ECPR Press).

Kriesi, H. (2018), 'Revisiting the populist challenge', *Politologický časopis-Czech Journal of Political Science*, 25(1): 5–27.

Laclau, E. (1977), *Politics and Ideology in Marxist Theory: Capitalism, Fascism, Populism* (London: New Left Books).

Laclau, E. (2005), *On Populist Reason* (London: Verso).

Lendvai-Bainton, N. and Szelewa, D. (2021), 'Governing new authoritarianism: Populism, nationalism and radical welfare reforms in Hungary and Poland', *Social Policy & Administration*, 55(4): 559–72.

Lieberman, R., Mettner, S. et al. (2019), 'The Trump presidency and American democracy: A historical and comparative analysis', *Perspectives on Politics*, 17(2): 470–79.

Lubbers, M. and Scheepers, P. (2002), 'French Front National voting: A micro and macro perspective', *Ethnic and Racial Studies*, 25(1): 120–49.

Mazzolini, S. and Borriello, A. (2021), 'The normalization of left populism? The paradigmatic case of Podemos', *European Politics & Society*, 23(3): 285–300.

McDonnell, D. (2006). 'A weekend in Padania: Regionalist populism and the Lega Nord', *Politics*, *26*(2): 126–32.

Meijers, M. J. and Zaslove, A. (2021), 'Measuring populism in political parties: Appraisal of a new approach', *Comparative Political Studies*, 54(2): 372–407.

Moffitt, B. (2015), 'How to perform crisis: A model for understanding the key role of crisis in contemporary populism', *Government and Opposition*, 50(2): 189–217.

Morlino, L. and Tarchi, M. (1996), 'The dissatisfied society: The roots of political change in Italy', *European Journal of Political Research*, 30(1): 41–63.

Mudde, C. (2004), 'The populist Zeitgeist', *Government and Opposition*, 39(3): 542–64.

Mudde, C. and Rovira Kaltwasser, C. (2013), 'Exclusionary vs. inclusionary populism: Comparing the contemporary Europe and Latin America', *Government and Opposition*, 48(2): 147–74.

Müller, J.-W. (2016), *What is Populism?* (Philadelphia: University of Pennsylvania Press).

Norris, P. (2005), *Radical Right: Voters and Parties in the Electoral Market* (Cambridge: Cambridge University Press).

Ostiguy, P. (2018), 'Populism: A socio-cultural approach', in C. Rovira Kaltwasser, P. Taggart et al. (eds.), *Oxford Handbook of Populism* (Oxford: Oxford University Press): 73–97.

Pappas, T. K. (2019), 'Populists in power', *Journal of Democracy*, 30(2): 70–84.

Pirro, A. L. P. and Stanley, B. (2022), 'Forging, bending, and breaking: Enacting the "Illiberal Playbook" in Hungary and Poland', *Perspective on Politics*, 20(1): 86–101.

Ramiro, L. and Gomez, R. (2016), 'Radical left populism during the Great Recession: Podemos and its competition with the established radical left', *Political Studies*, 65(15): 108–26.

Roberts, K. M. (1995), 'Neoliberalism and the transformation of populism in Latin America: The Peruvian case', *World Politics*, 48(1): 82–116.

Roberts, K. M. (2017), *Varieties of Capitalism and Subtypes of Populism: The Structural Foundations of Political Divergence in Northern and Southern Europe* (Florence: SNS Lunch seminar series' paper, 17/11/2017).

Rodrik, D. (2021), 'Why does globalization fuel populism? Economics, culture, and the rise of right-wing populism', *Annual Review of Economics*, 13: 133–70.

Rooduijn, M. (2018), 'What unites the voter bases of populist parties? Comparing the electorates of 15 populist parties', *European Political Science Review*, 10(3): 351–68.

Rooduijn, M. and Akkerman, T. (2017), 'Flank attacks: Populism and left-right radicalism in Western Europe', *Party Politics*, 23(3): 193–204.

Rooduijn, M., Van Kessel, S. et al. (2019), The PopuList: An Overview of Populist, Far-right, Far-left and Eurosceptic Parties in Europe, available at www .popu-list.org.

Ruth-Lovell, S. P. and Grahn, S. (2022), 'Threat or corrective to democracy? The relationship between populism and different models of democracy', *European Journal of Political Research*, 62(3): 677–98.

Salvati, E. (2019), 'Eurosceptic, Eurocritical or Euroconfused? An analysis of the Five Star Movement's voting behaviour in the European Parliament', *European Politics & Society*, 20(3): 296–314.

Sanders, K., Molina Hurtado, M. J. et al. (2017), 'Populism and exclusionary narratives: The "other" in Podemos' 2014 European Union election campaign', *European Journal of Communication*, 32(6): 552–67.

Schäfer, A. (2022), 'Cultural backlash? How (not) to explain the rise of authoritarian populism', *British Journal of Political Science*, 52(4): 1977–93.

Skonieczny, A. (2021), 'Trump talk. Rethinking elections, rethoric, and American foreign policy', *Politics*, 41(1): 127–34.

Spoon, J. J. and Klüver, H. (2019), 'Party convergence and vote switching: Explaining mainstream party decline across Europe', *European Journal of Political Research*, 58(4): 1021–42

Spruyt, B., Keppens, G. A. et al. (2016), 'Who supports populism and what attracts them to it', *Political Research Quarterly*, 69(2): 335–46.

Stanley, B. and Cześnik, M. (2019), 'Populism in Poland', in D. Stockemer (ed.), *Populism Around the World. A Comparative Perspective* (Cham: Springer).

Stavrakakis, Y. and Katzambekis, G. (2014), 'Left-wing populism in the European periphery: The Case of SYRIZA', *Journal of Political Ideologies*, 19(2): 119–42.

Stavrakakis, Y., Katsambekis, G. et al. (2017), 'Populism, anti-populism and the crisis', *Contemporary Political Theory*, 17(1): 4–27.

Taggart, P. (2004), 'Populism and representative politics in contemporary Europe', *Journal of Political Ideologies*, 9(3): 269–88.

Taggart, P. and Pirro, A. L. P. (2021), 'European populism before the pandemic: Ideology, Euroscepticism, electoral performance, and government participation of 63 parties in 30 countries', *Italian Political Science Review*, 51(3): 281–304.

Tarchi, M. (2015), 'Italy: the promised land of populism?', *Contemporary Italian Politics*, 7(3): 273–85.

Vadlamannati, K. C. and Grace, K. (2017), *Welfare Chauvinism? Refugee Flows and Electoral Support for Populist-right Parties in Industrial Democracies*. MPRA Paper No. 81816.

Vasilopoulou, S. (2009), 'Varieties of Euroscepticism: The case of the European extreme right', *Journal of Contemporary European Research*, 5(1): 3–23.

Vasilopoulou, S. (2018), 'The party politics of Euroscepticism in times of crisis: The case of Greece', *Politics*, 38(3): 311–26.

Vasilopoulou, S., Halikiopoulou, D. et al. (2014), 'Greece in crisis: Austerity, populism and the politics of blame', *Journal of Common Market Studies*, 52(2): 388–402.

van der Brug W. and Fennema, M. (2007), 'Causes of voting for the radical right', *International Journal of Public Opinion Research*, 19(4): 474–87.

Vittori, D. (2022), 'Threat or corrective? Assessing the impact of populist parties in government on the qualities of democracy: A 19-Country comparison', *Government & Opposition*, 57(4): 589–609.

Weyland, K. (2003). 'Neopopulism and neoliberalism in Latin America: How much affinity?', *Third World Quarterly*, 24(6): 1095–115.

Index

Please note that page references to Figures will be followed by the letter 'f', to Tables by the letter 't'.